Tome of Terror

Horror Films of the 1930s

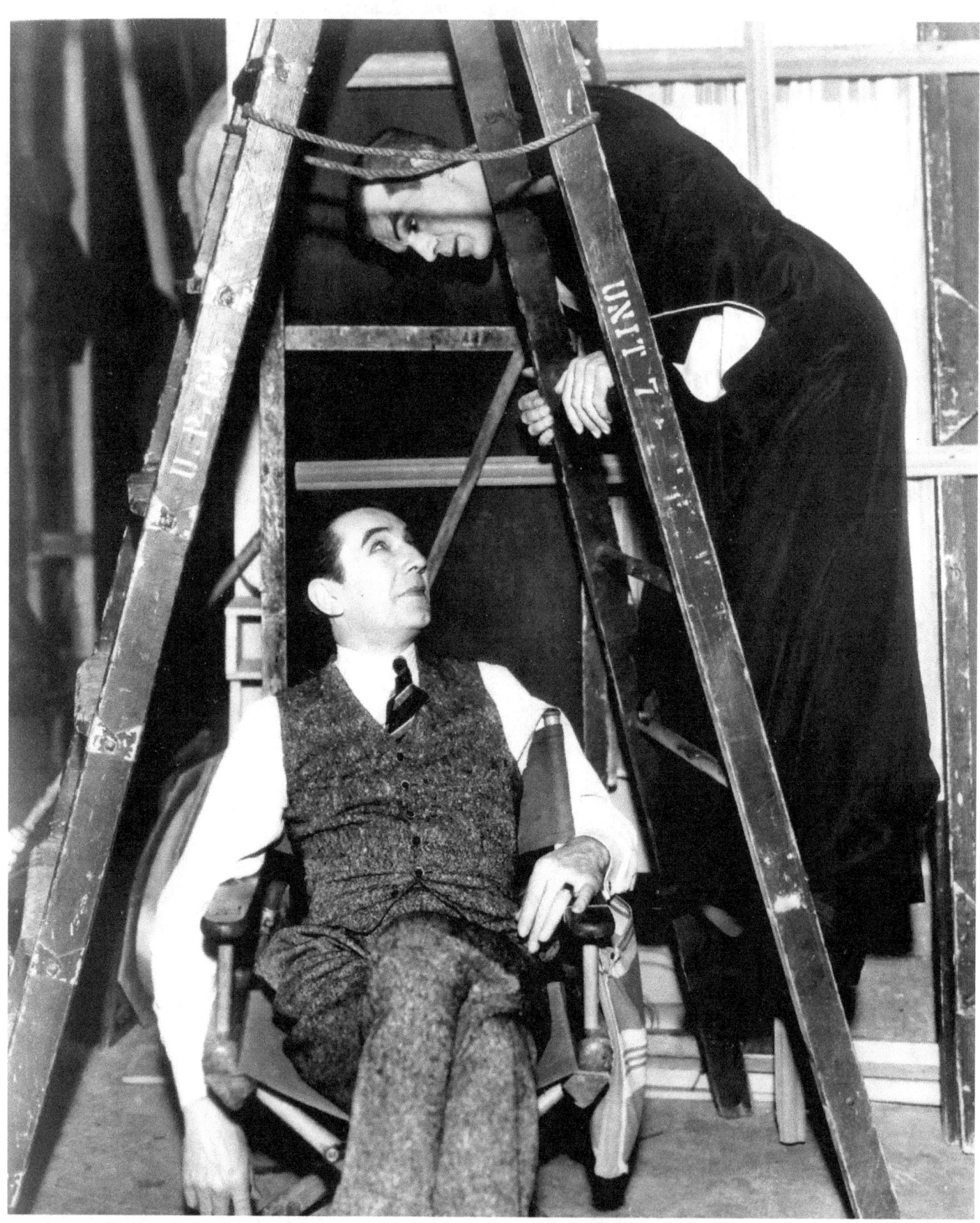

Boris Karloff and Bela Lugosi, two historic figures who reigned during the horror film decade of the 1930s, in a publicity shot between takes on the set of *The Black Cat* (1934)

Tome of Terror
Horror Films of the 1930s

by Christopher Workman
and Troy Howarth

Midnight Marquee Press, Inc.
Baltimore, Maryland, USA; London, UK

Acknowledgements

The authors would like to thank the following people for their contributions to and/or support of *The Tome of Terror*: Gary J. Svehla and Aurelia Susan Svehla, whose acceptance and support of the project has made its publication a reality; Mark Ege, whose tireless editorial efforts helped shape the individual reviews as well as the book as a whole; the Workman and Howarth families, without whose support the series could not have been written; Russ Lanier, for kindly donating some stills from his archive; Horace Cordier, Luigi Cozzi, Sandy Crabtree Brogdon, Jennifer Gantner, Salem Kapsaski, Mike Kenny, Samantha Little, Scott MacDonald, Melinda McCord, Steve and Rosetta Molden, August Ragone, Ian Regan, Matt Gemmell Robertson, Ellen Vass Sanderson, Brent Sweeting and Don and Angel Workman, who were kind enough to help spread the word.

Copyright © 2015 Christopher Workman and Troy Howarth
Interior layout by Gary J. Svehla
Cover Design by Aurelia Susan Svehla
Copy Editor Janet Atkinson

Without limiting the rights under copyright reserved above, no part of this publication may be reproduced, stored in or introduced into a retrieval system, or transmitted, in any form, or by any means (electronic, mechanical, photocopying, recording or otherwise), without the prior written permission of the copyright owner or the publishers of the book.

ISBN 978-1-936168-49-1
Library of Congress Catalog Card Number 2014956458
Manufactured in the United States of America
First Printing February 2015

To our parents—

Connie and Donnie Workman and Diane and Gary Howarth

Without whom we never would have been exposed
to so many great and classic films ...

Table of Contents

8 ....A Note on the Entries

9 ....Introduction

11 1930

20 1931

42 1932

87 1933

114 1934

140.....................1935

175 1936

204.....................1937

222 1938

235 1939

259.....................Index of Film Titles

A Note on the Entries

The entries in this volume are arranged in alphabetical order within the year of each film's production (to the best of our knowledge). Because many were released under different titles in different places, we have listed each under the title most often used in the United States. Alternate titles, if any, are noted beneath the primary title. There is also an Index of Film Titles in the back of this volume to help with cross-referencing. Articles such as *A*, *An*, or *The* have been excluded during the alphabetization process. For example, James Whale's classic *The Invisible Man* is listed in the year 1933 under the letter *I*. In some areas, however, it was released as *H.G. Wells' The Invisible Man*. Hence, the entry for that title begins like this:

The Invisible Man
aka **H.G. Wells' The Invisible Man**

The next line contains the name of the production company, whether the film is in b/w or color, its running time and country of origin. Because running times might vary from place to place, we have tried to include alternate running times (when known) in parentheses. As pertains to countries of origin, we have spelled them out in full except in the case of the United States, which we abbreviate as U.S. Hence, for *The Invisible Man*:

Universal; b/w; 71 min; U.S.

We have also included standard credit information. To conserve space, we generally list only the first letter of each position on the crew, and we have limited ourselves to only the most important credits. These break down as Director (*D:*), Scenarist (*S:*), Producer (*P:*), Cinematographer (*C:*), Music (*M:*) and Special Effects (*FX:*). For *The Invisible Man*, then, the credit line appears as:

D: James Whale; *S:* R.C. Sherriff, Philip Wylie, Preston Sturges; *P:* Carl Laemmle, Jr.; *C:* Arthur Edson; *M:* Heinz Roemheld; *FX:* John P. Fulton

The last line of each entry's credit segment lists the cast members. We have listed the primary stars of each film first, followed by those whose names might be of interest to genre aficionados. Unless the cast of a film is very small or the film itself is very important to the genre, we do not provide a complete cast list. (To do so would have grown the size of the volume, which is already lengthy at 200,000 words, by a considerable amount and made it an untenable publishing endeavor.) For *The Invisible Man*, we have the cast listed as such:

Cast: Claude Rains, Gloria Stuart, William Harrigan, Henry Travers, Una O'Conner, Forrester Harvey, Holmes Herbert, E.E. Clive, Dudley Digges, Harry Stubbs, Donald Stuart, Merle Tottenham, Walter Brennan, John Carradine, Dwight Frye

Finally, each review ends with the initials of the person who wrote it: CW for Chris Workman and TH for Troy Howarth.

Horror film icon Bela Lugosi as he appeared in Universal's *The Black Cat* (1934)

Introduction

The 1930s did not, as many film historians suppose, mark the birth of the horror genre in cinema. Horror had been around since the beginning, even though it was initially confined mostly to Europe and parts of Asia. What the 1930s did see, however, was the birth of American cinematic horror, a development so significant that it forever influenced the way viewers and filmmakers worldwide treated the genre. Before 1931, horror in the United States had largely been confined to the shadows, kept at bay by copious amounts of comic relief as aging spinsters, wisecracking heroes or threatened damsels fought off women-snatching gorillas, masked bank robbers in tacky costumes or disfigured megalomaniacs. Fright films had no place on the big screens of American theaters during this period; after all, the scarred visages of sons returning from the real-life terrors of the Great War were horrifying enough. What 1920s America needed was laughs, and the "horror" films of that time gave them plenty. The chief exception could be found in the work of Lon Chaney, the so-called "man of a thousand faces" and arguably the horror genre's first legitimate icon. Chaney's obsession with mental and physical disfigurement was enthusiastically received by audiences, but it is worth noting that even he tended to dilute pure horror with elements of human fragility (*The Phantom of the Opera*'s Erik, for example, wanted nothing more than to be loved), and the films in which he appeared routinely mixed the humorous and the melodramatic with the macabre.

The year 1931 was something of a watershed. Over a decade had passed since the end of the Great War, and Americans were ready to be frightened by the images projected on the big screen. No longer did horror have to be watered down, and no longer was humor its *raison d'etre*. The problem was that, being new to the game, American studios didn't know how to market horror as a genre. When the nation's first major supernatural thriller, Tod Browning's *Dracula*, was released in February of 1931, it was advertised as a macabre love story and released on Valentine's Day. The marketing ploy proved a smart one; women swooned for Bela Lugosi's urbane, charming Count Dracula, a vampire whose embrace meant ecstasy *and* terror, everlasting life and destruction of the soul.

The film proved such a success that some nine months later James Whale's superior *Frankenstein* followed, which made a horror icon out of its star, Boris Karloff. While not strictly supernatural, the frights it portrayed were definitely not of the "old dark house" variety that had been so popular during the late silent era. Though its empathetic tone was reminiscent of Chaney, there was nary a chuckle to be had. Rather, the film was grounded in a scientific world born of the Great War, where technological advancement could bring about death and destruction just as easily as it could ease the burden of travel and create domestic comfort. Director Whale gleefully piled on the ghastly imagery, and audiences of the time rewarded his strategy with massive ticket sales.

The twin successes of *Dracula* and *Frankenstein* forever changed the genre, ushering in a new era in which terror thrived. Helping set the stage was Paramount's *Dr. Jekyll and Mr. Hyde*, released on the last day of the year to critical acclaim and mass respectability; its star shared an Oscar for Best Actor at the following year's Academy Awards. Horror hadn't merely found success; it was considered art, deserving of the highest accolades.

None of this spelled an end to the lowbrow thrills and comedy relief of the past, it should be noted. For the next decade, both elements remained a big part of many genre films. To a great extent, however, they were rendered archaic by the release of Whale's iconic *The Old Dark House*, which lampooned the subgenre so well that any future entries from other studios and filmmakers—mostly from poverty row, since the only things an "old dark house" movie required were an obtuse, excitable old lady or two, a few cardboard sets and a good-looking hero and heroine—became artistically obsolete. So while they continued to be churned out (and at a faster rate than ever before), it was the heavier, more supernatural or scientific horrors that dominated. And among those, Whale and his home studio, Universal, was the master.

Not surprisingly, the years 1932 and 1933 saw a boost in the number of horror films being produced. Other major Hollywood studios wasted no time in jumping on the lucrative bandwagon built and popularized by Universal. Paramount offered up *Murders in the Zoo* and *Island of Lost Souls*; Fox gave audiences *Chandu the Magician* and *Trick for Trick*; Warner Brothers released *Doctor X* and *The Mystery of the Wax Museum*; MGM produced *Freaks* and *The Mask of Fu Manchu* and RKO chimed in with *The Most Dangerous Game* and what would become the greatest giant monster movie of all time, *King Kong*. But despite the success of most of these films, none of these companies was able to hit the heights of Universal, which had the likes of James Whale, Edgar Ulmer and Robert Florey at its disposal. Films such as *The Invisible Man*, *The Black Cat* and *The Bride of Frankenstein* staked out ever more daring territory, and other studios were simply unable to match Universal's knack for artistic innovation.

During this period, horror film conventions made their way into other genres. Westerns grew weirder than ever before. Mys-

Boris Karloff menaces Gloria Stuart in *The Old Dark House*.

Director James Whale (far right) and cinematographer John J. Mescall on the set of *The Bride of Frankenstein*

teries included fantastic elements. Melodramas became steeped in shadows. But despite the popularity of the horror boom, it wasn't to last. First came the Production Code. Created to head off the direction in which cinema was obviously headed, it threw buckets of cold water over what studios could show onscreen. Then Great Britain, fearful of the impact horror films would have on society, put into effect laws aimed at preventing their release altogether. And finally, parental groups, worried that their kids were sympathizing with the monsters society should have been (in their view) condemning, threatened studio boycotts if said studios continued producing films so-called decent people didn't like. It didn't help matters that the family who had founded Universal lost control of the studio to new owners hoping to emulate the classier output of MGM. One immediate result of all this was a watering down of film content, executed by the blue-noses during both pre- and post-production (*The Black Cat* and *The Bride of Frankenstein* were subjected to this radical tinkering even before the Laemmles lost Universal, though the directors of both still managed to sneak plenty of subversive elements past the censors), ultimately leading to a loss of steam as it pertained to outright fright-film production.

Horror refused to die, however; instead, it went underground for a while. Those films that had, just a few years before, become quaint in the face of Universal's dark onslaught experienced resurgence. The genre's conventions seeped even more noticeably into mysteries, comedies and melodramas. Boris Karloff terrorized *Charlie Chan at the Opera*; Bela Lugosi committed *Murder By Television*; Wheeler and Woolsey were *Mummy's Boys*; Tom Tyler tackled *The Phantom of the Range*; Robert Montgomery and Rosalind Russell got into enough *Trouble for Two* and Basil Rathbone offered Ann Harding *Love from a Stranger*.

In addition, much of the slack of outright horror product in the United States and Britain between late 1936 and 1939 was taken up by other nations. The genre thrived in Mexico and Japan, just as it had in Germany in the 1920s and in the United States in the early 1930s. And even at the height of the British clampdown on horror films, the nation produced its own barnstorming anti-hero in Tod Slaughter, whose Gothic melodramas set the tone for many a future Hammer production.

In 1939, with war raging in Europe and U.S. involvement imminent, Universal's new management decided to revisit their stable of classic monsters, though with a more kid-friendly bent. It was a smart move. *Son of Frankenstein* was a resounding success, and other studios followed suit, leading to a year that included such greats as *The Cat and the Canary* from Paramount, *The Hound of the Baskervilles* from Fox and *The Hunchback of Notre Dame* from RKO, as well as a slew of other popular efforts from Universal. The horror film was reborn for a new generation at a time when it was most needed to help society process the fears and frustrations of a world in peril. Crucially, these productions were accorded healthy budgets and A-list star actors, which in and of itself fended off ghettoization ... though a change was in the air that would come to fruition in the 1940s (a story we'll save for a future volume in our series).

While the 1930s do not represent the birth of the horror genre, the decade does represent the genre at its most formative. Not until the 1970s would it see another such year, and as it stands, the decade contains some of the most astounding, beautiful, eerie and influential horror films ever made. Without it, cinema would be a much different and far less intriguing institution.

Christopher Workman
Troy Howarth

1930

Alraune
aka **Daughter of Evil**
Oswald; b/w; 103 min; Germany

D/Co-P: Richard Oswald *S:* Charlie Roellinghoff, Richard Weisbach *Co-P:* Erich Pommer *C:* Gunther Krampf *M:* Bronislau Kaper

Cast: Brigitte Helm, Albert Basserman, Harald Paulsen, Agnes Straub, Bernhard Goetzke, Martin Kosleck, Kathe Haacke, Ivan Kombal-Samborsky, Liselotte Schaak, Paul Westermeier, Henry Bender, Elsa Basserman

Demented scientist Ten Brinken (Basserman) artificially inseminates a prostitute (Helm) in an attempt to create the ideal woman. The child, named Alraune, grows quickly to adulthood unnaturally and creates a sensation in polite society. All who fall in love with her meet early deaths, and things get even messier when Brinken himself develops an attraction to her.

This, the first sound version of Hanns Heinz Ewers' novel, followed Henrik Galeen's 1928 version, which also starred Brigitte Helm (*Metropolis*, 1927) in the title role. Though virtually impossible to see today, critics have noted that the 1930 *Alraune* falls short of Galeen's adaptation and, like so many early talkies, suffers from terminal verbosity.

In addition to Helm, the cast includes several noteworthy character actors. Albert Basserman (*The Red Shoes*, 1948) takes on the role essayed by Paul Wegener in the previous adaptation, while future B-movie heavy Martin Kosleck (*The Mummy's Curse*, 1944) makes one of his earliest screen appearances, albeit in a small role. Bernhard Goetzke, so memorable as the "weary death" of Fritz Lang's *Destiny* (1921), is also on board.

Cinematographer Gunther Krampf went on to shoot the Boris Karloff horror item *The Ghoul* (1933), while composer Bronislau Kaper later won Oscars for *The Chocolate Soldier* (1941) and *Lili* (1953), as well as being nominated for several others. Director Oswald made his final—and best—contribution to the genre with *Uncanny Stories* (1932), a blackly comedic remake of his silent horror film *Weird Tales* (1919).

Alraune's next cinematic outing was in 1952's *Unnatural*, featuring Hildegard Knef as the demonic Alraune and Erich Von Stroeheim as her creator. TH

L'Autre
aka **Le procureur Hallers**
Films Albatros; b/w; 95 min; France

D: Robert Wiene *S:* Johannes Brandt, Jean Guitton *C:* Nikolaus Farkas *M:* Artur Guttmann, Friedrich Hollaender, Will Meisel

Cast: Jean-Max, Colette Darfeuil, Suzanne Delmas, Florelle, Georges Colin, Henry Krauss, Charles Barrois, Bill Bocket, Alfred Pallon

Suffering from strange blackouts, Dr. Hallers (Jean-Max) manifests an evil alter ego.

German-born director Robert Wiene made two different versions of the Paul Lindt/Hippolyte Taine stage play *The Other*. The first was filmed in the German language with an all-German cast; this alternate version was shot in French with a mostly

A German advertisement for *Alraune*

French cast. The German version made its way to the United States under the title *The Other*, but the French adaptation failed to garner any exposure outside its intended country. The crew itself is mostly the same as in the German version, but the shorter running time hints at somewhat tighter pacing this time out.

Leading man Jean-Max was active from 1927 until 1961. He later had a key supporting-role in Abel Gance's horror-tinged anti-war picture, *J'Accuse* (1938). TH

The Bat Whispers
Schenk; b/w; 83 min; U.S.

D/S: Roland West *P:* Joseph M. Schenk *C:* Ray June (35mm); Robert H. Planck (65mm) *M:* Hugo Riesenfeld

Cast: Chester Morris, Chance Ward, Una Merkel, Richard Tucker, Wilson Benge, Maude Eburn, Grayce Hampton, Charles Dow Clark, William Bakewell, DeWitt Jennings, Spencer Charter, Gustav von Seyffertitz, Hugh Huntley, Sidney D'Albrook, S.E. Jennings

A dangerous criminal known as The Bat terrorizes the residents of a lonely old house in the countryside, but spinster Cornelia (Hampton) refuses to be frightened off and calls in the police to investigate. Detective Anderson (Morris) promises to apprehend the fiend, whom he believes to be in search of a bundle of cash recently stolen from a local bank.

The Bat, written by Mary Roberts Rinehart and Avery Hopwood, was a huge success on Broadway in 1920. Writer/producer/director Roland West first brought the play to the screen in 1926 as *The Bat*. For this, his 1930 remake, he re-titled the

Battered, terrified and fully armed, the men of *The Bat Whispers* hold their ground.

property *The Bat Whispers*, no doubt to emphasize the then-new innovation of sound. In addition to spoken dialogue, the film utilized the cutting-edge technology of the 65mm widescreen process. (Other early titles shot in 65mm include the musical *Happy Days*, 1929, and Raoul Walsh's Western hit *The Big Trail*, 1930, starring John Wayne).

Actually, *The Bat Whispers* was shot in two separate versions, the other being a standard-ratio 35mm edition done to ensure that profits wouldn't be impacted by theaters unequipped for 65mm. In both versions, one is struck by the mobility of the camera; West allows it to hurtle down hallways and to free fall from a great height before tracking through a window to join a scene in progress. It's all very showy and theatrical ... and frankly, it's also the film's saving grace. The story itself is creaky and predictable by modern standards, with performances encompassing both the unfunny comedic mugging of Maude Eburn and the heavy-handed posturing of Chester Morris.

Taken on a purely visual level, *The Bat Whispers* provides much to admire. West effectively utilizes conventional spooky-house lighting that when combined with sophisticated model work helps cut through the inherent staginess of the proceed-

A publicity photo for Roland West's *The Bat Whispers* shows the titular creature menacing Una Merkel and friend.

ings. He directed only one more feature, *Corsair* (1931), before retiring from directing and opening a restaurant with the financial assistance of his wife and actress Thelma Todd (with whom he was having an affair). His reputation plummeted when Todd was found dead in her car of carbon monoxide poisoning; West was one of many suspected of engineering her demise. TH

Botan dōrō
Teikine; b/w; length unknown; Japan
  D: Shuichi Yamashita
  Cast: Tasaburo Matsumoto, Tsuruko Matsuda

This early sound version of Sanyutei Encho's story is considered lost. It was produced by Teikine, a Japanese production company that got its start in the mid-1920s, only to disband in the early 1930s due to poor management and a string of box-office failures. This was one of their later films, followed up with *Oiwa Nagaya* (1931), an adaptation of the kabuki play *Yotsuya kaidan*.

Tsuroko Matsuda plays a mysterious, lantern-bearing woman who seduces a young samurai (Matsumoto). He has deserted his previous lover, causing her to wither away and die. In the end, the lantern-bearer is revealed to be none other than the dead lover's ghost, returned to extract revenge.

This was not the only adaptation of the tale to be filmed during the 1930s. At least two more versions existed, both bearing the same title: one in 1936, the other in 1937. CW

The Cat Creeps
Universal; b/w; 75 min; U.S.
  D: Rupert Julian, John Willard *S:* William Hurlbut, Gladys Lehman *P:* Carl Laemmle, Jr. *C:* Hal Mohr *M:* Heinz Roemheld
  Cast: Helen Twelvetrees, Raymond Hackett, Neil Hamilton, Lilyan Tashman, Jean Hersholt, Montagu Love, Lawrence Grant, Theodore von Eltz, Blanche Friderici, Elizabeth Patterson

Greedy relatives gather in a spooky old house for the reading of a will. Things get lively, however, when a homicidal maniac begins to eliminate the guests one by one.

Paul Leni's film of the John Willard stage play *The Cat and the Canary* (1927), though silent, is recognized today as the definitive adaptation. *The Cat Creeps* was the first talkie version and, title change aside, seems to have been as faithful to the original as the Leni adaptation was. This new version was most likely made chiefly to benefit from the addition of sound. But alas, without a director of Leni's vision and creativity at the helm, the film was, by all accounts, a comparatively dull affair.

The Cat Creeps marked the final directorial work of Rupert Julian, best remembered for shaping *The Phantom of the Opera* (1925), which had starred Lon Chaney. (Julian was known to be something of a preening dictator on the set, one who fancied himself an Erich Von Stroeheim, yet he lacked Stroeheim's formidable talent.) Reviews at the time were less than complementary; today, apart from a few surviving stills (and snippets of soundtrack archived at the University of California, Los Angeles), the film is considered lost.

The original playwright is listed as co-director, but how he split duties with Julian is anybody's guess. The cast includes a number of familiar faces, including Lawrence Grant (*Son of*

Frankenstein, 1939), Montagu Love (*The Last Warning*, 1929) and Jean Hersholt (*The Mask of Fu Manchu*, 1932). Leading lady Helen Twelvetrees was a somewhat popular actress at the time, but she found film work harder to come by after the mid-1930s. She committed suicide in Harrisburg, Pennsylvania in 1939, at the age of 49. TH

The Cat Creeps
aka **La voluntad del muerto**;
The Will of the Dead Man
Universal; b/w; 87 min; U.S./Mexico

 D: Enrique Tovar Avalos, George Melford *S:* William Hurlbut, Gladys Lehman, Baltasar Fernandez Cue *P:* Paul Kohner *C:* George Robinson *M:* Heinz Roemheld

 Cast: Antonio Moreno, Lupita Tovar, Andres de Segurola, Roberto E. Guzman, Paul Ellis, Lucio Villegas, Agostino Borgato, Conchita Ballesteros, Maria Calvo, Soledad Jimenez, Nicolas Ruiz

It was common practice in the early sound era to produce Spanish-language versions of significant studio fare. Dubbing had not yet been perfected, and producers were keen to take advantage of the Mexican/Latin American market. *The Cat Creeps* was one film given this bi-cultural treatment.

A comparison between the Spanish version of *Cat Creeps* and the far more famous Spanish version of Tod Browning's *Dracula* (1931) turns up several of the same names, including George Melford, George Robinson, Lupita Tovar, and Paul Kohner. Director Melford reached the pinnacle of his popularity directing the Spanish *Dracula* (also 1931), which many find preferable to Browning's version, though this is a debatable proposition. Cinematographer Robinson went on to establish himself as a major talent, his stylish photography enhancing such Universal horror films as *Son of Frankenstein* (1939) and *House of Dracula* (1945). Sexy and vivacious star Tovar eclipsed Helen Chandler between the competing versions of *Dracula* and no doubt made an interesting contrast to Helen Twelvetrees in the two versions of *The Cat Creeps* as well.

As for producer Kohner, creating Spanish-language variants of English-language product was something of a letdown for him. Universal president Carl Laemmle groomed him for better things, but when the old man decided to promote his namesake, Carl Laemmle, Jr., as his successor, Kohner's career was dealt a serious blow. He remained determined to outdo Laemmle, Jr., making his casts and crews study the rushes of the English-language version and encouraging them to improve upon it wherever possible. Given that Melford and Robinson were working from the rushes of the notoriously volatile but uninspired Rupert Julian, it seems safe to assume that their version of *The Cat Creeps* eclipsed it in terms of atmosphere and visual richness as

Notice the words "You'll laugh" come before "you'll shudder … you'll scream, making it clear that the emphasis is on humor, not horror, from *The Cat Creeps*.

well. In any event, like its English-language companion piece, the Spanish version of *The Cat Creeps* remains a lost film.

Male lead Antonio Moreno is best known to classic horror and science fiction film buffs as Carl in *Creature from the Black Lagoon* (1954). TH

The Gorilla
First National; b/w; 70 min; U.S.

 D: Bryan Foy *S:* B. Harrison Orkow, Herman Ruby *C:* Sid Hickox

 Cast: Joe Frisco, Harry Gribbon, Lila Lee, Walter Pidgeon, Purnell Pratt, Roscoe Karns, William H. Philbrick, Landers Stevens, Charles Gemora

In a spooky old house, a lunatic in a gorilla suit commits a series of bizarre murders.

Director Alfred Santell first filmed Ralph Spence's play in 1927. This, the first talkie adaptation, is—just like its predecessor—considered lost. It would seem that both movie adaptations opted for a mixture of humor and chills, though with plenty of extra wisecracking the second time around to take advantage of sound. Walter Pidgeon, soon to become a major Hollywood star, here returns from the original film's cast, albeit in a different role. Leading lady Lila Lee was a popular starlet of the period; among her many appearances was one opposite Lon Chaney in Tod Browning's *The Unholy Three* (1925).

The film is also noteworthy for an early appearance by actor Charles Gemora in a gorilla outfit. The Philippine actor milked a long-running career from this shtick, from 1928's *The Leopard Lady* to 1954's *Phantom of the Rue Morgue*.

Director Bryan Foy would later be nominated for a Best Documentary Oscar for 1951's right-wing *I Was a Communist for the FBI* (of which he was a producer), though he got his start in vaudeville as one of "the seven little Foys" (subject of 1955's biopic *The Seven Little Foys*, starring Bob Hope). Foy's directorial career never matched that of his career as a producer, and he hung up his megaphone for good in 1934.

Director Allan Dwan remade *The Gorilla* in 1939. TH

Ingagi
Congo; b/w; 75 min; U.S.

D: William Campbell *S:* Adam Shirk *P:* William Alexander, Nat H. Spitzer *C:* L. Gillingham, Ed Joyce, George Summerton, Fred Webster, Harold Williams *M:* Edward Gage

Cast: Sir Hubert Winstead, Daniel Swayne, Charles Gemora, Arthur Clayton, Louis Nizor

An expedition to the Congo investigates reports of gorilla-worshipping natives. When the intrepid explorers, led by Sir Hubert Winstead (playing himself), finds the tribe, it's right at the moment that a native virgin girl is being carted off, kicking and screaming, to become the bride of said revered gorilla (Gemora). Naturally, Sir Hubert and his men set out to rescue the woman.

This obscure cheapie has two principal points of interest. First, the film utilizes a great deal of Congo location footage, which gives it an air of exoticism. At a time when most films were studio bound, the notion of going to a far-off locale in the pursuit of realism was very novel. Second, the plot bears a resemblance to a much more famous "ape" epic, *King Kong* (1933)—though *Ingagi*'s ape is of normal size. In each, a damsel in distress is presented to a sacred ape as a gesture of appeasement, and a group of civilized types tries to retrieve her.

As it turns out, the similarity between the two films isn't coincidental. RKO picked up this independent production for distribution, and its success helped convince studio heads that *Kong* would be a viable property to develop.

Character actor Charles Gemora portrayed the ape, another early example of his iconic ape/gorilla performances. The cast is top-lined by real-life adventurer Sir Hubert Winstead, making his one and only film appearance. Nothing much is really known about Winstead, and any hopes he had of pursuing further film stardom were doubtless dampened when it became known that *Ingagi* was a load of hooey and not the anthropological documentary it purported to be.

Ingagi is today considered a lost film. A sequel of sorts, *Son of Ingagi*, followed in 1940. TH

Kaidan Kasane-ga-fuchi
Makino; b/w; length unknown; Japan

D: Buntaro Futagawa *S:* Yoshi Segawa *C:* Seizo Ishino

Cast: Kunitaro Sawamura, Tomoko Makino, Tsukie Matsura, Masaru Kogani

This was likely the first adaptation of Senyutei Encho's 1860 novel *Shinkei Kasane-ga-fuchi* to be produced in the 1930s, following at least three silent screen versions (one of which was the popular *Passion of a Woman Teacher*, in 1926, which experienced a positive reception in Europe). Unfortunately, little else in the way of information exists about this long-lost film other

The original poster for *Ingagi* focused on sexual titillation rather than chills.

than the cast and crew and the barest of plot outlines: A woman kills herself upon learning that her blind-masseur boyfriend is having an affair with one of her students, after which she rises from the grave to take revenge.

Kunitaro Sawamura's career was a long one, lasting from the late 1920s until 1960. He came from a family of actors that included brother Daisuke Kato and sister Sadako Sawamura. He died of a stroke in 1974.

Director Shozo Makino's production company released *Kaidan Kasane-ga-fuchi* on August 15, 1930, approximately two years after his death. CW

Midnight Mystery
RKO; b/w; 69 min; U.S.

D: George B. Seitz *S:* Beulah Marie Dix *P:* William LeBaron, Bertram Millhauser *C:* Joseph Walker

Cast: Betty Compson, Lowell Sherman, Raymond Hatton, Hugh Trevor, June Clyde, Ivan Lebedeff, Rita La Roy, Marcelle Corday, Sidney D'Albrook, William P. Burt

Gregory Sloane (Trevor) throws a party at his island castle off the coast of Maine. As a storm rages, he stages a fake murder to liven things up. But things get tense when a real dead body shows up. Gregory is blamed, and it's up to his fiancée, mystery novelist Sally Wayne (Compson), to clear his name.

This B-mystery's set-up is patently absurd, though the premise lends itself well to the typical "dark and stormy" aesthetic. The film had a previous incarnation as a stage play by Howard Irving Young, one forgotten today but successful enough at the time to prompt this cinematic adaptation. Director George B. Seitz went on to direct *The Thirteenth Chair* (1937) and finished out his career helming most of MGM's popular Andy Hardy series. Spunky Betty Compson had been nominated for an Oscar for *The Barker* (1928), but much of her talkie career was spent in quickie fare such as *Midnight Mystery*. She later appeared in the Bela Lugosi programmer *The Invisible Ghost* (1941).

Supporting player Lowell Sherman was at the heart of a real-life horror story—he was a guest at the raucous Labor Day party in 1921 at which Roscoe "Fatty" Arbuckle was accused of committing a violent sexual assault on actress Virginia Rappe that later allegedly caused her death. In addition to acting, Sherman worked extensively as a director. He was originally in charge of *Becky Sharp* (1935), though Rouben Mamoulian famously replaced him. He also oversaw Universal's dark fantasy *Night Life of the Gods* (1935). It was his final completed work, though he died of pneumonia a year before the film's release. TH

Le mystère de la Villa Rose
Les Établissements Jacques Haïk; b/w; 100 min; France

D: René Hervil, Louis Mercanton *S:* Louis d'Yvré, Pierre Maudru, Cyril Twyford *P:* Jacques Haïk *C:* Basil Emmott

Cast: Léon Mathot, Simone Vaudry, Louis Baron Fils, Hélèna Manson, Georges Péclet, Alice Ael, Jacques Henley, Dahlia, Jean Mercanton, René Montis

It's only fitting that a French production company filmed the second adaptation of A.E.W. Mason's 1910 mystery novel *At the Villa Rose*, given that the hero of the book is a French inspector named Hanaud. This particular version also shares a screenwriting credit with the same year's yet-to-be-released British adaptation *Mystery at the Villa Rose*. Cyril Twyford worked on the scripts for both productions, which explains why there are similarities between the two that aren't shared by the source novel.

The story concerns a fake medium who is befriended by a lonely widow (Ael) obsessed with spiritualism; when the old woman is murdered by someone seeking her jewels, the medium becomes the prime suspect and must help the inspector (Mathot) solve the crime.

Co-director Louis Mercanton was father to actor Jean Mercanton, who had a supporting role in the film, and stepfather to cinematographer Jacques Mercanton. He died of a heart attack in Paris, France in 1932, thus ending a distinguished cinematic

A Swedish poster for *Midnight Mystery*

career that included *Anne Boleyn* (1913) and *The Clairvoyant* (1923). René Hervil continued to direct for another six years before retiring; he died in Sartrouville, Yvelines, France in 1960. This was not his only horror film; in 1921 he had directed the dark comedy *Lord Arthur Savile's Crime*. Nor was this the first film to be co-directed by Mercanton and Hervil: That would be 1913's *Le Spectré du passé*.

Le mystère de la Villa Rose beat its British counterpart into theaters by approximately four months. CW

Mystery at the Villa Rose
aka **At the Villa Rose**
Julius Hagen; b/w; 78 min; Great Britain

D: Leslie Hiscott *S:* Cyril Twyford *P:* Julius Hagen, Henry Edwards *C:* Sydney Blythe *M:* John Greenwood

Cast Norah Baring, Austin Trevor, Richard Cooper, Barbara Gott, Francis Lister, Amy Brandon Thomas, Violet Farebrother

The Madam D'Auvray (Gott) has an obsession with spiritualism, which leads her to befriend and employ a medium named Celia Harland (Baring). Unknown to the old woman, however, there are people out there who are more than a little interested in her jewels. One night during a séance, she is murdered and her valuables taken. A detective (Trevor) interested in solving difficult puzzles is called in to investigate the case, and it isn't long before his brilliant mind unmasks the moronic culprit.

Mystery at the Villa Rose was based on a novel by A.E.W. Mason, which was first filmed under its original title *At the Villa Rose* in 1920. The year 1930 also saw a French production, released several months before this insipid little production hit theaters. The next and final adaptation, also titled *At the Villa Rose*, was released in 1940.

Though actor Austin Trevor received positive notices for his performance as Hanaud, the film quickly disappeared from theaters. No subsequent re-evaluation has found that it deserved any better. CW

The Other
aka **Der Andere**
Terra; b/w; 104 (90) min; Germany

D: Robert Wiene *S:* Johannes Brandt *C:* Nikolaus Farkas *M:* Artur Guttmann, Friedrich Hollaender, Will Meisel

Cast: Fritz Kortner, Kathe von Nagy, Heinrich George, Hermine Sterler, Ursula van Diemen, Eduard von Winterstein, Oskar Sima, Jules Falkenstein, Paul Bildt, Otto Stoessel, Emil Heyse, Hans Ahrens

Dr. Hallers (Kortner) suffers from blackouts, during which his debased alter ego runs amok.

First filmed by Max Mack in 1913, *The Other* was based on a stage play of the same name by Paul Lindau and Hippolyte Taine. The play, which was successful in Germany, took its cue from Robert Louis Stevenson's *The Strange Case of Dr. Jekyll and Mr. Hyde*. Yet whereas Stevenson's novella had a vague science fiction slant, the play is grounded in conventional realism; its protagonist does not undergo a literal physical transformation but simply suffers from a personality disorder.

Director Robert Wiene adapted the material himself, though the final scenario is credited to Johannes Brandt. Wiene, best remembered for the Expressionist milestone *The Cabinet of Dr. Caligari* (1919), was no stranger to fantastic cinema, though his uneven output has kept him out of the same league as, say, F.W. Murnau or Fritz Lang.

Leading man Fritz Kortner was a familiar face in many major German productions of the period, including Wiene's *The Hands of Orlac* (1924). The central role here provided the actor with a real chance to shine; he was more often cast in supporting roles, however, and remained in that capacity during his time in the film industries of Britain and the United States.

The Other was filmed in two separate versions, one German, the other French. The French version, *L'Autre*, was also released in 1930. TH

Paramount on Parade
Paramount; b/w-color; 102 (77) min; U.S.

D: Dorothy Arzner, Otto Brower, Edmund Goulding, Victor Heerman, Edwin H. Knopf, Rowland V. Lee, Ernst Lubitsch, Lothar Mendes, Victor Schertzinger, A. Edward Sutherland, Frank Tuttle *S:* Joseph L. Mankiewicz *P:* Jesse L. Lasky, Albert A. Kaufman, Adolph Zukor *C:* Harry Fischbeck, Victor Milner *M:* Howard Jackson

Cast: Warner Oland, Eugene Pallette, William Powell, Jack Oakie, Fay Wray, Clive Brook, Maurice Chevalier, Richard Arlen, Jean Arthur, William Austin, George Bancroft, Clara Bow, Evelyn Brent, Mary Brian, Nancy Carroll, Ruth Chatterton,

Philo Vance (William Powell) and Sherlock Holmes (Clive Brooke) in the "Murder Will Out" segment of *Paramount on Parade*.

Gary Cooper, Leon Errol, Stuart Erwin, Kay Francis, Richard Gallagher, Harry Green, Mitzi Green, James Hall, Helen Kane, Dennis King, Abe Lyman, Fredric March, Nino Martini, Mitzi Mayfair, Zelma O'Neal, Charles Rogers, Lillian Roth, Stanley Smith

In an attempt to emulate the success of MGM's *The Hollywood Revue of 1929* and Warner Brothers' *The Show of Shows* (both 1929), Paramount released *Paramount on Parade* to showcase its stars and directors. It was an anthology bearing numerous song and dance routines and the occasional two-color Technicolor flourish. By no means a horror film itself, *Parade*'s fifth segment is of interest to horror film historians, focusing as it does on Philo Vance (William Powell) and Sherlock Holmes (Clive Brook), hot on the trail of dastardly criminal mastermind Fu Manchu (Oland).

The film marked Oland's second appearance as the villainous Asian of Sax Rohmer's popular pulp novels. It beat the actor's third appearance as the infamous character (in *The Return of Dr. Fu Manchu*, 1930) into theaters by a mere two weeks. Of course, the purpose of including Fu Manchu at all was to drum up support among moviegoers for the franchise that Paramount had begun the previous year with *The Mysterious Dr. Fu Manchu* (1929). Rowland V. Lee, who had helmed that picture, was even brought in to direct the short segment in *Parade*. The strategy apparently worked, as *Return* was successful enough to spawn a follow-up, *Daughter of the Dragon* (1931), with Anna May Wong as the offspring of Fu Manchu. (Oland repeated his role as Fu, though the part was relatively small, possibly to avoid paying the actor his full rate.)

While Paramount released numerous versions of *Parade* in various foreign markets, a 102-minute cut was the standard American version until 1958, when Universal bought it for television syndication. Since then, a 77-minute cut (stripped of its partial Technicolor splendor) has been the one in general circulation. The UCLA Film and Television Archive has restored the missing scenes and color footage, though some portions of the sound remain absent. CW

Warner Oland as the vengeful Manchurian in *The Return of Dr. Fu Manchu*

The Return of Dr. Fu Manchu
aka **New Adventures of Dr. Fu Manchu**
Paramount; b/w; 73 min; U.S.
  D/P: Rowland V. Lee *S:* Florence Ryerson, Lloyd Corrigan *C:* Archie Stout
  Cast: Warner Oland, O.P. Heggie, Jean Arthur, Neil Hamilton, Evelyn Hall, William Austin, Margaret Fealy, Shayle Gardner, Evelyn Selbie, Tetsu Komai

At the funeral of Dr. Fu Manchu (Oland), Inspector Nayland Smith (Heggie) relates how the mad scientist exacted revenge on the families of those who killed his wife and son, and how the grandson of one of those men, Dr. Jack Petrie (Hamilton), managed to escape. Manchu, Smith says, committed suicide by ingesting poison. (In case you're wondering, all of this went down in *The Mysterious Dr. Fu Manchu*, 1930.) But unbeknown to Smith, Fu Manchu is quite alive, having in truth swallowed a substance that caused only the *appearance* of death. And now the Chinese madman, along with his assistant Chang (Komai), is at it again, hatching a plot to kill Petrie on the day of his wedding to Lia Eltham (Arthur) at the estate of the Ladies Bartley (Hall, Fealy). The ceremony, when it occurs, is indeed interrupted by murder, but it's Lia's poor Chinese servant Fai Lu (Selbie) who is done in rather than Petrie. Inspector Smith summons men from Scotland Yard to protect the estate grounds and the people thereon, but Fu Manchu's dacoits are already lurking about, and before long they've taken hostage both Lia and Lady Agatha. A note is delivered to the Bartley Estate calling on Petrie to give up if he wants to save the two women. But instead Smith impersonates Petrie, feigns surrender and is brought to the criminal mastermind's island lair, where he learns that his mind is to be erased by an ancient Chinese elixir. In the nick of time, however, Smith and Lady Agatha are rescued. Fu is shot in the process but manages to escape and take Lia with him. After a lot more talk and a few action sequences, he blows himself up while trying to orchestrate Petrie's suicide.

The film references some of the subplots—such as the "Call of Siva"—found in Sax Rohmer's original novels, but overall it bears little resemblance to the source material. Director Rowland V. Lee smartly makes the character of Fu Manchu more sympathetic than the Yellow Peril monster of Rohmer's books, thereby avoiding the type of controversy Rohmer's stories (and other film versions) elicited. In the sinophobic novels, the Oriental criminal's *raison d'être* is to dominate the Occidental West in order to "destroy" the "white races." In *Return*, Manchu's rage is humanized by the fact that he saw his family butchered by Britons (with whom he sided) during the Boxer Rebellion. Warner Oland's Fu (who chews the scenery here in a way that Oland did not in his classic turn as Charlie Chan later in the same decade) is not a mindless villain bent on world domination, but rather a man avenging the loss of those he most loved. Even as he chases down his last remaining enemy, he tries to avoid causing the deaths of other Caucasians (though he has no problem murdering fellow Chinese).

This was the last time the character was played sympathetically (he was revisited for laughs in Peter Sellers' last film, *The Fiendish Plot of Dr. Fu Manchu*, 1980). In the 1960s, Chris-

Publicity still from Paramount's second horror feature to star Warner Oland as a Chinese madman, here menacing actress Jean Arthur in *The Return of Dr. Fu Manchu*

Horror Films of the 1930s 17

Pauline Garon as she appeared in *Le Spectre Vert*

topher Lee portrayed the character as the arch villain Rohmer envisioned, in a series of films for producer Harry Alan Towers that began with 1965's *The Face of Fu Manchu*.

Evelyn Hall often played older English Dames of the classic sort in a film career that went from the late 1920s through the early 1930s. Here, she easily steals scenes from the less accomplished actors around her, particularly Jean Arthur and Neil Hamilton. Formidable character actor O.P. Heggie holds his own as Smith, however, and thankfully is given the screen time he deserves. Heggie made a name for himself as the blind hermit in James Whale's *The Bride of Frankenstein* in 1935 before dying the following year of pneumonia.

Return is a flawed work that bogs down increasingly as the story progresses. The problem isn't its performances or even its screenplay—which is pretty much the typical serial-type fare of the period (though in feature form)—but rather the direction of Lee, who had not yet developed his trademark style. The camera is parked in stationary mode throughout and shoots almost every scene through a static lens. Had Lee followed a more offbeat path—such as that traced by Roland West in *The Bat Whispers* the same year—he might have achieved a classic of cinematic adventure/horror. As it is, his film wastes its potential. To further hamper the proceedings, the budget here appears to be about half that of the previous outing. While *Mysterious Dr. Fu Manchu* is full of large and interesting sets, *Return*, which takes place in a few rooms in Bartley Estate or in Fu's lair, is not.

It is, in the end, a typical example of a studio hoping to make quick returns off a successful initial effort by going cheaper and hoping that audiences' love for the character will bring them back. It appears to have worked, and Paramount revisited Fu one more time with *Daughter of the Dragon* (1931), an even lower-budgeted effort without Rowland V. Lee at the helm. It remained for MGM and Boris Karloff to breathe everlasting life into the character with Charles Brabin's *The Mask of Fu Manchu* (1932). CW

Le Spectre Vert
MGM; b/w; length unknown; U.S./France
 D: Jacques Veyder S: Yves Mirande
 Cast: Andre Luguet, Jetta Goudal, Pauline Garon, Georges Renavent, Jules Raucourt, Andre Berley, Youcca Troubetzkov, Arnold Korff, Lionel Belmore, Andre Petit, Arthur Hurni, Sojin

Lord Montague's (Luguet) old military regiment is being killed off one by one. Sir James of Scotland Yard (Raucourt) determines to trap the killer by having all the regiment's surviving members gather at Montague's mansion.

This is the alternate, French-language version (the title translates as "The Green Ghost") of the Lionel Barrymore-directed *The Unholy Night* (1929). In the early days of sound, it was not uncommon to shoot different-language versions of a production. Between the late 1920s and the early 1930s, before dubbing and subtitling took over, a number of films—including Universal's *The Cat Creeps* (1930) and *Dracula* (1931)—were shot in different versions. But while it was typical for said versions to be given concurrent releases in their respective marketplaces, *Le Spectre Vert* didn't emerge in France until a year after the English-language version.

Of the actors involved in the two films, only Lionel Belmore and Japanese character actor Sojin appeared in both. The French-language version is believed to be lost, with surviving details sketchy at best. Given the staginess of Barrymore's version, one can only hope this one was a bit more cinematic. TH

The Unholy Three
MGM; b/w; 72 min; U.S.
 D: Jack Conway S: J.C. Nugent, Elliott Nugent P: Irving Thalberg C: Percy Hilburn M: William Axt
 Cast: Lon Chaney, Lila Lee, Elliott Nugent, Harry Earles, Ivan Linow, John Milhan, Clarence Burton, Crauford Kent

Ventriloquist Echo (Chaney) devises a devilish plan for a series of burglaries, and he enlists fellow sideshow performers Tweedledee (Earles) and Hercules (Linow) to assist. Calling themselves the Unholy Three, they set up a clever front for their criminality: Echo, with his ability to disguise himself both physically and vocally, pretends to be a harmless old woman; Tweedledee takes advantage of his tiny physique to impersonate a baby and Hercules takes on the role of the so-called baby's protective father. The "family" opens a bird shop and establishes itself as an upstanding part of the community. Little do the locals realize that the old woman and her cronies are preying on their rich customers, breaking into their homes at night and robbing them.

Tod Browning's silent film *The Unholy Three* (1925) was a huge moneymaker for MGM. The film paired director Browning with the studio's number one character star, Lon Chaney, and in the wake of its success the two stuck together for a string of perverse melodramas.

The advent of sound recording at first did not appeal to Chaney. Like others at the time, he expected sound films to be a short-lived novelty. When in 1930 Universal re-released Chaney's mammoth hit *The Phantom of the Opera* (1925) with sound effects added, the aural enhancements did not include Chaney's voice; he had steadfastly refused to record any dialogue to accompany his performance, ensuring that the Phantom himself remained silent. The wildfire success of talking films, however, soon caused Chaney to reconsider, and a sound remake of *The Unholy Three* seemed the perfect vehicle for him to make his talkie debut. Apart from being a remake of a proven success, here was a role that would enable Chaney to display his gifts for vocal imitation—something at which he was every bit adept as he was at creating new visages.

The opportunity came at a difficult time in the actor's life. During work on the railroad melodrama *Thunder* (1929), he had come down with a serious case of pneumonia, after which it was discovered that he was suffering from the advanced stages of lung cancer. But despite the toll that treatment took on his physical wellbeing, he nevertheless consented to top-line the second *Unholy Three*.

The revisitation establishes beyond a shadow of a doubt that Chaney could deliver perfect vocalizations. His work in it veers impressively from the timid understatement of Mrs. O'Grady to the tough guy, no-nonsense attitude of Echo. It's a thoroughly entertaining performance, one to make connoisseurs regret that his life and career were cut so tragically short.

Lon Chaney in his only talking picture, *The Unholy Three*

MGM sensibly brought back diminutive Harry Earles to repeat his role as Tweedledee, and though his heavy German accent makes it difficult at times to discern what he's saying, he is in fine form nonetheless. The interplay between him and Chaney is wonderfully dark and comedic, with the two actors clearly relishing every second of it.

Ivan Linow replaces the original's Victor McLaglen (who played Hercules). Linow isn't as accomplished a performer as McLaglen, but he does a competent job as the all-muscle-and-no-brains member of the gang. Lila Lee as Rosie, the girl Echo has his eye on, is attractive and vivacious, while Elliott Nugent (who co-wrote the screenplay with his father J.C. Nugent) does the best he can with the thankless role of Hector, Chaney's patsy.

It's unclear why Tod Browning wasn't brought back to direct the film, but most likely he was simply busy with Universal's *Dracula* (1931). In his place, MGM brought in studio hack Jack Conway. Conway's direction can't begin to compare with the economy and style Browning brought to the original, but he clearly studied the earlier version. He even repeats the memorable silhouette of the unholy three planning their wild scheme.

The overall film, while inferior to the first, certainly provides its own share of pleasures. Sadly, it was to be Chaney's last. He died of a throat hemorrhage just weeks after its release. TH

1931

The Bells
British Sound; b/w; 75 min; Great Britain
   D: Harcourt Templeman, Oscar M. Werndorff *S:* C.H. Dand *P:* Sergei Nolbandov *C:* Gunther Krampf, Eric Cross *M:* Gustav Holst
   Cast: Donald Calthrop, Jane Welsh, Edward Sinclair, O.B. Clarence, Wilfrid Shine, Ralph Truman

   This is one of at least three sound versions of the Leopold Lewis stage melodrama (adapted from a French play by Erckmann-Chatrian), which lead actor Sir Henry Irving had made a bona fide hit in November of 1871 (and which has been revived numerous times since).

   Donald Calthrop stars as the anti-Semitic burgomaster/innkeeper Mathias, who murders a wealthy Polish Jew and steals his fortune. Haunted by visions of the murdered man's ghost, Mathias learns that his victim's brother, along with an accompanying mesmerist, seeks an inquest. When Mathias himself is assigned to investigate the murder, his conscience finally drives him mad.

   Though some sources credit this film as a German production (perhaps because of the many Germans who made up its crew), it was produced entirely by British Sound Film Productions. It was shot in March 1931 in Grampians National Park near Melbourne in Victoria, Australia. From all accounts, the weather conditions were difficult, making the shoot slow going. On an interesting connected note, the film was banned in Germany during the Nazi regime.

   Cinematographer Gunther Krampf had worked on such silent German Expressionist horror films as *The Hands of Orlac* (1924) and *The Student of Prague* (1926). Just how much Expressionist influence there was on *The Bells* is impossible to know, since it has long been considered lost.

   Another version of Lewis' play was shot the same year in France and was released in English-language markets under the title *The Polish Jew*. CW

Chinatown After Dark
Like/Action; b/w; 56 (59) min; U.S.
   D: Stuart Paton *S:* Betty Burbridge *P:* Ralph M. Like *C:* Jules Cronjager
   Cast: Carmel Myers, Rex Lease, Barbara Kent, Edmund Breese, Frank Mayo, Billy Gilbert, Michael Visaroff

   Ralph (Mayo) is hired to deliver a valuable dagger to the Royal Chinese family of Lee Fong (Breese), but when he does, the lights go out. When they come back on, Fong has been murdered, and Ralph has disappeared. Enter Ralph's brother Jim (Lease), who is suspected by blundering cop Dooley (Gilbert) in the murder of Lee Fong. It all turns out to be a plot by the murderous Madame Ying Su (Myers) and her cohorts to steal a priceless jewel hidden within the dagger. Once the usual homespun adventures bring the film to a respectable running time, Jim and his new girlfriend (Kent), a white woman raised as an Asian, are allowed to live happily ever after.

   Chinatown After Dark is another of the many Yellow Peril thrillers that followed in the wake of Sax Rohmer's successful

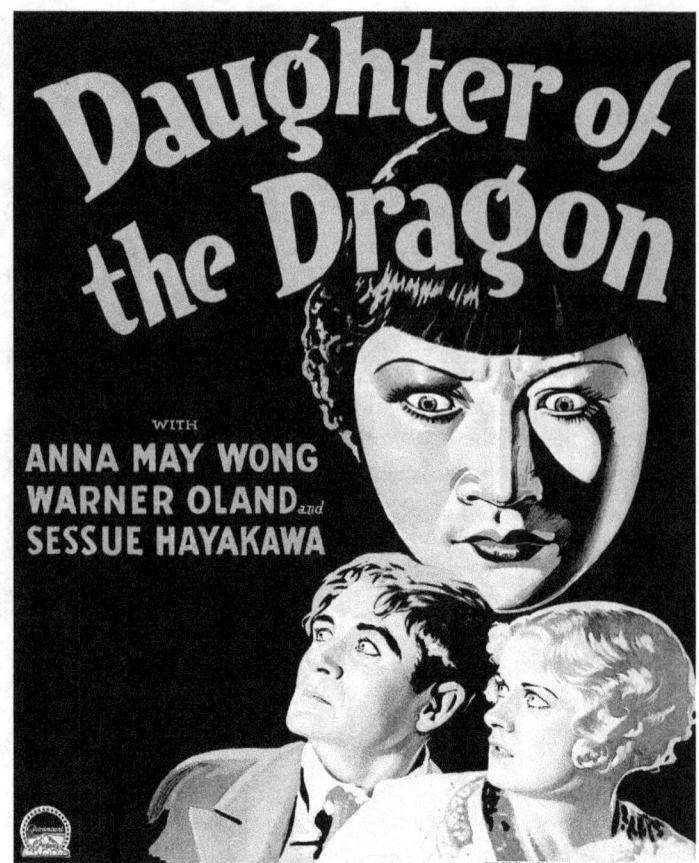

series of Fu Manchu novels, themselves the basis for numerous silent and early talking pictures. One of them, Paramount's *Daughter of the Dragon*, had been released in early September 1931 and appears to have been the impetus for *Chinatown*, which was shot quickly and released in mid-October. This cheapie knockoff suffers insurmountably by the absence of *Daughter's* talented Anna May Wong in the lead; instead, it has Carmel Myers at her wooden worst as the villainous Madame Ying Su.

   San Francisco-born Myers first acted in a bit part in D.W. Griffith's mega-production of 1916, *Intolerance: Love's Struggle Through the Ages*. From there she somehow garnered a major contract with Universal and went on to work with the likes of Rudolph Valentino. Some of the classic films in which she starred include *Beau Brummel* (1924), *Ben-Hur: A Tale of the Christ* (1925), *Camille* (1926) and *Sumuru* (1927). When it became painfully apparent, as it is here, that her talents didn't translate to talkie cinema, she was relegated to minor parts in mostly low-budget films. She did have roles in two early classic horror talkies, however: *Svengali* and *The Mad Genius* (both 1931).

   Rex Lease as *Chinatown*'s handsome hero is, amazingly, no better. Lease had begun his career in silent films after choosing acting over the ministry. Work in comedies and action adventures gave way to roles in cheap Westerns in the 1930s, and by the early '40s his career had waned to mostly unbilled parts in B-movies. That he got even those roles is surprising, given his inability to recite a single line of dialogue without either flubbing it entirely or pausing to recall what he's supposed to say next (a trait on full display in *Chinatown*).

   Barbara Kent as the heroine Lotus (!) and Billy Gilbert as Detective Dooley are just as bad. While Gilbert inexplicably

The beautiful Anna May Wong as the *Daughter of the Dragon*

went on to provide some genuinely funny comic relief in a number of movies, his mugging here is unbearable, making Abbott and Costello appear riotous by comparison. Frank Mayo gives a decent performance, but he's the only actor to do so.

Add to all this some flat direction from Stuart Paton, bland camerawork from Jules Cronjager and the complete lack of a music score, and *Chinatown After Dark* emerges as a breathtakingly boring strip of celluloid. The only positive, apart from Mayo, is that *some* of the minor characters are actually played by people of Asian descent. CW

A Dangerous Affair
Columbia; b/w; 75 min; U.S.

D: Edward Sedgwick *S:* Howard J. Green *C:* Ted Tetzlaff

Cast: Jack Holt, Ralph Graves, Sally Blane, Susan Fleming, Blanche Friderici, Edward Brophy, DeWitt Jennings, Tyler Brooke, William V. Mong, Fred Santley, Sidney Bracey, Charles Middleton, Esther Muir

Wally Cook decides to play a trick on cocky heiress Marjory Randolph by sneaking into her house and stealing her valuable necklace. The police, led by Lieutenant McHenry (Holt), are called in to investigate. But Wally and McHenry are old friends, and the lieutenant is talked into going along with the prank. McHenry stores the temporarily purloined item in his desk. The following evening he provides police protection at the Randolph mansion during the reading of a will. Marjory's rich uncle, it turns out, has left her everything, but the location of her late uncle's treasure is concealed in the stolen necklace. When Marjory becomes understandably frantic, McHenry fesses up to what has happened. The two go to McHenry's office and find that the necklace has been stolen, this time for real! McHenry enlists Wally to help him investigate the mystery that, several corpses later, is solved.

This B-mystery with "old dark house" trappings is virtually impossible to see today. A print is housed in the UCLA Film and Television library, but it has never been released for home viewing, and the film hasn't turned up on television in years. By all accounts, it's a lively if implausible little romp that piles on the creepiness during its scenes in the spooky old manor house.

Leading man Jack Holt led a life befitting his rugged good looks. Born in New York, he tried his hand at everything from gold mining to railroad work to cattle herding before he entered films in 1914. Not long after *A Dangerous Affair*, he moved smoothly from lead roles to solid character performances, remaining active in film until his death in 1951. Horror aficionados know him as the Commodore in Val Lewton and Jacques Tourneur's *Cat People* (1942) and as Jack Hart in Columbia's horror/gangster hybrid *Behind the Mask* (1932).

Director Edward Sedgwick was an efficient but uninspired journeyman. He finished out his career helming the likes of *Ma and Pa Kettle Back on the Farm* (1951) and guiding Lucille Ball and Desi Arnaz through a now-obscure big-screen version of *I Love Lucy* (1953). His most noteworthy contribution to the horror genre, however, was some uncredited action direction on Universal's *The Phantom of the Opera* (1925). TH

Daughter of the Dragon
Paramount; b/w; 70 min; U.S.

D/Co-S: Lloyd Corrigan *Co-S:* Monte M. Katterjohn, Sidney Buchman *C:* Victor Milner

Cast: Anna May Wong, Warner Oland, Sessue Hayakawa, Bramwell Fletcher, Frances Dade, Holmes Herbert, Lawrence Grant, Harold Minjir, Nicholas Soussanin, E. Alyn Warren

Stage performer Ling Moy (Wong) has been seeking her true father, but when she finally meets him, she discovers that he is none other than Fu Manchu (Oland). Fu tells his daughter about the deaths of her mother and brother at the hands of Britons during the Boxer Rebellion and devises a plan by which she will worm her way into the home of the final living Petrie, Sir John's son Robert (Fletcher). Young Petrie falls for Moy, sending his girlfriend Joan Marshall (Dade) into a heated jealousy.

Set 20 years after the events of *The Mysterious Dr. Fu Manchu* (1929) and *The Return of Dr. Fu Manchu* (1930), *Daughter of the Dragon* presents a continuity problem or three. Most glaringly, it's difficult to reconcile the Petries of this film with those of the previous two. The ages are all wrong, even if an additional 20 years hadn't been tacked on. Adding to the confusion, Nayland Smith is (presumably) dead, and none of the cast from the previous films—other than Oland—is anywhere to be seen. *Daughter*, it seems, is the cinematic bastard of the Fu Manchu family.

Director Rowland V. Lee had moved on by this time, leaving Paramount for the gangster-ridden streets of First National. The screenwriter of the previous films, Lloyd Corrigan, took over directing chores, and, despite *Daughter* being only his

Fredric March plays the vicious Mr. Hyde in Rouble Mamoulian's *Dr. Jekyll and Mr. Hyde.*

third directing job, he exhibits a surprising amount of skill. Fu Manchu's first onscreen appearance is a standout example. The villain's sinister voice is heard, next the man himself comes into view—out of focus in the background with his head out of frame—as he approaches Sir John Petrie (Herbert). Cinematographer Victor Milner's camera, under Corrigan's guidance, moves fluidly with the actors, and many shots are taken from above or at an angle, which makes for some impressively arresting images. Also to the good is the film's taut screenplay: It propels the action forward with seldom a dull moment, despite its continuity problems.

That's not to say the film is perfect. Swedish-born Oland (who credited his Asian appearance to his Mongolian grandmother) has too few scenes, though the steady presence of Anna May Wong helps compensate for this. She *is* perfect, bringing just the right amount of sensuality and sympathy to the daughter of Fu Manchu. British-born Bramwell Fletcher proves a likeable hero as Ronald Petrie. Though his career lasted into the 1960s, his time as a leading man was short-lived. His most famous role, as the man who awakens Im-Ho-Tep in *The Mummy* (1932), was also one of his shortest (he appears in the film's first five minutes and is gone thereafter). His other horror appearances include turns in *Svengali* (1931), *The Monkey's Paw* (1933) and *The Undying Monster* (1942). From the early 1950s on he was relegated to television.

Daughter of the Dragon is purportedly based on Sax Rohmer's novel *The Daughter of Fu Manchu*, to which it bears little resemblance. In Rohmer's book the character is known as Fah, not Luee; she had first been introduced in the third novel in the series, *The Hand of Fu Manchu* (1917). The character proved popular and a decade later received her own story, first published in *Collier's Magazine* in March 1930. Paramount paid Rohmer $20,000 for the rights and began shooting their adaptation in early 1931. The story itself was reprinted as a stand-alone novel to take advantage of the film's release on September 5.

Paramount's film was one of their more expensive efforts of the year, but Fu Manchu's daughter didn't have the kind of drawing power displayed by her father, and the company abandoned the series altogether after this release, leaving MGM to purchase the rights to the Rohmer stories and to borrow Boris Karloff from Universal. The result was the blood-and-thunder outing *The Mask of Fu Manchu* (1932). CW

Dr. Jekyll and Mr. Hyde
Paramount; b/w; 97 (82) min; U.S.
 D/Co-P: Rouben Mamoulian *S:* Samuel Hoffenstein, Percy Heath *Co-P:* Adolph Zukor *C:* Karl Struss *M:* Herman Hand, Rudolph G. Kopp, John Leipold, Ralph Rainger
 Cast: Fredric March, Miriam Hopkins, Rose Hobart, Holmes Herbert, Halliwell Hobbes, Edgar Norton, Tempe Pigott

Dr. Henry Jekyll (March) is a brilliant and innovative young scientist. Renowned for both his razor-sharp intellect and his philanthropic work with the poor, he stirs controversy among members of his profession by suggesting that it's possible to separate the evil side of human personality from the good. Determined to prove his assertion, he drinks a potion of his own creation and is transformed into a simian-like brute that calls himself Mr. Hyde. The monster is initially interested only in stirring things up a little, but over time he becomes increasingly sadistic. He brutalizes a young prostitute named Ivy Pearson (Hopkins), who had earlier attempted to seduce Jekyll. Afterward, the remorseful Jekyll attempts to comfort Ivy by assuring her that Hyde will never return, but as time goes on, he increasingly loses control over Hyde's appearances. Hyde winds up murdering Ivy, then setting his sights on Jekyll's fiancée, Muriel Carew (Hobart).

Robert Louis Stevenson's novella *The Strange Case of Dr. Jekyll and Mr. Hyde* has inspired numerous film adaptations, but it's the 1931 version—directed by Rouben Mamoulian and with an Oscar-winning dual performance from Fredric March—that remains the most acclaimed. Born in Russian-controlled Georgia to Armenian parents, Mamoulian established himself as an accomplished stage director before coming to Paramount to direct his first feature, *Applause*, in 1929. Unlike many early film directors, Mamoulian refused to allow the clunky sound recording equipment of the time to hinder his camerawork. *Applause*

This lobby card suggests the sexual thrust of Dr. Jekyll's dual persona—Fredric March and Miriam Hopkins are depicted.

displayed real visual flair and so impressed the studio heads at Paramount that he was retained for *City Streets* (1931) and *Dr. Jekyll and Mr. Hyde.*

Mamoulian approached *Jekyll*, his sole horror credit, with panache and enthusiasm, bringing with him all the creativity he could muster. He intelligently recognized that the film was a chance to wow audiences with effects trickery, and for this he turned to acclaimed cinematographer Karl Struss. Struss had amazed moviegoers with the spectacle of the curing of the lepers in *Ben Hur* (1925), and he brought his bag of tricks to transform Jekyll into Hyde on screen. He used (as he had in *Ben Hur*) a technique involving the use of red and green lighting to bring out detail in subtly applied red and green make-up (otherwise invisible on black-and-white film). This method enabled Fredric March to appear to transform right before the filmgoers' eyes. It was a remarkable effect for 1931 and remains impressive today; Italian cinematographer-turned-director Mario Bava utilized the same technique in *I Vampiri* (1957) and *Black Sunday* (1960).

It wasn't merely the story's potential for technical trickery that appealed to Mamoulian, however. He recognized the depth and substance of the material, which the superb adaptation by screenwriters Samuel Hoffenstein (*Phantom of the Opera*, 1943) and Percy Heath mined to great effect. At its heart, of course, the story of Jekyll and Hyde is a morality play, but Mamoulian would also come to see it as somewhat predictive of the drug culture of the 1960s.

The film sometimes feels a little too theatrical and florid, but its missteps are forgivable in light of its many pleasures. March's performances as Jekyll and Hyde can't avoid comparison to those of John Barrymore in the 1920 version. (Interestingly, Paramount originally approached Barrymore for this film, hoping to recapture the success of that earlier adaptation.) And while March's portrayal of Jekyll seems perhaps a bit too mannered to contemporary audiences, his Hyde remains the standard by which all other interpretations are judged. The character is initially impish and funny, more interested in playing pranks and having a few laughs than in causing any genuine harm. But each time he emerges, he becomes more grotesque in both appearance and demeanor. He doesn't stay funny for very long.

Mamoulian has artfully suggested that this Hyde isn't so much the simplistic evil side of Jekyll as he is the manifestation of animal urges, hence his devolved appearance. As such, it makes sense that Hyde isn't bloodthirsty and sadistic from the word go; a scene where he's unleashed by the sight of a cat heartlessly slaughtering a nightingale (a long-censored sequence finally restored to the film for its original home video release) brings the point home even more forcefully.

Wally Westmore's apish make-up reportedly caused no shortage of pain and discomfort for March (who is said as a result of it to have been hospitalized for weeks after shooting wrapped), but the actor was effusive in his praise for it when he was awarded the Academy Award for Best Actor, a prize he shared with Wallace Beery for *The Champ* (1932)—a rare instance of two people winning for the same category due to a tie. There wouldn't be another Oscar-winner for acting in a horror film until Kathy Bates won for *Misery* (1990).

Director Rouben Mamoulian sits down with his two leads for a publicity-photo meal, from *Dr. Jekyll and Mr. Hyde.*

The quality of March's performance is equaled by Miriam Hopkins' heartbreaking portrayal of Ivy. She's wonderfully sexy and earthy in her early scenes—the scene in which she strips in an attempt to seduce Jekyll is one of the stand-out erotic moments in horror history—but as she falls under Hyde's domination, she becomes a tragic shell of her former self. The final showdown between Hyde and Ivy, climaxing with her demise at Hyde's brutish hands, is one of the most potent scenes in any early horror film.

The remainder of the cast may pale a bit in comparison, but Rose Hobart (*The Mad Ghoul*, 1943), Holmes Herbert (*The Thirteenth Chair*, 1929), Halliwell Hobbes (*Sherlock Holmes Faces Death*, 1943) and Edgar Norton (*Son of Frankenstein*, 1939) do fine, solid work overall.

Mamoulian took advantage of the period's lax censorship to give the film ample edge, though it ran afoul of local censors and was brutally chopped upon its re-release in the mid-1930s. Some material, such as an admittedly too-long POV shot at the beginning of the picture, was trimmed to improve the pacing, while other material (notably the risqué seduction scene and Jekyll's reaction to the nightingale's death) was removed due to the stricter Production Code sensibilities of the time.

It was the abbreviated 82-minute cut that was in circulation for many years, and the film went on to endure even further misfortune. Metro-Goldwyn-Mayer bought the rights to it in order to prevent favorable comparisons with their own 1941 adaptation (starring Spencer Tracy) and effectively buried Mamoulian's picture for over 20 years. Even when it was rescued from presumed oblivion, it returned in its emasculated version. Fortunately, it's since been restored to more or less original form (only a few minor trims remain unaccounted for) and can today be viewed in what's effectively its full-strength cut.

While Mamoulian didn't return to the genre during the remainder of his distinguished career, he and March made a definite impact with *Dr. Jekyll and Mr. Hyde*; it remains for most the definitive version of Stevenson's novella. TH

Dracula
Universal; b/w; 75 min; U.S.

D/Co-S/Co-P: Tod Browning *Co-S:* Garrett Fort, Dudley Murphy *Co-P:* Carl Laemmle, Jr. *C:* Karl Freund

Cast: Bela Lugosi, Helen Chandler, David Manners, Edward Van Sloan, Dwight Frye, Herbert Bunston, Frances Dade, Joan Standing, Charles Gerrard, Moon Carroll, Michael Visaroff, Carla Laemmle, Geraldine Dvorak, Cronelia Thaw, Dorothy Tree

Real estate agent Renfield (Frye) is dispatched to Transylvania to complete the sale of some English property to the reclusive Count Dracula (Lugosi). The Count is hospitable, if decidedly odd, and Renfield falls under his demonic spell. Together, they return to England, where Dracula works to ingratiate himself into society and spread his vampiric influence among the populace. He sets his sights on Lucy (Dade), who falls ill, then dies from his bite—though she is subsequently seen roaming the countryside at night. When Lucy's friend Mina (Chandler) exhibits some of the same symptoms as did Lucy, Professor Van Helsing (Van Sloan) is called in to investigate. He recognizes Dracula as a vampire and sets out to destroy him.

Tod Browning's *Dracula* has fallen into disrepute over the years. Granted, the film hasn't aged as well as some of the other major horror titles of the period, notably James Whale's *Frankenstein* and Rouben Mamoulian's *Dr. Jekyll and Mr. Hyde* (both 1931). Yet one can easily argue that most of those other films would never have been made if it weren't for the box-office success of Browning's film. And while *Dracula* is inarguably a deeply flawed work, contemporary viewers and critics have often, while enumerating these flaws, overlooked both its significance in the history of the genre and its artistic merits.

Lest we forget: *Dracula* was the first unambiguously supernatural-themed horror film to be made in the United States. A look at fright fare from the silent era reveals that while European filmmakers like Paul Wegener (*The Golem: How He Came Into the World*, 1920) and F.W. Murnau (*Nosferatu*, 1922) had no qualms in explicitly dramatizing the unearthly in their films, American filmmakers had proven reluctant to do so; American horror films of the period were mostly either melodramas (*Phantom of the Opera*, 1925) or mysteries where apparently supernatural plot elements turned out to be not so fantastic after all (Browning's own *London After Midnight*, 1927). It was, for the time, a rather original and daring move to bring *Dracula* to American screens at all.

The project did not originate with Browning and producer Carl Laemmle, Jr. though; it was producer Paul Kohner who first saw the story's potential and convinced Universal president Carl Laemmle, Sr. to purchase the rights. Kohner saw the film as an ideal vehicle to reunite director Paul Leni and star Conrad Veidt, who had formerly collaborated on the Universal "super jewel" production *The Man Who Laughs* (1928). But when Leni passed away in 1929 and Veidt, self-conscious about his accent in the new age of sound cinema, returned to Germany, Laemmle settled on Lon Chaney as a suitable replacement. Unfortunately, the silent screen megastar died of cancer in 1930. It's widely held that Chaney at the time of his death had already signed a contract for and was set to play the part, but there's no real evidence to support such a claim. He was, when he died, under contract at Metro-Goldwyn-Mayer, and though possible, it seems unlikely that MGM would have loaned him out to a competing studio for a property that, as it happened, they had once half-heartedly attempted to secure for themselves. Bela Lugosi (who had already established a reputation in the United States playing *Dracula* on Broadway) was ultimately and famously given the role. The rest, as they say, is history.

Kohner's role in the creation of the film was abruptly minimized when Laemmle handed over control of Universal to his son as a 21st birthday present. Fortunately for eight decades of horror enthusiasts, Junior Laemmle was also drawn to the macabre, and he too believed in the project. When the dust finally settled, Kohner wound up with supervising duties for the alternate Spanish language version of the film.

Browning was brought on board to direct the American version due to his experience with horrific subject matter, yet the film's uneven quality has dogged the director's reputation for years. The fact that the film is not as strong as one might wish is not entirely Browning's fault, however. Part of the problem stems from a budget that was slashed from an ambitious "super jewel" prestige picture to a still A-level but smaller work. There's also evidence that the studio rushed the production, and Browning later maintained that control of the picture had been wrested from him during the editing process.

However disputable any of this may be, the existence of the film's hopelessly stagebound feel is not. Pulitzer Prize-winning author Louis Bromfield's initial and ambitious script was nixed in favor of a scaled-down approach, closer to the popular stage play by Hamilton Deane and John L. Balderston. The result reeks of generic drawing-room melodrama, with the limitations that the stiff material placed on Browning very apparent.

This isn't to say that the film is without charm. Most of the best stuff is at the beginning, however. Browning's staging in the opening half hour is crisp and efficient, with some impressive, stylistic flourishes—notably, the moody dolly shot that introduces Dracula in the castle's crypt and the crane shot that introduces the sanitarium where Renfield is imprisoned.

Bela Lugosi strikes a menacing pose as Count Dracula, threatening Lucy (Frances Dade), from *Dracula*.

This publicity photo from Universal stresses the seductive chills of its "macabre love story," featuring Lugosi and Helen Chandler.

After that, however, the pace slows considerably as *Dracula* settles into what is largely a series of filmed conversations; characters stand around talking about things that would have been much more interesting had they been visualized, and as they do so a fog of ennui rolls in. But though it's easy to blame Browning for not doing much with the material, in fairness to the director, one must note the Spanish version suffers from the same problem, despite its oft-proclaimed stylishness.

Bela Lugosi (1882-1956) remains the popular idea of how Dracula should be portrayed on screen. Later performances by everybody from Christopher Lee to Gary Oldman have their various merits, but it is Lugosi's interpretation that has embedded its way into popular culture. Lugosi brings a dark, wry humor to the character, the charmer who's clearly up to no good, and his otherworldly aura and deliberate delivery set the tone for the picture.

Lugosi campaigned hard for the role; too hard, in fact. Universal realized he was desperate to play the part at any price, and they took full advantage of that fact, hiring him for an insulting wage (reportedly $500 a week, which, even in 1931, was pathetic for the leading role in a major production, especially when one realizes that bland juvenile supporting actor David Manners took home considerably more). And while the film made Lugosi a star, it was also pretty much the peak of his career, with subsequent typecasting as vampire-like characters in embarrassing Z-grade horror films later taking him to pitiable depths unworthy of his talents.

The film offers additional standout performances, including Dwight Frye's as Renfield and Edward Van Sloan's as Van Helsing. Van Sloan seems a bit stodgy here compared to his other Universal performances of the period (including the film's first sequel, *Dracula's Daughter*, 1936), but he did establish a template for other actors to follow in playing the character. As far as Frye is concerned, he proved so convincing as the deranged fly-eating madman that he, too, found himself stereotyped for the remainder of his life, which was tragically cut short by a sudden heart attack in 1943.

Ultimately, regardless of its merits, the film paid off at the box-office. And this is no minor point; it was the film's tremendous financial success that encouraged Universal to follow it up with *Frankenstein* and scores of other horror films, many of which have become classics in their own right. *Dracula* may not be the most accomplished work of its director, nor the most compelling film in the first wave of Universal horror films, but it's still a watershed work that commands respect. TH

Drácula
aka **Dracula**; **Spanish Dracula**; **Dracula—The Spanish Version**; **The Spanish Version of Dracula**
Universal; b/w; 104 min; U.S.

D: George Melford *S:* Baltasar Fernández Cué *P:* Paul Kohner, Carl Laemmle Jr. *C:* George Robinson

Cast: Carlos Villarias, Lupita Tovar, Barry Norton, Pablo Alvarez Rubio, Eduardo Arozamena, José Soriano Viosca, Carmen Guerrero, Amelia Senisterra, Manuel Arbó

English solicitor Renfield (Rubio) travels to Transylvania to oversee the sale of some British real estate to Condé Drácula (Villarias), unaware that el Condé is a vampire. Once business is concluded, Drácula takes his casket of damp earth and travels to England, accompanied by the now-insane Renfield, who wants little more than to eat bugs and serve his new master. In London Drácula attends the opera, where he meets Dr. Seward (Viosca), the doctor's lovely daughter Eva (Tovar) and family friend Lucia (Guerrero). After victimizing Lucia, el Condé turns his bloodthirsty attentions to the beautiful Eva, but her lover Juan Harker (Norton) stands in the way. Thankfully, a guest in the Seward house, Professor Van Helsing (Arozamena), recognizes Drácula for the vampire he is.

During the silent era, the production of alternate-language versions of films was a straightforward process: Studios simply

An original lobby card for Universal's Spanish-language version of *Dracula,* featuring Carlos Villarias as Count Dracula (center)

Horror Films of the 1930s

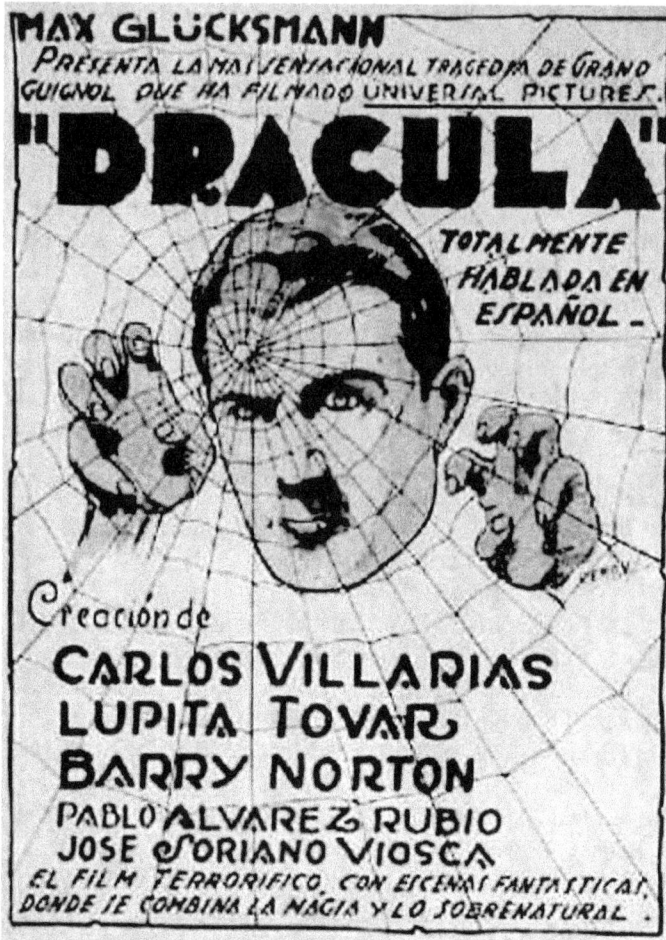

Spanish language newspaper ad for Universal's alternate version of *Dracula*, aimed at the Mexican market

replaced the language in the original title cards with the language of the area in which the film was playing. With the advent of sound in the late 1920s, however, this uncomplicated process was obviously no longer feasible. Studios were left to ponder just how to market their films in foreign-language territories, and they quickly hit upon the idea of shooting pictures in various-language versions simultaneously, utilizing a different cast of actors fluent in the desired second language. Such efforts included *Anna Christie* (1930) and *The Testament of Dr. Mabuse* (1933), among others.

Universal, at the time primarily a producer of B-films, was one of the first studios to apply this newfound strategy. They knew that Spanish speakers made up a large portion of the populace in the Southwestern United States, as well as in Central and South America and, of course, Spain. In 1930 they produced *East Is West* and *The Cat Creeps*, among others, in both English and Spanish, and the following year, at the same time as Tod Browning's famed *Dracula*, they shot *Drácula*, probably the most famous example of a 1930s alternative-language film.

Not long after purchasing the rights to Bram Stoker's novel *Dracula* (as well as its stage adaptation by John L. Balderston and Hamilton Deane), Carl Laemmle, Sr. decided—at the insistence of producer Paul Kohner—that the property was a good fit for a dual Spanish-English treatment. Czech-born Kohner was originally slated to produce both films, but once Carl Laemmle, Sr. gifted the studio to his son Carl Laemmle, Jr., Kohner was relegated to the Spanish-language version alone. This second version was to be shot on the same sets as the English-language version, but at night, after the cast and crew of the primary *Dracula* had gone home for the evening.

Affronted by his demotion, Kohner and director George Melford encouraged their crew to examine the dailies from the daytime shoots in an effort to top them with more atmospheric angles and shots. They were helped in this regard by superlative cinematographer George Robinson, who had been in the business since at least 1921 and would go on to shoot some of the most classic films in Universal's horror arsenal. Of the film's performers, only lead Carlos Villarias was allowed to view the other in-progress production, the better to imitate Bela Lugosi's mannerisms so viewers wouldn't notice when inserts from the Browning film were used for shots too complicated or expensive to be done twice. (It didn't work; Villarias was unable to match Lugosi's seminal style, and the footage with Lugosi remains glaringly obvious.) The rushes were not allowed to be seen by the rest of the cast as part of an effort to encourage them to give more sensual performances than their English-language counterparts. (According to an interview with lead actress Lupita Tovar, Spanish-speaking nations were less repressive about sexuality than the United States, and Kohner and Melford understood they would be able to get away with amping up the sexuality in the Spanish-language film.)

Unable to speak Spanish, Melford was forced to use an interpreter, Enrique Tovar Avalos, as his intermediary with the Latin cast (the crew was made up mostly of English speakers). Despite this obstacle, he developed a close relationship with his actors. It shows! The ensemble acting is more cohesive in *Drácula* than in *Dracula*, helping the Spanish version to develop a reputation as the better of the two films, with its director seeking to imbue its every moment with a uniquely eerie mood distinct from the stage-bound play on which it was based. Its biggest single downside, when compared to Browning's film, is that Villarias, while effective, is no Lugosi. (Nor was Pablo Alvarez Rubio an entirely effective replacement for Dwight Frye, though Lupita Tovar, who had starred in the Spanish version of *The Cat Creeps* the year before, was the perfect replacement for Helen Chandler.)

There are numerous, additional minor differences between the two versions. Aside from the Spanish version's more explicit sexuality (the women swoon passionately in the presence of Drácula, and they wear lower-cut dresses), the vampiric attacks are also more brutal. When Renfield cuts his finger with a knife, there is a copious amount of blood for a film of the period; and when he collapses after drinking drugged wine, it is Drácula's three brides—not el Condé himself—who fall upon him like beasts of prey. Later, when Drácula strangles Renfield and throws him over a stairwell, the act is fairly extensive in comparison to the same one in Browning's film, and there is a loud thud as Renfield's body hits the stone floor below. And when Drácula is finally staked through his Spanish … er, Hungarian heart, he does not, as does Lugosi in some prints of Browning's film, go silently; his anguished cries die down to a long, low moan before ending altogether.

Other relatively small changes act cumulatively to have a positive effect on the film. Whenever Drácula's casket is opened,

Carlos Villarias (with Lupita Tovar) made a less-than-convincing replacement for Bela Lugosi in the 1931 Spanish-language version of *Dracula*.

it invariably releases a mist that prefigures the appearance of el Condé. While en route to England, neither film hesitates to imply that Drácula feeds upon the life-blood of the ship's crew; but while the English-language version merely shows us the aftermath, the Spanish version has Drácula's hand reaching out from his coffin, then cuts to the terrified faces of his victims and then finally back to el Condé's leering countenance as he rises from his makeshift grave, the maniacal Renfield laughing insanely as he watches. Even today, the scene sends a shiver up one's spine.

Yet some of what makes Tod Browning's film so often fall flat does the same thing here: too much time is spent on conversation or with characters walking in and out of the same few rooms. And because it's so much longer, the draggy aspects of the Spanish version are felt even more acutely. To his credit, Melford at least attempts to liven up such scenes. For instance, when Van Helsing thrusts his mirror into Drácula's face, el Condé, rather than slapping the object away with his hand, smashes it with his cane. Other minor touches, such as camera angles or the way characters stand in relation to each other, frequently frame the action in such a way as to pronounce it rather than, as in Browning's version, to downplay it.

There is, incidentally, a wonderful touch as fledgling vampire Lucia is destroyed off screen; a scream is heard, and a large bird flies from its roost above the cemetery gates, after which Van Helsing and Harker exit. This cuts to a terrific shot of Carfax Abby, perched upon a cliff overlooking the ocean, which in turn serves as a transition to a shot of Drácula carrying Eva's inert body.

The Spanish version of *Dracula* proved a hit in Latin markets and influenced a whole generation of future Hispanic filmmakers to make their own horror films beginning in the late 1950s. Despite this, it was for decades considered a lost film. By the late 1980s most of its reels had been found, but it wasn't until film historian David J. Skal came upon the final, missing reel in Cuba that the complete film was finally restored.

Though the experience of filming *Drácula* was a resentful one for producer Kohner, he was able to claim one major triumph as a result: He fell in love with Lupita Tovar, and less than two years after the film was completed, the two were married. They remained so until his death in 1988. CW

The Drums of Jeopardy
aka **Drums of Jeopardy; Mark of Terror**
Tiffany; b/w; 66 (75) min; U.S.

D: George B. Seitz *S:* Florence Ryerson *P:* Phil Goldstone *C:* Arthur Reed *M:* Val Burton

Cast: Warner Oland, June Collyer, Lloyd Hughes, Clara Blandick, Hale Hamilton, Wallace MacDonald, George Fawcett, Florence Lake, Mischa Auer, Ernest Hilliard

The Drums of Jeopardy is the name of a valuable, rubied necklace because of its small, carved figures of natives holding drums. The treasure belongs to the Royal Petrov Family of Russia, a member of whom gives it to the beautiful Anya (Lake), while the two are having an affair. Later, when her lover rejects her and she kills herself, Anya's father, mad scientist Boris Karlov (Oland), vows revenge. During the Russian Revolution he becomes a Bolshevik leader, sending the Petrovs fleeing to the United States, but Karlov intercepts a correspondence stating their whereabouts. He follows them with vengeance on his mind.

The first half of *The Drums of Jeopardy* has action to spare, taking place in a number of interesting locations (a luxurious Russian estate, a ship bound for America, a New York City apartment). The film sags somewhat after that, however, as the setting changes to a large country estate. There, Karlov eliminates the Petrov family one by one, signaling each death with a piece of the eponymous necklace.

That's not to say some wonderfully morbid moments don't exist in the second half. There's a particularly masterful scene in which Prince Gregor (MacDonald) is thrown into a cellar and exposed to poison, with the camera focused on Karlov's face as he listens to the guttural screams from below. And the climax, in which Karlov tries to coerce Prince Nicholas (Hughes) into murdering the woman (Collyer) he loves, is taut, due largely to a script that successfully creates three-dimensional characters.

Based on the novel of the same name by Harold MacGrath, this 1931 adaptation of *The Drums of Jeopardy* was something of an upgrade from the typical Tiffany fare. A decent budget and superior art direction (the interiors are larger and more lavish than usual for the studio, while the windswept exteriors conjure a fair degree of creepiness) contribute to an opulent look. Of particular note visually is the dilapidated barn in which Karlov executes much of his horrible revenge.

Though George B. Seitz's direction, as noted above, loses steam during the second half of the picture, the performances remain strong throughout, particularly that of Warner Oland as mad scientist Boris Karlov. Less hammy than usual, Oland likely underplayed the part in an effort to differentiate the Karlov character from the actor's earlier Fu Manchu portrayals, which were no doubt thoroughly familiar to 1930s audiences.

That Oland's character's name here is so similar to horror icon Boris Karloff's is probably no coincidence; Karlov was introduced in MacGrath's 1920 novel, which became an immediate sensation and was adapted to Broadway not long thereafter. (The first film adaptation had come in 1923.) It's believed by some historians that a young and still-unknown William Henry Pratt took his screen name from the MacGrath character. CW

Frankenstein
Universal; b/w; 71 min; U.S

D: James Whale *S:* Garrett Fort, Francis Edwards Farragoh, John L. Balderston, Robert Florey, John Russell, John Huston *P:* Carl Laemmle, Jr. *C:* Arthur Edeson *M:* Giuseppe Becce, Bernhard Kaun *FX:* John P. Fulton

Cast: Colin Clive, Boris Karloff, Mae Clark, John Boles, Edward Van Sloan, Frederick Kerr, Dwight Frye, Michael Mark, Marilyn Harris, Lionel Belmore, Francis Ford

Henry Frankenstein (Clive) creates a human being by stitching together parts from dead bodies. The result (Karloff) is initially docile but exhibits murderous tendencies when provoked. Devastated by his perceived failure, Frankenstein attempts to redeem himself by destroying the monster, but it escapes and goes on a rampage.

Of all the adaptations of Mary Shelley's immortal novel *Frankenstein, or The Modern Prometheus* (1818), Universal's 1931 production remains the most iconic. British actor/director James Whale (1889-1957), riding the success of his theater triumph *Journey's End* (which he filmed in 1930), had his sights set on Hollywood success. Universal president Carl Laemmle, Jr., the eccentric Briton's biggest fan, signed Whale to a lucrative contract that, along with providing A-level budgets, gave the director the creative freedom he craved.

Waterloo Bridge (1931), a pre-Code exploration of prostitution in war-torn England, marked Whale's debut at Universal. It was a hit with both critics and audiences, and Whale was given the pick of his next project. A production of *Frankenstein* was on the schedule, and the director couldn't resist throwing his hat into the ring for it. The only problem was that it was entrusted to French émigré Robert Florey (1900-1979), who had already developed a treatment and had his eye on Bela Lugosi (hot off the success of *Dracula*, 1931) to play the pivotal role of the creature. Whale was none too concerned about any of this, however, and made it known to Laemmle that *Frankenstein* was his picture of choice. Florey was duly booted from the project—he was assigned another lower-budgeted horror, *Murders in the Rue Morgue* (1931), as a consolation prize—and Whale began work on a masterpiece.

Abandoning most of Florey's treatment, Whale worked with screenwriters Garrett Fort and Francis Edwards Farragoh to give the project his own personal stamp. The end result retained a handful of plot points from Florey's treatment, most notably the idea of the monster's anti-social tendencies arising from its criminal brain. Shelley's novel was more or less ignored, owing to the fact that much of John L. Balderston's original adaptation had derived not from the book but from the stage play by Peggy Webling.

Yet, whereas Tod Browning's *Dracula* signals its stage roots at every turn, the same cannot be said of *Frankenstein*. A look at Whale's earlier credits, in fact, reveals his steady growth as a stylist. The spare, stagy approach of *Journey's End* actually enhances its dramatic potency, but as filmmaking goes, it's

Creator (Colin Clive) and creation (Boris Karloff) meet in a tense sequence from director James Whale's masterful *Frankenstein*.

crudely functional at best. Following some uncredited work on *Hell's Angels* (1930) for Howard Hughes—it was Whale who handled the dramatic scenes, leaving Hughes free to obsess over the aerial battles—the director brought a more assured hand to the gritty *Waterloo Bridge*. *Frankenstein* exemplifies his rapid growth as an artist, an evolution that would culminate in *The Bride of Frankenstein* (1935) and *Showboat* (1936), proving Whale arguably the flashiest and most cinematic director in 1930s Hollywood.

He studied a number of Expressionist horror films from Germany—notably *The Golem: How He Came into the World* (1920) and *The Cabinet of Dr. Caligari* (1919)—in preparation for *Frankenstein*, and their influence can be seen throughout. The stylized settings, extreme visual contrasts and poetic imagery help transform Whale's film into one of the most stark and beautiful to be found anywhere in the horror genre. While there is a regrettable gaffe here and there—a few wrinkled backdrops, a pitiful dummy standing in for Colin Clive when he is thrown from the burning mill and a surprisingly sloppy moment wherein the sheet covering the reclining monster reveals that Karloff is wearing a pair of patent leather dress shoes—they are rendered irrelevant by the film's overall texture and quality.

Whale assembled an eclectic cast for the picture. Universal had wanted Leslie Howard as Henry Frankenstein and Bette Davis as his bride-to-be Elizabeth, but Whale had other ideas. He saw Frankenstein as an ideal fit for his friend and colleague Colin Clive, who had already scored a major triumph on both stage and screen as the neurotic, alcoholic Captain Stanhope in *Journey's End*. Whale also thought the role of Elizabeth better suited for Mae Clark, who had already impressed him in *Waterloo Bridge* (which, incidentally, featured Bette Davis in a minor role). Contemporary critics tend to chide Clive for being over the top, but doing so shows a degree of inattentiveness. Far from the hammy performance derided by detractors, Clive's is a sensitive accomplishment capturing both the character's overreaching ambition and eventual feelings of contrition. Clark's performance is less successful overall, though she is at times quietly effective.

The character of Victor Moritz, Frankenstein's friend and apparent romantic rival for Elizabeth's affections, was entrusted to silent superstar John Boles (*The Last Warning*, 1929). It's a middling part, but Boles does competently by it. Having already played Professor Van Helsing in *Dracula*, Edward Van Sloan was a logical choice to fill the role of Frankenstein's former instructor, the stern Professor Waldman. Comedic relief (of the blessedly low-key variety) is provided by Frederick Kerr as Frankenstein's wheezing and cantankerous father and Dwight Frye, another *Dracula* alum, who brings a darker strain of humor to his role as the sadistic hunchback Fritz.

Then there's the monster himself. There's much Hollywood lore surrounding the casting of Boris Karloff, but most of it doesn't stand up to close inspection. Taking events in chronological order, the fact that Bela Lugosi was originally approached to play the role is well known. Lugosi always maintained that he had turned the part down, thus opening the door for Karloff to come in (and swiftly eclipse Lugosi's popularity at the box-office). While this story offers an appealing mix of irony and romanticism, it doesn't appear to be entirely true. In point of fact, Whale did not approach Lugosi for the role that Karloff inherited. During Lugosi's involvement, Robert Florey was still running the show, and Florey's monster was to be just that: a monster, with empathy-eliciting mannerisms in short supply.

While Lugosi's version of events would have us believe that he felt himself too good for the role, it conjures up an even more unlikely image—that of Lugosi rejecting a role … any role! Even as he continued to ride on the success of *Dracula*, the proud Hungarian appeared in many a bargain-basement cheapie. Lugosi often carped that he didn't *want Frankenstein* because it required him to bury his handsome features beneath mounds of make-up; while vanity may have been on his mind, this doesn't explain why he took the considerably less showy role of the Sayer of the Law in Paramount's *Island of Lost Souls* (1932), which also required him to be unrecognizable beneath shaggy make-up. There's little doubt that Lugosi regretted not being in *Frankenstein*, but it seems likely that pride compelled him to make excuses sooner than admit a more likely reality: James Whale probably simply didn't want him in the film. Whale was aware of the success of *Dracula*, of course, and simply may have been unimpressed by it, an idea that would indicate he didn't feel any apparent need to ride on its coattails.

According to Whale himself, he wanted an unknown for the part—and 43-year-old bit player Boris Karloff fit the bill perfectly. Karloff had been struggling to make a name for himself as an actor, undertaking a variety of odd jobs (including driving a truck and performing other manual labors) to make ends meet. Just how he came to Whale's attention is as shrouded in mystery as Lugosi's exit from the picture; Karloff always maintained that Whale spotted him in the studio cafeteria (at the time he was shooting the gangster film *Graft*, 1931, for Universal), while others have suggested that Whale was impressed by his performance as a murderous convict in Howard Hawks' *The Criminal*

The title lobby card from *Frankenstein* focuses on Frankenstein's Monster rather than the scientist who created him.

Code (1930). In any event, it was a match made in movie heaven, and the role ultimately catapulted the actor to superstardom.

Despite heavy make-up and a lack of dialogue, Karloff delivers the nuanced performance that a Florey/Lugosi collaboration would have eschewed. Far from being the unfeeling brute of Florey's conception, Karloff—with Whale's guidance and approval—transformed the character into a lost child looking for parental acceptance. The monster's hideous looks brand him as something other than human and cause people to reject him on sight. (Whale exercised one instance of poor judgment in retaining the "criminal brain" angle of Florey's script, since the suggestion that the monster turns violent due to being treated poorly by the people around him was more than sufficient motivation for his rage.)

The hardworking Karloff certainly earned his paycheck on the film. The lead-based make-up and heavy costume—coupled with shooting in the midst of a sweltering summer and being required to do virtually all his own stunt work—took its toll on the actor, who suffered through it like a trooper. He never forgot the impact the character had on his career. And far from resenting the typecasting it later caused, he would refer to the monster as "my best friend."

It's easy to forget that audiences of 1931 were shocked by the brilliant make-up design of Jack P. Pierce (with the input of Whale, a trained commercial artist in his own right). The flat-topped visage, complemented by sunken cheeks and protruding electrodes, is so familiar today that even children who've never seen the film—let alone heard of Boris Karloff—can readily identify it. It's a remarkable effort, and the reason it works as well as it does is because it was designed for Karloff's gaunt physique; later, bigger-cheeked actors like Lon Chaney, Jr. and Bela Lugosi had a more difficult time pulling it off because they're facial structures were so completely different from Karloff's. Even Karloff never looked quite as impressive in the two sequels in which he appeared, *The Bride of Frankenstein* and *Son of Frankenstein* (1939); once his features began to fill out a bit, something of the haunting simplicity of his initial appearance was sacrificed.

Horror Films of the 1930s 29

Karloff brought pathos to his role as the sometimes benevolent, sometimes malevolent monster in *Frankenstein*.

That the film was subjected to censorship, some of it on its initial release, the rest upon its re-release in 1937, is well known. Clive's almost orgasmic exclamation, "Now I know what it feels like to be God!," the monster tossing a little girl (Marilyn Harris in an affecting performance) into a lake and various close-ups of the monster being tortured by Fritz were all cut; fortunately, these trims have since been reinstated in contemporary restorations of the film.

Laemmle's faith in Whale's abilities was, in the end, amply rewarded. *Frankenstein* proved to be a huge hit at the box-office, and many critics of the time were impressed. Whereas *Dracula*'s flaws have become more evident with the passing of time, *Frankenstein* still feels fresh and vibrant. It is not a perfect film—and Whale would soon outdo it—but it remains the definitive film version of Mary Shelley's tale, while, ironically, bearing little literal resemblance to it. TH

The Ghost Train
Gainsborough; b/w; 85 (72) min; Great Britain
 D: Walter Forde *S:* Lajos Biro, Sidney Gilliat, Angus MacPhail *P:* Michael Balcon, Phil C. Samuel *C:* Leslie Rowson
 Cast: Jack Hulbert, Cicely Courtneidge, Ann Todd, Cyril Raymond, Allan Jeayes, Donald Calthrop, Angela Baddeley, Henry Caine, Tracy Holmes, Carol Coombe

As passengers wait in a railway station for their train's departure, an old stationmaster attempts to make them leave by regaling them with local legends about the station being haunted. It turns out that the place is a front for a smuggling operation.

Arnold Ridley's play *The Ghost Train* made its debut on British radio in 1923 and proved popular enough to spawn several film adaptations. The first emerged in 1927 as a co-production between German and British companies. Michael Balcon was one of its producers, and he was also behind this, the first talkie adaptation, which is now considered lost.

The cast includes Jack Hulbert and his real-life spouse, Cicely Courtneidge. Hulbert's film career was spotty, but he was also a popular dancer for a time and joked in his later years that his career was murdered by the arrival of Fred Astaire. Courtneidge was better known for her stage work, which ultimately netted her the title Dame Commander of the Order of the British Empire. In 1966, she put in a memorable cameo in the all-star, horror-tinged farce *The Wrong Box* (1966). Sultry Ann Todd made one of her first screen appearances here as well; she went on to a lengthy film career and is best known today for her appearance in the 1945 classic, *The Seventh Veil*.

The screenplay for this particular adaptation of *The Ghost Train* passed through the hands of at least two writers who later worked with Alfred Hitchcock: Sidney Gilliat (*The Lady Vanishes*, 1938) and Angus MacPhail (*Spellbound*, 1945).

Two other adaptations of Ridley's play, both titled *The Ghost Train*, appeared in 1933. TH

The House of Unrest
aka **House of Unrest**
Associated Picture; b/w; 58 min; Great Britain
 D/S: Leslie Howard Gordon *P:* Seymour Hill *C:* Desmond Dickinson
 Cast: Dorothy Boyd, Malcolm Keen, Tom Helmore, Leslie Perrins, Hubert Carter, Mary Mayfren

A mansion on a Scottish island is the setting for this morbid mystery. A group of people gathers there, only to be killed off one-by-one by a mysterious killer seeking a valuable diamond.

Leslie Howard Gordon originally wrote *The House of Unrest* for the stage. It met with some success, which inspired him to adapt it to the big screen. A fairly routine piece, it was Gordon's first film as director. He directed only two more features in its wake.

Among the cast, the best-known performer is probably Tom Helmore, remembered today as the smooth-talking Gavin Elster in Alfred Hitchcock's masterpiece *Vertigo* (1958*). Unrest* was one of Helmore's earliest credits; he finished out a long and distinguished career with an appearance on Rod Serling's NBC-TV series *Night Gallery* in 1972. He passed away in 1995.

Leading man Malcolm Keen had previously played a detective in Hitchcock's *The Lodger: A Story of the London Fog* (1927). He was more active on stage than on screen. His son Geoffrey Keen went on to become a respected character actor in his own right, racking up the occasional horror and fantasy credit, including *Taste the Blood of Dracula* (1970) and *Holocaust 2000* (1977). TH

Immediate Possession
Starcraft; b/w; 42 min; Great Britain
 D: Arthur Varney-Serrao *S:* Brock Williams *P:* Harry Cohen
 Cast: Herbert Mundin, Dorothy Bartlam, Leslie Perrins, George Bellamy, Merle Tottenham, Joan Matheson

This rather short British comedy was an original take on the "old dark house" motif so prevalent during silent and early sound cinema. A real estate agent (Mundin) is assigned such a house to sell—and he has only 24 hours to do it. Unfortunately, the house is haunted, a fact that's impossible to hide from would-be buyers.

Released in February of 1931, around the same time as Universal's successful horror romance *Dracula* (which debuted on

Valentine's Day), *Immediate Possession* foreshadowed the spate of horror films kicked off by *Dracula* and James Whale's *Frankenstein* (1931).

The film appears to have been the only one from director Arthur Varney-Serrao (often listed simply as Arthur Varney) containing any degree of horror, muted as it was. Varney's career was relatively short and undistinguished; in fact, he may be more famous for his off-screen romancing of Canadian-born filmmaker Nell Shipman, who not only acted during the silent era, but also wrote, produced, directed and edited, a rarity for a woman of the period. CW

Law of the Tong

Kent; b/w; 54 (52, 56) min; U.S.

D: Lew (Lewis D.) Collins *S:* Oliver Drake *P:* Willis Kent *C:* William Nobles

Cast: Phyllis Barrington, John Harron, Jason Robards, Dot Farley, Mary Carr, Frank Lackteen, William Malan, Richard Alexander

This is an ugly picture. Though it makes the odd stab at humanizing some of its Chinese characters, it portrays the remainder as mostly degenerate killers. The action centers on pretty Joan (Barrington), who works in a dance hall-cum-brothel along San Francisco's waterfront. When drunken sailors threaten her, Denny (Harron) comes to the rescue and advises her to switch to a more respectable line of work. Shortly thereafter, she turns down a "dance" from a client, and the ensuing argument with her madam (Farley) results in Joan taking leave of her job. Now aimlessly unemployed, she wanders the streets of Chinatown, where she encounters a Western-garbed Chinaman named Charlie Wong (Robards). As they speak, unseen gunmen in a passing vehicle fire at him; he saves both himself and her before taking her back to his home for her continued safety. There, he confesses to Joan that he's a member of a Tong (a violent Chinese gang) that's smuggling illegal immigrants into the country. He also introduces her to other members of his gang, one of whom develops a crush on her, leading to a violent confrontation between Wong and him. Joan gets a new job at a local soup kitchen and again runs into Denny, whom she now learns is an undercover agent out to get the goods on her savior. In due course, Denny is captured by the Tong and sentenced to death. Joan pleads with Wong for Denny's life, police show up, and a rival Tong member stabs Wong. As he dies, his last act is to save Denny and Joan.

Despite the ever-threatening presence of the Tong, whose members skulk in the shadows throughout, watching unobserved, *Law of the Tong* is more interested in romantic exploits than in the story's horror potential. The film suffers further from uniformly bad performances, flat direction and camerawork and a meandering script that lengthens the film's short running time to no good end.

British horror-company Hammer tackled Chinese Tongs to greater success in 1960's *Terror of the Tongs*. CW

The Limping Man
aka Creeping Shadows

British International; b/w; 79 min; Great Britain

D/P: John Orton *S:* John Orton *M:* Colin Wark

Cast: Franklin Dyall, Arthur Hardy, Margot Grahame, Lester Matthews, Jeanne Stuart, Gerald Rawlinson, David Haw-

Fritz Lang's *M* presents a starkly realistic child murderer (Peter Lorre) who suffers from schizophrenia.

thorne, Charles Farrell, Henrietta Watson, Matthew Boulton, Percy Parsons

Disher (Dyall) moves into the estate he has inherited, but life there is anything but idyllic. Three ex-cons on whom Disher once informed terrorize him mercilessly. Threatening phone calls and various other happenings begin to drive the man insane, so he enlists a detective (Hardy) to investigate.

John Orton (sometimes billed as J.O.C. Orton) adapted this thriller from a stage play by Will Scott. It offers clichéd thrills and chills as its hapless protagonist is driven to the brink of insanity. Such "old dark house" thrillers were very common in the 1920s and 1930s (and beyond), reaching their apex with expatriate British filmmaker James Whale's masterful *The Old Dark House* (1932).

Franklin Dyall worked sporadically in films, but he was more comfortable on the stage. He was the father of the gaunt, sinister-voiced character actor Valentine Dyall, best remembered for a key supporting-role in *Horror Hotel* (1960). Lester Matthews was at the start of his long career in film and television when he starred in *The Limping Man*; he later relocated to the United States and appeared in such Universal horror movies as *The Raven* and *Werewolf of London* (both 1935) and *The Invisible Man's Revenge* (1944).

The Limping Man was filmed again by Cy Endfield in 1953. TH

M
aka Murderers Among Us; M—Eine Stadt sucht einen Mörder

Nero; b/w; 110 min; Germany

D/Co-S: Fritz Lang *Co-S:* Thea von Harbou *P:* Seymour Nebenzal *C:* Fritz Arno Wagner

Cast: Peter Lorre, Otto Wernicke, Gustaf Grundgens, Theodor Loos, Ellen Widmann, Friedrich Gnass, Fritz Odemar, Paul Kemp, Theo Lingen, Rudolf Blumner, Georg John, Franz Stein, Ernst Stahl-Nachbauer, Gerhard Bienert

Berlin is shocked by a series of gruesome child murders. The police search in vain for the killer, while the criminal underworld, unhappy with having its activities interrupted by the

Peter Lorre as the pedophile marked with the letter "M" for murderer, from *M*

manhunt, launches its own investigation. Unknown to anyone, the killer is Hans Beckert (Lorre), a lonely deviant acting on a psychotic compulsion he is powerless to control.

Like many silent-era pioneers, Fritz Lang was reluctant to make the leap to sound. His apprehension had an understandable basis—filmmakers the world over (and particularly in Germany) had spent the 1920s mastering the visual mechanics of cinematic storytelling, and the addition of sound, by complicating the product, created a potential for artistic regression. But while Lang's prediction proved accurate in many instances, he nonetheless made a smooth transition to the new technology. *M* marked his talkie debut, and his use of sound here is as imaginative as his geometrical sense of framing and camera movement.

The screenplay, by Lang and his wife/collaborator Thea von Harbou, draws inspiration from real-life murderer Peter Kurten, the so-called "Vampire of Dusseldorf." From February 1929 to March 1930, Kurten terrorized and at times murdered a variety of victims, only some of them children. The police had no luck in catching him until a young woman he'd raped led authorities to his apartment. Interviews with a police psychologist revealed Kurten to be a sexual deviant who derived sexual pleasure from his monstrous acts (one of his victims was stabbed 20 times simply because Kurten was having a difficult time reaching an orgasm). Kurten was put on trial in May 1931, and the German public breathed a sigh of relief when he was guillotined on July 2 of that same year. His exploits were recounted in *The Sadist*, a true-crime account by Dr. Karl Berg, first published in 1932, but the news-conscious Lang had his fictionalized account completed and in theaters well before then. *M* (production title: *Murderers Among Us*) was released on May 11, 1931 while the Kurten trial was still underway.

In many respects, *M* is a tricky film to pigeonhole. It's undeniably one of the earliest examples of the serial killer subgenre. It's also a thriller, a melodrama and something of a pseudo-documentary. Lang's filmmaking obsessiveness manifests in his detailed exploration of police techniques; time and time again, he spells out the minutiae of their investigation, revealing a keen interest in the particulars of their investigative techniques.

The director's use of moody *mis-en-scene* also pushes the film into proto-film noir terrain, though the noir subgenre had yet to fully form. He also makes excellent use of crosscutting to keep the story flowing. The film never remains in one plot strand long enough to get bogged down; it moves back and forth between the two major strands of the narrative (that of the police's investigation and that of the criminals'), while providing discreet glimpses of and insight into Beckert and his activities.

Throughout his career, Fritz Lang remained fixated on the concept of fate. *M*'s Hans Beckert is presented as a fundamentally decent man who cannot escape his psychosis. Lang presents the character sympathetically, and his film clearly condemns the idea of capital punishment. There's no doubt that Lang was appalled by the eventual execution of Kurten, though recognizing that the deranged killer was a menace to society who needed to be confined where he could do no further harm.

Peter Lorre (1904-1964) makes his film debut in the lead role, remaining one of the most impressive acting debuts on record. The actor is said to have clashed with the authoritarian Lang (seldom on good terms with his actors), yet the director later claimed to be in awe of the young man's talent, reportedly expressing regret that this film was their only collaboration.

The abbreviation of the title from *Murderers Among Us* to the simple, enigmatic *M* came about, Lang later claimed, due to political interference; he stated in interviews that the emerging Nazi party viewed the original title as a veiled insult. But the reality was probably much more mundane—film scholars speculate that there were simply too many films coming out with the word *Murder* in the title and that the renaming was an attempt to distinguish it from the pack.

Despite his then-misgivings over making a talkie, Lang often referred to *M* as his favorite film—and for good reason. While the director created a number of remarkable pictures, *M* is his masterpiece.

Joseph Losey remade the film in 1951, and Lang's own *While The City Sleeps* (1956) can be seen as something of an Americanized redo. TH

The Mad Genius
Warner; b/w; 81 min; U.S.
D: Michael Curtiz S: J. Grubb Alexander, Harvey Thew C: Barney McGill M: David Mendoza
Cast: John Barrymore, Marian Marsh, Charles Butterworth, Donald Cook, Luis Alberni, Carmel Myers, André Luguet, Frankie Darro, Boris Karloff (uncredited)

The club-footed Vladimir Ivan Tsarakov (Barrymore) makes his living as a puppeteer, though his lifelong fantasy is, impossibly, to be a dancer. When he spies a young boy, Fedor Ivanoff (Darro), running from his abusive father (Karloff), he's captivated by the boy's fluid motion. He takes the boy under his wing (in what we today would call an abduction) and over time transforms the youth into a great dancer. However, the adult Fedor (Cook) tires of Tsarakov's domineering control. And when he meets the beautiful Nana Carlova (Marsh), he rebels against

In *The Mad Genius*, John Barrymore (with Marian Marsh) plays an interesting variation on his previous role as Svengali in *Svengali*.

his mentor, prompting the jealous Tsarakov to arrange for Carlova to enter into an affair with Count Renaud (Luguet). In the end, Fedor breaks from Tsarakov's almost superhuman will, and a crazed ballet master kills Tsarakov.

Warner Bros. was so pleased with the terrific box-office returns of *Svengali* (1931) that the studio immediately followed up with this feature, reteaming the film's two leads, John Barrymore and Marian Marsh. But this time around the love of the deranged tutor is aimed at a young male dancer rather than an adult female singer. It was a daring if necessarily ambiguously presented plotline, its deniability buttressed by having Tsarakov encourage his male protégé to sexually entertain a bevy of women. But though the "father" allows his "adopted son" the physical company of females, he attempts to block Fedor from any heterosexual emotional intimacy, viewing it as a threat to their own relationship.

John Barrymore brings the same intensity to his role as the Russian Tsarakov that he had to his roles as *Dr. Jekyll and Mr. Hyde* (1920), Captain Ahab in *Moby Dick* (1930) and the aforementioned *Svengali*. His line delivery is impeccable, as when he first sees Fedor and explains that, like the Golem fashioned from mud or the Frankenstein monster brought to life by man, "I will create my own being—that boy! ... I will mold him, I will pour into him my genius, my soul. In him all my dreams, all my ambitions will be fulfilled." There is a mad gleam in his eye as he speaks, and the light on his face creates sinister shadows. From even this early stage, it is clear that he is obsessed with the boy and will stop at nothing to control him.

But unfortunately, while Barrymore's performance is spot on, that of Donald Cook is not. This is most obvious when he plays against the talented Marian Marsh, who breathes three-dimensional life into Nana Carlova. Cook's two-dimensionality in these scenes provides the film's only indisputable sour notes.

The Mad Genius was an early talkie, made when producers were just beginning to realize the potential of music to enhance drama in sound films. While most of the music here is produced by onscreen sources, a background score by David Mendoza is also used, intermittently and to good effect, to stress a number of arousing or poignant moments. More of this sort of thing, in fact, would have gone a long way in providing the film with the pep it sometimes lacks.

Director Michael Curtiz had begun a film career in Austria more than two decades before, and he went on afterwards to a major Hollywood career, most notably with the classic *Casablanca* (1942). He was, however, no stranger to horror either before or after *The Mad Genius*, amassing writing or directing credits for such genre fare as *Alraune* (1918), *Drakula halála* (1921), *Doctor X* (1932) and *Mystery of the Wax Museum* (1933), among others. He had a knack for shadow play and lighting, and his Eastern European Expressionist background isn't lost on his American product. CW

Murder at Midnight
Tiffany; b/w; 69 min; U.S.

D/Co-S: Frank Strayer *Co-S:* W. Scott Darling *P:* Phil Goldstone *C:* William Rees *M:* Val Burton

Cast: Aileen Pringle, Alice White, Hale Hamilton, Robert Elliott, Clara Blandick, Brandon Hurst, Leslie Fenton, William Humphrey, Tyrell Davis, Aileen Carlyle, Kenneth Thomson, Robert Ellis

A parlor game turns deadly when Mr. Kennedy (Thomson) accidentally shoots his secretary Channing (Ellis) with live ammunition. Kennedy is found dead shortly thereafter, an apparent suicide. Inspector Taylor (Elliott) determines to get to the bottom of the matter, even as the bodies keep piling up.

Murder at Midnight is a strictly formulaic "old dark house" murder mystery. Director Frank Strayer (1891-1964) was born in Altoona, Pennsylvania and entered films as a bit player and assistant director. He made his directorial debut with *An Enemy of Men* (1925) and worked prolifically thereafter in a variety of genres. Horror buffs will best remember him for his stylish B film *The Vampire Bat* (1933), starring Lionel Atwill, Melvyn Douglas and Fay Wray, but he found his greatest commercial success guiding Chester Morris through the *Blondie* series, based on the comic strip of the same name. Overall, Strayer made several contributions to the horror genre, but none came close to matching *The Vampire Bat*, leading one to conclude that that film's appeal has to do less with its direction than with its excellent cast.

Murder at Midnight is by no means a disaster, but neither is it very interesting. The hackneyed plot and clichéd characterizations give one a sense of *déjà vu*, and stodgy pacing

Promotional ad sheet for Frank Strayer's otherwise dull *Murder at Midnight*

makes the film feel much longer than it really is. Even so, Strayer manages a few stylistic touches, including an early instance of point-of-view camerawork that momentarily implicates the audience in a murder about to be committed.

The cast is comprised largely of minor players, but genre fans will enjoy seeing the lugubrious Brandon Hurst (*White Zombie*, 1932) in yet another shifty butler role. Screenwriter W. Scott Darling later provided the script for Universal's *The Ghost of Frankenstein* (1942). TH

Murder by the Clock
Paramount; b/w; 75 min; U.S.
  D: Edward Sloman *S:* Henry Myers *C:* Karl Struss
  Cast: William "Stage" Boyd, Lilyan Tashman, Irving Pichel, Regis Toomey, Sally O'Neil, Blanche Friderici, Walter McGrail, Lester Vail, Martha Mattox, Frank Sheridan, Frederick Sullivan

Adapted from a story by Rufus King and the play based on it by Charles Beahan, *Murder by the Clock* is Paramount's answer to Universal's *Dracula* (1931), which it followed into theaters by a mere five months.

Leaving her mentally challenged son Phillip (Pichel) high and dry, the widow Mrs. Endicott draws up a will bequeathing her massive fortune to her alcoholic nephew Herbert and his gold-digging wife Laura (Tashman), though they can only collect their inheritance if they live in her palatial mansion. Laura entices her husband into murdering the old woman and pinning the blame on Phillip, then convinces her lover, Thomas Hollander (Vail), to strangle her husband. Herbert survives the attack, as well as a second one, only to be frightened to death by what appears to be the spirit of his murdered aunt. Meanwhile, Phillip escapes from jail and, at Laura's prompting, murders Thomas. Now all Laura has to do to get away with murder is charm Lieutenant Valcour (Boyd) into taking her side.

With output every bit as visually interesting as that of James Whale, Tod Browning or Edgar Ulmer, silent film director Edward Sloman brings a high level of creativity to *Murder*, especially for what is essentially a so-so script (one of its more original ideas has old Julia Endicott so terrified of being buried alive that she has a horn placed within her tomb to alert those outside that she still breathes). A remnant of the early talkie era, the

Lilyan Tashman as the gold-digging wife in *Murder by the Clock*

film's spooky atmospherics—including a creepy graveyard, an art deco tomb and a lavish old dark house—holds the viewer's interest throughout. And as the candles burn low and the evening wears on, Sloman piles on incident after horrible incident, proving that we don't need vampires, werewolves or Frankenstein's Monster to make a gripping horror movie. Greedy relatives with a lust for blood, in the right hands, are more than enough.

While Myer's script in and of itself would have the film be little more than a redo of *The Bat Whispers* (1930) or any number of silent-era mysteries (*The Bat*, 1926; *The Cat and the Canary*, 1927), Sloman's filtering of the entire affair through a horror lens lends it a far greater credence. When Julia is murdered, for instance, he focuses on the stealthy shadow, arms outstretched and ready to choke, creeping up behind her. And then there's the ghostly death mask Julia uses to scare Herbert to death, along with skulking figures aplenty lurking about the murky graveyard.

Sloman effectively convinces the audience that old Julia Endicott may very well be prowling the grounds as either a mistakenly buried victim of somnambulism or a spirit returned from the grave. There's also a drug that may revive the dead and a late-night seduction in a graveyard that ends with one person disappearing into an above ground crypt's secret passage. Sloman, one might say, throws in everything *and* the kitchen sink.

Lilyan Tashman is a *tour de force* as the conniving and seductive Laura Endicott, who loves no one but herself and will stop at nothing to be both rich and free of the constraints of a man. She plants murder in the head of every male she meets and damn well gets away with it until she tries it once too often, this time with a man too smart to be fooled by her slinky charms. Her skin-tight gowns cling to her lithe body with alluring feline elegance, and she plays the "helpless woman" card with evil precision, a praying mantis that devours the men who fall for her.

Tashman's star was on the rise in the early 1930s, as evidenced by her steady ascent from supporting cast to female lead despite her ill-fated lesbian relationship with the then-powerful Greta Garbo. In 1925 she married gay actor Edmund Lowe to hide her many same-sex affairs, and the two remained married until her death in 1934, at age 37, of cancer. Her funeral was attended by Mary Pickford, Jack Benny and Eddie Cantor (who delivered her eulogy), among many others, and some 10,000 fans and curiosity seekers attended her Brooklyn, New York service at the Temple Emanu-El on Fifth Avenue, which resulted in injuries when an unruly crowd toppled a gravestone. Her last film, *Frankie and Johnnie* (1936), was released two years after her death. It should also be noted that *Murder by the Clock* was not her only horror film; she had an important role in Universal's lost horror feature of 1930, *The Cat Creeps*.

While *Murder*'s cast as a whole does just fine, its other truly noteworthy performance is that of Irving Pichel as the dimwitted anti-hero Phillip. He leers and grins his way into horror film history, adding a touch of pathos to the dark proceedings. It was Pichel's first role in a horror film and became something of his signature. As both an actor (*Dracula's Daughter*, 1936) and a director (*The Most Dangerous Game*, 1932), he went on to become very familiar with the genre. Tall and imposing, he had a unique face and deep voice that landed him in grim roles time and time again.

Murder by the Clock also sports a romantic entanglement between a cop (Toomey) and a maid (O'Neill). Never fully developed, the subplot provides a measure of comedy relief to ease the tension created by the film's onslaught of grisliness. Still, it's that almost unending barrage of terror that makes the film an unsung classic of early 1930s horror, one deserving of a reappraisal.

William Boyd (*Night Life of the Gods*, 1935), who stars as Lieutenant Valcour, should not be confused with the Western actor of the same name. To differentiate them, the former frequently inserted the moniker "Stage" between his first and last name. CW

Oiwa nagaya
Teikine; b/w; length unknown; Japan
　　D: Kyotaro Namiki
　　Cast: Sumiko Suzuki, Seizaburo Kawazu

This appears to have been the first film adaptation of Tsuruya Nanboku IV's 1825 play *Yotsuya kaidan* to be shot in the 1930s. Like two previous adaptations, it starred popular Japanese actress Sumiko Suzuki as Oiwa, the poor but devoted wife of a samurai. When her husband meets the beautiful Oume, the daughter of a rich landowner, he forsakes his wife for her. After he disfigures and kills Oiwa and marries his mistress, he winds up face to face with an indescribable horror from beyond the grave.

The film's title translates as *Oiwa Tenant*. Suzuki returned to the role one final time in 1937's *Irohagana yotsuya kaidan*, a remake of a film in which she had starred in 1927. CW

The Phantom
Supreme; b/w; 62 min; U.S.
　　D/S: Alan James P: Louis Weiss C: Jack Draper
　　Cast: Guinn "Big Boy" Williams, Allene Ray, Niles Welch, Tom O'Brien, Sheldon Lewis, Wilfred Lucas, Violet Knights, William Gould, William Jackie, Bobby Dunn, Billie Griffith, Rodney Hildebrand, Horace Murphy

A killer known as The Phantom escapes from prison and threatens the life of the district attorney (Lucas). Strapping reporter Dick Mallory (Williams) and his fiancé Ruth (Ray), who happens to be the D.A.'s daughter, try to find the criminal before he can carry out his death threat. Their search takes them to a creepy insane asylum where the presiding doctor (Gould) is planning some unorthodox brain experiments.

The Phantom is a veritable catalogue of "old dark house"/mad scientist serial trappings, albeit in feature form. The only thing missing is a man in a gorilla outfit, and the presence of one wouldn't have hurt the proceedings any. Little good can be said of this wretchedly acted, abysmally directed affair. There's plentiful comedic relief, true, but none of it is funny, though the odd unintentional laugh might erupt as the actors struggle with their lines as they—barely—manage to avoid knocking over the furniture.

Leading lady Allene Ray was a popular fixture in silent-era serials, but her career came to a halt not long after entering talkies. It's easy to see why; she may well have been a fetching ingénue in her day, but the arrival of sound clearly didn't work to her advantage. Her line readings are appalling enough to earn her the distinction of being *The Phantom*'s worst actor, which is no mean feat.

A cast that can be considered watchable only when compared with someone of her ilk surrounds her. Sheldon Lewis in particular manages to be grating as well as mediocre; once the star of the "other" 1920 version of *Dr. Jekyll and Mr. Hyde*, he repeats his scuttling bogeyman routine here, and it's no more effective than it was a decade before.

Writer/director Alan James amassed a number of credits between 1916 and 1943, most of them in the Western genre. He clearly had no affinity for mystery or horror and *The Phantom* suffers accordingly.

The film tries (kind of) to be a wild and wooly combination of humor, horror and cliffhanger-style thrills. Unfortunately for the viewer, it's never funny in the appropriate places, it's never persuasively frightening and it can hardly be described as exciting. TH

The Phantom of Paris
aka Chéri-Bibi
MGM; b/w; 74 (72) min; U.S.
　　D: John S. Robertson S: Bess Meredyth, Edwin Justus Mayer, John Meehan C: Oliver T. Marsh

Cast: John Gilbert, Leila Hyams, Lewis Stone, Jean Hersholt, C. Aubrey Smith, Natalie Moorhead, Ian Keith, Alfred Hickman

French journalist Gaston Leroux is most famous for his 1911 novel *Le Fantôme de l'Opéra*, but he wrote numerous other bestselling books as well. Most were detective novels starring sleuths strikingly similar to Poe's Inspector Dupin, and one of these clones, named Chéri-Bibi, had a primary career as a professional magician. He appears to have made his big-screen debut in 1914 in the obscure French film *Les premières aventures de Chéri Bibi*, with Emile Keppens in the title role. In a second little-known French outing, 1919's *The New Dawn*, José Davert portrayed Chéri-Bibi.

In 1930 MGM took an interest in elevating the character to feature-film status, assigning the role to the Man of a Thousand Faces, Lon Chaney. Chaney had proved his mettle in the talkies with an astounding performance in *The Unholy Three* (1930), where he not only spoke but did so in several different voices. And *The Phantom of Paris* would have required him to emote from under various make-ups, the very talent with which he had gained fame.

Unfortunately, Chaney died of a throat hemorrhage, and silent-era superstar John Gilbert was given the role. Once Rudolph Valentino's leading rival for the hearts of women (and a man or two), Gilbert's career had hit the skids around 1926, allegedly due to an incident related to his near-marriage to Greta Garbo. The story goes that when she abandoned him at the altar, MGM studio head Louis B. Mayer cracked a crude joke about her. It has been claimed that Gilbert struck Mayer, who in turn vowed revenge. While the veracity of this anecdote is difficult to verify, it does provide a plausible explanation as to why Gilbert was suddenly relegated into lesser roles in minor films despite being one of MGM's highest paid stars. At any rate, Chaney's death and Gilbert's casting shifted *The Phantom of Paris* to second-string status.

The first such film from a major producer, *Phantom* aimed to capitalize on the then-in-vogue theme of Houdini-like magicians. The story concerns Chéri-Bibi's infatuation with a woman named Cecil (Hyams). Cecil's father, Bourrelier (Smith), does not approve of the two's proposed engagement, and when he is murdered, a previously overheard argument between him and Chéri-Bibi makes the magician the prime suspect. Chéri-Bibi is put into a heavily secured jail cell, but he escapes to clear his name and avenge the murder of his fiancée's father.

Actor/director John S. Robertson had found fame a decade earlier when he brought Robert Louis Stevenson's *Dr. Jekyll and Mr. Hyde* (1920) to the big screen with Broadway star John Barrymore as both the kindly Dr. Jekyll and the sinister Mr. Hyde. But while that film has atmosphere in spades, Robertson here seems so intoxicated by the wonders of synchronized sound that he lets much of the tale's potential ambiance drift away. The first reel of *Phantom* is packed with wordy displays of Chéri-Bibi's magical prowess (clearly a holdover from the original casting of Chaney). While this is apparently aimed at getting the audience to identify with Chéri-Bibi, it serves to drag the film down. A well-shot prison sequence and a few scenes set in an old country house admittedly provide some welcome relief from all the talk, but the proceedings are ultimately drowned in chatty theatrics. Rather than the full-throttle horror film *Phantom* wants so clearly to be, it emerges as a mystery without much mystery, a drama with little drama and an adventure with little sense of adventure. And on top of it all, the ending is inexplicably rushed.

It should be noted that none of this is Gilbert's fault; he actually acquits himself nicely in a role intended for someone else. By the time of *Phantom*, his career had pretty much wound down. His first talking film after his rumored tiff with Mayer had been *His Glorious Night* (1929), in which his voice drew derisive laughter from audiences. (His daughter has alleged that Mayer altered Gilbert's voice to make it higher than normal.) Garbo herself attempted to stoke Gilbert's career by getting him cast as her male love interest in *Queen Christina* (1932). And while that performance was acclaimed, his very next film, *The Captain Hates the Sea* (1934), bombed. A raging alcoholic, Gilbert died of a heart attack that same year at the still-youthful age of 36.

The Phantom of Paris is a justifiably forgotten film today, but it is not without its merits. Too bad its worth derives more from what went on behind the scenes than from any goings-on in front of the camera.

A smattering of additional magician-themed films followed *Phantom* into theaters, most made by rival Fox (*The Spider*, 1931; *Chandu the Magician*, 1932; and *Trick for Trick*, 1933). The next film to star Leroux's character was the minor French effort *Chéri-Bibi* in 1938. CW

The Polish Jew
aka **Le juif polonaise**; **Polish Jew**; **The Bells**
Franco-American Film Company; b/w; 85 min; France

D: Jean Kemm *S:* Pierre Maudru *C:* Paul Cotteret, Robert Lefebvre

Gaston Leroux's famous detective Chéri-Bibi (Emile Keppens) is brought to the big screen in *The Phantom of Paris*, with Leila Hyams.

Cast: Harry Bauer, Mady Berry, Georges La Cressonnière, Simone Mareuil, Lucien Dayle, Geo Laby, Louis Pré Fils, Raymond Gardanne, Raymond Turgy, Jules Maurice, Jules Maurier

Based directly on Émile Erckmann and Alexandre Chatrian's original French play rather than Leopold Lewis' English adaptation, *The Polish Jew* concerns a town mayor and innkeeper named Mathias (Bauer), who is also the town burgomaster. When a rich but nomadic Jew arrives at the inn amid the sound of sleigh bells, Mathias sees an opportunity to dig himself out of debt. He murders the Jew and steals his money. Years later, Mathias has moved on with his life and forgotten about the incident, until the subject of the killing comes up over dinner one evening. Mathias faints and in his delirium has a nightmare in which his victim's ghost visits him. To make matters worse, the Polish Jew's son arrives in town and falls in love with Mathias' daughter.

In an ironic note, actor Harry Bauer died at Nazi hands in 1943 while in Germany to shoot a film. His wife was Jewish and suspected of spying, and the Gestapo tortured him for information. Though he was eventually released, he ended up dying as a result of his injuries.

The Polish Jew wasn't released in the United States until September of 1937 and is frequently but erroneously cited as having been produced that same year. CW

The Speckled Band
Wilcox; b/w; 49 min; Great Britain
   D: Jack Raymond *S:* W.P. Lipscomb *P:* Herbert Wilcox *C:* Freddie (F.A.) Young
   Cast: Raymond Massey, Athole Stewart, Lyn Harding, Angela Baddeley, Nancy Price, Marie Ault, Franklyn Bellamy, Ivan Brandt, Stanley Lathbury, Charles Paton, Joyce Moore

Violet Stonor (Moore) dies mysteriously, but just before expiring, she whispers the phrase "speckled band" to her devoted sister Helen (Baddeley) who, though devastated by the death, can't help but notice that their crass stepfather, Dr. Grimsby Rylott (Harding), seems strangely unmoved. Fearing that her own life may be in danger, Helen visits Sherlock Holmes (Massey) to discuss the matter. Holmes, intrigued by the dying words, agrees to investigate the situation. Despite admonitions from Rylott to steer clear, the sleuth persists in nosing around and comes to suspect that the doctor has indeed murdered his stepdaughter.

The Adventure of the Speckled Band is, along with *The Hound of the Baskervilles*, one of the more horror-tinged Sherlock Holmes stories. Published by Sir Arthur Conan Doyle in 1905, it was reportedly the author's own favorite of all his Holmes adventures. It's certainly a clever piece of writing with a memorable twist, not to mention a vivid villain in Dr. Grimsby Rylott. It's curious that it hasn't been adapted nearly as often or as devotedly as *Hound*.

The Speckled Band is an early British talkie that tinkers with Doyle's particulars but retains the heart of the story. If one can overlook the slightly ridiculous conceit of Holmes and a frazzled secretary using then-modern technology to consolidate information, the film shapes up as an efficient little piece of entertainment.

Raymond Massey (1896-1983) makes a commendable Holmes. He was at the beginning (his third screen credit) of a

Publicity shot of Raymond Massey, who starred as Sherlock Holmes in the horror-tinged *The Speckled Band*

long and distinguished career; a year later he appeared as the semi-heroic Philip Waverton in James Whale's masterful *The Old Dark House* (1932), and he went on to star in everything from Fritz Lang thrillers (*The Woman in the Window*, 1944) to sensitive dramas for Elia Kazan (*East of Eden*, 1955). His greatest career success was his portrayal of President Abraham Lincoln in *Abe Lincoln of Illinois* (1938), a role he revisited in one of his last pictures, the all-star Cinerama epic *How the West Was Won* (1962).

From a physical perspective, Massey was an ideal match for Holmes; with his lean frame and hawk-like visage, he closely resembles illustrator Sidney Paget's conception in the original *Strand Magazine* publication of the stories. And while this film requires Massey to be off-screen for long stretches, he makes the most of the time he's there, coming off as supercilious, witty and at times even melancholy about his own inability to fit into society.

Athole Stewart portrayed Dr. Watson. Stewart was, like Massey, a relative newcomer to the screen. He died in 1940 at the rather young age of 61. One of his last roles was as a reverend in Michael Powell's excellent wartime thriller *The Spy in Black* (1939), starring Conrad Veidt.

Dr. Grimsby Rylott is played by Lyn Harding, a Welsh character actor who is further connected to the Sherlock Holmes saga by portrayals of Professor Moriarty in several of the Arthur Wontner films, including *The Triumph of Sherlock Holmes* (1937) and *Murder at the Baskervilles* (1937). Harding is an imposing presence, though his leaden acting style makes it blindingly obvious from the first reel that he's most likely the killer.

The Spider is one of several Fox horror films to focus on a magician (in this case played by Edmund Lowe) battling evil.

Somewhat stodgily directed by Jack Raymond, the film benefits from the moody cinematography of Freddie Young. Young went on to become one of Britain's top cinematographers, renowned today for his artful, Oscar-winning work on such David Lean epics as *Lawrence of Arabia* (1962), *Doctor Zhivago* (1965) and *Ryan's Daughter* (1970). His lighting makes the most of the Gothic architecture of Rylott's sinister abode, thus enhancing the film's horror/mystery look. TH

The Spider
Fox; b/w; 59 min; U.S.

Co-D/FX: William Cameron Menzies *Co-D:* Kenneth MacKenna *S:* Barry Conners, Phillip Klein *P:* William Sistrom *C:* James (Wong) Howe *M:* Carli Elinor, R.H. Bassett, Hugo Friedhofer, Glen Knight

Cast: Edmund Lowe, Lois Moran, El Brendel, John Arledge, George E. Stone, Earle Foxe, Manya Roberti, Howard Phillips, Purnell Pratt, Jesse De Vorska, Kendall McComas, Ruth Donnelly

The Great Chatrand (Lowe) is a stage magician and hypnotist. During one of his performances, there is an attempted murder in the audience. When he's implicated in the crime, he uses his skills to unmask the real culprit.

Based on a play by Lowell Brentano and Fulton Oursler, adapted by screenwriters Barry Conners and Phillip Klein into a tightly paced blend of magic, mystery and horror, *The Spider* is part of an unofficial trilogy involving the magic arts; the other two were *Chandu the Magician* (1932, also written for the screen by Conners and Klein) and *Trick for Trick* (1933).

William Cameron Menzies is best remembered for his Oscar-winning work on the epic *Gone with the Wind* (1939), but in his earlier days he co-directed both *The Spider* and *Chandu*. The two films also share star Edmund Lowe and cinematographer James Wong Howe. Lowe was a popular leading man in his day, though his career was on the wane by the time he top-lined here. He's far more likable and energetic in *The Spider* than he is in *Chandu*, heading a cast that, while not offering anything as colorful as Lugosi's scene-stealing villain, still proves the stronger of the two. Howe, for his part, creates some fabulous images in *The Spider*, most notably the ghostly apparitions that appear as part of Chatrand's attempt to scare the villain into betraying his identity.

The film's 59-minute running time is another plus. If it had been much longer, it likely would have overstayed its welcome. As it is, despite some clumsy comedy relief by El Brendel and Kendall McComas (as wisecracking members of the audience), *The Spider* slips through as an artfully crafted B-movie.

The 1945 remake bears almost no similarity to this version, transforming the narrative into a hardboiled noir thriller with the usual bunch of tough guys and double-crossing dames. TH

Svengali
Warner; b/w; 81 min; U.S.

D: Archie Mayo *S:* J. Grubb Alexander *C:* Barney McGill *M:* David Mendoza *FX:* Fred Jackman

Cast: John Barrymore, Marian Marsh, Donald Crisp, Bramwell Fletcher, Carmel Myers, Luis Alberni, Lumsden Hare, Paul Porcasi

As the title suggests, this first sound film adaptation of George Du Maurier's *Trilby* focuses on Svengali, the musical virtuoso obsessed with the virginal Trilby O'Farrell. The tale begins by presenting the libidinous title character, an unkempt, filthy, mesmeric fiend who seduces young woman and then, after fleecing them, drives them to suicide. One can't help but no-

Svengali (John Barrymore) is a musician and composer who longs for the love of Trilby, from *Svengali*.

tice the similarity between this Svengali and film portrayals of real-life Russian holy man Rasputin.

After the set-up, the story proper begins: Svengali (Barrymore) and his servant Gecko (Alberni) go to the apartment of the Laird (Crisp) and Taffy (Hare) to beg for money. There they meet a charming artist's model named Trilby (Marsh). While changing her clothes to pose for Svengali (whom she believes is rich), Trilby breaks into song. Though her voice is untrained and weak, Svengali hears in it a potential for greatness. After he leaves, Little Billee (Fletcher, a year before he was immortalized as the archaeologist driven insane by the sight of the walking dead in Universal's *The Mummy*, 1932) walks in and falls instantly in love with her. But when next he sees her, Svengali has her in his hypnotic control (under the guise of banishing her headaches) and thus prevents her and Little Billee from becoming an item.

Though it gets off to a slow start (35 minutes, to be exact), hampered in part by some overzealous comedy relief, *Svengali* picks up once Barrymore cuts loose as the demonic villain. Archie Mayo's direction is flawless, as is Barney McGill's superb camerawork. In the film's most famous sequence, a cloudy-eyed Svengali looks out his bedroom window and mentally summons Trilby. The camera pans from behind the mesmerist, cuts to a close-up of his glazed eyes, then pulls back from his face. On its way out the window of his attic apartment, the camera turns around to view the Parisian skyline (done up with an Expressionist flourish by art director Anton Grot), then flies over the rooftops to Trilby's apartment. Her balcony doors blow open, the camera enters and focuses on her bed and she begins to twist in the throes of a nightmare. Cut to Svengali, watching from a distance, followed by a shot of the awakened and now-entranced Trilby. When next we see Svengali, it's as Trilby enters his room: He sits in a wooden chair in the background of the shot, a perched raven's silhouette over his head, while Trilby stands in the foreground. Mayo cuts to Trilby's face, then to a close shot of Barrymore from below as he pets his black cat. Direction, cinematography, editing and set design blend perfectly to create a delirious sense of claustrophobic terror.

After staging her fake suicide in the River Seine, Svengali whisks Trilby away and, using his supernatural power over her, makes her a great opera star. Years later, during a performance in England, Little Billee spies her leaving an opera house. At that moment, Svengali briefly loses control over her (due to a heart palpitation). She comes to her senses, recognizes Little Billee and runs to him. But when Svengali's palpitation is over, Trilby again falls under his control. Little Billee vows to get Trilby back, but in the end she dies uttering Svengali's name while Svengali, whose heart has been weakened over the years by the strain of controlling Trilby, has a heart attack and expires.

The film is sexually candid for the period. While the Laird bathes, Svengali plays "God Save the Queen" knowing that the man will stand out of respect. There are several flashes of suggested nudity, and one might wonder what exactly the friendship between the Laird and Taffy entails, given that they not only share an apartment but that one should watch the other as he bathes (on the same note, when Billee reveals to the roommates his love for Trilby, their reaction suggests a disinterest in women that Billee is encouraged to share). Later, when Little Billee

A publicity shot of John Barrymore as the evil hypnotist Svengali

rushes into an art school class, he finds a naked Trilby posing for the students; Mayo suggests her nudity via some startlingly daring camera angles.

Mayo (1891-1968) has often been called a journeyman director, but his filmography suggests an artisan of a higher order. Though he began his career as an actor, he began making silent, two-reel comedies in the mid-teens. By the time the silent era closed, he had graduated to A-list features for the fledgling Warner Bros. studio.

While *Svengali* was one of his more famous early sound efforts, it was the success of his Bette Davis/Leslie Howard vehicle *The Petrified Forest* (1936) that guaranteed his place in film history. In casting a little-known theater actor named Humphrey Bogart as the lead villain, Mayo created an overnight sensation. He went on to direct several more films that are rightly considered classics, including *The Adventures of Marco Polo* (1938) and *A Night in Casablanca* (1946). But after the failure of the stylish *Angel on My Shoulder* (1946), which was intended to reignite America's love affair with Paul Muni, Mayo effectively retired from directing. He emerged only once more, in 1958, to produce the anti-communist *The Beast of Budapest*. He died of cancer in Mexico in 1968.

In 1931 John Barrymore was a major star who had made a successful transition from the silents to sound, and his casting as Svengali was something of a coup. Trilby was much harder to cast, however. Originally, Barrymore wanted his wife at the time, actress Dolores Costello (daughter of the famous filmmaker Maurice Costello), to play the part, but she was more interested in nurturing Barrymore's daughter, to whom she'd recently given birth. A nationwide search to fill the role brought Marian Marsh to Barrymore's attention. Marsh had had several small roles in major films, and she had already screen tested for the role of Trilby by the time Barrymore noticed her (she resembled his wife, and it has been alleged that the two had a short-lived affair during filming).

Reviews of Marsh's performance in *Svengali* were mixed, but audiences took to her. The film was a box-office success, and Warner followed it up six months later with another pairing of Barrymore and Marsh in *The Mad Genius* (1931). That film, released in November, likewise concerned an insane musician obsessed with the talent of a young person in his care (this one a male). Marsh played the love interest that tears the two apart. That film wasn't nearly as successful as its predecessor, however, and when Marsh tried flexing her muscle at Warner as Bette Davis had recently done, her option was dropped. She found herself adrift in poverty row productions before signing a contract with Columbia in 1935. There she appeared in *The Black Room* (1935) with Boris Karloff, but when her contract ended the following year, it was back to the bargain bin, working in such features as *Murder by Invitation* (1941). She retired from the movie industry in 1942, though she did a handful of television appearances in the late 1950s. After marrying entrepreneur Cliff Henderson in 1960, she dedicated herself to charity work, focusing mainly on conservation, an interest she maintained until her death in 2006.

Like so many adaptations of Du Maurier's Gothic horror novel before it, this *Svengali* makes no mention of its central villain's religious beliefs (in the book, he's Jewish), no doubt in deference to the growing anti-Semitism of the time.

On an interesting side note, actor Bramwell Fletcher, who plays the boyishly handsome and heroic Little Billee, later married Barrymore's daughter Diana. CW

Vampyr
aka **Vampyr—Der Traum des Allan Grey; Adventures of David Gray; Castle of Doom; Not Against the Flesh; The Strange Adventure of David Gray; The Vampire; Vampyr, ou l'étrange aventure de David Gray**
Tobis; b/w; 73 min; Germany, France

D/Co-S/Co-P: Carl Th. (Theodor) Dreyer *Co-S:* Christen Jul *Co-P:* Julian West *C:* Rudolph Mate *M:* Wolfgang Zeller

Cast: Julian West, Maurice Schutz, Rena Mandel, Sybille Schmitz, Jan Hieronimko, Henriette Gerard, Albert Bras, N. Babanini, Jane Mora, Georges Boidin

Allan Grey (West) is obsessed with the supernatural. His search for vampires leads him to a mansion inhabited by an elderly lord (Schutz) and his two daughters, Leone (Schmitz), who is bedridden with an unknown malady and Gisele (Man-

A memorable shot from Carl Dreyer's Expressionistic *Vampyr*.

Allen Grey (Julian West) is buried alive in *Vampyr*'s most striking sequence.

del). An unknown killer strikes the lord dead as Leone grows ever weaker, all the while being attended to by a mysterious doctor (Hieronimko) who appears to be in league with an old hag (Gerard). Grey at length deduces that the old woman is a vampire and the doctor her soulless companion.

Danish-born Carl Theodor Dreyer (1889-1968), revered by many as one of cinema's finest filmmakers, first dabbled in the macabre with *Leaves from Satan's Book* (1921), but *Vampyr* is certainly his most significant contribution to the genre and remains one of the most genuinely dream-like pictures ever made. It came about following his silent artistic triumph *The Passion of Joan of Arc* (1928). Dreyer decided to do a film grounded in the dark realm of the supernatural. Given the popularity at the time of the Hamilton Deane stage adaptation of *Dracula*, vampirism was a logical choice of subject matter. Dreyer drew inspiration not from Stoker, however, but from another Irish-born author, J. Sheridan Le Fanu.

Le Fanu's classic novella *Carmilla*—about an implicitly lesbian vampire who feeds on a succession of pretty young women—served as Dreyer's starting point. Yet precious little of Le Fanu's story is evident in *Vampyr*, which in truth is far less concerned with plot than with ambience. The film is deliberately difficult to follow; shot through a haze of fog and soft-focus filters, it effectively duplicates the oft-attempted (but seldom realized) disorientation common to nightmares. The characters are intended to be ciphers with neither depth nor detail. Dreyer doesn't expect viewers to care about Allan Grey; rather, he is bent on making the audience share the protagonist's strange journey.

The character of Grey is portrayed by Julian West, whose real name was Nicolas de Gunzburg. West, a real-life baron, made his name as an editor-in-chief of the still-extant *Town & Country* magazine. He had money and connections, and in exchange for financing the picture, he got to star in it. The majority of the supporting cast is similarly non-professional, the exceptions being Maurice Schutz and Sybille Schmitz, cast respectively as the ill-fated lord and his ailing daughter.

The film was Dreyer's first talkie picture, and he clearly approached the new technology gingerly. Much of the film plays out without dialogue, and its use of intertitles to provide exposition is little removed from silent film. Yet, by not being weighed down by the stationary mechanics of live sound recording, Dreyer and cinematographer Rudolph Mate accessed a greater visual dexterity than is found in a typical talking film of its vintage. *Vampyr* is at heart a stream of striking images, its pace slow and deliberate. Its plot is deliberately obscure and elliptical as it builds to its most celebrated set piece, in which Grey imagines that he is being buried alive. Dreyer's use of subjective camera makes the scene simultaneously claustrophobic and poetic.

Not surprisingly, given the film's arty and original tone, it flopped. Given that his previous film, the aforementioned *Joan of Arc*, had also lost a bundle, the innovative director had a hard time finding continued film work. In fact, Dreyer didn't do another feature until *Day of Wrath* (1943), while Le Fanu's story wouldn't be adapted again until Roger Vadim's stylish *Blood and Roses* (1960).

Vampyr's sparse dialogue was recorded in German, French and English (with the English edition only partially completed). The German version is generally recognized as the most desirable and complete, though it inexplicably changes the hero's first name to David. After being available for years only in a battered print with oversized English subtitles, it can today be easily found in more-or-less pristine condition.

Vampyr remains one of a handful of films that can be called truly unique. It contains imagery that, once seen, can never be forgotten. TH

Director of *What a Night* ... Monty Banks with wife Gracie Fields

What a Night

British International; b/w; 58 min; Great Britain

D/P: Monty Banks *S:* Syd Courtenay, Lola Harvey

Cast: Leslie Fuller, Molly Lamont, Frank Stanmore, Charles Paton, Syd Courtenay, Ernest Fuller, Molly Hamley-Clifford, Nina Olivette, Lola Harvey

Not to be confused with *What a Night* (1928) or *Oh, What a Night!* (1935), British International Pictures' *What a Night* is typical for its time and country of origin in that its focus is more on humor than chills. A lonely traveler holes up in an inn reputed to be haunted, but instead of squaring off with a supernatural entity, he encounters a burglar who's using the place as a hideout, hoping that its ghostly reputation will scare off authorities.

The film's screenwriters, Syd Courtenay and Lola Harvey, appear in supporting acting roles. The reliable Monty Banks, a pseudonym for Mario Bianchi, who was born in Cesena, Italy, in 1897, directed. Banks had been a popular onscreen comedian during the silent era, but with the coming of sound his thick Italian accent put a damper on his acting career, resulting in him switching to directing. That occupation was also derailed when Great Britain declared Italians to be enemies of the state and began a process of interning them during World War II. Banks and his wife, Gracie Fields, escaped to Canada and then to the United States, where they remained until after the war. They retained both Italian and U.S. citizenship. Banks died in January 1950 of a heart attack. CW

1932

After Dark
Parker/Fox; b/w; 44 min; Great Britain
 D: Albert Parker S: R.J. Davis, J. Jefferson Farjeon P: Hugh Perceval C: Geoffrey Faithfull
 Cast: Horace Hodges, Hugh Williams, Grethe Hansen, George Barraud, Henry Oscar, Ian Fleming, Polly Emery, Arthur Padbury, Lucille Lisle

This dull "old dark house" movie spends its first 15 minutes (one-third of its running time) setting up its central plot: A young man (Williams) returns home from abroad and finds that the emeralds he was carrying have been stolen by a man (Fleming) he had met on the trip. With the aid of the thief's niece (Hansen), he tracks the precious gems to a spooky old mansion in the country, where they've been placed inside a grandfather clock.

Unfortunately, the potential suspense of the situation is strangled in its crib by some stunningly unfunny comedy, mostly involving an old codger and a young boy whose bumbling antics never fail to draw one's attention away from anything else that is going on. Nor is the film's story as coherent as the above synopsis might make it sound, perhaps because the lengthy stage play on which it's based was cut down to 44 minutes of screen time; all the major characters are still there, but not enough of anything else. There are too many people and incidents squeezed into too short a time, with little of it developed beyond what's barely necessary to propel the storyline forward. The script, which was adapted by R.J. Davis from Joseph Jefferson Farjeon's play, utilizes enough of its source's conversations that Farjeon gets a co-writing credit for dialogue; but the screenplay is the sort of mess that any self-respecting writer would have yanked his name from it without a second thought.

Taking advantage of the country's quota rule, *After Dark* was produced by the British arm of Fox. That rule tightly fixed the ratio of American to British films playing in Britain's theaters to keep U.S. product from flooding the British film industry. In practice, though, the law proved a double boon to the major American studios, who simply opened small production facilities in England and took advantage of the nation's tax breaks to make short, cheap movies—which were then presented on a double bill with their much bigger-budgeted American counterparts.

The film has no idea what it wants to be—crime, drama, romance, comedy, or horror—and as such doesn't achieve much of anything apart from boring its audience. The script is, in a word, dreadful. But as is the general trend with British films of the era, *After Dark*'s performances are by and large outstanding (though Hugh Williams does come across as a younger, paler Colin Clive). The female lead, Grethe Hansen, is especially good, making one wonder why her career never took off. She was under contract to Gainsborough at the time but loaned out to Fox for this sole production (a fact that is alluded to twice in the film's opening credits). Despite her obvious talent, most of her roles ended up being uncredited bit parts in minor films.

On the flip side, *After Dark* gave stage actor Henry Oscar his first movie role, and he went on to become a major player in British film and television. While few of these proved to be of

Original one-sheet for *The Amazon Head Hunters* emphasizes the gruesome, also adding a tad bit of nudity to attract further attention.

the horror persuasion, the actor did have parts of various sizes in *The Man Behind the Mask* (1936), *The Terror* (1938), *The Greed of William Hart* (1948), *The Spaniard's Curse* (1958) and *The Brides of Dracula* (1960). CW

Amazon Head Hunters
aka **Au pays du scalp**
Universelle; b/w; 75 min; Belgium/France
 D: Marquis de Wavrin S: Irene Kuhn P: Sol Lesser M: Maurice Jaubert
 Cast: Marquis de Wavrin, Fred Shields

This is a sensationalist pseudo-documentary—obviously influenced by Joseph Conrad's classic novel *Heart of Darkness* (1899)—in which the Marquis de Wavrin (playing himself) investigates the disappearance of a friend in the Amazon, where his fear that headhunters are to blame turns out to be well-founded.

Born Comte Robert Frédéric de Wavrin de Villers au Tertre in Belgium in 1888, de Wavrin later fell under the spell of South America. His travels to the continent piqued his fascination with the people and their customs, and he played the role of intrepid explorer and amateur documentarian in the hopes of bringing more awareness to that part of the world. *Amazon Head Hunters* was the last of his attempts in this direction—he had been making documentaries on the subject since 1924—but it was the first one to embrace the creepier elements of the culture, what with its fixation on head hunters and their rites.

Following the muted response to the film, de Wavrin gave up filmmaking, but he remained passionately involved in South American culture, donating materials to his favorite museums in Paris and Brussels until his death in 1971. TH

L'Atlantide
Nero/Societé Internationale; b/w; 94 (89) min; Germany/France

D: G.W. Pabst *S:* AlexandreArnoux, Jacques Deval, Hermann Oberländer, LadislausVajda *P:* Seymour Nebenzahl, Romain Pinés *C:* Joseph Barth, EugenSchüfftan *M:* Wolfgang Zeller

Cast: Brigitte Helm, Pierre Blanchar, Tela Tchai, Georges Tourreil, Vladimir Sokoloff, Mathias Wieman, Jean Angelo, Florelle, Gertrude Pabst, Rositta Severus-Liedernit

After the successful 1928 re-release of *Missing Husbands* (the 1921 film adaptation of Pierre Benoit's *L'Atlantide*, 1919), German filmmaker G.W. Pabst made three film adaptations of Benoit's novel (in three different languages) in a single year. All three starred Brigitte Helm as the beautiful Queen of Atlantis, who lures men from the outside world to her throne, uses them for a short while and then kills them, keeping their gold-encrusted bodies on display in a grisly underground museum.

This version was made in cooperation with French studio Societé Internationale, with a mostly French-speaking cast. The same year Pabst also made the German-language *Queen of Atlantis*, with a mostly German cast, and the English-language *Mistress of Atlantis*, with a mostly British and German cast. Each film had a native speaker contribute to its screenplay, and all three were shot partly on location in Nigeria, with the internal shots done on massive sets constructed in Germany.

While this adaptation is generally unknown in North America, it is considered something of a classic in France, where it is readily available on home video. CW

The Barton Mystery
Paramount/British-Dominion/Wilcox; b/w; 76 min; Great Britain

D: Henry Edwards *S:* Walter Hackett *P:* Herbert Wilcox *C:* Stanley Rodwell

Cast: Ursula Jeans, Ellis Jeffreys, Lyn Harding, Ian Swinley, Wendy Barrie, Joyce Bland, Tom Helmore, O.B. Clarence, Franklyn Bellamy, Wilfred Noy

This talkative 1932 thriller is the second film based on Walter Hackett's 1917 play *The Barton Mystery* and was shot at Elstree Studios, London. Lyn Harding, who had starred in the original 1920 film adaptation of the play, returns as Beverly Barton, a man of shady repute who has in his possession some incriminating letters. After a visit by a young man hoping to retrieve the letters, Beverly is found shot to death in his apartment. Suspicion falls on the young man, of course, and a psychic is engaged to hold a séance and ferret out the real killer.

While predominantly an actor in British cinema from the teens through the 1950s, Henry Edwards (1882-1952) also had stints as writer, director and producer. Though his career was generally horror-free, he did produce *Mystery at the Villa Rose* (1930) and star in *Green for Danger* (1946). CW

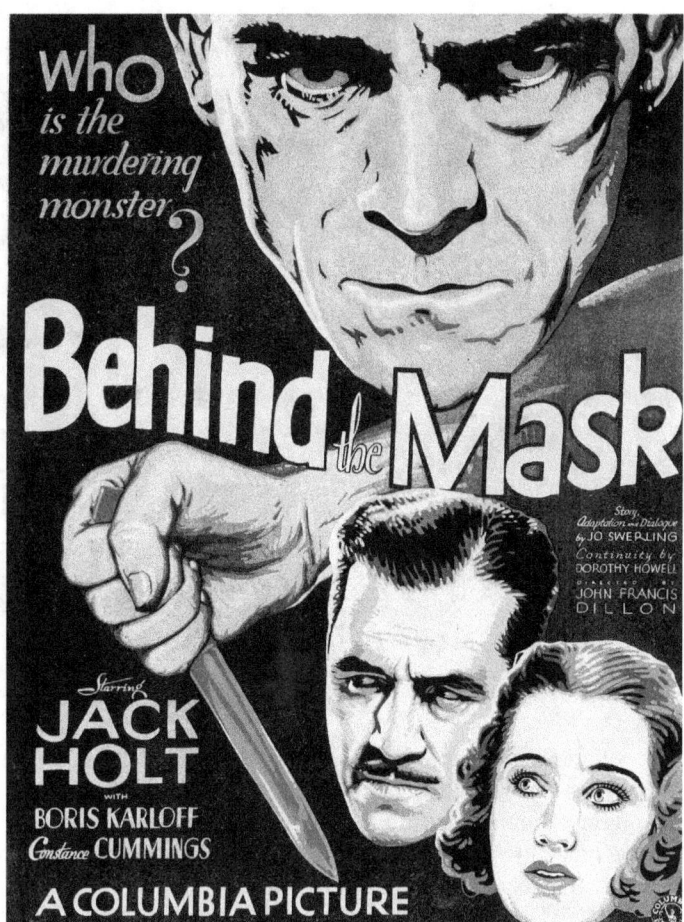

Shot before *Frankenstein* but released afterwards, *Behind the Mask*'s one-sheet poster emphasizes the presence of Boris Karloff, who only had a minor role in the movie.

Behind the Mask
aka **The Man Who Dared**; **Secret Service**
Columbia; b/w; 69 (70) min; U.S.

D: John Francis Dillon *S:* Jo Swerling, Dorothy Howell *P:* Harry Cohn *C:* Ted Tetzlaff

Cast: Jack Holt, Constance Cummings, Boris Karloff, Edward Van Sloan, Claude King, Bertha Mann, Willard Robertson

With the success of *Frankenstein*, which was released in November 1931, Boris Karloff shot to cinematic superstardom. As a result, several films on which he'd worked prior to *Frankenstein* were rushed into theaters with his name prominently featured. One such film was Columbia's *Behind the Mask*, which was released in February 1932. While it had been originally conceived as a minor crime picture, its redone advertising campaign stressed Karloff's presence and accentuated plot elements involving a mad scientist (played, appropriately enough, by Edward Van Sloan, who had starred as Professor Waldman in *Frankenstein* and as the saintly Professor Van Helsing in *Dracula*, 1931). The surprise here is that, despite the studio's original intent for the film, it really does come off as an outright work of horror, with some of the most morbid dialogue ever vocalized at that point in cinema history.

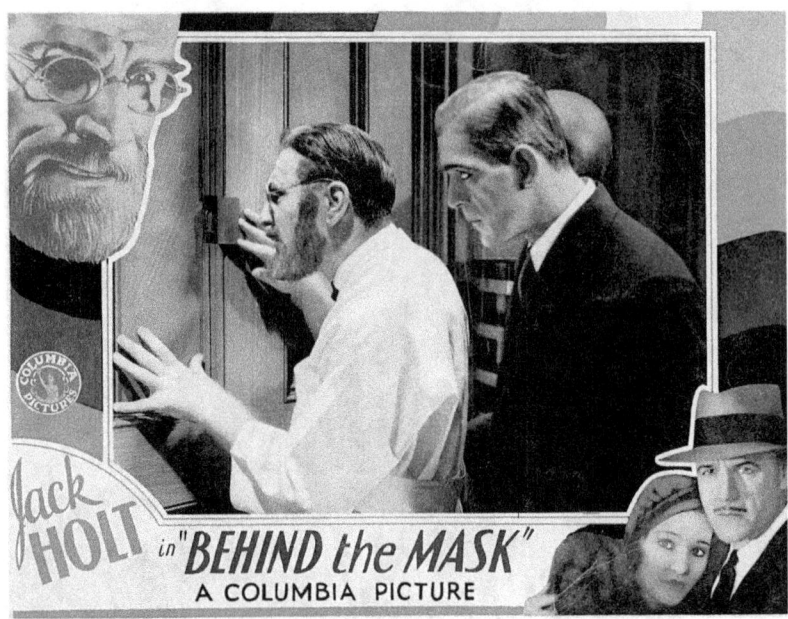

An original lobby card for *Behind the Mask* features horror stars Edward Van Sloan and Karloff.

Rugged leading man Jack Holt stars as Jack Hart, a federal agent who dons the guise of criminal Quinn to infiltrate a drug-smuggling gang headed up by Jim Henderson (Karloff). Henderson reports to a mysterious figure known only as Mr. X (Van Sloan), who secretly runs a hospital where the gang's enemies are murdered and narcotics smuggled in their caskets. But while posing as Quinn, Hart must gain the trust of Arnold (King), a gang member being threatened by Mr. X because he's believed to be an informer. And while holing up in Arnold's house, Hart falls in love with Arnold's daughter, Julie (Cummings).

Mask isn't perfect, but it manages to find its most stable ground when it's on horror footing. While Holt is suitably dashing as the hero and Karloff is strong in his relatively minor role, it's Edward Van Sloan, appearing in no less than three disguises, who steals the picture. His final turn as the mysterious Mr. X, decked out in a surgeon's outfit as he threatens Hart's life with a scalpel, adds an extremely disturbing touch to an otherwise mostly so-so product. Never before had a doctor's operating outfit cloaked its wearer in such palpable menace. Van Sloan's line delivery stresses the threat in every syllable. "The pain whilst I am cutting through the outer layers of skin will not be unendurable. It is only when I commence to carve on your vital organs that you will know you are having … an experience," he tells Holt, before explaining that there comes a point when pain turns into ecstasy. His Mr. X is a truly creepy figure, and the fact that he runs a hospital of death instead of saving lives makes him all the more terrifying. Van Sloan may have made a powerful hero, but the actor was clearly just as at home with diabolical roles as he was playing kindly, resourceful old men.

On April 4, 1934, two years after the release of *Behind the Mask*, director John Francis Dillon died of an apparent heart attack at the still-youthful age of 49. He left behind a large but minor body of work, most of it in the silent era.

Russian-born screenwriter Jo Swerling (1893-1964) based the film's script on his own unpublished story, *In the Secret Service*. His name isn't much remembered today, but the films he wrote certainly are. They include the classics *Pennies from Heaven* (1936), *The Westerner* (1940), *Blood and Sand* (1941), *The Pride of the Yankees* (1942), *Lifeboat* (1944) and *Leave Her to Heaven* (1945), among many others. He also contributed to *Gone With the Wind* (1939) and *It's a Wonderful Life* (1946). In 1952, he won two Tony Awards for his work on the stage musical *Guys and Dolls*.

While many critics don't find *Mask* horrific enough to suit them, the ad line says it all: "A Slinking Fiend—Skulking Figure—Mad Murder!" True, the film invokes clichés commonly associated with action/adventure and melodrama. But it still manages enough horror to qualify for inclusion in that scariest of genres. CW

Castle Sinister
Delta; b/w; 50 min; Great Britain
D/S/P: Widgey R. Newman
Cast: Eric Adeney, Haddon Mason, Wally Patch, Ilsa Kilpatrick, Edmund Kennedy

According to most available plot synopses, this lost British horror film concerned a mad scientist, Professor Bandov (Adeney), who, believing that certain glands can bring about the rejuvenation of human tissue, attempts to place the brain of a woman into the body of an ape. A *Bioscope* review from April 6, 1932 asserts that the film's focus was on its young hero (Patch), trapped on a large country estate during a windstorm—which, one can assume, belongs to the aforementioned misguided scientist. There's also a beautiful young woman on hand to supply the requisite romantic interludes and imperiled flight.

By all accounts, this was one of the few outright horror films made in Britain during the early sound era (others include *The Bells*, 1930; *The Face at the Window*, 1932 and *The Ghoul*, 1933). Most British horror films of that time tended to be either uneasy horror-mystery hybrids or horror comedies. And while *Castle Sinister*'s plot seems far from original (there had been numerous silent films before it with the same basic storyline), its focus does appear to have been on chills.

Jonathan Rigby, in his excellent book *English Gothic*, purports that *Castle Sinister* was released too early to have been influenced by the emergence of Hollywood's now-famous horror product, yet the fact that it appeared a whole year after the release of Universal's classic *Dracula* (1931)—and that it was a quota quickie quickly released after what was probably a rushed shooting schedule—suggests otherwise. Rigby's assertion that its plot was largely influenced by Fox's now-lost *The Wizard* (1927), however, appears to be on the money.

Newman's next horror film is the equally lost *The Unholy Quest* (1934), while another unrelated film titled *Castle Sinister* was released in 1948. CW

Chandu the Magician
Fox; b/w; 71min; U.S
Co-D: Marcel Varnel, *Co-D/FX:* William Cameron Menzies *S:* Barry Conners, Phillip Klein *C:* James (Wong) Howe *M:* R.H. Bassett, Peter Brunelli, Louis De Francesco, Glen Knight

Cast: Edmund Lowe, Irene Ware, Bela Lugosi, Herbert Mundin, Henry B. Walthall, Weldon Heyburn, June Lang, Michael Stuart, Virginia Hammond, Nigel De Brulier, John George, Charles Stevens, Dick Sutherland

Chandu (Lowe) is adept in the art of yoga. He can perform such miraculous acts as teleportation and mesmerism, though he's morally bound to do so only for mankind's benefit. When he learns that the villainous Roxor (Lugosi) has procured a death ray, he takes action to prevent the madman from achieving world domination.

The success of Universal's *Dracula* and *Frankenstein* (both 1931) prompted other studios to hop on the horror bandwagon. Paramount released *Dr. Jekyll and Mr. Hyde* (1931), Warner delivered *Doctor X* (1932) and MGM unleashed the controversial *Freaks* (1932). Fox Film Corporation (later 20th Century Fox) was a bit cautious about joining the pack, and its own foray into fright watered down the horror with a dose of Saturday matinee kiddy fare. Still, *Chandu the Magician*—based on a then-wildly-popular radio serial by Harry A. Earnshaw, Vera M. Oldham and R.R. Morgan and featuring Gayne Whitman in the title role—shrewdly secured its horror "street cred" by casting Bela Lugosi as the evil Roxor. The Hungarian-born actor would later find major studio work hard to come by, but at this point he was still at the peak of his popularity. And, frankly, the film would likely be long forgotten were it not for Lugosi's presence, along with that of cinematographer James Wong Howe and co-director/FX whiz William Cameron Menzies.

The screenplay is unremarkable—pure cliché—although it does pack a lot of quickly paced action into its 71 minutes. Its general air of innocent good-natured fun gives away the fact that children were its target audience (although there is a hint of pre-Code naughtiness on display when pretty blonde June Lang is put on the white-slavery auction block wearing nothing but a revealing slip). It's impossible to take any of it seriously, but Lugosi is fine as an imposing and believable menace.

His performance shines all the more when set against the rest of the cast. Edmund Lowe is wooden and unconvincing as Chandu; he lacks the otherworldly quality that the role requires, and he doesn't seem interested in trying to achieve it. He later amassed a number of credits in mainstream fare—appearing in the all-star *Dinner at Eight* the following year, and top-lining Universal's obscure "old dark house" thriller *The Great Impersonation* (1935)—but he proves disposable here. Similarly, Irene Ware, best known for her vacuous turn in *The Raven* (1935), fails to muster much believability as an imperiled princess, while Herbert Mundin provides only humor-free comic relief.

On the plus side, future Academy Award-winning cinematographer Howe (*Hud*, 1963) gives the film the look of a major production. His silky lighting and mobile camerawork make for some striking images; the rapid dolly flying through the winding tunnels of Roxor's lair remains impressive even today.

Menzies—revered by science fiction buffs for his paranoid classic *Invaders from Mars* (1953), though he netted his Oscar for the design on *Gone with the Wind* (1939)—is credited only as co-director, but there's no doubt that he contributed to the frequently impressive set designs and special effects.

Then there's Marcel Varnel, chiefly responsible for staging the dialogue-laden scenes that are, plainly put, a chore to

Bela Lugosi poses a threat to Irene Ware in this lobby card from Fox's *Chandu the Magician*.

sit through. Interestingly, when reviewer Val Guest declared in an English publication that if he couldn't write a better picture himself, he'd be thoroughly ashamed, Varnel saw the review and took Guest up on his contention. Guest penned *No Monkey Business* (1935) for the director and continued writing for him for some time before striking out to direct on his own. Today horror and science fiction aficionados revere Guest for such pictures as *The Quatermass Xperiment* (1954) and *The Day the Earth Caught Fire* (1961).

Chandu's success spawned a cheapie sequel in serial form, *The Return of Chandu* (1934), which was later reissued as two features—chapters one through four as *The Return of Chandu* (1934) and Chapters 5 through 12 as *Chandu on Magic Island* (1935). The producers of the low-budget follow-up learned from Fox's casting misstep and put a more compelling actor in *Return*'s lead role: Bela Lugosi. TH

Condemned to Death
Twickenham; b/w; 75 min; Great Britain

D: Walter Forde *S:* H. Fowler Mear, Bernard Merivale, Brock Williams *P:* Julius Hagen *C:* Sydney Blythe,

Cast: Arthur Wontner, Gillian Lind, Gordon Harker, Cyril Raymond, Jane Welsh, Norah Howard, Edmund Gwenn, Griffith Humphreys, T. Gordon Blythe, James Cunningham, Gilbert Davis, Bernard Brunel, H. St. Barbe West

Inspired by the James Dawson and George Goodchild play *Jack O'Lantern*, *Condemned to Death* is a remarkable little quota quickie that was meant to cash in on Britain's then-fresh interest in American horror films. After a jury condemns a criminal to death, the convicted man hypnotizes the judge, Sir Charles Wallington (Wontner), into murdering the jurors. As the corpses accumulate, a Scotland Yard inspector (Raymond) works to crack the case.

The film's mixture of horror and melodrama prefigures the work of George King and Tod Slaughter by a couple of years and the work of Britain's famed Hammer Film Productions by two and a half decades. Arthur Wontner, who played the judge, is better remembered today for playing Sherlock Holmes in the film series that preceded Basil Rathbone's. Wontner's other horror films include *Murder at the Baskervilles* (1937), *The Terror* (1938) and *Three Cases of Murder* (1955). CW

The Crooked Circle
Astor/Sono Art/World Wide; b/w; 59 (68, 70, 76) min; U.S.
  D: H. Bruce Humberstone *S:* Ralph Spence, Tim Whelan *P:* William Sistrom *C:* Robert B. Kurrle
  Cast: Zasu Pitts, James Gleason, Ben Lyon, Irene Purcell, C. Henry Gordon, Raymond Hatton, Roscoe Karns, Burton [Berton] Churchill, Spencer Charters, Robert Frazer, Ethel Clayton, Frank Reicher, Christian Rub, Tom Kennedy

The Crooked Circle is a largely forgotten footnote in horror-film history. The morbid mystery begins in the underground chamber of a hooded, black-robed group known as, yes, The Crooked Circle, professional criminals who play at occultism, swearing their loyalty over a human skull while making pronouncements of death against those who threaten them. They perform a ritual in which each draws a card from the skull, with the lucky winner assigned the assassination of one of their enemies, in this case one Colonel Wolters (Churchill), who is a member of a group of criminologists known as The Sphinx Club. Wolters has arranged a meeting of the club at his manor house to install psychic Swami Yoganda (Gordon) as the group's new head, replacing Brand Osborne (Lyon). Everyone, good and bad guy alike, gathers at the predictably old, predictably dark house. Horror turns to humor and then becomes horror again before ending on a humorous note ... or something like that.

Much of the film is dull, but it does have its moments, such as the first appearance of the Renfield-like Old Dan (Rub), caretaker of the estate. He warns heroine Norah Rafferty (Pitts) that the house is haunted by a sad and vengeful ghost who plays the violin in anticipation of disaster—and indeed, shortly after hearing that violin play its first mournful tune, Captain Wolters disappears, then turns up apparently dead before vanishing again. The house itself is nicely done, a distinguished and relatively creepy setting, though there are long stretches in which its potential goes unutilized. It's equipped with secret panels leading to cobwebbed passages, of course, as well as with moving skeletons. There's also a skulking hermit (Hatton) and a swooning damsel-in-distress, along with a jittery housemaid and scaredy-cat cop whose frightened shenanigans get stale quickly. (To the filmmakers' credit, at least the audience is spared the usual scared African American servant usually found in horror and mystery films of the period.)

The often-flat mix of comedy and horror seems fated when one learns that Florida-born Ralph Spence (1889-1949) wrote the screenplay; he had authored the classic and oft-filmed stage play *The Gorilla*. A title-card writer during the silent era, Spence gained a reputation as a film doctor, a man who could transform a mediocre screenplay into cinematic gold, making him something of the Frank Darabont of his day. He usually did this by adding humorous touches, and by the time the sound era rolled around, he was regularly working with Wheeler and Woolsey or Laurel and Hardy, earning film credits galore and scads of money (allegedly as much as $5 a word, a princely sum in the 1920s and '30s). Spence's last film credit was for *Plainsman and the Lady* (1946), which was based on one of his stories, though he had retired from the industry a couple of years earlier. He died three years later of a heart attack, leaving a mass of editing and writing credits. His many horror films included *On Time* (1924), *The Gorilla* (1927, 1930, and 1939), *Tomorrow at Seven* (1933), *Sh! The Octopus* (1937) and *The Smiling Ghost* (1941), the last one for which he went uncredited.

Adding to *Crooked Circle*'s entertainment value are minor performances by various character actors popular at the time, including C. Henry Gordon (who played a similar role in *Thirteen Women* the same year), Raymond Hatton (*The Devil-Stone*, 1917), Berton Churchill (*The Avenger*, 1933), Spencer Charters (*The Raven*, 1935), Robert Frazer (*Daughter of the Tong*, 1939) and Frank Reicher (*Before Dawn*, 1933). CW

The Death Kiss
K.B.S.; b/w; 71 (75) min; U.S.
  D: Edwin L. Marin *S:* Gordon Kahn, Barry Barringer *P:* E.W. Hammons *C:* Norbert Brodine *M:* Arthur Lange
  Cast: David Manners, Adrienne Ames, Bela Lugosi, John Wray, Vince Barnett, Alexander Carr, Edward Van Sloan, Harold Minjir, Barbara Bedford, Al Hill, Harold Waldridge

An actor is murdered while doing the final scene of a film, and he was romantically linked to the wives of numerous people connected to the production. Studio writer Franklin Drew (Manners) decides to play amateur detective and uncover the identity of the killer, much to the chagrin of the lead detective (Wray).

This ad for *The Death Kiss* focuses on Lugosi's fearsome presence, making the film appear more horror oriented than it actually was.

This cheapie is a perennial favorite of public domain aficionados. Despite its poverty row production values, it provides a glimpse into the world of 1930s filmmaking—and reunites three of the lead actors from Tod Browning's *Dracula* (1931).

Much was made at the time of Bela Lugosi's presence in *The Death Kiss*, but in truth he doesn't get a chance to contribute a great deal. He's tasked with skulking around looking sinister, which was no great stretch for the actor. Edward Van Sloan, who had played Professor Van Helsing in the earlier film, is given a few good moments and figures memorably in the climax, though he was cast in a minor role as a director.

It is David Manners, however, who is expected to carry the show. Based on his wooden turn as Jonathan Harker in *Dracula*, one might at first consider this cause for alarm. It's largely forgotten, though, that the Canadian-born actor proved engaging and capable in much of his lesser-known work—which, thankfully, includes this. He gives a highly competent performance as the smarmy writer-turned-private detective. It was one of few leading roles he ever landed, playing his usual second-fiddle to Boris Karloff in *The Mummy* the same year.

Director Edwin L. Marin, an efficient hack who would wind up churning out close to 60 features, made his debut with this picture. His direction is none too creative, but he does a capable job of keeping the film moving.

The Death Kiss is certainly not a disagreeable way to spend 70-plus minutes. Its story is reasonably engaging, its revelation of the killer's identity manages to surprise and, while it's not so much a horror film as a murder mystery, its cast and set-up should be of mild interest to horror enthusiasts. TH

Dr. Jekyll and Mr. Hyde

Vance; b/w; 10 min; U.S.
  D/P/S: William Vance
  Cast: William Vance

Dr. Jekyll (Vance) concocts a formula that isolates the evil side of the human personality. Using himself as a guinea pig, he unleashes the wild and depraved Mr. Hyde (also Vance).

This amateurish short subject was the debut of actor/producer/director William Vance. A college friend and associate of Orson Welles, Vance went on to co-direct Welles' first work behind the camera, *The Hearts of Age* (1934). That film flopped and immediately faded into obscurity. And while Welles had mastered filmmaking by the time he made his official debut with *Citizen Kane* in 1941, Vance never really did. Following his one-shot collaboration with Welles, he left cinema, eventually finding a niche directing TV commercials.

The film has vanished from circulation; if a copy exists anywhere today, it is likely in someone's private collection. TH

Doctor X

Warner/First National; both b/w and color versions; 76 min; U.S.
  D: Michael Curtiz *S:* Robert Tasker, Earl Baldwin *P:* Hal B. Wallis, Darryl F. Zanuck *C:* Ray Rennahan (Color version), Richard Towers (Black-and-white version) *M:* Bernhard Kaun *FX:* Fred Jackman, Jr.
  Cast: Lionel Atwill, Lee Tracy, Fay Wray, Preston Foster, John Wray, Harry Beresford, Arthur Edmund Carewe, Leila Bennett, Robert Warwick, George Rosener, Willard Robertson, Thomas E. Jackson, Harry Holman, Mae Busch, Tom Dugan

The Moon Killer, a shadowy figure who cannibalizes his victims, terrorizes New York City. Reporter Lee Taylor (Tracy) is determined to crack the case, and he sets his sights on the mysterious Dr. Xavier (Atwill) as a suspect. Following his hunch to Xavier's secluded mansion, he discovers the doctor conducting an experiment in his own effort to find the murderer.

Based on a stage play by Howard W. Cornstock and Allen C. Miller, *Doctor X* is noteworthy as the first horror film to be shot entirely in two-color Technicolor. Most color films before it were hand-stenciled (*The Haunted Castle*, 1897, for example), though Charles Urban shot the now-lost *Dr. Jekyll and Mr. Hyde* (1913) using his own Kinemacolor process, and Universal's *Phantom of the Opera* (1925) had a color masquerade ball sequence in the midst of its black-and-white. Warner Bros-First National had signed a deal with Technicolor for access to a newly improved two-strip color process, which, like Urban's process, favored red and green hues. The palette of available tints lent itself well to the surreal and macabre, and *Doctor X* utilized it to the hilt.

Warner clearly had reservations about diving into the genre; the film was conceived and marketed as a mixture of horror and comedy *a la The Cat and the Canary* (1927). Like many films of its type from the period, the comedy relief can be a bit overbearing. Most of the attempted levity comes from Lee Tracy in the central role of ace-reporter Lee Taylor, and one's reaction to

big screen's first authentic scream queen. She gets to scream here, too, but far less effectively; she is put upon—twice—to simply walk onscreen and over-react to the sight of her father doing something shady.

Indeed, the film has more than a few awkward moments, and the story, if dwelt upon, doesn't make a great deal of sense. Yet it manages a consistent level of odd style. Director Michael Curtiz (1886-1962) had earlier dabbled in the horror genre with a now-lost version of *Alraune* (1918). His greatest success came a decade after *Doctor X*, when he scored an Oscar for directing *Casablanca* (1942). His work here gives away his formative professional years in the European film scene, and he makes terrific use of odd camera angles and indirect lighting.

The color photography by Ray Rennahan is wonderfully unnatural, evoking (whether intentionally or not) the look of faded comic panels. Interestingly, Warner simultaneously shot a black-and-white version, just in case the cost of color processing ended up proving prohibitive. Though this alternate version is no longer in circulation, it is said to have utilized mostly the same takes as the color release. (Reportedly, a separate cinematographer positioned his camera next to the Technicolor model and shot the same material at the same time.)

The film's success inspired Warner to reteam Curtiz, Atwill, and Wray for another color horror film, *The Mystery of the Wax Museum*, the very next year. What many mistake as a belated follow-up, *The Return of Dr. X* (1939) has no real connection to this film. That film cast Humphrey Bogart as a *different* mysterious Dr. X, back from the dead and needing regular blood transfusions to remain alive. TH

Tracy's wise-guy, rat-a-tat performance will contribute a great deal to his or her response to *Doctor X* as a whole. While some will doubtlessly find Tracy sporadically amusing, the film works best when it forgoes laughs and focuses on the horror.

The script is surprisingly risqué for its time and country of origin. Its plot incorporates elements of drug addiction, cannibalism and rape; and Tracy's character even visits a brothel (where he makes a lame attempt at picking up one of the women). The film's cannibalism isn't graphic, of course, but descriptions of the killer's proclivities are wonderfully lurid.

Doctor X also marks the genre debut of one of horror's most beloved character stars, London-born Lionel Atwill (1885-1946), who had made his stage debut in 1905 and quickly established himself as a matinee idol (and talented theatrical director) on both sides of the Atlantic. He moved into film work in 1918 and, unlike many of his theatrical contemporaries, immediately realized and embraced the possibilities of the medium. With his piercing eyes and sonorous delivery, he quickly became a favorite heavy to cinemagoers—a role the actor relished.

In the first of three horror films in which they appeared together, Atwill is paired with Fay Wray (1907-2004), here cast as his daughter. Wray would famously find her greatest success being menaced by *King Kong* (1933), and she was arguably the

The Face at the Window
Real Art; b/w; 52 min; Great Britain
D: Leslie Hiscott *S:* H. Fowler Mear *P:* Julius Hagen *C:* Sydney Blythe
Cast: Raymond Massey, Eric Maturin, Isla Bevan, Claude Hulbert, Henry Mollison, A. Bromley Davenport, Harold Meade, Dennis Wyndham, Charles Groves

This is the first sound-era film adaptation of F. Brooke Warren's phenomenally successful stage play *The Face at the Window*. It followed two silent adaptations (1919, 1920), both of which carried the same title. Relatively obscure today, this version has been eclipsed by Tod Slaughter's barnstorming adaptation of 1939.

Raymond Massey stars as a Parisian detective on the trail of a murderous bank robber who kills night watchmen with a poison-dispensing ring. In the end, it takes the revival of a murder victim (a current of electricity is used to stimulate his muscles to animation) to reveal that the killer is none other than Count Fournal (Maturin).

Canadian-born Massey went on to a respectable career in Hollywood, starring alongside the likes of Errol Flynn (*Santa Fe Trail*, 1940), Cary Grant (*Arsenic and Old Lace*, 1944), Gary Cooper (*The Fountainhead*, 1949), Gregory Peck and Susan Hayward (*David and Bathsheba*, 1951) and James Dean (*East of Eden*, 1955), among many others. CW

Fantômas
Braunberger-Richebé; b/w; 79 (91, 62) min; France

D/Co-S: Paul Fejos *Co-S:* Anne Mauclair *P:* Pierre Braunberger, Roger Richebé *C:* J. Peverell Marley

Cast: Thomy Bourdelle, Tania Fédor, Jean Worms, George Rigaud, Anielka Elter, Roger Karl, Maurice Schutz, Gaston Modot, Marie-Laure, Jean Galland, Philippe Richard, Georges Mauloy, Paul Azaïs

Created in 1911 by novelists Marcel Allain and Pierre Souvestre, Fantômas may be pop literature's first anti-hero, a sociopathic serial killer who murders in a variety of sadistic ways and often takes on the identities of those he dispatches. That such a character so quickly captured the public imagination indicates just how rapidly the literary transition from Gothic horror to modern-day crime novel caught on. The film rights to the character were swiftly snatched up by popular French silent-film director Louis Feuillade. Feuillade followed the novels' ingenious approach to the character by serializing his filmed exploits. He also toned down the character's murderous exploits, recreating him as something of a hero for the disenfranchised.

For this *Fantômas*, the first talkie film adaptation, director Paul Fejos (*Lord Arthur Saville's Crime*, 1920; *Queen of Spades*, 1922) went all the way back to the first novel. He sets the first half of his film in the dark and Gothic confines of an old chateau on a stormy night, where the elderly Marquise de Langrune (Marie-Laure) has invited her friends and family to witness the transaction of a significant amount of money, brought to her by Lord Beltham (Worms). During the night, Fantômas (Galland), bedecked in black and apparently knowledgeable of the chateau's many hidden passages, brutally murders the Marquise and steals the money, prompting his nemesis Inspector Juve (Bourdelle) to enter the case.

The first portion of the film is amazingly faithful to its source material, but once it steps into the daylight world of crime and espionage, it strays—and in doing so becomes much less interesting, despite the occasional murder. And unfortunately, Fantômas himself, often seen clad in a skin-tight black suit and mask, is more goofy-looking than chilling (though the sequence in which he murders the Marquise is one of the film's highlights).

Howling wind, blazing candles, secret passages and mysterious, black-gloved hands cutting telephone wires or appearing out of secret passages set the film's first half well within horror territory. There's an undeniable debt to Universal's silent classic *The Cat and the Canary* (1927), which should come as no surprise given that in 1927 Fejos was not only housed at Universal, he also directed the horror film *The Last Performance* for the company.

The next film adaptation of the venerable character came in 1937, with two more appearances in the 1940s. In the 1960s, the character got his most popular big-screen incarnation in a series of movies made in response to the success of Dr. Mabuse's 1960 German revival by director Fritz Lang. CW

Freaks
aka **Forbidden Love**; **Nature's Mistakes**; **The Monster Show**
MGM; b/w; 64 min; U.S.

D/Co-P: Tod Browning *S:* Willis Goldbeck, Leon Gordon, Charles MacArthur, Edgar Allan Woolf *Co-P:* Irving G. Thalberg, Harry Rapf *C:* Merritt B. Gerstad

Cast: Wallace Ford, Olga Baclanova, Harry Earles, Leila Hyams, Henry Victor, Roscoe Ates, Daisy Earles, Rose Dione, Daisy Hilton, Violet Hilton, Schlitze, Johnny Eck, Josephine Joseph, Frances O'Connor, Peter Robinson, Olga Roderick, Koo, Prince Randian, Martha Morris, Elvira Snow, Jenny Lee Snow, Angelo Rossitto, Elizabeth Green, Edward Brophy, Matt McHugh, Michael Visaroff

Tod Browning's controversial *Freaks* is set among the denizens of a traveling circus. Together with strongman Hercules (Victor), a trapeze artist named Cleopatra (Baclanova) hatches a scheme to con midget Hans (Harry Earles) into believing that

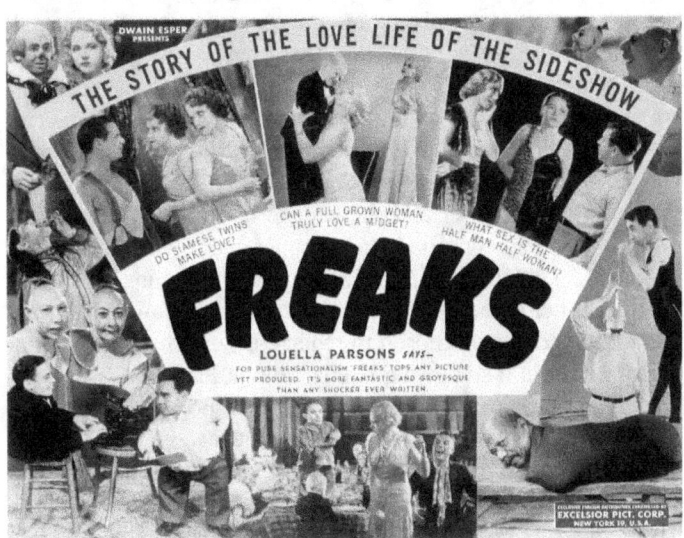

Hercules (Henry Victor) and Cleopatra (Olga Baclanova), the normal people, become the real villains of *Freaks*, not little person Hans (Harry Earles).

she's in love with him. Despite Hans' engagement to another midget named Frieda (Daisy Earles), he's duped into marrying Cleopatra, who then begins to slowly poison him. Her plan is to kill him without arousing suspicion and then, after inheriting his fortune, run off with Hercules.

During the making of *The Unholy Three* (1925), diminutive actor Harry Earles brought the film's director, Tod Browning, a short story titled *Spurs*. Providentially, Tod Robbins, who wrote the novel upon which *The Unholy Three* is based, wrote *Spurs*. The story appealed to Earles because it offered a leading role to a little person. And with its circus backdrop and tale of mutilation and revenge, it also fit the dark sensibilities of Browning, whose varied career had included a stint on the carnival circuit. He arranged for Metro-Goldwyn-Mayer—then his home studio—to purchase the rights as a vehicle for another *Unholy* co-star named Lon Chaney. When Chaney died of a throat hemorrhage related to lung cancer in 1930, the project went into hiatus.

Later, riding high on the success of *Dracula* (1931)—which he directed while on loan to Universal—Browning revisited the idea of bringing *Spurs* to the screen. He approached MGM producer Irving G. Thalberg, who was likewise interested in tapping into the public's newfound interest in horror. When Browning pitched *Spurs*, the producer worried that it might be too horrific. Yet the go-ahead was given, and the project, once commenced, morphed into *Freaks*.

The director cast the widest array of sideshow performers ever assembled in a single venue. The "normal" characters proved more problematic to cast, however. The role of Cleopatra was assigned to Myrna Loy, then under contract to MGM, but the script repulsed her and she begged to be released from the project. Thalberg complied, then cast her in the even more overtly sadistic *The Mask of Fu Manchu* (1932), playing the kinkiest role of her career as Fu Manchu's nymphomaniac daughter. Olga Baclanova was chosen to replace Loy, perhaps due to her performance in a somewhat similar role in Paul Leni's impressive *The Man Who Laughs* (1928). Correspondingly, the part of good-hearted Venus was originally slated for Jean Harlow, a major box-office draw due to *Hell's Angels* (1930) and *Public Enemy* (1931). At the last second, however, Leila Hyams (*Island of Lost Souls*, 1932) took her place.

The loss of major star power doubtless diluted the film's potential box-office, but nobody could have anticipated the public's revulsion to *Freaks* or the lingering impact it would have on Browning's career. (Reviews in general were similarly vitriolic.) The film didn't merely flop; it was, rather, a rare instance of controversy keeping audiences away rather than drawing them in. Browning never recovered from the drubbing; just as *Dracula*'s success put him at the top of the heap, *Freaks* ended up destroying his career.

The British censor was sufficiently horrified to ban the picture outright, and it encountered serious difficulties in the United States as well. The 90-minute preview version, after going over poorly, was cut drastically and partially reshot. A disclaimer was also grafted onto the film's beginning, citing the filmmakers' "humility" in the face of the *abnormal* "blunders of nature" contained in the film. Nobody bought it.

Regrettably, the film survives only in its truncated, watered down form. But even in this form, it remains a remarkable achievement. Though undeniably crude and at times even awkward, the film does present a sincerely compassionate portrait of "otherness." Seen today, it's hard to understand why audiences were so outraged. If anything, Browning is to be commended for the pains taken to depict the "freaks" as human beings. In showing the sideshow performers as having real lives, loves, miseries and dreams, he humanizes them in a genuinely striking manner.

It is intentionally obvious, in fact, who the "freaks" of the film really are; the "normal" Cleopatra and Hercules are as vile and twisted a pair of characters as one can find in a Hollywood film of this vintage. Browning takes advantage of pre-Production Code laxity to paint their relationship in purely sexual terms. ("How do you like them?" Cleopatra posits, supposedly inquiring about how the muscle man likes his eggs, but the fact that she does so while thrusting her breasts at him leaves no doubt as to what she's really asking.) Browning's contempt for the couple is evident throughout, as is his delight at the vengeance wreaked upon them at the end of the picture.

The precise process of that revenge is obscure—if not completely incomprehensible—in the surviving cut of the picture; Cleopatra ends up a legless, scarred "chicken woman," the very

Director Tod Browning poses with the chicken woman on the set of *Freaks*.

sort of sideshow "freak" she had previously mocked. Hercules simply disappears in the edited version, but in the preview cut, he too was on display—singing castrato in a new sideshow exhibit. (Obviously, the suggestion of genital mutilation was too over-the-top for audiences of the time.)

Freaks is not a perfect film. Due largely to the recutting, the continuity gets a bit jumbled at times, and the retooled ending is far too sentimental. There are also some awkward performances, but it helps to remember that the cast is mostly comprised of amateurs; that Browning got what he did out of them is a testimony to his skill with actors. The film remains one of the most distinctive titles in the history of cinema (horror or otherwise). Its reputation has grown over the years, winning over generations of new admirers.

Many filmmakers have openly paid homage to the film, ranging from the grotesquerie of Alejandro Jodorowsky's *El Topo* (1971) to the apocalyptic vision of Werner Herzog's *Even Dwarfs Started Small* (1970) and the nightmare imagery of David Lynch's *Eraserhead* (1977). More recently, the teleseries *South Park* and Martin Scorsese's groundbreaking *The Wolf of Wall Street* have made reference to Browning's now-classic work of art. Browning didn't live to see any of this—he passed away in 1962 after years of self-imposed seclusion—but the fact that the project which had ruined his career has gone on to so much acclaim is a touching vindication in itself. TH

The Frightened Lady
aka **Criminal at Large**
British Lion; b/w; 87 (70) min; Great Britain
D: T. Hayes Hunter *S:* Angus MacPhail, Bryan Edgar Wallace *P:* Michael Balcon
Cast: Emlyn Williams, Cathleen Nesbitt, Belle Chrystall, Norman McKinnel, Gordon Harker, Cyril Raymond, D.A. Clarke-Smith, Percy Parsons, Finlay Currie, Julian Royce, Eric Roland

Lady Aisla (Chrystall) is invited to stay with Lord Lebanon (Williams) and his domineering mother, Lady Lebanon (Nesbitt). Lady Lebanon lets it be known that she wants her son to marry Aisla, but the young woman isn't in the least interested. The plot thickens when two other visitors are strangled, and after an attempt on Aisla's life, Chief Inspector Tanner (McKinnel) unmasks the culprit.

Edgar Wallace published his novel *The Frightened Lady* in 1932, and this first cinematic adaptation hit theaters soon after. Michael Balcon, who took over Ealing Film Studios six years later and guided it into producing classics in a range of genres, including comedy (*Kind Hearts and Coronets*, 1949) and horror (*Dead of Night*, 1945), produced the film.

Uninspired journeyman T. Hayes Hunter directed *The Frightened Lady*. He is best remembered today for helming the Boris Karloff vehicle *The Ghoul* (1933), which, as is the case here, displays his lack of affinity for the horror genre.

Interestingly, *Lady*'s script was adapted by none other than Wallace's son, Bryan Edgar Wallace, who went on to become a popular thriller writer himself. Assisting in crafting the script was Angus MacPhail (1903-1962), a screenwriter whose lasting claim to fame is his affiliation with Alfred Hitchcock. Some film historians credit MacPhail with devising the beloved "MacGuffin" plot device that figured so prominently in the Master of Suspense's movies (in essence, the MacGuffin is an all-important but deliberately vague plot point that sets the action in motion).

Welsh writer/actor/director Emlyn Williams makes his cinematic acting debut in *Lady* as the spineless Lord Lebanon; his later performing credits include Hitchcock's *Jamaica Inn* (1939) and the interesting, artsy horror title *Eye of the Devil* (1966). He is best known, however, for writing the hit play *Night Must Fall* (1935), in which he played the quietly maniacal male lead. It was filmed several times, most famously in 1937 and 1964.

Cathleen Nesbitt portrayed *Lady*'s domineering mother and would later essay a key role in Hitchcock's final feature, *Family Plot* (1975). Her horror credits include *Chamber of Horrors* (1940) and *The Haunting of Julia* (1977), and she also repeated her role as Lady Lebanon in the live BBC TV broadcast of *The Case of the Frightened Lady* in 1938.

Finlay Currie later appeared in *The 49th Parallel* (1941) and *I Know Where I'm Going!* (1945) for Michael Powell and Emeric Pressberger, respectively, and *Great Expectations* (1946), for David Lean. He also lent solid support to the atmospheric Boris Karloff chiller *Corridors of Blood* (1958).

The Frightened Lady was remade several times in all; in addition to the BBC broadcast, other versions appeared in 1940 (as *The Case of the Frightened Lady*), 1963 (as *The Indian Scarf*, part of the series of German-made *krimis* based on Wallace) and 1983 (another British TV version, again titled *The Case of the Frightened Lady*). TH

Geheimnis des blauen Zimmers
aka **Secret of the Blue Room**
Engels & Schmidt; b/w; 73 min; Germany
D/P: Erich Engels *S:* Arnold Lipp *C:* Hugo von Kaweczynski *M:* Heinz Letton
Cast: Theodor Loos, Else Elster, Hans Adalbert Schlettow, Wolfgang Staudte, Peter Wolff, Oskar Sima, Gerhard Dammann, Paul Henckels, Betty Bird, Reihold Bernt, Bernhard Goetzke

The mysterious blue room of a German castle is reputed to be haunted. Looking to impress Irene (Elster) and thus win her affections, Axel (Schlettow), Frank (Staudte) and Thomas (Wolff) take a mutual dare: Each will spend a night alone in the blue room, and whoever emerges unscathed will vie for Irene's hand in marriage. The agreement is hatched in the spirit of fun, but when Thomas disappears on the first night and Frank is killed on the second, the enjoyment quickly fades.

Based on a story by Erich Phillipi, this obscure German production has vanished, though it remains noteworthy for inspiring three U.S. remakes by Universal Studios—*Secret of the Blue Room* (1933), *The Missing Guest* (1938) and *Murder in the Blue Room* (1944). The first remake, helmed by German émigré Kurt Neumann less than a year after this film's release, seems to have followed the original with the most fidelity; the screenplay for that film, written by William Hurlbut (*The Bride of Frankenstein*, 1935), even recycles most of the character names.

The cast of the German original includes Theodor Loos, a popular presence in German films of the period; he can also be seen as the sinister doctor who tempts *The Student of Prague* (1935). Director Erich Engels (not to be confused with Erich Engel, who specialized in heavier fare) never made much of a name for himself, even within the confines of his native Germany. TH

Get That Girl
Talmadge/Mercury; b/w; 61 (67) min; U.S.

D: George Crone *S:* Charles R. Condon *P:* Richard Talmadge *C:* Harry Jackson, Jack Stevens

Cast: Richard Talmadge, Shirley Grey, Fred Malatesta, Carl Stockdale, Lloyd Ingram, Geneva Mitchell, Victor Stanford,

After being followed to the train station by three heavies (one of them in drag), Ruth Dale (Grey)—an heiress to a large estate—comes to believe that her suitor, an innocent salesman named Dick (Talmadge), is involved in something shady. After she alerts the police to her suspicions, her pursuers get Dick out of the way long enough to kidnap her. They take her to a gloomy asylum presided over by the mad Dr. Tito (Malatesta) and his wife Nedra (Mitchell), who try in vain to force her to sign over her inheritance to them. When Dick tracks her down and tries to rescue her, he's captured and taken to Tito's laboratory. Nedra, who finds Dick attractive, offers to free him on the condition that she gets to come along. But their plan is interrupted by her husband, whose particular mad experimentation, it turns out, involves turning people (mostly beautiful women) into mannequins! The police arrive in search of Dick, and while they're occupied with the doctor, Nedra and Dick escape—right into their arms. Dr. Tito sees this as his cue to turn Ruth into a mannequin, but Dick gives the police the slip and saves her.

Get That Girl is fast moving and fun, though it has plot holes aplenty. Producer/actor Richard Talmadge (real name: Sylvester Metzetti), who stars as Dick, began his career in the silent era as a stunt actor. After moving to Hollywood, he became popular in his own right, but a high-pitched voice killed his acting career with the majors when cinema transitioned from silents to talkies. He responded by producing his own vehicles, often casting himself as the acrobatic male lead, and *Get that Girl* was one of these. Part of its appeal lies in Talmadge's ability to do multiple daring stunts in long, unedited takes. Too bad the action scenes are somewhat undone by the goofy cinematography, which is a bit too Keystone Cops to completely work.

Talmadge was born in Germany in 1892. Barnum and Bailey brought him to the United States and presented him, along with his two equally athletic brothers, as the Mazetti Troupe. He worked as a stunt double for Douglas Fairbanks before becoming an actor himself. He died of cancer in Carmel, California in 1981.

Primarily an action flick, *Get That Girl* doesn't really become horror until the nature of the doctor's experiments is revealed. It also utilizes typical comedy relief, with one bit involving an old deaf lady and a Tarot reading actually managing to be funny.

Shirley Grey, a bit player under contract to Paramount for a brief period, was something of a scream queen during the mid-1930s, even starring in Hammer Film Productions' first feature-length stab at horror, *Phantom Ship* (1935). Not liking the direction in which her career was going, however, she retired that same year. *Get That Girl* requires little from her other than the odd scream here and there. CW

Ghost Valley
RKO; b/w; 54 min; U.S.

D: Fred Allen *S:* Adele S. Buffington *P:* Harry Joe Brown *C:* Ted McCord *M:* Max Steiner, Arthur Lange

Cast: Tom Keene, Merna Kennedy, Kate Campbell, Mitchell Harris, Ted Adams, Harry Bowen, Harry Semels, Ernie Adams, Bill Franey, George 'Gabby' Hayes, Jack Kirk, Tom London, Buck Moulton, Al Taylor, Slim Whitaker

Corrupt Judge Drake (Harris) and his henchman Gordon (Adams) are looking to bilk Jane (Kennedy) out of her inheritance. A charismatic stranger (Keene) comes to the rescue.

Ghost Valley is an early example of the horror-Western hybrid. Though the subgenre never really caught fire, a number of similar titles followed over the ensuing years, culminating in such noteworthy entries as Antonio Margheriti's *And God Said to Cain* (1970) and Clint Eastwood's *High Plains Drifter* (1973). The ads for *Ghost Valley* promised the "Chills of a Mystery Shocker, Thrills of a Wild Western, Combined in a double-barreled ACTION ATTRACTION," a reminder that it's often not entirely wise to place too much stock in advertising. The horror elements—a spooky abandoned mining town and a little haunted house action—are there but relatively low-key. At its core, the film is very much a B-grade Western, indistinguishable from many others of the period (though production company RKO had access to better production resources and personnel than, say, Monogram or Republic).

Vienna-born music director Max Steiner entered cinema in 1929 and was near the beginning of his long and distinguished career here; the following year he composed the groundbreaking soundtrack for RKO's *King Kong*, and in later years he netted Oscars for *The Informer* (1935), *Now, Voyager* (1942) and *Since You Went Away* (1945). His scores for *Gone with the Wind* (1939), *Casablanca* (1942) and *Life with Father* (1948) were given further nominations. He remained a prolific presence until the 1960s, with the latter part of his career spent working in the medium of television. He died in 1971.

The film's stunts were the work of Yakima Canutt. A former rodeo rider, he broke into films around 1910 and eventually became a long-time stunt double/personal friend to John Wayne. He's best remembered today, however, for staging the chariot race in William Wyler's Oscar-winning *Ben-Hur* (1959).

John Wayne as he appeared in the horror oater *Haunted Gold.*

The cast is top-lined by Tom Keene, star of many low-budget oaters of the 1930s and '40s. Keene never clicked with the public in the same way as John Wayne or even Lash LaRue, and while reasonably famous, Keene's star never quite ignited. One of his last credits was as Colonel Tom Edwards in Ed Wood's infamous *Plan 9 from Outer Space* (1959). By contrast, George "Gabby" Hayes, seen here sans his trademark scruffy beard, became a hugely popular fixture in Hollywood Westerns until he retired from the screen in 1951. TH

Haunted Gold

Warner; b/w; 58 min; U.S.

D: Mack V. Wright *S:* Adele S. Buffington *P:* Leon Schlesinger *C:* Nicholas Musuraca

Cast: John Wayne, Sheila Terry, Harry Woods, Erville Alderson, Otto Hoffman, Martha Mattox, Blue Washington

A wonderfully lurid opening credit sequence ripped right from Universal's *Dracula* (1931) telegraphs from the get-go that *Haunted Gold* is a byproduct of Hollywood's Golden Age of horror films.

The 1931-1932 period saw the birth of more horror-influenced films than at any time before it. The worldwide success of *Dracula* and *Frankenstein* (also 1931) put interest in the dark and moody at an all-time high, and producers scrambled to rework mainstream fare into products palatable to horror audiences. This typically involved adorning conventional mysteries with "old dark house" trappings or an accursed "Hindoo" jewel. Even Westerns were dressed up in monster suits more frequently than they had been in the past, as is the case with this early talkie oater starring John Wayne himself, his horse Duke, and his African American sidekick Blue Washington.

As if the animated bats and black-clad figure of death in the opening credits weren't enough to establish the spooky tone, the film begins on a dark and stormy night. Wolves howl in the background as Musuraca's camera prowls the deserted dirt streets of a ghost town, the doors of its haunted buildings flapping in the wind. Eyes peer from a narrow slit behind an old painting, keeping watch as an outlaw gang awaits the return of one of their own. But the only men to ride into town this night are John Mason (Wayne) and Clarence Washington Brown (Washington), who pass an eerie cemetery en route and encounter a riderless horse. On the horse is pinned a note from a phantom, threatening death to anyone who breeches the confines of the Sally Anne Mine.

Director Wright goes further to establish the film's horror bona fides; shadowy shapes abound, along with secret passages, a mysterious figure in black, cobwebs, rats, a haunted mine and creepy, zombie-like servants—most of it set in, yes, an old dark house. There's even a scene in which an organ is played (atop which sits the statuette made famous in the original *The Maltese Falcon*, 1931).

Mason has come to call on Janet Carter (Terry), co-owner of the mine. She fears that something sinister is afoot, and boy is she right. But unfortunately for horror fans, the thrills dissipate as mundane Western hijinks take over ... though not before Washington gets to do the standard bug-eyed "scared" routine, a sure-fire knee-slapper in the 1930's and '40's if its prevalence in the cinema of that time is any indicator. After a couple of horse chases and fist fights, it's all revealed to have been a plot to scam the mine, which still contains gold, from its rightful owner.

Haunted Gold was one in a series of low-grade Westerns shot by Warner Bros. and starring John Wayne, released during 1932 and 1933; shortly thereafter, Wayne's contract with the company ended, and he wandered through a forest of grade-Z

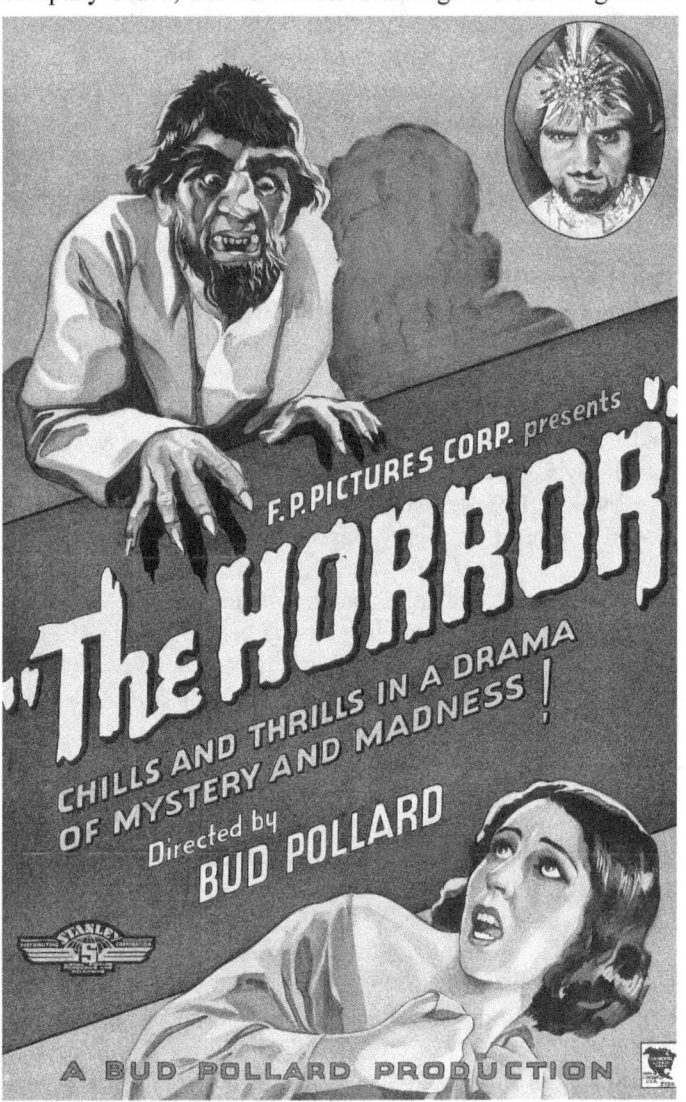

Westerns before finding everlasting fame in John Ford's *Stagecoach* (1939), which was produced by Walter Wanger for United Artists but today resides, interestingly enough, at the very company that had let Wayne go.

A remake of the silent weird Western *The Phantom City* (1928), *Haunted Gold* uses plenty of stock footage from the original, mostly of Ken Maynard and his horse Tarzan standing in for Wayne and his horse Duke in long shots. CW

The Horror
aka **The Monster; John the Drunkard**
Pollard/F.P. Pictures; b/w; 70 min; U.S.

D/P: Bud Pollard *S:* Basil Smith *C:* Dal Clawson *M:* William David

Cast: Leslie King, Jimmie Kelo, Ilene Myers, Reed Brown, Jr., Gus Alexander, John Gray, Raja Rabold, Nyreda Montez

This routine "old dark house" story reportedly featured a damsel in distress (Myers), a mysterious killer and an ape-like monster.

Producer/director Bud Pollard was active through the 1930s and '40s, but he wasn't particularly productive, and his work is long since forgotten. Some sources list him as the first president of the Screen Director's Guild, but the official DGA database lists King Vidor in that capacity (from 1936 to 1938).

The Horror's cast doesn't include any familiar names, which doubtless contributes to its obscurity. Though reissued in the 1940s as *John the Drunkard* (the film was altered considerably to cater to the time's trendy interest in alcoholism, with the horror angle greatly reduced), all incarnations of the film have since disappeared from view; as a result, it is believed to be lost. TH

The Hound of the Baskervilles
Gaumont British; b/w; 75 min; Great Britain

D/Co-S: V. Gareth Gundry *Co-S:* Edgar Wallace *P:* Michael Balcon *C:* Bernard Knowles

Cast: Robert Rendel, Frederick Lloyd, John Stuart, Reginald Bach, Heather Angel, Wilfrid Shine, Sam Livesey, Henry Hallett, Sybil Jane

Sherlock Holmes (Rendel) and Dr. Watson (Lloyd) are employed to protect Sir Henry Baskerville (Stuart) from a family curse.

This second British adaptation of the popular Sir Arthur Conan Doyle mystery (the first having been filmed in 1921) is noteworthy chiefly for the fact that its screenplay was co-authored by Edgar Wallace. London-born Wallace (1875-1932) was a journalist, playwright and screenwriter, as well as a novelist responsible for a series of lurid murder mysteries. These novels found tremendous success and would later be filmed as a long-running series of macabre thrillers in Germany, known as krimis. As a screenwriter, his most significant contribution was the scenario of the original *King Kong* (1933), though little of his input was actually used.

There's something oddly fitting about Wallace adapting Doyle's most popular thriller to the screen, but the film's poor box-office performance indicates that it probably missed the mark; Phil Hardy's *The Overlook Film Encyclopedia: Horror* describes it as "thoroughly pedestrian." The visual materials are

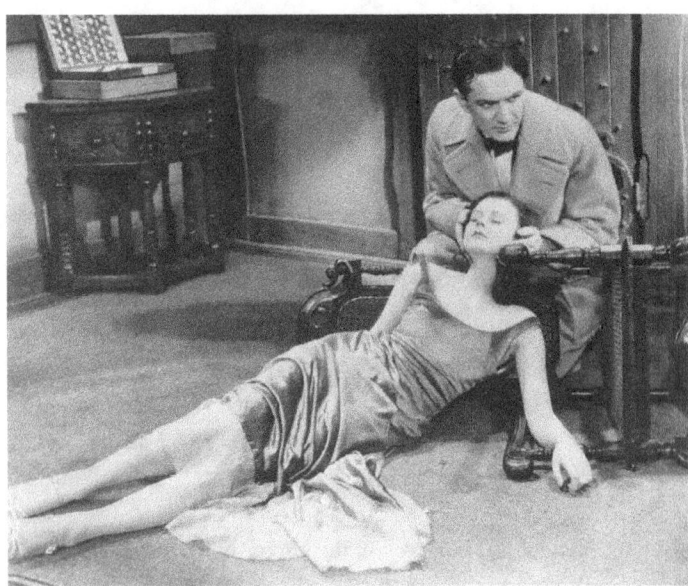

Sherlock Holmes (Robert Rendel) has his hands full in *The Hound of the Baskervilles*.

reportedly still intact, but the soundtrack is considered long lost. The film remains difficult to see in any form.

Character actor Robert Rendel portrayed Holmes, while Frederick Lloyd played Watson. Neither actor, career-wise, carved much of a niche, and it seems that this is the only time they portrayed these particular literary creations. John Stuart played Sir Henry, who later developed into a stern character actor visible in numerous films in the 1950s and '60s. Fans of the horror genre may remember him best as the coroner in Hammer's remake of *The Mummy* (1959).

Heather Angel, who stars as Sir Henry's love interest, later appeared in such classic Universal horror fare as *The Mystery of Edwin Drood* (1935) and Fox's *The Undying Monster* (1942). Director V. Gareth Gundry had previously contributed to the screenplay of James Whale's first solo work as a film director, *Journey's End* (1930), but his own credits as director are very limited and stop cold after his version of *Hound*. TH

The Intruder
Allied; b/w; 66 min; U.S.

D: Albert Ray *S:* Frances Hyland *P:* M.H. Hoffman, Jr. *C:* Tom Galligan, Harry Neumann *M:* Abe Meyer

Cast: Monte Blue, Lila Lee, William B. Davidson, Gwen Lee, Arthur Housman, Sidney Bracey, Harry Cording, Mischa Auer, Wilfred Lucas, Lynton Brent, John Beck, Allan Cavan

A man is murdered aboard a cruise ship, and a hardboiled detective (Davidson) launches an investigation. When a storm hits and the ship begins to sink, the detective rounds up his suspects and herds them onto a lifeboat. The motley crew of survivors ends up on a desert island populated by a mysterious stranger (Auer), his pet gorilla and the skeletal remains of several erstwhile inhabitants.

The Intruder is, if nothing else, a masterpiece of audacity. The convoluted plot doesn't make a lick of sense, and when the action shifts from ship to desert island, amid settings that make *Gilligan's Island* look like high-dollar entertainment, the lunacy amps up to a breathtaking degree. Mischa Auer, a Russian-born

Spooky publicity shot demonstrating the shadowy cinematography of Karl Struss, along with hero and heroine Richard Arlen and Leila Hyams, in *Island of Lost Souls*

character actor who made a number of Z-grade film appearances (*The Monster Walks*, 1932, for instance) before graduating to more distinguished fare, here portrays the "Wild Man," apparently so called due to his penchant for letting fly with sub-Tarzan jungle calls. Toss in some skeletons (to whom Auer refers by name) and an uncredited extra in a tacky gorilla outfit, and it all adds up to a wacky good time.

The performances lack conviction, but so what? At least Auer and burly Harry Cording (familiar from such Universal fare as *The Black Cat*, 1934, *The Wolf Man*, 1941 and *The House of Fear*, 1945) provide a homey feel. And Arthur Housman adds some stupid amusement as the obligatory drunken passenger; he went on to a successful career playing drunks, slurring and stumbling his way through everything from the Laurel and Hardy short *The Live Ghost* (1934) to James Whale's lavish *Show Boat* (1936).

Director Albert Ray was at the tail end of his career with *The Intruder*; he'd done most of his work in the silent era, and his filmography yields little in the way of familiar titles (though he did direct *The Thirteenth Guest* in 1932). He also did some acting and, as a screenwriter, contributed to a number of films, including *Charlie Chan in Reno* (1939). He doesn't display anything directorially remarkable here, but he does keep the action flowing at a decent pace.

Mystery buffs will likely be disappointed by the garbled conclusion—hats off to anybody who actually understands the final explanation, though its incoherence does add to the film's loopy appeal. TH

Island of Lost Souls
Paramount; b/w; 70 (67) min; U.S.

D: Erle C. Kenton S: Philip Wylie, Waldemar Young C: Karl Struss M: Arthur Johnston, Sigmund Krumgold FX: Gordon Jennings

Cast: Charles Laughton, Richard Arlen, Leila Hyams, Bela Lugosi, Arthur Hohl, Kathleen Burke, Stanley Fields, Paul Hurst, Hans Steinke, Tetsu Komai, George Irving, John George

Stranded on an island somewhere in the South Pacific, Edward Parker (Arlen) discovers that disgraced scientist Dr. Moreau (Laughton) rules the place like a tyrant while conducting experiments on the locals. After considerable snooping, he learns that the doctor's work involves vivisecting animals and giving them human traits. Together with Moreau's rebellious assistant Montgomery (Hohl), the two—along with other guests of Moreau—devise an escape plan.

H.G. Wells remains to this day a highly influential and oft-read science fiction author. While best known for his speculative fiction classics, he also wrote extensively in other areas, including hard science and history. His 1896 novel *The Island of Dr. Moreau* is science fiction as social commentary, a surreal exploration of the horrors of animal vivisection. It was an instant success at the time of its publication and remains in print today.

Paramount's choice of Waldemar Young to co-write *Moreau*'s screenplay was inspired. Young had long been a favorite of director Tod Browning, under whose tutelage he crafted the most perverse and outlandish scenarios of the silent era, most notably *The Unknown* (1927). Here he joins literary forces with gifted science fiction novelist Philip Wylie, best remembered by contemporary readers for *When Worlds Collide* (1933, co-written with Edwin Balmer) and *Gladiator* (1930), the latter often cited as inspiration for comic book characters Superman and Doc Savage. Young and Wylie together crafted a wonderfully macabre interpretation of Wells' novel, one that eschewed the moral posturing of the book in favor of a more dispassionate, and thus more disturbing, tone.

To direct, Paramount selected Erle C. Kenton (1896-1980), a capable journeyman who had by this point racked up more

An original lobby card from *Island of Lost Souls* demonstrates the conflict between the Panther Woman (Kathleen Burke) and two "manimals."

Charles Laughton, as Dr. Moreau, turns beasts into men (and women!) in *Island of Lost Souls*.

than 50 screen credits beginning in the silent era. He would later dig in at Universal, bringing style and economy to such B-grade fright films as *The Ghost of Frankenstein* (1942) and *House of Dracula* (1945). *Island of Lost Souls* is arguably his finest film; its pacing is brisk, the shocks pack a wallop and he gets terrific performances from his actors. Credit, however, must be shared with ace cinematographer Karl Struss (*Dr. Jekyll and Mr. Hyde*, 1932), whose evocative lighting and gracefully mobile camerawork makes *Lost Souls* one of the most vivid horror films of its period.

Charles Laughton, fresh from James Whale's *The Old Dark House* (1932), is at his perverse best as Dr. Moreau (though Wells—who hated the film—objected to the reduction of his novel's central character to a mere sadist). Kenton's direction keeps Laughton's legendary excesses in check; the actor's wonderfully perverse line readings and facial expressions remain believably chilling throughout.

Richard Arlen makes a likable hero, while Kathleen Burke (Lionel Atwill's faithless wife in the same year's *Murders in the Zoo*) is seductive as Lota the Panther Woman, one of Moreau's few successful experiments. Burke makes Lota endearing, sympathetic and sexy. (It's interesting to note that the character did not appear in Wells' original book, yet a female character much like her has appeared in every film adaptation.) Burke was cast after winning a nationwide contest for the part.

Only a couple of years after balking at the idea of playing the Frankenstein monster (due to the character's heavy make-up), Bela Lugosi is here virtually unrecognizable (under Wally Westmore's superb make-up) as the Sayer of the Law. His distinctive vocalizations are readily identifiable, of course, as are his trademark eyes. His work here is a fine characterization by an underappreciated actor, one that proves him capable of eliciting audience empathy even from beneath layers of cosmetic cover.

The film moves beautifully to its violent climax, which carries a disturbing charge even today. For years it was banned in parts of the United States, and it didn't see a U.K. theatrical release until 1958. Wells' story has been officially filmed twice more, first in 1977 (with Burt Lancaster as a more humane Dr. Moreau) and again in 1996 (with a bizarre Marlon Brando dominating the proceedings), both under the title *The Island of Dr. Moreau*. TH

Kongo
aka **Conga**
MGM; b/w; 86 min; U.S.

D: William J. Cowen *S:* Leon Gordon *C:* Harold Rosson

Cast: Walter Huston, Lupe Velez, Conrad Nagel, Virginia Bruce, C. Henry Gordon, Mitchell Lewis, Forrester Harvey, Curtis Nero

"Deadlegs" Flint (Huston) has established himself as a living god among the superstitious natives of a small African village. A former magician, he lost the use of his legs in a fight with Gregg (Gordon), who at the time was having an affair with Flint's wife. Since then, Flint has been biding his time in the jungle, constructing his revenge. He has engineered a life of drug addiction and prostitution for Gregg's illegitimate daughter, Ann (Bruce), whom he now brings to his commune so he can gloat to Gregg (who is trading ivory in the area). But there's something Flint doesn't know about Ann's heritage.

Tod Browning's *West of Zanzibar* (1928) was the kinkiest of his collaborations with Lon Chaney, and this talkie remake attempts to outdo it in terms of shock value. Based, as was the Browning film, on Chester DeVonde's 1926 Broadway play

The young heroes (Virginia Bruce and Conrad Nagel) of *Kongo*, a remake of Lon Chaney's perverse *West of Zanzibar*

Kongo (1926), the Cowen version retains the play's title and stars Walter Huston, who played the central role on the stage.

Huston is the film's greatest asset, with his performance as the vengeful Flint beautifully realized. The future Oscar-winner (for a supporting role in his son John Huston's masterpiece, *The Treasure of the Sierra Madre*, 1948) plays a character who starts out in thoroughly despicable terrain but transforms convincingly as he realizes the wrongness of his actions. The supporting cast includes the sexy Lupe Velez, as memorable here as she was in Browning's *Where East is East* (1929).

Director William J. Cowen crafted only a handful of pictures between 1928 and 1934, though he lived until 1964. He reportedly had a distinguished military career, having served in World War I. And while his body of work as a director is mostly unimpressive, *Kongo* plays out briskly and efficiently. Cowen is also to be commended for not drawing back from the seedier elements of the story. The film revels in suggested drug addiction, alcoholism and sexual perversity, and it packs a definite frisson by doing so.

Ultimately, *Kongo* isn't as accomplished as the Browning original, but it's a worthwhile curio for fans of Golden Age horror films. TH

Love and Death
aka **Amore e Morte**
Aurora; b/w 94 min; Italian/U.S.

D/S/P: Rosario Romeo *C:* Alfred Gandolfi, Nick Rogelli *M:* E. Aversano

Cast: Rosario Romeo, Carmelina Romeo, Antonino Ruggeri, Ada Ruggeri, Rafael Bongini, Clara Diana, Angelo Gloria, Guglielmo Onofri, G. Perez, F. Perez, A. Fratellone, F. Colombo, L. Busacco

The Agro family suffers under the weight of an ancient curse, due to the indiscretions of its ancestors. Yet Ruggerio Agro (Romeo) heedlessly carries on the debauched family tradition of seducing local women. When one of his lovers dies, the girl's father vows revenge on Ruggerio for soiling her name.

A melodrama with horror trappings, *Love and Death* is today virtually impossible to see. The film, though in the Italian language, was shot in New Jersey. The filmmakers recruited members of a Sicilian-American theatrical troupe to perform in the picture, which was aimed at Italian-American viewers.

Producer/writer/director/star Rosario Romeo was the creative force behind the film, which failed to generate much interest in its target demographic or anywhere else. It is the only film credit to be found for either Romeo or anyone else involved. Presumably, its commercial failure prompted the participants to return to their more successful theatrical careers. TH

The Mask of Fu Manchu
MGM/Cosmopolitan; b/w; 68 min; U.S.

D: Charles Brabin, Charles Vidor *S:* Irene Kuhn, Edgar Allan Woolf, John Willard *P:* William Randolph Hearst *C:* Tony Gaudio *M:* William Axt *FX:* Warren Newcombe, Kenneth Strickfaden

Cast: Boris Karloff, Lewis Stone, Karen Morley, Charles Starrett, Myrna Loy, Jean Hersholt, Lawrence Grant, David Torrence

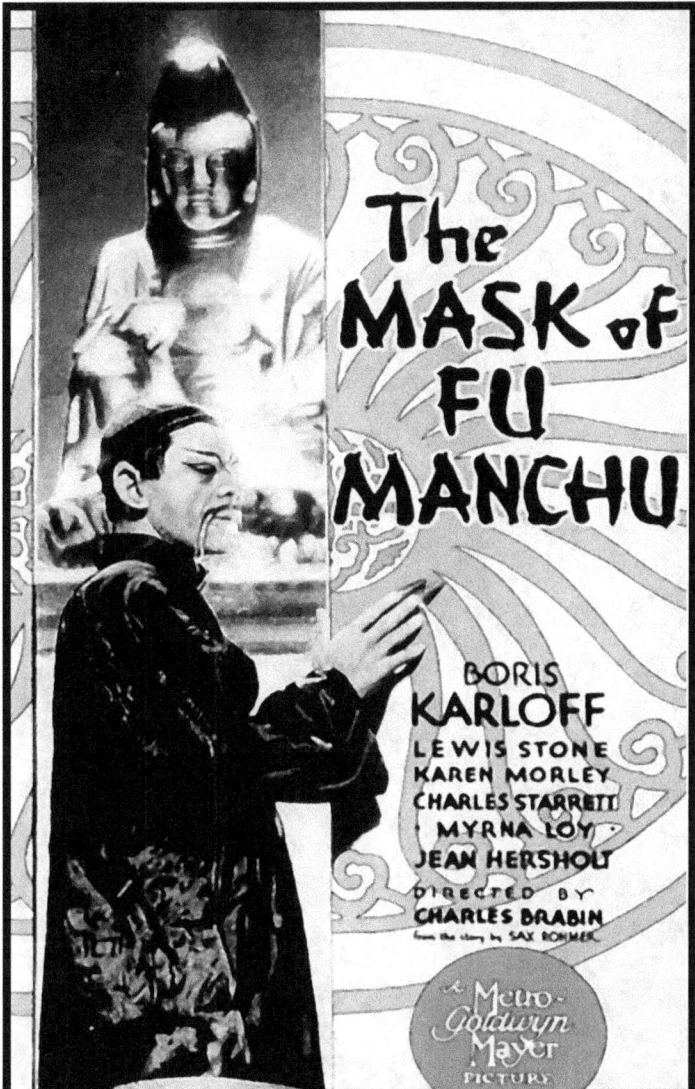

With the success of Universal's *Dracula* and *Frankenstein* (both 1931) having kick-started the horror genre, executives for what was then the world's leading film company, MGM, decided that it was high time for the studio to re-enter the market it had neglected (apart from the subdued *The Unholy Three* in 1930) since Lon Chaney's silent-era heyday. Their first attempt, Tod Browning's lyrical *Freaks* (1932), proved too controversial; it was met with opposition everywhere it was released and banned in many areas, leaving the red-faced studio to heavily trim the picture and lease it out to small-time exploitation producer Dwain Esper (*Maniac*, 1934) for exhibition at roadshows and burlesques.

Intent on not dropping the ball twice, MGM turned to newspaper tycoon William Randolph Hearst's Cosmopolitan Pictures for their next effort. Cosmopolitan had formed in 1918 as an adjunct to Paramount after United Artists refused to allow Hearst into that particular venture. (Hearst had hoped to make a star of his mistress, actress Marion Davies.) Paramount had seen the opportunity to work with Hearst as a cash cow, given the free-publicity potential of his many popular magazines and newspapers. But disagreements arose between Hearst and Paramount over receipts from block-booking (the practice of distributing multiple films, sight unseen, to independent theaters; it was out-

Fu Manchu (Boris Karloff) resides over a feast fit for the gods in *The Mask of Fu Manchu*.

lawed by the United States Supreme Court in 1948), leading Cosmopolitan to sever its ties with the bigger company. Hearst moved operations from New York City to Hollywood and there took MGM up on its offer, agreeing to produce films with the giant studio.

Meanwhile, the rights to infamous character Fu Manchu lapsed at Paramount (where he had been the basis for three films released between 1929 and 1931, all of them starring Warner Oland). Author Sax Rohmer sold the rights to his next novel in the series, *The Mask of Fu Manchu*, to Hearst's *Cosmopolitan* magazine for publication in serial form during the summer of 1932. That *Cosmopolitan* should become Fu's new home was apt given Hearst's anti-Asian xenophobia—his publishing empire had almost single-handedly mainstreamed the terms "yellow peril" and "yellow terror" into U.S. culture. Well-versed in the magic of cross-promotion, Hearst snapped up the film rights to Rohmer's latest tale with the intention of immediately adapting it to film. Shrewdly, he planned the fall release of the film to coincide with the release of the serial in novel form.

Only one hurdle remained: His studio didn't have a script. Cosmopolitan went through three writers as the production date neared, including playwright John Willard (author of the classic play *The Cat and the Canary*, 1922), but when filming began, the script was still under construction. Presumably it was completed during production, though by whom is anyone's guess.

Charles Vidor was hired to direct the film. Vidor, whose real name was Károly Vidor, was a relative newcomer to the industry, a Jewish immigrant from Hungary who had directed only one prior film, the 1929 short *The Bridge*, which he adapted from Ambrose Bierce's classic short story *An Occurrence at Owl Creek Bridge* (1890). A critical and commercial hit, its success prompted Cosmopolitan to hand him MGM's second major horror entry of 1932.

The question remained, who was to portray Fu Manchu? MGM had considered Boris Karloff, who was then under contract to Universal, for the role of Rasputin in their big-budget epic *Rasputin and the Empress* (1932). But when they realized that they could get John Barrymore (and his siblings Lionel and Ethel, to boot) for the film, they passed on Karloff, assuming that the trio of Barrymores would make *Rasputin* a shoo-in success. (They were mistaken; the film was a resounding flop). The *Rasputin* role now a done deal, Karloff was approached to portray the sinister Dr. Fu Manchu instead. This involved persuading Universal to lease him out for the role, which the studio did without hesitation, no doubt believing (correctly) that it would enhance Karloff's reputation as the King of Horror and thus benefit Universal's own future productions with the actor.

Beauteous RKO contract player Myrna Loy was chosen to play Fu's nymphomaniac daughter, having previously portrayed the half-caste villainess in that company's *Thirteen Women* (1932). (Little did anyone know that only two years later, her turn as Nora in MGM's *The Thin Man* would make her a Hollywood superstar.) Cast as *Mask*'s heroine was Karen Morley, an up-and-comer who had made her mark in the classic *Scarface* earlier that year and had also starred in the same year's sublime *The Phantom of Crestwood*.

None other than Clark Gable was considered for the male heroic lead, but when it became clear that the shoots for MGM's *Red Dust* (1932) would not be finished on schedule, he was removed from consideration in favor of a former college football player named Charles Starrett (*Murder on the Campus*, 1933), who had entered cinema in 1926 as an extra in a football-themed movie titled *The Quarterback*. Though he was no Clark Gable, Starrett proved himself leading man material and by 1930 was working opposite the likes of Carole Lombard and Miriam Hopkins.

Mask's remaining roles were filled with a bevy of solid MGM contract players, including Lewis Stone (*The Phantom of Paris*, 1931) as Sir Nayland Smith, Jean Hersholt (*The Cat Creeps*, 1930) as Dr. Von Berg and Lawrence Grant (*Daughter of the Dragon*, 1931) as Sir Lionel Barton. And in keeping with the racism of the day, several uncredited black and Asian actors were cast as Fu Manchu's minions and victims.

With the casting complete, the film went into production on August 6, 1932, but was almost immediately halted when the top brass at MGM decided abruptly that Vidor was not a good fit for the material. Charles Brabin replaced him, but on his way out the door, Vidor fell in love with romantic lead Karen Morley, and the two soon married. Vidor went on to become one of Hollywood's most important directors, shaping such classic productions as *A Song to Remember* (1945), *Gilda* (1946), *Hans Christian Andersen* (1952) and *Love Me or Leave Me* (1955). He died of a heart attack in Vienna, Austria in 1959, after completing work on his last film, *Song Without End* (1960).

Brabin had been working in the industry since the early 1900s—he started out at Edison Studios—directing numerous silent films, including such horror efforts as *The Necklace of Rameses* (1914) and *The Raven* (1915), marrying silent screen vamp Theda Bara along the way. His arrival on the set of *The Mask of Fu Manchu* was fortuitous given that he had just been booted as director of the aforementioned *Rasputin and the Empress*. His competent hand, combined with the atmospheric cinematography of future Oscar-winner Tony Gaudio, resulted in a gem of 1930s horror, albeit with the racist slant so common at the time.

The story begins with Sir Nayland Smith (Stone) entrusting Sir Lionel Barton (Hersholt) with the task of finding the tomb of Genghis Kahn before its contents, which have the power to unite Asian hordes in opposition to the "white man," fall into the hands of the fiendish Dr. Fu Manchu (Karloff). While on his mission, Barton is kidnapped, and his daughter Sheila (Morley) vows to comb the Gobi Desert herself in search of both tomb and father. She joins an expedition headed by her fiancé, Terry Granville (Starrett), and they discover the tomb—which, it turns out, houses the mask and sword with which the original Genghis Kahn conquered all of Asia. Granville attempts to throw Fu Manchu off the scent by delivering a fake mask and sword to him and for his efforts is taken captive, whipped, offered to Fu Manchu's daughter Fah Lo See (Loy), drugged and sent back to camp to lead the rest of the expedition into the evil Oriental's trap. In the meantime, Nayland Smith discovers and infiltrates Fu Manchu's desert lair. He's likewise captured and then sentenced to death by crocodile. He breaks free and saves the rest of the cast from the ignoble madman's equally ignoble clutches.

The Mask of Fu Manchu was released in late November 1932, approximately one month after shooting wrapped, and is one of the most wildly provocative and audacious horror films of its period, thanks largely to a heavy dose of gratuitous sex and violence. When Granville is taken captive, his shirt is torn off and his bare torso whipped by Fah Lo See's near-naked, muscled black servants as she watches in horny anticipation, crying, "Faster! Faster!" He is then taken to a bedchamber where she coos over his unconscious body before stealing a kiss as her father watches voyeuristically from the shadows. After the obligatory fade to black, the villainous doctor prepares Granville for his hypnotic drugging by having the captive stripped down to a loincloth and bound to a table, while the above-referenced crew of shirtless Africans stands guard.

The film's violence, which ranges from stabbings and whippings to shootings and threatened impalement, is every bit the match of its sexual content. At one point a severed hand, a warn-

Myrna Loy plays the daughter of the dragon in *The Mask of Fu Manchu*.

ing to all who would stand in the way of Fu Manchu's plans, falls from a tree to the feet of the unsuspecting Granville. Moments such as these no doubt contributed to the enforcement of stronger rules by the Production Code only two years later. (Even during its pre-Code run, *Mask* was heavily censored almost everywhere it was shown and in some locales was not shown at all.)

Today's viewer, however, is more likely to squirm over the film's racism than its sex and violence. It's impossible to read *Mask* as anything but a swipe at the world's entire Asian population. When Smith explains to Barton the threat that Fu Manchu poses, he puts it thus: "Should Fu Manchu put that mask across his wicked eyes and take that scimitar in his bony, cruel hands, all Asia rises. He'll declare himself Genghis Khan come to life again and lead hundreds of millions of men to sweep the world!"

At another point, Sheila refers to her captor as a "hideous yellow monster." (Of course, Asians are presented as the *true* racists, as when Fah Lo See gushes to her father about Terry's handsomeness and Fu Manchu retorts, "for a white man.") The fear of miscegenation also looms large, as when a worried Smith asks Granville: "Do you suppose for a moment that Fu Manchu doesn't know we have a beautiful white girl here with us?" or when Fu delivers this inspirational speech to his underlings as they ponder the trussed-up Sheila, laid out in preparation for her sacrifice to the gods: "Would you all have maidens like this for your wives? Then conquer and breed! Kill the white man and take his women!"

The film's ubiquitous bigotry, in fact, led to some static from the Japanese American Citizens League when *Mask* was re-released in the early 1970s as part of MGM's Triple Shock package (along with *Dr. Jekyll and Mr. Hyde*, 1931 and *Mark of the Vampire*, 1935). The League, apparently not above a little bigotry of its own, blasted the film for depicting Fu Manchu as an "ugly, evil homosexual with five-inch fingernails while his daughter is a sadistic sex fiend ..." If they were led to assume Fu's sexual preference based on his lisp, then it displays, among other things, an ignorance of how Karloff naturally spoke. Similarly, if the group was basing the assumption on Fu's rather fetching wardrobe, it was deliberately ignoring China's (and Japan's) rich cultural history. The fact is nothing suggests that Fu Manchu is homosexual, apart from, barely arguably, Karloff's intentionally campy performance. And if that's the giveaway, then one must explain how else an A-list actor would be expected to tackle a role with such blazingly goofy dialogue. (It has been asserted that Karloff and co-star Myrna Loy ruined a take or two with fits of laughter at lines they were expected to recite.)

Still, the fuss resulted in the excision of much of the re-release version's racist dialogue and the general disappearance of the original prints. When MGM and Warner released the film to home video in 1992, one such edited print was used for the transfer. The full film wasn't available again until the early 2000s, when a complete print was thankfully unearthed.

Today *The Mask of Fu Manchu* can be appreciated for the tasteless yet engaging little masterpiece that it is. Despite its garishness and hole-riddled script—both of which offer up their own little nuggets of enjoyment—the film benefits from breezy direction and impressive sets, the latter by Cedric Gibbons and Kenneth Strickfaden. Karloff looks great in make-up created by Cecil Holland, who evidently felt the need to compete with Universal's more famous make-up man Jack Pierce. And the actors, it must be acknowledged, give it their all; Karloff and Loy in particular are a delight, if a somewhat guilty one.

Ultimately, MGM's attempts at mining horror gold resulted in a string of box-office failures—*The Mask of Fu Manchu*, *Rasputin and the Empress* and *Kongo* (1932) included. Realizing that their bread was better buttered with more down-to-earth stuff, the company focused on racy sex dramas until the Production Code put a kibosh on those as well, at which point the studio shifted to the safety of light-hearted romantic comedies and serious costume dramas.

Of course, none of this made any difference to Sax Rohmer, whose deliciously vile character continued to enjoy success in novels, radio, serials and television ... and at the movies. CW

Midnight Warning
Mayfair; b/w; 63 min; U.S.
D: Spencer Gordon Bennet *S:* John T. Neville *P:* Cliff T. Broughton, George W. Weeks *C:* Jules Cronjager *M:* Lee Zahler
Cast: William Boyd, Hooper Atchley, Claudia Dell, John Harron, Huntley Gordon, Lloyd Whitlock, Phillips Smalley, Lloyd Ingraham, Henry Hall, Lon Poff, Art Winkler

When an unknown assailant takes a shot at Dr. Walcott (Atchley), Private Investigator Bill Cornish (Boyd) investigates. He deduces that the shot came from the home of Enid Van Buren (Dell), and he uncovers a link between the incident and the sudden disappearance of Enid's brother.

Based on the same urban legend—a disappearance at the 1893 Chicago World's Fair—that inspired *The Moonstone of Fez* (1914), *So Long at the Fair* (1950) and an episode ("Into Thin Air") of *Alfred Hitchcock Presents*, *Midnight Warning* is a well-paced murder mystery with a macabre finale not found in the tale's other versions: the imperiled heroine goes bananas in a creepy morgue filled with shroud-covered cadavers.

The cast includes John Harron, the wimpy hero of *White Zombie* (1932), but stage veteran William "Stage" Boyd takes the lead role; his biography is more interesting than the film. Born in New York City in 1889, Boyd established himself in

the theater scene early in life and began tinkering in the film business in 1913. A series of arrests for public drunkenness and drug possession put an end to his acting career shortly after it began. His antics also damaged the career of another actor with the same name. Best known for his performances as Hopalong Cassidy, it's said that the other Boyd's lucrative contract with RKO was terminated the day after it was signed when news of one of bad-Boyd's arrests made the papers. (A judge at one point tried to help "Hopalong" Boyd by forcing *Midnight Warning*'s Boyd to adopt the moniker William "Stage" Boyd.)

"Stage" Boyd passed away from a liver ailment in 1935, while the "other" Boyd continued to work into the mid-1950s before passing away in 1972. TH

Mistress of Atlantis
aka **The Lost Atlantis**
Nero; b/w; 81 (77) min; Germany/Great Britain
D: G.W. Pabst *S:* Hermann Oberländer, Miles Mander, Ladislaus Vajda *P:* Seymour Nebenzahl, W. Lowenberg *C:* Ernst Kömar, Eugen Schüfftan *M:* Wolfgang Zeller

Cast: Brigitte Helm, John Stuart, Tela Tchai, Gustav Diessl, Florelle, Georges Toureil, Gertrude Pabst, Wladimir Sokolow, Mathias Wieman

This is an alternate-language version of director G.W. Pabst's *Queen of Atlantis* (1932), with Scottish-born John Stuart (*The Hound of the Baskervilles*, 1932; *The Black Abbot*, 1934) filling Heinz Klingenberg's role as Lieutenant Saint-Avit. Here the actors speak in English (indeed, many of them were Englishmen), while *Queen* was done in German. An introduction by a British radio announcer was also tacked onto the beginning, providing a backdrop for this fanciful tale set in a still-extant vestige of Atlantis in the mountains of northern Africa (where much of the film was shot).

Based on Pierre Benoit's hugely successful and controversial novel *L'Atlantide* (first published in 1919 and first filmed in 1921), *Mistress of Atlantis* kicks off with Lieutenant Saint-Avit (Stuart) and fellow officer Captain Morange (Diessl) being waylaid by African natives in the mountain deserts of the French Sahara. Morange disappears, and after collapsing from exhaustion while searching for him, Saint-Avit is carried to a lost civilization's underground lair (done up in the finest 1930s art deco). The place belongs to Antinéa (Helm), the beautiful descendant of Atlantean royalty, who has a good thing going with a series of men kidnapped from the outside and brought to her for her amusement. (When she tires of them, she hooks them on drugs and disposes of them, embalming their bodies and displaying the remains in glass cases—an aspect of the story spelled out in the novel but only hinted at here.)

As one would expect from Pabst, the audience's first look at Antinéa is stunning. As the camera glides toward her, she turns her head, revealing her smooth, gorgeous profile. Her hair is fashioned like that of Maria, Fritz Lang's robotrix from *Metropolis* (1927) who, need it be said, was also played by the exquisite Brigitte Helm. Helm is quietly seductive here, winning the heart of her captive as well as the audience by beating him in a game of chess. And despite the evil deeds of her character, she retains a fair amount of sympathy throughout.

Too bad, then, that the film moves too slowly to hold one's interest for long, and the horror set pieces—the discovery of a skeleton half-buried in the sand, the funeral procession for one of Antinéa's victims—are simply too far apart to conjure much dread. A pall of twisted sexual obsession lingers over the proceedings, culminating in Saint-Avit's murder of Morange when the latter spurns Antinéa's advances. Still, even during its down times, Pabst adorns the film with superb set design and costumes.

The same year that *The Mistress of Atlantis* and *Queen of Atlantis* were shot, Pabst also made a French version titled, like the 1921 film adaptation, *L'Atlantide*. CW

The Monster Walks
aka The Monster Walked
Like; b/w; 57 min; U.S.

D: Frank R. Strayer *S:* Robert Ellis *P:* Cliff P. Broughton *C:* Jules Cronjager *M:* Jean de la Roche, Charles Dunworth, Lee Zahler

Cast: Rex Lease, Vera Reynolds, Mischa Auer, Sheldon Lewis, Martha Mattox, Sidney Bracey, Sleep 'N Eat (Willie Best)

Ruth Earlton (Reynolds) is called back to her family estate for the reading of her recently departed father's will. But as the night unfolds, a murderous ape menaces her repeatedly.

There's little to recommend this Poverty Row item. Though director Frank R. Strayer has the interesting *The Vampire Bat* (1933) and *Condemned to Live* (1935) to his credit, he seems to be on autopilot here. Static camerawork and dismal acting make *The Monster Walks* seem far older than it is. As others have noted, were it not for the soundtrack, one might easily mistake it for a not-particularly-good silent melodrama. The usual clichés are shamelessly paraded—a spooky house, a stormy night, sinister servants, a murderous ape—but Strayer does nothing of interest with them.

Even at 57 minutes, the pace drags interminably. Scenes heavy with dialogue are played out in static long shots, and the cast apparently believes that it's on a stage, emoting for the benefit of the back row. Russian-born character actor Mischa

Auer (who does much better as a remorseful hunchback in *Condemned to Live*) is particularly abominable as the sinister housekeeper's even more sinister son, while Willie Best (at this point in his career still credited as "Sleep 'N Eat") mugs continuously as the stereotypical frightened black servant.

But the mugging falls as flat as everything else in the movie. The only mildly effective moment—tellingly, the only time in the film that the camera actually moves a bit!—is when a hairy hand emerges from the wall as the heroine sleeps (though even this is a steal from any number of previous films and is therefore nothing new). TH

The Most Dangerous Game
aka **The Hounds of Zaroff**
RKO; b/w; 63 (78) min; U.S
.*D:* Ernest B. Schoedsack, Irving Pichel *S:* James Ashmore Creelman *P:* Merian C. Cooper, David O. Selznick *C:* Henry Gerrard *M:* Max Steiner *FX:* Lloyd Knechtel, Harry Redmond, Jr., Vernon L. Walker
Cast: Leslie Banks, Joel McCrea, Fay Wray, Robert Armstrong, Noble Johnson, Steve Clemente, Oscar "Dutch" Hendrian, William B. Davidson, Clarence Linden "Buster" Crabbe (uncredited)

Bob Rainsford (McCrea) gets shipwrecked on a small island and makes his way through a dense forest to a castle—the only sign of civilization in evidence. There he meets Count Zaroff (Banks), a disgraced Russian expatriate who has fled his country and established a private sanctuary on the island. Soon, Rainsford learns that he's not the only guest of the odd but hospitable Zaroff; an earlier shipwreck has also stranded Eve Trowbridge (Wray) and her brother Martin Trowbridge (Armstrong). The amicable Count speaks at length about his passion for hunting but neglects to mention at first that his prey of preference is human beings.

First published in *Collier's Weekly* in January of 1924, Richard Connell's short story *The Most Dangerous Game* was an instant hit with both critics and readers. Today it remains the author's most celebrated and influential work. Inevitably, the tale caught the eye of producer/director team Merian C. Cooper (1893-1973) and Ernest B. Schoedsack (1893-1979). The two had met in the Ukraine following their WWI military service, and their shared affinities for both adventure and filmmaking led to a partnership that yielded several documentaries (including 1925's *Grass*) and a noteworthy 1929 adaptation of A.E.W. Mason's adventure novel *The Four Feathers*.

The two developed their film adaptation of *Game* in tandem with their mega-production *King Kong* (1933). Pre-production on the massive *Kong* was already underway, thus minimizing the prep work needed to bring its co-project to screen life. The smaller film also promised to be a comparatively simple production, one not requiring the extensive special effects work of its companion.

The project ran into difficulties when RKO slashed *Game*'s already-small budget in half. To their credit, Cooper and Schoedsack made the most of what was left on the table. The script was of necessity trimmed and condensed, and it's doubtless partly due to this that *Game* emerges as one of the most taut and exciting horror films of the 1930s. The studio enlisted Irving Pichel to tackle the hands-on aspects of directing, dealing with the actors and the dialogue (Pichel was also an actor, most noted for his performance as the zombie-like Sandor in Universal's *Dracula's Daughter*, 1936), which left Schoedsack to focus on the technical aspects of the production.

Relative newcomer Bruce Cabot was the first choice for the role of Count Zaroff, but Leslie Banks (1890-1952), whose face had become partially paralyzed during WWII, fills the villainous part perfectly. Banks had already established himself on the British stage and had recently made his American theater debut in *Game*'s stage version, titled *The Hounds of Zaroff*. While he apparently performed in George Fitzmaurice's lost 1921 silent film *Experience*, *Game* marks, for all practical purposes, his cinematic debut. His biggest star turn came two years later as the lead in Alfred Hitchcock's *The Man Who Knew Too Much* (1934), but *Game* is arguably his finest film work. He later offered a variation on the performance in the Edgar Wallace thriller *Chamber of Horrors* (1940).

The heroic Rainsford is very well played by a young Joel McCrea, who went on to become a major star. His potential is in full evidence here, and he makes for a terrific foil for the sadistic Zaroff. Likewise, Fay Wray is her classic self as the imperiled Eve. Her horror trifecta—*Game*, *Doctor X*, and *The Mystery of the Wax Museum*—plucked her from obscurity and instantly cemented her scream queen status, with the release of *King Kong* the following year shooting her into the Hollywood stratosphere. Wray's *Kong* co-star Robert Armstrong is in unexceptional but decent form as her brother, an irritating drunkard who becomes an addition to Zaroff's trophy room.

Game benefits from an exciting score by Max Steiner. Indeed, the presence of a full orchestral soundtrack is unusual in a film of this vintage, and one can argue that it was Steiner's work here, as well as in *Thirteen Women* (1932) and *Kong*, that helped establish the value of music scores in talking pictures.

The film encountered some difficulties during its preview screening. Audience members were reportedly ap-

This poster for *The Most Dangerous Game* tries to do for Leslie Banks' eyes what *Dracula* did for Lugosi's.

Leslie Banks plays the evil Count Zaroff in *The Most Dangerous Game.*

palled by a too-explicit depiction of Zaroff's hobby, resulting in approximately 15 minutes worth of cuts. Though the footage has never resurfaced, surviving stills do give an idea of what was cut. Despite this, some surprisingly violent footage made it into the final cut, including a gruesome moment in which Eve finds her brother's head in a jar of formaldehyde.

The Most Dangerous Game remains a classic of its kind, a potent production often imitated (both officially and unofficially; among the latter, 1994's *Surviving the Game* with Rutger Hauer and Ice-T is worthy of note) but never duplicated. In 1943 the radio series *Suspense* produced its own version, with Orson Welles as Zaroff and Joseph Cotten as Rainsford. In 1945 RKO lensed its own second take on the story, titled *A Game of Death,* under the auspices of director Robert Wise. Unfortunately, it had none of the class Wise brought to his Val Lewton-produced horror films of the same period. TH

The Mummy
Universal; b/w; 73 min; U.S.

D: Karl Freund *S:* John L. Balderston *P:* Carl Laemmle, Jr., Stanley Bergerman *C:* Charles Stumar *M:* James Dietrich *FX:* John Fulton

Cast: Boris Karloff, Zita Johann, David Manners, Edward Van Sloan, Arthur Byron, Bramwell Fletcher, Noble Johnson, Kathleen Byron, Leonard Mudie, James Crane, Henry Victor (scenes deleted)

English archaeologists unearth the mummy of Egyptian high priest Im-Ho-Tep (Karloff), which comes to life when a member of the team (Fletcher) reads aloud the sacred words of life. Ten years later the resurrected being, masquerading as a scholar named Ardath Bey, leads an expedition to the tomb of Princess Ankh-es-en-Amon (Johann). It's Im-Ho-Tep's plan to revive his beloved Princess, but he discovers that she's already been reincarnated as Helen Grosvenor (Johann again).

Universal's *The Mummy* was developed from *Cagliostro,* a screen treatment by writer Nina Wilcox Putnam. In Putnam's tale, an Egyptian mystic stays alive for thousands of years by injecting himself with nitrates. Changing identities as needed throughout the centuries, he eventually emerges in modern-day San Francisco and sets his sights on a society woman with whom he has fallen in love. Producer Carl Laemmle, Jr. recognized that Putnam's basic set-up was a winner and hired John L. Balderston (who co-wrote the play used as the basis for *Dracula,* 1931) to fashion it into a screenplay. The finished script, retitled *Undead,* bore only a superficial resemblance to its inspiration. Producers Laemmle and Bergerman renamed the project *The Mummy* and sensibly molded it into a showcase for Universal's newest master of menace, Boris Karloff.

Karloff, a year after *Frankenstein* (1931) and fresh from the MGM camp-fest *The Mask of Fu Manchu* (1932), was subjected to yet another arduous make-up regimen. In addition to the eight hours a day required for the bandaged look, there were also lengthy sessions to transform him into wrinkled, cadaverous Ardath Bey. The amazing Jack Pierce rose to the occasion, providing a pair of memorable looks for what is unquestionably one of Karloff's finest performances. Im-Ho-Tep/Ardath Bey seems at first glance more overtly villainous than Karloff's other famed characterizations (notably the Frankenstein monster), but closer attention reveals that here, too, is an instance of the actor giving complex, empathetic depth to a well-written character. There's a deep sadness to his centuries-old romantic obsession with Princess/Helen, and his portrayal of Im-Ho-Tep in the guise of Ardath Bey is a masterpiece of understatement. He seldom raises his voice or moves much, the suggestion being that his ancient body is too frail for such activities, yet his intensity is unflagging throughout. It's a *tour de force* from an actor who too often found himself in vehicles unworthy of his extraordinary talents.

The Mummy also marked the directorial debut of the great German cinematographer Karl Freund. Freund had established himself in Germany while still in his 30s, photographing such classics as F.W. Murnau's *The Last Laugh* (1924) and Fritz Lang's *Metropolis* (1927). He was a pioneer of the moving camera, and his shadowy, suggestive lighting techniques helped define horror's aesthetic even as it formed. By his early 40s he was

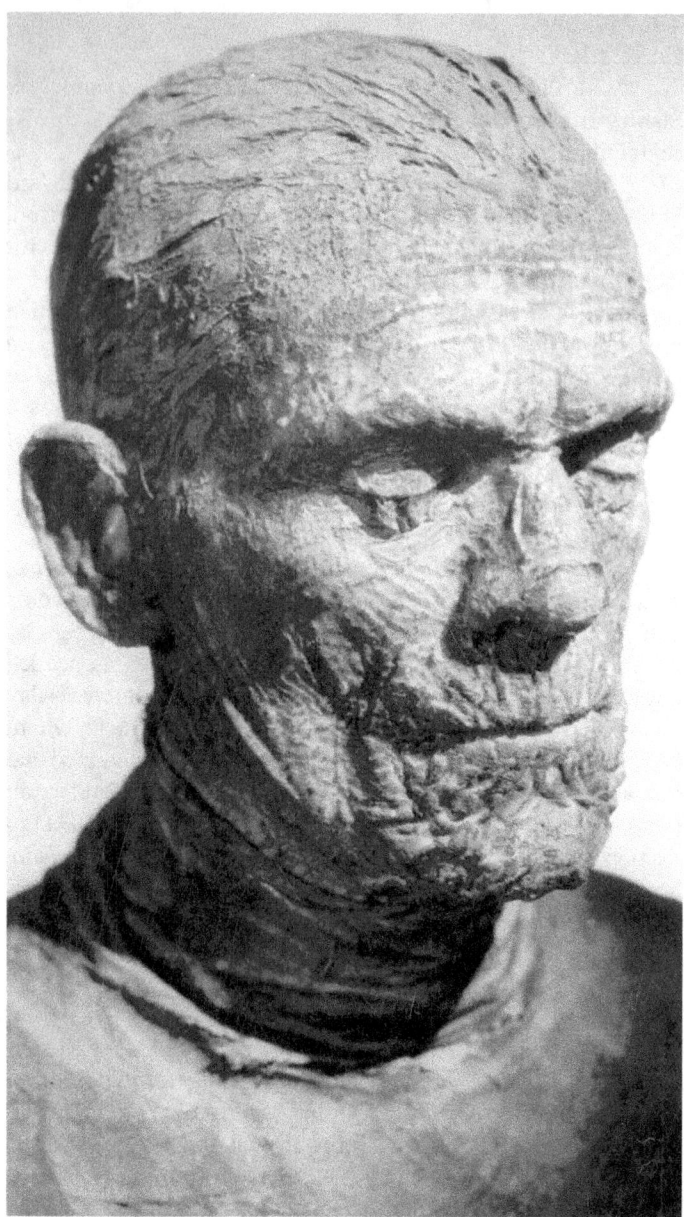

Boris Karloff under Jack Pierce's moody make-up for *The Mummy*

working in the United States, where he photographed *Dracula* (1931) and *Murders in the Rue Morgue* (1932). Here he brings just the right air of gravity to the proceedings. *The Mummy* is unique among early horror films in that it contains not a glimmer of comedy—there are no stammering servants, frightened maids or pompous asses to provide a tension-relieving chuckle. Freund's restrained approach is nowhere more evident than in the celebrated scene of Im-Ho-Tep's resurrection. The camera captures Karloff's flickering eyes and his hand dropping from his chest to his side. Then there's a jumpcut to that same hand reaching into the frame to pick up the scroll of life. Another jumpcut follows, to a trail of bandages dragging across the floor as the incredulous archaeologist who witnesses it all goes mad with laughter. It's a bravura sequence, more for what it implies than for what it shows. Freund was pressured by Laemmle to display the animated mummy completely, but Freund opted to deny the audience that particular payoff, going instead for the suspense of the not quite seen.

Of all the 1930s and '40s Universal horror classics, *The Mummy* is the closest to the silent fever dreams of German cinema (no surprise, of course, given that Freund had a hand in so many of Germany's horror films). In addition to the striking framing and camerawork, Charles Stumar's chiaroscuro lighting adds weight to even the most seemingly innocuous of scenes. Stumar continued with Universal, doing work on *The Raven* and *Werewolf of London* (both 1935) before his death in a plane crash that same year. He is at times confused with his brother John Stumar, likewise a cinematographer, who worked until the late 1940s and died in 1962.

The supporting cast can't help but pale in comparison to Karloff, but leading lady Zita Johann holds her own as Helen/Princess Ankh-es-en-Amon. Though Balderston had suggested Katherine Hepburn for the role (the mind reels!), Johann proves a perfect fit. The Hungarian-born actress is striking to look at, though slighter of build than most leading ladies of the period. She worked in only a few films, taking a very long break from the mid-'30s until her final appearance in 1986's *Raiders of the Living Dead*. She passed away in 1993 at age 89.

David Manners (Jonathan Harker in *Dracula*, 1931) is his usual wooden self as the romantic leading man, but Edward Van Sloan (both *Dracula* and *Frankenstein*, 1931) adds another solid characterization to his filmography as the wise Professor Muller. It's a character not far removed from his famed portrayal as Van Helsing in *Dracula*, but his performance here is less theatrically mannered than his work in Tod Browning's film.

Speaking of *Dracula*, much has justly been made of *The Mummy*'s ties to that picture. In addition to the involvement of Freund, Manners and Van Sloan in both productions, Balderston's screenplay borrows much from *Dracula* (with which he was also, after all, creatively involved). In both films, very old supernatural monsters set their sights on a damsel; an elderly professorial type possesses knowledge that saves the day and religious symbols are used to subdue the menace (a crucifix in *Dracula*, an amulet in *The Mummy*).

Some have speculated that Freund—irritated by Browning's stagy direction of *Dracula*—set out consciously to surpass that earlier film. It's a plausible theory, given Freund's reputation for arrogance. And, despite the merits of Browning's film (and keeping in mind that he was generally a far better director than *Dracula* indicates), one must admit that Freund comes out on top in such a hypothetical movie match-up. *The Mummy* is one of the great horror films not just of the early '30s, but of all time.

A belated sequel, *The Mummy's Hand* (starring Tom Tyler in the title role), appeared in 1940, and it kicked off a series of progressively less-interesting entries starring Lon Chaney, Jr. In 1959, Britain's Hammer Film Productions produced a Technicolor version of *The Mummy* starring Peter Cushing and Christopher Lee; despite the title, it was more of a summation of the 1940s sequels than a remake of the original. A more literal remake, titled *The Mummy Lives* (1993), (mis)cast Tony Curtis in the Karloff role. And the more recent franchise initiated by *The Mummy* (1999) has more in common with Steven Spielberg's razzle-dazzle *Raiders of the Lost Ark* (1981) and its sequels than with Freund's suspenseful, romantic, low-key masterpiece. TH

Murder at Dawn
Big 4; b/w; 52 (62) min; U.S.

D: Richard Thorpe *S:* Barry Barringer *P:* Burton L. King, John R. Freuler *C:* Edward Kull *FX:* Ken Strickfaden

Cast: Josephine Dunn, Jack Mulhall, Eddie Boland, Marjorie Beebe, Martha Mattox, Mischa Auer, Phillip Smalley, Crauford Kent, Frank Ball, Alfred Cross, George Reed

Danny (Mulhall) and Doris (Dunn) want to get married and are off to obtain the blessing of her father, Professor Farrington (Ball). They take along with them a married couple, Freddie (Boland) and Gertrude (Beebe), as chaperones, arriving at Farrington's Gothic estate just as he perfects his greatest invention, the DXL Accumulator, a device that can harness the power of the sun and thus free the world's "wage slaves." (How exactly one will bring about the other is never spelled out.) The obligatory thunderstorm erupts, Farrington's friend Judge Folger (Smalley) is murdered, the professor disappears and a mysterious stranger arrives and takes control of the situation. Dead bodies turn up and disappear with alarming frequency, and the culprit turns out to be a rival who needs Farrington's formula to make his own accumulator work.

Murder at Dawn is the only horror film made by Big 4, which normally specialized in Westerns. Its moderate success resulted in founder John R. Freuler forming a separate division to focus mostly on mysteries and thrillers (with an occasional Western thrown in for good measure), but the company petered out by the end of the following year.

The one striking thing about the film is not its hybridization of horror, comedy and mystery—which was common at the time—but its inclusion of a strong science fiction element. Freuler wisely sought out the services of Ken Strickfaden to create Dr. Farrington's outlandish (and outlandish-looking) invention; Strickfaden had designed the laboratory equipment for James Whale's *Frankenstein* the previous year, but here he's severely limited by budget constraints, with the DXL Accumulator paling in comparison to Dr. Frankenstein's way cooler and larger apparatus. Still, the accumulator makes for an interesting touch in an otherwise typical thriller of the time.

Thorpe's direction is torpid, despite an occasional flash of creativity. He fails to establish the necessary atmosphere, in spite of superimposing the opening credits over the image of a shadowy figure and the occasional secret passage echoing with thundering sound effects. It's hard to believe that from so unimpressive a beginning, Thorpe went on to make minor classics for major studios, including a number of Tarzan films for MGM. His other horror credits include *The Secrets of Wu Sin* (1932) and *Night Must Fall* (1937), as well as *Strange People* (1933), *Green Eyes* and *Secret of the Chateau* (both 1934), the latter for Universal. Thorpe, who was a relative newcomer at the time *Murder at Dawn* was produced, wasn't helped by an atrocious script from Barry Barringer (*One Glorious Day*, 1922) that ultimately makes little sense of the proceedings. Not helping matters any are the performances, which are rote imitations of the work of better actors. Jack Mulhall (*The Rogues Tavern*, 1936) would like nothing more than to be David Manners' John Harker in *Dracula* (1931), while Frank Ball (*Border Phantom*, 1936) wants really badly to be Edward Van Sloan's Professor Van Helsing. Comic relief Eddie Boland, by the same token, does his best to out-Marx Groucho Marx but fails to elicit a single laugh. The only people to stand out at all—and that's merely because of whom they're acting against—are Mischa Auer (*Sinister Hands*, 1932) and Martha Mattox (*The Cat and the Canary*, 1927), who repeat their roles from Frank Strayer's marginally more interesting *The Monster Walks* (1932), which was released to theaters only a week before *Murder at Dawn*. CW

Murders in the Rue Morgue
Universal; b/w; 61 min; U.S.

D/Co-S: Robert Florey *Co-S:* Tom Reed, Dale Van Every, John Huston *P:* Carl Laemmle, Jr. *C:* Karl Freund *FX:* John Fulton

Cast: Bela Lugosi, Sidney Fox, Leon Waycoff, Bert Roach, Betsy Ross Clarke, Brandon Hurst, D'Arcy Corrigan, Noble Johnson, Arlene Francis, Charles Gemora

After being dropped from Universal's planned adaptation of *Frankenstein* (1931) in favor of James Whale, Robert Florey was given another opportunity to craft a horror film for the studio. In an evident attempt to outdo Whale's film, Florey imbues his *Murders in the Rue Morgue* with a surprising amount of violence, sexual titillation and controversial science. (The film's advertising slogan focused on the bestial sexuality of the story when it teased, "Innocent Beauty—this was her wedding eve. On the wall a shadow ... the beast was at large grinning horribly, cruelly. What was her fate?") And on the whole, this envelope-pushing mishmash really works!

Based loosely on Edgar Allan Poe's short story, first published in *Graham's Magazine* in 1841, *Murders* has Dr. Mirakle

Sidney Fox and Leon Ames with Bela Lugosi as Dr. Mirakle in *Murders in the Rue Morgue*

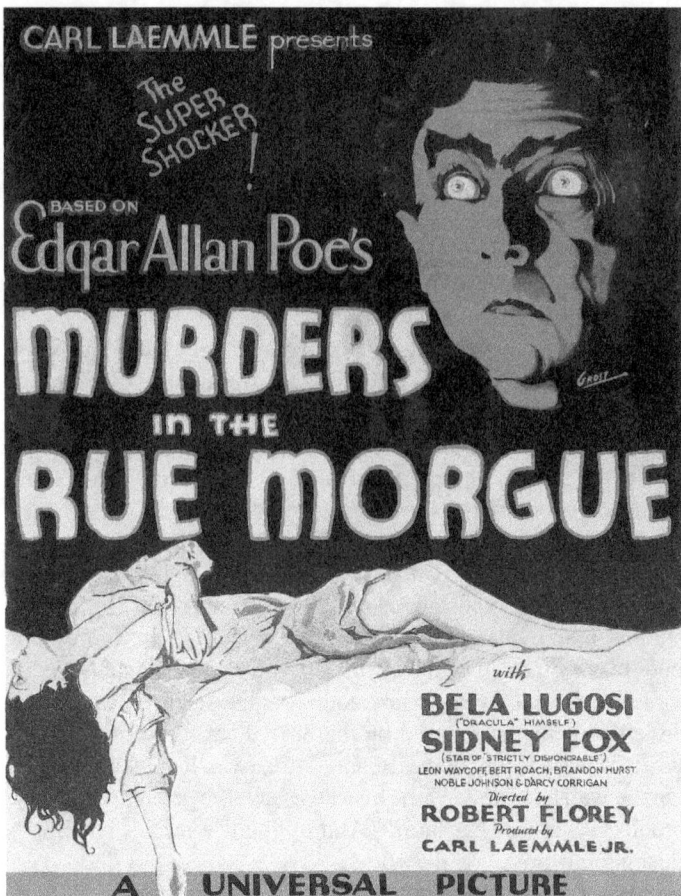

(Lugosi) injecting women with non-human primate blood in an attempt to prove that all life sprang up via the process of descent with modification (better known as evolution). After explaining the pertinent science to a group visiting his fairground show (and the audience, of course), Mirakle goes out at night and picks up a "woman of the streets" who's just been victimized during a fight between her pimp and a client. The doctor has her bound to a cross during a torturous attempt to meld her blood with that of his gorilla Erik (Gemora). The experiment fails, and Mirakle goes into angry hysterics, shouting that the woman has "rotten blood" and that her "beauty was a lie." The assertion that the woman suffers from some sort of venereal disease is more than implicit. But her very sexual activity is what makes her a fallen woman and worthy of what happens next in the eyes of Mirakle. Mirakle's assistant Janos (Johnson) callously cuts her body free and drops it into the sewer below the mad doctor's lab, where it will be allowed to float into the Seine (footage of the prostitute being stabbed to death was deemed too violent by Carl Laemmle and excised before the film's release).

Concluding that what he really needs is the blood of a virgin, Mirakle targets beautiful young Camille L'Espanaye (Fox), who is dating medical student Pierre Dupin (Waycoff). The move is a big mistake, as Dupin has already taken it upon himself to investigate a series of prostitute murders in which the victims' blood is contaminated by an unknown element. (The detective in Poe's story is named C. Auguste Dupin, apparently making Pierre a close relation.) Mirakle nonetheless sends Erik to claim the young woman, and while there the beast also kills Camille's mother (Clarke) and stuffs her in the chimney. A scene lifted directly from Poe's story follows, in which various neighbors testify that the killer spoke in different languages ... Danish, German, Italian, and so forth. Sloppy police work results in the arrest of Dupin, while at the same time Mirakle prepares to inject Camille with ape's blood. Luckily, the beast Erik, which has fallen in love with Camille, offs Mirakle before carrying his beloved up to the Parisian rooftops, where he is done in by the just-released Dupin.

Florey's film borrows heavily from Robert Wiene's 1919 classic *The Cabinet of Dr. Caligari*, with Lugosi's fairground showman Mirakle a thinly disguised Caligari and Gemora's ape man a clear stand-in for Conrad Veidt's somnambulist. The older film's silent German Expressionist motif is intentionally evoked by Charles D. Hall's impressive sets; though placed in 1845 Paris, the film depicts a dark fairytale world where buildings are obtuse rather than angular, becoming a three-dimensional conception of the weird, painted backdrops of classical Expressionism. Florey was no stranger to such forms of artistic expression, as one can see in his early films *The Love of Zero* and *Johann the Coffinmaker* (both 1927), *The Life and Death of 9413–A Hollywood Extra* (1928) and *The Hole in the Wall* (1929).

The contributions of German émigré Karl Freund's (*Dracula*, 1931) superb and inventive camerawork should also not be overlooked. In one striking instance, Freund even attaches his camera to a swing while Camille is pushed back and forth by Dupin. The effect is disconcerting and in perfect keeping with the mood Florey is intent on establishing, one of intense and delirious horror. (That mood is threatened only when Florey trots out the probably inevitable, ham-fisted comic relief.)

The film's distinctive look is further enhanced by the make-up mastery of Jack Pierce. Lugosi's Mirakle sports a foppish hairdo and a massive black unibrow, while African American actor Noble Johnson, credited as "Janos, The Black One," appears anything but black, with his hair and facial features hidden beneath layers of make-up that make him look European in descent.

Lugosi gives one of the best performances of his career as the demonic Dr. Mirakle. It was a particularly good year for the actor, having also starred in the masterful low-budget indie *White Zombie*, where he played Voodoo enthusiast Murder Legendre. As Mirakle, Lugosi gets ample opportunity to leer and shout, yet comes across as genuinely menacing rather than unintentionally campy as in so many of his other appearances.

Most of the supporting players are likewise engaging, with Waycoff a likeable hero and Fox a vivacious and appealing heroine. As Dupin's roommate Paul, Bert Roach is a little less interesting, crossing the line at times between mediocrity and mild annoyance. More interesting is the fact that the woman of the streets is played by a young Arlene Francis, who years later found success on network television, at one point hosting her own program, *The Arlene Francis Show*, in 1957.

Some have accused *Murders in the Rue Morgue* of anachronism in its presentation of the theory of evolution 15 years before the publication of Charles Darwin's *On the Origin of Species*, but in truth, theories of evolution had been around for years before Darwin's breakthrough book. Competing theories had been posited by the likes of Jean-Baptiste Lamarck, Immanuel Kant and Darwin's own grandfather Erasmus Darwin, though it was Charles Darwin who finally struck upon the correct mecha-

Lugosi and Charles Gemora, who plays the murderous gorilla (seen in the background), from *Murders in the Rue Morgue*

nism—natural selection—by which the process works. What may be more surprising than the presentation of the theory itself is that the film approaches it in a positive manner, as is evidenced by the following exchange between Dupin and Paul:

> Dupin: Did you pay attention to what he [Mirakle] said?
> Paul: You mean about us being the product of evolution?
> Dupin: Yes ... Has it occurred to you that he might be right?
> Long pause.
> Paul: Eat your lunch.

Though Paul (who is presented as a buffoon throughout) can't grasp the theory and therefore dismisses it, the hero Dupin clearly believes. And it's his belief in scientific facts that enables him to discover just what Mirakle is up to.

Interestingly, Erik the Ape Man is referred to within the film as variously a baboon, a gorilla and an ape; in close shots, a very real chimpanzee portrays him, while full body shots clearly utilize a man in a gorilla costume. An uncredited Charles Gemora portrayed Erik; he first played an apish primate in *The Leopard Lady* (1928). It was a shtick for which he found lasting fame (within movie studio circles) and to which he returned in *Do Gentlemen Snore?* (1928), *Seven Footprints to Satan* (1929), *Ingagi*, *Bear Shooters*, *The Unholy Three* and *The Gorilla* (all 1930), *Ghost Parade* (1931), *Seal Skins*, *The Chimp*, *Hawkins and Watkins Inc.* and *The Savage Girl* (1932), *Nature in the Wrong* and *Sing, Bing, Sing* (1933), *Bum Voyage* (1934), *Gum Shoes* (1935), *Swiss Miss* (1938), *The Monster and the Girl* and *Road to Zanzibar* (1941), *Two Weeks to Live* (1943), *Gildersleeve's Ghost* (1944), *Who Killed Doc Robbin* (1948), *Africa Screams* (1949), *White Witch Doctor* (1953) and *Mardis Gras* (1958). He also played the part in the next adaptation of Poe's story, Roy Del Ruth's *Phantom of the Rue Morgue* (1954).

Perhaps because of its in-your-face violence, relatively explicit references to sexual matters and sympathetic treatment of the theory of evolution, Florey's adaptation of Poe's story was a failure at the box-office, prompting Universal to drop both him and Lugosi. In the years since, however, the film has come to be considered one of *the* classics of 1930s horror cinema. CW

Mystery Ranch
aka **Death Valley**; **The Killer**
Fox; b/w; 55 min; U.S.
D: David Howard S: Alfred A. Cohn P: Sol M. Wurtzel C: Joseph August, George Schneiderman M: Hugo Friedhofer
Cast: George O'Brien, Cecilia Parker, Charles Middleton, Charles Stevens, Forrester Harvey, Noble Johnson, Roy Stewart, Betty Francisco, Russ Powell

Opening with a murder set to classical music (by the chronically unacknowledged Hugo Friedhofer, whose scores for 1940's *The Mark of Zorro* and 1946's *Gilda*—among more than 100 others—went similarly uncredited), *Mystery Ranch* evokes horror from the get-go. It was released in the year following Universal's twin successes with *Dracula* and *Frankenstein* (both 1931). A pre-Code offering, its gruesome approach to Old West violence wouldn't be revisited until the heyday of the Spaghetti Western in the mid-1960s (though without the Gothic trappings found here).

Based on the novel *The Killer* by Stewart Edward White, *Mystery Ranch* has Henry Steele (Middleton), a piano-playing madman, aggressively driving out homesteaders while holding captive a beautiful young woman named Jane (Parker), with whose home he's become obsessed. Not one to commit murder himself, he sends out his renegade Apache and mute servant Mudo (Johnson) to do his dirty work. Onto the scene rides the heroic Bob Sanborn (O'Brien), there to end Steele's stranglehold on the valley. When Bob meets Jane, he finds himself just as obsessed with her as Steele is, and a game of wits ensues with the girl as the prize. (One guess as to which man Jane prefers.)

Produced by Fox, director David Howard's adaptation of White's novel is anything but a second-string oater, despite its short running time. It's a fairly unique and well-done piece of cinema, playing fast and loose with Western conventions to create a Western/Gothic horror hybrid that actually works. Mudo, his tongue severed as a boy after he was accused of lying, is a sort of Frankenstein's Monster-like figure doing the bidding of his vile master, while Steele is the sort of killer who came to prominence in the horror/thriller genre in the 1990s: vastly intelligent, entirely cold blooded and completely insane. Add to this the director's talent for action and set-up, as well as cinematographers August and Schneiderman's virtuoso use of chiaroscuro lighting and deep shadows, and the tension couldn't be any more palpable.

The viewer is introduced to Steele's ranch in the midst of a pounding thunderstorm, the silhouette of a murder victim hanging by the neck, the body perfectly framed in a dining room window. It's precisely the sort of touch that, along with its overall technical excellence, makes *Mystery Ranch* possibly the most successful of the early "weird" Westerns. It knows what it wants to do and just does it; there are no singing cowboys or funny sidekicks, no obvious stunt work or cheap theatrics to water down the central story.

Character actor Charles Middleton was no stranger to playing villains; he may be best remembered for his role as Ming the Merciless in Universal's *Flash Gordon* programs. Predominantly a Western actor, he took time out on a fairly regular basis to star in horror features, including *Tomorrow at Seven* (1933), *Mystery of Marie Roget* (1942), *The Black Raven* (1943) and *The Strangler of the Swamp* (1946).

Lead George O'Brien became a star of Westerns during the silent era and rode that fame right into the 1960s. *Mystery Ranch* appears to have been his only horror appearance (unless one considers his early, uncredited bit part in *The Ghost Breaker*, 1922). Celia Parker went on to find fame as Marian Hardy in the Andy Hardy film series, while Noble Johnson was typecast as exotic types in numerous horror films of the period, including *Black Waters* and *The Mysterious Dr. Fu Manchu* (both 1929), *East of Borneo* (1931), *Murders in the Rue Morgue*, *The Most Dangerous Game* and *The Mummy* (all 1932), *King Kong* and *The Son of Kong* (1933), *She* and *Dante's Inferno* (both 1935), *Mummy's Boys* (1936), *The Ghost Breakers* (1940), *The Mad Doctor of Market Street* (1942) and *A Game of Death* (1945). Though Johnson was African American, he portrayed numerous different races, from Latin American to Chinese, on the big screen. He retired from acting in 1950 and died at the good old age of 96. CW

The Night Rider
Supreme/Weis/Artclass; b/w; 54 (72) min; U.S.
D: Fred Newmeyer *S:* Harry P. Crist *P:* Louis Weiss, Alfred T. Mannon *C:* James R. Diamond
Cast: Harry Carey, Elinor Fair, George F. Hayes, Julian Rivero, Jack Weatherby, Nadja, Tom London, Walter Shumway, Bob Kortman, Cliff Lyons

When a man called The Stranger (Carey) rides into a generic Old Western town, its inhabitants fear that he may be the notorious outlaw Jim Blake. It turns out, however, that he's a federal officer named John Brown, there to apprehend The Night Rider, a mysterious black-clad criminal stalking the area and robbing the locals. Brown enlists the help of two men, a tourist known as Altoony (Hayes) and a hired hand named Valdez (Rivera), both of whom provide far more comic relief than assistance. Brown takes a job as foreman on a ranch owned by Barbara Rogers (Fair) in hopes that it will bring him closer to the nighttime raider. He learns of a deserted mine near the ranch and suspects that it might be the Night Rider's lair. The plot, such as it is, thickens when he finds that a hidden passage runs from Barbara's house to the mine.

While not as overtly horrific as some of the other weird Westerns of the time (such as *Haunted Gold*, *Mystery Ranch* and *Tombstone Canyon*, all 1932), *The Night Rider* has a handful of striking moments, most notably its shots of the dark-robed villain riding his equally dark horse through the desolate evening countryside. The story itself, on the other hand, is too clichéd to generate much frisson, and the performances are par for the poverty row course. Nor does its mercifully short running time compensate for its lack of action and overwhelming talkiness (with much of the latter blazingly and offensively stupid). And the mystery's solution, when it at long last arrives, illuminates more plot holes than it ties loose ends.

Harry P. Crist was a pseudonym for writer/director Harry Fraser. Though he didn't direct *The Night Rider*, his dull hand

Boris Karloff is mute servant Morgan in James Whale's darkly humorous *The Old Dark House*.

is all over it. Many film historians believe that William Nigh (*The Strange Case of Dr. Rx*, 1942) provided uncredited directorial assistance to Fred Newmeyer, a hack who, as evidenced here, took whatever work he could get. Among Newmeyer's few interesting credits are the lost 1925 horror opus *Seven Keys to Baldpate* and the 1935 Lon Chaney, Jr. thriller, *A Scream in the Night*.

The Night Rider was remade twice, first as *Desert Phantom* in 1935 and then as *The Range Busters* in 1940. CW

The Old Dark House
Universal; b/w; 71 min; U.S.
D: James Whale *S:* Benn W. Levy *P:* Carl Laemmle, Jr. *C:* Arthur Edeson *M:* Bernhard Kaun
Cast: Boris Karloff, Melvyn Douglas, Charles Laughton, Ernest Thesiger, Lillian Bond, Raymond Massey, Gloria Stuart, Eva Moore, Brember Wills, Elspeth Dudgeon

Three travelers—Roger Penderel (Douglas), Philip Waverton (Massey) and Margaret Waverton (Stuart)—are stranded in a strange house in the Welsh countryside during a violent thunderstorm. The inhabitants of the house include Horace Femm (Thesiger), his sister Rebecca (Moore) and a mute servant named Morgan (Karloff). As the evening unfolds, another pair of refugees from the weather, Sir William Porterhouse (Laughton) and his chorus-girl girlfriend Gladys (Bond), join them. The storm builds steadily, as does the tension, while the unwelcome guests

Lovely Gloria Stuart is menaced by Karloff's Morgan in *The Old Dark House.*

learn that the house has other inhabitants, including a 102-year-old, bed-ridden patriarch (Dudgeon) and a pyromaniac older brother, Saul (Wills), who is confined to his room.

J.B. Priestley (1894-1984) conceived his 1927 novel *Benighted* as a shocker. It was a big hit in Britain and later in the United States (where it was published under the title *The Old Dark House*). In the wake of the commercial success of *Dracula* (1931) and *Frankenstein* (1931), Universal head Carl Laemmle, Jr. was on the lookout for additional properties that would make good thrillers on the big screen. He thought Priestley's novel a great catch and sensibly assigned James Whale to direct. Whale had scored a major artistic triumph with *Frankenstein* but was then pushed into directing a now-forgotten minor comedic melodrama titled *The Impatient Maiden* (1932). He'd found that project tedious and uninteresting, which no doubt contributed to the finished film's mediocrity.

Conversely, he accepted *The Old Dark House* with enthusiasm. But whereas Priestley's novel was intended seriously, Whale approached the film with tongue planted firmly in cheek. Collaborating with acclaimed screenwriter Benn W. Levy (who had in 1931 worked with Whale on *Waterloo Bride* and who would later contribute uncredited material to Whale's 1936 mystery comedy *Remember Last Night?*), Whale infuses *House* with a sense of sardonic humor. The film is loaded with witty visual touches and priceless dialogue, and there are a few wonderfully vivid moments of horror and suspense amid its mostly comedic tone.

Scenes of conflict are staged and edited with real tension and energy; the final battle of wits between Penderel and the unleashed Saul, for example, is legitimately unsettling and suspenseful. The sequence in which Rebecca Femm terrorizes Margaret is equally noteworthy; Whale alternates grotesque, distorted images of Rebecca with shots of the young woman's frightened face. The result is both disturbing and darkly funny at the same time. That the scene peaks with the elderly woman grabbing at the younger's breasts is unexpected, but not really surprising when one considers Whale's propensity for pushing the envelope. His caustic, cynical sensibility is likewise reflected by the presence of Roger Penderel and Horace Femm. Penderel is a mouthpiece for Whale's Wilde-like wit, while Femm's mocking views on religion dovetail with those of the director, who was openly homosexual and atheist.

To the inattentive viewer, the film may come off as stagey—it's confined to a single, albeit elaborate, set for most of its running time, and there's much more talk than action—but Whale's direction is far more cinematic than theatrical. His choice of camera angles and movements adds an air of effortlessness to the work, and it transcends the feel of filmed theater in a way that so many of its contemporaries (*Dracula*, for instance) do not.

Laemmle conceived of the film as a vehicle for the studio's new master of menace, Boris Karloff. But Whale had other ideas; he had by this point become somewhat jealous of his star discovery, resenting the fact that Karloff received so much of the attention for *Frankenstein*. Friends and associates recalled years afterward that Whale often turned his bitchy wit toward the actor, and at times during the filming of *The Old Dark House*, he sadistically forced the older man to repeatedly redo difficult scenes. By casting Karloff as the mute, brutal Morgan, Whale satisfied Universal's desire to use the actor while at the same time pushing him into the background with a relatively small role. (The studio nonetheless gave Karloff top billing—with the single-name, all-caps treatment—and featured him prominently in the advertising campaign. In addition, a Producer's Note in the film informs viewers that he's indeed the same actor who portrayed "the mechanical monster in Frankenstein.")

Jealousy aside, Whale does afford Karloff some wonderful moments—be it peering through the door to welcome the guests or cradling the dead Saul in his arms. Karloff's role as Morgan isn't shaded enough to allow him any real sense of pathos, but as a purely physical presence, he's terrifically effective.

A last-minute substitution for Russell Hopton, Melvyn Douglas is ideal as the cynical Penderel. He became a major leading man for a time before evolving into one of Hollywood's most distinguished and reliable character actors and ultimately winning two Best Supporting Actor Oscars (for 1963's *Hud* and 1979's *Being There*) before his death in 1981 at the age of 80. He

Melvyn Douglas and Gloria Stuart huddle in fear as they try to survive *The Old Dark House.*

In this original lobby card, notice how Universal shadowed out the lower portion of Karloff's face to heighten his fear factor.

wrings the wit out of his every line of dialogue, and in the final reel proves endearing as a brave man of action.

The film also marked the Hollywood debuts of three other distinguished performers: Ernest Thesiger, Raymond Massey and Charles Laughton. It's the cadaverous Thesiger (1879-1961) who steals *House* from his co-stars. As the effete and blasphemous Horace Femm, he gets the best lines ("As my sister hints, there are, I'm afraid, no beds," or his immortal "Have a po-tato!"). He'd go on to appear in many popular films, but at this point he was still a virtual unknown. Whale had worked with him on stage in Britain, and had him brought to the United States to play the role of Femm. The two collaborated again on *The Bride of Frankenstein* (1935), which gave Thesiger his most famous screen appearance as the venal Dr. Pretorius.

Canadian-born Raymond Massey had already played Sherlock Holmes in *The Speckled Band* (1931), but he wouldn't find major success until he played Abraham Lincoln in Robert E. Sherwood's play (and the 1940 film) *Abe Lincoln in Illinois*. He makes the most of a rather dull role, effectively holding his own amongst the gifted ensemble. In an interesting footnote, Massey later portrayed a villain in *Arsenic and Old Lace* (1944) who has had facial reconstruction surgery and now looks like a bizarre mixture of Boris Karloff and the Frankenstein monster.

Charles Laughton (1899-1962) was already an established stage presence in his native Britain and on the threshold of film stardom. His portrayal of the Yorkshire-born Sir William Porterhouse teeters on the edge of self-parody, but Laughton infuses the character with touching flashes of humanity, notably when Porterhouse recalls the death of his beloved wife after business associates snubbed him. Laughton is possibly the most openly human and lovable character in the film—not so caustic as Penderel, but livelier and more interesting than Philip. He later scored an Oscar of his own for his portrayal of the title character in *The Private Life of Henry VIII* (1933). Despite being homosexual, he married actress Elsa Lanchester, who dual-roled for Whale (as author Mary Shelley and the title character) in 1935's *The Bride of Frankenstein*.

Gloria Stuart, later to be nominated for an Oscar for James Cameron's epic *Titanic* (1997), makes the first of several appearances for Whale; she later appeared in *The Kiss Before the Mirror* and *The Invisible Man* (both 1933).

It has long been known that Whale and cinematographer Arthur Edeson carefully studied Paul Leni's *The Cat and the Canary* (1927) prior to making *The Old Dark House*. Watching the two films back to back removes all doubt that while Whale borrowed certain elements (notably the looming shadows and long corridors with billowing curtains), he nevertheless made *House* his own. Its tone is far less jocular and more perverse than that of Leni's film, with the menace far more physical and threatening.

Because of a legal dispute between the film's producer and J.B. Priestley's estate, the film was out of circulation for many years, until a film archivist and fan raised the money to purchase the rights directly. It made its home video debut in the 1990s and has been readily available ever since.

As a blend of humor and horror, *House* has never been bettered. Even Whale's more celebrated *The Bride of Frankenstein* feels a bit forced in comparison. Hammer Film Productions and Columbia Pictures shot another version of Priestley's novel (under the same title) in 1963. Directed and co-produced by William Castle, it pales next to the original—or films in general, for that matter. TH

The Phantom Express
Majestic; b/w; 70 min; U.S.

D: Emory Johnson *S:* Laird Doyle, Emory Johnson *P:* Irving C. Franklin, Donald M. Stoner, Emory Johnson *C:* Ross Fisher

Cast: William Collier, Jr., Sally Blane, J. Farrell MacDonald, Hobart Bosworth, Axel Axelson, Lina Basquette, Eddie Phillips, Robert Ellis, Claire McDowell, David Rollins, Tom O'Brien, Huntley Gordon, Brady Kline, Jack Pennick, Jack Mower, Allan Forrest

A railway runs into trouble when several of its trains are involved in accidents with a so-called phantom train. Bruce Harrington (Collier, Jr.), the ne'er-do-well son of the railroad's head, goes into action to discover what is behind the wrecks.

Despite its title, this briskly paced B-movie barely qualifies as horror. That aside, and despite a final twist that's fairly easy to guess, director Emory Johnson does a reasonable job of keeping the action chugging along. Johnson spent the better part of his career as a character actor; as a director, he guided only a handful of titles, of which *The Phantom Express* was the last. Indeed, the film proved to be his penultimate title in any capacity—he made an inglorious return to acting with an uncredited bit part in *I Wanted Wings* (1942), starring Ray Milland and William Holden—before retiring permanently. He passed away in 1960, a long-forgotten veteran of the silent era.

Phantom's cast performs capably enough, though William Collier, Jr. proves an uninspiring protagonist. A large reason for this is the two-dimensional nature of the character he plays—Bruce is cocky and aimless and only moved into action because he's making a play for the film's leading lady (Sally Blane). Blane—the lesser-known sister of actress Loretta Young—is photogenic but similarly hamstrung by ill-defined characterization.

Special effects work includes some competently executed miniatures, but the big action scenes lack impact. As time-killers go, one could do worse, but genre fans looking for thrills may well find *The Phantom Express* a bit lacking. TH

The Phantom Fiend
aka **The Lodger**
Twickenham; b/w; 62 min; Great Britain
D: Maurice Elvey *S:* H. Fowler Mear, Miles Mander, Paul Rotha *P:* Julius Hagen *C:* Basil Emmott, William Luff *M:* W.L. Trytel
Cast: Ivor Novello, Elizabeth Allan, Jack Hawkins, A.W. Baskcomb, Barbara Everest, Shayle Gardner, Peter Gawthorne, Kynaston Reeves, Drusilla Wills, Anthony Holles, George Merritt, Molly Fisher, Andreas Malandrinos

A psychotic murderer who calls himself the Avenger terrorizes London. The police are unable to catch a lead as the killings continue with eerie efficiency. Against this backdrop, Mr. and Mrs. Bunting (Baskcomb and Everest) decide to lease out one of their rooms for extra income. The mysterious Michel Angeloff (Novello) moves in, and in due time the Buntings begin to fear that he may be the Avenger. That fear increases when it becomes obvious that their daughter Daisy (Allan) is infatuated with him.

Marie Adelaide Lowndes' 1913 novel *The Lodger*—a thinly disguised take on the exploits of Jack the Ripper—had already been filmed to great effect by Alfred Hitchcock in 1927 as *The Lodger: A Story of the London Fog*. With the emergence of sound, however, it was determined that the story was ripe for an updating. But while the producers were successful in getting Ivor Novello to reprise his role as the mysterious title character, they were not able to secure the services of Hitchcock to direct. In his place, Maurice Elvey was brought in. Elvey had previously directed the 1921 version of *The Hound of the Baskervilles*, generally considered a thoroughly pedestrian treatment of the source material. The same can be said of *The Phantom Fiend*, which pales considerably in comparison to Hitchcock's original film.

Ivor Novello may or may *not* be Jack the Ripper in *The Phantom Fiend*, the second screen adaptation of Marie Lowndes' play.

Fiend also suffers from some unduly melodramatic performances, notably that of Novello. Hitchcock had managed to keep Novello's histrionics under control in the earlier version, but here the actor consistently goes over the top. More mediocrity permeates the performance of a young Jack Hawkins. This was only his second screen appearance—following his debut in *Birds of Prey* (1930)—and the qualities that went on to make him one of England's most distinguished character actors are, to be kind, not evident here. On the positive side, Elizabeth Allan (*Mark of the Vampire*, 1935) outshines her co-stars as the intelligent and resourceful damsel in distress.

The film displays a little life during its final section but is for the most part a stagy and unexciting thriller. Lowndes' story was remade again as *The Lodger* in 1944 and 2009; the former of these, directed by John Brahm, is arguably the most successful adaptation of the story to date. The story was also shot in 1953 under the title *The Man in the Attic*, which starred Jack Palance, and as a 1965 episode in the television series *Armchair Mystery Hour*. And Hammer Film Productions ripped the idea off for *Room to Let* (1950), which was based on a strikingly similar play by Margery Allingham. TH

The Phantom of Crestwood
RKO; b/w; 76 min; U.S.
D: J. Walter Ruben *S:* Bartlett Cormack *P:* Merian C. Cooper, David O. Selznick *C:* Henry Gerrard *M:* Max Steiner
Cast: Ricardo Cortez, Karen Morley, Anita Louise, Pauline Frederick, H.B. Warner, Mary Duncan, Sam Hardy, Tom Douglas, Richard Gallagher, Aileen Pringle, Ivan Simpson, George E. Stone, Robert McWade, Hilda Vaughn, Gavin Gordon,

A woman named Jenny Wren (Morley) blackmails a former lover (Warner) into arranging a party at his cliffside estate. The invitees? The list includes other socially upstanding men who have had "improper" relationships with Wren and from whom she intends to extort money. But after she makes several high-powered enemies and the party winds down, she's terrorized by the apparent ghost of a young man with whom she had once had a relationship and driven to suicide. She's murdered, and a raging thunderstorm causes a mudslide that traps the guests on the estate with the killer. Enter Gary Curtis (Cortez), a thug who has come to relieve Jenny of some incriminating letters but who instead has to solve the murder lest it get pinned on him.

The Phantom of Crestwood began life as a multi-part radio play hosted by announcer Graham McNamee, the biggest name in the field at the time, on NBC. Two screenwriters, J. Walter Ruben and Bartlett Cormack, concocted the story with an eye toward its finale being produced as a big-screen movie, thus forcing listeners, if they wanted to learn the solution to the mystery, into theaters to get it. Cormack was enlisted to write the film and Ruben to direct it. Fans of the radio show were invited to submit a solution to the story's mystery and submit it to NBC for various prizes, with the final winner possibly dictating the conclusion to the climactic film. (This was done entirely for publicity purposes. None of the selections was chosen as the film's conclusion; *Crestwood*, in fact, was pretty much completed by the time the radio play and contest were done.)

RKO produced the film, the company forming in 1929 when Radio Corporation of America (RCA) and Film Booking

Old dark houses containing old dark corridors like this one were a staple in early sound horror films such as *The Phantom of Crestwood*. Pictured are Anita Louise and Pauline Frederick.

Office of America (FBO) joined forces. The plan was to bring together the two most then-popular mediums of entertainment, radio and cinema, under a single umbrella company. Included in the deal was the Keith-Albee-Orpheum theater chain, in which the company's films were to be shown, and Pathé Studios, which provided additional production resources.

The Phantom of Crestwood is a prime example of RKO's successful exploitation of the two mediums by appealing to both markets simultaneously. The film debuted in October of 1932, just in time for Halloween. The tag line for the ad campaign shouted out in all caps, "WHO KILLED JENNY WREN?" prefiguring by 45 years the famous "Who shot J.R.?" campaign for television's *Dallas*.

Reviews of *Crestwood* were positive, which is not surprising given the expert way in which director Ruben handles the subject matter. Not content with just another "old dark house" thriller, he fills his movie with original directorial flourishes, particularly during the many flashback sequences. Unjustly, his reputation never surpassed the level of a journeyman, partly because he was more interested in writing and producing than in directing, and partly because he died of heart failure a mere two days after his 43rd birthday (allegedly brought about by the stress he went through while producing William Dieterle's historically inaccurate *Tennessee Johnson*, 1942).

Ruben's success at making a visually appealing picture is abetted by cinematographer Henry Gerrard's mobile camera, which prowls down dark corridors in a manner reminiscent of Karl Freund's best work and 20 years before Floyd Crosby did the same for Roger Corman. For its part, Cormack's script provides enough twists and turns to keep the viewer guessing until the film's satisfying conclusion.

The Phantom of Crestwood also boasts superior lead performances. Ricardo Cortez's Gary Curtiz appears to be a dry run for his one go-around as Perry Mason in *The Case of the Black Cat* (1936), while a young Karen Morley (*The Mask of Fu Manchu*, 1932) keeps tongue firmly in cheek as she prances around the screen, deliciously bitchy as the duplicitous Jenny Wren.

H.B. Warner (*Stark Mad*, 1929), Ivan Simpson (*Maid of Salem*, 1937), Mary Duncan (*Thirteen Women*, 1932), George Stone (*The Face Behind the Mask*, 1941) and Gavin Gordon (*Mystery of the Wax Museum*, 1933) turn in capable supporting performances, but the real knockout is Pauline Frederick as the killer. Though she's all but forgotten today, Frederick was a popular stage actress on Broadway before she made a successful transition to film in 1915. She was one of a handful of silent screen actresses who had the chops to move to talkies, but by the 1930s her poor health limited the number of roles she could take. Her final film was *Thank You, Mr. Moto* (1937); she died the following year of asthma. Her performance as the wonderfully named Faith Andes in *Crestwood* is entirely natural in the manner of later actresses such as Emma Thompson and Judi Dench, making her premature demise all the more regrettable.

Shot and released before the Production Code's stringent rules about what could be shown on film, *Phantom* provides enough violence and sexual innuendo to fill several pictures. Murders are shown onscreen, and there are not one but two suicides. Wren's dresses are lower cut than they would have been had the film been released a mere two years later, and the fact that she has slept with multiple married men is stated rather than implied. Yet somehow the film managed to escape the censorship that fettered the same year's *Thirteen Women* (1932).

Buoyed by the mild success of *The Phantom of Crestwood* and other films of its ilk, RKO executive producer David O. Selznick and associate producer Merian C. Cooper pushed ahead with an aggressive slate of high- and low-brow films aimed at every market. The plan worked, and after the success of the following year's *King Kong*, the studio found itself in the big leagues.

As for Jenny herself, she still registers an occasional blip on the cultural radar; one of her more recent appearances was as the title character in an oddly sympathetic 2005 Paul McCartney song, based on Wren's first appearance in Charles Dickens' novel, *Our Mutual Friend*. CW

Queen of Atlantis
aka Die Herrin von Atlantis
Nero; b/w; 87 min; Germany

D: G.W. Pabst *S:* Herman Oberländer, Ladislaus Vajda *P:* Seymour Nebenzahl *C:* Ernst Körner, Eugen Schüfftan *M:* Wolfgang Zeller

Cast: Brigitte Helm, Heinz Klingenberg, Gustav Diessl, Vladimir Sokoloff, Tela Tchai, Florelle, Mathias Wieman, Georges Tourriel, Gertrude Pabst

In 1919 Peirre Benoit garnered terrific sales throughout Europe with his second novel, *L'Atlantide*, but the success was not without controversy. After a French literary supplement accused Benoit of plagiarizing his story from H. Rider Haggard's novel *She: A History of Adventure* (first serialized in 1886 and 1887), Benoit sued the magazine. The similarities between the two novels being quite strong, he not only lost the case but was also ordered to reimburse the court for its costs (though, in his defense, it seems likely that Benoit derived his novel from tales he'd heard during his childhood in French Algeria). Still, despite—or because of—the publicity generated by the scandal, Benoit's book sales remained strong. And in 1921 it was adapted to the big screen under its original title; the film was released in the United States under the seedier name *Missing Husbands*.

When that first adaptation was re-released in 1928, it proved wildly successful, leading German filmmaker G.W. Pabst to begin work on his own version. Realizing that translating talkies into foreign languages takes more than exchanging title cards, he shot three different versions virtually simultaneously in German, French, and English. Each had mostly its own cast, though they all shared Brigitte Helm, who'd become a European superstar after appearing in Fritz Lang's *Metropolis* (1927) and Henrik Galeen's *Alraune* (1928).

While both the film *Queen of Atlantis* and the novel *L'Atlantide* are predominantly science fiction/fantasy yarns, the tale veers into horror terrain in its story of the queen (Helm) of an Atlantean remnant holed up in a French Saharan mountain. She lures outside males into her lair to seduce, kill and embalm them, then puts them on display. CW

Rasputin and the Empress
MGM; b/w; 121 min; U.S.

D: Richard Boleslavsky *S:* Charles MacArthur *P:* Bernard H. Hyman, Irving Thalberg *C:* William Daniels *M:* Herbert Stothart

Cast: John Barrymore, Ethel Barrymore, Lionel Barrymore, Ralph Morgan, Diana Wynyard, Tad Alexander, C. Henry Gordon, Edward Arnold, Gustav Von Seyffertitz, Mischa Auer, William Boyd

The first film to detail the relationship between Grigori Yefimovich Rasputin and the last of Russia's Romanov Dynasty came in 1917, the year after Rasputin's death. In 1918, the Bolsheviks executed Tsar Nicholas Romanoff II, his wife Alexandra, their five children and their four servants, further enhancing the situation's already high drama quotient. The real-life story of these tragic events (which bookended the Russian Revolution) was still ripe for the cinematic picking in 1932, and MGM head Irving Thalberg decided it was time for his studio to have a crack at it.

Thalberg hired noted novelist and playwright Mercedes de Acosta, a friend of Rasputin's principal assassin Prince Yusupov, to script *Rasputin and the Empress*, the "true story" behind the Russian Revolution. Obviously influenced by 1917's *Rasputin, The Black Monk*, Thalberg insisted that de Acosta add a fictional scene in which Rasputin rapes the prince's wife. De Acosta refused, warning Thalberg that Prince Yusupov would sue for libel should such a derogatory sequence be presented. Her cautious integrity was rewarded with a position as the first in a series of fired or rejected writers, followed by Ben Hecht, Robert E. Sherwood and Lenore J. Coffee. Finally, Charles MacArthur turned in a script with the rape of the princess as a key component. Thalberg didn't completely throw legal caution to the wind, however; he and MacArthur made a token effort to cover themselves by changing the names of Prince Yusupov and his wife Irene to Prince Paul Chegodieff and Natasha (how that ruse worked out for them is touched upon below).

To enhance the film's chances for success, MGM hired the famous Barrymore siblings—John, Ethel and Lionel—to star.

John, Ethel and Lionel Barrymore in MGM's big budget exercise in historical horror, *Rasputin and the Empress*.

Never before had they been in a film together, and their often volatile relationships (the first was a drunk, the second a self-righteous prig and the third hooked on painkillers[1]) reportedly made for a tumultuous shoot. Noted director Charles Brabin (*The Mask of Fu Manchu*, 1932) was brought in to oversee things, but ongoing clashes with Ethel (she referred to him as *Mr. Theda Bara*[2], the silent-screen superstar to whom Brabin was married) resulted in his removal from the picture. And though he goes uncredited on the final print, much of the footage he shot remains in the film.

Brought in to replace Brabin was Richard Boleslavsky, who had been born in Poland when it was still a part of the Russian Empire. A former Broadway actor, Boleslavsky was at the time an up-and-coming director in Hollywood; he went on to helm such major features as *The Mystery of Mr. X* and *The Painted Veil* (both 1934), *Les Misérables* (1935) and *Three Godfathers* and *The Garden of Allah* (both 1936) before an untimely heart attack took him, at age 47, in 1937. But Boleslavsky also had a difficult time keeping the Barrymores in check. At one point Lionel, who believed that his brother John was attempting to steal a scene by placing his hand on him while Lionel delivered his dialogue, stormed off the set, only to call the director and threaten to "lay a hand" on John should John touch him one more time.

In the interest of the film's verisimilitude, MGM approached J. Stuart Blackton, the former head of American Vitagraph, and acquired Blackton's privately owned footage of Russian military parades and apropos outbreaks of civil violence. This stock footage was incorporated throughout *Empress*, giving it the unmistakable aura of authenticity. Add to that a big budget, lavish sets and costumes and a seven-month shooting schedule, and the film easily qualifies as epic in scope.

The film begins at the tercentenary celebration of the House of Romanov, but the festivities hide a growing unrest within a country where Nicholas II (Morgan) and his wife Alexandra (Ethel Barrymore) lack the skills to rule effectively—leaving underlings free to execute peasants without trial over the smallest of infractions. Prince Paul Chegodieff (John Barrymore) understands that if things don't soon change within the court of the

Royal Family, disquiet will erupt into revolution. Against this backdrop, young Tsarevitch Alexai (Alexander) falls down and is injured. Nicholas and Alexandra learn that their son is a hemophiliac, but the royal doctors are unable to do anything to help him. An unhinged-looking monk (Lionel Barrymore) named Rasputin arrives on the scene, introduces himself to the Tsarina, and convinces her that he can cure the boy using mystical powers. She leaves Rasputin alone with her son, and the monk places the boy under hypnotic control, willing him into health and at the same time prompting him to shun the affection of everyone but his mother and the monk. Soon, the mad holy man has the entire Romanov household beholden to him. He also manages to place spies and acolytes throughout government in an attempt to take control of Russia. Suspecting what Rasputin is up to, Prince Paul shoots him, but a bulletproof vest keeps the monk from harm. In retaliation, Rasputin rapes Paul's wife Natasha (Wynyard), who is also the governess of the Romanov children. After learning of the assassination attempt, Nicholas discharges Paul, who takes it upon himself to remove Rasputin once and for all. In the meantime, Alexandra learns that Rasputin has attempted to seduce her daughter Maria. The monk is dismissed from court, and shortly thereafter, Paul has him poisoned and beaten. Rasputin refuses to die (shouting that if he does so, Russia will die with him), so Paul drags him to the river and drowns him. The narrative concludes much later, during the Bolshevik Revolution, with an exiled Nicholas II, Alexandra and children being shot to death by Communist captors in the cellar of a country estate.

After the film's release in 1932, the real-life Prince Yusupov and his wife did indeed sue MGM for libel in both Britain and the United States. When the British court found in the married couple's favor and awarded them over $127,000, MGM, fearing a similar result in the U.S., settled with the Yusupovs for anywhere from $250,000 to $1,000,000[3] (depending upon whose account one chooses to believe). The studio then pulled the film from circulation, cut the rape sequence and added the words "Fictional Character" to the opening credits behind the names "Prince Chegodieff," "Natasha" and others. This hubbub led to the practice, still the norm today, of placing statements in film credits asserting that the film is a work of fiction and is not in any way intended to be construed as real, and that if there is any similarity to actual persons or events, it's entirely coincidental.

The rape scene was originally placed approximately 67 minutes into the film; in the recut version, the scene begins but fades to black. After Paul's attempted assassination of Rasputin, the monk, still alive and well, returns to his rooms where Natasha awaits him. He enters through the door, the screen goes dark and Natasha's voice can be heard to say, "I heard a shot." Rasputin responds, "Yes, my daughter," to which Natasha responds, "It was Paul." Here the scene ends, but, oddly, what originally came next still appears in the film's trailer. "We're going to punish him," Rasputin says of Paul to Natasha, "you and I." She backs away in fear as he approaches her, a leer on his bearded face. She tries to escape but he grabs her; she screams as his back blocks the shot and the scene fades. It's pretty obvious what's going on.

Additionally, attentive viewing reveals the scriptwriter's original intent. Before the bowdlerized scene, Natasha supports and defends the holy man, but after it her mood indisputably shifts. She clearly fears Rasputin, and later in the film blocks him when he attempts to sexually exploit the Grand Duchess Maria. Additionally, in each of the two scenes in which Rasputin and Natasha interact after the rape, there is a sudden jump cut in mid-conversation. Something has obviously been removed and, in context, it seems highly likely that references to the rape were cut to avoid audience confusion (not to mention further legal action on the part of the Yusupovs). Unless one assumes that the rape occurred, Natasha's change in heart toward Rasputin (not to mention the jump cuts) makes no sense.

The reworked *Rasputin and the Empress* got a wide release in March of 1933, but audience reception was lukewarm. The film retains a strikingly horrific tone even after MGM's butchery. From Rasputin's use of hypnosis to control others to his sadistic mental torture of Alexai, director Boleslavsky manages to create some chilling—and at times overtly sexual and violent—images. Most effective is the death of Rasputin, which dramatizes one of Yusupov's many contradictory accounts of the incident. Rasputin is first fed enough poisoned chocolate to kill several men. Then Paul brutally beats him until his hair and beard are matted with blood (given the period in which the film was made, the latter is a shocking bit of Grand Guignol). Even more emotionally vivid are the film's final images of the Romanovs, being led downstairs to their deaths in a dank cellar by the very people they believe will keep them safe. But none of this can top the sequence in which Alexai is forced to watch in extreme close-up a lowly ant set upon and kill an "aristocratic" fly, a clear metaphor for the peasant mob that's about to rise up and pull down the aristocratic Romanov dynasty.

While most of the performances are very good (except for Ethel Barrymore, who doesn't seem to have realized that the silent era was over), it's Lionel Barrymore and Tad Alexander who steal the show. Barrymore portrays Rasputin as the disgusting creep he was; comparisons of his appearance here with photographs of his real-life counterpart reveal just how much alike they looked. Belching, spitting and chewing his way through the film, Barrymore convincingly sports unkempt hair and fake beard with the palpable aura of a person who never bathes and has terrible breath. (There's no doubt that it isn't entirely because he's scary when other people shrink from him). Making the performance all the more remarkable was the fact that Barrymore was frequently high throughout the long shoots[4] (after, ironically, having beaten out fellow addict Bela Lugosi for the role).

Rasputin and the Empress came a year after Barrymore won the Academy Award for Best Actor for 1930's *A Free Soul*. One of the most sought-after actors of his generation, he also appeared in such classics as *Grand Hotel* and *Dinner at Eight* (both 1932*)*, *Treasure Island* (1934), *Camille* (1936), *You Can't Take It With You* (1938), *It's a Wonderful Life* (1945), *Duel in the Sun* (1946) and *Key Largo* (1948). His horror film appearances include *The Bells* (1925), *West of Zanzibar* (1928), *The Unholy Night* (1929), *The Mark of the Vampire* (1935) and *The Devil Doll* (1936). Though his film career began in 1908, he worked right up until 1953, a year before his death from a heart attack. In addition to acting, he wrote a novel and a bestselling autobiography. He was also a member of ASCAP, composing several songs and one-act operas. When his friend Lon Chaney died in 1930, he was one of the pallbearers.

The Romanov family prepares to be executed in the controversial *Rasputin and the Empress*.

Tad Alexander as Alexai manages to convey a number of different emotions, from boyish excitement to abject terror. This appears to have been only his third film; and while he worked afterward in several other minor pictures, his only other film of note was Phil Rosen's 1934 adaptation of the classic Louisa May Alcott novel *Little Men*.

Also interesting in an important role is Ralph Morgan, who gives a nicely understated performance as Nicholas II. Morgan brought respectability to any role he took, later providing class to many a B-grade horror film, including *Trick for Trick* (1933), *The Mad Doctor* (1941), *Night Monster* (1942), *Weird Woman* and *The Monster Maker* (both 1944), *The Monster and the Ape* (1945) and *The Creeper* (1948).

And while it's been alleged that he was drunk on set most of the time[5], John Barrymore's performance as the rather bland hero is quietly effective.

With its mostly good performances, lavish sets, beautiful costumes and stunning directorial flourishes, it's a shame that *Rasputin and the Empress* has garnered a reputation as something of a cheat. In whatever version, it should be more accurately regarded as an unsung masterpiece awaiting rediscovery. CW

[1] Peters, Margot. *The House of Barrymore*. New York: Knopf, 1990. p. 340. Print.

[2] Nissen, Axel. *Actresses of a Certain Character: Forty Familiar Hollywoood Faces from the Thirties to the* Fifties. North Carolina: McFarland, 2007. p. 27. Print.

[3] Peters, Margot. *The House of Barrymore*. New York: Knopf, 1990. p. 345. Print.

[4] Peters, Margot. *The House of Barrymore*. New York: Knopf, 1990. pp. 326-327, 337, 438, 571. Print.

[5] Peters, Margot. *The House of Barrymore*. New York: Knopf, 1990. p. 344. Print.

Rasputin, Demon with Women
aka **Rasputin, Dämon der Frauen**; **Rasputin**
Gottschalk Tonfilm; b/w; 82 min; Germany

   D: Adolf Trotz *S:* Ossip Dymow, Adolf Lantz, Conrad Linz *P:* Ludwig Gottschalk *C:* Curt Courant *M:* Wladimir Metzl, Fritz Wenneis

   Cast: Conrad Veidt, Paul Otto, Hermine Sterler, Kenneth Rive, Alexandra Sorina, Karl Ludwig Diehl, Ida Perry, Charlotte Ander, Elza Temary, Brigitte Horney, Bernhard Goetzke, Franziska Kinz, Marian Chevalier, Heinrich Heilinger, Edith Meinhard

   Grigori Rasputin (Veidt) is a simple priest with a taste for wine and women. He also possesses an uncanny ability to heal the sick and infirm. When called upon to cure Czar Nicholas' (Otto) ailing son, he gains access to a lavish lifestyle suited to his extravagant tastes. But in time he runs afoul of the royal family, and a plot is hatched to dispose of him.

   The true story of Grigori Rasputin (1869-1916) has inspired numerous melodramas, none of which has really come to grips with his complex persona or the circumstances surrounding his ascent to power and subsequent demise. Many believe that he ruled the Russian empire from behind the scenes, manipulating Nicholas II and his wife Alexandra into doing as he wished. He's viewed by most as both a healer and/or a charlatan, whose desire for power led him to a grisly demise.

   His story was told as early as 1917, a scant year after his murder, in the lost silent film *Rasputin, The Black Monk*, starring Montagu Love. Threats of legal action squelched the possibility of a frank and honest presentation of his life (an issue that persisted as late as 1965, when Hammer's lurid *Rasputin: The Mad Monk* cast Christopher Lee in the role).

   1932 would see the next two cracks at the story. And while Metro-Goldwyn-Mayer's lavish *Rasputin and the Empress* remains the most revered version—thanks in no small part to the casting of John, Lionel, and Ethel Barrymore in the same film for the first time—the far more obscure German production, *Rasputin, Demon with Women*, is certainly interesting enough in its own right.

   Having already played the crazed Ivan the Terrible in Paul Leni's *Waxworks* (1924), Conrad Veidt was an ideal choice for the part of Rasputin, and to no one's surprise he delivers a memorable performance. He presents his character as a free spirit, sensually indulgent but also with a strong religious sensibility. It's a strikingly sympathetic portrayal of a traditionally vilified figure.

   It's also a take on the role consistent with the vision of director Adolf Trotz, who takes the Russian royal family to task for using and abusing Rasputin. The finale in particular drives this point home as the priest unknowingly devours poisoned chocolate and wine. The viewer feels no sense of triumph, but rather one of distaste for the cowardly and venal conspirators. For Rasputin one feels sympathy as his murderers hasten his demise by riddling his prone body with bullets.

   Trotz creates both moodily effective interiors and magnificent snow-bound exteriors. He also employs editing techniques unusual in a talkie as early as this. This was one of his final works—his filmography comes to an end in 1936. With its moody cinematography and elaborate art direction, it indisputably resembles a Gothic horror tale, though its emphasis on melodrama keeps it from lurching completely into horror terrain. TH

The real-life Rasputin provided the impetus for a number of horror films, including *Rasputin, Demon with Women*.

The River House Ghost
Warner/First National; b/w; 52 min; Great Britain

   D: Frank Richardson *S:* Scott Darling *P:* Irving Asher *C:* Basil Emmott

   Cast: Florence Desmond, Hal Walters, Joan Marion, Mike Johnson, Shayle Gardner, Earle Stanley, Helen Ferrers

   Many believe the River House mansion to be haunted, but Flo (Desmond) doesn't believe it. She sets out to discover what's going on and uncovers a syndicate plot to scare off the property's prospective buyers.

   The River House Ghost is yet another variation on the *fake* haunted house theme. Writer Scott Darling and director Frank Richardson don't bring much creativity to the proceedings, which are dominated by picturesque comedienne Florence Desmond. Born in London, Desmond found early success as a music hall performer and continued to impress audiences with lively impersonations throughout her career. Film stardom proved more elusive, and with vehicles like *The River House Ghost* it's easy to see why. She remained active in films, off and on, until 1969 and died in 1993 at the age of 87.

   Darling later lengthened his name to W. Scott Darling and contributed to some fine horror and suspense items produced by Universal Pictures, including *The Ghost of Frankenstein* and *Sherlock Holmes and the Secret Weapon* (1942). He also penned the Mr. Wong films (starring Boris Karloff) for Monogram Pictures and had a hand in some of the Roland Winters-starring entries in the Charlie Chan series. TH

Satanas
aka **Satan**
Nepomuceno; b/w; length unknown; Philippines
   D: Jose Nepomuceno
   Cast: Alma Bella, Rosa Del Rosario, Carlos Padilla, Sr., Billy Surot Viscara

As far back as 1905 foreigners shot films in the Philippines. Samuel Ilagas directed the first true Filipino film, *Country Maiden*, in 1919. Still, it wasn't until the early 1930s that the country's film industry really took off. *Satanas* appears to have been the very first horror film to originate from the Philippines. Two others quickly followed, one in the same year, the other in 1933, a result of the impact of Universal's *Dracula* and *Frankenstein* (both 1931) on overseas markets.

Long considered lost, little is known about *Satanas* apart from it containing the acting debut of Rosa Del Rosario. Some sources list it as having been shot in color, though this seems unlikely; it's also said that it was shot in Tagalog, English, and Spanish, which is even more unlikely, as *Ang Aswang* (1933) appears to have been the Philippines' first sound picture, and it was shot after this.

Del Rosario returned for the second Filipino horror film, *Tiyanak* (1932). She was only nine years old when she was cast in *Satanas* as the daughter of the Alma Bella and Carlos Padilla characters. Born to an American father and Filipina mother, Del Rosario—real name: Rose del Rosario Stagner—was the leading actress of the Filipino film industry from the 1930s into the 1950s. She also had parts in a couple of U.S.-made movies, including *Anna and the King of Siam* (1946). She died in 2005 of a heart attack at the age of 88. CW

Secrets of the French Police
aka **Mysteries of the French Secret Police**
RKO; b/w; 59 min; U.S.
   D: Edward Sutherland *S:* Samuel Ornitz, Robert Tasker *P:* David O. Selznick *M:* Max Steiner
   Cast: Frank Morgan, Gregory Ratoff, Gwili Andre, Arnold Korff, John Warburton, Rochelle Hudson

Moloff (Ratoff), a half Russian/half Chinese general who also operates as a spy and is being investigated by a French police detective (Morgan), has struck upon a brilliant way to amass a great fortune—specifically, the estate of Russian Tzar Nicholas II. In a small French pub, he has met a young woman named Eugenie (Andre), a flower girl of Russian descent, whom he believes he can pass off as Nicholas' youngest daughter Princess Anastasia, long believed to have survived the massacre of her family on July 17, 1918. The one person Moloff needs to convince more than any other is Anastasia's uncle (Nicholas' brother), Grand Duke Maxim (Korff). However, after inviting Maxim to his Gothic chateau, Moloff finds the man unwilling to believe that Eugenie is anything other than a young girl of Russian heritage who bears no relation whatsoever to himself or any other royalty. In response, Moloff has Maxim killed, as he has already done to a couple of other people who might have exposed his plan.

A flower girl (Gwili Andre) is led to believe she is the last-living descendent of the Romanov dynasty in *Secrets of the French Police*.

A little-seen film, *Secrets of the French Police* is a curious mixture of Yellow Peril action and outright horror. A year before *The Mystery of the Wax Museum* (1933) made it fashionable (and possibly added as a result of a leak at Warner Bros.), Moloff tortures, experiments on and murders people before encasing their corpses in wax to serve as interior decoration for his home (the chateau was fashioned from sets left over from *The Most Dangerous Game*, 1932, as were many of the costumes). In a manner reminiscent of *Svengali* (1931), Moloff holds Eugenie under his spell via hypnosis. When things finally fall apart and it becomes clear that his plan will not succeed, Moloff decides to add Eugenie to his home's décor.

At less than an hour, this film (which begins in the sinister terrain of a graveyard) borrows liberally from many major films of the period, including MGM's *Rasputin and the Empress*, which was released some nine months prior. Morgan adds a touch of class to the proceedings as the police detective investigates the murder of a friend and colleague, and Moloff is a suitably malicious take on *The Most Dangerous Game's* literary villain Count Zaroff.

Secrets further courted success by incorporating elements of an event making headlines at the time. That event, which had occurred a decade earlier but had become increasingly well known over the intervening years, involved a young woman by the name of Anna Anderson. Anderson, who had been committed to an insane asylum in the early 1920s, claimed to be none other than Princess Anastasia. In a time before DNA, and with no known site to mark the Tsar's family grave, there was little chance of either refuting or corroborating Anderson's story. Over the next four decades she alternated homes between Europe and the United States, attended to by devotees who believed her dubious claims. (An earlier film from 1928, *Anastasia: The Tsar's False Daughter*, also dealt with this case.)

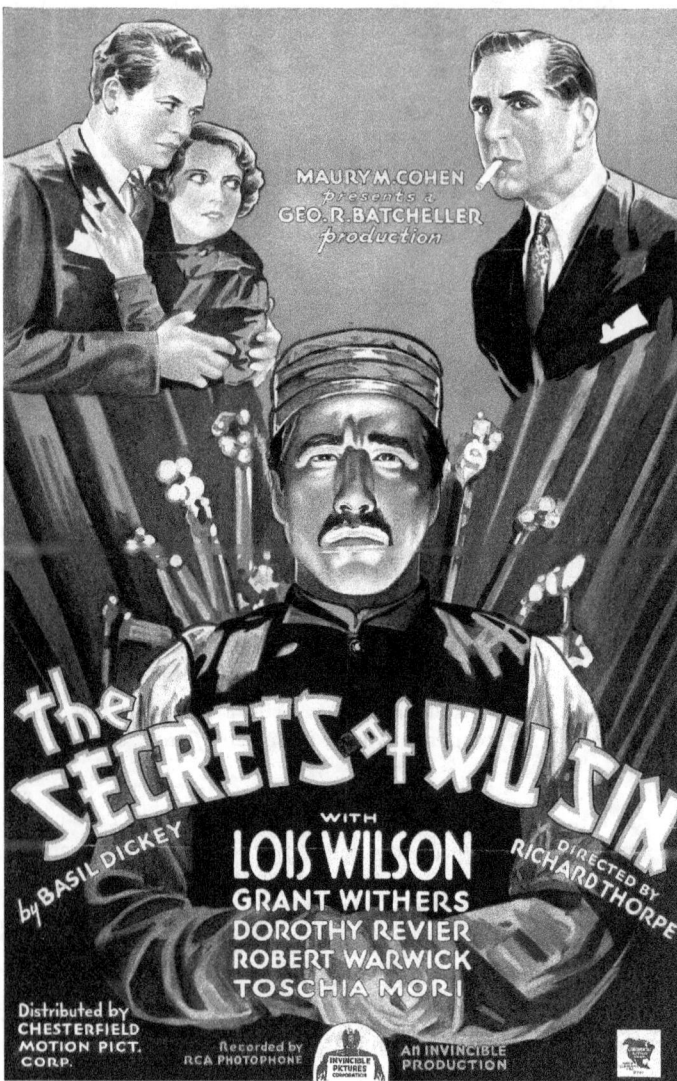

On an interesting historical note, the gravesite for the Tsar's family was finally located in 1991, and in March of 2009 it was conclusively established that young Anastasia had indeed suffered the same fate as her parents and siblings—she was indisputably among the family and servants who were taken by Bolsheviks to a cellar, lined up, shot and stabbed until dead. The faces of the victims were then crushed to make identification difficult, and the bodies were buried in a forest in Ekaterinburg, Russia to await the day, almost a century later, when they would find real peace. CW

The Secrets of Wu Sin
aka **Secrets of Wu Sin**
Invincible; b/w; 65 min; U.S.
　D: Richard Thorpe *S:* Betty Burbridge, Basil Dickey, William J. McGrath *P:* George R. Batcheller *C:* M.A. Anderson
　Cast: Lois Wilson, Grant Withers, Dorothy Revier, Robert Warwick, Tetsu Komai, Toshia Mori, Richard Loo, Luke Chan, James Wang, Eddie Boland

After he prevents writer Nona Gould (Wilson) from killing herself, editor James Manning (Withers) gives her a job at his newspaper. She takes it upon herself to investigate illegal Chinese immigration in San Francisco's Chinatown, despite the fact that the story is assigned to Eddie Morgan (Boland). What she uncovers is a plot by wealthy Roger King (Warwick) to smuggle cheap labor into the country with the help of Tong (Chinese gang) leader Wu Sin (Komai). Wu Sin orders Manning—who is engaged to King's daughter Margaret (Revier)—murdered, but the attempt backfires. Wu Sin commits suicide, and King and his daughter skip town aboard the same ship they had used to transport the illegals.

One of many examples of the Yellow Peril subgenre, *The Secrets of Wu Sin* offers yet another variation on Sax Rohmer's venerable literary creation, the insidious Dr. Fu Manchu, though the film does present a number of sympathetic portrayals of Asians, a rare thing during that period. (Compare it, for instance, to Cosmopolitan and MGM's *The Mask of Fu Manchu*, made the same year.) Too bad that various romantic subplots take precedence over the action.

Director Richard Thorpe went on to provide a greater sense of balance between romance, mystery and horror with such films as *Secret of the Chateau* (1934) and *Night Must Fall* (1937) before going on to direct some of cinema's arguable classics, including *Vengeance Valley* (1951), *Ivanhoe* (1952) and the Elvis Presley movies *Jailhouse Rock* (1957) and *Fun in Acapulco* (1963).

Actress Lois Wilson (1894-1988) began her career in 1915 playing a young character named Beatrix in a series of comedy shorts. Hers was a prolific career that lasted until 1955, when she retired from film and television after a brief stint on the daytime CBS soap opera *Guiding Light*. CW

Shin Yotsuya kaidan
Shochiku; b/w; length unknown; Japan
　D: Houtei Nomura
　Cast: Emiko Yagumo, Joji Oka, Yukiko Tsukuba, Kashichi Shimada

The title of this 1932 adaptation of the famous 1825 kabuki play translates as *New Version of the Ghost Story of Yotsuya*, and it offers a twist on the oft-filmed tale. Whereas the play deals with a Samurai so obsessed with a landowner's beautiful daughter that he forsakes his wife, here that wife, the beautiful Minekichi (Yagumo), is far more central to the story. Minekichi is a Geisha who falls in love with a fellow actor (Oka), only to be betrayed by him. She is then killed in a mysterious fall down some stairs, during which her face is horribly disfigured. She goes on to rise from the grave, her face a twisted mask of horror, and take revenge on the man who caused her death.

Actor Joji Oka also wrote scripts under the name Shozo Nakamizo (*Tetsu no tsume*, 1951). CW

Sinister Hands
Willis Kent; b/w; 65 min; U.S.
　D: Armand Schaefer *S:* Oliver Drake *P:* Willis Kent *C:* William Nobles
　Cast: Mischa Auer, Jack Mulhall, Phyllis Barrington, Crauford Kent, Louis Natheaux, Gertrude Messinger, Lloyd Ingraham, James P. Burtis, Phillips Smalley, Helen Foster, Lillian West, Fletcher Norton, Bess Flowers, Russ Coller

Wealthy entrepreneur Richard Lang (Smalley) has alienated his friends and family by trying to control their lives. His wife (West), who may be having an affair, is funneling a great deal of money to a fortune teller/medium named Swami Yomurda

(Auer). The Langs' daughter Betty (Messenger) is cavorting with a gangster (Natheaux). Richard's secretary (Flowers) has been stealing from him, and his good friend (Ingraham) suspects him of having an affair with *his* wife (Barrington). All of them, along with a few others who bear not-so-secret grudges against the man, come to his not-so-old-or-dark house for a somewhat improbable party ... complete with a séance presided over by Swami Yomurda. The lights go out, and someone who appears to be left-handed stabs Lang with a dagger. Detective Captain Devlin (Mulhall) and his bumbling assistant Jimmy Burtis (Watkins) jump on the case, but not soon enough to prevent a second murder—that of Richard's butler (Norton), a former criminal with a penchant for spying, who had been on the verge of revealing the murderer's identity.

As a boring murder mystery with typical 1930s horror trappings, *Sinister Hands* is exactly what one expects of a vintage Poverty Row chiller. Willis Kent, who was better known for formula oaters, produced, though he did occasionally, with varying degrees of success, veer into other genres.

While no one in the cast really stands out, Mischa Auer (*The Intruder*, 1933) as the ominous swami gets a dry run here for many a later performance. Two other cast members directed films during the silent era: Lloyd Ingraham (*At the Sign of the Jack O'Lantern,* 1922) and Phillips Smalley (*Oh! You Mummy*, 1914).

Sinister Hands' director, Armand Schaefer, was at his best when creating action set pieces (which, unfortunately, is not what he's doing here). He is best known for having directed two John Wayne serials, *The Hurricane Express* (1932) and *The Three Musketeers* (1933). CW

Six Hours to Live
aka 6 Hours to Live
Fox; b/w; 72 min; U.S.

D: William Dieterle S: Bradley King C: John F. Seitz

Cast: Warner Baxter, Miriam Jordan, John Boles, George F. Marion, Halliwell Hobbes, Irene Ware, Beryl Mercer, Edward McWade, John Davidson, Edwin Maxwell, Dewey Robinson, Torben Meyer

Paul Onslow (Baxter) believes that a new trade agreement is motivated solely by corporate greed and that it will have a negative effect on the small European nation in which he lives. When he's found strangled to death, scientist Otto Bauer (Marion) uses an invention with which he's revived dead animals to bring Paul back to life. The catch? Paul's miraculous revival will only last for six hours. He has that short period of time to track down the person who murdered him.

An early talkie sci-fi/horror film, *Six Hours to Live* foreshadows a host of similar films from Warner and Columbia—most of them starring Boris Karloff—made in the latter part of that same decade and the first part of the next. Those films generally concern the "scientific" revival of an executed man and the avenging of his death. Titles include *The Walking Dead* (1936) and *The Man They Could Not Hang* (1939), among others.

Six Hours gave German director William Dieterle a chance to hone skills that would come in handy later in his career, when he oversaw the production of such Hollywood classics as *The Story of Louis Pasteur* (1936), *The Life of Emile Zola* (1937), *The Hunchback of Notre Dame* (1939), *The Devil and Daniel Webster* (1941) and *Salome* (1953). CW

Strangers of the Evening
aka The Hidden Corpse
Quadruple; b/w; 70 (66) min; U.S.

D: H. Bruce Humberstone S: Stuart Anthony, Warren Duff P: Samuel Bischoff C: Arthur Edeson M: Val Burton

Cast: Zasu Pitts, Lucien Littlefield, Eugene Pallette, Tully Marshall, Miriam Seegar, Theodore von Eltz, Warner Richmond, Harold Waldridge, Mahlon Hamilton, Alan Roscoe, William Scott, Charles Williams, James P. Burtis, Francis Sayles

When bodies disappear from the city morgue, Detective Brubacher (Pallette) is called in to investigate. The plot thickens when a man (Littlefield) suffering from amnesia shows up to report a murder he's not sure he didn't commit himself.

Strangers of the Evening blends attempted humor, suspense and a dash of the morbid to create a truly bewildering witch's brew. The plot, lifted none-too-cleanly from a book by Tiffany Thayer (author of the novel that became the basis for another twisted production, RKO's *Thirteen Women*, in 1932), is hopelessly convoluted. Production values are poor, and none of the actors manages to rise above the sea of mediocrity created by H. Bruce Humberstone's efficient but unimaginative direction. Worse still is the plentiful lame humor; it's hard to believe that the assorted wisecracks and sight gags elicited much of a chuckle even in their day, and they have not aged well. On the plus side, there is at least some impressively creepy lighting courtesy of Arthur Edeson (*Frankenstein*, 1931).

Director Humberstone went on to make some of the best Charlie Chan mysteries for Fox (*Charlie Chan at the Opera*, 1936, for one), so it seems likely that inadequate resources and the aforementioned lousy screenplay hindered him here. *Stranger*'s cast includes Zasu Pitts, whose screen career stretched from 1917 until 1963; her last credit was a small role in 1963's all-star mega-comedy *It's a Mad, Mad, Mad, Mad World*. Co-star Lucien Littlefield had earlier appeared in *Seven Keys to Baldpate* (1929), while rotund character actor Eugene Pallette later achieved cinematic immortality as Friar Tuck in Michael Curtiz and William Keighley's *The Adventures of Robin Hood* (1938). TH

Tangled Destinies
Mayfair; b/w; 56 min; U.S.

D: Frank Strayer *S:* Edmund T. Lowe *P:* Ralph M. Like *C:* Jules Cronjager *M:* Lee Zahler

Cast: Gene Morgan, Doris Hill, Glenn Tryon, Sidney Bracey, Vera Reynolds, Ethel Wales, Monaei Lindley, Syd Saylor, Lloyd Whitlock, James B. Leong, William P. Burt, Henry Hall, William Humphrey

An airplane is forced to land to evade an approaching storm. The landing area is desolate, and the passengers and crew take refuge in a spooky, deserted manor. While there, several of them are murdered before the mystery of who is doing so is solved.

This hopelessly creaky "old dark house" murder mystery brings nothing new to the table. The bland cast performs as if in an amateur summer stock production, and director Frank Strayer (*The Ghost Walks*, 1934) brings little of the stylistic flair that distinguishes some of his other B-horror work.

Screenwriter Edmund T. Lowe also worked on Strayer's *The Vampire Bat* (1933) and in later years contributed to the Universal monster rallies *House of Frankenstein* (1944) and *House of Dracula* (1945). German-born cinematographer Jules Cronjager also worked with the director on *The Monster Walks* (1932), though *Tangled Destinies*' myriad blackouts make it seem as if most of the film unfolds in total darkness.

The disparate—and desperate—collection of characters includes the obligatory shady Asian, whose presence provides the butt of some offensively crass dialogue ("Where's that slant-eyed chink?"). Even at a running time of less than an hour, *Tangled Destinies* overstays its welcome. TH

Is Dr. Mabuse (Rudolf Klein-Rogge) man or spirit? From Fritz Lang's *The Testament of Dr. Mabuse.*

The Testament of Dr. Mabuse
aka **Das Testament des Dr. Mabuse**; **Dr. Mabuse's Testament**; **The Crimes of Dr. Mabuse**
Nero; b/w; 120 min; Germany

D/Co-S: Fritz Lang *Co-S:* Thea von Harbou *P:* Seymour Nebenzal *C:* Fritz Arno Wagner, Karl Vash *M:* Hans Erdmann *FX:* Ernst Kutzmann

Cast: Rudolf Klein-Rogge, Otto Wernicke, Oscar Beregi, Sr., Gustav Diessl, Wera Liessem, Karl Meixner, Theodor Loos, Rudolf Schundler, Oskar Hocker, Theo Lingen, Hadrian Maria Netto, Camilla Spira, Georg John, Paul Bernd, Henry Pless, Adolf E. Licho, Klaus Pohl, Ludwig Stossel

Infamous villain Dr. Mabuse (Klein-Rogge) is confined to an insane asylum where, after years of unresponsiveness, he suddenly begins to write. At first his scrawlings seem incoherent, but as asylum head Professor Baum (Beregi, Sr.) examines them, he comes to realize that the notes are Mabuse's "testament," a guidebook to crime and anarchy. In the process, Baum is drawn in by Mabuse's powerful will, which drives him to do Mabuse's bidding even after the criminal mastermind dies. Inspector Lohmann (Wenicke) is called in to investigate the ensuing crime wave.

While Fritz Lang was one of the greatest filmmakers in the history of cinema, his own accounts of how his films came into being—along with his versions of most things—are best taken with a grain of salt. He repeatedly told interviewers that he was reluctantly forced to direct this sequel to his silent epic *Dr. Mabuse, The Gambler* (1922), yielding only when he realized that he could use the archetypal evildoer as a veiled device for attacking the then-rising Nazi party. According to scholar David Kalat, however, the truth of the matter went more like this: while preparing his first sound picture *M* (1931), Lang corresponded with Norbert Jacques, the creator of Mabuse. It was Lang who asked Jacques to come up with a new spin on the character so that he could be revisited in a sound film. But the scenario Jacques developed into a novel called *Mabuse's Colony* didn't suit Lang, who felt that overall it lacked the urgency and suspense of the original.

Picking what little he liked about Jacques' treatment and discarding the rest, Lang (along with wife/collaborator Thea von Harbou) wrote the screenplay for what became *The Testament of Dr. Mabuse*. The resulting film ran afoul of German censors—it wasn't released there until 1961—though Lang's account of his meeting with Ministry of Propaganda head Dr. Josef Goebbels was, like so many of the director's stories, enhanced for dramatic effect. Still, *Testament* remained Lang's last German film until 1959, when producer Artur Brauner lured him back to his homeland for a color remake of his script "The Indian Epic," a pulp adventure in two parts (*The Tiger of Eschnapur*; *The Indian Tomb*), which had been filmed against his wishes by Joe May in 1921.

While *Dr. Mabuse, The Gambler* had covered so much ground that it was split into two parts, *The Testament of Dr. Mabuse* condenses its action into a comparatively short two hours. The pace is tight, though the film was still deemed too long by American distributors and cut down to 75 minutes for a dubbed, English-language edition (*The Crimes of Dr. Mabuse*). Lang was furious about the cuts and the damage they inflicted

Dr. Mabuse drives his victims to commit crimes, including murder, in *The Testament of Dr. Mabuse*, with Rudolf Klein-Rogge and Oscar Beregi, Sr.

on the film's reputation. Not until the complete German-language edition resurfaced in the 1970s did the film regain stature as one of Lang's most accomplished works.

Testament is noticeably more macabre than its predecessor, which feels like more of a straightforward crime serial in comparison. The possession angle is literally depicted by Lang, who later came to believe that his approach was too heavy handed. Be that as it may, little doubt remains that Mabuse's ghostly image (his post-autopsy skull dissected, revealing the criminal brain within) is among the most striking in Lang's filmography.

The emphasis here is less on the crimes themselves than it was in the first *Mabuse*, thus allowing the character of Inspector Lohmann to come to the foreground. Interestingly, Lohmann is a holdover from Lang's *M*, in which he pursued child murderer Hans Beckert (wonderfully played by Peter Lorre). Rotund Otto Wernicke plays the character in both films, linking *Testament* to *M*, even though the films are not narratively connected.

Working with cinematographer Fritz Arno Wagner (*Nosferatu—A Symphony of Terror*, 1922), Lang creates some notably vivid imagery. From the opening sequence in which disgraced Detective Hoffmesiter (Meixner) spies on Mabuse's gang to the final, chilling conclusion, the visuals hold a tremendous grip on the viewer. Even the obligatory romantic subplot involving reluctant gangster Thomas Kent (Diessl) and naïve Lilli (Liessem) doesn't dilute the film's tension. And, as he had in *M*, the director makes excellent use of sound, constructing set pieces that simply couldn't have been done in the silent idiom. The result is that *Testament* is in many respects the most overtly spooky film Lang ever made.

Following the German censorship debacle over the film, Lang retreated to France and made *Lilliom* (1934) before heading to the United States. His first U.S. production, *Fury* (1936), was marked by heated clashes with producers, an experience that came to typify his tenure in Hollywood, where he simply couldn't command the same respect and authority he'd attained in Germany.

Lang revisited the character of Dr. Mabuse for his final film *The Thousand Eyes of Dr. Mabuse* (1960), which kicked off a series of Mabuse films from various directors.

The director's edit of *Testament* received its world premiere in Budapest in 1933. While the film has appeared in various versions over the years, it can easily be acquired today at more or less its original running time. The little that remains missing subtracts nothing from the film's basic structure or continuity. TH

Thark
Wilcox/British and Dominions; b/w; 79 min; Great Britain
 D: Tom Walls S: Ben Travers P: Herbert Wilcox C: Freddie Young
 Cast: Tom Walls, Ralph Lynn, Robertson Hare, Mary Brough, Claude Hulbert, Joan Brierley, Gordon James, Evalyn Bostock, Beryl de Querton, Marjorie Corbett, Miles Malleson

Based on a 1927 stage play by Ben Travers (who also wrote the script for this film adaptation), *Thark* is yet another comedy done up in horror trappings. Set in a standard-issue old dark house called Thark Manor, it concerns the sale of that manor by real estate agent Sir Hector Benbow (Wells) to one Mrs. Todd (Brough). When Mrs. Todd suspects that the house is haunted, Benbow and some friends spend a night in the place to find out for themselves.

Tom Walls, who starred in about as many films as he directed (and, in this case, did both), directed *Thark*. A member of the Aldwych Theater group, he was often involved with the comedic stage plays of Ben Travers, usually starring Ralph Lynn and Robertson Hare. In 1929 the group made the leap to the big screen, though many of their films appear to have been mere theatrical productions put to film.

Two of *Thark*'s characters are named Hook and Death, leading one to suspect that the film's humor was neither highbrow nor witty. CW

Thirteen Women
RKO; b/w; 73 (60) min; U.S.
 D: George Archainbaud S: Bartlett Cormack, Samuel Ornitz P: David O. Selznick C: Leo Tover M: Max Steiner
 Cast: Irene Dunne, Myrna Loy, Ricardo Cortez, Jill Esmond, Mary Duncan, Kay Johnson, Florence Eldridge, C. Henry Gordon, Peg Entwistle, Harriet Hagman, Wally Albright

A remarkable little film in that it foreshadows the slasher subgenre of the early 1980s, and in particular *The House on Sorority Row* (1983), *Thirteen Women* deals with the strange deaths of a group of former sorority sisters, most of whom have sent off to have their horoscopes read by Swami Yogadachi (Gordon). Little do they know that the swami is being manipulated and sometimes hypnotically controlled by a mysterious Eurasian named Ursula (Loy) with an axe to grind. Ursula's final target is Laura (Dunne), whom Ursula hopes to destroy through her young son Bobby (Albright). It turns out that Ursula was raped by a group of Caucasian sailors when she was 12 years old and, to avoid future attacks, later hoped to integrate into society by passing as white. However, once in school, she was found out and tormented by a group of 12 malicious sorority sisters. They eventually forced her departure from academia and shattered her

Myrna Loy is the half-caste killer avenging her ill treatment by sorority sisters in the heavily censored *Thirteen Women*.

dreams of integration. Now she's picking them off one-by-one in creative ways that play on the fears of each. In a strange bit of directorial creativity, each death is marked by the image of a bright star shooting toward the camera. Tover's cinematography is top-notch and foreshadows similar work from Nicholas Musuraca for Val Lewton in the 1940s. All in all, it is a surprisingly daring little horror programmer.

While it's difficult to decipher whether the film was ahead of its time in its presentation of a Eurasian as the angry victim of a hate crime or whether it was simply presenting a racist tract during a period when tensions between the United States and Asia were on the increase, it's easy to see why *Thirteen Women* received a scant release in 1932 and an only marginally larger one the following year. It wasn't until the careers of Dunne and Loy took off (Loy also starred as Fu Manchu's nymphomaniac daughter in *The Mask of Fu Manchu* the same year, before finding success two years later in *The Thin Man*) that it received a wide release, though it was severely cut by censors, losing almost 15 minutes of footage and dropping a couple of characters.

The controversial novel by Tiffany Thayers in 1931 became the basis of the film. (Thayers also founded the Fortean Society, devoted to the ideas of iconoclastic writer Charles Fort.) A lesbian subplot involving Hazel Cousins (Entwistle) was changed to mariticide in the film version. Ricardo Cortez (pseudonym of Jewish actor Jacob Krantz), hot off the heels of *The Maltese Falcon* (1931), took the role of Sergeant Clive. Though he's far from the film's main player, he nevertheless received top billing.

Perhaps more interesting—and (in)famous—than the film itself is the story of 24-year-old Peg Entwistle, whose only film role was that of Hazel Cousins in *Thirteen Women*. On the night of September 18, 1932, just two days after the film's premiere, a drunken Entwistle, depressed that she wasn't immediately being offered more and bigger roles, climbed a workman's ladder to the top of the letter H in the famous HOLLYWOODLAND sign (which in 1949 became the famous HOLLYWOOD sign) atop Mount Lee in Griffith Park, and leapt to her death. At the foot of the sign was her purse, in which she had left a suicide note that read, "I am afraid I am a coward. I am sorry for everything. If I had done this a long time ago, it would have saved a lot of pain. P.E." After plunging 50 feet, she died from complications related to a shattered pelvis, though her body wasn't found for some three days afterwards. The body battered beyond recognition, authorities ran ads in several newspapers in the hopes that someone would step forward to identify her. Finally, recognizing her initials and knowing that his own niece had disappeared on the evening the woman was believed to have jumped from the sign, Entwistle's uncle provided the necessary information to identify her. Thus did Lillian Millicent "Peg" Entwistle enter the Hollywood lexicon forever.

Although perhaps apocryphal, it has been reported that the day after Entwistle's death, a letter arrived at her home offering her the role of a suicidal woman in an upcoming stage play. Interestingly—and this is *not* apocryphal—Peg was also for a short time the stepmother of future actor Brian Keith. CW

The Thirteenth Guest
aka **Lady Beware**
Monogram; b/w; 69 min; U.S.
  D: Albert Ray *S:* Frances Hyland, Arthur Hoerl *P:* M.H. Hoffman *C:* Tom Galligan, Harry Neumann
  Cast: Ginger Rogers, Lyle Talbot, J. Farrell MacDonald, Paul Hurst, Erville Alderson, Ethel Wales, James Eagles, Crauford Kent, Eddie Phillips, Frances Rich, Phillips Smalley

Marie Morgan (Rogers) fears for her life after a killer targets members of her family; intrepid criminologist Phil Winston (Talbot) comes to her rescue.

In essence an "old dark house" murder mystery, *The Thirteenth Guest* rattles along at an acceptable pace under the uninspired direction of Albert Ray (*The Intruder*, 1931), who includes plenty of clichés such as secret panels, a cackling villain and hidden treasure. The film starts off with a bang and on the surface seems to anticipate *Psycho* (1960) by almost 30 years, but an awful plot contrivance pops out of nowhere and takes the wind out of those particular sails.

Guest remains chiefly notable as one of Ginger Rogers' earliest screen vehicles. The Missouri-born singer/dancer/actress entered movies in 1930 and, after toiling for a time in B-pictures such as this, established herself as a major Hollywood star. She's best remembered today for her numerous musical pairings with Fred Astaire, so her presence in an obscure genre title such as this will no doubt come as an interesting surprise for many.

Despite a flawed screenplay, the cast performs capably, and the film obviously isn't without nostalgic appeal. In addition to Rogers as the imperiled heroine, the cast includes Lyle Talbot as the sardonic criminologist who falls in love with her. Born in Pittsburgh, Pennsylvania, Talbot was one of the founding members (along with Boris Karloff, David Manners and many others) of the Screen Actors Guild. He appeared in numerous B-films of the 1930s and '40s (including horror-oriented fare like *Torture Ship*, 1939), worked in some of Edward D. Wood, Jr.'s most notorious pictures (*Glen or Glenda*, 1953, and *Plan 9 from Outer Space*, 1959) and later routed his career to popular TV shows of the '50s (*Ozzie and Harriet*), '60s (*The Beverly Hillbillies*), '70s (*Charlie's Angels*) and '80s (*Newhart*).

He and Rogers play well off each other here. Ray, Rogers and Talbot re-teamed the following year for *A Shriek in the Night* (1933). TH

Tiyanak
aka **Child Monster**; **Tianak**
Nepomuceno; b/w; length unknown; Philippines
  D: Jose Nepomuceno
  Cast: Rosa del Rosario

This is the second horror film shot in the Philippines. It starred a very young Rosa del Rosario, who returned for the remake in 1953.

In Philippine legend, when a baby dies without receiving its baptismal rites (or when a baby is born to a woman impregnated by a demon, or when a fetus is aborted), the infant's spirit goes to limbo and there becomes an evil spirit called a tiyanak. After returning to the earthly realm, these unfortunates take on impish form and feast on the flesh of the living. It was once believed that when people traveled in the woods or in the mountains, they should steer clear of wailing babies, for surely those babies were the tiyanaks in human form. Should anyone pick them up, they'd assume their true shape and devour all who beheld them. But while the legend also states that the only way to defeat a tiyanak is by turning its clothes inside out (?), this lost 1932 film substituted a crucifix for that purpose.

The next Filipino horror film, *Ang Aswang* (1933), was the country's first sound feature and dealt with a flesh-eating, witch-like creature. CW

Tombstone Canyon
K.B.S.; b/w; 62 min; U.S.
  D: Alan James *S:* Earle Snell, Claude Rister *P:* Burt Kelly, Samuel Bischoff, William Saal *C:* Ted McCord
  Cast: Ken Maynard, Cecilia Parker, Sheldon Lewis, Frank Brownlee, Jack Clifford, George Gerwing, Lafe McKee,

Tombstone Canyon is so-called because the Phantom Killer (Lewis) allegedly haunts it (his piercing cry portends death). Into this milieu rides Ken (Maynard), after receiving a letter claiming that information about his unknown parentage lies somewhere near the mysterious canyon, but as he approaches the area, he's attacked by a gang hoping to steal his horse. He fights back and wounds one of the men, later recognizing his attackers at a saloon in town. They're part of a gang headed up by Alf Sykes (Brownlee) and including Sykes' son Clem (Gerwing), but the men have an ironclad alibi as to their whereabouts when Ken was attacked, and the Sherriff (Peil, Sr.) refuses to arrest them. Meanwhile, a mysterious figure in a black cloak is killing off members of Sykes' gang one by one.

Given the popularity of horror films in the early 1930s, it was inevitable that horror elements would make their way into other genres. Thus did a short-lived subgenre of weird Westerns emerge, usually featuring masked phantoms and/or haunted ranches. Examples include *Haunted Gold* (1932) starring John Wayne and *Smoking Guns* (1933) starring Ken Maynard. *Tombstone Canyon* is a fairly typical entry, with the scarred phantom here turning out to be the hero's father (whose face was bashed in by Sykes and his cronies years before to prevent identification of his body after he'd been "killed").

Cecelia Parker (famed as Marian Hardy in the Andy Hardy films) provides the love interest, and Lafe McKee plays her father, Colonel Lee. And naturally, Maynard's horse Tarzan receives a credit. *Canyon* was made on an ultra-low budget, but with popular star Maynard on the payroll, it didn't matter. Maynard had been packing in fans of Westerns since the early 1920s; though hated by most of his co-stars, he was liked by audiences who knew nothing of his behind-the-scenes alcoholic tirades.

Director Alan James is better known as a writer; as a director he didn't achieve much. As *Tombstone* proves, he particularly stank at directing action sequences, whether they involved fisticuffs or horseback chases. Though he inexplicably worked almost exclusively in Westerns, he did direct the 1931 horror film *The Phantom* under the name Alvin Neitz (and proved to be no better at horror movies than he was at oaters).

In this particular instance, the writing is on a par with the direction. Claude Rister conceived the unoriginal story, while the dialogue, courtesy of Earle Snell, is frequently laughable, with enough unsubtle double-entendres to keep the most ardent anti-Western viewer in stitches. Snell remained a writer well into the 1950s, though he never escaped—or perhaps chose to remain in—the Western genre.

The film's production company K.B.S. (named from the initials of its three primary producers) was formed specifically to produce films for Maynard. World Wide distributed its output, with its audacious icon of an apparently topless woman holding

A portmanteau of horror stories done up in Expressionistic style, in *Uncanny Stories*

two large globes over her (presumably much smaller) breasts. On one globe was the word "World" and on the other the word "Wide." CW

Uncanny Stories
aka **Unheimliche Geschichten; Der Unheimliche; Fünf unheimliche Geschichten; Five Sinister Stories; Ghastly Tales; Tales of the Uncanny; The Living Dead; Suicide Club**
G.P.; b/w; 89 min; Germany

D/Co-S/Co-P: Richard Oswald *S:* Heinz Golderg, Eugen Szatmari *P:* Gabriel Pascal *C:* Heinrich Gartner *M:* Rolf Marbot, Bert Reisfeld

Cast: Paul Wegener, Harald Paulsen, Roma Bahn, Mary Parker, Gerhard Bienert, Paul Henckels, John Gottowt, Eugen Klopfer, Maria Koppenhofer, Erwin Kalser, Franz Stein, Gretel Berndt

Uncanny Stories is a three-episode anthology revolving around a mad scientist named Morder (Wegener). In the first section, Morder murders his wife when her pet cat disrupts one of his experiments; a journalist, Frank (Paulsen), overhears her screams and alerts the police. They interrogate Morder, who gives himself away and is sent to an insane asylum. In Part Two, Morder helps organize a rebellion of the inmates and takes control of the madhouse. Then, in the final episode, Morder uses the asylum as a cover for his suicide club, in which people with more daring than common sense play dangerous games of chance.

Austrian-born director Richard Oswald first directed a version of *Uncanny Stories* (known as *Unheimliche Geschichten* in its native Germany) in 1919. Starring Conrad Veidt and released in the United States as *Weird Tales*, it was a fairly straightforward exercise in the macabre, framed by a contrived vignette involving dummies in a waxworks museum. For the 1932 sound remake, Oswald dispenses with the wraparound story—though it does rear its head briefly before the final fade-out—and shifts the tone from the horrific to the darkly comedic. The result is vastly superior to the creaky original, though not without its own share of shortcomings.

Since the film can easily be viewed as a send-up of Expressionist horror cinema, the casting of Paul Wegener in the central role is a major coup. Who better than the man behind *The Golem: How He Came into the World* (1920) to be put up to Oswald's funhouse mirror? Wegener is his usual imposing self, and his exaggerated gestures and facial expressions are put to particularly good use in this context. But like so many anthologies—including the original version of this one—the film is ultimately uneven despite its central performance.

The opening segment, freely adapted from Edgar Allan Poe's *The Black Cat*, is by far the most impressive. Oswald makes terrific use of Expressionist imagery—lots of looming shadows and weird camera angles—to heighten the mood while subtly commenting on the artificiality of the Expressionist movement. The reveal of the wife's body in the wall is genuinely ghoulish, and there's a wonderful chase through a darkened waxworks.

Things hit a downturn during the sketch-like second segment, loosely based on Poe's *The System of Dr. Tarr and Professor Fether*. The episode is much too brief to be very effective, though it's more overtly comedic and helps push the film further into the realm of the absurd. More successful is the final segment, based on Robert Louis Stevenson's *The Suicide Club*, which details how Wegener has taken over the asylum and opened an elaborate society for daredevils. The Art Deco sets are put to good use, and Wegener presides over the tortures with wild-eyed enthusiasm.

Oswald never topped this, his finest film. He continued to direct pictures until 1951 and passed away in 1963. *Uncanny Stories* was re-released in the United States in 1940 as *The Living Dead*, in an edited version that sought to remove the more obvious comedic content. TH

The Wayne Murder Case
aka **A Strange Adventure; Wayne Murder Case**
Chadwick; b/w; 60 (62) min; U.S.

Co-D/Co-S: Hampton Del Ruth *Co-D:* Phil Whitman *Co-S:* Lee Chadwick *P:* I.E. Chadwick *C:* Leon Shamroy

Cast: Regis Toomey, June Clyde, Lucille La Verne, Jason Robards Sr., William V. Mong, Eddie Phillips, Dwight Frye, Nadine Dore, Alan Roscoe, Isabel Vecki, Harry Myers, Eddy Chandler, Fred Toones (Snowflake)

When family members gather for the signing of patriarch Silas Wayne's (Mong) will, he is mysteriously murdered before their eyes, despite the presence—requested by Silas—of two police officers (Chandler, Myers) and a doctor (Robards) in the room. Detective Sergeant Mitchell (Toomey) is duly called in to investigate. His job is hampered by newspaper reporter "Nosey" Toodles (Clyde), who threatens to write a story exposing the police as buffoons if she isn't allowed to hang around and put in her two cents. The sort-of romantic duo quickly decides upon a prime suspect, the old man's nephew Claude (Phillips), but his murder prompts them to rethink the matter. The fact that each of Silas' family members had reasons for wanting him (and Claude) dead doesn't make their investigation any easier.

The Wayne Murder Case is a standard, 1930s Z-grade mystery with horror asides. It hasn't an ounce of atmosphere, and it's bogged down by its lack of a music score. Nothing in the film delivers on the promise of the opening credits, which play out nicely over a painted backdrop of a sinister, shrouded phantom. There's a smattering of interesting touches, particularly a shot of the silhouette of the hung-by-a-noose Claude, as well as a superfluous subplot about a cursed diamond and a need-to-pay-the bills performance by red-herring Dwight Frye as another of Silas' creepy nephews.

The mystery's solution is obvious to everyone but the cast from almost the beginning, and the knife-wielding killer is a tad on the stupid side, pointlessly wandering the corridors of the crowded, not-so-dark old house in a hooded robe. He even takes a break at one point just to frighten servant Jeff (an African American character actor called Snowflake—get it?). Apparently, skulking about murdering people isn't stimulating enough.

Fred "Snowflake" Toones began his career at the tail end of the silent era and spent a large portion of it under contract to Republic Pictures, who shuffled him into comedic bit parts in many of the low-budget oaters of the day. He retired in 1951 and died in 1962 while still in his 50s. Among his more noteworthy appearances was a bit role in the Barbara Stanwyck and Fred MacMurray Christmas classic *Remember the Night* (1940).

The Wayne Murder Case was originally released as *A Strange Adventure* on November 20, 1932. It wasn't until it was re-released several years later by Monogram that it was retitled *The Wayne Murder Case*, after a line spoken by "Nosey" Toodles at the film's conclusion. It is under this second name that the film is most readily available today. CW

White Zombie
Halperin; b/w; 67 min; U.S.

D: Victor Halperin *S:* Garnett Weston *P:* Edward Halperin *C:* Arthur Martinelli *M:* Abe Meyer, Guy Bevier, Gaston Borch, Nathaniel Dett, Hen Herkan, H. Maurice Jacquet, Leo Kempinski, Hugo Risenfeld, Xavier Cugat *FX:* Howard A. Anderson

Cast: Bela Lugosi, Madge Bellamy, Robert Frazer, John Harron, Joseph Cawthorn, Brandon Hurst, George Burr MacAnnan, Clarence Muse, Frederick Peters, Annette Stone, John Printz, Dan Crimmins, Claude Morgan, John Fergusson, Velma Gresham

The mysterious Murder Legendre (Lugosi) turns Madeline (Bellamy) into a zombie at the behest of corrupt plantation owner Charles Beaumont (Frazer), who has fallen in love with her and wants to steal her away from her fiancé. But Beaumont has second thoughts when he sees the soulless being she becomes. And Legendre, it turns out, has plans of his own.

With the mammoth box-office success of *Dracula* (1931), Bela Lugosi became inextricably linked to horror. The independently-made *White Zombie* was a perfect follow-up. It's considered the first authentic zombie film—though its concept of zom-

bies as a product of Haitian folklore is quaint when compared to the Romeroesque flesh-eaters that dominate the genre today.

Based on a 1928 stage play called *Zombie*, the film was produced by Edward Halperin, who commissioned his brother Victor to direct. The Halperins rented studio space at Universal (thus enabling them to reuse sets from *Dracula*), and the film was rushed into existence in the space of a mere 11 days.

In the end, though, *White Zombie*'s low-budget and brisk shooting schedule contributed to a pretty remarkable (if accidentally so) achievement. The crudeness and wooden acting on display evoke a magical atmosphere more reminiscent of Carl Theodor Dreyer's *Vampyr* (1931) than the Universal horrors on which it was seeking to piggyback. And while initial reviews were decidedly mixed, the film has maintained a strong cult following over the intervening decades.

And, yes, deservedly so. There's a wonderful fairy tale ambience to much of the film, with some moody, magnificent images—zombies silently working in the sugar mill as processing machinery groans in the background, the living dead stalking slowly yet relentlessly across a bleak nighttime landscape and Legendre's hypnotic eyes reflected in a glass of wine are among the most notable. Cinematographer Arthur Martinelli layers on the shadows with joyful abandon, and the result is both eerie and oddly delicate, evoking a feel similar to a Brothers Grimm story. Abe Meyer's soundtrack is an equally invaluable component of the spooky atmosphere; indeed, the use of sound (and silence) is remarkably sophisticated for an early talkie.

The film, whether intentionally or not, reflects Depression Era distrust of the wealthy. Legendre is the ultimate evil businessman, robbing workers of their will for the sake of cheap labor. *White Zombie* also taps into 1930s America's xenophobia, depicting the plight of an innocent couple abroad, duped by an evil foreign menace with a sinister accent.

In this original lobby card, Bela Lugosi as Murder Legendre holds possessive power over Madge Bellamy, from *White Zombie*.

While Halperin and Martinelli would collaborate on future projects—including the horror films *Supernatural* (1933) and *Revolt of the Zombies* (1936)—they would never again approach the clumsy splendor of this particular film. Bela Lugosi harbored conflicted emotions over *White Zombie* for the remainder of his life; although proud of the film and his work in it, he regretted the low sum of money he accepted ($800 is popularly cited, but accounts vary) in light of the film's box-office success. But all else aside, Murder Legendre stands today as one of Lugosi's meatiest roles. Especially when compared to his overtly theatrical work in *Dracula*, the actor seems both confident and relaxed here; he doesn't exactly exude subtlety, of course, but much of the joy in watching him in films like this is seeing him go for broke. He has, frankly, some magnificent moments in *Zombie*, squeezing magic from clunky, frequently innuendo-laden dialogue. ("I have taken a fancy to *you*, Monsieur!" he says to Beaumont, and means it.)

The same praise cannot be laid upon the supporting cast. Madge Bellamy, demonstrating why she failed to make a successful transition from the silent era, is disastrous as Madeline. Her stiff line delivery and blank expressions make her appear zombie-like even before Legendre has taken control of her. Her fiancé is played by John Harron, another silent film veteran who, looking distractingly like an over-earnest Stan Laurel and stuck with the least rewarding role in horror iconography—the concerned love interest—fails to generate much heat or interest or anything else. Robert Frazer, later to appear in such poverty row horrors as *The Vampire Bat* (1933) and *Black Dragons* (1942), is way too ham-fisted as the anti-hero Beaumont. Joseph Cawthorn provides comic relief, but his constant requests for a match make one yearn for his entry into the ranks of the silent undead.

Fortunately, however, Lugosi is allowed to dominate the proceedings, and whenever he's the center of the action (or during the frequent stretches when Halperin allows the film to proceed without dialogue), *White Zombie* is a wonderful experience. Debates about socio-political content are all well and fine, but in the end it's a short, creepy little fairy tale, told in a simple and entertaining fashion. TH

Lugosi in *White Zombie*

1933

Ang Aswang
aka **The Witch**; **The Vampire**
Manila Talkatone; b/w; length unknown; Philippines
 D: George Musser
 Cast: Celia Burgos-Xerxes, Monang Carvajal, Patring Carvajal, Mary Walter

Existing records indicate that *Ang Aswang* was not only one of the Philippines' earliest horror films, it was also the country's first talking feature. It was shot in the Austronesian language Tagalog, which is spoken by about 22 million Filipinos; some of the film's characters, however, apparently spoke Spanish and English as well.

The plot concerned an aswang, a vampiric witch of Filipino legend. Belief in the aswang arose during the Spanish occupation of the islands between the early 1500s and late 1800s. The presence of the occupiers during those times forced rebels from the coasts inward to the mountainous regions. The Spaniards took to claiming that these runaways were in fact demonic beings who had wings, bloodshot eyes, mangy hair and that they changed shape at will to disguise themselves.

Unfortunately, only four titles from pre-World War II Philippines exist today (most of them were destroyed during Japanese occupation), but this is not one of them. CW

Before Dawn
aka **Death Watch**
RKO; b/w; 60 min; U.S.
 D: Irving Pichel *S:* Garrett Fort, Ralph Block, Marion Dix *P:* Shirley C. Burden *C:* Lucien Andriot *M:* Max Steiner
 Cast: Stuart Erwin, Dorothy Wilson, Warner Oland, Dudley Digges, Gertrude Hoffman, Oscar Apfel, Frank Reicher, Jane Darwell

On his deathbed, bad guy Joe Valerie (Reicher) confesses to Dr. Cornelius (Oland) that, years earlier, he stole a million dollars and stashed it in the creepy old mansion of one Mrs. Marble (Darwell). Mrs. Marble gets wind of the confession and starts searching for the loot, but after a terrifying visitation by the gangster's ghost, she falls down her stairs and dies. At the same time, undercover police officer Dwight Wilson (Erwin) arrests Patricia Merrick (Wilson), a clairvoyant he suspects is a charlatan. Patricia offers to prove her innocence by psychically aiding Wilson in an investigation. She then has a vision of Mrs. Marble's death, and the investigator takes her and her medium father (Digges) to the old house to clear up the matter. While the trio is there, Doctor Cornelius arrives, pretending to be interested in the case (though he's really in search of the hidden money himself). He winds up throwing Mrs. Marble's housekeeper Mattie (Hoffman) down a well in the cellar, but Patricia and Dwight figure out what he's up to. Dwight and Cornelius fight, and Cornelius falls to his death down the very same well.

Actor Irving Pichel, who directed *Before Dawn*, was no stranger to horror. Best known for his performance as Sandor in the 1936 classic *Dracula's Daughter*, he also starred in *Murder by the Clock* (1931) and co-directed (with Ernest B. Schoedsack) *The Most Dangerous Game* (1932). Pichel was gifted with solid directorial skills, and he brought a strong sense of atmosphere to

everything he touched. On *Before Dawn* he worked closely with cinematographer Lucien Andriot to create a wonderful sense of doom and gloom amid the shadows of Mrs. Marble's old dark house.

Also contributing to the film's high quality is a script written primarily by Garrett Fort, who had crafted the silent horror film *On Time* (1924) and co-written Tod Browning's genre-building *Dracula* (1931). Fort went on to write the aforementioned *Dracula's Daughter*, Tod Browning's horror swan song *The Devil-Doll* (1936) and Paramount's 1941 fright flick, *Among the Living*.

Before Dawn benefits from some very good performances, including that of Warner Oland, still in his pre-Charlie Chan days, as the villain. (His portrayal here is very much a sinister take on the character he would later make his own.) Rounding out the cast are the likewise first-rate Stuart Erwin (*Paramount on Parade*, 1930), Dorothy Wilson (*The Last Days of Pompeii*, 1935), Gertrude Hoffman (*The Ape*, 1940), Oscar Apfel (*Tomorrow at Seven*, 1933), Frank Reicher (*The Crooked Circle*, 1932) and Jane Darwell (*The Devil and Daniel Webster*, 1941). CW

Before Midnight
Columbia; b/w 63 minutes; U.S.
 D: Lambert Hillyer *S:* Ralph Quigley *C:* John Stumar
 Cast: Ralph Bellamy, June Collyer, Betty Blythe, Arthur Pierson, George Cooper, William Jeffrey, Joseph Crehan, Otto Yamaoka

Inspector Steve Trent (Bellamy) is faced with a murder in which the victim had predicted his own death.

Before Midnight was the first in a short series of Inspector Trent thrillers produced by Columbia Pictures. *The Crime of Helen Stanley*, *One is Guilty* and *Girl in Danger* followed, all produced and released in 1934. Of the four, only *Before Midnight* bears any connection to the horror genre; the others are straightforward B-mysteries.

The series gave Ralph Bellamy (1904-1991) a chance to occupy center stage, though his character was not well-drawn enough to allow him to truly shine. Not long after the series, Bellamy moved successfully to second-fiddle status. He found his niche as the nice guy who doesn't get the girl, losing out romantically to Cary Grant and other major stars in such comedic fare as *The Awful Truth* (1937) and *His Girl Friday* (1940), netting his only Oscar nomination (for Best Supporting Actor) in the former. (He did receive a Lifetime Achievement Academy Award in 1987.)

He also played key roles in such 1940s Universal classics as *The Wolf Man* (1941), *The Ghost of Frankenstein* and *The Great Impersonation* (both 1942). After retreating to stage and television for much of the 1950s and '60s, he made a triumphant return to the big screen in Roman Polanski's 1968 masterpiece, *Rosemary's Baby* (and inexplicably turned down the John Huston part in Polanski's *Chinatown,* 1974). His final foray into horror territory came with an appearance in the color reboot of *The Twilight Zone* in 1986. He turned in a fish-out-of-water performance, best forgotten, in the moderately successful *Disorderlies* (1987), sharing the screen with old-school rappers The Fat Boys. His final cinematic outing was in the Richard Gere/Julia Roberts romantic comedy *Pretty Woman* (1990). He died the following year.

Director Lambert Hillyer did much of his work in B-Westerns, but he also helmed two of Universal's more underrated 1930s horror classics—*Dracula's Daughter* and *The Invisible Ray* (both 1936). Hillyer's economy and skill help to make *Before Midnight* a breezy piece of unpretentious (if unoriginal) entertainment, as they later did with *One is Guilty*. TH

The Crying Woman
aka **La llorona**
Eco; b/w; 60 (73) min; Mexico

D: Ramón Peón *S:* Fernando de Fuentes, Carlos Noriega Hope, A. Guzman Aguilera

Cast: Ramón Pereda, Virginia Zurí, Carlos Orellana, Adriana Lamar, Esperanza del Real, Alberto Martí, Paco Martínez, María Luisa Zea, Alfredo del Diestro, Conchita Gentil Arcos, Antonio R. Frausto, Victoria Blanco, Manuel Dondé

While walking down a street, a man hears an unearthly wailing, suffers a heart attack and dies. Cut to a hospital operating room, where we meet Dr. Ricardo de Acuna (Pereda), who wants desperately to get home to his wife Ana María (Zurí) and his son in time to celebrate the latter's fourth birthday. Later, after the birthday party has ended, Ana Maria's brother, Don Fernando de Moncada (Martínez), takes Ricardo to the library to alert him that many of the family's male children have suffered a horrible fate just after turning four. Don Fernando produces an old book and reads Ricardo the story of Ana (Lamar) who, during the Elizabethan Age, was in love with Roderigo (Martí), the father of her four-year old son. When Roderigo rejected her for another woman, she stabbed her son and herself to death and has spent the centuries since as a spirit, wailing in agony over her loss. While Don Fernando tells the tale, a skulking figure bearing an ancient-looking ring (the same one worn by Ana in the story) stalks Ricardo's young boy. Ricardo dismisses Fernando's tale and departs, and shortly thereafter Fernando is murdered and his book stolen by the stalking figure. Ricardo finds his brother-in-law's body just as Ana María is terrorized and their son kidnapped by the mysterious figure, escaping into a secret passageway. Ricardo follows and rescues the child, but the villain gets away. When a second book is found, another story from the family's strange past is learned. This one involves a Native American woman named La Malinche (Zea) who, hundreds of years earlier, assisted Cortés in his conquest of Mexico; she also bore his male child but had the babe stolen from her by Conquistadors as she was locked away in prison. While incarcerated, she obtained a knife and killed herself. A fellow Indian woman stole her ring (again, the same one worn by the present-day killer) from her dead body as her spirit left her body and, as in the first story, commenced centuries of wandering the Earth, crying mournfully. Back in present-day 1930s Mexico, the hooded figure finally nabs the boy but, as he's about to stab him on a sacrificial Aztec altar, is shot by the police. The killer is then revealed to be a female family servant, whose spirit, like those who died centuries before her, now rises into the air, a shrill cry arising from her ghostly lungs.

The story of La llorona (or "the crying woman") was a cautionary tale warning girls against premarital sex and alerting them to the wiles men work in pursuing it. The tale originated in the Spanish-speaking colonies of North and South America. In the original parable, La llorona was a promiscuous woman who, rejected by the man she loved because she had children (who may or may not have been his), killed them in an attempt to snag him. When he rejected her anyway, she killed herself, thus damning her spirit to wander eternity crying for her lost children. The tale has a counterpart in North America's urban legends of "crybaby bridges," where the wails of murdered infants thrown from bridges can be heard.

The story of La llorona is a well-known one, adapted numerous times in Mexican cinema, with this 1933 presentation being the first. The most famous version came in 1960 and was also titled *The Crying Woman*, while a 1963 version titled *The Curse of the Crying Woman* seems to have been influenced more by Mario Bava's *Black Sunday* (1960) than by native folklore.

Obviously aping the style of Universal horror films of the day, and in particular the Spanish version of *Dracula* (1931), this first *Crying Woman* is a surprisingly complex film. The script is sprinkled with healthy doses of Mexican history, native superstition and Catholicism. The sparsely decorated period sets are more than made up for by the beautiful—and accurate—costume design. What is most refreshing about the film is that, at a time when most "old dark house" movies (and this most definitely belongs in that subgenre) relied on the setting alone to provide the chills, *The Crying Woman* goes all out to establish the supernatural in its attempts to scare its audience. Its creepy flashbacks provide relief from its uninteresting "eerie mansion" setting, riddled with secret panels and hidden passageways.

Why the filmmakers opted to depict two very different origins of the wailing woman before adding a third when wrapping up the then-modern story is up for debate, but it works despite—or possibly even because of—its seemingly contradictory structure.

Two of the film's stars, Ramón Pereda (who played Dr. Ricardo de Acuna) and Adriana Lamar (who played Ana Xicontencatl), were a real-life married couple. They frequently starred opposite each other.

While *The Crying Woman* was released in Mexico in May of 1933, it wasn't screened in the United States until July 1935. CW

Excess Baggage
Real Art; b/w; 59 min; Great Britain

D: Redd Davis *S:* H. Fowler Mear *P:* Julius Hagen *C:* Sydney Blythe

Cast: Claud Allister, Frank Pettingell, Sydney Fairbrother, Rene Ray, Gerald Rawlinson, Viola Compton, O.B. Clarence, Maud Gill, Finlay Currie, Minnie Rayner, Ruth Taylor, Charles Groves

Colonel Murgatroyd (Allister) is out hunting when he accidentally shoots his superior officer. Believing the man to be dead, he stuffs the body into a trunk with the intent of disposing of it in a river. The trunk gets mixed up with a look-alike and is collected by a woman who is staying at a house reputed to be haunted. The "dead" man awakens, and zaniness ensues.

This farcical British comedy works in horror elements—apparent death, ghosts and a haunted house—but it's all treated with tongue planted firmly in cheek. Leading man Claud Allister entered films in 1929; one of his first credits was as Algy Longworth in that same year's Oscar-nominated *Bulldog Drummond*, starring Ronald Coleman as the titular sleuth. Allister revisited the role in *The Return of Bulldog Drummond* (1934) and *Bulldog Drummond at Bay* (1937). His most noteworthy horror credit was the small role of Sir Aubrey in Universal's classic *Dracula's Daughter* (1936).

Director Redd Davis had an unremarkable career behind the camera, which lasted from 1932 to 1942. *Excess Baggage* was his only work in the horror genre. TH

The Flaming Signal
Berke/Imperial; b/w; 58 (64) min; U.S.

Co-D: George Jeske *Co-D/S:* Charles Edward Roberts *P:* William Berke *C:* Irving Akers *M:* Lee Zahler

Cast: Flash, John Horsley, Marceline Day, Noah Beery, Henry B. Walthall, Armelita Geraghty, Mischa Auer (Manu), Francisco Alonso, Anya Gramina, Jane'e Olmes

Jim Robbins (Horsley), pilot of *The Spirit of '76*, sets off from Los Angeles on the first leg of a flight around the world. He hadn't planned on taking his dog Flash, but the improbably intelligent canine swipes a parachute and stows away. Once aloft, the two lose radio contact with the mainland while flying through a storm near the island of Hawaii; the plane is struck by lightning, catches fire and crashes into the ocean. The plucky Flash parachutes to safety, pulls his master ashore unharmed and alerts nearby bathing beauty Sally James (Day) to their plight. Sally gets dressed and introduces the newcomers to her father, a Christian missionary (Walthall). Preacher and daughter then take their guests to the island's only bar, which is owned by evil European Otto Von Krantz (Beery). Von Krantz runs a scam in which he hires natives to pearl dive in dangerous waters, after which his buxom bartender (Geraghty) relieves them of their meager pay at his bar. The ever astute Flash quickly perceives that something isn't right with Von Krantz, but when he attempts via growls to alert the comparatively dull-witted Jim, he succeeds only in irritating the con man, who tries to whip him. Later, when Von Krantz rapes the daughter of native chief Manu (Auer), Manu responds by ordering Von Krantz to leave the island. Von Krantz, in turn, kills the chief. The natives perform a ritual that brings their chief back to life, but Flash ties up the story's loose ends and saves the day.

This may all sound like a lot of stupid fun, but it isn't. Even at a mere 58 minutes, *The Flaming Signal* goes on way, way too long, due mostly to its excessive use of lengthy stock footage clips (crowds gathering to watch air shows; airplanes performing; natives diving for pearls; sea life fighting and feeding, etc.). Its sole undeniably well-done portion, oddly, is the rape scene, which signals the film's origins in the period before the Forces of Good stepped up to enforce decency standards. When the chief's daughter comes upon Von Krantz during a search for her beau, the villain traps her in his room, picks her up and squeezes her tightly while she objects profusely as the scene fades out. It's the film's only engaging segment; apart from that accidental moment of real drama, *The Flaming Signal*—with its awful rear-screen projection and sped-up shots of natives running—is unengaging even as camp, though there *is* a wonderfully lurid moment when the "heroic" Flash tears out the villainous Von Krantz's throat while his barmaid watches in horror.

While *Signal* has all the elements (minus Lon Chaney) of a Tod Browning jungle opus, it's neither *West of Zanzibar* (1928) nor *The Most Dangerous Game* (1932). It does, however, mark dog-idol Flash's talkie debut, following his work in MGM's silent comedy *Honeymoon* (1928). He went on to star in several films during the 1930s, often receiving top billing. He shouldn't be confused with either the ubiquitous Rin-Tin-Tin or Disney TV's animated canine crime-fighter Flash, both of whom are different Wonder Dogs entirely.

Sharing the screen with Flash is John David Horsley in his first starring role. Horsley makes little of the opportunity, walking through the part with no hint of emotion. On the other hand, character actors Noah Beery (*Mystery Liner*, 1934), Mischa Auer (*Sucker Money*, 1933) and Henry B. Walthall (*Stark Mad*, 1929) acquit themselves admirably in roles that don't deserve it.

Marceline Day (1908-2000), who played the character of Sally (called "Molly" in the credits for no discernable reason), was the sister of actress Alice Day. Marceline's career in film began in 1924; while she was a major star by 1925, the coming of sound shuffled her into a forgotten series of low-budget programmers. She retired not long after starring in *The Flaming Signal* and refused thereafter to speak about her career as an actress. It should be noted that her most famous role was in that Holy Grail of lost movies, Tod Browning's *London After Midnight* (1927), which also starred Lon Chaney. CW

Forging Ahead
Cohen; b/w; 49 min; Great Britain
 D: Norman Walker *S:* Brandon Fleming *P:* Harry Cohen
 Cast: Margot Grahame, Gary Marsh, Anthony Holles, Clifford Heatherley, Clifford Makeham, Melville Cooper, Edgar Norfolk, Edith Saville

A supposedly haunted house is, in fact, a front for a gang of criminals!

Forging Ahead is one of way too many entries in the "phony haunted house" subgenre. Based on the novel *Easy Money* by K.R.G. Browne, it was very much a second-feature property designed for British audiences. The film's sense of humor and short running time didn't garner it much of a release outside of the United Kingdom, and it remains obscure today.

Director Norman Walker entered the film industry in 1926 after a stint in the British Army. He remained active until shortly before his death in 1963, but he never established himself as anything other than competent. Leading lady Margot Grahame worked with such distinguished filmmakers as John Ford (*The Informer*, 1935), Robert Siodmak (*The Crimson Pirate*, 1952) and Otto Preminger (*Saint Joan*, 1957), but her lead roles were generally confined to B-fare such as this. TH

The Ghost Train
City Film; b/w; length unknown; Hungary
 D: Lajos Lazar *S:* Laszlo Bekeffi
 Cast: Jeno Torzs, Marika Rokk, Oscar Beregi, Sr., Lajos Ihasz, Zoltan Maklary, Margit Ladomerszky, Sandor Pethes, Ica Bodo, Gabor Kertesz, Ferenc Turay

An apparently haunted train station turns out to be a front for a smuggling ring.

It's interesting that Hungary and Romania contributed so few films to the horror and fantasy genres during the 1930s, yet both created versions—in the same year, no less—of Arnold Ridley's popular play *The Ghost Train*. Both films credit the same screenwriter, Laszlo Bekeffi. Each title has a distinct cast and credit list (apart from Bekeffi), so it doesn't seem likely that a single film is being mistaken for two. But apart from credit information, little is known about either of these two particular films.

Ridley's play received its next adaptation in 1937 as one of the first BBC-TV plays. The Will Hay comedy *Oh, Mr. Porter!* (1937) drew uncredited inspiration from (read: was a rip-off of) the play, while the next big-screen adaptation was done in the Netherlands in 1939. TH

The Ghost Train
aka **Trenul fantoma**; **The Phantom Train**
Hunnia; b/w; length unknown; Romania
 D: Jean Mihail *S:* Laszlo Bekeffi, Victor Eftimiu *C:* Istvan Eiben *M:* Mihaly Eisemann, Deszo Szenkar
 Cast: Tony Bulandra, Gheorghe Storin, Lisette Verea, Stroe Atanasiu, Renee-Annie, Dida Solomon-Calimachi, Marcel Enescu

A sinister conductor who warns that the station is haunted scares off passengers awaiting their train.

This is one of two 1933 European versions of Arnold Ridley's play *The Ghost Train*. The story was an instant hit in Britain when it debuted in 1923, and the first of many film adaptations was done in 1927. Just how much any of these early versions played up the horror angle is unknown since, while only the 1931 adaptation (the first talkie version) is officially lost, none of them—including those from 1933—are accessible for viewing. TH

The Ghoul
Gaumont-British; b/w; 77 min; Great Britain
 D: T. Hayes Hunter *S:* Rupert Downing, Leonard Hines, Roland Pertwee, John Hastings Turner *P:* Michael Balcon *C:* Gunther Krampf *M:* Louis Levy, Leighton Lucas
 Cast: Boris Karloff, Cedric Hardwicke, Ernest Thesiger, Anthony Bushell, Dorothy Hyson, Kathleen Harrison, Harold Huth, Ralph Richardson, D.A. Clarke-Smith

On his deathbed, Professor Morlant (Karloff) instructs his servant Laing (Thesiger) to bury him with his sacred Egyptian jewel, swearing that if his instructions are not followed, he will return from the grave to seek vengeance. Laing, though wary, decides that such a thing isn't possible and steals the jewel instead of burying it.

The history of *The Ghoul* is an illustration of the hype that can develop around a "lost" film. It received a fair amount of

The resurrected Moriant (Boris Karloff) goes on a rampage and attacks Ernest Thesiger in *The Ghoul*.

publicity during its production because it marked Karloff's return to the British film industry. Having found international fame and fortune playing the monster in *Frankenstein* (1931), the actor's return to his homeland to carry a native film was considered by many to be quite a big deal. The movie came and went quickly, though, and for decades afterwards stills showing Boris Karloff's superb make-up (the work of Heinrich Heitfeld) were thought to be all that was left of the film. Horror fans decided that *The Ghoul* was a lost classic, but when it finally resurfaced in the 1980s, many people's expectations were dashed.

Not that the film is a complete waste—the talent involved pretty much precludes that—but it does fall short of delivering on the promise of those moody stills. The script, based on a novel and play by Dr. Frank King, gives Karloff scant opportunity to display his considerable gifts as an actor. He does indeed look wonderfully sinister, and his impassioned performance steals the scene in which he swears vengeance if his wishes are not obeyed. But then he dies and remains off-screen throughout the film's weak mid-section. Things do pick up some when he at last lumbers from his tomb, but though he is given one or two memorable moments—notably a gruesome scene in which he carves an Egyptian symbol into his bare chest—he otherwise does little more than skulk around frightening people. It's a role that requires him to be menacing and little else.

The supporting cast fares somewhat better. It's surprising to see so many distinguished actors crammed into this kind of film. As the shady lawyer Broughton, Cedric Hardwicke (1893-1964) makes his first of several horror film appearances. Already an established stage actor in Britain, he started film work in earnest in 1931 with the title role in *Dreyfus*, which dealt with the famous Dreyfus affair. He was knighted in 1934 and thereafter made his way to Hollywood, where he specialized in character roles. He's marvelously sinister in *The Ghoul*, looking very much like an Expressionist take on a Dickens character as he gives the film's stand-out performance.

Ernest Thesiger plays Karloff's unfaithful assistant; the two had previously co-starred in James Whale's *The Old Dark House* (1932) and would reteam to much greater effect in Whale's *The Bride of Frankenstein* (1935). Thesiger pulls out all the stops here—including a clubfoot and Scottish burr—but the part simply isn't worthy of his talents. Anthony Bushell—who became a television director of minor repute, with the occasional foray onto the big screen, such as Hammer's 1961 horror adventure *The Terror of the Tongs*—makes a brusque and unlikable hero, while Kathleen Harrison (best remembered as Scrooge's cleaning woman in the 1951 version of *A Christmas Carol*) provides some unfunny comedic relief.

Making his film debut is Ralph Richardson (1902-1983), cast as a parson with a trick up his sleeve. He ended up with the most consistently distinguished career of any of *The Ghoul*'s participants, knighted in 1947 and twice nominated for an Oscar (including a nod for his final performance in *Greystoke: The Legend of Tarzan*, 1983). The role doesn't give him a lot to do, but the young actor brings needed charm and vitality to the film. He didn't return to horror until relatively late in his career with the tongue-in-cheek *The Wrong Box* (1966) and *Whoever Slew Auntie Roo?* (1971). He also provided the first cinematic face of E.C. Comics' cadaverous Cryptkeeper in *Tales from the Crypt* (1972).

Cinematographer Gunther Krampf (*The Hands of Orlac*, 1924) brings plenty of flair to the lighting, but his efforts are

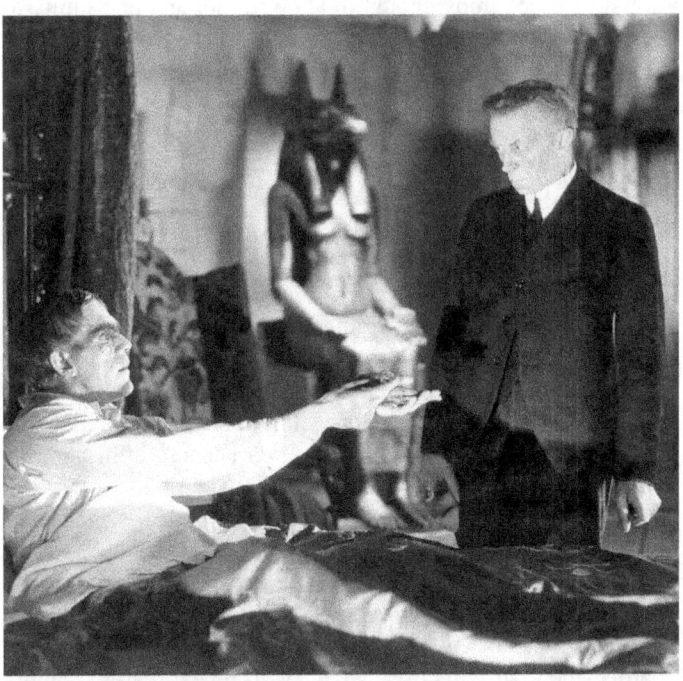

Professor Moriant (Boris Karloff) provides his servant (Ernest Thesiger) with instructions that will enable him to rise from the dead in *The Ghoul*.

undercut by the pedestrian direction of T. Hayes Hunter. It's a sad indicator of Hunters' lack of feeling for the material that he allows the film to become bogged down in a reel of tedium after Karloff's final scene.

The film has no connection to another horror film titled *The Ghoul* (1974), which featured Peter Cushing. TH

The Invisible Man
aka **H.G. Wells' The Invisible Man**
Universal; b/w; 71 min; U.S.

D: James Whale *S:* R.C. Sherriff, Philip Wylie, Preston Sturges *P:* Carl Laemmle Jr. *C:* Arthur Edson *M:* Heinz Roemheld *FX:* John P. Fulton

Cast: Claude Rains, Gloria Stuart, William Harrigan, Henry Travers, Una O'Conner, Forrester Harvey, Holmes Herbert, E.E. Clive, Dudley Digges, Harry Stubbs, Donald Stuart, Merle Tottenham, Walter Brennan, John Carradine, Dwight Frye, Bert Young

Herbert George Wells was born on September 21, 1866 to a lower middle class family in Kent, England. His father was a shopkeeper and his mother a former domestic servant. Despite his high intelligence and interest in writing, Wells was enrolled in a cheap private school, which he later said was structured to prepare students for trade occupations. After an accident put an end to his father's short-lived attempt at a cricket career, the lad was pulled out of school and placed in an apprenticeship as a draper. Around this same time, his mother went back to work as a maid under the condition that she be provided a place to live without her husband or four children. Wells' parents separated but never divorced.

His mother was a devout Protestant, but the young Wells appears to have been more heavily influenced by his father's independent and scientifically oriented worldview. After failing at a series of jobs, Herbert, while still young, became a teacher, a job he did not enjoy, though it allowed him an opportunity to continue his education. He also joined a debate group, where he learned about and became devoted to socialism. After receiving a Bachelor's Degree in Zoology, he launched a career writing fiction; it was during this period that he wrote some of his most famous and astounding science fiction, including *The Time Machine* (1895), *The Island of Doctor Moreau* (1896), *The Invisible Man* (1897), *War of the Worlds* (1898), *The First Men in the Moon* (1901), *The Food of the Gods* and *How It Came to Earth* (1904), among others.

The Invisible Man was originally serialized in the magazine *Pearson's Weekly* before being published in novella form later the same year. It concerns a mysterious, bandaged traveler who shows up at the Coach and Horses Inn in a remote English village, where he inspires gossip and rumor because of his strange appearance and secretive experiments as, simultaneously, a series of robberies besets the town. One morning the innkeeper and his wife, Mrs. Hall, believing their tenant to be away, enter his room and find his clothes spread over the floor, after which the room's furniture comes alive as though possessed by a poltergeist. Later, when the innkeeper confronts the bandaged boarder, the man pulls off his clothes to reveal that he's invisible. It turns out that he is a poor young medical student named Griffin who, intent on making a splash in the scientific com-

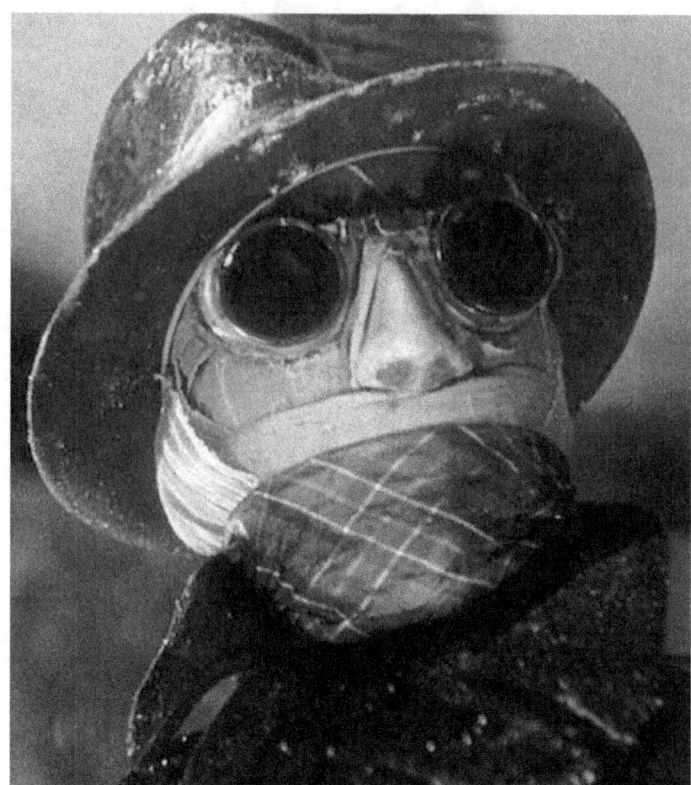

Claude Rains stars as the invisible one in *The Invisible Man*

munity, has developed a formula that affects light refractivity on the human body, though it only works in people with an albino condition like himself. Unfortunately, the chemical—for which he has failed to create an antidote—also causes a degeneration of mental stability. Before long Griffin is committing murder with reckless abandon and plotting to take over the world.

The Invisible Thief (1909), by Ferdinand Zecca and Segundo de Chomón, was the first film adaptation of Wells' story. Having stripped away the horror inherent in Wells' book, probably in an attempt to avoid a lawsuit because they hadn't purchased the film rights, it bore scant resemblance to its source material and concerned a petty thief, obsessed with Wells' book, who develops a serum to make himself undetectable by human eyes.

The novella did not receive another adaptation, official or unofficial, until the rights were optioned by Universal as a possible vehicle for Boris Karloff, who had become a superstar in 1931 after his appearance as the Monster in James Whale's masterful *Frankenstein*. There the project went through a series of directors, including Robert Florey (*Murders in the Rue Morgue*, 1932) and Cyril Gardner (*Doomed Battalion*, 1932), as well as such screenwriters as Garrett Fort (*Dracula's Daughter*, 1936), John Huston (*The Maltese Falcon*, 1931) and John Balderston (*The Mummy*, 1932), with draft after draft getting turned down by the studio's head brass. Many of these attempted adaptations were based as much on Philip Wylie's 1931 novel *The Murderer Invisible*—the film rights to which Universal had also purchased—as they were on Wells' classic. Life was finally breathed into the near-dead project when Universal's most beloved director, James Whale, showed interest.

Born in Dudley, England in 1889 to a large, impoverished, working class family, the artistic Whale escaped his dreary life

Una O'Conner appears as the barmaid harrassed by Rains in *The Invisible Man*.

by joining the British Army after the outbreak of the Great War. During his time as a prisoner of war, he developed an interest in acting and stage direction. Afterward, with the success of the London stage play he directed, *Journey's End,* under his belt, Whale moved to the United States to work on Broadway in New York City and later to Hollywood to adapt the play as a motion picture. The film's success paved his way to Universal, where he directed *Waterloo Bridge* (1931), also based on a play set during wartime. Ecstatic at the results, the Laemmles gave Whale his choice of scripts for a follow-up feature, and he chose *Frankenstein* (1931).

Whale heavily reworked the story, going back to silent German Expressionism for inspiration. It was a smart choice: His third feature film was yet another hit for both director and studio. The Laemmles were so happy with the man that they gave Whale creative control over all future projects produced by the studio (a setup that lasted until the Laemmles lost control of Universal by 1936).

Whale followed his first horror film up with another, the oddly comical *The Old Dark House* (1932), casting in major character roles multiple veterans of the British stage with whom he'd previously worked. Seeing that horror pictures were a cash cow and that Whale had a knack for such dark fare, Universal head Carl Laemmle, Jr. urged the company's star filmmaker to direct a sequel to *Frankenstein*, but the director initially refused. Instead, he selected *The Invisible Man*, a project that had been languishing in development limbo, as his next picture.

To help him craft a screenplay Whale imported writer R.C. Sherriff, the same man who had written *Journey's End*, from their native England. Like the other writers who had previously tackled *The Invisible Man*, Sherriff went through a series of outrageous treatments. But after rereading Wells' book, he realized just how filmable the novel actually was. He did add a few touches to make it more commercial, including a love interest for Griffin and a recast of the novel's Kemp character into a villainous foil. He also borrowed a leaf from Wylie's *The Murderer Invisible* by bringing front-and-center the invisible man's megalomania. The final script owed as much to Whale's *The Old Dark House* as it did to the director's *Frankenstein*; *The Invisible Man*'s screenplay is a heady mix of campy humor and unadulterated horror.

As R.C. Sherriff and James Whale honed the script, Universal was having issues with its prospective star, Boris Karloff. It has long been rumored that Karloff refused to play the part because his face wouldn't be seen onscreen for longer than a few seconds. But in fact, in the two years since the release of *Frankenstein*, Karloff *had* become a major celebrity. He had starred in a requisite number of hit films, however, and a clause in his contract, based on a form created by Universal before the Great Depression hit, stipulated that he was to receive a jump in pay beginning in 1932 (which might explain why Universal was so quick to loan him out to other studios). Karloff waived the increased fee for the first applicable film on the condition that it would go into effect with the second one. That film would have been *The Invisible Man*, but Universal refused to honor their agreement with Karloff, and the actor opted out. Nor was Karloff the only person to walk. Chester Morris, who had been cast as Kemp, also refused to play his part, purportedly after reading the script and finding it objectionable!

Whale offered the role of Griffin to Colin Clive, who had played the title role of the doctor in *Frankenstein*, but the British actor was unable to do the project, leaving Whale in a bit of a bind. While looking at old screen tests, he came across one of Claude Rains, who had thus far acted in only one film, a 1920 silent feature. Despite the fact that Rains' test was viewed as terrible by virtually everyone who had ever seen it, Whale cast him as Griffin, insisting that it was the stage actor's "intellectual" voice that was important. He then cast American actor William Harrigan as Kemp. Gloria Stuart, who had previously starred in *The Old Dark House*, was cast as the invisible man's love interest. Contract players filled out most of the remaining roles.

The film went into production in June of 1933, was completed in August and released theatrically in November of the same year. The plot follows the original novel fairly closely, with a bandaged stranger (Rains) appearing one snowy night at an inn in Iping, England. His mysterious appearance arouses the suspicions of the innkeeper (Harvey) and his wife (O'Conner), and their nosiness eventually results in the stranger revealing himself as an invisible man. He then goes on a murderous rampage, planning world domination and bringing his erstwhile lab partner Dr. Kemp into his schemes. Things get ugly, however, when the traitorous Kemp rats him out and is murdered for it.

The film utilized then state-of-the-art special effects by John Fulton and superlative camerawork by Arthur Edson to create several realistic tableaux in which objects move about by themselves, powered by an unseen man. And it was this aspect of the film, its groundbreaking special effects, on which Universal's marketing campaign focused.

The film was met with immediate critical applause and commercial success everywhere it played and has long been regarded as a premiere classic of both the horror and science fiction genres. Even H.G. Wells, disappointed by Paramount's film adaptation of his novel *The Island of Doctor Moreau*, was generally pleased this time around.

The film certainly helped the careers of Whale, Rains, Sherriff and Fulton. Whale went on to make *The Bride of Frankenstein* (1935) and *Showboat* (1936) before new heads at Universal yanked his creative control. Rains became a major star, not only in horror films (*The Man Who Reclaimed His Head*, 1934; *The Mystery of Edwin Drood* and *The Clairvoyant*, both 1935; *The Wolf Man*, 1941 and *Phantom of the Opera*, 1943) but also in films of other genres (*The Adventures of Robin Hood*, 1938; *Mr. Smith Goes to Washington*, 1939; *Here Comes Mr. Jordan*, 1941; *Casablanca*, 1942; *Mr. Skeffington*, 1944; and *Angel on My Shoulder*, 1946; among many others). R.C. Sherriff became one of the most important screenwriters in Hollywood, turning out such classics as *The Four Feathers* and *Goodbye, Mr. Chips* (both 1939), *Mrs. Miniver* (1942) and *Odd Man Out* (1947). And John P. Fulton went on to do the effects for approximately 250 films, including virtually all of Universal's 1930s and '40s horror films as well as such classics as *The Naked Jungle*, *Rear Window* and *White Christmas* (all 1954), *The Ten Commandments* (1956) and *Vertigo* (1958).

Of course, the box-office receipts from *The Invisible Man* alone weren't enough for Universal. By the end of the decade, they had put the first in a long line of sequels before the camera. The first two follow-ups, *The Invisible Man Returns* and *The Invisible Woman*, were released in 1940, with *Invisible Agent* (1942), *The Invisible Man's Revenge* (1944), *Abbott and Costello Meet Frankenstein* (1948) and *Abbott and Costello Meet the Invisible Man* (1951) following.

Yet, none of these subsequent works came anywhere near to comparing to James Whale's original production, a masterpiece of black humor and horror that reintroduced one of the world's greatest character actors, Claude Rains, to motion pictures. To call it groundbreaking is an understatement; it set new standards for special effects cinematography that, for at least a while, trumpeted substance over style without sacrificing one iota of either. CW

Japanese King Kong
aka **King Kong Made in Japan; Wasei Kingu Kongu**
Shochiku; b/w; length unknown; Japan
D: Torajiro Saito *S*: Akira Fushimi *C*: Yoshio Taketomi
Cast: Yasuko Koizumi, Takeshi Sakamoto, Kotaro Sekiguchi, Nagamasa Yamada, Isamu Yamaguchi

Released in October 1933, this appears to have been Japan's answer to RKO's hugely successful *King Kong*, which had been released in the United States the preceding March and gone worldwide in April. RKO's mega-production featured stellar special effects by Willis O'Brien and Marcel Delgado, making a whopping $2 million dollars in its initial run, a fact that one supposes would have inspired Shochiku to create this short imitation.

Shochiku's film is today considered lost, with only a single still from it known to exist. That still features a man in a hairy ape-like costume straddling the rooftops of two connected buildings; in his hand he holds a doll representing a living woman. Sound familiar?

Film historians have debated for years whether this film was really ever made. Not only are Japanese sources firm on this point, however; so, too, are film historians who have made it

Kong on the attack against a Pteranodon in *King Kong*

their life's work to study Japanese cinema. For instance, August Ragone gives it mention in his book *Eiji Tsuburaya: Master of Monsters* (Chronicle Books, 2014).

Director Torajiro Saito's (1905-1982) career began in the silent era. While he was known mostly for comedies, he also dabbled in horror, as can be seen in 1929's *Modern Kaidan: 100,000,000 Yen* and 1954's *Weak-kneed from Fear of Ghost Cat*. A writer and editor as well, he made his last film, *Dare yori-mo kane o aisu*, in 1961.

While *Japanese King Kong* may have been the first daikaiju (or giant monster) movie made in Japan, it was (quite famously) far from the last. Two more King Kong films followed in the late 1930s, *King Kong Appears in Edo* and *Edo ni arawareta Kingu Kongu* (both 1938). Like their predecessor, both are considered lost today. And, of course, with 1954's *Gojira* (aka *Godzilla*), from Japan's famed Toho Studios, the mother of all homegrown Japanese giant monsters made its big-screen debut. CW

King Kong
aka **The Ape**; **Kong**; **The Eighth Wonder**; **The Beast**; **King Ape**
RKO; b/w; 104 (100) min; U.S.
Co-D/Co-S/Co-P: Merian C. Cooper *Co-D/Co-P:* Ernest B. Schoedsack *Co-S:* Ruth Rose, Edgar Wallace, Leon Gordon *C:* Eddie Linden, J.O. Taylor, Vernon Walker *M:* Max Steiner *FX:* Willis O'Brien, Marcel Delgado, Harry Redmond, Jr., Harry Redmond, Sr.
Cast: Fay Wray, Robert Armstrong, Bruce Cabot, Frank Reicher, Sam Hardy, Noble Johnson, Steve Clemente, James Flavin, Merian C. Cooper, Ernest B. Schoedsack, Madame Sul-Te-Wan, Victor Wong

In the early 1900s, a rumor circulated that an Indonesian island controlled by the Dutch was home to some sort of giant "land crocodile." In time, the director of a zoological museum in Java got hold of the skin of just such a reptile, which he declared a new species of lizard, *Varanus komodoensis*. At over nine feet long, it was allegedly a small sample, with some specimens—he

A French movie poster for *King Kong*

was told—reaching 20 feet long. But even the relatively small sample was larger than any previously known animal of its ilk and must have seemed positively prehistoric in nature.

The topic of giant reptiles on Komodo Island faded from public scrutiny until, over a decade later, a young explorer, hunter and collector named W. Douglas Burden heard a lecture on the subject. He was instantly intrigued and convinced the New York Museum of Natural History to fund an expedition to Komodo to hunt for both living and dead oddities. In 1926, with little formal education but much real-life expedition experience, Burden, along with his actress wife (the only woman on board), set sail with a small team in search of the elusive and possibly even mythical giant lizard of Komodo and whatever else they might find.

After a detour through China, they finally docked along the shore of the remote island. On their first day on land, they spotted massive birdlike footprints with heavy drag marks between them, left in the mud along a shallow pool. They also spotted evidence of large water buffalo and, later that same day, obtained irrefutable proof of the existence of the Komodo dragon, as Burden came to call it. Through his field glasses, he spied a long, black lizard slinking through the grass on a hill half a mile away. Over the next few days, he and his team captured two living specimens. They shot and tagged 12 others, several of which were stuffed and remain mounted in the New York Museum of Natural History to this day.

W. Douglas Burden was a good friend of another famous explorer, Merian C. Cooper, who had by the late 1920s produced two exotic documentaries. While numerous legends have arisen around the persona of Cooper (many of them created by Cooper himself), it is known for certain that, in 1927, he read Burden's account of the Komodo dragon discovery in the Dutch East Indies. The thought of a recently discovered island inhabited by previously unknown giant reptiles sparked a brainstorm, but at the time he had access to neither the backing nor the production facilities he would need to explore the possibilities of the theme, so he let the whole thing slip to the back of his mind.

In 1928, while shooting *The Four Feathers* in Africa, Cooper became obsessed with gorillas. A scenario gestated in his mind in which an expedition comes across a large gorilla that falls for the sole woman in the group, abducts her and is forced to fight prehistoric lizards (similar to Komodo dragons, of course) to keep her safe. Eventually, the beast is captured and taken to civilization where, unable to adjust to captivity, it dies. Cooper pitched the idea to Paramount, which had released his last three films, but the studio passed.

Still, all was not lost. In 1931 David O. Selznick was hired by fledgling company RKO to turn its sagging fortunes around. The studio, yet to have a major hit, had been placed in receivership. One of Selznick's first moves was to hire Cooper for help in sorting out which proposed projects should be developed. Cooper immediately stopped production on a prehistoric adventure titled *Creation*, believing the story to be fairly dull, despite the fact that several of Willis O'Brien's effects sequences had already been filmed. (The effects were of the stop-motion variety, where stationary models are moved bit-by-bit and filmed frame-by-frame, creating the illusion of motion.) As befitted his background and interests, Cooper selected scripts that mixed exotic adventure with a dash of romance and sometimes horror; these included *The Most Dangerous Game* and *The Phantom of Crestwood* (both 1932), as well as *The Monkey's Paw* (1933). He also approached Selznick with the idea of producing his long-dwelt-upon project.

Kong, standing atop the Empire State Building, is attacked by planes in the groundbreaking *King Kong*.

Kong chews on a native in this once censored scene from *King Kong*.

Realizing that he could use stop-motion monster footage from the abandoned *Creation* project—and that Willis O'Brien would be on hand to shoot more as needed—Selznick greenlighted the film. As Cooper's scenario was fleshed out, Kong the gorilla became fantastically big, and his Skull Island foes went from being Komodo dragon-like lizards to equally large antediluvian monsters. The public's interest in dinosaurs had grown since Roy Chapman Andrew's much-publicized discovery of dinosaur eggs in Mongolia in the early 1920s, and the first major film to use stop-motion to bring the beasts not only to life but also to civilization, *The Lost World* (1925), had been a silent blockbuster. And that film's real star had been its special effects man—one Willis O'Brien.

Knowing that a movie is ultimately only as good as its script, Cooper hired one of the most successful novelists of his day, mystery writer Edgar Wallace, to craft the screenplay. Wallace turned in a first draft, titled *The Eighth Wonder*, shortly thereafter, and Cooper suggested changes. But on February 10, 1932, Wallace unexpectedly died of pneumonia. Several other writers were brought in to polish what had been left behind, but it wasn't until Cooper gave the rewriting task to longtime friend Ruth Rose that things began to congeal. This was also about the time that the film's title was changed simply to *Kong*.

To keep costs down, Cooper opted to shoot much of the film's jungle footage on the already-built set of *The Most Dangerous Game* and to import many of that film's cast and crew over to the *Kong* production. Robert Armstrong and Fay Wray, among others, made the jump. But Joel McCrea was unable to oblige, allegedly due to a demand for more money than RKO was willing to shell out, and the role of adventurous hero Jack Driscoll was given to Bruce Cabot. Such cinema stalwarts as Frank Reicher and Noble Johnson also came aboard. To direct, Cooper chose his old friend and ally Ernest B. Schoedsack, with whom he'd worked on several projects in the past, including the aforementioned *Game*.

Principal photography on *Kong* began in May of 1932 and lasted through January of 1933. Though stop-motion remained the order of the day for the special effects sequences, there were several large prehistoric-animal hands, feet and heads created to share the screen with human actors in live-action sequences. Max Steiner was hired to compose the film's score, and the title was changed to the now-legendary *King Kong*. After several post-production reshoots and much polishing of the effects sequences, the completed film was finally exhibited for distributors in March. After test audiences reacted negatively to a sequence in which men fall from a log into a canyon and are devoured by giant spiders, Cooper ordered that the scene be heavily edited. The altered film debuted at two New York City venues—Radio City Music Hall and The RKO Roxy—on March 2, 1933, and then moved to Grauman's Chinese Theater in Hollywood, California, before going worldwide in April.

Showings were sold out everywhere, and for good reason: The film was both epic in scale and massively entertaining. Nothing like it had ever been made before. Audiences flocked to it, awed and horrified in equal measure. Even the critics loved it.

The tale begins on the rundown freighter SS *Venture*, docked in the Hudson River. A documentary movie producer, Carl Denham (Armstrong), has found a map to a little-known island in the East Indies. He has hired the *Venture* to carry him and his crew there to shoot a movie, but he needs an actress to play the female lead. As luck would have it, a scene or two later he happens to be walking through Times Square just as a beautiful, down-and-out young woman named Ann Darrow (Wray) is hassled by a shopkeeper for attempting to steal an apple. One decent meal later, she agrees to accompany Denham's expedition.

Once all are aboard and the ship has set sail, Denham reveals that they are headed to an island with a skull-shaped mountain and a large wall separating the native islanders from the island's interior. When they get there, they find the natives preparing to sacrifice a woman to the native god Kong. But when the natives see Ann, they decide that she's a much better choice. They go for her, but Denham and his men get her back onto the boat in the nick of time. Nonetheless, the natives are relentless; that night, they sneak aboard, kidnap her, and take her back to the island. There, they fetter her to an altar just inside the giant wall and close the enormous door. The ground trembles, the treetops move, and out of the forest stalks a gargantuan (as in 40 feet tall) gorilla, which takes the helpless Ann back into the jungle, where it fights off the prehistoric monsters that want to make a meal of his new bride. The remaining expedition members follow and retrieve her, triggering events forever etched in horror film history.

Due in part to a lengthy and expensive marketing campaign that included the publication of a novelization (possibly the world's first based on a movie), radio programs, magazine advertisements and more, the film was a phenomenal success worldwide. By grossing approximately $1,700,000 in 1933 alone (its budget was around $670,000), the film pulled RKO out of receivership and turned the company into a powerhouse. *King Kong* was also re-released numerous times in the ensuing decades, grossing massive amounts of money each time out. In fact, a successful outing in the early 1950s led to the production of *The Beast from 20,000 Fathoms* (1953), a myriad of "giant monster" imitations, and a science fiction boom that lasted over a decade.

A scene that never happened! Kong squares off against a Stegosaurus, part of RKO's marketing campaign for *King Kong*.

To the surprise of no one involved in the production, *King Kong*'s real stars were O'Brien's special effects creations: a Stegosaurus, a "Brontosaurus," a Tyrannosaurus rex, an Elasmosaurus, a Pteranodon, and a giant vulture, along with an array of large snakes, bugs and lizards. The Stegosaurus, Tyrannosaurus rex and Pteranodon were all fairly realistic in their presentations and were more or less appropriately sized. Sequences involving a huge, two-horned prehistoric mammal known as an Arsinoitherium and a frilled, horned dinosaur known as a Styracosaurus were also reportedly shot (the former possibly for O'Brien's aborted *Creation*) but never used.

Of the animals that do appear in the film, the taxon "Brontosaurus" has since fallen into disuse in accordance with the scientific rules for genus and specie nomenclature. Othniel Charles Marsh named the creature "Brontosaurus," and he also named Apatosaurus under the belief that the two animals were distinct (although closely related) types. According to the rules of scientific nomenclature, if two members of the same genus or specie are named separately, the first published name is the correct one. Therefore, the more common name of "Brontosaurus" was eliminated in favor of the less common Apatosaurus. (It didn't help clarify things when the first reconstruction of a "Brontosaurus" was given the head of a Camarasaurus and the feet of a Diplodocus.)

King Kong adds to the "Brontosaurus" confusion by depicting it as a vicious meat eater. It was actually an herbivore, without the tooth or jaw structure needed to grab a man in its mouth and fling or devour him. Nor did the beast live in lakes or swamps, though this was a common misbelief at the time of shooting. The actual body and size of the animal is otherwise fairly accurate.

One of the film's most dramatic scenes has King Kong squaring off against a bipedal, carnivorous dinosaur. This dinosaur, simply called "The Meat Eater" in the film's script, has been labeled both an Allosaurus and a Tyrannosaurus rex by various sources. It's true that the animal has three fingers on its forelimbs, as does Allosaurus. However, it should be noted that, at the time, no forelimbs had ever been discovered for T-rex or any of its close relatives, and so it was mistakenly believed among paleontologists that the predator was indeed three-fingered. One should also note the shape of the animal's skull and body is modeled after paleoartist Charles Knight's famous Tyrannosaurus rex painting, still on display at the Chicago Field Museum. (Most of the exotic, prehistoric animals in the film, in fact, are based on artwork from Knight.) Given all this, and the animal's extreme size and bulk, it appears that T-rex is the better of the two guesses.

As Kong enters his cavernous lair with Ann in tow, he engages in a fight with a huge Elasmosaurus. In real life, Elasmosaurus was a water-dwelling reptile, a type of Plesiosaur—the animal many cryptozoologists believe still haunts the chilly waters of Loch Ness in Scotland—with a long neck and a squat, turtle-like body. It had flippers rather than clawed hands and feet to propel itself forward through the water. Why the filmmakers behind *King Kong* chose to present it so inaccurately when so many of the other animals evidence an almost rabid attention to detail is a mystery.

One more tidbit apropos to dinosaurs: In the sequence in which Cabot's Driscoll is trapped in a shallow cave, he is threatened by a reptilian creature with only two forelimbs, no hind limbs and a body that tapers into a serpent-like tail. That creature was originally supposed to be an Aetosaur, a large, heavily armored herbivorous reptile from the late Triassic period. But after RKO balked at the cost of the some of the effects, it was decided to cut costs by cutting the animal down in size. This was accomplished by reducing the number of its limbs by two, which lowered both the expense of the model and the amount of work needed to animate it.

A year after *King Kong* was released, the Production Code, which had been adopted by the industry in 1930 to govern moral content in films, began to be strictly enforced. With its original release coming before the actual implementation of the rules, *King Kong* suffered little in the way of cuts (apart from those demanded by Cooper himself). However, when the film was re-released in 1938, it had to adhere to the Code, which meant the excision of a fair amount of footage. Gone were images of Kong stomping on and chewing natives, dropping a woman to her death and stripping off a portion of Ann Darrow's dress before sniffing his fingers! (These cuts inadvertently made Kong far more sympathetic than he had been in the original edit of the film.) What was left of the film was then darkened so that the sight of blood during the battle with the T-rex would be obscured. This version of the film remained in circulation for decades, until Janus Films finally located a more complete print. Today, all of the offensive scenes (with the exception of the feast of spiders originally snipped by Cooper) have been restored and made a part of every home-entertainment release since the late 1980s. The dark tinting has likewise been removed. As a result, the film has never looked better than it does today, thanks to the magic of high-definition!

Even before *King Kong* was released, RKO and producer Cooper knew they had a hit on their hands. They immediately went into preproduction on a sequel, the far more kid-friendly

The Son of Kong, which was released later the same year, just in time for Christmas. *Son* wasn't the success of its predecessor, but that didn't stop RKO and other filmmakers from visiting "giant ape" territory again and again. RKO's own *Mighty Joe Young* was released in 1949, and Toho Productions of Japan got in on the action when they spliced the character into their Godzilla series with *King Kong vs. Godzilla* (1962). The mid-1960s saw the production of an animated television series, and the year 1977 brought a full-fledged remake that tanked at the box-office (yet still spawned a sequel). In 2005 Peter Jackson tried his hand at an adaptation for Universal, one that paid better (though still inferior) homage to the original classic.

Despite these efforts (and more, no doubt, in the future), no director, producer or film studio has ever been (or likely ever will be) able to capture the magic that was the original masterpiece known as *King Kong*. CW

The Monkey's Paw
RKO; b/w; 58 min; U.S.

D: Wesley Ruggles, Earnest B. Schoadsack *S:* Graham John *P:* David O'Selznick *C:* Leo Tover *FX:* Lloyd Knechtel, Vernon L. Walker, Linwood Dunn *M:* Max Steiner

Cast: C. Aubrey Smith, Ivan Simpson, Louise Carter, Bramwell Fletcher, Betty Lawford, Winter Hall, LeRoy Mason, Nigel de Brulier

After his friend Sergeant Major Tom Harris (Smith) tells a shocking tale about a Hindu fakir who gave him a monkey's paw alleged to have the power to grant three wishes, John White (Simpson) steals the mummified talisman. He promptly wishes for 200 pounds, then learns that his son (Fletcher) has been killed in his workplace while telling his co-workers about the paw, laughing so hard in the process that he fell into some machinery and was mangled to death. As next of kin, however, Mr. and Mrs. White receive a compensation of 200 pounds. Mrs. White (Carter) then makes the brilliant move of taking the paw and wishing her son back to life. Sure enough, there's a familiar knocking at the front door. But Mr. White, afraid that his son has returned in mangled form, takes the paw and wishes the young man back into the grave. When Mrs. White opens the door, nobody is there.

When the first cut of this film didn't meet the desired running time, additional footage was shot, much of it directed by Earnest B. Schoedsack. A prologue was added telling of the paw before it fell into Sergeant Harris' hands: Nura (Quartero), a female native of India, uses it to wish for true love but instead receives death (this freshly written portion was trimmed before release). An "it was all a dream" ending was also added.

The film drew mostly positive reviews and was moderately successful. Today only portions of it are known to exist. CW

Murder on the Campus
aka **The Campanile Murders; On the Stroke of Nine**
Chesterfield; b/w; 69 (73) min; U.S.

D: Richard Thorpe *S:* Andrew Moses *P:* George R. Batcheller *C:* M.A. Anderson

Cast: Shirley Grey, Charles Starrett, J. Farrell MacDonald, Ruth Hall, Dewey Robinson, Maurice Black, Edward Van Sloan, Jane Keckley, Richard Catlett

Based on the novel *The Campanile Murders* by Whitman Chambers, *Murder on the Campus* is a decent murder mystery from Poverty Row studio Chesterfield. It concerns Charles Starrett as newspaper journalist Bill Bartlett, who is obsessed with Lillian Voyne (Grey), a nightclub performer working her way through school. He accuses her of loving Malcolm Jennings, star athlete and chime player. When a shot rings out from a bell tower (or, in Italian, a "campanile") on the college campus, Bartlett watches the building's entrance until the police arrive to discover the body of Jennings shot to death inside. The death is quickly ruled a homicide despite the fact that no living person is found inside with the body, and Bartlett and the police are left to figure out how the murder occurred. Voyne quickly becomes suspect number one, but after a few more murders occur, Bartlett discerns the truth.

Fairly straightforward with just the right atmospheric touches, *Murder on the Campus* is marred somewhat by its poor lead performances. Shirley Grey was capable of better work (see *Circumstantial Evidence*, 1935), but here she pretty much walks disinterestedly through her part. Leading man Charles Starrett's lack of interest is matched by her lack of enthusiasm. Starrett had been a college football star "discovered" by fellow actor Richard Dix in 1926. Starrett found small acting roles in the silent era, and by the early 1930s his star was on the rise. In 1932 he portrayed the object of Fu Manchu's nymphomaniac daughter's affection in *The Mask of Fu Manchu*, but it was as the Western hero Durango Kid for Columbia that he found lasting fame. He retired from acting in the early 1950s when Columbia ceased production on its flailing Western series; he died of cancer in 1986, just a few days before his 83rd birthday.

Grey and Starrett are outdone by J. Farrell MacDonald (*The Phantom Express*, 1932) as a police captain and Edward Van Sloan (*Behind the Mask*, 1932) as a professor and amateur sleuth. Ruth Hall (*The Three Musketeers*, 1933), Maurice Black (*She Done Him Wrong*, 1933) and Jane Keckley (*Curtain at Eight*, 1933) round out the cast, all of them offering performances superior to the juvenile leads. It's Van Sloan, not surprisingly, who manages to steal the picture from pretty much everyone else.

Director Richard Thorpe went on to make the grisly MGM classic *Night Must Fall* (1937). CW

Murders in the Zoo
Paramount; b/w; 62 min; U.S.

D: A. Edward Sutherland *S:* Philip Wylie, Seton I. Miller *P:* E. Lloyd Sheldon *C:* Ernest Haller *M:* Karl Hajos, Sigmund Krumgold

Cast: Lionel Atwill, Charles Ruggles, Gail Patrick, Randolph Scott, Kathleen Burke, John Lodge, Harry Beresford

Zoologist Eric Gorman (Atwill) is insanely jealous of his beautiful wife Evelyn (Burke). While on an expedition in the Orient to pick up specimens for his menagerie, he discovers that she has kissed another man—and reacts by sewing his mouth shut. On the boat trip back to the U.S., he catches her becoming friendly with fellow passenger Roger Hewitt (Lodge). Once home, he utilizes the animals in his zoo to dispose of Roger and to ward off further potential infidelities as they crop up.

This memorably kinky pre-Code item is an ideal showcase for Lionel Atwill who, though second-billed to Paramount funny

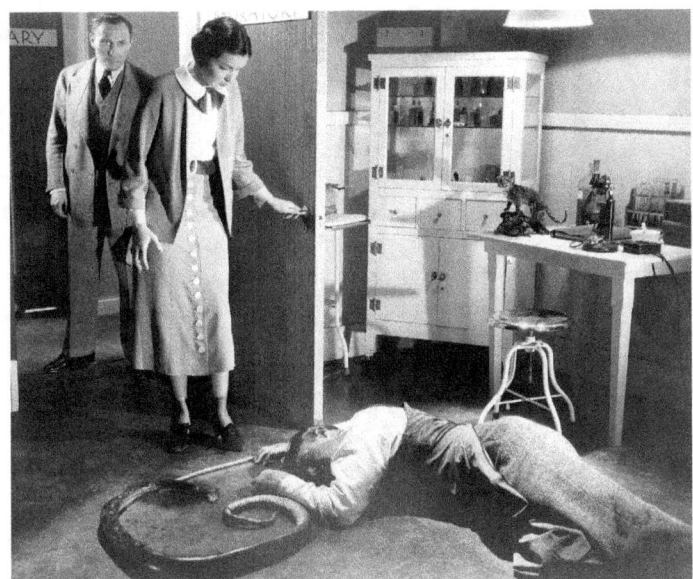

Lionel Atwill terrorizes Gail Patrick and Randolph Scott in *Murders in the Zoo*.

man Charlie Ruggles, indisputably steals the picture. A gleeful sadistic streak is in evidence throughout, from the opening shot of Atwill sewing shut a victim's mouth to the final image of a character being crushed by a python.

If *Murders* never makes it to the level of disturbing perversity evidenced in *Island of Lost Souls* (1933) or *The Black Cat* (1934), it's nevertheless pretty strong stuff for its period. This is surprising at first glance, given that the director wasn't a dark visionary *a la* Edgar G. Ulmer or Tod Browning, but rather comedy specialist A. Edward Sutherland. Sutherland racked up a number of credits between 1925 until his retirement in 1961, but apart from this film, his only horror-related titles are borderline—*Secrets of the French Police* (1932) and *The Invisible Woman* (1940). He spent most of his career helping create such popular comedies as *International House* (1933) and *The Flying Deuces* (1939), and a playful directorial wit is sporadically evident here; in the opening titles, for instance, the main actors are listed alongside animals meant to reflect the personalities of the characters they play.

Philip Wylie (best known for co-authorship, with Edwin Balmer, of the 1933 novel *When Worlds Collide*) was primary screenwriter here. Given his contribution to *Island of Lost Souls*, it's a safe bet that most of the nastiness on display can be laid at his doorstep. Still, Sutherland can be credited for attacking the edgy material with an unsavory (and thoroughly entertaining) ferocity.

The gifted Atwill, needless to say, has a field day here. He squeezes every drop of venom from each double entendre, and his every glance carries a perverse charge that speaks volumes. He is well matched by the striking Kathleen Burke, who played Lota the Panther Woman in the aforementioned *Island of Lost Souls* and was, simply put, one of the most silkily seductive actresses of the period. Randolph Scott is stuck with the thankless task of playing the square-jawed lead, and while he doesn't embarrass himself, neither does he display the charisma that would in time make him a major star. Top-billed yet overshadowed, Charlie Ruggles plays a nervous press agent working for the

Director Michael Curtiz (with script in hand) on the set of *The Mystery of the Wax Museum* with Lionel Atwill sitting at the bench

zoo who manages a few amusing moments without breaking the morbidly riveting spell being cast around him.

At a brisk 62 minutes, the film can hardly be accused of overstaying its welcome—and indeed, for most of its running time, *Murders in the Zoo* is one of the best lesser-known horror films of the 1930s. TH

The Mystery of the Wax Museum
aka **Mystery of the Wax Museum**; **Wax Museum**
Warner/First National; color; 77 min; U.S.

D: Michael Curtiz S: Carl Erickson, Don Mullaly P: Henry Blanke C: Ray Rennahan M: Bernhard Kaun, Cliff Hess

Cast: Lionel Atwill, Fay Wray, Glenda Farrell, Frank McHugh, Allen Vincent, Gavin Gordon, Holmes Herbert, Arthur Edmund Carewe, Edwin Maxwell, Thomas E. Jackson, DeWitt Jennings, Matthew Betz, Monica Bannister

London, 1921: Ivan Igor (Atwill) has a falling out with business partner Joe Worth (Maxwell). Worth is worried over the fact that they are deeply in debt and hatches a scheme to make some quick cash: set fire to their waxworks museum and collect on the insurance. Igor is appalled by the idea, pointing out that the wax figures are his life's work. Worth knocks him unconscious and sets the place alight. Igor is badly burned in the blaze.

New York City, 1933: Igor relocates and opens a new waxworks exhibit; visitors are struck by how lifelike the sculptures are and Igor is celebrated as a great artist. The opening of the

museum coincides with a series of strange disappearances throughout the city, however, and reporter Florence Dempsey (Farrell) begins to suspect a connection.

Reuniting many of the creative personnel from *Doctor X* (1932), *The Mystery of the Wax Museum* marks Warner Bros.-First National's second attempt to one-up Universal by releasing a horror film in color. The two-strip Technicolor process is used to garish advantage but, despite some memorable highlights, the overall product is less successful than the group's previous outing.

A large part of the problem is that the wisecracking reporter hero—or in this case heroine, as played by Glenda Farrell—is just plain grating this time around, with any progress toward building atmosphere repeatedly shot down by her annoying presence. Watching her in action makes one long for even the slight level of charm exhibited by Lee Tracy in the earlier picture. And it doesn't help that this film's variety of locales robs it of the claustrophobic sense that infuses *Doctor X*.

Mystery, then, while by no means unworthy, is nevertheless something of a disappointment, this despite a great performance by Lionel Atwill, who is clearly having the time of his life, particularly during the final reel when his evil intentions are at last unveiled.

Fay Wray is not much of a presence here, since her role is kept small to conserve screen time for Farrell's alleged witticisms. Wray does a capable job, but apart from the scene in which she realizes that Igor isn't what he pretends to be—thus leading to the wonderful unmasking scene, comparable to that in *The Phantom of the Opera* (1925)—the film doesn't give her much to do. The supporting cast includes fine character actors Holmes Herbert (*Dr. Jekyll and Mr. Hyde*, 1932) and Arthur Edmund Carewe (another hold-over from *Doctor X*, in one of his last roles before suffering a stroke that led him to suicide).

Director Michael Curtiz and cinematographer Ray Rennahan, also alumni of the earlier film, do a fine job of setting the mood. Born in Hungary, where he got his start directing pictures (including *Alraune*, 1918), Curtiz also made a number of silent features in Germany before immigrating to the United States. His time in Germany clearly influenced his sense of composition and shadow play, both of which are notable here. The shadowy atmospherics and lurid use of color give the film plenty of stylistic punch. The imaginative art direction by Anton Grot also contributes to the film's visual appeal.

Mystery was considered lost for many years but re-emerged in the 1980s; its reputation having been built up as something of a lost masterpiece, it received a cool reception among modern viewers, many of whom were disappointed by the constant comic intrusions. Even so, the film's introduction of a popular horror mainstay—the deranged artist using wax to hide his victims' bodies—went on to inspire two remakes (both titled *House of Wax*, in 1953 and 2005, respectively) and a number of imitations, ranging from the ridiculous (*Nightmare in Wax*, 1969) to the sublime (*A Bucket of Blood*, 1959). TH

Night of Terror
aka **He Lived to Kill; Terror in the Night**
Foy/Columbia; b/w; 64 (61, 65) min; U.S.
D: Benjamin Stoloff S: Beatrice Van, William Jacobs, Lester Nielson P: Bryan Foy C: Joseph A. Valentine

Cast: Bela Lugosi, George Meeker, Tully Marshall, Bryant Washburn, Edwin Maxwell, Wallace Ford, Sally Blane, Gertrude Michael, Mary Frey, Matt McHugh

"Mad Murdering Menace!" proclaimed Columbia's original one-sheet for *Night of Terror*, an interesting 1930s horror film fatally flawed by the time's inescapable comedy relief. Based on playwright Willard Mack's story *The Public Be Damned*, it begins with a silly sequence in which fortune-teller Sika (Frey) gazes into her crystal ball at the film's opening credits. Things then move on to a young couple waxing romantic beneath a lover's moon as a hideous, leering monstrosity (Maxwell) drops from the trees behind them. There's a scream, the scene fades

Degar (Lugosi) confronts the startled Tom Hartley (Wallace Ford) in *Night of Terror*.

to black and then the viewer meets a group of high-society types complaining about a local maniac who stabs his victims to death. It's also noted that said maniac lingers somewhere along the road near Rinehart Estate, where the remainder of the film's action takes place.

After this morbid introduction, the film settles into well-shot unevenness. A young scientist by the name of Arthur Hornsby (Meeker) plans on being buried alive. His aim? To prove to the scientific community that he has invented a formula that will prevent death by asphyxiation. But on the evening before his stunt is to be performed, his girlfriend Mary Rinehart (Blane) is warned by servant Sika that death is soon to visit. And sure enough, the shaggy-maned killer murders Mary's wealthy father Richard (Marshall) and the gravedigger responsible for removing the dirt from Hornsby's burial spot. The arrival of relatives (Washburn, Michael) and the obligatory wisecracking reporter, Tom Hartley (Ford), who is there to cover the premature burial (and who also happens to be in love with Mary), further muddies matters. More murders follow—one of them during a spooky séance. A school of red herrings, including Bela Lugosi as a turbaned swami with a knack for muttering dire statements, stand around looking sinister without doing much to persuade the audience of their possible guilt. And with the "It's the person you least suspect" rule firmly in place, the real killer is all too obvious all too early in the proceedings.

Night of Terror isn't a classic, but neither is it anywhere near the worst of its ilk. Its biggest influence appears to have been Universal's 1930 horror opus *The Cat Creeps*, itself a fairly faithful remake of the same studio's 1927 *The Cat and the Canary*. As such, *Terror* offers the standard trappings of the "old dark house" subgenre: an old dark house (natch), murder, psychics, naturally a séance, a maniacal killer and a premature burial. When the film's on straight horror film terrain, it's actually pretty good (and Benjamin Stoloff's direction is certainly up to the task of creating a sense of claustrophobic terror). But the curse of the breed, bad comedy relief (Wallace Ford's painfully unfunny lead character and a jittery and ghost-obsessed African American chauffeur are the worst, but they are far from the only culprits), runs the overall effort aground a few times too many.

One of the more interesting aspects of *Night of Terror* is its unconventional ending. Once it is revealed that the maniac is not responsible for the murders at the Rinehart Estate (why he was lurking around there in the first place is never addressed), he slinks out of the shadows to warn audiences against revealing the ending. Intended to be funny, it comes across as inane instead. It should also be noted that character Mary Rinehart is a reference to Mary Roberts Rinehart, the novelist and playwright responsible for *The Bat* (1926).

Night of Terror was an unfortunate predictor of Bela Lugosi's future career path, pretty much marking the beginning of his decline. For the next couple of decades, the majority of Lugosi's roles would be either fairly large ones in really bad, low-budget movies for Monogram and PRC or fairly small ones in B-pictures from bigger companies like Universal and RKO. Though he's not terrible here, he's shuffled into a part too small for his oversized persona and comes out all the worse for it, despite receiving top billing, no doubt on the laurels of his work for Universal.

A publicity photo of Bela Lugosi from *Night of Terror*. While Lugosi received top billing, he actually had little to do in the film.

Comedy specialist Benjamin Stoloff directed only two more horror films in his career, *Super Sleuth* (1937) and *The Mysterious Doctor* (1943). Both were, like *Night of Terror*, smaller affairs for A-list companies—*Sleuth* for RKO and *Doctor* for Warner Bros.—but neither did anything for his career. He made only a few more films during the remainder of the 1940s before retiring from cinema altogether.

Night of Terror was one of Columbia's few horror outings during the early to mid-1930s (others included the ill-fated but fun *Black Moon*, 1934, starring Fay Wray, and the terrific *The Black Room*, 1935, starring Boris Karloff). Weighed down by its brevity, it wasn't a big moneymaker for the company, which pretty much left horror alone until the late 1930s, when it shuffled Boris Karloff into a series of "man-revived-from-dead-seeks-revenge" pictures. CW

The Phantom Broadcast
W.T. Lackey; b/w; 72 min; U.S.

D: Phil Rosen *S:* Tristram Tupper *P:* William T. Lackey *C:* Gilbert Warrenton

Cast: Ralph Forbes, Vivienne Osborne, Arnold Gray, Gail Patrick, Guinn "Big Boy" Williams, George Hayes, Paul Page, Pauline Garon, Rockliffe Fellowes, Harland Tucker, Carl Miller, Mary MacLaren, George Nash, Althea Henley

Grant Murdock (Gray) is a successful radio crooner. He is also a fraud; his golden voice is really that of his accompanist/manager Norman Wilder (Forbes). Norman is a club-footed hunchback who, as such, is deemed unworthy of celebrity. The fact that Grant gets all the fame, money and women understandably chafes Norman, and when Grant is murdered, Norman is the prime suspect. (It probably doesn't help his case that, though he denies being the one responsible, he admits that he was planning to kill Grant anyway.) Norman gets away from the police but is shot in the process. Dying slowly, he uses his last hours to unmask the real killer.

Director Phil Rosen does a competent job of keeping things going, despite the fact that the film consists mostly of stagy dialogue scenes in interior locations. Rosen went on to direct Lionel Atwill in *The Sphinx* (1933) and Bela Lugosi and John Carradine in *Return of the Ape Man* (1944), both of which are considerably more charming if no less preposterous than this outing.

Screenwriter Tristram Tupper later wrote the Boris Karloff vehicle *Night Key* (1937). His scenario for *The Phantom Broadcast* relies heavily on the novelty of radio, which may well have worked for audiences in 1933. Seen today, however, it's hopelessly dated and predictable.

Ralph Forbes gives a decent performance as the lovelorn, hunchbacked impresario; he went on to portray the ill-fated Sir Hugo Baskerville in *The Hound of the Baskervilles* (1939). Gail Patrick is passable as an implicitly "immoral" woman, but 1933's *Murders in the Zoo* better served her.

Monogram distributed the film. It is a studio fondly remembered today for its Poverty Row cheapies, including a series of Bela Lugosi programmers in the 1940s. TH

Profanation
aka **Profanación**
Indo-América; b/w; length unknown; Mexico
D: Chano Urueta
Cast: Julio Villareal, Graciela Muñoz Peza, Fernando A. Rivero, Matias Santoyo, Isidro D'Olace

This was the first feature-length film directed by genre specialist Chano Urueta, whose career lasted into the 1970s and included several of wrestler/actor Blue Demon's excursions into the supernatural.

In ancient Mexico an Aztec chief wearing a cursed jade necklace dies and is buried with the object still around his neck. At some point afterward, the necklace is stolen from his grave. In 1933 Julio (Villareal), with full knowledge of the object's sinister history, purchases it for his wife Graciela (Peza). Graciela puts it on and falls for Julio's pianist brother Fernando (Rivero). She gives Fernando the necklace, which he puts on just before a piano recital during which he dies. Julio, obsessed with suspicions of having been cuckolded, becomes a cocaine addict. He digs up Fernando's body and finds the necklace adorning the corpse. He takes the body home, places it at a piano and puts on one of his brother's recordings. His wife walks in, freaks out and admits her infidelity.

Though *Profanation* was shot and presumably released in Mexico in 1933, it wasn't released in the United States until January of 1934. CW

Quest of the Perfect Woman: The Vampire of Marrakesh
Hammer; b/w; 9 min; Britain/Morocco
Credits unknown
Cast: Tom Terriss

"Is there such a thing as a perfect woman? Perhaps not where civilization has created artificial values, but in the more primitive countries where simplicity and nature rule supreme, may not such a rarity be found? And so Tom Terriss has started on a world search and, accompanied by his friend Jimmy, we find him in the barbaric city of Marrakesh in the heart of Morocco." So begins *Quest of the Perfect Woman: The Vampire of Marrakesh*, an early short film from Hammer Pictures.

Tom (Terriss) and Jimmy are searching for the perfect woman in an ancient mountain village between Morocco and the Sahara desert, a walled settlement of beautiful minarets and other striking architecture of Islamic origin. For no discernable reason, the film flashes back to an incident involving narrator Terriss' discovery of a topless woman sunbathing by a pool in Marrakesh. Her eyes (among other things) tempt him, and he follows her indoors past a bevy of beautiful babes who apparently make a living serving as decoration. By the time he catches up with the topless sunbather, she's relaxing on a divan. She gives him a drink from her chalice, which, it turns out, contains drugged wine. He duly passes out and awakens to find that his hostess is a vampire. She attacks him, he passes out again, and this time he reawakens in a road. Back to the present: Terriss professes to Jimmy that they are not going to find the perfect woman in Morocco, and off they go to look for her elsewhere.

While the film does not appear on any of Hammer's official filmographies (at the time of this writing), it seems likely that it is from the same production company that made horror a byword in British cinema from the 1950s to the 1970s. There is little question that *Quest of the Perfect Woman* is a British production; its leads are British and it contains a number of naked female breasts, something American filmmakers didn't dare display until the 1960s. It also makes sense that Hammer would have been "dipping a toe" into cinema with short films in 1933, considering that the studio's first official full-length feature, *The Public Life of Henry IX*, was shot less than two years after *Quest of the Perfect Woman*. All that said, however, some Hammer historians contend that this Hammer was not that Hammer, which wasn't registered until late the following year.

British-born Tom Terriss got his start as the lead in Herbert Blaché's 1914 horror film *The Chimes*, which was based on a story by Charles Dickens. He followed it up the same year with a performance in another Dickens adaptation, *The Mystery of Edwin Drood*, which he also wrote and directed. Although he went on to star in only a few films, including the Charlie Chaplin comedy *Sunnyside* (1919), he directed several more. By the end of the silent era, his career was pretty much over, though he lived until 1964. While he isn't credited with directing *Quest of the Perfect Woman*, it seems reasonable to conclude that he had some behind-the-scenes hand in its production. CW

Secret of the Blue Room
Universal; b/w; 65 min; U.S.
D: Kurt Neumann *S:* William Hurlbut *P:* Carl Laemmle, Jr., Henry Henigson *C:* Charles Stumar *M:* Heinz Letton

Cast: Lionel Atwill, Paul Lukas, Gloria Stuart, Edward Arnold, Onslow Stevens, William Janney, Robert Barrat, Muriel Kirkland, Russell Hopton, Elizabeth Patterson, Anders Von Haden, James Durkin

While celebrating the birthday of Irene von Helldorf (Stuart), three prospective suitors hatch a plan to vie for her hand in marriage. Taking inspiration from a story told by the girl's father (Atwill), Captain Brink (Lukas), Frank Faber (Stevens) and Thomas Brandt (Janney) agree to each spend a night in her family castle's blue room, which has been sealed for 20 years following a spate of murders there. The idea is to impress Irene, but Thomas vanishes during his overnight stay. When Frank insists on taking his turn anyway, he's killed, and Police Commissioner Forster (Arnold) is called in to investigate.

Erich Engels' *Geheimnis des blauen Zimmers* (1932) was the inspiration for this uncredited remake from Universal Pictures. The basic plot—a group of suitors putting on a show of bravery to woo a pretty girl—is nothing original, but in the hands of director Kurt Neumann and this gifted ensemble, it works pretty well. German-born Neumann (1908-1958) first entered the American film industry directing German-language versions of Hollywood pictures. He eventually established himself as a competent talent, and *Secret of the Blue Room* was his first English-language crack at the horror genre. Best remembered for directing the original version of *The Fly* (1958), he committed suicide in 1959 after the death of his beloved wife.

Blue Room doesn't offer too many surprises to the experienced mystery buff, but Neumann does a commendable job of keeping things interesting. His coverage is economical but stylish, and together with cinematographer Charles Stumar (*The Mummy*, 1932), he gives the film the look of a classic Universal horror picture. The presence of some familiar sets by Charles "Danny" Hall adds yet more to the film's creepy ambience.

The cast is excellent. Top-billed Lionel Atwill, sidelined somewhat during the picture's second half, is his usual suave and sinister self (though there's never really any doubt of his red herring status). Gloria Stuart's role doesn't compare to her work for James Whale in *The Old Dark House* (1932) and *The Invisible Man* (1933), but she makes an intelligent and photogenic heroine. Hungarian-born Paul Lukas (*The Lady Vanishes*, 1938) is likewise in fine form as the hero of the piece, bringing sophistication and gravitas to the kind of role that someone like David Manners would have been at a loss to bring to life. Edward Arnold (*The Devil and Daniel Webster*, 1941) is appropriately no-nonsense as the police commissioner, while Onslow Stevens (*House of Dracula*, 1945) makes a fine impression as the somewhat cocky and arrogant murder victim.

Ultimately, the film belongs to the "old dark house" murder mystery genre, the kind of material popularized in pictures like Paul Leni's *The Cat and the Canary* (1927). *Blue Room* isn't really a blood-and-thunder Universal horror, *per se*, but with its recycling of "Swan Lake" over the titles, the presence of Atwill acting suspiciously and its array of immaculately rendered and shadowy set designs, it certainly has the feel and texture of one. TH

The Shadow
Real Art; b/w; 71 min; Great Britain
D: George A. Cooper *S:* Terence Egan, H. Fowler Mear *P:* Julius Hagen *C:* Sydney Blythe
Cast: Henry Kendall, Elizabeth Allan, Felix Aylmer, Jeanne Stuart, Cyril Raymond, Viola Compton, John Turnbull

A blackmailer known as The Shadow is terrorizing England. His *modus operandi* is to threaten his wealthy victims with exposure of their scandalous secrets—unless, of course, they pay an exorbitant amount to keep their skeletons securely in their closets. When a police inspector (Turnbull) on The Shadow's trail suffers a fatal encounter, it's up to Scotland Yard, assisted by novelist/amateur detective Reggie Ogden (Kendall), to unmask the villain. But what does Ogden know that he isn't telling? Suspects gathered in an old mansion may find out, if The Shadow doesn't do them in first.

The Shadow has nothing to do with the famed fictional character Lamont Cranston, created by Walter P. Gibson and most famously portrayed on radio by Orson Welles. Instead, the viewer is here treated to a forgettable stroll through a forest of clichés, watching poorly drawn characters in a rambling mansion being stalked by a cloaked assassin. And while director George A. Cooper (not to be confused with the crab-faced character actor who crops up in such Hammer horror films as *Nightmare*, 1963, and *Dracula Has Risen from the Grave*, 1968) handles the material with efficiency, the film lacks atmosphere; the seasoned mystery buff will have little difficulty guessing the identity of the villain.

The cast includes Elizabeth Allan (*Mark of the Vampire*, 1935) as the damsel in distress and Felix Aylmer (*The Mummy*, 1959) as a stuffy police commissioner. The actors perform capably, but the film's air of *déjà vu* becomes suffocating. Still, it's well paced, reasonably entertaining and far from the worst in the long run of "old dark house" murder mysteries that flooded screens in the 1920s and '30s. TH

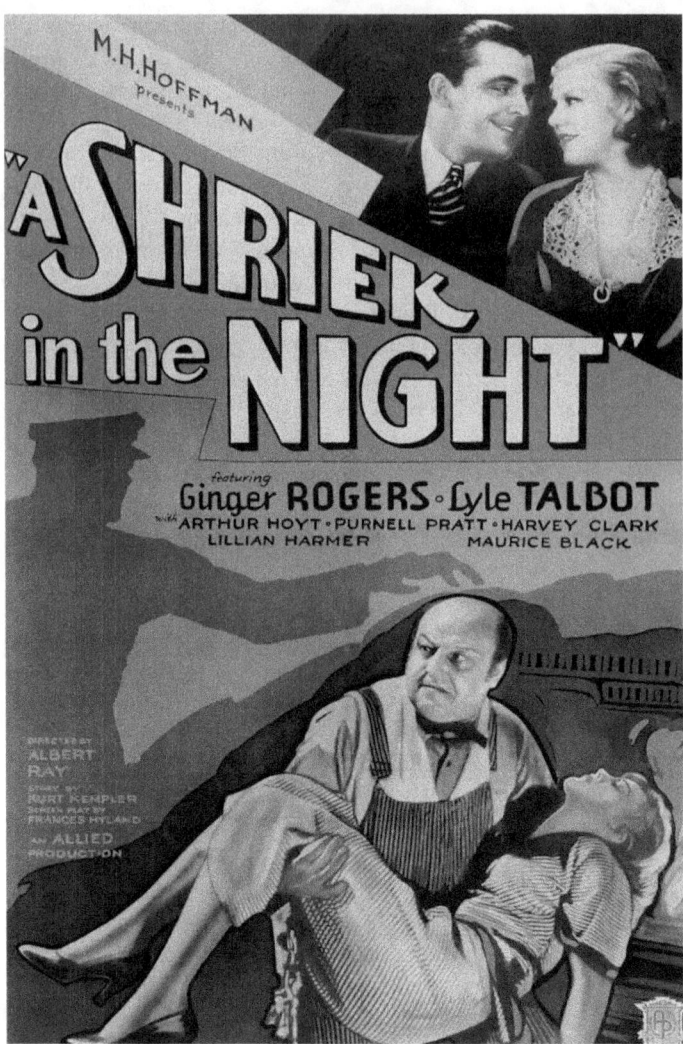

A Shot in the Dark
Real Art; b/w; 53 min; Britain

D: George Pearson *S:* H. Fowler Mear *P:* Julius Hagen *C:* Ernest Palmer

Cast: Dorothy Boyd, O.B. Clarence, Jack Hawkins, Michael Shepley, Davy Burnaby, A. Bromley Davenport, Russell Thorndike, Hugh E. Wright, Henrietta Watson, Margaret Yarde, Jack Vyvian

This dire little work from Britain's Real Art studios, based on a novel by Gerard Fairlie, featured O.B. Clarence as a minister-turned-sleuth who investigates sinister doings at a creepy mansion. The plot concerns a miserly old man (Davenport) who gathers his relatives for the reading of his will. Not surprisingly, he's murdered (during, yes, a terrible thunderstorm), but before the gramophone recording of the will can be played, Reverend Makehan (Clarence) destroys the machine with an unfortunately misdirected golf ball. The hunt then begins for the old man's murderer, whom Makehan correctly suspects is a member of the family.

This appears to have been the first film based on a work by Fairlie, most of whose novels are now forgotten. An Olympic athlete for a time, he also enjoyed a brief but moderately successful Hollywood screenwriting career. Among his works for the big screen were the scripts for *Alias Bulldog Drummond* and *Charlie Chan in Shanghai* (both 1935). Interestingly, he was the basis for the character Bulldog Drummond, and when Drummond's creator, Sapper (pseudonym for H.C. McNeile), died in 1937, Fairlie continued the series of novels on his own.

Short-lived star Dorothy Boyd took first billing over the film's hero, O.B. Clarence, despite the fact that her only previous horror appearance had been in Leslie Howard Gordon's *The House of Unrest* (1931). She'd begun film acting during the silent era but easily made the transition to sound and often starred, as here, in low-budget quota quickies, films made to meet Britain's requirement that a certain percentage of movies shown in the nation be domestically produced. Boyd saw her last film released in 1940, though she lived until 1996.

Among *A Shot in the Dark*'s minor cast was Russell Thorndike, the actor/novelist who created the adventurous Dr. Syn, a pirate and smuggler masquerading as a physician in a small coastal village in Britain. That character inspired such horror films as *Doctor Syn* (1937) and *Captain Clegg* (1962).

This *Shot* should not be confused with a 1935 horror film of the same name, that one from Chesterfield Studios. CW

A Shriek in the Night
Allied; b/w; 66 min; U.S.

D: Albert Ray *S:* Frances Hyland *P:* M.H. Hoffman, Jr. *C:* Tom Galligan, Harry Neumann *M:* Abe Meyer

Cast: Ginger Rogers, Lyle Talbot, Harvey Clark, Purnell Pratt, Lillian Harmer, Arthur Hoyt, Louise Beavers

When Mr. Harker falls to his death, Inspector Russell (Pratt) suspects that Harker's secretary, Pat Morgan (Rogers), is involved. But nosy reporter Ted Kord (Talbot) discovers that Pat is, in fact, also a reporter. When he steals her information and puts it into his column, she is furious, but he charms her into helping him uncover the killer's identity. As the killings—each preceded by a macabre calling card—continue, Pat and Ted piece together the evidence that unmasks the murderer.

Following their collaboration on the "old dark house" thriller *The Thirteenth Guest* (1931), director Albert Ray and stars Ginger Rogers and Lyle Talbot reunited for this brisk but uninspired offering. The film was Rogers' final foray into B-genre territory; that same year she rose to prominence in *Gold Diggers of 1933* and *Flying Down to Rio*.

Ray and Talbot weren't so lucky. Director Ray helmed a further handful of unremarkable titles, retiring in 1939 and dying in 1944. Talbot found screen infamy in Ed Wood's *Glen or Glenda* (1953) and *Plan 9 from Outer Space* (1959).

A Shriek in the Night is a pleasant enough time killer, though its horror elements are minor and its central mystery is fairly easy to guess. The finale in which the killer traps Rogers and tries to outwit the police (who are too slow on the uptake to realize that the killer is under their very noses) is staged with theatrical flair. Otherwise, the picture suffers dialogue-heavy exposition and wisecracking comedy relief. Thankfully, Rogers is at least permitted to play something other than the fainting airhead typical of the genre; her Pat Morgan is notably cunning and resourceful. TH

Smoking Guns
aka **Doomed to Die**
Maynard/Universal; b/w; 62 min; U.S.

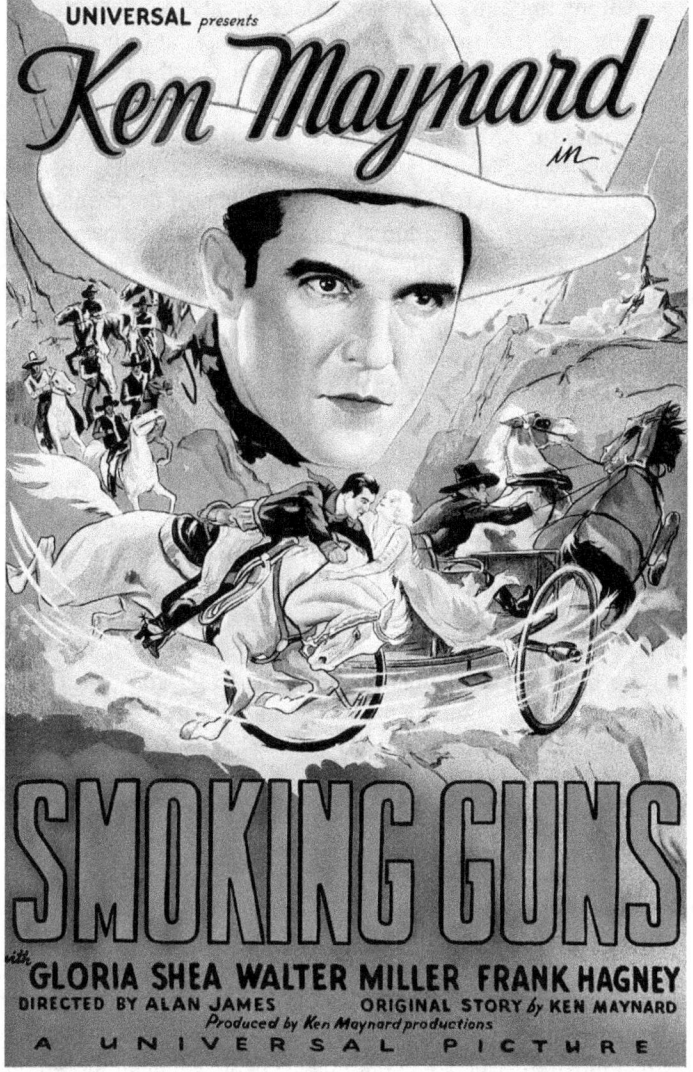

D: Alan James *Co-S:* Nate Gatzert *Co-S/P:* Ken Maynard *C:* Ted McCord

Cast: Ken Maynard, Gloria Shea, Walter Miller, Harold Goodwin, William Gould, Bob Kortman, Jack Rockwell, Edward Coxen, Slim Whitaker, Martin Turner, Etta McDaniel

Few Western stars were as obsessed with melding the oater and horror genres as Western star Ken Maynard, who was despised by Hollywood's brass even as he maintained a bevy of undiscerning fans. Universal gave Maynard complete control over his material, but his choice of odd scripts and his ability to alienate his associates created static with his boss, Carl Laemmle, Jr. After he produced and starred in the ten-gallon clunker *Smoking Guns*, Maynard was fired and forced into the wilderness of independent production. His fame and popularity was such, however, that he went on to form his own production company and hack up a few more sub-par offerings.

Smoking Guns is a throwback (an inferior one, as impossible as that might seem) to Maynard's earlier weird Westerns, which include *The Haunted Ranch*, (1926), *The Phantom City* (1928) and *Tombstone Canyon* (1932). After being framed for murder, Ken Masters (Maynard) flees to South America (thanks to some home-movie footage shot by Maynard himself, who took that particular vacation on Universal's dime). A ranger named Dick Evans (Miller), apparently unaware that his jurisdiction doesn't extend to the Southern Hemisphere, comes looking for Masters and finds him, though in the process he gets himself bitten on the leg by an alligator. Masters saves the poor guy from gangrene by cutting the leg off, but the ranger, unwilling to face the indignity of a one-legged life, shoots himself in the head. Realizing his own resemblance to the guy (unlike the film's creators, who failed to note that the two actors looked nothing alike), Masters returns to the Lone Star State, pretending to be Evans as he searches for the man who framed him. Luckily for him, none of Evans' acquaintances notices the difference.

The film doesn't really delve into horror terrain until its last reel or so, when Maynard returns to find his home a ramshackle mess now believed to be haunted. Filled with the obligatory hidden passages, the house does indeed turn out to be occupied, not by a ghost but by a madman who turns out to be Masters' insane father.

None of this makes a whole lot of sense, but fortunately it's the sort of dreck that doesn't need to. Maynard's preposterous storyline is augmented by Alan James' god-awful direction. The result is a grade-Z masterpiece. For those with a taste for ineptness run amok, *Smoking Guns* is cruddy filmmaking at its best … er, worst … er, best! CW

The Son of Kong
aka **Son of Kong**
RKO; b/w; 70 min; U.S.

D/Co-P: Ernest B. Schoedsack *S:* Ruth Rose *Co-P:* Merian C. Cooper *C:* Eddie Linden, J.O. Taylor, Vernon Walker *M:* Max Steiner *FX:* Willis O'Brien, Harry Redmund, Jr., Juan Larringa

Cast: Robert Armstrong, Helen Mack, Frank Reicher, John Marston, Victor Wong, Ed Brady, Noble Johnson, Clarence Wilson, Lee Kohlmar, Steve Clemente

Even before the completion of their epic *King Kong* (1933), producer Merian C. Cooper and director Ernest B. Schoedsack had begun pre-production for this sequel entitled *The Son of Kong*. It picks up immediately where its predecessor left off but with an emphasis on romance, melodrama, action and humor rather than horror; its status as a horror film is purely a matter of guilt by association with its more famous and much tenser predecessor.

Showman Carl Denham (Armstrong) is having problems: Giant ape Kong's assault on New York City—which occurred during the climax of the previous film—has resulted in numerous lawsuits aimed in Denham's direction. He skips town and heads for the East Indies, seeking redemption in the possibility that another great discovery will prompt all to be forgiven. Unfortunately, the ship on which he's traveling is mutinied by a motley crew headed by duplicitous companion Nils Helstrom (Marston), the man who had originally sold Denham the map of Skull Island. They set the producer adrift in a tiny row boat, along with a beautiful stowaway (Mack) whose father has been murdered by Helstrom, the ship's captain (Reicher) and its Chinese cook (Wong). But after flexing muscles he doesn't have, Helstrom is likewise thrown overboard, to be rescued by the very group he just betrayed. They make their way to Skull Island and there encounter a large albino gorilla, the apparent offspring of the original Kong. Unlike his father, however, Little Kong is

Robert Armstrong and Helen Mack nurse a wounded Baby Kong in *Son of Kong*.

friendly; he proves, in fact, to be the perfect ally for the group as they do battle with the island's prehistoric creatures.

The second film's much smaller budget (about one-third that of its predecessor) necessitated some cutbacks. *Son* features far fewer characters, greatly reduced special effects and a much shorter running time than did *King Kong*. The head brass at RKO also demanded that the film be finished in time for a Christmas 1933 release, resulting in a compressed shooting schedule and far less time to get the complicated and time-consuming effects completed. All of this was much to Cooper's chagrin. And as if to add insult to injury, during the film's shoot, effects man Willis O'Brien's estranged wife shot and killed their two sons before shooting herself (she survived and lived her life out in a hospital where, a couple of years later, she died from cancer and a tuberculosis infection). The same year his children were murdered, O'Brien (called Obie by his friends) dated another woman who ended her life by jumping from the top of a hotel after discovering she also had cancer.

The Son of Kong's budget constraints aren't entirely detrimental to the film, however; the lowered resources prompted a greater focus on character development, particularly for Denham and his orphaned love interest (called Helene in the film but Hilda in the opening credits). The resulting product emphasizes human interaction over dinosaur action. Thus actors—not FX—are the film's primary stars, with Helen Mack (*She*, 1935) stealing the show as the melancholic Helene, whose reaction to the loss of her father and subsequent co-dependence on the steely but kind-hearted Denham pave the way for the film's disheartening climax.

None of this is to say that Armstrong (*The Most Dangerous Game*, 1932) isn't good; he's terrific, in fact, along with the rest of the cast. John Marston (*The Mayor of Hell*, 1933) is wonderfully seedy as the villainous Helstrom, leaving one to wonder why he was so often relegated to uncredited bit parts during his 18-year career. Frank Reicher (*The Mummy's Ghost*, 1944) is perfectly controlled as the stoic captain, and Victor Wong (*Hair-Trigger Casey*, 1936) is his usual likeable self, playing the stereotypical Asian cook.

Among the film's more impressive effects sequences is one involving a Styracosaurus, a type of Ceratopsian (a horned dinosaur from the Cretaceous period) that chases the captain, the cook and the villain into a cave. The model for the animal had been created for *King Kong* and may even have appeared in a scene that was eventually jettisoned. In any case, it's utilized here to perfect effect. The stop-motion model of the prehistoric reptile is fairly accurate, though in real life it would have been about six feet tall at the hips and about 18 feet in length from its snout to the tip of its tail; it's also given the correct number of spikes on its frill, six in all, and a single nose horn. And while the barbed dinosaur was in real life a plant eater, it would likely have had no problem in defending itself had it felt threatened, as appears to be the case here when Captain Englehorn shoots at it while it grazes.

A regrettable sequence involving a cave bear, more correctly called Ursus spelaeus, follows. Cave bears became extinct before the end of the last ice age, but not before causing much grief to Neanderthals and early Homo sapiens. They grew slightly larger than the largest bears known today, with a build similar to the modern brown bear (their nearest relative). The film has the beast chase Denham and Helene to the top of a rocky ledge before being subdued by the smaller Little Kong. From this point on, the effects take on a rushed appearance, except for when Little Kong is onscreen.

The day after the battle with the cave bear, a Nothosaurus, a largely sea-dwelling reptile that resembled a smaller and less cumbersome Sauropod, or long-necked dinosaur, attacks Little Kong. Nothosaurs were not dinosaurs, though they lived during the first period in dinosaur evolution, the Triassic. Here, the Nothosaurus has Sauropod-like features, making it resemble an awkward cross between an Apatosaurus and a dragon. It is also much too large; in real life, the average Nothosaurus was about 13 feet in length. Some paleontologists believe that animals akin to Nothosaurus may have been the ancestors of the plesiosaurs.

The final prehistoric animal given any kind of screen time at all is a Cretaceous-period Elasmosaurus, a long-necked, sea-

Baby Kong battles a dragon-like sauropod in *Son of Kong*.

the film, including Kong historian Ray Morton, tend to use the name Kiko when referring to the "little guy."

Son of Kong was by no means a bomb, but it was hardly the blockbuster that its ambitious and classic parent film was. Today it's relatively forgotten, lost in the shadow of its groundbreaking precursor. Yet, despite its issues, it has plenty to offer discerning viewers and is an interesting exercise in modern-day mythological storytelling. CW

The Sphinx

Monogram; b/w; 63 min; U.S.

D: Phil Rosen, Wilfred Lucas (uncredited) *S:* Albert DeMond *P:* Albert S. (Sid) Rogell *C:* Gilbert Warrenton *M:* Abe Meyer

Cast: Lionel Atwill, Sheila Terry, Theodore Newton, Paul Hurst, Luis Alberini, Robert Ellis, Lucien Prival, Lillian Leighton, Paul Fix

Jerome Breen (Atwill) is accused of strangling several stockbrokers. The only snag is that Breen is a deaf mute, and the murderer was heard speaking during the crimes. Intrepid reporter Jack Burton (Newton) is convinced that Breen is faking his disability and sets about trying to outwit him. Breen is acquitted, and when he begins romancing Burton's girlfriend Jerry Crane (Terry), Burton fears for her life.

dwelling plesiosaur believed by many to be the inspiration for the Loch Ness Monster sightings. An Elasmosaurus had also been present in the original *King Kong* and was one of the few creatures in that film to be presented incorrectly. Here, all the audience sees of the creature is its long neck, head and upper back, all of which appear to be much more accurate than last time around, though the neck is a bit too thick and not quite long enough (and in reality would not have been as bendable as shown here).

The "Brontosaurus" from *King Kong* also makes a very brief appearance, raising its head out of the water during the climactic flooding and disintegration of Skull Island.

As noted above, the film's budget was not the only reason for the poor quality of some of the special effects sequences. In addition to the personal tragedies he was facing, Willis O'Brien also found himself in conflict with Cooper and Schoedsack, who wanted more creative control over the effects. (This may explain why the Nothosaurus and Elasmosaurus look as much like fantastical beasts—such as dragons and sea serpents—as they do the very real animals on which they were based.) As O'Brien's interest in the project began to wane, so too did his time on set; he also found an ingenious way to get the last laugh on his bosses. During the scene in which Denham and Helene bandage Little Kong's injured middle finger, the albino gorilla quite plainly flips off the camera—and, by extension, Cooper and Schoedsack.

Though the film's script identified the son of Kong by name as Kiko (a shortened form of <u>Ki</u>ng <u>Ko</u>ng), the characters in the film refer to him as Little Kong, a ploy duplicated by RKO's publicity department at the time. However, modern-day fans of

Lionel Atwill is something of a rarity among horror stars. He embraced his bad-guy typecasting without complaint, and while many of the films in which he appears aren't worthy of him, he never seems to have considered himself superior to the material. Unlike virtually any other horror actor, there are no examples of him walking through a role out of disinterest or hamming it up to show his contempt. Thus, as a rule of thumb, it's safe to assume that if Atwill is involved in a picture—be it big or small, in a role flashy or subdued—*he* at least will be worth watching.

This generalization certainly applies to *The Sphinx*, a cheapie murder mystery produced by Poverty Row outfit Monogram Pictures. (Monogram later cast the likes of Bela Lugosi, John Carradine and George Zucco, as well as Atwill, in a slew of grade-Z mad scientist schlock pieces; this is one of their earlier forays into the genre.) And while it's not technically a horror film, Atwill's leering performance warrants its inclusion in any book dedicated to the genre.

The British thespian clearly relishes playing a character whom everybody knows to be guilty yet who has an unshakable alibi. The role requires him to remain mute for much of the running time—the fact that the actor clearly didn't know sign language is glossed over by camera angle trickery—but his presence dominates the proceedings anyway.

Theodore Newton is the film's Achilles heel as the inevitable wisecracking, tough-guy reporter. He goes beyond a mere lack of charisma into the realm of annoyance, inadvertently making it all the more credible that the never-speaking Breen would too easily woo the pretty heroine (Sheila Terry in a competent performance) from him.

The film's title is reporter Burton's nickname for the murderer; the word "Sphinx" is derived from the Greek word for "strangle," something both the murderer and the mythical monster have done to their victims. While it seems a bit of a stretch that Newton's dullard character would be literate enough to make that particular connection, the producers were no doubt going for a catchy title.

And, to be fair, once the film gets past the cutesy interplay between Newton and Terry, it settles down to business in a reasonably efficient manner. Phil Rosen's direction is unimaginative but competent; he later directed one of Monogram's most notorious horror pictures, *The Return of the Ape Man* (1944), which some sources claim Wilfred Lucas, bit part character actor and part-time director, had a hand in as well.

Among the nondescript supporting cast, two most familiar faces stick out: Lucien Prival, cast as Atwill's interpreter, played a snooty butler in James Whale's *The Bride of Frankenstein* (1935). Paul Fix, as one of Atwill's victims, later specialized in cowboy and hoodlum roles, as well as appeared in such horror fare as Universal's *Black Friday* (1940). TH

Strange People

Chesterfield; b/w; 64 min; U.S.

D: Richard Thorpe *S:* Jack Townley *P:* George R. Batcheller *C:* M.A. Anderson *M:* Abe Meyer

Cast: Hale Hamilton, John Darrow, Gloria Shea, Wilfred Lucas, Lew Kelly, Michael Visaroff, Jane Keckley, Jack Pennick, Mary Foy, Walter Brennan, Frank LaRue, Stanley Blystone, J. Frank Glendon

Attorney J.E. Burton (Hamilton) summons the 12 jurors responsible for an innocent man's execution to a creaky old mansion. There he attempts to illustrate the flaws of the judicial system by arranging a fake murder, but things get sticky when the intended "victim" turns up—and he's really dead!

This low-budget item from Chesterfield gets a boost by utilizing Charles "Danny" Hall's impressive sets from James Whale's masterful *The Old Dark House* (1932). That coup gives the film an A-budget gloss that, though the story is hackneyed and unbelievable, at least makes it look good.

Director Richard Thorpe was still a few years away from his later success at MGM, where he directed *Night Must Fall* (1937), among other notable titles. Here he keeps the third-rate material moving at a good clip, and the end result is livelier than the typical creepy murder mystery of the period.

The supporting cast includes Walter Brennan, who revisited Universal's Hollywood studios the following year for a bit part in Whale's *The Invisible Man* (1933). His career caught fire a few years down the line, and before it was over he had netted three Oscars for best supporting actor. Michael Visaroff is also on hand to play the mysterious caretaker; horror buffs will remember him as the wide-eyed innkeeper at the beginning of Tod Browning's *Dracula* (1931). TH

Sucker Money
Kent/Progressive; b/w; 59 min; U.S.

D: Melville Shyer, Dorothy Reid (aka Dorothy Davenport) *S/P:* Willis Kent *C:* James Diamond

Cast: Mischa Auer, Phyllis Barrington, Earl McCarthy, Ralph Lewis, Fletcher Norton, Mae Busch, Mona Lisa, Al Bridge, J. Frank Glendon, Anita Faye, Kit Guard, Harry Todd

Billed as "an exposé of the PSYCHIC RACKET: a True Life Photoplay," *Sucker Money* tells the tale of a newspaper reporter, Jimmy Reeves (McCarthy, billed here as McCarty), who is assigned the job of exposing a phony spiritualist who's bilking rich people out of their money. Reeves answers a newspaper ad placed by Swami Yomurda (Auer) seeking the services of an actor. In the process, he meets the beautiful Clare Walton (Lewis), whose banker father is smitten with the swami's purported abilities. The reporter lands the position, which entails pretending to be a dead relative of one of Yomurda's clients. This plants Reeves smack dab in the middle of the swami's despicable doings, most of which center on relieving Walton of his savings. When the swami gets wind of what's going on with Reeves, he takes the journalist captive and hypnotizes Clare into helping him procure another $20,000 of her father's money.

Chock full of séances, mesmerism and murder, *Sucker Money* has all the right ingredients but none of the atmosphere needed for a horror film. It does itself in by revealing too much too early, leaving no mystery to be solved. The impoverished sets (the massive television-set device that Yomurda uses to deceive his victims is sublimely ridiculous) and lackadaisical direction also fall flat, leaving only the cast's surprisingly good performances to give the picture what little panache it has.

Ralph Lewis (1872-1937), who portrays banker John Walton, began his acting career on the stage sometime around the turn of the 20th century. He quickly graduated to Broadway and from there was lured to the big screen by Reliance, a producer of mostly dramatic short films. After being "discovered" by D.W. Griffith, Lewis was cast in important roles in *The Avenging Conscience, or: Thou Shalt Not Kill* and *The Birth of a Nation* (both 1914), and *Intolerance: Love's Struggle Through the Ages* (1916). His career ended at age 65, Thanksgiving 1937; he was struck and killed by a car driven by mogul Jack Warner's personal chauffeur. Lewis' other horror films include *Dante's Inferno* (1924), *The Death Kiss* (1932) and *Mystery Liner* (1934).

Lewis wasn't the only member of *Sucker Money*'s cast to meet a tragic demise. Indiana-born Earl McCarthy, whose career had also begun in the silent era, died the same year *Sucker Money* was produced, in 1933, at the young age of 26. A former dancer, he was struck down by a massive heart attack. *Sucker Money* appears to have been his only horror-oriented film.

Phyllis Barrington's short-lived career, on the other hand, was steeped in low-budget horror, including *Law of the Tongs* (1931), *Sinister Hands* (1932) and *The Murder in the Museum* (1934). And lead villain Mischa Auer had a long career mostly playing sinister swami/foreigner types. CW

Supernatural
Paramount; b/w; 64 min; U.S.

D: Victor Halperin *S:* Garnett Weston, Harvey Thew, Brian Marlow, Sidney Salkow *P:* Edward Halperin *C:* Arthur Martinelli

Soon to be executed Ruth (Vivienne Osborne) is protected by Dr. Houston (H.B. Warner) as Roma (Carole Lombard) and Grant (Randolph Scott) look on in *Supernatural*.

Cast: Carole Lombard, Allan Dinehart, Vivienne Osborne, Randolph Scott, H.B. Warner, Beryl Mercer, William Farnum, Willard Robertson, George Burr MacAnnan, Lyman Williams

Notorious strangler Ruth Rogen (Osborne) is sentenced to die in the electric chair for murdering three of her lovers. Dr. Houston (Warner) believes that when a killer is put to death, any copycat killings thereafter are the work of the executed person's spirit in a second person's body. Houston goes to Ruth and asks her if he can have her body after death to test his theory. Though reluctant at first, the prison warden (Robertson) convinces her that it might just present her with an opportunity to live again. Meanwhile, Roma Courtney's (Lombard) brother John (Williams) dies, leaving her a fortune. She receives a missive from a phony spiritualist named Paul Bavian, who claims to have a beyond-the-grave message from John. Unknown to Roma, Bavian is a murderer who kills with a poison ring; he was also once in cahoots with the late Ruth Rogen, though he betrayed her to the police to save his own skin.

Roma agrees to a séance conducted by Bavian, and her boyfriend Grant Wilson (Scott) comes along. During the séance, John's "ghost" (in reality a death mask created by Bavian) accuses Nick Hammond (Farnum), the estate manager, of murdering him and trying to steal the estate. Grant ends the proceedings; afterwards he and Roma walk in on Dr. Houston's experiment on the body of Ruth Rogen. Ruth's spirit tries and fails to enter Roma's body, but a second séance gives her another shot. This time she takes control of Roma, after which she exacts a terrible vengeance on her betrayer.

In the wake of the success of *White Zombie* (1932), the Halperin Brothers were presented an opportunity to enter the big leagues. They were contacted by Paramount, who, prompted by Universal's success with *Dracula* and *Frankenstein* (1931), wanted to bolster their efforts in the lucrative horror market (having already scored one hit with *Island of Lost Souls*, 1932). The studio offered the brothers the use of an up-and-coming leading lady, one Carole Lombard. Lombard, who'd gotten her

A possessed Carole Lombard goes after her lover, Randolph Scott, in *Supernatural*.

start in silent pictures, was a hot property, though the consensus among producers was that she was only as good as her leading men, an opinion that would change when Howard Hawks cast her in 1934's *Twentieth Century*. But while it was indeed a casting coup for the Halperins, Lombard's terrific performance is simply not enough to completely redeem a so-so script and mediocre direction. The film's central conceit had been done to death during the silent era, and Lombard was viewed by audiences of the time as too sweet and charming to be taken seriously in such a dark, complex and compelling role.

Supernatural has gone down in history as something of an artistic bust, a shoddy follow-up to a surreal horror masterpiece of the early talkie era. But while it's true that *White Zombie* is a much better and more fluid picture—one that *Supernatural* looks nothing like—that doesn't make the latter film a total dud. No, *Supernatural* isn't what one would expect from the Halperins, but it's exactly what one would expect from Paramount. Glossiness and high production values abound, and it is an entertaining if ultimately forgettable diversion, as long as one doesn't dive into it expecting *White Zombie II*.

The film's lack of success ensured that the Halperins were cast from the big leagues they'd barely broke into; they remained jobless for the next three years. In 1936 they put together the ultra-low-budget *I Conquer the Sea*, and when that film also failed to make money, they made a beeline back to the subject matter for which they were known. But *Revolt of the Zombies* (1936) likewise failed to impress much of anyone, and by the early 1940s both brothers had left the industry for good.

One of the film's most interesting sequences is its opening credits, which present lightning flashes superimposed over a stormy sea, with the cherubic singing of holy throngs in the background. Quotes from holy men of various religious persuasions are offered: "Treat all supernatural beings with respect … but keep aloof from them!" (Confucius) "We will bring forth the dead from their graves." (Mohammed) And finally, "… and He gave His 12 disciples power against unclean spirits to cast them out …" (Matthew) It's an engaging start, even if the film that follows doesn't really follow through on its promise.

Starring opposite Carole Lombard was Randolph Scott, who became one of Hollywood's most sought-after leading men after paying his dues in such minor horror thrillers as *Murders in the Zoo* (1933) and *Rocky Mountain Mystery* (1935). CW

The Thirteenth Candle
Warner/First National; b/w; 68 min; Great Britain
 D: John Daumery *S:* Brock Williams *P:* Irving Asher *C:* Basil Emmott
 Cast: Isobel Elsom, Arthur Maude, Gibb McLaughlin, Louis Heyward, Louis Goodrich, D.A. Clarke-Smith, Winifred Oughton, Claude Fleming, Charles Childerstone, Hilliard Vox

A dinner party hits the skids when the host turns up dead. Various guests and relatives fall under suspicion before the real culprit is finally revealed.

This B-mystery has enough Gothic atmosphere to qualify as horror. Like the various versions of *The Cat and the Canary* (1927) and *Secret of the Blue Room* (1933), it pits a variety of unsavory characters against one another in a creepy mansion. It's all pretty old hat, and the film has more or less faded from view, though it is not regarded as a lost title.

Director John (nee Jean) Daumery was born in Belgium, and he began his film career in 1930, directing French-language versions of American films for First National. He eventually branched into English-language fare, and he made his way to the U.K. in 1932. He died in 1934 at the far-too-young age of 35.

Leading lady Isobel Elsom specialized in haughty high society snobbery. She spent much of the latter part of her career doing guest bits on television, but she also scored such film credits as the remake of *Love from a Stranger* (1947), Alfred Hitchcock's minor courtroom drama *The Paradine Case* (1947) and George Cukor's Oscar-winning *My Fair Lady* (1964).

The Thirteenth Candle also contains an early appearance from Louis Hayward, later to become a popular leading man in such fare as James Whale's *The Man in the Iron Mask* (1939) and Fritz Lang's *House by the River* (1950); he also racked up a few horror appearances, including the lead in *The Son of Dr. Jekyll* and a smaller part in *Terror in the Wax Museum* (1973). TH

Tomorrow at Seven
Jefferson; b/w; 61 min; U.S.
 D: Ray Enright *S:* Ralph Spence *P:* Joseph I. Schnitzer, Samuel Zierler *C:* Charles Schoenbaum *M:* David Broekman
 Cast: Chester Morris, Vivian Osborne, Frank McHugh, Allen Jenkins, Henry Stephenson, Grant Mitchell, Charles Middleton, Oscar Apfel, Virginia Howell, Cornelius Keefe, Edward LeSaint, Gus Robinson

Mystery novelist Neil Broderick (Morris) puts his expertise to the test by investigating a killer known as The Black Ace, whose perverse *modus operandi* is to alert his victims beforehand by sending each an Ace of Spades marked with the exact time of his or her impending death. Broderick is convinced he can uncover the killer's identity, amassing in the process material for a new best seller.

A damsel (Vivienne Osborne) about to be in distress in *Tomorrow at Seven*.

The set-up is far from original—a cocky writer tries to best the police—but *Tomorrow at Seven* emerges as a pleasant, unpretentious time killer. It benefits from a fine cast, including Chester Morris (*The Bat Whispers*, 1930) as the smarmy amateur detective and Vivienne Osborne (*The Phantom Broadcast*, 1933) as a spunky and determined heroine. Henry Stephenson (*The Adventures of Sherlock Holmes*, 1939) lends solid support as the killer's latest potential target.

Despite all that, the comic stylings of Frank McHugh (*Mystery of the Wax Museum*, 1933) and Allen Jenkins (*Sh! The Octopus*, 1937) will put off many contemporary viewers. The two dominate too many scenes as a pair of bumbling policemen trying to solve the mystery, and while they manage an amusing moment here and there, there's little doubt that their constant mugging detracts from the atmosphere. (Interestingly, there seems to be something of a homosexual relationship between the two, though some might argue that this is a contemporary reading of the film's subtext.)

Screenwriter Ralph Spence is best remembered for his stage hit *The Gorilla*, which was adapted officially and unofficially on numerous occasions, including as *The Gorilla* (1927, 1930, and 1939) and the aforementioned *Sh! The Octopus*.

Director Ray Enright got his start writing material for Mack Sennett and spent most of his directorial career helming comedies. TH

Trick for Trick
Fox; b/w; 67 (69) min; U.S.

D: Hamilton McFadden *S:* Howard J. Green *C:* L.W. O'Connell *M:* Samuel Kaylin *FX:* William Cameron Menzies

Cast: Ralph Morgan, Victor Jory, Sally Blane, Tom Dugan, Luis Alberni, Edward Van Sloan, Clifford Jones, James Burtis, Adrian Morris, Willard Robertson, Herbert Bunston

At once a murder mystery, action adventure and horror film, the obscure *Trick for Trick* was Fox's attempt at recreating the success of *Chandu the Magician* (1932) on an even lower budget. William Cameron Menzies, who co-directed *Chandu*, does the effects work here, guiding rival magicians Azrah (Morgan) and La Tour (Jory) as they battle it out with supernatural abandonment. While occasionally fun to watch, any threat of genuine tension is strangled at birth by that bane of '30s horror/suspense cinema, cornball comedy relief.

Trick begins with the discovery that the recent drowning death of Azrah's assistant Evelyn Maxwell (never seen in the film) was, in fact, a murder. He sets his sights on tracking down the culprit (whose identity is blazingly apparent to everyone but the cast), and there's a lot of—at times impressive—magical mayhem on tap as he pursues the obvious. Everything but the kitchen sink is thrown at the viewer, including a murderous Chinaman, a dwarf and a psychic. To seal the deal, for horror fans at least, Edward Van Sloan shows up as Mr. Russell, an attendee at a séance.

The play on which the film is based was a dud, but Fox, having purchased the rights before it opened, went ahead with the film adaptation, which received mostly negative attention and was withdrawn shortly after release. The film has never surfaced on home video, though at least one print is known to be extant.

Director Hamilton McFadden (1901-1977) is more famous for his Charlie Chan productions—*The Black Camel* and *Charlie Chan Carries On* (both 1931), *Charlie Chan's Greatest Case* (1933) and part of *Charlie Chan in Paris* (1935). As an actor, McFadden had parts in *Charlie Chan in Reno* (1939) and *Charlie Chan in Rio* (1941), not to mention a small, uncredited role in the Michael Shayne mystery, *Michael Shayne: Private Detective* (1940). CW

The Vampire Bat
aka **Blood Sucker**; **Forced to Sin**
Majestic; b/w; 62 min; U.S.

D: Frank R. Strayer *S:* Edward T. Lowe, Jr. *P:* Phil Goldstone, Larry Darmour *C:* Ira Moran *M:* Mischa Bakaleinikoff, Charles Dunworth

Cast: Lionel Atwill, Fay Wray, Melvyn Douglas, Maude Eburn, Dwight Frye, Robert Frazer, George E. Stone, Rita Car-

Fay Wray is menaced by Lionel Atwill once again in *The Vampire Bat*.

lyle, Lionel Belmore, William V. Mong, Stella Adams, Harrison Greene

In the sleepy German village of Kleinschloss, a string of murders has the locals terrified. Inspector Karl Brettschneider (Douglas) rejects village gossip concerning vampires, despite the fang marks on the throats of the victims and the fact that they all have been drained of blood. Working with Dr. von Niemann (Atwill), Karl is determined to prove that the problem is not supernatural. Meanwhile, the villagers become convinced that the slow-witted Herman (Frye) is the one responsible.

Like *White Zombie* (1932), this independent, low-budget production utilized already-existing sets at Universal Studios. The combination of these atmospheric settings by Charles "Danny" Hall with the moody cinematography by Ira Moran gives *The Vampire Bat* atmosphere to spare. This is an especially good thing as one encounters the jumbled screenplay, written by Edward T. Lowe, Jr. (Interestingly, Lowe wound up his career working with Universal, where he wrote such pictures as *Sherlock Holmes and the Secret Weapon*, 1942, and the last two serious entries in the initial series of *Dracula*, *Frankenstein* and *Wolf Man* pictures: *House of Frankenstein*, 1944, and *House of Dracula*, 1945.) Lowe's script for *Vampire* is structured as something of a mystery, though it's far too predictable to generate much suspense. And the revelation of Dr. von Niemann's role in the murders is even further diluted by the ludicrous science-fiction appearance of a sponge-like creature, representing the mad doctor's creation of life.

Needless to say, the plot doesn't bear close scrutiny; it is, however, not without its pleasures for horror aficionados. Lionel Atwill is at his shifty best as von Niemann. And while the script works hard to fool the viewer with a depiction of the character as a beloved humanitarian, there's never any doubt that he's up to no good. Part of the fun in a film of this nature is in watching a magnetic presence like Atwill sink his teeth into the absurd material. The finale, in which he reveals his crazy plan, requires him to spout clichéd gibberish ("I have lifted the veil!"), though he makes it work.

As in Warner's *Doctor X* (1932) and *The Mystery of the Wax Museum* (1933), Atwill is again paired with Fay Wray, a horror/fantasy icon known for her role in *King Kong* (1933). She isn't required to do much this time out, but she's typically fresh and down-to-earth in her portrayal.

The distinguished Melvyn Douglas, making his second horror/suspense appearance within the space of a year (following James Whale's superior *The Old Dark House*, 1932), plays her love interest. Douglas was at this point on his way to becoming a major star. He eventually developed into one of the most dependable and acclaimed elderly character actors in the business—though he would mostly steer clear of horror and suspense films until Roman Polanski's darkly comedic and disturbing *The Tenant* (1976). In *Vampire Bat*, he does a fine job as an eccentric, unlikeable character—too dense to see the truth, yet too arrogant to admit that he is on the wrong track.

Robert Frazer as Atwill's devoted lab assistant is far less melodramatic here than he was in *White Zombie*, while Dwight Frye does a rather touching variation of his portrayal as Renfield in *Dracula* (1931) as the bat-loving simpleton Herman. The Universal feel is further enhanced by the presence of Lionel Belmore, familiar to classic horror buffs for his roles in *Frankenstein* (1931), *Son of Frankenstein* (1939) and *Ghost of Frankenstein* (1942).

Director Frank R. Strayer employs some surprisingly mobile camerawork, including some crane shots that show off the sets, but the finale is clumsy and abrupt. His subsequent credits would include *The Ghost Walks* (1934) and *Condemned to Live* (1935), but he would find his greatest success directing numerous films in Columbia's *Blondie and Dagwood* franchise. TH

Voodo
Lesser; b/w; 36 min; U.S.
    D/Co-P: Faustin Wirkus *Co-P:* Sol Lesser
    Cast: unknown

This short documentary focuses on the exploits of Faustin Wirkus, a U.S. Marine Corps sergeant who was stationed in Haiti in 1925. While there, Wirkus befriended the natives and became familiar with their culture as well as their religion of voodoo. The natives grew so fond of him that they named him King Faustin I and made him an honorary ruler. He oversaw the island for three years but eventually grew nostalgic for his old life and returned to civilization.

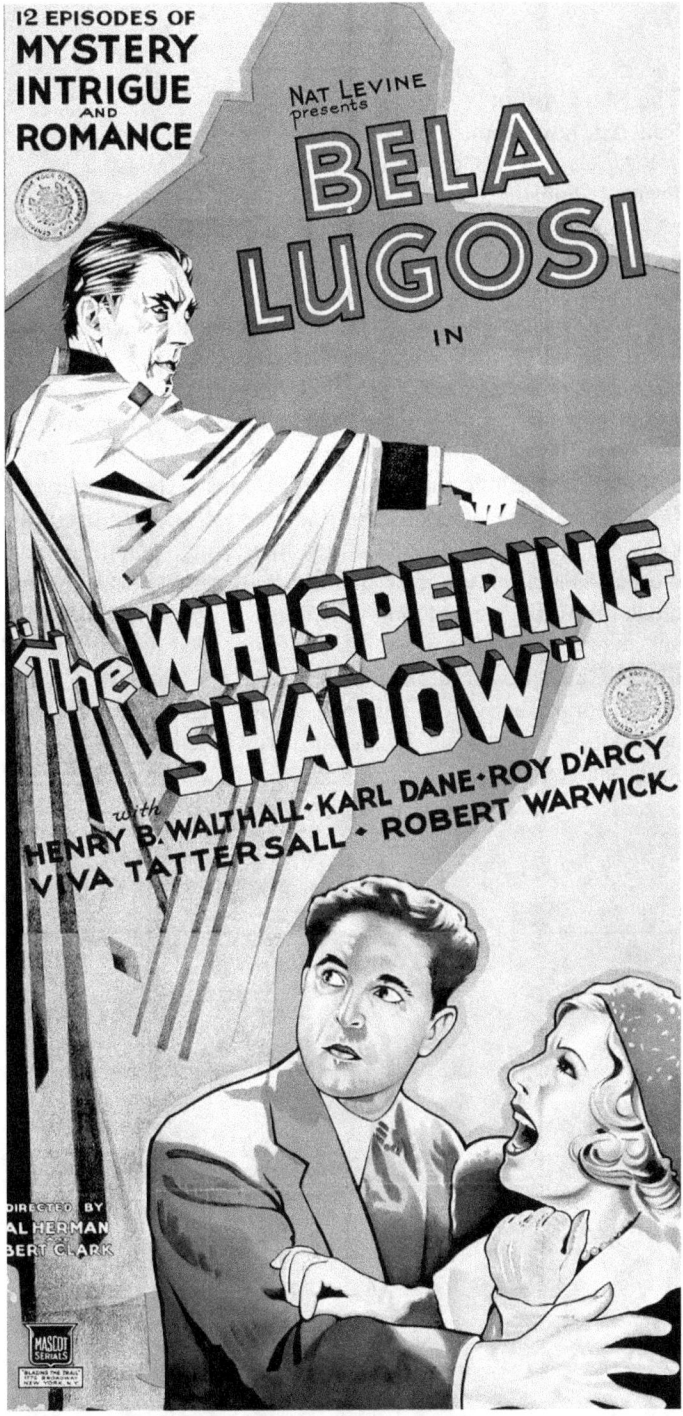

Recognizing that his adventures were unusual, Wirkus decided to make a few bucks from them with this film. The end result is only horror by association, but it fit into the burgeoning interest in voodoo and the living dead prompted by the success of the independent horror hit *White Zombie* (1933). Wirkus co-produced *Voodo* and, for all intents and purposes, directed it as well. Co-producer Sol Lesser, who also released the picture, had a hand in the release of another early horror-ish documentary, *Amazon Head Hunters* (1932).

Additional credits for *Voodo* are difficult to find. TH

The Whispering Shadow
Mascot; b/w; 12 chapters (224 min); U.S.
  Co-D/Co-S: Colbert Clark, Albert Herman *Co-S:* Wyndham Gittens, Norman S. Hall, George Morgan, Barney A. Sarecky *P:* Nat Levine *C:* Edgar Lyons, Ernest Miller *M:* Lee Zahler
  Cast: Bela Lugosi, Viva Tattersall, Malcolm McGregor, George J. Lewis, Henry B. Walthall, Robert Warwick, Ethel Clayton, Roy D'Arcy, Karl Dane, Lloyd Whitlock, Bob Kortman, Lafe McKee

Jack Forster (McGregor) and Detective Robert Raymond (Warwick) team up to bring down a criminal mastermind known only as The Whispering Shadow. The mysterious evildoer shows up at the damnedest times, using radio and television waves to kill those who cross him. A number of people are among the suspects, including one Professor Strang (Lugosi), the curator of a creepy wax museum.

The Whispering Shadow is chiefly of note as Bela Lugosi's first appearance in a serial. Little is required of him here other than skulking about and looking mysterious, and the fact that his thinly drawn character steals this show is telling. He went on to appear in *The Return of Chandu* (1934) and *The Phantom Creeps* (1939), and while neither of those efforts is exactly good, *The Whispering Shadow* is far, far worse. Bad comedic relief, sped-up fight scenes and obvious stunt doubles rule *Shadow*'s day, and the performances of Lugosi's co-stars run the gamut from the awful to the really awful.

Leading man Malcolm McGregor's work stands out, though only barely, as the worst. His wooden delivery provides some "so bad it's good" amusement, but not nearly enough to carry 12 (rather lengthy) episodes. His portrayal of the intrepid Jack Forster, in fact, makes one realize just how personable somebody like David Manners (the resident 'stiff' at Universal who went up against Lugosi in *Dracula*, 1931, and *The Black Cat*, 1934) really was.

Directors Colbert Clark and Albert Herman made a career out of undistinguished fare like this, and the cheapjack production values afforded by production company Mascot are on a par with everything else in this enterprise. Diehard serial or Lugosi buffs will want to check it out, no doubt, but others would do well to steer clear. TH

1934

The Black Abbot
Real Art; b/w; 56 min; Great Britain

D: George A. Cooper *S:* Terence Egan *P:* Julius Hagen *C:* Ernest Palmer

Cast: John Stuart, Judy Kelly, Edgar Norfolk, Richard Cooper, Drusilla Wills, Farren Soutar, Cyril Smith, Davina Craig, Earl Grey, Ben Welden, John Turnbull

The sinister Black Abbot allegedly haunts a spooky old house adjoining an abandoned monastery. A gang of thieves takes advantage of the tall tale by kidnapping the house's new owner in the hopes of extorting some quick money from him.

The title and some elements of the plot seem lifted from a 1926 Edgar Wallace novel of the same name, but in fact *The Black Abbot* was adapted from *The Grange Mystery* by little-known pulp author Philip Godfrey. Interestingly, Godfrey also worked as a character actor, and his credits in that capacity include the Wallace adaptation *The Return of the Frog* (1938). In any event, this *Abbot* is one of many so-called haunted house films of the period wherein crooks use rumors of ghosts to mask their criminal activities. This plot device was hackneyed well before this film came along, and the script here is as stale as any in the subgenre.

Director George A. Cooper helmed a number of unremarkable programmers between 1921 and 1941; he also directed the "old dark house" chiller *The Shadow* (1933). Scottish-born leading man John Stuart had previously played the hapless Sir Henry in *The Hound of the Baskervilles* (1932) and went on to portray stuffy authority figures in such genre titles as *The Mummy* (1959) and *The Village of the Damned* (1960).

The Black Abbot—properly adapted from Wallace source material—was later filmed in 1963 as part of Rialto's popular series of krimis. TH

The Black Cat
aka **The House of Doom**; **The Vanishing Body**
Universal; b/w; 66 min; U.S.

D/Co-S: Edgar G. Ulmer *Co-S:* Peter Ruric *P:* Carl Laemmle, Jr. *C:* John J. Mescall *M:* Heinz Roemheld

Cast: Boris Karloff, Bela Lugosi, David Manners, Jacqueline Wells, Lucille Lund, Egon Brecher, Harry Cording, Henry Armetta, Albert Conti

It was a logical and inevitable step for Universal to team its two biggest horror stars, Bela Lugosi (*Dracula*, 1931) and Boris Karloff (*Frankenstein*, 1931). *The Black Cat* was the first of three such vehicles produced by the studio over the course of three years and the only one in which both men worked as equals; the second of the three, *The Raven* (1935), was generally Lugosi's picture, while the third, *The Invisible Ray* (1936), belonged firmly to Karloff. *Cat* is by far the best of the three and was upon its release the most commercially successful; it was, in fact, Universal's biggest hit of 1934. It was also riddled with not-so-veiled references to adultery, incest, pedophilia, homosexuality and necrophilia, as well as an overt depiction of Satanism and a portrayal—albeit in silhouette—of a man being flayed alive. In short, it was exactly the sort of film that prompted, less than two months later, a massive tightening of the Motion Picture Production Code.

"Suggested by" Edgar Allan Poe's short story of the same name (first published in *The Saturday Evening Post* in August of 1843), Edgar G. Ulmer's film emulates Robert Florey's lurid *Murders in the Rue Morgue* (1932) with its onscreen portrayal of violence and sexual sadism. But while *Rue Morgue* stayed somewhat in the Poe ballpark, Ulmer readily admitted that his own invocation of the author was solely to draw in viewers, with *Cat*'s story quite obviously having nothing to do with Poe's. And frankly, the manner in which Vitus Werdegast's ailurophobia is worked into the film is the single most forced aspect of a screenplay that's otherwise as intellectual as it is daring.

The Black Cat begins with young mystery writer Peter Alison (Manners) and his new wife Joan (Wells) traveling via the Orient Express toward their honeymoon destination of Visegrad, Hungary. A conductor informs them that their compartment has been inadvertently double-booked, and the strange Dr. Vitus Werdegast (Lugosi) joins the couple. He explains that he's on his way to visit a "friend," an Austrian architect named Hjalmar Poelzig (Karloff). Couple and doctor wind up disembarking at the same station and taking the same bus, which crashes and kills the driver. The three take refuge in Poelzig's home, where the couple learns that Werdegast and Poelzig have been bitter enemies since the Great War. Werdegast was in the military, and

while he was called to battle, Poelzig claimed the doctor's wife and daughter as his own. The wife is now dead (though Poelzig continues to "love" her, honoring her memory by displaying her actual body in his basement) and the daughter has become the architect's latest consort. (Lest the audience not get it, Ulmer includes a shot of the two in bed together.) To strain things even further, it turns out that Poelzig worships Satan, and Peter and Joan have the misfortune to be stranded in his house on a night that calls for a—presumably virgin—human sacrifice (leaving one to conclude that Peter and Joan have yet to consummate their union).

Ulmer's picture stands apart from Universal's usual horror fare, including the seminal work of James Whale, in that, while Gothic at heart, its approach to the genre is jarringly modern. Nowhere to be found are the looming, creaky castles with their ornate and cobwebbed interiors, deep shadows and winding corridors. Ulmer's world of horror is art-deco minimalist and soaked in bright light. Architect Poelzig has built his shiny Bauhaus home of paned glass over the graves of countless Hungarian soldiers slaughtered due to his betrayal. It's haunted not by literal ghosts, but by the horrible deeds that have gone on around, beneath and within its walls. And the man responsible (named after famed German architect and set designer Hans Poelzig, with whom Ulmer claimed to have worked on the set of *The Golem: How He Came into the World* in 1920) has sold his soul to the Devil—or, at least, to the *idea* of the Devil. When he recites his Latin incantations, they are the stuff of nonsense (a concession to censors, though one wonders who took umbrage to the original invocations and pressed the issue). Poelzig's chants, when translated, yield such philosophical gems as "With a grain of salt a brave man may fall, but he cannot yield," and "To err is human. The wolf may change his skin, but not his nature. Truth is mighty and will prevail." There's also the jarringly original: "By fruit, not by leaves, judge a tree," and "Every madman thinks everybody mad." How flattered the Devil must have been to have such wisdom attributed to him.

Yet Lugosi's educated psychiatrist Werdegast isn't exactly a morally superior alternative to Poelzig; there's every indication that he too has at least a passing acquaintance with dark powers. When Joan behaves strangely after being drugged due to an injury received during the bus accident, the doctor explains, "It is perhaps the narcotic ... Sometimes these cases take strange forms. The victim becomes, in a sense, mediumistic, a vehicle for all the intangible forces in operation around her." When Peter calls Werdegast out on this line of reasoning ("Sounds like a lot of supernatural baloney to me," he says), Werdegast responds, "Supernatural, perhaps; baloney, perhaps not!"

Neither before or after this film (not even in his star turn as *Dracula*) did Lugosi so perfectly blend manner and dialogue as he does here, with his thick accent perfect for a character of Eastern European origin. His reaction when Werdegast is shown the body of his long-dead wife is nothing short of masterful; Lugosi's eyes tear up, his voice falters; the film becomes his, and only his, for that moment. It's a definitive rebuke to the notion that he was incapable of dramatic depth.

Karloff is no less excellent as Poelzig. In an evenly paced, menacing performance, the actor maintains a dignified air whether playing chess for Joan's life or preparing to sacrifice

A publicity shot of Bela Lugosi terrorized by the deadly shadow of the cat, for *The Black Cat*

her on an unholy altar. (In a particularly striking moment, Ulmer pauses the music—which until that moment has been almost continuous—as Karloff enters the room in which the sacrificial ceremony is to be held, flanked by his followers and bedecked in majestic satanic adornments.) He looks magnificent throughout, dressed in square-cut black, his hair smoothed back from a high, gray widow's peak; his eerily restrained look evidences make-up genius Jack Pierce in top form.

Others worthy of note are Jacqueline Wells (who also went by the pseudonym of Julie Bishop) and Lucille Lund. Wells approaches Joan Allison in perfectly naturalistic terms, while Lund—who later claimed that after she rebuffed Ulmer's sexual advances, he made her remaining days on the set miserable—plays the part of Werdegast's daughter with the childlike innocence so essential to the part.

Universal's resident horror hero David Manners (1900-1998), who had similar roles in *Dracula* and *The Mummy* (1932), turns in one of his best performances here as the cheeky Peter Allison. He comes across as boyish and confident, with an air of assurance that had grown even stronger by the time of his next horror film, *The Mystery of Edwin Drood* (1935). The young actor, after being discovered by James Whale, had appeared in that director's *Journey's End* in 1930. He wandered afterwards from studio to studio before finally settling in at Universal, where he became a short-lived house star. After helping form the Screen Actors Guild and retiring from the movie business in the latter part of the 1930s, he returned to stage acting while moving onto

A publicity shot of Boris Karloff juxtaposed against the same shadow of the cat, for *The Black Cat*

a ranch with his male partner, where he lived until his partner's death in the late 1970s. The reclusive Manners himself died in 1998, having also found success as a writer.

Ulmer's direction on *The Black Cat* is simultaneously delirious and controlled. The Czech-born director (1904-1972) began his film career as a set designer; following the great F.W. Murnau to the United States, he worked on that director's famous *Sunrise* in 1927 before making the leap to directing his own two-reelers. In 1933 he made his first feature, *Damaged Lives*, which wallowed in the consequences of sexual "immorality" in the form of venereal disease. It was a low-budget affair released directly to foreign markets, produced by Columbia under the name Weldon for audiences less uptight than those in North America.

Damaged Lives led Ulmer to a deal with Universal and participation in *The Black Cat*. Yet the film's massive success and critical approval couldn't save Ulmer's career from a private scandal involving the Laemmles themselves. As a result of an affair with the wife of Carl Laemmle's nephew, Ulmer was banned from the studio system and forced to work in the wilderness of poverty row. Yet he made a name for himself nonetheless, bringing style and sophistication to the most lowbrow projects, including blaxploitation (*Moon over Harlem*, 1939), film noir (*Detour*, 1945), science fiction (*The Man from Planet X*, 1951) and sexploitation (*The Naked Venus*, 1958). He died of a stroke in 1972, with most of his accolades coming posthumously.

In perfect imitation of Karl Freund's cinematography for *The Mummy*, John J. Mescall's camera glides down the cellar halls and up the winding iron stairwells of Poelzig's "masterpiece of construction" ("built," Werdegast says, "over a masterpiece of destruction"). Though Mescall's early films contain none of the fluid camerawork that would make him famous, his later Universal horror films almost always do. Among his most famous work is James Whale's *The Bride of Frankenstein* (1935), as well as Whale's film adaptation of the musical *Showboat* (1936). After departing Universal in the late 1930s, Mescall bounced from studio to studio, shooting unremarkable films that are mostly forgotten today, though he did receive an Academy Award nomination in 1942 for *Take a Letter, Darling* (1942). His other genre credits include *The Leopard Lady* (1928), *Night Life of the Gods* (1935) and the Roger Corman science fiction/horror hybrid *Not of This Earth* (1957).

The Black Cat is a rare example of a film whose virtues so outweigh its faults that it has gone down in history as a perfect horror film. Not only is it one of the best of its decade, it's one of the best ever made, and that's saying something in a genre that includes the likes of the aforementioned *Frankenstein*, *The Body Snatcher* (1945), *Psycho* (1960), *Rosemary's Baby* (1968) and *The Texas Chain Saw Massacre* (1974). CW

Black Moon
Columbia; b/w; 68 min; U.S.

D: Roy William Neill *S:* Wells Root *P:* Harry Cohn *C:* Joseph August

Cast: Jack Holt, Fay Wray, Dorothy Burgess, Cora Sue Collins, Arnold Korff, Clarence Muse, Lumsden Hare, Eleanor Wesselhoeft, Madame Sul-Te-Wan, Laurence Criner, Henry Kolker

A racist rant, *Black Moon* depicts black culture as a corruptive force threatening a far more enlightened European way of life. Its story concerns a woman named Juanita (Burgess), a New York socialite who has grown strangely cold toward her husband and daughter, becoming obsessed with the pounding of drums. Believing it the best thing for her, husband Stephen (Holt) sends her, along with their daughter Nancy (Collins), secretary Gail (Wray) and nurse Anna (Wesselhoeft) to Juanita's family plantation on San Christopher Island. Unknown to him, however, Juanita's parents had been sacrificed there by a voodoo cult when she was only two years old, and a black woman had instructed the then-child in the fine points of human sacrifice. Now the sound of voodoo drums calls her to take her place as high priestess of that same cult. Gruesome murders occur, all at the hands of blacks, whom it is revealed have tried no fewer than six times to murder all the whites on the island. Anyone opposed to Juanita's rise to power is summarily dispatched: the plantation foreman is stabbed in the back, a radio operator is hung and Nurse Anna is thrown into a pit. Then, when Stephen himself arrives on the island, the blacks revolt and Juanita prepares to sacrifice Nancy.

One of the last films made by Columbia before the Production Code set stringent guidelines for cinema content, *Black Moon* is—racism aside—not without artistic merit. Set to a soundtrack of pounding drums and the occasional hum of native singing, the film builds steadily and tensely to its shocking climax. The graphic sacrifice of a native girl and a shot of Stephen's blood-covered hand after a murder are striking examples of what filmmakers could get away within the early days of "talkie" cinema. Some critics have found complaint with a sub-

plot involving Gail's love for Stephen, but it provides the perfect counterbalance to the central plot, allowing relief from the tension without use of the more conventional (and hackneyed) comedy relief.

Roy William Neill's direction, though not perfect, does demonstrate why he was later chosen to shape entries in Universal's Sherlock Holmes series—starring Basil Rathbone and Nigel Bruce—and to helm the studio's first monster pairing, *Frankenstein Meets the Wolf Man* (1943).

Moon's performances are solid, with the female leads (Dorothy Burgess, Fay Wray) in particular standing out. Burgess infuses her villainous voodoo priestess with emotional complexity, while Wray is pitch-perfect as the priestess' foil. Jack Holt ultimately saves the day, but he can't take the picture away from his more believable female co-stars. The only actors to come up short are the African Americans, who are foiled by stereotypical writing.

Black Moon is far from a forgotten masterpiece, but neither is its obscurity warranted. Lying somewhere between *White Zombie* (1932) and *I Walked With a Zombie* (1943), it is a film awaiting a much-merited reappraisal. CW

Chloe, Love Is Calling You
aka **Chloe**
Trop/Pinnacle; b/w; 54 min; U.S.

D: Marshall Neilan *P:* J.D. Trop *C:* Max Stengler *M:* Erno Rapee, George Henninger

Cast: Olive Borden, Reed Howes, Mollie O'Day, Frank Joyner, Georgette Harvey, Jess Cavin, Gus Smith, Richard Huey, Philip Ober

Old voodoo priestess Mandy (Harvey) returns to her former bayou home to avenge herself on Colonel Gordon (Joyner), the man who lynched her husband a decade and a half before. She brings along her teenage daughter Chloe (Borden), who believes she is possibly part white, and her daughter's strapping young boyfriend Jim Strong (Ober, a Caucasian playing a black man without the aid of the usual blackface make-up). And though Strong loves Chloe, Chloe believes she can do better, even after her beau rescues her from an alligator. She develops an attraction to Wade Carson (Howes), Colonel Gordon's employee. Things get even livelier when Gordon (and Chloe) discovers that Chloe is his daughter, a white girl kidnapped at birth and raised by Mandy as her own.

One of several blaxploitation horror films centered on voodoo that were produced during the 1930s (others included *Ouanga*, 1935, and *The Devil's Daughter*, 1939), *Chloe, Love Is Calling You* was culled from the popular 1927 ballad "Chloe (Song of the Swamp)" by Gus Kahn and Neil Moret, which contains the line "Love is calling you." What sets *Chloe* apart from its peers is superior direction from one-time A-lister Marshall Neilan (*The Bottle Imp*, 1917), who'd had by this time major careers as a writer, producer, director and actor. The action scenes (particularly Jim's underwater battle with an alligator and his fight with a would-be killer) are harrowing and exciting, despite the film's almost non-existent budget. Too bad there aren't more such scenes, as the film is otherwise given to a surfeit of talk. Considering the director's many writing credits, some historians have suggested that Neilan wrote the script for *Chloe*, and while that's highly possible, there's no evidence to verify it.

It would be easy to dismiss *Chloe* as a racist rant, but there are sympathetic touches to be found within. Her husband having been lynched by a mob of whites motivates Mandy's villainy for one thing. Her kidnapping of Chloe is likewise rendered somewhat less vile when the viewer learns that it was a response to the death of her own daughter, whose body is buried near the old woman's cabin. There's also the "black" character of Jim Strong, perhaps the most sympathetic in the film, with an unrequited love for Chloe that spurs him to sacrifice himself on her behalf. And the heroic Wade Carson begins to fall for Chloe even while believing her to be at least part black.

All that said, however, the film *is* crammed full of stereotypes, from blacks sticking pins into voodoo dolls to the standard "scared darkie" routine (a black man reaches into a bag and is frightened by a harmless frog, prompting him to exclaim "Great Jehovah! Great Jehovah!"). There's also the matter of Chloe's longings for a white man, urges that she seems to believe are proof of her real racial make-up. And, of course, there's her unabashed elation at learning that she's the white daughter of a rich plantation owner.

Chloe was actress Olive Borden's last film. She'd been a major star for Fox during the 1920s but left the studio over a salary dispute. Afterward, despite the occasional acting job, she failed to make the leap from silents to talkies. She joined the

Claude Rains and Fay Wray star as a young married couple whose happiness is threatened by his newly acquired supernatural abilities, in *The Clairvoyant*.

WACS during World War II and worked as a nurse. Once the war ended, she failed to find suitable employment, became an alcoholic and died at the age of 41 in a Los Angeles, California mission. CW

The Clairvoyant
aka **The Evil Mind**
Gaumont; b/w; 69 (81) min; Great Britain

D: Maurice Elvey S: Charles Bennett, Bryan Edgar Wallace P: Michael Balcon C: Glen MacWilliams M: Arthur Benjamin

Cast: Claude Rains, Fay Wray, Mary Clare, Ben Field, Jane Baxter, Athole Stewart, C. Denier Warren, Felix Aylmer, Donald Calthrop, Margaret Davidge, Carleton Hobbs, Romilly Lunge, Graham Moffatt, Jack Raine, D.J. Williams

The Great Maximus (Rains) holds stage shows in which he fakes (poorly), with the aid of his wife Rene (Wray), an ability to read people's minds. But during one presentation, his wife is locked outside of the auditorium. Spurred on by a strange woman (Baxter) in the audience, Maximus is suddenly, weirdly able to tell a man in the crowd the contents of a letter in the man's pocket. Later, while on a train journey with his wife and parents, Maximus spies that same woman and has a premonition that the train is about to meet with disaster. Pulling the emergency brake, he, his family and the strange woman—who, it turns out, is named Christine Shawn and happens to be a journalist for the *Daily Sun*, a newspaper owned by her father—all depart the train, even as the crew refuses to heed his warning and the train resumes its trip. Just as predicted, the train derails with tragic results. Shortly thereafter, a newspaper somehow gets wind of the incident and hires Maximus as its resident fortune-teller. But he finds that he lacks the ability to foresee much of anything—until he again encounters Christine. His abilities grow stronger the more he's in the mysterious woman's presence, resulting in him pulling away from his wife and toward Christine's waiting arms. But then, when he forecasts the deaths of hundreds in a mine disaster, the mine owners ignore him, ordering their men to continue working in dangerous conditions. Maximus personally goes to the mine and implores the workers to stop what they're doing, but they refuse out of fear of losing their jobs. When the disaster occurs as predicted, Maximus is blamed for inducing panic and causing the accident that led to the fatalities. The public turns against him, and he is brought up on criminal charges.

The Clairvoyant's producer Michael Balcon formed his own film distribution company, Victory Motion Pictures, in the early 1920s. He went on to work for Gainsborough, staying with that studio as it evolved into Gaumont. By the mid-1930s, he had established himself as a major player in the British film industry and an aggressive filmmaker with an eye for successful material. He green-lit some of the classics of early British cinema, including Alfred Hitchcock's *The 39 Steps* (1935). He also took a young Michael Powell under his wing, molding him into the auteur he later became.

It is unknown who at Gaumont first came upon Ernst (Ernest) Lothar's novel *The Clairvoyant*, but it was Balcon who wisely decided to develop it. He assigned the treatment to Charles Bennett, a playwright who eschewed much of the novel's hackneyed plot in favor of a more original story (though both source and adaptation revolved around the titular clairvoyant). Once the story treatment was approved, Bryan Edgar Wallace, son of bestselling British novelist Edgar Wallace (who had died not long before), came aboard and helped Bennett craft the screenplay. Like his father, Wallace was a big name in the literary field and was popular enough to attract filmgoers merely through his heavily advertised involvement.

Maurice Elvey, possibly the most prolific director in British film history, was assigned to helm the project. He must have seemed a good bet for the venture, given his history with dark subject matter, including 1913's *Maria Marten, or The Murder in the Red Barn* and the bizarre mix of religion and fantasy, *The Wandering Jew* (also 1934).

Claude Rains, a worldwide success after his star turn in James Whale's 1933 blockbuster *The Invisible Man*, was cast in *The Clairvoyant* as Maximus. Selection of the female lead was both a fluke and a no-brainer; scream queen Fay Wray (*The Most Dangerous Game*, 1932; *King Kong*, 1933) happened to be in England at the time shooting *Alias Bulldog Drummond* (aka *Bulldog Jack*) for Gaumont. She was immediately offered the role of Rene, Maximus' wife, and she accepted without hesitation. (It's amazing that both of these Hollywood A-listers agreed to appear in such a low-budget effort; one can only surmise that they were drawn to its superior script.)

Once the film was completed, a new issue arose. Gaumont was unsure quite how to market what was basically a melodrama with scattered moments of subdued horror. With the recent success of John Barrymore's *Svengali* (1931) still on everyone's mind, the company hacked up this bizarre ad line: "Ruled by a female Svengali, he tortured women with his world prophecies!" Anyone seeing the picture after reading this nonsense would likely have been disappointed, as the film actually takes a very low-key approach to its central character's gift/curse. Still, *The Clairvoyant* was a moderate success in Great Britain. When it got to the United States, however, its Hollywood distributors were even more stymied as to how to market the film. They wound up cutting 12 minutes of comedy and drama, leaving the darker elements intact and retitling the result *The Evil Mind*. This version failed to find much of an audience, though years later it garnered something of a cult following after it became a staple of late-night television in the 1960s and '70s.

While far from perfect, the film (in either version) has a lot going for it. The script, as stated above, is first-rate, focusing on character development and human interaction while rendering the psychic aspects of the tale almost secondary. There are also superb performances from all involved. Rains excels in his portrayal of a man torn between his love for his wife and the power he derives from the presence of another woman. And Fay Wray (having already acted in well over 50 films by this point) does well just being her customary, sweet-natured self. Add to this supporting performances by Mary Clare (*The Lady Vanishes*, 1938; *The Night Has Eyes*, 1942), Jane Baxter (*The Man Behind the Mask*, 1936) and Athole Stewart (*Doctor Syn*, 1937), as well as well-done lesser appearances by Felix Aylmer (*The Mummy*, 1959), Donald Calthrop (*Love from a Stranger*, 1937) and Graham Moffatt (*Oh, Mr. Porter!* 1937; *Ask a Policeman*, 1938) and *The Clairvoyant* emerges as a dramatic *tour de force* that succeeds despite, rather than because of, Maurice Elvey's sober direction.

Not that said direction is entirely without merit, given the way Elvey unnaturally highlights Maximus' eyes (similar to

The stalking figure of Death awaits at least one of these terrified onlookers in *Death Takes a Holiday*.

Dracula, 1931) as the seer makes his predictions, and the skillful structure of a scene in which Maximus sees something sinister in his own future, followed by his own mother's untimely death. But Elvey's style is, at its heart, simply too subtle for a film of this nature.

Had someone of James Whale's talent and stature directed it, *The Clairvoyant* might survive today as one of the most important horror films of the 1930s. As it stands, it's a great story brought down to the level of being a merely good film by a director who doesn't quite know how to handle it. CW

Death Takes a Holiday
Paramount; b/w; 79 min; U.S.

D: Mitchell Leison *S:* Maxwell Anderson, Gladys Lehman *P:* E. Lloyd Sheldon *C:* Charles Lang *M:* Bernhard Kaun, Milan Roder, John Leipold *FX:* Gordon Jennings

Cast: Fredric March, Evelyn Venable, Guy Standing, Katharine Alexander, Gail Patrick, Helen Westley, Kathleen Howard, Kent Taylor, Henry Travers, G.P. Huntley, Otto Hoffman, Anna De Linsky, Hector Sarno, Phillips Smalley, Frank Yaconelli

In his native Italy, Alberto Casella (1891-1957) was a stage actor who tried his hand at writing. He hit pay dirt with *La Morte in Vacanza*, a play in which Death takes the form of a prince to infiltrate the house of a nobleman and learn why people love life so much. He meets a young woman who, conversely, takes life way *too* seriously. The two fall in love, and she agrees to leave the material world to be his consort.

The play was a hit when it was staged in Florence in 1924. From there it made its way to Broadway, in an English adaptation by Walter Ferris retitled *Death Takes a Holiday*. With lead roles essayed by Philip Merivale (who had gotten his start in the 1914 film adaptation of *Trilby*) and Rose Hobart (who went on to star in 1931's *Dr. Jekyll and Mr. Hyde* opposite Fredric March), the stage production ran for 180 days to enthusiastic acclaim and packed houses. It was revived in 1931, at which time Paramount optioned the film rights. Following a couple of years in development limbo (several writers worked on the screenplay), director Mitchell Leison selected the project as the follow-up to his 1933 debut, *Cradle Song*. He imported much of the cast from *Song*, including Evelyn Venable, Guy Standing, Gail Patrick and Kent Taylor. Paramount's premiere star, Fredric March, was given the male lead.

The film begins with Duke Lambert (Standing), his family and guests attending a carnival. As they travel home afterward, a frightening shadow floats over them, portending an automobile accident in which they narrowly escape death. Back at his villa, Lambert expresses hope that his son Corrado (Taylor) will marry the beautiful Grazia (Venable), daughter of a princess (Howard). He's clearly concerned more with money than with his offspring's happiness, for Grazia is a downer, obsessed with death and prone to fainting at the merest hint of malevolence. After everyone else goes to bed, Lambert sits pondering the day's events. None other than Death pops up and wants to know why everyone's so afraid of him. When Lambert doesn't answer to the Grim Reaper's satisfaction, the latter announces that he is going to take the form of a human for three days to figure it out. By a stroke of luck, a prince who was planning to visit the Duke has just passed away, unbeknownst to any of the Duke's guests.

Oscar-winning actor Fredric March took on the role of Death in *Death Takes a Holiday*.

The newly deceased body gives Death the perfect vehicle for infiltrating the household.

The visit begins, in the process providing the world with three days without a single death. Though Death has warned Lambert not to tell a soul who he is, the Duke gathers the household and instills in them such a fear of Prince Sirki that they could hardly be expected not to catch on. As things progress, Death, aroused by his newfound physicality, becomes smitten with the morbid Grazia. And when she departs for a while, he's left to cope with two young maids, Rhoda (Patrick) and Stephanie (Westley), who see the prince as husband material. These fresh experiences teach Death that love is an all-pervasive and important human emotion. Finally, when Grazia returns and learns who Prince Sirki really is, she offers to be his bride and to walk in the shadows with him for all eternity. He accepts, things return to normal for the world and the couple lives happily ever after, given the circumstances.

Paramount chose a marketing campaign for the film that was similar to Universal's for the 1931 film *Dracula* (which had been advertised as a macabre love story). "No one can die," the original one-sheet proclaimed, "while he makes love!" Another ad screamed, "HE LIVED FOR THREE DAYS … AND LOVED FOREVER!" Even the dialogue within the film, understanding to what it owed its existence, references the Universal classic when Prince Sirki, given the opportunity to taste alcohol for the first time, says, "I have never tasted [slight pause] … wine [longer pause] … of your country."

Death was a critical and commercial hit, though today its success seems due less to its artistry than to its crossover appeal; it's a concoction of romantic melodrama, fantasy, horror and comedy (although the stabs at humor aren't enough to pierce the gloom and depression that hang over the proceedings like a funeral pall). Its biggest single flaw is the presence of Evelyn Venable (*Double Door*, 1934), whose hysterical and maudlin line delivery steals the show, though not in a good way.

Still, there are some exceptional stretches of dialogue. "You seem to come from a distant place," Grazia tells Prince Sirki. "When I'm with you, I see depths in your eyes that are like the worlds I visit in sleep. And beneath your words is a sound I've heard in dreams. When you leave me, the light goes from the sky. You're like the mystery that's just beyond sight and sound, always just beyond reach, something that draws and frightens." Also effective are the special effects sequences by Gordon Jennings, particularly in Death's first and final appearances as he steps from or blends into the shadows, his entire body covered by a black burial shroud.

Male lead Fredric March had developed his style in the silent era and on Broadway (to which he later returned and won two Tony awards); his early performances were wrought with a heavy style similar to Venable's, which (thank God) he eschewed as he entered the 1940s. In *Death Takes a Holiday*, he alternates between precise control and unadulterated ham, a not entirely unsuccessful mixture. Nominated for five Academy Awards during the course of his career, he won two: one for the aforementioned *Dr. Jekyll and Mr. Hyde* (making him the first actor to ever win an Oscar for a horror film portrayal) and another for *The Best Years of Our Lives* (1946).

Death proved such a massive commercial success that in 1937 it was adapted as an hour program for the Lux Radio Theater, with March reprising his role as Death/Prince Sirki and his real-life wife Florence Eldridge playing Grazia. In 1958 Paramount sold the rights to *Death* and numerous other films to MCA; and when MCA merged with Universal in 1962, the rights came under Universal's control. In 1971 the company remade the film for television with Melvyn Douglas and Myrna Loy before giving it another big-screen go-round in 1998 as *Meet Joe Black* with Brad Pitt and Anthony Hopkins. The latter met with critical indifference and less than stellar box-office receipts, despite some praise for Brad Pitt in the tweaked role of Death/Joe Black. CW

Le Diable en bouteille
aka **The Devil in the Bottle**
ACE; b/w; 95 min; Germany/France
  D: Heinz Hilpert, Reinhart Steinbicker *S:* Serge Veber, Liselotte Gravenstein, Kurt Heuser *P:* Raoul Ploquin *C:* Fritz Arno Wagner *M:* Theo Mackeben
  Cast: Kathe von Nagy, Pierre Blanchar, Gina Manes, Paul Azais, Gabriel Gabrio, Roger Karl, Marguerite de Morlaye, Suzy Pierson, Georges Malkine, Roger Legris, Daniel Mendaille, Bill Bocket, Henri Richard, Gaston Mauger

This is the French version of Germany's *Love, Death and the Devil* (1934). Like its German counterpart, it's a melodramatic rendering of author Robert Louis Stevenson's short horror tale *The Bottle Imp* (1891), about a man who purchases a bottle that grants wishes but requires its owner to sell it for less than its purchase price (or else be eternally damned). Both films shift the story's emphasis away from supernatural horror toward dramatic fantasy. But while the German version is known for a single scene in which actress Brigitte Horney sings a Theo Mackeben song, the French version isn't known for anything.

Kathe von Nagy repeats her role from the counterpart film, but the rest of the cast is comprised of French thespians. The crew (directors Hilpert and Steinbicker, cinematographer Wagner, and scorer Mackeben) remains mostly the same.

Interestingly, some of the names of the characters are the same as those in the 1917 silent U.S. film version (as opposed to those in Stevenson's actual story). The film is often cited as having been produced in 1935, which is incorrect. CW

Double Door
Paramount; b/w; 75 min; U.S.

D: Charles Vidor *S:* Gladys Lehman *P:* E. Lloyd Sheldon *C:* Harry Fischbeck

Cast: Evelyn Venable, Mary Morris, Anne Revere, Kent Taylor, Sir Guy Standing, Colin Tapely, Virginia Howell, Halliwell Hobbes, Frank Dawson, Helen Shipman, Leonard Carey, Ralph Remley, Burr Caruth

When her younger brother Rip (Taylor) announces his engagement to beautiful but struggling nurse Anne (Venable), Victoria Van Brett (Morris) stops at nothing to prevent the union. She cuts Rip out of the will and imprisons Anne in the secret room where the Van Brett father was previously found dead. Victoria then creates a web of deceit to ensure that Anne stays locked away without anyone discovering her presence.

The film's credits include the hyperbolic assertion, "The play that made Broadway gasp!" An adaptation of Elizabeth McFadden's stage production, *Double Door* was allegedly based on the real-life exploits of the Wendell Family, New York socialites, privileged—and wealthy—enough to keep their sinister doings from the public (despite occasional police involvement). Elitist 5th Avenue residents of New York City gave the play the cold shoulder, and it closed not long after opening. Hollywood came knocking soon thereafter, though, and wisely turned the Big Apple's rejection of the play into a selling point.

The movie itself is an interesting horror entry along the lines of *What Ever Happened to Baby Jane?* (1962) and *Hush ... Hush, Sweet Charlotte* (1964); Mary Morris assumes the sort of role later taken on by the likes of Bette Davis and Joan Crawford. Add a spooky turn-of-the-century mansion to the mix and you've got a blood-and-thunder example of the *Grand Guignol* school of horror.

Both Mary Morris and Anne Revere reprise their stage roles here, Morris as mean-spirited Victoria and Revere as weakling sister Caroline—insane after doing some time in the secret room, courtesy of Victoria. CW

Drums O'Voodoo
aka **Louisiana; She Devil**
Sack; 70 min; b/w; U.S.

D: Arthur Hoerl *S:* Augustus Smith *P:* Alfred N. Sack, Louis Weiss *C:* J. Burgi Contner, Walter Strenge

Cast: Laura Bowman, Augustus Smith, Morris McKenny, Lionel Monagas, Edna Barr, Alberta Perkins, A.B. DeComathiere, Fred Bonny, Sam Baker, James Davis, Theresa Harris, Paul Johnson, Pedro Lopez, Bennie Small, Trixie Smith

The "secrets" of voodoo are revealed ...

Old Mrs. Van Brett (Mary Morris) will do anything to prevent her younger brother's marriage to Anne (Evelyn Venable), in *Double Door*.

The posters for *Drums O'Voodoo* promise an epic battle between "Saturday Sinners and Sunday Saints," but this flea-bitten independent production offers only a hollow exposé of voodooism. Director Arthur Hoerl is best known for *Tell Your Children* (1936), which attained full infamy on the Midnight Movie circuit under the title *Reefer Madness*. That film provided a hysterical, reactionary take on the dangers of marijuana, and a similar approach informs *Drums*. It's one of only a few productions that appear to have been inspired by the success of Victor Halperin's horror hit *White Zombie* (1932), though it failed to match that picture in either quality or box-office earnings.

Augustus Smith adopted *Drums O'Voodoo* from his own stage play. It was one of a handful of titles Smith wrote for the screen. He also worked off-and-on as an actor (often under the name Gus Smith) and among his acting credits is another early, schlock voodoo picture, *Chloe, Love Is Calling You* (1934). TH

The Ghost Walks
Invincible; b/w; 65 min; U.S.

D: Frank R. Strayer *S:* Charles S. Belden *P:* Maury M. Cohen *C:* M.A. Andersen

Cast: John Miljan, June Collyer, Richard Carle, Henry Kolker, Johnny Arthur, Spencer Charters, Donald Kirke, Eve Southern, Douglas Gerard, Wilson Benge, Jack Shutta, Harry Strang

Desperate playwright Prescott Ames (Miljan) invites Broadway producer Herman Wood (Carle) to his country home for the weekend, the better to schmooze him into backing Ames' new play. On the way there, however, a thunderstorm results in a fallen tree blocking their passage. At Ames' suggestion, the two take refuge in the nearby old dark house of Dr. Kent (Kolker), who has assembled various guests already, including a woman named Beatrice (Southern) whose husband was murdered in the home's dining room the year before and who claims she can communicate with his spirit. The evening takes a downturn at dinnertime when a mysterious spot of blood appears on the tablecloth. Then the lights go out and a ghostly face appears, and when the lights come back on, Beatrice is gone. Wood flees the room, and Ames congratulates the group on an acting job well done. The whole thing, you see, has been nothing more than the first act of Ames' latest play, done for the benefit of an unknowing Wood. But uh-oh … when they let Wood in on the charade and go to fetch Beatrice, they find that she really has been murdered. They learn that a serial killer known as Professor Twitterly (Charters) has escaped from a nearby asylum and taken refuge in the house. And now Wood refuses to believe any of it, insisting that it's all still part of the play.

Director Frank Strayer took on *The Ghost Walks* with a trio of horror films already under his belt. The first, *Murder at Midnight* (1931), was a minor—and very typical—mystery, while the second, *The Vampire Bat* (1933), had the good fortune of landing Fay Wray (*King Kong*, 1933) and Lionel Atwill (*The Mystery of the Wax Museum*, 1933) for its lead roles. The third, *Tangled Destinies* (1932), was yet another entry in the "old dark house" subgenre.

While *The Ghost Walks* is part of that same subgenre, it ups the horror ante a little (repeat: a little); too bad Strayer was so disinterested in the subject matter that he directed cinematographer M.A. Andersen's camera to remain static for the first two-thirds of the film, leaving things to hinge on a predominantly second-rate cast and a tiresome script by Charles S. Belden (who was responsible for the play on which the aforementioned *The Mystery of the Wax Museum* and its remakes were based, as well as some uncredited work on *Dracula's Daughter*, 1936).

The major performances are so wooden that it's hard to see why fictional producer Wood would ever consider funding Ames' play. Eve Southern (*The Haunted House*, 1928) deserves a posthumous Razzie for her haunted Beatrice, whose flat enunciation of every line is excruciating—the character's demise actually bumps the film's production values up a notch. Southern retired from acting a few pictures after this; she placed the blame on a car accident that left her with a broken back, but seeing her here makes one wonder whether she didn't simply leap at an opportunity to escape an embarrassing career choice.

Thankfully she's somewhat canceled out by the terrific Richard Carle (*The Witching Hour*, 1934) as the disbelieving producer. Carle was known for playing grumpy old men, a role he performs to perfection here, striking all the right notes while humiliating his hopelessly outgunned co-stars. The only other actor to give anything like a quality performance is Spencer Charters as the maniacal Professor Twitterly. He manages to be both comical and chilling, and his final scene is a little *tour de force*.

The last 20 minutes or so of *The Ghost Walks* seem spliced on from a different, better film. Andersen's camera at last moves, prowling the corridors and dark rooms of the estate, while Strayer's direction achieves some fairly atmospheric—if predictable (clutching hands, lurking shadows and screaming maidens)—touches. None of this really saves the picture, but things do go out on a happy note as Wood agrees to produce the struggling playwright's new piece of crap. CW

Green Eyes
Chesterfield; b/w; 68 min; U.S.

D: Richard Thorpe *S:* Andrew Moses *P:* George R. Batcheller *C:* M.A. Anderson *M:* Abe Meyer

Cast: Charles Starrett, Shirley Grey, John Wray, Arthur Clayton, Claude Gillingwater, William Bakewell, Dorothy Revier, Alden Chase, Ben Hendricks, Jr., Aggie Herring, Elmer Ballard, Edward Keene

Steven Kester (Gillingwater) is killed during a masquerade party, and it's up to a hardboiled cop (Wray) and a wisecracking amateur detective (Starrett) to figure out "who done it."

Based on the novel *The Murder of Steven Kester*, written by Harriette Ashbrooke in 1931, this is an enjoyable B-murder mystery with macabre elements. Amid the usual array of red herrings—each fishier than the last—director Richard Thorpe manages some genuinely entertaining touches. There's also a pretty high body count, as well as pre-Code suicide that would surely have gotten the film into hot water had it been released a year later.

Thorpe went on to direct the classic *Night Must Fall* (1937), though he found his greatest success with overstuffed MGM

fanfare of the 1950s such as *Ivanhoe* (1952) and *The Prisoner of Zenda* (1953). His direction here is crisp and efficient. Though saddled with an overly talky screenplay, Thorpe gets along fine, enlivening individual scenes with agitated camerawork and judicious cutting. *Green Eyes* shapes up as a decent time killer, thanks in no small measure to his stylish sense of direction.

The cast is headed by popular '30s leading man Charles Starrett, best known to horror buffs for his wooden turn in MGM's deliriously kinky *Mask of Fu Manchu* (1932). He's in better form here, and he manages some wry and amusing comments of the smartass variety. He gets solid support from John Wray (*Doctor X*, 1932) as the no-nonsense police inspector. TH

House of Danger
Peerless; b/w; 65 min; U.S.

D: Charles Hutchison *S:* C.C. Cheddon, Jack Natteford *P:* Sam Efrus *C:* Henry Kruse

Cast: Onslow Stevens, Janet Chandler, James Bush, Desmond Roberts, Howard Lang, Nina Guilbert, Tove Linden, Roy Rice, Stan Scharling

Don Phillips (Stevens) pretends to be the injured boyfriend of a woman named Sylvia (Chandler), who fears that the same person who murdered her boyfriend's father will also kill her. Everyone—Sylvia and the boyfriend's family included—buys the ruse. As he plays amateur detective, Don narrowly escapes being murdered.

This rather preposterous mystery thriller with "old dark house" overtones gets a boost from Onslow Stevens' performance. Stevens (1902-1977) had a long and varied career on stage and film, though lasting fame proved elusive. Cast most often in character roles, he's best remembered by horror buffs for his performance as the kindly Dr. Edelmann, who transforms into a Hyde-like killer when he is infected by the blood of Dracula (John Carradine) in *House of Dracula* (1945). His career was eventually derailed by alcoholism, and he died in a nursing home in California of complications caused by a broken hip, coupled with the onset of pneumonia. The coroner concluded that foul play was involved in his injury, but a culprit was never named. At the time of *House of Danger*, however, he was still a handsome and charismatic young actor.

The film's basic set-up is too contrived to take seriously. One must buy the idea that Don just happens to look just like the man he's pretending to be and accept that the family falls for the deception because he's been abroad for a long time—but at least it's vigorously staged, and Stevens does manage to help keep the far-fetched tale afloat.

Stevens' co-star Janet Chandler is certainly easy on the eyes, and she delivers a capable performance. Even more so than Stevens, she is stuck with an impossible role, that of a wide-eyed naïf who fails to recognize that the man she loves is not really the man she loves.

The supporting cast, without exception, is colorless. Director Charles Hutchison had been a presence in the film scene since 1914. He amassed more credits as an actor than a director, and *House of Danger* makes it easy to see why.

Ultimately, one hates to be too tough on a film of this ilk. It doesn't pretend to be something grand or elaborate, and as a B-mystery thriller it indeed has its moments. Though not by any stretch memorable, it's certainly far from the worst of its type. TH

House of Mystery
aka **The Ape**; **The House of Mystery**; **The Curse of Kali**
Monogram; b/w; 62 min; U.S.

D: William Nigh *S:* Albert DeMond *P:* Paul Malvern *C:* Archie Stout

Cast: Ed Lowry, Verna Hillie, John Sheehan, Brandon Hurst, Joyzelle Joyner, Fritzi Ridgeway, Clay Clement, George "Gabby" Hayes, Dale Fuller, Harry C. Bradley, Irving Bacon, Mary Foy, Sam Godfrey

Based on Adam Hull Shirk's creaky play *The Ape*, *House of Mystery* opens in 1913 in British-controlled India. During an expedition, drunken archaeologist John Prendergast "accidentally" kills a sacred monkey while raiding a secret Hindu temple of Kali (pronounced incorrectly throughout as Kay-lie and, though a goddess, referred to the whole time as "him"). He's threatened by the high priest but saved by an exotic temple dancer named Chandra (Joyner, billed—no kidding—as Laya Joy), though not before having a curse placed upon him. Prendergast escapes to the United States, changes his name to Pren, takes Chandra as his mistress and lives in anonymity off his stolen treasure. Twenty years later, Pren and Chandra are tracked down by several of the expedition's backers, who insist on their fair share of the riches. The claimants are invited to the Pren estate, where Pren, now confined to a wheelchair, promises to do right by them, then fills them in on the curse of Kali. It seems that Pren has already shared part of his fortune with two of his backers, who died as a result of the curse. Now, Pren wants the newcomers to stay in the house for one week before deciding whether they really want to risk claiming their share. But the party doesn't last long; various guests are predictably murdered, the first (Fuller) by an apparent gorilla and the second (Hayes) while wearing a gorilla suit.

Alternately interesting (the opening scenes), boring (much of what goes on in the old dark house setting) and downright funny (a séance in which the spirit of Pocahontas is called forth), *House of Mystery* is exactly what one expects from Monogram. Not much use is made of its well-done sets, while most of the film takes place in Pren's library/study. The solution to the mystery is obvious from the very beginning (a flaw not neutralized by stating such in the dialogue at the film's conclusion). And though aspects of it seem to have influenced Hammer's far superior *The Reptile* (1966), there's not much going for it otherwise.

Even worse, the comic relief is painfully unfunny. The worst offender is radio star Ed Lowry as an insurance representative who also becomes the inadvertent hero. Some critics have pointed to Joyzelle Joyner's turn as Chandra as *Mystery*'s standout performance, but her role is so undemanding that it's difficult to get a handle on how well she really does with it. The film is notable mostly for the presence of George Hayes in a bit part as a buffoon who tries to steal the treasure from Pren's vaults but dies for his efforts. He'd already acted in many movies by this time, and he went on to star in numerous Westerns under the name "Gabby" Hayes.

House of Mystery was remade by the same director under the title *The Ape* in 1940; that version, also produced by Monogram, starred Boris Karloff and bears no resemblance whatsoever to its predecessor. CW

Jane Eyre
Monogram; b/w; 62 min; U.S.

D: Christy Cabanne *S:* Adele Comandini *P:* Ben Verschleiser *C:* Robert Planck

Cast: Virginia Bruce, Colin Clive, Beryl Mercer, David Torrence, Aileen Pringle, Edith Fellows, John Rogers, Jean Darling, Lionel Belmore, Jameson Thomas, Ethel Griffies, Claire Du Brey, William Burress, Joan Standing, Richard Quine

This early Monogram attempt at respectability begins in an old dark house on a stormy night as a young Jane Eyre (Darling, giving an atrocious performance) hides from her stepsiblings. Falsely accused of theft, she's shipped off to the Lowood Orphanage for Girls by her wicked stepmother. There she has her golden locks chopped off, among other degradations brought about largely by her refusal to admit what's blazingly obvious to the audience: She's a nasty little brat.

Years pass and she grows into a beautiful young woman (Bruce, trying to best Darling's bad performance but not quite pulling it off). Weirdly, she becomes a teacher at the orphanage. As willfully obstinate and insulting as ever (despite the screenplay's attempt to portray her as sympathetic), she's dismissed for rudeness to the headmaster and takes a job as governess at Thornfield Manor. She takes care on the way to her new position to be boorish to her carriage driver, and when she first encounters her new boss Edward Rochester (Clive, hamming it up a year before his star turn in *The Bride of Frankenstein*), she makes sure to insult him (although, to be fair, she's at first unaware who he is). Then, in a moment of transcendent irony, she dresses down Rochester's servant Grace Poole, calling the old woman "disagreeable."

At this point, thankfully, the young governess falls in love with the subdued older Rochester and starts to mellow out a bit. Things get tense again when Jane's evenings take to being interrupted by frightening screams originating in the attic. The servants brush it off, but Jane knows that something's up. Later, just when she decides to leave Thornfield Manor and Mr. Rochester forever, Rochester pops the big question. No sooner does a starry-eyed Jane say "yes" than Rochester's crazy wife Bertha (Du Brey)—she of the screams in the attic—escapes from her upstairs prison and ruins everything. This time Jane really does split, evading Mr. Rochester when he follows.

Rochester gives up the chase, returns to Thornfield and finds that the house has been set alight by the missus, who dies in the fire (which also temporarily blinds him). When Jane gets word that the coast is clear, she dumps her new beau, a minister named Rivers, and returns to Thornfield, declaring her undying devotion to her soul mate, adulterer and kidnapper Rochester.

Director Christy Cabanne condenses Charlotte Brontë's lengthy 1847 Gothic romance into a mere 62 minutes, jettisoning subtlety in the process (though he does find room for an interminable musical number). Yet despite *Jane Eyre*'s brief running time, it is not a short film; it moves at a turtle's pace, the tedium broken only by a few unintentionally funny moments.

Some of the film's most annoying scenes (and that's one stiff competition) involve Rochester's ward Adele, whose "adorable kid" routine leads one to hope that her accidental fall about halfway through the film will finish her off (it doesn't). And though the plotline is fairly faithful to Brontë's original work, it does soften Rochester's character a tad by having him attempt to procure an annulment from his nutty wife before he decides to remarry.

Having begun his film career in the silent era working for the likes of D.W. Griffith, Cabanne was relegated to the confines of poverty row after the coming of sound, working mostly for companies like Monogram, Tiffany, and PRC. His one claim to respectability may be the Universal horror classic *The Mummy's Hand* (1940), which set the standard for all mummy films to follow.

The next cinematic version of *Jane Eyre* (1944), starring Orson Welles and Joan Fontaine, is considered *the* classic adaptation. CW

The Living Dead
aka **The Scotland Yard Mystery**; **The Case of the Missing Coffins**
Alliance; b/w; 64 min; Great Britain
  D: Thomas Bentley *S:* Frank Miller *P:* Walter C. Mycroft *C:* James Wilson
  Cast: Sir Gerald Du Maurier, George Curzon, Grete Nataler, Belle Chrystal, Leslie Perrins, Walter Patch, Henry Victor

When several heavily insured men die under mysterious circumstances, Inspector Stanton (Du Maurier) is placed on the case. He turns to Dr. Masters (Curzon) for assistance, but quickly comes to suspect the doctor of being involved in the macabre scheme.

Originally released in Britain under the more prosaic title *The Scotland Yard Mystery*, this British B-movie places a by-the-numbers whodunit within an impressively conceived mad scientist motif. Distinguished stage actor Sir Gerald Du Maurier—son of author Georges Du Maurier (*Trilby*, 1894) and father of acclaimed novelist Daphne Du Maurier (*Rebecca*, 1938)—carries the film and proves far more comfortable in the cinematic medium than many stage thespians who make the jump to the big screen. His performance here is warm and witty, and the character's willingness to bend the law in order to uphold it makes him infinitely more interesting than the typical doddering police figures in British films of the period. Sadly, Du Maurier made few film appearances (and passed away not long after his performance here).

George Curzon played the villainous Dr. Masters very heavy-handedly, and he went on to impress in the title role of Tod Slaughter's *Sexton Blake and the Hooded Terror* (1938). The character of Masters evokes Dr. Jekyll; both are seemingly decent men of medicine, yet each harbors a dark secret. But while Jekyll oversteps moral boundaries in search of a greater good, Masters is at heart a selfish bastard. And while the revelation of his involvement in the murders can be seen coming from miles off, things do get entertainingly silly when the denouement (in the form of a potion that brings on a state of living death) finally arrives.

The rest of the cast is none too impressive one way or the other, though note should be made of the presence of Henry Victor, better known for his role as the womanizing Hercules in Tod Browning's *Freaks* (1932).

Director Thomas Bentley has a difficult time getting things started, but if one can endure the stagy, clichéd and "veddy British" opening reels, there are rewards aplenty as the second half of the picture unfolds. And one would have to be a congenital stone-face to not smile at the film's final *bon mot*, though to quote it here would be to rob the first-time viewer of a moment of genuinely cheesy enjoyment. TH

The Love Captive
Universal; b/w; 63 min; U.S.

D: Max Marcin *S:* Karen DeWolf, Max Marcin *P:* Carl Laemmle, Jr., E.M. Asher *C:* Gilbert Warrenton

Cast: Gloria Stuart, Nils Asther, Paul Kelly, Alan Dinehart, Renee Gadd, Russ Brown, Virginia Kami, John Wray, Ellalee Ruby, Addison Richards, Robert Greig, King Baggot (uncredited)

Alice Trask (Stuart) falls in love with charismatic hypnotist Dr. Alexis Collender (Asther). She breaks the news to her fiancé, Dr. Norman Ware (Kelly), who decides that he cannot prevent Alice from following her heart but at the same time starts investigating Collender's background. He learns that Collender uses hypnosis to cure patients of various ills and is highly thought of as a result. Ultimately, it's revealed that Collender has been using his talents to control Alice.

The Love Captive was one of the films that made Universal contract player Gloria Stuart antsy to leave the studio. The beautiful and talented young actress had enjoyed her work for the studio's ace director James Whale, who'd guided her through *The Old Dark House* (1932), *The Kiss Before the Mirror* and *The Invisible Man* (both 1933), but subsequent assignments, including this one, were both unchallenging and undistinguished. Her work in *The Love Captive*, admittedly, paid a bill or two, but it didn't help her career much. The film today languishes in obscurity, a forgotten knock-off of hypnosis-themed fare like *Svengali* (1931).

The supporting cast includes the Danish-born and debonair Nils Asther as the shady hypnotist. While Asther's brooding good looks made him a popular leading man in the 1920s and '30s, he eventually descended into character roles as more conventional all-American performers came to the fore during World War II. Among his more notable forays into the genre are turns as a swami in Universal's *Night Monster* (1942) and as an inspector in Edgar G. Ulmer's *Bluebeard* (1944). Buried in *Captive*'s supporting cast is one-time star King Baggot, who had starred in Universal's *Dr. Jekyll and Mr. Hyde* (1913) but by this time was reduced to unbilled bit parts.

Director Max Marcin wrote the play *The Humbug* upon which this film was based. He directed only a handful of films, of which this was the last, but he did enjoy a prolific career as a writer for the theater and radio. His most enduring contribution was the *Crime Doctor* radio series, which was adapted during the 1940s into a series of B-films by Columbia. TH

Love, Death and the Devil
aka **Liebe, Tod und Teufel**; **The Devil in a Bottle**; **The Imp in a Bottle**; **Zwei auf Hawai**; **Das unsterbliche Glück**; **Der gläserne Fluch**
UFA; b/w; 150 min; Germany

D: Heinz Hilpert, Reinhart Steinbicker *S:* Liselotte Gravenstein, Kurt Heuser *P:* Karl Ritter *C:* Fritz Arno Wagner *M:* Theo Mackeben

Cast: Brigitte Horney, Kathe von Nagy, Albin Skoda, Karl Hellmer, Aribert Wascher, Erich Ponto, Paul Dahlke, Rudolf Platte, Josef Dahmen, Hans Kettler, Karl Hannemann, Oskar Sima, Albert Florath

Brigitte Horney became a household name in her native Germany after singing "So oder so ist das Leben" in this, the first sound adaptation of Scottish author Robert Louis Steven-

son's classic horror short story *The Bottle Imp* (1891). The film was made under the supervision of Joseph Goebbels, who headed up the Nazi propaganda machine. Though it contained fantastic elements, particularly a magical bottle that houses the devil and grants its owner his or her fondest wishes, only to afterwards damn his or her soul, it focused more on melodrama than the supernatural. It eschewed the shadowy and angular Expressionism so prevalent in silent German horror cinema in favor of a more realistic approach, one that, if not entirely successful on an aesthetic level, helped make the film hugely popular with European audiences at the time. Today it's pretty much forgotten (calling it the most famous film version of Stevenson's story—which it indeed is—isn't saying much), except for the scene in which Horney sings Theo Mackeben's song about the ups and downs of life (notably covered by Hildegard Knef several decades later).

Horney (1911-1988) began her career as a stage actress, but after UFA's *Love, Death and the Devil*, her claim to German cinema superstardom was such that she was at length given what became her most famous role: that of Empress Katherine the Great in Josef von Baky's *Münchhausen* (1943). She was very good friends with Joachim Gottschalk, a fellow actor who had been ostracized for taking his Jewish wife to a Nazi function, and bravely attended his funeral after he and his family committed suicide to escape the Gestapo. She later left Germany and became a U.S. citizen. She also may have been the inspiration for Bridget von Hammersmark, the fictional actress/singer/spy in Quentin Tarantino's *Inglourious Basterds* (2009).

A French version of *Love, Death and the Devil*, titled *Le Diable en bouteille* (1934) and starring a predominately French cast, was shot back-to-back with this German production, utilizing much of the same crew. Strangely, both the German and French adaptations retained many of the changes made for the 1917 U.S. silent film version, rather than focus entirely on Stevenson's original story. CW

The Man Who Reclaimed His Head
Universal; b/w; 80 min; U.S.

D: Edward Ludwig *S:* Jean Bart, Samuel Ornitz, Barry Trivers (uncredited) *P:* Carl Laemmle, Jr. *C:* Merritt P. Gerstad *M:* Heinz Roemheld *FX:* John P. Fulton

Cast: Claude Rains, Joan Bennett, Lionel Atwill, Juanita Quigley, Henry O'Neill, Henry Armetta, Wallace Ford, Lawrence Grant, William B. Davidson, Norman Ainsley, Ted Billings, Valerie Hobson, Edward Van Sloan

Paul Verin (Rains) is a Pacifist who writes for a radical publication. His treacherous editor Henry Dumont (Atwill) steals his articles and publishes them as his own, but Paul lives with this by reminding himself that the word of peace is still being spread. When Paul is drafted into war, Dumont puts the moves on the writer's beautiful wife Adele (Bennett). The would-be Casanova gets more than he bargained for when the wordsmith-cum-warrior returns from the front a very changed man.

Jean Bart, born Marie Antoinette de Sarlabous, was an American screenwriter and playwright whose work has mostly fallen into obscurity. Among her most successful plays was *The Man Who Reclaimed His Head*, which did reasonably well on Broadway. In it, a grotesque-looking Pacifist is driven to hysteria and murder by an unscrupulous rival. The New York production was instrumental in making its star Claude Rains a major name in the American theater. When Bart's play was brought to the screen in 1934, Universal was sensible enough to retain both her services and those of Rains. The film deviates from the play in its presentation of the hero (the idea of a hunchbacked, dwarfish leading man was a bit too much for the studio to stomach, despite its successful horror outings) but retains the original work's anti-war message.

In many respects, the film is similar to Abel Gance's *J'Accuse* (1919), though decidedly less horrific in the pursuit of its theme. Truth be told, *The Man Who Reclaimed His Head* isn't really a horror film at all—it's a drama, albeit one with a memorably grisly finale. But Universal's marketing approach, as well as the film's inclusion in the Shock Theater package of horror titles sold to television in the 1950s (which introduced a younger generation to some vintage horror), has ensured the film's stubborn linkage to the genre.

Claude Rains gives one of his finest performances as Pacifist hero Paul Verin. Though the script goes to great lengths to make him something of a bleary-eyed patsy, Rains' charm and charisma give the character depth throughout. His gradual change from optimistic activist to homicidal avenger is, through the actor's nuanced presentation, achieved without resort to cheap melodramatics.

Joan Bennett (*Suspiria*, 1976) is also effective here in one of her earliest screen appearances. She does a fine job with the somewhat underdeveloped character of Verin's doting wife, who is there mostly to provide a final motivation for Verin's mental collapse. She remains touchingly—if occasionally unbelievably—devoted to her husband even when hit on by Lionel Atwill's rich and prestigious Henry Dumot.

Lionel Atwill is at his best as the sleazy Dumont. With his "cat that ate the canary" grin and pompous demeanor, he provides an ideal counterpart to Rains' Verin. The supporting cast includes Wallace Ford (*Freaks*, 1932), Valerie Hobson (*The Bride of Frankenstein*, 1935) and Edward Van Sloan (*Dracula*, 1931), all appearing briefly with the latter two unbilled.

Chief among the film's scattered flaws is the disastrous performance by child actress Juanita Quigley as Verin's daughter. She's clearly meant to ooze adorable but instead runs the gamut between irritating and grating, causing the film to suffer terribly when her cutesy antics take center stage.

Director Edward Ludwig, a veteran journeyman whose career dates back to 1920, doesn't bring much panache to the proceedings, but he keeps the film moving at a decent pace. And while things at times teeter dangerously close to camp, *The Man Who Reclaimed His Head* is, on the whole, a potent and memorable work. The film is worth seeking out for fans of Universal horror movies and classic films in general. TH

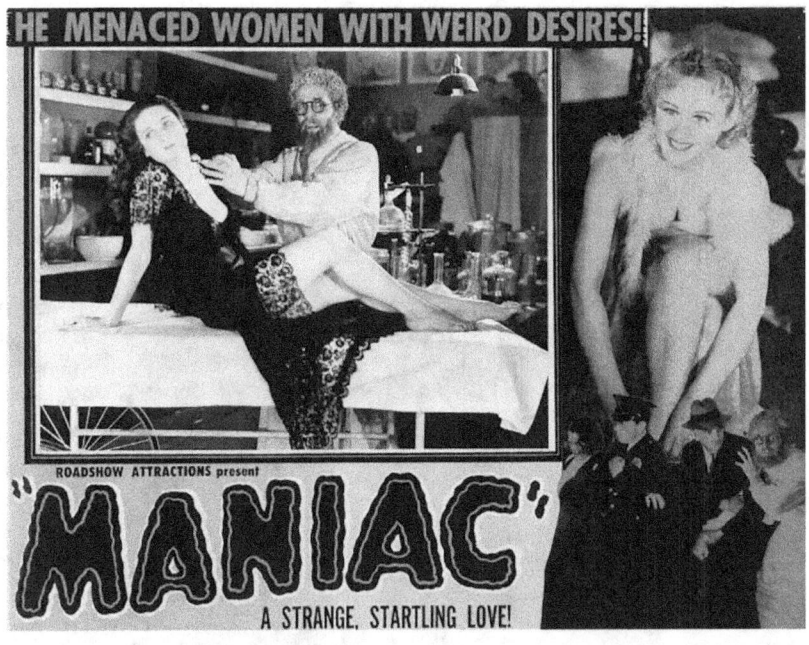

Maniac
aka **Sex Maniac**
Hollywood; b/w; 51 min; U.S.

D/Co-P: Dwain Esper *S/Co-P:* Hildegarde Stadie *Co-P:* Louis Sonney *C:* William Thompson

Cast: Bill (William) Woods, Horace Carpenter, Ted Edwards, Phyllis Diller, Theo (Thea) Ramsey, Jenny Dark, Marvel (Marvelle) Andre, Celia McCann, John P. Wade, Marion (Marian) Blackton, Satan the Cat (uncredited)

Midway though *Maniac*, a seasoned police inspector informs his co-workers that, "Doctors and scientists often have some queer things on their minds."

So, obviously, did the creative minds behind the film. The story concerns one Don Maxwell (Woods), a vaudeville actor with a talent for make-up and impersonation, who is hiding out from the law. He finds refuge as an assistant to Dr. Meirschultz (Carpenter), a crazed doctor with a bad German accent and an obsession with reviving the dead. Maxwell's terror at working with corpses makes him a less than desirable assistant, particularly after the two successfully revive a suicide victim. And when the doctor orders him to likewise kill himself so as to be similarly revived, Maxwell panics and instead kills Meirschultz. He attempts to cover his tracks by assuming the doctor's identity and taking over his psychiatric practice, as his escalating anxiety sparks a series of mental conditions (spelled out for the viewer in a series of graphic inserts and enhanced by clips from the 1922 film *Haxen* and Fritz Lang's 1924 *Seigfried*). Maxwell mistakenly injects a patient (Edwards) with adrenaline, and the patient's wife (Diller), having just discovered Meirschultz's body, blackmails Maxwell into turning her spazzed-out husband into an obedient zombie. The effort to do so does not go well, nor does anything else as the "doctor's" madness escalates until he is apprehended and put away.

Maniac was released on September 11, 1934 and distributed by Roadshow Attractions on the tent show/burlesque house circuit. It stands up today as a bizarre (and fun) little curio, a precursor to the work of Ed Wood but with fewer dull patches. As is the case with the worst/best Wood films, there's no question that *Maniac*'s high entertainment value is purely accidental and not the sort that its makers intended. The film's Z-grade acting (with some of the cast obviously reading from cue cards), its breathtaking technical ineptness and its rambling, goofball screenplay (cobbled together by Esper's wife Hildegarde Stadie from bits of Poe's *The Black Cat*, Shelley's *Frankenstein*, du Maurier's *Trilby*, Stevenson's *The Strange Case of Dr. Jekyll and Mr. Hyde* and God knows what else) somehow, through no fault of its own, creates a near-flawless dreamlike atmosphere. The film plays out as equal parts farce and nightmare, spiced up with the unsavory (grave-robbing, animal mutilation) and a heapin' helpin' of prurient content (sexual assault, gratuitous boobies). It wasn't until David Lynch's masterful *Blue Velvet* (1986) that a piece of cinema *deliberately* conjured this sort of atmosphere, albeit far more jarringly.

Like the Espers' better-known film *Marihuana: Weed with Roots in Hell* (1936), *Maniac* is a lip-smacking sleazefest done up as an Important Statement on a Dire Social Problem. Its forward, which scrolls up the screen, is classic crap psychology, circa the 1930s:

> The brain is indeed the instrument of thinking, but the mind is the skillful player that makes it give forth the beautiful harmony of thought. It is because of the disastrous results of fear-thought not only on the individual but on the nation, that it becomes the duty of every sane man and woman to establish quarantine against fear. Fear is a [psychological] disease, which

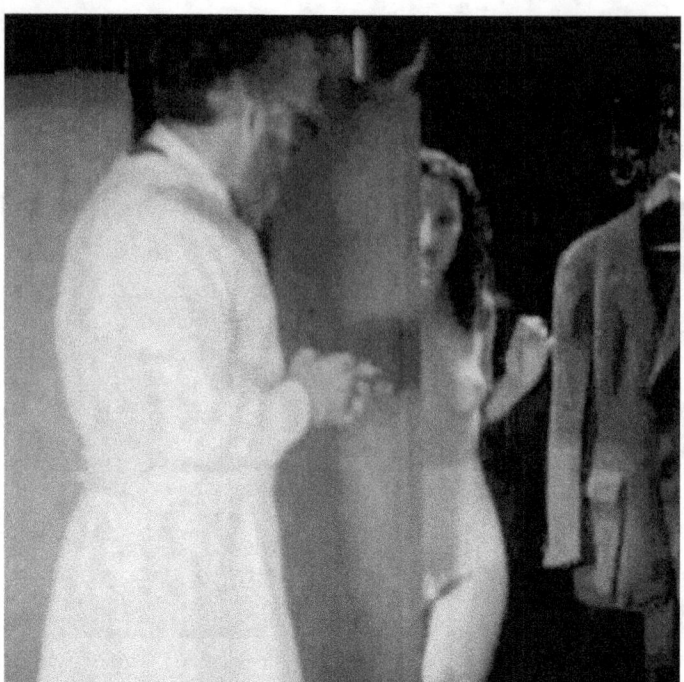

A shockingly candid moment from Dwain Esper's lurid, hypnotic *Maniac*

is highly contagious and extraordinarily infectious. Fear-thought is most dangerous when it masquerades as forethought. Combat fear by replacing it with faith. Resist worry with confidence.

(The quote is from Dr. William S. Sadler, psychiatrist, theologian and debunker of the paranormal who was also, somewhat paradoxically, an elder statesman of sorts in the Chicago-based Urantia Movement. He contributed to the famed "Urantia Book," purportedly a collection of "received" metaphysical and philosophical writings from various spirit guides.)

After an additional assurance that "The Chicago Crime Commission made a survey of 40,000 convicted criminals and found them all suffering from some mental disease," the film proper kicks in. From the get-go, the dialogue is both clunky beyond description and delivered in a tone that suggests hypnosis. This early exchange between Doctor Meirschultz, Maxwell and Satan the Cat (black, of course, although he does turn into a lightly colored tiger during one memorable shot), while likely not intended as such, provides a bit of irony to get things rolling:

Maxwell: It's horrible, I tell you. Working on the dead, trying to bring back life! It's not natural! You with your weird ideas! Haven't I stood here and nursed dying dogs, and even that miserable cat?
Satan (affronted): Hiss!
Maxwell: And for what? For a measly roof and food. Because you took me in when I was down and out!
Doctor (dismissively): Once a ham, always a ham! You? An actor?

That last line could easily have been assigned to any member of *Maniac*'s cast at any point during the film and been as equally effective.

William (here "Bill") Woods' portrayal of the hapless Don Maxwell is his only known onscreen work. He went from fictional make-up whiz to actual make-up artist (alternating between "Bill" and "William" as a first name and "Wood" and "Woods" as a last, tossing his middle initial "D" in now and then). He worked on such lowbrow mainstream cinematic fare as the Bob Hope vehicle *The Paleface* (1948) and *Samson and Delilah* (1950) and in television on episodes of *Have Gun Will Travel*, *Bat Masterson* and *I Spy*, among others.

Some sources assert that Marian Blackton (sister of *Maniac*'s assistant director and daughter of animation pioneer J. Stuart Blackton) appears here in male drag. That isn't the case, though there is the odd fact that Blackton, Ramsey and Andre are billed in the credits with masculinized variations of their given female names.

The "Phyllis Diller" who portrays Mrs. Buckley is not the famous wild-haired comedienne, who would have been 17 or so at the time of *Maniac*'s production. CW

The Medium
Test; b/w; 38 min; Great Britain
D/Co-S: Vernon Sewell *Co-S:* Michael Powell *P:* Jose Levy, Walter Tennyson
Cast: Barbara Gott, Nancy O'Neill, Shayle Gardner, Richard Littledale, Ben Welden, Sandra Lawson

A sculptor murders his wife and hides her body in one of his statues. It's up to a psychic to uncover the awful truth.

Adapted from a Grand Guignol play by Pierre Mills and C. Vylars titled *L'angoisse* (*Anxiety*), *The Medium* has long been considered a lost film. It is chiefly of note as writer/director Vernon Sewell's first work in the horror genre. Sewell (1903-2001) made his directorial debut with the German-made *Morgenrot* (1933), with *Medium* his second effort—and the first to be made in his native England.

The short subject format seems to have suited a scenario adapted from a Grand Guignol sketch, and the plot apparently contained some appropriately grisly elements. The backstory of a haunted dwelling investigated by a psychic obviously appealed to Sewell, who used the same set-up for three of his later horror films: *Latin Quarter* (1945), *Ghost Ship* (1952) and *House of Mystery* (1960).

Sewell's uncredited co-writer was a young Michael Powell, and he returned the favor by lending uncredited assistance on Powell's first major success, *The Edge of the World* (1939). TH

Menace
Paramount; b/w; 57 min; U.S.
D: Ralph Murphy *S:* Chandler Sprague, Anthony Veiller *P:* Bayard Veiller *C:* Benjamin Reynolds
Cast: Gertrude Michael, Paul Cavanagh, Henrietta Crosman, John Lodge, Ray Milland, Berton Churchill, Halliwell Hobbes, Robert Allen, Forrester Harvey, Montagu Love, Arletta Duncan, Gwenllian Gill

A group of friends in Kenya begs one of its numbers, a dam-builder named Freddie Bastion (Milland), to join their card party. He does so, but when an impending thunderstorm starts to look dangerous, he departs. He flies his plane through the storm to the home of his two sisters, which has been built below the newly

erected dam he's overseeing. But as he approaches his destination, he discovers that the dam has burst in the downpour and his sisters' house has washed away. Distraught that his siblings are apparently dead, he kills himself by flying his plane directly into the floodwaters. Years later the three surviving friends—Helen Chalmers (Michael), Colonel Leonard Crecy (Cavanagh) and Norman Bellamy (Churchill)—receive death threats from someone claiming to be Freddie's brother Timothy, who, it seems, has escaped from an insane asylum and blames them for Freddie's death. Fearful, the three gather, along with a group of Freddie's alleged friends and relatives (and a new butler) at a home in Santa Barbara. There they find a menacing note attached to a knife announcing Timothy's presence. They realize he's passing himself off as a member of their group, which proves to be a real problem since no one has any idea what he looks like. The lights go out; the cars are tampered with; the phone line is cut. Murder ensues, and an undercover police detective reveals himself in an effort to force Timothy to do likewise.

Menace is one of many horror films produced in the early to mid-1930s by Paramount Pictures and is easily identifiable as such by its unique look and slick production values. Philip MacDonald (1900-1980), one of the premiere English mystery authors of the time, provided the story on which the movie was based. Indeed, MacDonald's reputation was so strong that not only did he often adapt his own work for the big screen (*The Mystery of Mr. X*, 1934, for instance), he also contributed original scripts to the Charlie Chan and Mr. Moto film series as well as made uncredited contributions to the screenplay of Universal's *The Bride of Frankenstein*. Among his best-known works are *Patrol* (the basis of both a 1929 film and John Ford's 1934 *The Lost Patrol*, starring Boris Karloff), *The List of Adrian Messenger* and the novelization of MGM's hugely successful *Forbidden Planet* (1956).

Part of *Menace*'s charm, apart from an entertaining script that keeps the audience guessing until the very end, is Ralph Murphy's in-your-face direction, most evidenced by a particularly violent onscreen murder. The film came just as the Production Code was beginning to enforce its new rules governing onscreen violence, a policy that went into effect in July 1934. *Menace* was released in November of that year, and the aforementioned homicide indicates that someone was asleep at the switch when appraising it for general release. The oversight works to the film's advantage; it's a beautifully shocking moment, and *Menace* would have been a bit less ... menacing, without it.

The performances are generally good, including one from a young Ray Milland in the small role of suicidal pilot Freddie Bastion. CW

The Moonstone
Monogram; b/w; 45 min; U.S.
   D: Reginald Barker *S:* Adele Buffington *P:* Paul Malvern *C:* Robert Planck
   Cast: David Manners, Phyllis Barry, Gustav Von Seyffertitz, Jameson Thomas, Herbert Bunston, Charles Irwin, Elspeth Dudgeon, John Davidson, Claude King, Olaf Hytten, Evelyn Bostock, Fred Walton, John Power, Harold Entwistle, A.C. Henderson

The Herncastle Moonstone, a diamond originally taken from a sacred idol in India, is to be delivered to heir Anne Verinder (Barry) by family lawyer Franklin Blake (Manners). Some say the stolen stone is cursed, but Anne is more preoccupied with the return of Franklin, who happens to be her beau. A cast of red herrings assembles at the spooky Verinder Manor on a stormy evening, among them Carl Von Lucker (Seyffertitz, looking strangely younger here than in many of his earlier films), who is owed money by Anne's father Sir John Verinder (Bunston) and Yandoo (Davidson), a sinister ex-Hindu swami who is also Franklin's protector and confidante. When the moonstone vanishes and Sir John is found unconscious, everyone becomes a suspect, and Inspector Cuff (Irwin) shows up to solve the crime.

A fairly typical horror-mystery of the period, this version of *The Moonstone* is the most famous film adaptation of Wilkie Collins' oft-filmed 1868 novel of the same name. There had been numerous film adaptations and knock-offs during the silent era (beginning as early as 1909), but this was the first and only theatrical talkie version (several television adaptations came later). Unfortunately, Monogram's bargain-basement treatment trims the novel to the bone while updating its setting to the then-present. The film is thus of a kind with other cheap—though sometimes effective—1930s adaptations of Victorian era horror/mysteries, including Monogram's own *Jane Eyre* (1934) and Universal's *The Mystery of Edwin Drood* (1935).

In an effort to give the film a Universal feel, Monogram hired leading man David Manners (*Dracula*, 1931) to play the heroic Franklin Blake. Manners does a good job with the part, coming across as likeable and sincere opposite the charming Phyllis Barry (*The Invisible Menace*, 1938) as Anne. Gustav Von Seyffertitz (*She*, 1935) is likewise good as the vile Von Lucker. Herbert Bunston (*The Monkey's Paw*, 1933), Charles Erwin (*Kongo*, 1932) and Elspeth Dudgeon (*Sh! The Octopus*, 1937) round out the mostly adept cast. Only John Davidson (*The Devil Bat*, 1940) as Christian convert Swami Yandoo falls short.

Unfortunately the performances are pitted against thoroughly pedestrian direction from Reginald Barker (*Seven Keys to Baldpate*, 1929). Canadian-born Barker (1886-1945) directed a number of silent features before parlaying that success into a few sound features. He died of a heart attack in Los Angeles, California, a decade after shooting his last film, 1935's *Forbidden Heaven*. CW

The Murder in the Museum
aka **Murder in the Museum; The Five Deadly Vices**
Progressive; b/w; 65 min; U.S.

D: Melville Shyer *S:* F.B. Crosswhite *P:* Willis Kent *C:* James Diamond

Cast: Henry B. Walthall, John Harron, Phyllis Barrington, Tom O'Brien, Joseph W. Girard, Symona Boniface, Donald Kerr, Sam Flint, John Elliott, Steve Clemente

Set in the Sphere Museum, which isn't really a museum at all but a venue for freak shows, *The Murder in the Museum* concerns the slaying of a councilman (Flint) intent on shutting the shows down. But rather than taking the heat off the place, the killing sets a police commissioner (Girard) and a newspaper journalist (Harron) to poking around the establishment as they investigate a slew of suspects.

Much has been made of the similarities between *The Murder in the Museum* and a host of Tod Browning productions from the silent and early talkie eras, but beneath the surface, the former and latter are nothing alike. Whereas Browning's films (*The Unknown*, 1927; *Freaks*, 1931) were often thoughtful contemplations on the fragile nature of the human ego, *Murder* is a cheap whodunit with elements of sexploitation, and not a very entertaining one, either.

The only potentially interesting aspect of *Murder* to film connoisseurs is the presence of Henry B. Walthall in the cast, which he headlines despite essaying a supportive role to young lead John Harron. Walthall had been a major star of the silent era, but by the time the talkies came along, he was relegated to supporting parts in mostly minor productions. Still, he amassed an amazing number of screen credits with many horror films among them, including *The Sealed Room* (1909), *Rose O'Salem Town* (1910), *The Avenging Conscience: or 'Thou Shalt Not Kill'* (1914), *Ghosts* and *The Raven* (both 1915), *The Marriage Chance* (1922), *London After Midnight* (1927), *Stark Mad* (1929), *Chandu the Magician* (1932), *The Whispering Shadow* and *The Flaming Signal* (both 1933) and *The Devil Doll* (1936). He worked right up until his death by influenza in June of 1936, with his last three films being released posthumously.

The show's lead, John Harron, has the spotlight yanked from him by Walthall's commanding performance. Harron was

Sneaky goings-on in *The Murder in the Museum.*

never really star material and had gotten into movies mostly because of his older brother Robert, a silent film star who had died in 1920 in a "shooting accident" that many scholars believe was suicide. John's career didn't last long; shoehorned into low-budget films, he never found lasting success and died at the age of 36 in 1939, shortly after being diagnosed with spinal meningitis. CW

Mystery Liner
aka **The Ghost of John Holling**
Monogram; b/w; 62 min; U.S.

D: William Nigh *S:* Wellyn Totman *P:* Paul Malvern *C:* Archie Stout

Cast: Noah Beery, Astrid Allwyn, Edwin Maxwell, Gustav von Seyffertitz, Ralph Lewis, Cornelius Keefe, Zeffie Tilbury, Boothe Howard, Howard Hickman, Jerry Stewart, George Hayes, George Cleveland, John Maurice Sullivan

Based on Edgar Wallace's novel *The Ghost of John Holling*, *Mystery Liner* is an insignificant espionage thriller that wants to be a horror movie. The ship on which it is set is equipped with "old dark house" secret passages and lab equipment straight out of *Frankenstein* (1931). There's also a deranged captain, a couple of murders, a bit of science fiction (a remote control gadget and a television-like device on which messages can be transmitted), and, in the center of it all, the sinister red herring doings by the likes of Gustav von Seyffertitz and the villainy of Edwin Maxwell.

Professor Grimson (Lewis) has created the S505, a tube (!) that guides ships remotely from long distances. He wants to test its capabilities, and Captain Holling (Beery) agrees to allow him to use his ship for the experiment. But before they set sail, the captain goes insane, is placed in an asylum and escapes, after which the professor is brutally attacked and his neck broken. The ship sets sail nonetheless with a motley crew aboard, including a horny old woman, Granny Plimpton (Tilbury), whose attempts to find a lover provide the film's only intended humor. Soon the spectral Holling is skulking about and the replacement captain is murdered (his neck likewise broken), with more violence still to come. In the end, the person the viewer is meant to least suspect (and is therefore most likely to suspect) is indeed the culprit: the representative of a nameless foreign power who means to steal the S505, but only after confirmation that it actually works.

Despite its advertising campaign—"The Ghost of a Former Captain … A Maniac at Large on Shipboard! … Murder after Murder! … A Masterless Ship Plowing the Fog-Enshrouded Seas!"—the film is a whole helluva lot less interesting than it sounds. The pace is exceedingly slow, though inadvertently funny dialogue as the following livens things up occasionally:

> Professor Grimson: My work is now finished, Watson. It is now up to S505.
> First Officer: What is S505?
> Professor Grimson: The … uh … tube controls the energy, which will operate it by radio.
> First Officer: It's uncanny, professor.
> Professor Grimson: It's science.

Even Granny Plimpton seems fed up by the tedium, commenting (at the film's 52-minute mark) that "… [I was] never so bored in all my life …" Right after that point, the film does come to life with a few minutes of excitement before the end titles roll; but unfortunately, it's too little too late.

William Nigh had had a promising beginning in the silent era, even directing the likes of Lon Chaney (in *Mr. Wu* in 1927) for MGM. But his inability to draw convincing performances from actors in the sound era kept him floundering almost entirely in B-movies. Most of his horror output was for Monogram (*House of Mystery* and *The Mysterious Mr. Wong*, both 1934; *The Ape*, 1940, and *Black Dragons*, 1942), though he did shoot one very minor horror film for Universal (*The Strange Case of Dr. Rx*, 1942). Without a clue as to how to establish mood, effectively pace action or coach dialogue, the success or failure of his films was always predicated entirely upon the quality of the scripts he shot. He was never as bad as fellow Monogram director William Beaudine, but neither were his films ever as entertaining. CW

The Mystery of Mr. X
aka **Mystery of Mr. X; The Mystery of Mister X**
MGM; b/w; 84 min; U.S.

D: Edgar Selwyn, Richard Boleslawski *S:* Howard Emmett Rogers, Philip MacDonald, Monckton Hoffe *P:* Lawrence Weingarten *C:* Oliver T. Marsh *M:* William Axt

Cast: Robert Montgomery, Elizabeth Allan, Lewis Stone, Ralph Forbes, Henry Stephenson, Forrester Harvey, Ivan Simpson, Leonard Mudie, Alec B. Francis, Charles Irwin, Olaf Hytten

A string of murders has Scotland Yard baffled; all the victims have been run through with a sword cane and left with a chilling calling card signed by "Mr. X." Jewel thief Nick Revel (Montgomery) falls under suspicion, as do his associates "Hutch" Hutchinson (Simpson) and Joe Palmer (Harvey). Looking to clear his name, Nick investigates on his own in the hopes of unmasking the mysterious Mr. X.

Adapted by Philip MacDonald from his novel *The Mystery of the Dead Police*, *The Mystery of Mr. X* is a brisk and efficient murder mystery. The film gets a tremendous boost from Robert Montgomery, who gives a scene-stealing performance as the charming jewel thief turned amateur detective. A few years later, Montgomery likewise did a terrific job as a homicidal maniac in *Night Must Fall* (1937), though today he is best remembered as a light comedic leading man in less imposing fare.

The excellent supporting cast includes Lewis Stone (*The Mask of Fu Manchu*, 1932) as yet another impatient authority figure, Elizabeth Allan (*Mark of the Vampire*, 1935) as the resourceful damsel in distress and Forrester Harvey (*The Wolf Man*, 1941) as a cabbie who falls under suspicion. And there's just enough London fog and characters scuttling around in the dark to maintain a creepy atmosphere throughout.

Director Edgar Selwyn was at the end of his short and none-too-distinguished directorial career at the time of this film. He directed sporadically from 1929 until 1934 but found far more success as a writer. His handling of the material here is brisk and effective, but he may have had help from an uncredited Richard Boleslawski, who was brought in for some unspecified retakes. Sometimes billed as Richard Boleslavski, he was responsible for a number of prestigious pictures for MGM, including *Rasputin and the Empress* (1932), starring John, Lionel and Ethel Barrymore, *Les Miserables* (1935), starring Charles Laughton and Fredric March and *Clive of India* (1935), starring Ronald Coleman and Colin Clive. TH

The 9th Guest
aka **The Ninth Guest**
Columbia; b/w; 65 min; U.S.

D: Roy William Neill *S:* Owen Davis, Garnett Weston *C:* Benjamin H. Kline *M:* Louis Silvers

Cast: Donald Cook, Genevieve Tobin, Hardie Albright, Edward Ellis, Edwin Maxwell, Vince Barnett, Helen Flint, Samuel S. Hinds, Nella Walker, Sidney Bracey

Eight strangers spend the night together in a penthouse apartment. None of them has any idea who has invited them, but during the course of the evening a strange voice on the radio informs them that, before the night is through, they will all be dead. The group then bands together to thwart their unseen assailant.

This B-murder mystery with horror overtones was based on the novel *The Invisible Host* by Gwen Bistow and Bruce Manning which, first published in 1930, is a thinly disguised knockoff of Agatha Christie's venerable tale *Ten Little Indians*. Director Roy William Neill here proves adept at building tension and making the most of his limited settings; he went on to helm some of the most impressive horror and suspense items of the 1930s and '40s. He is best remembered for his stylish work on 11 of the 14 Sherlock Holmes films that starred Basil Rathbone and Nigel Bruce. *The Ninth Guest* isn't among his best work, but it does show Neill honing his skill as a storyteller and a stylist. The following year the director was back at Columbia guiding Boris Karloff through one of his finest performances in *The Black Room*.

Leading man Donald Cook later had a featured role in James Whale's lavish *Showboat* (1936) and toplined Universal's final and least horrific version of *The Secret of the Blue Room* (1933), the humor-tinged *Murder in the Blue Room* (1944).

Guest's supporting cast includes Samuel S. Hinds, a busy character actor who was later menaced by Karloff and Bela Lugosi in *The Raven* (1935) before playing James Stewart's father in *It's A Wonderful Life* (1946). TH

The Phantom of the Convent
aka **Il fantasma del convento; Ghost of the Convent**
FESA; b/w; 85 min; Mexico

D: Fernando De Fuentes *S:* Juan Bustillo Oro, Fernando De Fuentes, Jorge Pezet *P:* Jorge Pezet *C:* Ross Fisher *M:* Max Urban

Cast: Enrique del Campo, Marta Ruel, Carlos Villatoro, Paco Martinez, Victorio Blanco, Francisco Lugo, Beltran de Heredia, Agustin Gonzalez, Jose Ignacio Rocha

Eduardo (Villatoro) and his wife Cristina (Ruel) are journeying through the forest with their friend Alfonzo (del Campo) when they become lost. They meet up with a monk (Blanco), who gives them sanctuary at a nearby convent. While there, their personalities change for the worse. Cristina tries to seduce Alfonso, and the travelers bicker amongst themselves. More weirdness transpires as the evening goes on.

The Phantom of the Convent was one of the earliest horror films to emerge from the Mexican film industry. While Mexico didn't really make its mark in the genre until the international success of *The Vampire* (1957), early titles such as this and *The Crying Woman* (1933) demonstrated a genuine flair for the macabre.

The Phantom of the Convent was directed by Fernando De Fuentes, a key figure in the early days of Mexican cinema who remained active in the country's fantasy film scene until the early 1960s. One of his last credits was the Lon Chaney vehicle *Face of the Screaming Werewolf* (1964), for which he contributed to the screenplay. De Fuentes was plainly influenced by German Expressionism via the Universal horror films that were flooding the marketplace when *Phantom* was made.

Despite a low budget and primitive production techniques (the film industry in Mexico was still struggling to get on its feet in light of the devastation wrought by the Mexican Revolution), *Phantom* offers rich visuals and a nice, gloomy atmosphere.

The next major Mexican horror film was *Two Monks* (1934). TH

Picture Brides
Allied; b/w; 59 (66) min; U.S.

D: Phil Rosen *S:* Adele Buffington *P:* M.H. Hoffman *C:* Harry Neumann, Tom Galligan

Cast: Dorothy Mackaill, Regis Toomey, Dorothy Libaire, Alan Hale, Will Ahern, Harvey Clark, Mary Kornman, Esther Muir, Mae Busch, Gladys Ahern, Fred Malatesta, Viva Tattersall, Al Hill, Michael Visaroff, Brooks Benedict, Franklin Parker, Larry McGrath, Jimmy Aubrey

Four tarnished women—Mame (Mackaill), Flo (Muir), Gwen (Busch) and Lena (Tattersall)—and a girl named Mary Lee (Libaire), who's just looking for a job—arrive at the Brazilian river village of Lottogrosso, where the evil Von Luden (Hale) co-owns and runs the Standard Diamond Mine. The women (except for Mary Lee) are mail-order brides. Knowing what could happen to the innocent Mary Lee at the hands of the lecherous bachelors, Mame gives the young girl her picture bride card, thus marking her as taken by Dave Hart (Toomey), a ruggedly handsome miner who also happens to be on the lam from an embezzlement conviction.

When the ladies first go ashore, they are distressed by the conditions there, prompting Gwen to proclaim, "My word! There isn't anything here but tattooed women and snake charmers," to which Mame replies, "*We're* the snake charmers, baby, if you get what I mean." Mary, who it seems is not only innocent but also vapid, asks, "Aren't there any white people around here?"

She quickly learns that it isn't the non-whites she should fear, for immediately after posing her insipid question, the newcomers encounter Von Luden, who's in the process of shooting a native in cold blood because the man demanded to be paid for his work. Still alive, the worker is about to be tossed into an alligator-infested swamp, but good-hearted criminal Dave insists that he be taken to Doc Rogers (Clark) and fixed up.

Repulsed and turned on in equal measure by Von Luden, Mame offers to marry him. At the same time, Dave refuses to wed Mary without having even seen her. This leaves Mary available for Von Luden, who decides he prefers the virgin to the tramp. Happily, however, when Dave sees Mary for the first time, he quickly changes his mind.

Later, when Mary's dress is accidentally torn, she is taken to a bedroom to mend it. There, Von Luden attacks her. Mame overhears Mary's screams and alerts Dave, who breaks down the door and takes on Von Luden. As the two duke it out, the feisty Mame steps in and knocks out the bad guy. The next day Von Luden, aware of Dave's fugitive status, summons the police. From here things only get worse.

Picture Brides is one of a number of sleazy jungle pictures produced in the 1930s, but with its focus on sexual obsession and depravity, it owes more to Tod Browning's silent horror film *West of Zanzibar* (1928) than it does to its tamer contemporaries. The most shocking scene comes when the doctor's daughter Mataeo (Kornman), after being gussied up by Mary and Mame to celebrate her 18th birthday, is attacked, raped and murdered by Von Luden. (This scene is missing from the 59-minute print of the film, though it's clear where it occurs: After Mataeo approaches Von Luden and announces that she's now a woman, the scene fades to black and changes abruptly, cutting her off in mid-sentence.)

The film is based on the play *Red Kisses* by Charles E. Blaney and Harry Clay Blaney and is actually an entertaining, if seedy, mixture of adventure, horror and romance. Former silent film cinematographer Phil Rosen took on the directing chores, lending the film a glossy look it would have lacked had it been helmed by someone of lesser talent.

The actors acquit themselves well, though top-billed Dorothy Mackaill as the tough but softhearted Mame grabs the attention from everyone else every time she shows up on screen. Mackaill had been both a Ziegfeld Follies girl and a screen star during the silent era. Despite her good looks, mellifluous voice and charming presence, she remained mired in low-budget B-pictures once talkies caught on. She made her last film in 1937. In her later years she moved to Hawaii, where she appeared in two episodes, four years apart, of the television series *Hawaii Five-O*. She died there in 1990 of kidney failure. CW

The Return of Chandu
Sol Lesser; b/w; 15 chapters; U.S.

D: Ray Taylor *S:* Barry Barringer *P:* Sol Lesser *C:* John Hickson *M:* Abe Meyer, Charles Dunworth, Francis Gromon, Hen Herkan, Felix Mills, Josiah Zuro

Cast: Bela Lugosi, Maria Alba, Clara Kimball Young, Lucien Prival, Dean Benton, Jack Clark, Josef Swickard, Wilfred Lucas, Cyril Ambrister, Murdock MacQuarrie

Princess Nadji (Alba) finds herself in danger when the black magic cult of Ubasti decides that she's the reincarnation of their long-dead queen. The cult kidnaps her with the aim of awakening the queen's spirit in Nadji's body. It's up to the intrepid Chandu (Lugosi) to prevent this diabolical reincarnation from taking place.

Secret agent Frank Chandler (aka Chandu) sprang into being in 1932 as the eponymous character in a Los Angeles radio drama. Written by Harry A. Earnshaw, Vera M. Oldham and R.R. Morgan, KHJ radio's *Chandu the Magician* was unapologetic hokum designed to thrill children and undiscerning adults. The series' immediate and enormous popularity inspired Fox to

This time out Bela Lugosi gets to play the hero in the serial thriller, *The Return of Chandu*.

give it the feature-film treatment, and the commercial success of *Chandu the Magician* (1932) in turn inspired this quickie serial follow-up.

But whereas the first filmed *Chandu* came from a major studio and employed state-of-the-art special effects, this outing isn't nearly as polished. The producers of *Return* did make one major improvement, however, by replacing the rather dull Edmund Lowe with Bela Lugosi (the villainous Roxor in the first film) as the heroic magician. Lugosi, neither leering nor skulking about, clearly has a ball here; relishing his rare opportunity to play a valiant man of action, he emerges as an engaging and charming hero. (The supporting cast, regrettably, isn't up to his standard, with Maria Alba proving particularly dreadful as Princess Nadji.)

The film makes good use of standing sets from *King Kong* (1933)—horror movie enthusiasts will instantly recognize the huge doors that framed Kong's attack on the Skull Island village—but overall looks poverty stricken when compared to the Fox feature. And while there's indisputably plenty of action, it all becomes a bit redundant after a while, with too many abductions and rescues to keep track of.

The 15-chapter serial was eventually re-edited into two separate features: a stand-alone edit of *The Return of Chandu* (1934), and *Chandu on Magic Island* (1935). Chapters one through four of the serial went into the first film, while the remaining 11 episodes were edited into the second. Sharp-eared viewers will recognize that the soundtrack—comprised mostly of stock music—includes snippets also used in the golden age classics *White Zombie* (1932) and *The Vampire Bat* (1933). TH

Return of the Terror
First National; b/w; 65 min; U.S.

D: Howard Bretherton *S:* Peter Milne, Eugene Solow *P:* Samuel Bischoff *C:* Arthur L. Todd *M:* Bernhard Kaun

Cast: Lyle Talbot, Mary Astor, John Halliday, Frank McHugh, Robert Barrat, Irving Pichel, George E. Stone, J. Carrol Naish, Frank Reicher, Robert Emmett O'Connor, Renee Whitney, Etienne Giardot, Maude Eburne, Charley Grapewin,

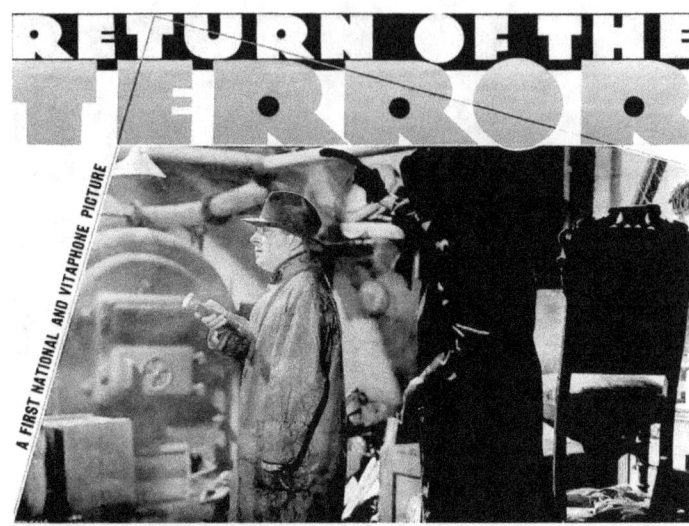

An original lobby card from *Return of the Terror* depicts the mysterious killer with a fetish for calling cards.

George Humbert, Edmund Breese, George Cooper, Cecil Cunningham, Frank Conroy, Howard C. Hickman, Lorena Layson, Harry Seymour, Philip Morris, Bert Moorhouse, Eddie Shubert

Dr. John Redmayne (Halliday), dubbed The Terror by the press, is put on trial for murder. Redmayne denies that he poisoned his patients but admits that he committed one mercy killing. On the advice of his lawyer Daniel Burke (Pichel), he pleads insanity and is sentenced to confinement in his own sanitarium. After several months of incarceration, however, Redmayne begins to actually go insane while, simultaneously, a fresh series of killings occur, each accompanied by a note signed "The Terror."

Edgar Wallace's hit play *The Terror* made it to the silver screen in 1928 as the first all-talking, feature-length horror film. It did well, and First National, who produced the picture, decided to capitalize on its popularity with this follow-up. *Return*'s story is only marginally connected to the events of the first film, though once again a mysterious killer with a fetish for calling cards is on the loose. The clever scenario plays on perceived insanity in a way that foreshadows later film noir classics, including Samuel Fuller's *Shock Corridor* (1963).

Like its more-famous predecessor, *Return of the Terror* has long been considered lost. This is particularly regrettable given its interesting array of character actors, many of whom are familiar to fans of golden age horror cinema. Frank Reicher (*King Kong*, 1933), Irving Pichel (*Dracula's Daughter*, 1936), J. Carrol Naish (*House of Frankenstein*, 1944) and Frank McHugh (*Mystery of the Wax Museum*, 1933), among others, were in its cast.

Wallace's story got its next cinematic go-around in the British-made *The Terror* (1938). TH

Secret of the Chateau

Universal; b/w; 66 min; U.S.

D: Richard Thorpe *S:* Albert DeMond, Harry Behn, Llewellyn Hughes *P:* Lou L. Ostrow *C:* Robert H. Planck *M:* Abe Meyer, Heinz Roemheld, Oliver Wallace

Cast: Claire Dodd, Alice White, Osgood Perkins, Jack La Rue, George E. Stone, Clark Williams, William Faversham, Ferdinand Gottschalk, DeWitt Jennings, Helen Ware, Frank Reicher, Alphonse Ethier, Morgan Brown, Olaf Hytten

Inspector Marotte (Gottschalk) investigates a series of murders linked to an original Gutenberg Bible. Suspicion falls upon Julie Verlaine (Dodd), who indeed plans to steal the bible, though her dishonesty stops short of murder. Julie, in turn, suspects that Paul (Williams) is the guilty party. She pays a visit to Paul's chateau, where a number of suspicious characters happen to be assembled.

Universal's *Secret of the Chateau* is yet another mystery-thriller masquerading as a horror film. Lumped together with "authentic" horror films (*Frankenstein* and *Dracula*, 1931) and borderline entries (*The Man Who Reclaimed His Head*, 1934) in the now-famous *Shock Theater* television syndication package in the 1950s, the film is of interest chiefly to completists. The original ad mats promised the kind of thrills one associates with a more overtly morbid thriller, such as *The Cat and the Canary* (1927), but *Chateau* merely offers up a pretty standard cross-and-double-cross crime scenario in which everybody has a secret.

Performances are professional, if not particularly inspired. Osgood Perkins stars as one of many red herrings. Two years prior to this, Perkins had sired a son, Anthony, who later followed in his father's footsteps. But alas, the younger Perkins' success arrived far too late to impress his father, who passed away in 1937 at age 45 from a massive heart attack.

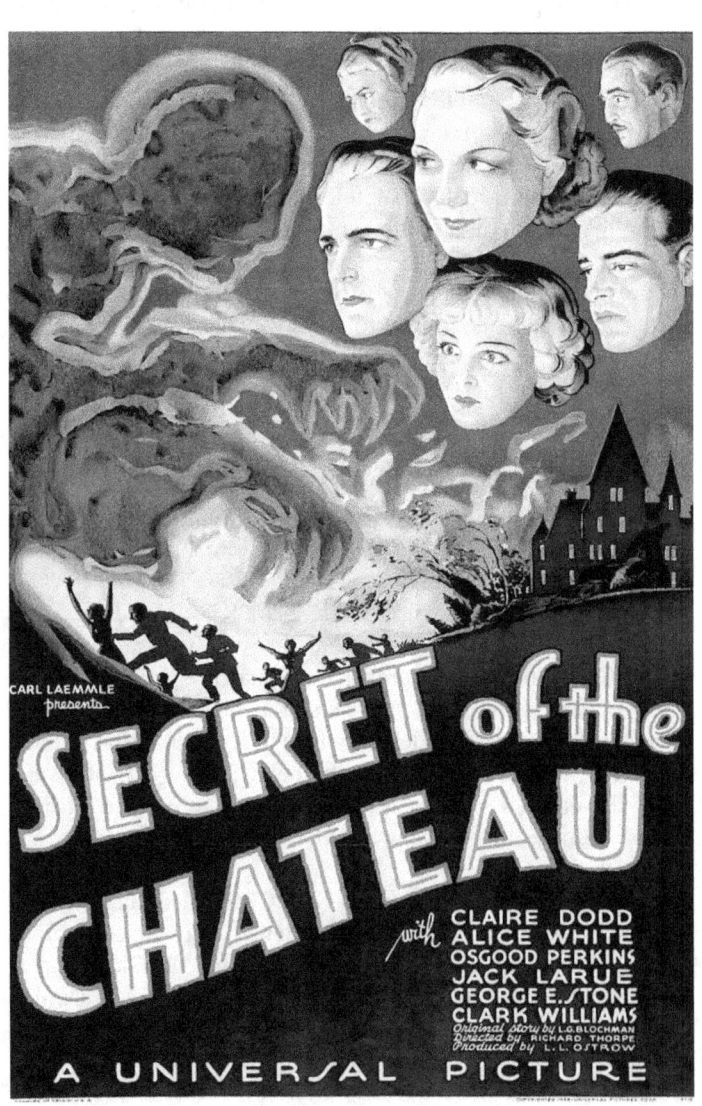

Director Richard Thorpe was a prolific talent, active from 1923 until 1967. Though never regarded as top-of-the-line, he was a dependable journeyman who always brought his films in on time and budget. His best-known title is the first screen version of *Night Must Fall* (1937), which provided him with far more appetizing material to work with than did *Secret of the Chateau*. TH

The Secret of the Loch
aka **The Loch Ness Mystery**
Wyndham; b/w; 72 (80) min; Great Britain
 D: Milton Rosmer *S:* Charles Bennett, Billie Bristow *P:* Ray Wyndham *C:* James Wilson *M:* Peter Mendoza
 Cast: Seymour Hicks, Nancy O'Neil, Gibson Gowland, Frederick Peisley, Eric Hales, Ben Field, Hubert Harben, Stafford Hilliard, Rosamund John, Robb Wilton, John Jamieson, Elma Reid

The monster of Loch Ness as seen in *The Secret of the Loch*

The first sighting of a creature in the vicinity of the River Ness, which feeds the famous Loch Ness in Scotland, was allegedly by St. Columba in the 6th century. The account, which had Columba repelling the "water beast" with the sign of the cross, first appeared in *Vita Columbae*, written by St. Adomnán of Iona, a century after it purportedly took place. Adomnán's recounting placed the beast squarely in the realm of the metaphysical, a demonic manifestation tamed by the power of faith.

No more was heard of the creature until 1933, when a couple claimed to have seen a large, long-necked monster cross the road in front of their car, move through the brush and vanish into the water of Loch Ness. Their account was published in a local newspaper the following month, around the same time that a motorcyclist maintained that he nearly hit the same creature while out riding late one evening. No one could precisely describe the animal's means of locomotion on ground, but the stories conjured images of prehistoric plesiosaurs, marine reptiles with long necks, sharp teeth for eating fish and paddles and a tail for locomotion in water.

Plesiosaur fossils had been discovered in England over a century before, and there were specimens gracing the halls of museums around the world by the early 1900s, so it doesn't seem to be a stretch that people claiming to have seen a monster in the loch would describe it in plesiosaur-like terms. There's also the matter of 1933's worldwide release of RKO's *King Kong*; one of the Skull Island monsters was a "Brontosaur," a long-necked dinosaur believed at the time to live in water, and another an "Elasmosaur," a plesiosaur inaccurately depicted as having arms, legs, clawed hands and feet and living on land. *Kong*'s massive success likely fed the spate of sightings of giant, antediluvian monsters, Scottish and otherwise.

After the initial sightings at the loch, tourists hoping to see the beast, or possibly to photograph or film it, began to scour the shoreline, spurring sensational headlines that in turn drew more tourists. And by 1934, the search for the so-called Loch Ness monster had gained such renown that British movie producer Ray Wyndham realized the potential of a *King Kong* of his own.

Wyndham was no high-powered movie producer; he was a small-time player in the industry, after a quick buck by milking Britain's quickie quota rule. He'd made only a couple of films when he approached powerhouse playwright Charles Bennett to compose a story treatment. Bennett did so, taking care not to include too many scenes that would require special effects; in that spirit he went back to Sir Arthur Conan Doyle's bestselling novel *The Lost World* (1912) for inspiration, drawing from its story of a grumpy professor trying to prove the existence of living *dinosauria* and the reporter who provides his link to the rational world.

Given its small budget, it's no wonder that former actor Milton Rosmer—as opposed to an up-and-comer like Alfred Hitchcock or Michael Powell—was chosen to direct. Rosmer was a competent specialist who'd been working since the silent era, but he wasn't much of a stylist. While never as prolific as his contemporary Maurice Elvey, he was every bit as unoriginal and the finished product here attests to that, though a few of his following projects (*Maria Marten, or The Murder in the Red Barn*, 1935; *Goodbye, Mr. Chips*, 1939) did manage to exhibit a bit of artistic growth.

The Secret of the Loch begins with a fictionalized extract from the *Daily Mail* of October 19, 1933, which states, "Whether people believe in the existence of a Loch Ness Monster or not, Highlanders are convinced that the watery depths harbor some fantastic, and abnormal creature." The action then begins with a man running through the woods toward a small tavern while apprehensive people gather children and livestock into homes and barns. The man rushes into the pub and yells, "Boys, boys! I've seen it!" The *it* in question was the head of a long-necked beast poking from the mire of the loch's waters. As he gives his account, something akin to a howl emanates from outside the pub, after which Professor Heggie (Hicks) bursts through the front doors, insisting that a prehistoric animal does indeed reside in the loch.

That's a promising enough start, but unfortunately, it's all downhill from there. Too much of the film's running time is spent following Professor Heggie as he talks about proving the existence of a dinosaur—to wit, a Diplodocus, though he can't pronounce the word correctly—in the loch's waters. He believes that blasting operations (!) have opened an underground cavern and hatched a prehistoric egg therein, and though he presents

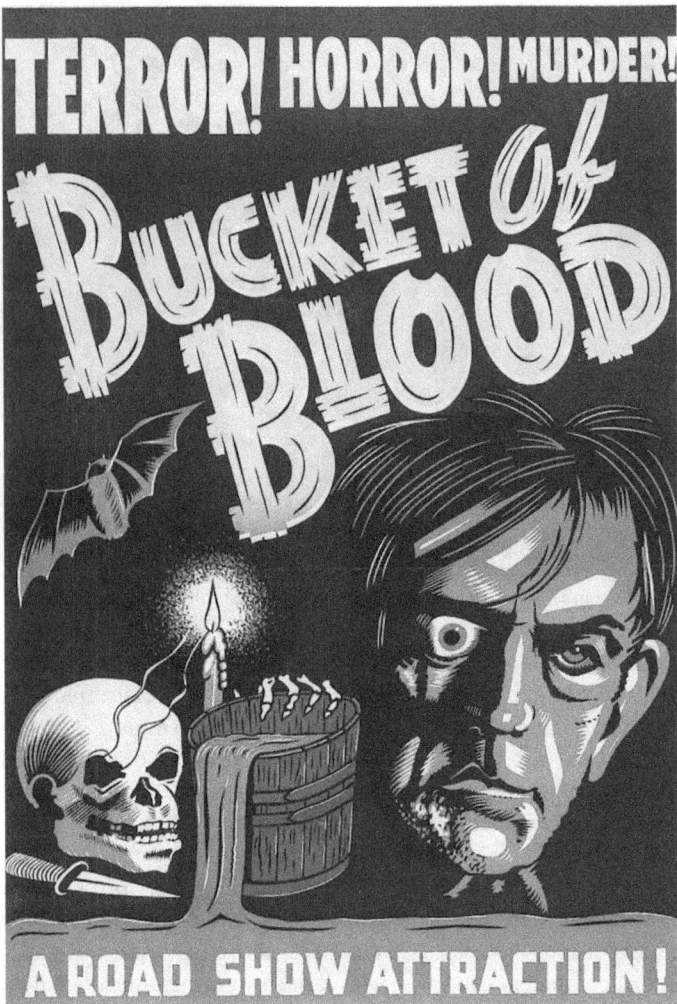
A Du-World reissue one-sheet poster for *The Tell-Tale Heart*

no scientific evidence for his ravings, reporter Jimmy Anderson (Peisley) wants the story for his paper. When Heggie refuses to cooperate, the handsome young reporter resorts to romancing the professor's beautiful granddaughter Angela (O'Neil), with another way-too-long chunk of the film being dedicated to their screwball courtship.

It isn't until the final reel that the monster is unveiled, and what an underwhelming monster it is—an iguana that looks nothing like a Diplodocus or a Plesiosaur or anything, really, other than an iguana, its size enhanced via miniatures and rear-screen projection. And even when this beastie gets to devour someone, the monster's mayhem is done offscreen, lessening the moment's potential coolness.

The film, which was released in May of 1934, got something of a coincidental publicity boost when, a month before, a then-unnamed surgeon produced a picture he claimed to have taken of the beast. The image showed a small, reptilian head sitting atop a long neck rising out of the water. (It's since been proved to be a fake.) But even this tabloidish tidbit didn't help the film for long; word got out quickly that *The Secret of the Loch* was talk, talk and more talk. And not only did the film flop in its native Great Britain, it couldn't find a distributor in the usually reliable United States or Australia either (though an edited version later made the late-night television rounds in both countries).

None of this is to say that *Secret* is entirely without merit. The film's photography is sharp, particularly in the external scenes (some of which are actually well-integrated stock footage), and the set direction is nice. One scene was even filmed in the paleontology department of a museum, with the bones of a prehistoric mastodon or mammoth in full view, providing a bit of verisimilitude to the proceedings.

The performances are likewise good, especially Seymour Hicks as Professor Heggie. Hicks had gotten his start as Ebenezer Scrooge in the 1913 film *Old Scrooge*, a role he repeated on the stage many times and in a second film, *Scrooge*, in 1935. Though he was only in about 25 movies between 1913 and 1949, his many stage performances and authored plays got him a Knighthood in 1935. He died of influenza in April 1949.

Yet, strong performances, nice sets and solid photography aren't enough to make up for a dreary and unexciting script that tells rather than shows the viewer what's going on. And it's for that reason that cinema's very first appearance of The Loch Ness Monster is all but forgotten today.

The Secret of the Loch's one claim to fame may be that it was edited by David Lean, who went on to become one of Britain's most important, award-winning directors. CW

Shivers
Columbia; b/w; 20 min; U.S.
D/S: Arthur Ripley *P:* Jules White *M:* Louis Silvers
Cast: Harry Langdon, Dick Elliott, Chester Gan, Florence Lake, Louise Vincenot

Ichabod Somerset Crop (Harry Langdon) earns his living writing mysteries. But when he moves into a haunted house to find inspiration, the experience nearly proves the death of him.

Shivers offers yet another variation on the tired old formula of a skeptic confronting his skepticism in a haunted house. A comedy short, it was designed to showcase the talent of star Harry Langdon, whose popularity had been steadily waning since the late 1920s. He broke into films relatively late in life following a successful stint in vaudeville and had found widespread popularity in a string of silent comedies, several of which were directed by a young Frank Capra. Allegedly, Langdon grew jealous of sharing praise with the likes of Capra and opted to strike out on his own. Whatever his motivation, his solo efforts were less than stellar, and a series of self-produced box-office bombs tarnished his reputation for good. Even so, he remained active in cinema until his death in 1944, at the age of 60.

Like many of Langdon's vehicles, *Shivers* has faded into obscurity. The film should not be confused with David Cronenberg's feature debut of the same title, which was released in the United States as *They Came From Within* (1975). TH

The Tell-Tale Heart
aka **Bucket of Blood**
Hurst/Clifton; b/w; 53 (55) min; Great Britain
D: Brian Desmond Hurst *S:* David Plunkett Greene *P:* Harry Clifton *M:* John Reynders
Cast: Norman Dryden, John Kelt, Yolande Terrell, Thomas Shenton, James Fleck, Colonel Cameron, Tom Shenton

A young man (Dryden) murders his uncle (Kelt) and believes that he has gotten away with it. But in the end his guilty conscience does him in.

Long before helming what many believe to be the definitive version of Charles Dickens' *A Christmas Carol* (1951), Brian Desmond Hurst cut his teeth on B-grade programmers. *The Tell-Tale Heart* was his directorial debut, though reviewers of the time didn't perceive much potential talent behind the camera. The Irish-born filmmaker later made his mark with the World War II propaganda picture *The Lion Has Wings* (1939), but he was never the most prolific of filmmakers; between 1934 and 1962, he directed a mere 26 titles.

The script hews closely to Edgar Allan Poe's short story, but the arch performances and slim production values smother any spark of mood or atmosphere. The cast is comprised of theatrical performers, most of whom never acted in the movies again. Yolande Terrell, as the young woman who catches the protagonist's eye, did go on to play a supporting role in Arthur Woods' superb *They Drive by Night* (1938), but even she made only a handful of film appearances.

The film was issued in the United States as *Bucket of Blood* (1934), but there is no connection between it and Roger Corman's witty *A Bucket of Blood* (1959). Poe's story got its next cinematic go-around with Jules Dassin's short subject, *The Tell-Tale Heart*, produced in 1941 by MGM. TH

Terror Aboard
aka Dead Reckoning
Paramount; b/w; 69 (63) min; U.S.

D: Paul Sloane *S:* Robert Presnell Sr., Manuel Seff, Harvey F. Thew *P:* William LeBaron *C:* Harry Fischbeck *M:* Herman Hand, John Leipold

Cast: John Halliday, Charles Ruggles, Shirley Grey, Neil Hamilton, Jack La Rue, Verree Teasdale, Stanley Fields, Leila Bennett, Morgan Wallace, Thomas E. Jackson, William Janney, Paul Hurst, Frank Hagney Clarence Wilson, Paul Porcasi, Bobby Dunn, Kit Guard, Peter Hancock

Upon emerging from a dense fog, a cargo ship comes upon a passenger liner traveling in circles as if unmanned. The captain of the cargo ship assembles a team and boards the liner, only to find that it's littered with dead bodies. He finds a tattered radiogram announcing that the "Bankrupt Police" (a branch of law enforcement apparently international in scope) is seeking the arrest of the liner's owner for grand larceny and forgery. The narrative then fades to the moment when the liner's owner, Maximilian Kreig (Halliday), received the message from his radio operator (Janney). Kreig asks the operator whether a group of nearby islands is occupied. When he gets the answer he wants (some of them aren't, he learns), he shoots the operator in cold blood and then sets about isolating his fiancée Lili Kingston (Grey) from the other passengers, his goal being for the two of them to escape to a deserted island and live unimpeded by the law. Oh, and for additional insurance, he wants everyone else on the boat dead, a goal he partially accomplishes by turning the passengers against one another (though he's not above committing murder himself when opportunity permits). His plan is threatened, however, by the inopportune (and too improbable to be accidental—but at least the film is sensible enough to point this out) arrival of Lili's ex, a pilot named Jim Cowles (Hamilton). When Cowles admits his desire to win Lili back, it drives Kreig even madder.

Halliwell's Film, Video & DVD Guide mistakenly describes *Terror Aboard* as a "fair murder mystery," despite the fact that it's anything but (to the audience, anyway). What it is is a largely forgotten gem, an explicit exercise in voyeuristic sadism from the pre-Code era. Film buffs have referred to *Terror Aboard* as the *Friday the 13th* (1980) of its time, a fairly accurate appraisal of a film that wouldn't be bested in the body count arena until Mario Bava's *Twitch of the Death Nerve* (1971) almost 40 years later. Like that later film, *Terror* presents a barrage of shootings and stabbings, along with deaths by drowning, freezing, poisoning and hanging. One of the film's most disquieting moments comes early, when the radio operator is offed: There's a close up of the unsuspecting victim, with his murderer out of frame. A shot is heard, and the viewer is left to wonder for a moment whether Kreig has just committed suicide. The operator sits blankly for a moment, stunned, before his white jacket becomes stained with seeping blood! It's not the sort of sequence one expects in a film of this vintage, and it's certainly an example of the sort of thing that spurred the Production Code the following year to institute new, stronger rules governing what could be shown onscreen.

Paul Sloane was first and foremost a writer, but beginning in 1925 he tried his hand at directing. *Terror Aboard* appears to have been his only attempt at a horror film, and what a stylish and well-conceived attempt it is—outside of some noxious comedy relief from Charles Ruggles and a nitwit, man-crazy maid. It's an exercise in cathartic brutality that makes no bones about its *raison d'etre*; people die in ways assorted and creative (a scene in which most of the ship's crew is bumped off *en masse* is particularly clever).

Perhaps because of the film's lowbrow, guilty-pleasure nature, Sloane doesn't seem to have been offered much work afterward. He retired from the industry not long after *Terror*, except for an unsuccessful comeback attempt in 1950. He died of a heart attack in New York City in 1963.

Among the film's cast are a bevy of noteworthy performers, including Neil Hamilton (best known as Commissioner Gordon in ABC's 1966-1968 *Batman* teleseries) and scream queen Shirley Grey. On the strength of her performance here and in *Get That Girl* (1932), Grey was shuffled into a series of second-rate horror features; in 1935, she had the distinction of being the female lead in the very first Hammer horror film, *Phantom Ship*. Little more than a rehash of *Terror Aboard*, that film had a similar body count (though without the onscreen violence and with superstar Bela Lugosi in an important role).

Purchased by Universal in 1958 for television syndication and currently residing in their library, Paramount Pictures produced *Terror Aboard* at a time when the company was trying to cash in on the horror craze ignited by Universal with *Dracula* and *Frankenstein*. To that end, Paramount produced and released *Dr. Jekyll and Mr. Hyde* (1931), *The Barton Mystery* and *Island of Lost Souls* (both 1932), *Murders in the Zoo* and *Supernatural* (both 1933), *Double Door, Menace,* and *The Witching Hour* (all 1934) and *Rocky Mountain Mystery* (1935), among others, after which, due to pressure brought on by the British horror film ban and by industry watchdog groups in the United States, the company's fright excursions went underground, more often than not dressing up as mysteries or gangster films.

As a savory little bonus, *Terror Aboard* features one of the most blatant, brilliant *deus ex machina* conclusions in film history. CW

The Third Clue
Fox; b/w; 72 min; Great Britain
D: Albert Parker *S:* Frank Atkinson, Michael Barringer, Lance Sieveking *P:* Ernest Gartside *C:* Alex Bryce

Cast: Basil Sydney, Molly Lamont, Robert Cochran, Alfred Sangster, C.M. Hallard, Raymond Lovell, Adela Mavis, Frank Atkinson, Ernest Sefton, Ian Fleming, Quentin McPhearson, Eric Fawcett, Bruce Lester, Mabel Terry-Lewis, Noel Dainton, Rani Waller

Two years after his mildly horrific *After Dark* (1932), director Albert Parker returned to the genre with *The Third Clue*, a quota quickie offering from the British branch of Fox. This time around, however, Parker didn't feel the need to cocoon the horror in a dimwitted comic plot about stolen gems. This isn't to say that there aren't stolen gems in *Clue*—they're the backbone of the plot, in fact—but this time out they are most uncomically, if somewhat drearily, cursed. Cursed jewels were hardly an original concept in 1934, having been done as recently as Gaumont's *The Ghoul* (1933) and Monogram's *The Moonstone* (1934). And though the humor of that time has tended to date badly, including such humor in *Clue* couldn't have made it much stiffer than it is.

The tale begins in the old dark house of Mark Clayton (Fleming) during a nasty thunderstorm, as a group of Indians (Hindus, not Native Americans) tries to force Clayton to reveal the location of the jewels they say belong to their goddess. Clayton refuses, his captors do him in and with his dying breath he asks his brother to give the goodies to his son—though he dies just before he's able to reveal where on the estate grounds the jewels have been hidden.

What follows is a typical mishmash of greedy would-be heirs, matching murderous wits with Indians and a gang of thieves, all crossing and double-crossing one another to procure the gems for themselves. It all takes place among the obligatory hidden passages, with none of it very interesting. The almost nonstop musical score doesn't help move the film any; nor does its running time, which is about 10 minutes longer than the average quota quickie.

The Third Clue was based on the novel *The Shakespeare Murders* (1933), written by Neil Gordon, a pseudonym (one of several) for an Indian-born Scotsman named A.G. Macdonell. Macdonell's most famous book was *England, Their England* (also 1933), which won the James Tait Black Award.

One of *The Third Clue*'s scenarists, Frank Atkinson, also had a small part in the film as a two-bit hood named Lefty. Better known as an actor than as a screenwriter, he had parts in approximately 150 films while having written only 10. CW

Two Monks
aka **Dos monjes**
Proa; b/w; 85 min; Mexico
D/Co-S: Juan Bustillo Oro *Co-S:* José Manuel Cordero *Co-P:* José San Vicente, Manuel San Vicente *C:* Agustin Jiménez *M:* Max Urban

Cast: Magda Haller, Víctor Urruchúa, Carlos Villatoro, Emma Roldán, H. Beltran de Heder, Emma Roldan, Albert Miquel, Manuel Noriega, Manuel Bernaldez, José Cortés, Conchita Gentil Arcos, Hugo Taboada, Sofia Haller

While not a horror film per se, *Two Monks*' use of Expressionist sets and direction definitely tips it in that direction. Over the years it has come to be regarded as an example of Mexican fantasy cinema, due in large part to its inclusion in Phil Hardy's *The Overlook Film Encyclopedia: Horror* (1993).

Set within a spooky monastery, the film concerns two monks who once loved the same woman. It begins with a scene, daring for its time, in which one monk attempts to bludgeon the other with a crucifix. We then learn, via two flashbacks, why the pair became monks and have such a deep-seated hatred of each other. The first monk, Javier (Villatoro), recounts how, in his early days, he and his mother took in the needy young Ana (Haller) when she was kicked out by her father. Javier and Ana fell in love, but he caught her in an embrace with his then-best friend (and current fellow monk) Juan (Urruchúa). The two men fought, and during the struggle Juan accidentally shot and killed Ana. The second flashback tells the same story from Juan's perspective. He claims that he and Ana had been involved long before she met Javier, but they had become separated. Her subsequent affair with Javier, Juan claims, was mere pretense on her part. She was in fact planning on leaving Javier when the ugliness occurred. Not surprisingly, Juan at first maintains that it was Javier's actions that led to Ana's death. When Juan does at length admit his own guilt, Javier plays on an organ a musical composition he wrote for Ana. At the height of his performance, however, he suffers an attack of dementia and drops dead.

Released in Mexico in November of 1934 and in the United States in January of 1935, *Two Monks* can be seen as something of a Gothic forerunner to Akira Kurosawa's much more famous—and straightforward—*Rashomon* (1950) in that it illustrates the fluidity of truth based on who's telling the story.

Born in Mexico City in 1904, Juan Bustillo Oro began his career as a screenwriter toward the end of the silent era. His scripts for *El compadre Mendoza* and *The Phantom of the Convent* (both 1934) cleared his path to a successful directing career. He continued making films in Mexico until his retirement in 1969 and died in 1989 in his beloved birthplace.

His next horror film was *The Mystery of the Ghastly Face* (1935). CW

The Unholy Quest
Newman, Wyer and Hopkins; b/w; 57 min; Britain
D/S: R.W. Lotinga (Widgey R. Newman) *P:* Widgey R. Newman, Reginald H. Wyer

Cast: Claude Bailey, Terence de Marney, Christine Adrian, John Milton, Harry Terry, Ian Wilson

A Crusader (of the medieval, Roman Catholic variety), who has returned from the dead, terrorizes a group of people.

This quota quickie was the work of producer/writer/director Widgey R. Newman. Newman (sometimes billed, as he is here, as R.W. Lotinga) entered films in 1926. His ambition exceeded his business ability, however, and he filed for bankruptcy in 1931. He relinquished control of his self-named production company, Widgey R. Newman Ltd., and sold off the rights to

its films in order to pay off creditors. To his credit, he did forge ahead afterward and set up a second production company, Delta Pictures, under whose banner he made a horror film titled *Castle Sinister* (1932). The "Newman, Wyer and Hopkins" studio that released *The Unholy Quest* was apparently formed soon afterward.

Given the "lost" status of both *Quest* and *Sinister*, it's impossible to ascertain how much flair Newman displayed for the genre, but reviews of the period were none too favorable. As a gossipy aside, it's worth noting that for years R.W. Lotinga and Widgey R. Newman were presented to the public as two separate people; it has been postulated that Newman utilized the pseudonym as a means of keeping some of his income secret from his wife, whom he divorced in 1934.

Newman died in 1944 at the age of 43. TH

The Witching Hour
Paramount; b/w; 64 min; U.S.

D: Henry Hathaway *S:* Anthony Veiller *P:* Bayard Veiller *C:* Ben Reynolds

Cast: Sir Guy Standing, John Halliday, William Frawley, Judith Allen, Tom Brown, Olive Tell, Richard Carle, Ralf Harolde, Purnell Pratt, Frank Sheridan, Gertrude Michael, Ferdinand Gottschalk, John Larkin

A bizarre courtroom drama with supernatural overtones, *The Witching Hour* has psychically gifted Jack Brookfield (Halliday) inadvertently hypnotizing weak-minded Clay Thorne (Brown) into killing Brookfield's enemy, a criminal heavy named Frank Hardmuth (Harolde) who wants a take in Jack's gambling business. Because the case seems so open and shut, no lawyer will take it, and it's up to Clay's mother to convince a former judge (Standing) to represent her son. During the trial, the judge/defender arranges for an attempted murder—orchestrated by mesmerism—to take place in the courtroom!

Based on a 1907 play by Augustus Thomas, *The Witching Hour* (filmed twice before, first in 1916 and again in 1921) suffers from the talkative, unsubtle handling that plagues so many 1930s stage-to-screen adaptations (see *Dracula*, 1931, for what may be the most egregious example). There is little action and nothing of interest visually; only talk … followed by more talk. The performances are decent but require nothing of the actors other than that they deliver their dialogue with a minimum of conviction. The final denouement—that Clay is set free because it's proven in court that he killed another human being because of accidental hypnotic suggestion—is ridiculous in the extreme. At least a cat's eye ring, telepathy and a haunting apparition add a little bit of juice to the proceedings.

Henry Hathaway (1898-1985) went on to direct some of the most famous Westerns ever made, including *Brigham Young* (1940), *The Shepherd of the Hills* (1941), *Garden of Evil* (1954), *North to Alaska* (1960), segments of *How the West Was Won* (1962), *The Sons of Katie Elder* (1965), *Nevada Smith* (1966) and *True Grit* (1969). He also dabbled in film noir, offering up *The House on 92nd Street* (1945), *Kiss of Death* (1947) and *Call Northside 777* (1948), among others. Little of the style that made his later films so outstanding is on display in *The Witching Hour*, and it remains a forgotten item today. CW

The Woman Condemned
Progressive; b/w; 66 min; U.S.

D: Mrs. Wallace Reid (Dorothy Davenport) *S/P:* Willis Kent *C:* James Diamond *M:* Lee Zahler

Cast: Claudia Dell, Lola Lane, Richard Hemmingway, Jason Robards, Mischa Auer, Paul Ellis, Douglas Cosgrove, Sheila Bromley, Louise Beavers, Tom O'Brien, Neal Pratt

Newspaper reporter Jerry Beall (Hemmingway) falls for beautiful Barbara Hammond (Dell). When Barbara is accused of murdering radio star Jane Merrick (Lane), Beall sets out to clear her of the charges.

This is one of those melodramas that tries to pass itself off as a horror film. All the right elements are certainly there—a mad doctor, shady surgery, a ghostly vision—but they're revealed to be of decidedly innocuous origin; as such, the film anticipates by some three decades the formula popularized by the animated series *Scooby Doo*. The characters frown and skulk with conviction, but the final reveal is far too garbled to make much sense, let alone pack any dramatic impact.

Director Dorothy Davenport, billed here as Mrs. Wallace Reid (her husband, Wallace Reid, died of morphine addiction in 1923, but she continued to use his name on occasion), helmed a handful of films between 1923 and 1934. *The Woman Condemned* was her last outing as director. She was far more prolific as an actress, amassing over 100 credits in that capacity. Her writing career was even longer lasting, and she remained active as a scenarist until the 1950s. She died in 1977.

The supporting cast includes acclaimed stage actor Jason Robards, who later fathered Oscar-winner Jason Robards, Jr. Robards, Sr. went on to give good performances in the Val Lewton horror classics *Isle of the Dead* (1945) and *Bedlam* (1946), but he's not at his best in *The Woman Condemned*. Like much of the rest of the cast, his performance suffers from hammy overemoting. Russian character actor Mischa Auer (*Sinister Hands*, 1932; *Condemned to Live*, 1935) plays a shifty doctor who may or may not be mad. TH

1935

The Beast of Borneo
Far East; b/w; 63 (61) min; U.S.
 D/P: Harry Garson *S:* Alfred Hustwick, Frank J. Murray *C:* Lewis W. Physioc
 Cast: Mae Stuart, John Preston, Eugene Sigaloff, Alexander Schonberg, Doris Brook, Val Durran, John Peters

Playing like a throwback to the silent era (complete with title cards explaining changes in action or setting), *The Beast of Borneo* is the bastard stepchild of Universal's lurid jungle melodrama *East of Borneo* (1930). Harry Garson, who'd done on-location second-unit work for *East*, dipped into its unused stock footage—particularly close-ups of a male orangutan—to flesh out this independent cheapie.

A thick-tongued Russian baddie, Dr. Boris Borodoff (Sigaloff), believes that in order to prove his own theory of evolution, he must extract the glands from an orangutan. (How exactly this will do the trick is left unclear.) But when his supplier fails to deliver the desired primate, the doctor takes his own expedition to the jungles of Borneo to procure a few. There he meets area expert Bob Ward (Preston), a hunter who refuses to guide the expedition because he opposes vivisection (though he apparently has no problems killing the region's wildlife). Borodoff's beautiful blonde assistant Alma Thorne (Stuart), however, sexes it up and seduces Bob into acting as their guide. All goes reasonably well until it becomes obvious that the two are falling in love, at which time Borodoff's resentment toward Bob reaches a new intensity. Things come to a head after Borodoff, in the process of capturing a large male orangutan, pushes Bob's Asian assistant Darmo (Durran) into the beast's net, where it crushes the man to death. Bob, in response, rediscovers his opposition to vivisection and blocks Borodoff's plans to operate on the creature. They fight, Bob is bested, and the beast of Borneo escapes, dragging the guide along. Alma helps rescue him, though, and in the end the doctor is killed by the very animal on which he had hoped to experiment.

A mixture of action/adventure, melodrama and subdued horror, *The Beast of Borneo* is undone not by its schizophrenic nature but by its astoundingly cheap production values, which include obvious stock shots, terrible use of rear-screen projection and drama club acting. The adult orangutan—which looks more like an ape or a gorilla—is a man in a suit so cheap that it's wisely kept out of full view, hidden in the shadows or behind foliage (which actually adds a little charm to the film). The most (okay, the only) impressive scene is when the beast is attacked by a large snake and kills it, but even here the impact is dampened by the god-awfulness of the entire enterprise.

The horrific elements of the film were hyped in its ad campaign, which promised a "Mad scientist on [a] quest for gorilla glands!" and said of the love story that it was the "weirdest triangle ever filmed!" *The Beast of Borneo* was director Harry Garson's swan song, though he didn't live to see it receive a major release. He died in the 1938, with the film receiving its widest distribution in the 1940s.

Garson may be better known for his relationship with volatile silent film star Clara Kimball Young. Young had caused a bit of a controversy in the second decade of the 20th century

Bob Steele, the hero of *Big Calibre*, was a major Western star in the late 1920s and early 1930s.

when she left her husband James Young for heavyweight producer Lewis J. Selznick. When that relationship went south, she jumped ship in favor of film exhibitor Garson, who immediately decided he wanted to be a producer and director with Clara as his muse. One evening, while leaving the Astor Theater in New York City, Garson was attacked by a knife-wielding James Young, whose marriage to Clara had yet to be dissolved. Garson survived the attack and went on to direct numerous silent-era films, most of them starring Clara but few of them successful. His lack of skill in setting up shots and in drawing competent performances from his actors was infamous, and when Clara was offered a contract with Paramount, it was with the stipulation that Garson not be allowed to participate in her work. (She rejected the contract.) Eventually the two separated, and Garson spent the rest of his career doing second-unit work and directing and producing for Poverty Row studios. CW

Big Calibre
Supreme; b/w; 58 min; U.S.
 D/Co-S: Robert N. Bradbury *Co-S:* Perry Murdock *P:* A.W. Hackel *C:* John Alton, William Hyer
 Cast: Bob Steele, Peggy Campbell, Forrest Taylor, John Elliott, Georgia O'Dell, William Quinn, Earl Dwire, Frank Ball, Si Jenks

Mixing elements of horror and science fiction, *Big Calibre* is easily one of the weirdest Westerns ever made. After his father is murdered by a gas bomb and $60,000 stolen from him, Bob Neal (Steele) discovers a local mad scientist, Otto Zenz (William Quinn, billed here as "Bill"), committed the deed. Zenz, realizing that Neal is on his trail, tries unsuccessfully to kill Neal with a second gas bomb, then leaves town in search of safer pastures. A series of additional murders and thefts leads Neal to the beautiful June (Campbell), whose father was among the victims. A lecherous individual named Bentley (Taylor) who, it turns out, is in cahoots with a sinister man named Gadski, pressures June romantically. While hiding out in a cave on her property, Neal figures out why Bentley is so eager to marry the girl—the cave is full of valuable marble deposits. The action culminates in a masquerade ball, where Gadski, done up as a vampiric hunchback with sharp canine fangs, is exposed as none other than the fugitive Zenz!

While by no means a great film, *Big Calibre* is nonetheless a fast-moving and fun one, with Bob Steele turning in his usual professional performance. Steele, born Robert Adrian Bradbury in Portland, Oregon in 1907, got his start in movies in 1920, teaming with his brother Bill in the cleverly titled *The Adventures of Bob and Bill*. Signing with F.B.O. Studios in the late 1920s, he was rechristened Bob Steele and shuffled into a string of successful Westerns. Though mostly remembered for those films, he did manage to get cast in some classic productions, including *Of Mice and Men* (1939), *The Big Sleep* (1946), *McLintock!* (1963) and *Hang 'Em High* (1968). His relatively few horror appearances include roles in *Border Phantom* (1936), *Revenge of the Zombies* (1943) and *The Atomic Submarine* (1960). He died in 1988 from complications related to emphysema. CW

The Black Room
aka The Black Room Mystery
Columbia; b/w; 68 min; U.S.

D: R. (Roy) William Neill *S:* Henry Myers, Arthur Strawn *C:* Allen G. Seigler *M:* R.H. Bassett, Milan Roder, Louis Silvers *FX:* Jack Cosgrove, Roy Davidson

Cast: Boris Karloff, Marian Marsh, Robert Allen, Thurston Hall, Katherine DeMille, John Buckler, Henry Kolker, Colin Tapley, Torben Meyer, Edward Van Sloan

Somewhere in 19th century Austria or thereabouts, twin barons Anton (Karloff) and Gregor (Karloff) grow up under an ancient family curse, which warns that the younger brother will one day murder the older in order to usurp power. The prophecy creates a rift between the brothers, and Anton—the younger by a few minutes—moves abroad rather than live with a brother who distrusts him. In his absence, Gregor treats the villagers with contempt while luring a number of young women to his castle for his sadistic amusement. Years later, he invites Anton to let bygones be bygones and rejoin him. The naïve younger brother accepts the offer at face value, but doesn't live to regret it; Gregor murders him almost immediately and stores the body in the castle's "black room." He then takes on Anton's identity in order to ingratiate himself to the locals who, it seems, have had just about enough of Gregor's antics.

Though produced on a B-movie budget, *The Black Room* has all the attributes of an A-level production. Director Roy William Neill (1887-1946) wasn't properly appreciated in his day, but critics today often point to him as a model of B-movie efficiency and craftsmanship. The British director entered the film industry as an actor in 1916, making his directing debut with *The Girl, Glory* in 1917. He became a U.S. citizen and thereafter found his most enduring success by guiding Basil Rathbone and Nigel Bruce through 11 of Universal's Sherlock Holmes films. The director's artful sense of framing, combined with a keen ability to bring a picture in on time and under budget, made him a favorite at Universal, where he also saved the troubled production of *Frankenstein Meets the Wolf Man* (1943).

The Black Room marks Neill's third foray into the horror genre (after *The Ninth Guest* and *Black Moon*, both 1934), and his talents are evident throughout. Apart from being singularly handsome and polished, the film moves at the brisk pace one as-

sociates with his later Sherlock Holmes pictures. The story itself is an ironic meditation on the futility of trying to escape fate, with a palpable air of doom hanging over twin brothers Gregor and Anton from the moment they are born.

Karloff gives a *tour de force* performance—two of them, in fact. The brothers are completely opposite: Gregor is slovenly, cruel and hateful toward everybody and everything, while Anton is impeccably groomed, warm-hearted and fond of people and animals. Karloff carefully shades both characters, portraying each as a three-dimensional human being. Gregor is—along with the perverse Satanist Hjalmar Poelzig in Edgar G. Ulmer's remarkable *The Black Cat* (1934)—one of the few thoroughly disagreeable characters the actor ever played, and his performance is pitch-perfect.

The supporting cast—including Katherine DeMille, the adopted daughter of director Cecil B. DeMille, later to marry actor Anthony Quinn—is more than capable. And Edward Van Sloan (Karloff's co-star in *The Mummy*, 1932, though he is best remembered as Dr. Van Helsing in *Dracula*, 1931, and *Dracula's Daughter*, 1936) makes a cameo appearance as the doctor who announces the birth of the twins.

Neill and cinematographer Allen G. Seigler (*The Devil Commands*, 1941) make the most of the imposing sets; and the special effects work allowing Karloff to act against himself (ranging from the use of convincing doubles to some then-intricate split screen work) is of a high caliber.

Some sources list the film's running time at 75 minutes, but the current version runs only 68 minutes; it could be that some

post-production tinkering is responsible for the discrepancy, with at least one plot strand (Gregor hinting that he will have his revenge on a servant who betrayed him) going nowhere in the current edit. At any rate, the film's flaws are far outweighed by its virtues. *The Black Room* remains one of the outstanding horror films of the 1930s. TH

The Bride of Frankenstein
aka **Bride of Frankenstein**; **The Return of Frankenstein**
Universal; b/w; 75 min; U.S.

D/Co-P: James Whale *S:* William Hurblut *Co-P:* Carl Laemmle, Jr. *C:* John J. Mescall *M:* Franz Waxman *FX:* John P. Fulton

Cast: Boris Karloff, Colin Clive, Ernest Thesiger, Valerie Hobson, Elsa Lanchester, O.P. Heggie, Una O'Connor, E.E. Clive, Gavin Gordon, Douglas Walton, Dwight Frye, Lucien Prival, Reginald Barlow, Mary Gordon, Anne Darling, Ted Billings, John Carradine, Maurice Black, Helen Jerome Eddy, Elspeth Dudgeon, Joan Woodbury, A.S. "Pop" Byron, Norman Ainsley, Josephine McKim, John George, Walter Brennan, Neil Fitzgerald

On a stormy night in a Swiss chateau, Mary Godwin (Lanchester) regales Lord Byron (Gordon) and Percy Shelley (Walton) with the further exploits of her literary creation, the Frankenstein Monster (Karloff). The creature, she informs them, was not destroyed in the burning windmill that ended her previous account. Rejected anew by its maker Henry Frankenstein (Clive) and harassed by the simple frightened villagers, it flees into the woods. There, it stumbles upon the abode of a blind hermit (Heggie) and learns to talk before two locals happen by and drive it off again. It then falls in with the decadent Dr. Pretorius (Thesiger), an ex-mentor of Dr. Frankenstein, and the two kidnap Frankenstein's wife and blackmail him into creating a female companion for the creature.

Following the commercial success of *Frankenstein* (1931), the story department at Universal got to work developing a sequel. But they hit a brick wall early on when director James Whale, the man responsible for *Frankenstein*'s resounding success, declared that he wanted no part of a second outing. Production Head Carl Laemmle, Jr. dogged Whale for years, during which the eccentric filmmaker continued to dabble in the macabre, reteaming with Boris Karloff for *The Old Dark House* (1932) and guiding Claude Rains (in his film debut) through *The Invisible Man* (1933). And while Laemmle did reluctantly assign German émigré Kurt Neumann (*Secret of the Blue Room*, 1933) to direct *The Return of Frankenstein*, he knew full well that Neumann lacked Whale's dramatic flair. As the project became mired in pre-production, Laemmle considered chucking it altogether, convinced that any *Frankenstein* sequel without Whale's guidance would be stillborn.

The impasse broke in 1934, when Whale expressed a keen interest in bringing John Galsworthy's very British courtroom melodrama *One More River* to the screen. Universal's producers were just as keenly uninterested in the project, and Laemmle realized that a major bargaining chip was being thrown his way. He offered Whale direction duties on *One More River*—even sweetening the deal by assigning it A-budget status—if the director agreed to follow it with a sequel to *Frankenstein*. Whale at last caved, and after the release of his pet project (which did respectable business), he enlisted playwright William Hurlbut to help him hammer out a screenplay for the follow-up to his most famous work.

The director found ridiculous the idea of the monster surviving the collapse of a burning windmill (its means of demise at the end of *Frankenstein*); therefore, he approached the film as, in his words, "a hoot." He let the creature live, of course, and used that unlikelihood to kick off a full-blown satire of horror movie conventions, changing the title to *The Bride of Frankenstein* as he mined Shelley's novel for fresh inspiration. (The novel actually has Frankenstein begin work on a mate for his creation, though he aborts the undertaking midway to the goal.)

The film's fanciful prologue, in which the authoress and her companions muse over the story and its stormy reception by the publishers, originally contained a great deal of suggestive dialogue. The censors pruned much of it, creating in the process some awkward cuts and continuity issues; still, it does start the film off on the sardonic note Whale was aiming for.

Frankenstein's Monster courts his less-than-enthused bride (Elsa Lanchester) in the classic *The Bride of Frankenstein*.

The film is far from a flat-out comedy, however. Whale sprinkles shocks and sorrow amid the humor, despite the censors' curtailment of an originally quite imposing level of violence. And the director does manage to artfully vary the tone of the film; pathos shares the screen with absurdity, and horror is interspersed with elaborate flights of fantasy. Some critics have suggested that it's all too much to take in, but be that as it may, there's no denying the skill and artistry at work here. As evidenced by *The Old Dark House* and *The Invisible Man*—and the more obscure films he made in the interim—Whale had continued to grow as an artist following *Frankenstein*. His camerawork became more assured and his eye for design more daring, so that by the time of *Bride* he was able to dazzle the audience consistently.

Nearly the entire film (apart from a few exteriors) was shot on sound stages, and Whale consistently utilizes that artificiality to heighten the fantastic tone. The director—a confirmed atheist—also appropriates Christian imagery in ways that, while obvious to anyone who's paying attention, can also elude conscious notice. Much has been made of the vulgar nature of the scene in which the monster is crucified by the villagers, yet it can just as easily be taken as a valid commentary on the way that misfits have time after time been tormented and vilified by "God-fearing" mobs.

Whale at times moves the camera with wild abandon, utilizing rapid editing and expressive lighting to heighten the mood. This combination of techniques is most impressive in the celebrated "birth" of the creature's bride, which actually manages to outdo the impressive parallel scene in the original film. The use of canted angles, exaggerated lighting and quick cutting is positively euphoric, an effect underscored by Franz Waxman's remarkable musical score.

In his return to the role that made him a star, Boris Karloff (billed simply as "Karloff," a sign of his box-office standing) is nothing short of remarkable. (The actor had gained some weight since the previous film, forcing Jack P. Pierce to modify the make-up accordingly as he added the scars and singed hair caused by the fire in the mill.) The actor argued bitterly with Whale over whether the monster would speak (though this element is cribbed directly from the novel). The actor's misgivings are not evident in the film, however. Karloff employs a hoarse, halting delivery that masks his own distinctive lisp and, despite his concerns, enhances rather than damages the monster's mystique. The footage of the monster talking with the blind hermit (another borrowing from the novel, albeit with some modifications) is as moving as anything in the first feature.

Colin Clive also returns as Henry Frankenstein, though the second time around his role is somewhat marginalized. The neurotic actor's addiction to alcohol had taken a tremendous toll on his frail disposition by this time, and at 35 years old he looks surprisingly drawn and unhealthy. He does a respectable job regardless, but his best years were clearly behind him. He died a mere two years after the release of *Bride*, at a far too young 37.

Clive's laborious performance isn't helped by his interaction with Ernest Thesiger, who steals every scene he's in as the perverse Dr. Pretorius. There's some indication that Bela Lugosi was originally considered for the role (by the studio, at least; Whale doesn't seem to have been much of a fan), and at any rate

Dr. Pretorius (Ernest Thesiger) presents Dr. Frankenstein (Colin Clive) with their joint creation, in *The Bride of Frankenstein*.

it's well documented that Claude Rains was Whale's preference for the part. Thesiger is an inspired second-choice, an absolute delight, whether disarming the monster with charm ("Have a cigar. They're my only weakness!") or slyly suggesting an inclination toward necrophilia (when examining the body of a recently exhumed woman, he quips, "I hope her bones are firm!").

For the dual role of Mary Godwin and the eponymous Bride, Universal first sought the services of Brigitte Helm, star of both the 1928 and 1930 versions of *Alraune* and best remembered as the robotrix Maria in Fritz Lang's *Metropolis* (1927). When that fell through, Whale settled on Elsa Lanchester, the wife of friend and *Old Dark House* cast member Charles Laughton. Lanchester is appealingly pixyish as the author, and her bird-like movements, coupled with Pierce's Nefertiti-inspired make-up, created a genre icon.

O.P. Heggie is memorable as the blind hermit who offers the monster its only real experience of affection, while John Carradine and Walter Brennan can be glimpsed in smaller roles.

The casting falters somewhat as regards Valerie Hobson and Una O'Connor. The 17-year-old Hobson simply isn't up to the task of playing Elizabeth, creating embarrassment on those occasions when she is required to emote. As for O'Connor, whose shrieking harridan routine effectively enlivened Whale's *The Invisible Man*, she has her moments, but is an onscreen irritant at least as often. One suspects that Whale used her for his amusement alone. She is, at any rate, allowed too great a presence in the picture.

Bride's reputation as an unassailable masterpiece has come under fire in some circles. While the film indeed has its technical problems, most of them are due to post-production tinkering. Apart from the aforementioned matter of the clumsily censored prologue, the studio had issues with Whale's overall vision for

the piece. The director had originally ended the film on a downbeat note, and Universal balked, fearing damage to the franchise. Reshoots were done with Whale's reluctant participation; an arbitrarily happy ending was cobbled together in which the monster, having a change of heart, allows Henry and Elizabeth to go free. The alteration creates a continuity flub—the overhead shot of the lab going up in smoke clearly shows Henry cowering against the wall, while the reshoot footage has them both running down the stairs to safety.

The deletion of a subplot in which Karl (Frye) frames the monster for murders he himself commits was also a misstep. In the finished film the murders remain but there's no indication that Karl is responsible, unfairly making it look as though the creature is a bloodthirsty fiend.

Some have criticized the sequence illustrating Pretorius' successful creation of homunculi. And true, one could argue that it's self-indulgence on Whale's part ... yet somehow it actually works. It's a witty little episode in its own right, and it lets the audience see that Pretorius' methods are more akin to black magic, as Frankenstein terms it, than they are to the scientific leanings of his younger, more idealistic colleague.

Whatever its faults, *The Bride of Frankenstein* undeniably occupies a special niche in horror history. It's as personal an exploration of the fantastic and the macabre as Whale's *The Old Dark House*, and, as a pure visual extravaganza, it has few equals; it is also a film of rich substance and emotional resonance, quite deserving of its reputation as a masterpiece. TH

The Burgomeister
aka **Flames of Conscience**; **Hypnotized**; **The Burgomaster**
Southwell; b/w; 56 min; Australia

D/P: Harry Southwell *S:* Denzil Batchelor *C:* George Heath *M:* Isador Goodman

Cast: Janet Johnson, Muriel Meredith, Lily Molloy, Harry Southwell, Stan Tolhurst, Gabriel Toyne, Ross Vernon

This is the final 1930s film version of Leopold Lewis' *The Bells*, a stage play adapted from Émile Erckmann and Alexandre Chatrian's French play *Le Juif Polonaise* (The Polish Jew). Though adapted numerous times from 1911 to 1935, it is largely forgotten today, known by some as the play that made a star of British thespian Sir Henry Irving.

The Burgomeister was the second film adaptation of *The Bells* to have been directed by Harry Southwell (the first was the 1925 British-Belgium co-production entitled, yes, *The Bells*). This incarnation of the story concerns an innkeeper/burgomaster who murders a traveling Jew for his money, only to have his conscience, triggered by a mesmerist, drive him insane. It was known as *Flames of Conscience* in Great Britain and was also released under the title *Hypnotized* in its native Australia. CW

Charlie Chan in Egypt
Fox; b/w; 73 min; U.S.

D: Luis (Louis) King *S:* Robert Ellis, Helen Logan *P:* Edward T. Lowe, Jr. *C:* Daniel B. Clark

Cast: Warner Oland, Pat Paterson, Thomas Beck, Rita Cansino, Stepin Fetchit, Jameson Thomas, Frank Conroy, Nigel de Brulier, Paul Porcasi, Arthur Stone, James Eagles, Frank Reicher, George Irving, Anita Brown, John Davidson

In the early 1900s literary fiction about nefarious Asians was all the rage, thanks largely to Sax Rohmer's insidious Dr. Fu Manchu, a Chinese madman intent on destroying "the white race." By 1923, novelist Earl Derr Biggers had had enough. His protest of the time's pop xenophobia took the form of the intelligent, friendly and caring Charlie Chan, a Chinese American detective who was the polar opposite of the Yellow Peril then threatening Occidentals from page and screen.

The first film adaptation of the instantly popular character was 1926's 10-part Pathé serial *The House Without a Key*, followed by Universal's *The Chinese Parrot* (1927). Each cast a Japanese actor in its lead role, and for some reason neither was very successful. Fox was the next major company to try their hand at the character, with a Korean Chan in 1929's *Behind That Curtain*. Deathly dull, it too was unsuccessful. Then Fox tried again with Swedish actor Warner Oland—who was in fact of Mongolian descent on his Russian grandmother's side (and had already played Asian in a series of Fu Manchu movies for Paramount). Unfortunately his first Chan film, *Charlie Chan Carries On* (1931), is now lost, but at the time it hit pay dirt, and Fox immediately signed the actor to a series of Chan mysteries. Chan proved so cinematically successful that he outlasted both actor and studio affiliation and continued through the 1940s. The character's intelligence, self-effacing sense of humor and humble manner was pointedly unthreatening to white audiences. And while his stilted Pidgin English was as racist a portrayal then as it is now, it must be remembered that in the 1930s U.S. relations with both China and Japan were tense, yet here was an Asian character not only leading an American picture—he was the *hero*!

Universal had proved (with 1931's *Frankenstein* and *Dracula*) that there was big money to be made in horror pictures, yet, as the decade progressed, a British clampdown on "objectionable" content—in particular, its mid-thirties ban on horror films—reached well across the pond. Before the ban, many studios emulated Universal with their own horror offerings (Paramount made *Murder by the Clock*, 1931, for example; RKO produced *King Kong* and a sequel, both 1933; and Columbia offered *Black Moon*, 1934, among others). But Fox, for some reason, hadn't jumped on that bandwagon; it had only a trio of dull outings (1932's *Chandu the Magician* being the best known of them) to its horror name. And those films, with their magicians, turbans and death rays, weren't really very frightening, even to the kiddies who watched them at matinee shows.

Curiously, at around the same time U.S. studios were catering (on the surface, anyway) to the British ban as well as to parental watchdog groups who insisted that horror films were dangerous, they also began pushing the limits of what could be shown on screen. Fox got belatedly on board, spicing up mundane mystery fare with the macabre, enhancing its income with "non-horror horror films" that tap-danced around those censors and watchdog groups. *Charlie Chan in Egypt* was one of these, and it was successful enough that Fox continued putting Chan through his horror paces for a few years thereafter.

Honolulu private detective Charlie Chan (Oland), working for a French archaeological society, travels to Egypt to investigate why artifacts from the tomb of Ameti are turning up in museums around the world. There, he discovers that the head of the tomb's excavation has been murdered. While everyone else seems to think it was due to a curse placed upon the tomb by Ancient Egyptian priests, Chan doesn't buy it.

Sounds like a straightforward mystery, right? Not hardly. The influence of Karl Freund's *The Mummy* (1932) permeates *Egypt* from the very first scene, in which Professor Arnold (Irving) and his crew break into Ameti's tomb, only to have the first man who pokes his head into the darkened vault killed by an unseen hand.

Nor is lifting plot points from Freund's classic the end of it; director Louis King also apes Freund's directorial style as his camera glides ominously over creepy Ancient Egyptian artifacts. Recycled horror touches permeate the entire picture, from the discovery (using X-rays) of a modern—and very dead—body stuffed into an old sarcophagus, to an appearance by the goddess Sekhmet, her baleful eyes glowing in the dark of the crypt. The actors likewise seem to be imitating the cast of Universal's fright classic; James Eagles, who plays the first murder victim's son Barry, is a skinnier version of Bramwell Fletcher, the archaeologist driven mad by the sight of a shambling mummy in the earlier film.

Despite the resemblance, Eagles' performance isn't anywhere near the quality of Fletcher's. Frankly, he mars *Egypt*, though not nearly as unforgivably as Stepin Fetchit, who plays

Rita Hayworth (credited as Rita Cansino) stands next to Warner Oland in *Charlie Chan in Egypt*.

a bumbling, scared black servant with the unfortunate name of Snowshoes. It's difficult to understand how anyone—in any time period—could have found this racist cornball routine funny, yet here it is for all to see … and be annoyed by.

Faring not quite as badly, but badly enough, is Pat Patterson as the film's distressed heroine Carol Arnold. She screams, wilts and faints at every opportunity, proving to all concerned that women are indeed the weaker sex. If her flighty performance is dismissable as stereotypical tripe—and it is—her real life story was far more interesting. A year before the release of *Charlie Chan in Egypt*, she had married noted actor Charles Boyer (*Gaslight*, 1944). In 1939 she retired from acting, allowing her husband to continue to bring home the bacon from his work in films and on television. In the mid-70s, Pat was diagnosed with cancer, and two days after her death on August 23, 1978, Boyer, unable to continue living without her, committed suicide.

Oland's performance, in contrast with most of those around him, is spot on, as is Frank Conroy's as Professor Thurston. There's also an impressive appearance, in a small but seductive role, by Rita Cansino, who later changed her name to Rita Hayworth.

It isn't for the performances, then, that *Charlie Chan in Egypt* should be watched. Nor is the central mystery, with evidence that doesn't really lead to the final solution and plot holes aplenty, all that interesting. No, the film's merit derives from the sense of horror that oozes from nearly every frame. This is without a doubt every bit as horror-oriented as any number of Universal films from the same period, though its reputation as a straightforward mystery has tended to obscure this wonderful fact.

It didn't take long for the quick-witted detective to again come face to face with the stuff of horror, in *Charlie Chan's Secret*, *Charlie Chan at the Circus* and *Charlie Chan at the Opera* (all 1936), the latter opposite Boris Karloff as a Phantom-like madman. CW

Circumstantial Evidence
Chesterfield; b/w; 68 min; U.S.

D: Charles Lamont *S:* Ewart Adamson *P:* George R. Batcheller *C:* M.A. Anderson

Cast: Chick Chandler, Shirley Grey, Arthur Vinton, Claude King, Dorothy Revier, Lee Moran, Carl Stockdale, Eddie Phillips, Edward Keane, Robert Frazer, Huntley Gordon, Lew Kelly

After a jury renders a guilty decision in a murder case, condemning a possibly innocent man to death on flimsy evidence, a reporter named Jim Baldwin (Chandler) sets out to end the use of circumstantial evidence in criminal trials. He enlists the aid of his friend Fred Stevens (Vinton), unaware that Stevens—who is in love with Baldwin's fiancé, courtroom artist Adrienne (Grey)—secretly hates him. Stevens is also something of a womanizing sadist, a pro at seducing married women and who adorns his home with human skulls and mummified bodies. He plots to use Baldwin's cause to rid himself of his rival and take Adrienne for himself. Their agreed-upon plan is to stage a counterfeit crime, in which Stevens' murder is faked and for which Baldwin will be sentenced to death based on circumstantial evidence. Then, the scheme goes, Stevens will reveal himself, and circumstantial evidence will be exposed to the world as the bane of fair trials everywhere. What Baldwin doesn't know, of course, is that Stevens intends to play dead indefinitely.

The plot proceeds … and an argument between the two is staged, and Baldwin makes sure to be seen afterward lurking around a party hosted by Stevens. Then a fire is set, with one of Stevens' skeletons used as a stand-in for his charred corpse. But then, uh-oh, a real body is found in the rubble along with the skeleton. It turns out that Stevens really was murdered, and Baldwin, who has meticulously set himself up, is arrested, convicted of murder and sentenced to die. It is left to his friends to prove his innocence.

Taking advantage of the debate about capital punishment raging in the United States at the time, *Circumstantial Evidence* has its liberal heart in the right place but suffers in its, shall we say, *execution*. Its script espouses an anti-death penalty viewpoint at every turn (most explicitly, by having Baldwin rail to the courtroom about the evils of circumstantial evidence just before he's sentenced to death). But while it wants to be taken seriously as a plea for a more civilized criminal justice system, it's held prisoner (sorry) by its low budget and bad theatrics.

Screenwriter Ewart Adamson's interest in darker themes came to more gruesome fruition the following year with *The Walking Dead* (1936), which cast Boris Karloff as a man convicted of a murder he didn't commit, who, after being returned to life by scientific means, slaughters the criminals responsible for his death.

Charles Lamont directed *Evidence*, and Lamont later worked for Universal, overseeing various Abbott and Costello, Ma and Pa Kettle and Francis the Talking Mule outings. Among these were several horror-comedy hybrids, including *Abbott and Costello Meet the Invisible Man* (1951), *Abbott and Costello Meet Dr. Jekyll and Mr. Hyde* (1953), *Abbott and Costello Meet the Mummy* (1955) and *Francis in the Haunted House* (1956). Lamont had been directing since the early 1920s and was a professional journeyman whose work was well paced and usually interesting. He is remembered as an actor's director, a verdict

(sorry) borne out by the performances in *Circumstantial Evidence*. He coaxes realistic portrayals from Chick Chandler, a future television player, and Shirley Grey, who starred in Hammer's first horror film, *Phantom Ship*, the same year *Evidence* was released.

In 2003, a very similar picture, *The Life of David Gale*, was released to critical acclaim, though it tanked at the box-office. CW

Condemned to Live
aka **Demon of Doom**; **Life Sentence**
Invincible; b/w; 65 min; U.S.

D: Frank R. Strayer *S:* Karen DeWolf *P:* Maury Cohen, Max Alexander, Arthur Alexander *C:* M.A. Anderson *M:* David Broekman, Charles Dunworth

Cast: Ralph Morgan, Maxine Doyle, Pedro de Cordoba, Russell Gleason, Mischa Auer, Lucy Beaumont, Carl Stockdale,

Barbara Bedford, Robert Frazer (misspelled as Frazier), Ferdinand Schumann-Heink, Hedi Shope, Marilyn Knowlden

A series of vampiric murders plagues a small village in 19th-century Europe. The villagers believe that a supernatural agent is responsible and that they are powerless against the attacks. Kindly Professor Kristan (Morgan) searches for a rational solution but is repeatedly set back by odd nighttime headaches and blackouts, followed by memory lapses and exhaustion. He comes to suspect that he may be the fiend everybody is seeking, and he confides his fears to his old friend Dr. Bizet (de Cordoba). Along with Kristan's faithful servant Zan (Auer), Bizet maintains a constant eye on the professor to determine whether the suspicions are sound.

Following his flawed but interesting *The Vampire Bat* (1933), director Frank R. Strayer helmed this second Poverty Row variation on the vampire myth, with results far less accomplished than those of his earlier effort. *Condemned*'s problems spring almost entirely from the overly wordy screenplay by Karen DeWolf, who in her attempt to capture period dialogue manages ludicrously purple prose instead. The film moves from one needlessly wordy set piece to the next, with only an occasional—and welcome—stretch of silence. It doesn't help that the direction here is even less adventuresome than it was in *Bat*; the camera remains mostly stationary, and long, dreary stretches play out in prolonged master shots.

Admittedly the film does contain some interesting ideas and innovations. Its depiction of vampirism as an illness separates it from the more overtly fanciful and supernatural machinations of *Dracula* (1931) and others of its ilk. The fact that the protagonist is effectively cursed from birth (his mother apparently having been bitten by a vampire bat while pregnant with him) lends the proceedings a tragic dimension, and the finale in which Kristan and his assistant commit suicide would in a better film be quite jarring (no doubt the strict Hayes Code, which frowned upon suicide, saw the act as justifiable in this context).

In the end, *Condemned*'s inept writing and lazy direction bury any significant merit the film might contain. Whatever impact the film manages for some is undoubtedly due to the sincere performances by Ralph Morgan, Pedro de Cordoba and Mischa Auer. Morgan does a commendable job in the central role, even if one has to struggle to believe the film's assertion that he is not yet 40 years of age. The less successful brother of actor Frank Morgan (best remembered for playing *The Wizard of Oz*, 1939), Ralph appeared in several B-horrors in the '40s, including the Poverty Row thriller *The Monster Maker* (1943) and Universal's semi-classic *Night Monster* (1942). One of his few classy roles came in 1938 as a man accused of murder in James Whale's *Wives Under Suspicion* (1938), a low-budget remake of the director's 1933 *Kiss Before the Mirror* (which, interestingly, had cast Frank in the same role Ralph reprised).

Gaunt character actor de Cordoba, familiar to modern horror enthusiasts for Tod Browning's *The Devil Doll* (1936) and Robert Florey's *The Beast With Five Fingers* (1946), brings a similar surprising conviction to his role as Morgan's slow-witted but well-meaning assistant. Russian-born Auer had earlier played the lead in the grade-Z horror film *The Monster Walks* (1932) and later found a measure of success with small roles in higher profile pictures. While *Condemned* weighs him down with some none-too-convincing hunchback make-up, he manages moments of genuine pathos.

Like *The Vampire Bat*, *Condemned to Live* makes extensive use of standing sets at Universal Studios. One interesting result is that the scenes of villagers storming through the streets can't help but remind one of *Frankenstein* (1931). TH

The Crime of Dr. Crespi
Liberty/Republic; b/w; 63 min; U.S.

D/P: John H. Auer *S:* Lewis Graham, Edwin Olmstead *C:* Larry Williams

Cast: Erich von Stroheim, Dwight Frye, Paul Guilfoyle, John Bohn, Harriett Russell, Geraldine Kay, Jean Brooks, Patsy Berlin, Joe Verdi, Dean Raymond

The credits for *The Crime of Dr. Crespi* claim, somewhat dubiously, that the tale was "Suggested by Edgar Allan Poe's *The Premature Burial*," which was first published in the *Philadelphia Dollar Newspaper* in 1844. The film opens with a POV shot, a street view from within an ambulance as it races toward the Taft Clinic, where one Andre Crespi (von Stroheim) is chief surgeon. Crespi harbors a bitter resentment toward another doctor, Stephen Ross (Bohn), who long ago stole the woman (Russell) Crespi loves. In fact, it is Dr. Ross, having just been injured in a car crash, who is in the ambulance. Seeing his opportunity, Crespi plots a terrible revenge; he administers to Ross a serum he has developed, one that induces the appearance of death, and then has his rival buried alive. But one of Crespi's assistants, Dr. Thomas (Frye), suspects that his boss is up to something, and he and another doctor (Guilfoyle) disinter the victim. What nobody foresees is Ross' return to mobility, a development he utilizes to exact a vengeance of his own.

Unfortunately, despite some interesting subjective shots (including an image from within Ross' coffin as the dirt is shoveled into the grave), the film, while certainly watchable, isn't nearly as engaging as its like-themed contemporaries *Mad Love* and *The Raven* (both also from 1935). Von Stroheim, generally a good performer, doesn't hold a candle to the love-crazed antics of Peter Lorre and Bela Lugosi in those films. Nor does it help that director Auer focuses his camera squarely and clumsily on Von Stroheim's face every time Crespi obsessively wigs out.

A period photo showing the marquee of a theater playing *The Crime of Dr. Crespi*

A teaser ad for *Dante's Inferno*

Von Stroheim, a German émigré, hated the film, calling it "The Crime of Republic" (though it was actually shot by Liberty Pictures before the company folded and what was left of the studio purchased by Republic, who distributed the film). Yet his over-the-top performance gives the film one of its few true *raisons d'etre*. *Crespi* was Von Stroheim's first horror film (though his turn as the mad ventriloquist in *The Great Gabbo* in 1929 certainly came close), and he followed it the next year by contributing to the script for Tod Browning's *The Devil Doll*, perhaps in a failed effort to garner a starring role in that film. He worked in only three additional horror movies (*The Lady and the Monster*, 1944; *The Mask of Diijon*, 1946 and *Unnatural*, 1952), all of them fairly small and forgettable affairs.

The actor was born in 1885 in Vienna, in what was then Austria-Hungary, to a Jewish hat maker. Upon his 1909 arrival in the United States, he concocted an elaborate biography claiming to be a member of the Austrian aristocracy. In 1912 he moved in with Margaret Knox (who later became his wife for a year), who encouraged his talents and helped him learn English. He worked as a novelist, scenarist and director, but his real love was acting, his knack, which is evidenced here and there even in *Crespi*, as in a terrific sequence in which he gloats over his paralyzed victim. After a period of respectable work lasting into the mid-1940s, Von Stroheim moved to France and shot a couple of films there. Though he returned to Hollywood for the occasional bit part, he remained a French citizen, dying there of cancer in 1957. One of his last significant roles was as Ludwig van Beethoven in Sacha Guitry's *Napoleon* (1955).

The presence of Universal supporting player Dwight Frye also lends *Crespi* some allure. Frye had seen his fortunes wane over the years; he had, during the early 1920s, been busy on Broadway, but after moving to Hollywood to star in films, he became lost amid the crowd of young people looking for work at the big studios. It wasn't until he was cast in the role of Renfield in Tod Browning's 1931 classic *Dracula* that he found real fame, though it proved to be a mixed bag. While his most famous performances thereafter were still-remembered juicy characters (Wilmer Cook in *The Maltese Falcon*, 1931; Herman in *The Vampire Bat*, 1933; Fritz in *The Bride of Frankenstein*, 1935), most of his career consisted of uncredited bit parts with only a line or two of spoken dialogue (*The Invisible Man*, 1933; *The Great Impersonation*, 1935; *The Road Back*, 1937; *The Ghost of Frankenstein*, 1942 and *Frankenstein Meets the Wolf Man*, 1943, among many others). Though he desperately wanted to star in comedies (as he had on stage), studios refused to give him the opportunity, typecasting him instead as dimwits and sadistic types. He eventually accepted a job at Douglas Aircraft, working nights in support of the war effort, to ensure that his wife and son were properly clothed and fed. Finally, in 1944, he was cast in an important non-horror role as President Woodrow Wilson's Secretary of War in the biopic *Wilson*. He suffered a fatal heart attack before filming commenced and died at the still-youthful age of 44. Strangely, in *The Crime of Dr. Crespi*, Frye was given just the sort of role that could have led to more, playing it straight as a doctor who is not only the film's hero but also gets the girl. Yet he walks through the part with little hint of interest, opting for a level of brevity not called for in the script.

It's easy to dismiss director John H. Auer as a hack, but he manages some crafty sequences in *Crespi*, such as a scene in which the zombie-like Ross stumbles toward a nurse working at her station in the hospital hall. The cheesiness of the threadbare set is somewhat offset by interesting lighting; sinister shadows upon the walls call to mind the look of German Expressionism.

More scenes like this would have played in the film's favor, yet it still retains a sort of obvious, surreal charm. The presence of a child's skeleton in Dr. Crespi's office is a particularly noteworthy touch, portending the much later work of David Lynch. CW

Dante's Inferno
Fox; b/w; 89 min; U.S.

D: Harry Lachman *S:* Philip Klein, Robert M. Yost *P:* Sol M. Wurtzel *C:* Rudolph Maté

Cast: Spencer Tracy, Claire Trevor, Henry B. Walthall, Alan Dinehart, Scotty Beckett, Robert Gleckler, Rita Cansino, Gary Leon, Willard Robertson, Morgan Wallace, Astrid Allwyn, Don Ameche, Oscar Apfel, Yakima Canutt, Ray Corrigan, Barbara Pepper

Not so much a horror film as a glossy piece of exploitation, this *Dante's Inferno* owes much to Fox's earlier (silent) film of the same name. The big difference is that, while the 1924 production frequently inserted visions of Hell into its modern story of a greedy businessman who would go as far as to engineer a friend's suicide to get what he wants, the 1935 version (mostly) eschews the fire and brimstone as it heaps on the staid melodrama.

Spencer Tracy stars as Jim Carter, a greedy entrepreneur with a hankering for Pop McWade's (Walthall) carnival sideshow, which is based upon the narrative of Dante's *Inferno*. Carter marries McWade's daughter Betty (Trevor) and winds up in full control of the operation. A building inspector (Robertson) pronounces the amusement park unsafe, and Carter bribes the man to keep his mouth shut. When the place collapses, however, Carter is prosecuted and his wife leaves him. Carter's next business venture is a cruise ship portentously named *Paradise*. He displays the same disregard for human safety as he did at the carnival, and due to his negligence a fire breaks out in the hold. In the ensuing panic, many people—both passengers and crew—die. Contrite, Carter confesses to Betty that he has made his own hell, and all is forgiven.

The most (perhaps only) notable sequence in the film is its 10-minute presentation of Hell; coming late in the proceedings, it kicks off the narrative wrap-up with some astonishing eye candy. Parts of it come directly from the 1925 film, while other portions—apparently influenced by the paintings of Gustave Doré—are original (director Harry Lachman was himself a painter and fan of the great French artist).

Inferno includes an early, brief appearance by future glamour girl Rita Hayworth, billed as Rita Cansino. During production, Tracy is said to have frequently showed up to work drunk (when he showed up at all), at one point even destroying much of one set in particular in an alcoholic rage. This, not surprisingly, prompted the revocation of his Fox contract, after which he moved to MGM and became a major star.[1]

The film was partly inspired by the SS *Morro Castle* disaster of the previous year. While en route from Cuba to New York City in September of 1934, the ship encountered severe fog and heavy rain. The bad weather reached its apex on the night of

September 7, when conditions grew so terrible that most people retired to their cabins. The ship's captain died of a heart attack not long after taking supper, and the ship's reins passed to Chief Officer William Warms.

Around 3:00 am the next morning, a fire broke out in a storage locker and within 20 minutes engulfed much of the ship, shutting down power, ending radio contact (though a single S.O.S. did make it out) and leaving both passengers and crew in complete darkness. Unable to get to the rescue boats, some jumped overboard, a bad decision given the increasingly turbulent waters being created by a developing Nor'easter. Rescue ships arrived late but then left early after misreading the gravity of the situation. The Coast Guard allegedly refused to dispatch floatplanes until the local media reported bodies washing ashore along the New Jersey coast. All in all, nearly 140 people died, and the incident led to the creation of major new safety regulations aboard cruise ships.

Unfortunately, this particular *Dante's Inferno* is nowhere near as interesting as the incident that helped give birth to it. CW

[1.] Russo, William. "Dante's Inferno: Tracy's Trial By Fire." *Spencer Tracy Fox Film Actor: The Pre-Code Legacy of a Hollywood Legend.* Ed. Brenda Loew. Newton, MA: New England Vintage Film Society, 2008. p. 182. Print.

The Dead Speak
aka **Los muertos hablan**
Films de Mexico; b/w; length unknown; Mexico

D/Co-S: Gabriel Soria *Co-S:* Emilio Fernández *P:* José Luis Bueno *C:* Jack Draper *M:* Mario Talavera, Max Urban

Cast: Julián Soler, Amelia de Ilisa, Manuel Noriega, Miguel Arenas, Aurora Cortés, Isidro D'Olace, Jorge Mondragon, José Eduardo Pérez, Godofredo de Velasco, Ricardo Carti, Manuel Buendia, Gilberto González, Paco Martinez, David Valle González

The Dead Speak is a melodrama with elements of horror and science fiction. Based on a novel by Pedro Zapiain, it trades on the fantastic idea, dating from the days of Jack the Ripper, that the human retina retains the image of the last thing a person sees before death. Professor Jiménez (Noriega) supports this notion and is mocked for his belief while one of his students, Eduardo (Soler), supports him in the face of public ridicule. Eduardo is in

Johnny Mack Brown, far right, starred in many Westerns in the 1930s and 1940s.

love with Marta (de Ilisa), but her father (Arenas) is reluctant to bless their betrothal, largely due to Eduardo's relationship with Professor Jiménez. One evening while attempting to steal a body for Professor Jiménez' experiment, Eduardo is shot by police. He drags himself to the professor's lab, where the professor calls Marta, who shows up just in time to be the last thing Eduardo sees before he dies. A photograph of the young man's retinas reveals that Professor Jiménez's goofball theory is in fact correct, and the professor's name is redeemed. A university lecture hall is posthumously dedicated to Eduardo, his attempt at body-snatching apparently forgiven.

The title *The Dead Speak* is a bit hyperbolic, given that Eduardo never speaks after his death. The film wasn't the first to contain the idea that retinas are nature's own photographic film (complete with developing and printing ability). That canard was first advanced in the French film *The Last Look*, which was shot by Pathé in 1909.

Manuel Noriega was something of a horror celebrity in his native Mexico during the 1930s, starring in such films as *Two Monks* (1934), *The Mystery of the Ghastly Face* (1935), *The Macabre Trunk* (1936) and *The Super Madman* (1937). Born in 1880, he entered the movies in 1907 and amassed over 200 credits as an actor while also writing, directing and producing a few titles. He died in 1961, shortly after his last uncredited bit role in *Macario* (1960). CW

Desert Phantom
Supreme; b/w; 65 min; U.S.

D: S. Roy Luby *S:* E.B. Mann, Earl Snell *C:* Bert Longenecker

Cast: Johnny Mack Brown, Sheila Manors (Sheila Bromley), Ted Adams, Karl Hackett, Hal Price, Nelson McDowell, Charles King

Billy Donovan (Brown) visits a small Texas town, hoping to sell the locals some guns and ammo. While there, he becomes intrigued by Jean Halloran (Manors), a lovely cowgirl being threatened by a mysterious figure known as The Phantom. She believes this Phantom to be a supernatural presence. Billy doesn't buy the spook angle, though, and quits his job to protect her on the ranch. There he has run-ins with Jean's paraplegic stepfather (Hackett) and a local bandit known as Salazar (Adams), with whom he has an unpleasant history.

Desert Phantom is a thinly disguised remake of *The Night Rider* (1932), which starred Harry Carey and George "Gabby" Hayes. But while the original was only moderately weird, this version incorporates eerie elements in the form of a possibly supernatural menace. The film overall isn't distinguishable from any number of other low-budget Western/horror films of the period. The dialogue is as stilted as the acting (when Billy says that he just saw something "queer," Jean asks, "Did it look like a phantom?"), and there are the obligatory cliffhanger thrills and barroom brawls, along with the occasional atmospheric nighttime exterior shot.

Johnny Mack Brown went from all-American athlete in college to a short career in movies in the 1930s. His lead performance in King Vidor's *Billy the Kid* (1930) led to work in a few B through Z-grade Westerns, usually for smaller outfits like Monogram and Supreme Pictures. (It was Supreme, in fact, that gave birth to *Desert Phantom*.) Brown also starred in *Branded a Coward* (1935), which is sometimes incorrectly cited as another horror/Western hybrid.

S. Roy Luby directed over a hundred films, mostly oaters. His pseudonyms include Roy Claire, Roy S. Luby, Roy Luby, Sol Luby and Russell Roy. He worked with such then-popular leads as Bob Steele, Ray "Crash" Corrigan, and, of course, Johnny Mack Brown.

The *Night Rider/Desert Phantom* story got another go-around with 1940's *The Range Busters*, which retained the Phantom angle. TH

The Florentine Dagger
Warner; b/w; 69 min; U.S.

D: Robert Florey *S:* Tom Reed, Brown Holmes *P:* Harry Joe Brown, Hal B. Wallis, Jack L. Warner *C:* Arthur L. Todd *M:* Leo F. Forbstein, Bernhard Kaun

Cast: Donald Woods, Margaret Lindsay, C. Aubrey Smith, Henry O'Neill, Robert Barrat, Florence Fair, Frank Reicher, Charles Judels, Rafaela Ottiano, Paul Porcasi, Eily Malyon, Egon Brecher, Herman Bing, Henry Kolker

Juan (Woods) is the last descendant of the infamous Borgia clan. Haunted by his family's bloody legacy, he seeks comfort in the arms of his girlfriend, Florence Ballau (Lindsay). When her father (O'Neill), who forbids them to marry, is found dead with a Florentine dagger in his chest, Juan worries that he may be the killer.

Based on a novel by Ben Hecht, *The Florentine Dagger* is a more-macabre-than-usual entry in Warner Bros' *Crime Club* series. In addition to a scenario that sneaks a few subversive elements past the censors of the time (most notably, the notion of a murderer getting away with his or her crime), the film benefits from the stylish direction of Robert Florey. Florey spent much of his career making the most out of underfunded B-movie fare such as this, and his Expressionistic visual touches infuse the film with the requisite creepy mood.

Dapper character actor C. Aubrey Smith is in fine form as the kindly doctor who attempts to help Juan, but Donald Woods is miscast—and seems to know it—in the lead role. Still, the film manages to hold one's interest, less because of its predictable scenario than the mood and atmosphere it conjures. TH

The Great Impersonation
Universal; b/w; 66 min; U.S.

D: Alan Crosland *S:* Eve Green, Frank Wead *P:* Edmund Grainger *C:* Milton Krasner *M:* Heinz Roemheld, Clifford Vaughan *FX:* John P. Fulton

Cast: Edmund Lowe, Valerie Hobson, Wera Engels, Murray Kinnell, Henry Mollison, Esther Dale, Brandon Hurst, Ivan Simpson, Spring Byington, Lumsden Hare, Leonard Mudie, Claude King, Frank Reicher, Harry Allen, Dwight Frye

While on expedition in Africa, disgraced Brit Sir Everard Dominey (Lowe) runs into Baron Leopold (also Lowe). The two men, it's revealed, once went to the same school, where their physical similarity was a frequent source of confusion. Unknown to Sir Everard, Baron Leopold is working for a foreign government, hoping to undermine Britain in a forthcoming global conflict. He arranges for Everard to have an "accident," then takes his place and returns to Britain to wreak his sabotage. There, he contends with a neurotic wife (Hobson) and an eerie, possibly haunted, manor house.

Edward Phillips Oppenheim (1886-1946) was a popular English writer. Though his name is today largely forgotten, connoisseurs of spy fiction recognize him as the author of the brilliant 1920 novel *The Great Impersonation*, first filmed by George Melford (director of the Spanish version of *Dracula*, 1931) in 1921.

For this, Hollywood's second crack at the story, Universal and producer Edmund Grainger played the "spooky atmospherics" angle for all it was worth. Truth be told, however, *Impersonation* is an odd amalgam of spy thriller and "old dark house" mystery. The typical horror buff is bound to be somewhat disoriented during the opening scenes, which reek of political intrigue. Once the film moves to Britain, however, it wades waist-deep into familiar, if banal, Universal horror territory.

The spooky old manor house, replete with sinister servants and a haunted bog, evokes comparisons to *The Cat and the Canary* (1927) and *The Old Dark House* (1932), though it's closer at heart to Sir Arthur Conan Doyle's *The Hound of the Baskervilles*. That the film never really comes together is due almost entirely to the rather uncertain direction by Alan Crosland. Crosland was a prolific talent during the silent era (among his most enduring titles were *Don Juan*, 1926, starring John Barrymore, and *The Jazz Singer*, 1927, notable as the first feature-length film to contain recorded dialogue), but he failed to make a smooth transition to talkies. *Impersonation* was one of his last films. Crosland and cinematographer Milton Krasner (an Oscar-winner for *Fate is the Hunter*, 1964, though he also photographed many of Universal's horror B-movies in the 1940s) create some suitably creepy tableaux—notably a mysterious hand holding a knife, which menaces Lowe while he sleeps—but there's simply something missing. In his hesitant attempt to meld two types of film, Crosland achieves not a synthesis but something closer to cinematic schizophrenia.

Edmund Lowe (*Chandu the Magician*, 1932) does a competent job in his dual roles, while Valerie Hobson (*The Bride of Frankenstein*, 1935) is wasted as Sir Everard's unbalanced wife.

A Mexican poster for *Lucrezia Borgia*

The supporting cast includes horror stalwarts such as Brandon Hurst (*White Zombie*, 1932) and Frank Reicher (*King Kong*, 1933). Dwight Frye appears briefly in a thankless cameo, basically unrecognizable beneath a shaggy beard.

A minor, flawed entry in the Universal horror canon, *The Great Impersonation* nonetheless has a degree of charm (and it does manage at least one genuinely surprising plot twist). Oppenheim's story was again filmed (by John Rawlins) in 1942, though that version made no attempt to integrate any elements of horror. TH

Lucrezia Borgia
aka **Lucrèce Borgia**
Compagnie du Cinema; b/w; 93 min; France

D/Co-S: Abel Gance *Co-S:* Léopold Marchand, Henri Vendresse *P:* Henri E. Ullman *C:* Roger Hubert, Boris Kauffman

Cast: Edwige Feuillère, Gabriel Gabrio, Maurice Escande, Roger Karl, Aimé Clariond, Philippe Hériat, Jacques Dumesnil, Max Michel, Louis Aymond, Jean Fay, René Bergeron, Gaston Modot, Antonin Artaud, Marcel Chabier, Georges Prieur, Louis Perdoux, Josette Day

The Borgia Family rose to Italian dominance in 1492 when Rodrigo Borgia was elected Pope. Taking the name Alexander VI, he acknowledged at least four illegitimate children and used his station to ensure their rise to power. Son Giovanni was made Duke of Gandia, while another son, Cesare, was appointed Archbishop of Valencia. To maintain a secure grip on the governance of assorted papal and city-states, daughter Lucrezia was pimped out in marriage to various men in families of power. The youngest son Gioffre was also pressed into marriage to the daughter of an influential family; that woman later became the sexual consort of several of the Borgia men.

Lucrezia's part of the family tree was subject to a fair amount of grafting. When she and Cesare decided that her first marriage was politically useless, her husband was forced to annul the union, signing papers admitting to impotency (though not before accusing his wife of incest with her father and older brother). After the annulment, Lucrezia gave birth to a son, which may have been Cesare's or the Pope's messenger Perotto's. Lucrezia then married Alfonso of Aragon, who was considered attractive. Cesare seems to have been jealous of him, a situation probably complicated by a bout of syphilis that pockmarked Cesare's face, a turn-off to his sister that also prompted him to wear a mask when in public. At any rate, after Lucrezia bore his child, Alfonso was attacked by Cesare's men and, while recovering, mysteriously strangled. Lucrezia's third marriage, to Alfonso d'Este, was also her longest, though neither was faithful to the other. She died in 1519 after giving birth to her eighth child.

Far from being a historical treatise, Abel Gance's *Lucrezia Borgia* was crafted to revisit the success of his more famous *Napoleon* (1927), which had by 1935 already garnered classic status. (The novel by Alfred Schirokauer was the basis of *Lucrezia*, not any sort of factual research.) The film's excesses, while arguably the major reason to watch it, also got it banned in several countries around the world and heavily cut in several others.

Its sympathetic focus on Lucrezia (Feuillère) as a victim of her notorious brother Cesare (Gabrio) and his scheming friend Nicolo Machiavelli (Clariond)—who is writing his famous book *The Prince* as the film unfolds—is forced, to say the least, but remains trashy fun. Cesare will stop at nothing to gain power, killing his own homosexual brother Jean (Escande) and threatening his father, Pope Alexander VI (Karl). Gioffre, on the other hand, is nowhere to be found.

After forcing Lucrezia's first husband, the Duke of Milano (Dumesnil), to admit impotency and agree to an annulment, Cesare forces his sister into a second marriage to a man he later murders. Juiciest of all is the film's climactic sequence, where Cesare admits his love for his sister and the jealousy with which he has regarded her various marriages and illicit love affairs. In an act of torturous cruelty, he reveals to Lucrezia the burial place of the men she's loved, all of whom Cesare has had murdered and interred together. Still, in the end it's Lucrezia who outlives her siblings, and she exits life hoping to be remembered as a patron of the arts rather than for her (mis) deeds.

Yet, if the title character, indisputably one of history's most beautiful villainesses, is whitewashed to the point of sappiness, the film she inhabits is anything but. Not only does her brother poison, stab and torture his way to political success, but he rapes every woman who suits his fancy. The number of exposed breasts (with at least one full frontal female nude on display) must surely have raised eyebrows even in the director's native France. After all, the year 1935 was a socially conservative one as a worldwide Depression crushed European economies and

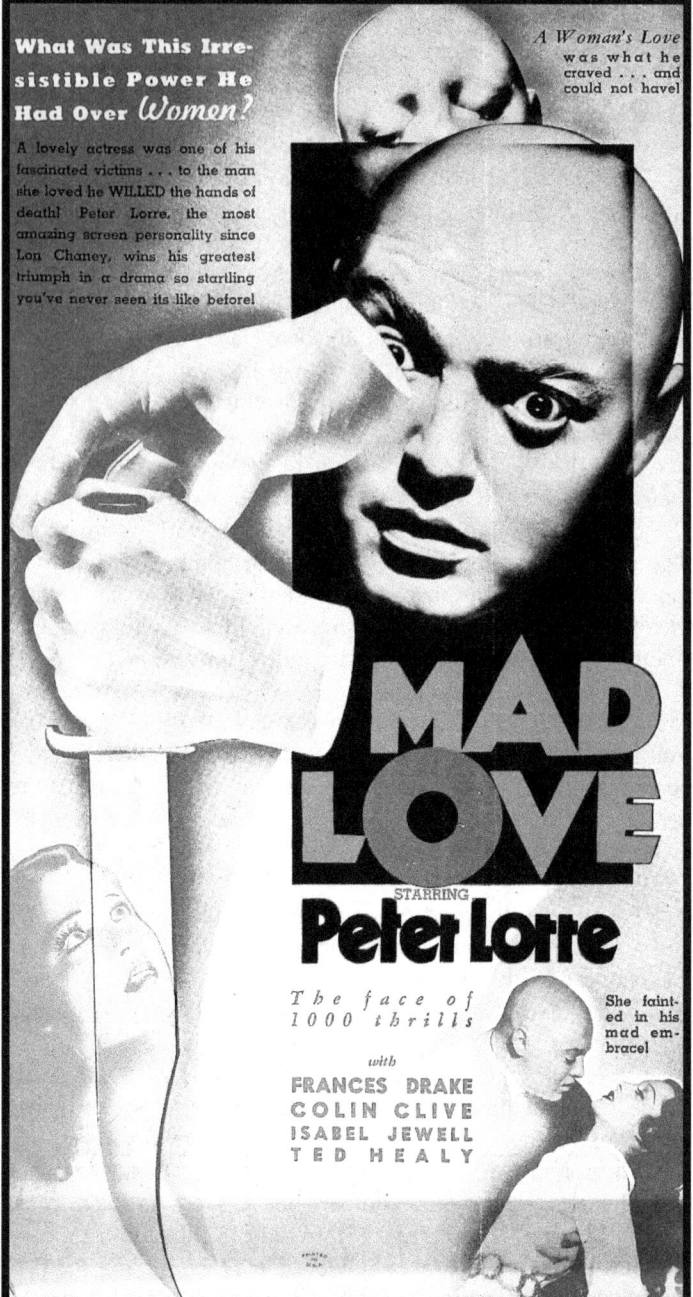

Hitler's Nazis gathered, ready to decimate anyone who didn't agree with their particularly nasty brand of ethics and religious virtue.

Lucrezia Borgia emerges as quite the bawdy little soap opera, with performances that tend toward the melodramatic. Yet it undeniably maintains a resonant power throughout. The one moment in which Gance uses music to heighten the mood (before which the movie is almost entirely music free) is a potent one. The camerawork is consistently superb, and while the sets and costumes are at times a bit lacking, the film remains visually attractive. It shows what Rowland V. Lee might have accomplished with *Tower of London* (1939) had he not been constrained by Universal's fear of the very sex and violence it sought to exploit.

Ultimately, Gance's film is as much a horror movie as it is a costumed spectacle. It's far from perfect, but it does have something to offer those curious about European cinema at a time when the United States was beginning to stunt its own cinematic creativity. CW

Mad Love
aka The Hands of Orlac
MGM; b/w; 68 min; U.S.

D: Karl Freund *S:* John L. Balderston, P.J. Wolfson, Guy Endore, Leon Wolfson, Edgar Allan Woolf, Gladys von Ettinghausen, Leon Gordon *P:* John W. Considine, Jr. *C:* Chester Lyons, Gregg Toland *M:* Dimitri Tiomkin

Cast: Peter Lorre, Colin Clive, Frances Drake, Ted Healy, Sara Haden, Edward Brophy, Henry Kolker, Keye Luke,

Dr. Gogol (Lorre) is a brilliant surgeon who is obsessed with actress Yvonne Orlac (Drake), a performer at the Theater du Grand Guignol in Paris. Though she rejects his advances, she turns to him when her husband, famous concert pianist Stephen Orlac (Clive), finds his hands badly injured in a train wreck. Gogol transplants onto Stephen the hands of Rollo the Knife Thrower (Brophy), a recently executed murderer. The performer recovers but is plagued by violent impulses, and Gogol takes advantage of the situation by making another play for Yvonne.

Robert Wiene had already filmed Maurice Renards' 1920 novel *Le Mains d'Orlac* as *The Hands of Orlac* (with German great Conrad Veidt in the title role) in 1924. But despite the popularity of both book and film, no further movie versions were done until this one by cinematographer-turned-director Karl Freund. In adapting the story, writer Guy Endore (whose novel *The Werewolf of Paris*, 1933, is *the* touchstone lycanthropy-themed literary work) altered the text considerably to accommodate Lorre's screen persona. (The character of Dr. Gogol is actually not present in the novel, which centers on Orlac's inner conflicts over the origin of his new hands.)

Mad Love marks the Hollywood debut of Peter Lorre, who had chilled audiences as a pedophilic murderer in Fritz Lang's *M* (1930) before moving to Britain and making a villainous splash in Alfred Hitchcock's *The Man Who Knew Too Much* (1934). Lorre's ability to evoke empathy for disagreeable characters is on full display here. Like Lon Chaney in so many silent melodramas, Gogol is an oddball outsider, lusting for an unattainable woman. Lorre shaved his head for the role, and his odd features mesh beautifully with Freund's stylized aesthetic.

Departures from the novel push the title character somewhat into the background, though Colin Clive—in one of his last roles before his death from alcoholism in 1937—brings plenty of nervous intensity to the role as it is. He compares well to Veidt in the earlier version and easily bests Mel Ferrer in the same role in *The Hands of Orlac* (1960).

Frances Drake, who is wonderful as Yvonne, completes the trio of strong central performances. She appeared in only one other horror film—as Boris Karloff's neglected wife in *The Invisible Ray* (1936)—and a few unremarkable comedy and mystery releases. One wonders at her relative obscurity today. Not only is she photogenic, she is also a nuanced and gifted performer.

The film is disrupted at times by the arbitrary inclusion of comedy relief by Ted Healy, who portrays a reporter representing the U.S. press in Paris. Overall, however, Freund's handling of the material is as superb as it was in *The Mummy* (1932).

Colin Clive and Frances Drake star as lovers facing a seemingly insurmountable object, the impulse of his hands to murder with knives, in *Mad Love*.

Mad Love was his final bow as a director; he thereafter returned exclusively to cinematography. His later career found him working in television, where he developed the three-camera style of shooting sitcoms for *I Love Lucy* (1951-1956).

Thematically, *Mad Love* bears some striking similarities to the same year's *The Raven*, which also starred Bela Lugosi as a demented surgeon in love with an unattainable woman. Yet the two films are night and day in terms of execution: *The Raven* aims for crude shocks and lumbers under pedestrian direction, whereas *Mad Love*, despite some clumsy humor, is a work of cinematic art. The film's rich cinematography is courtesy of Chester Lyons and the great Gregg Toland, the latter revered for his work on Orson Welles' *Citizen Kane* (1941). Freund had tried to get Toland to shoot the entire picture, but MGM balked at his request and assigned Lyons to the picture. The director reportedly spent more time tinkering with the lighting than working with his actors, however, and when Toland was eventually brought in for some additional photography, the two men clashed. Regardless, the collaborative effort between them results in one of the most visually pleasing horror films of its decade.

1995's flat romantic comedy drama *Mad Love* has no connection to this masterpiece. TH

Maria Marten, or The Murder in the Red Barn
aka Murder in the Red Barn; Murder in the Old Red Barn
King; b/w; 58 (70) min; Great Britain

D: Milten Rosmer *S:* Randall Faye *P:* George King *C:* George Stretton *M:* Leo T. Croke

Cast: Tod Slaughter, Sophie Stewart, D.J. Williams, Eric Portman, Clare Greet, Gerard Tyrell, Ann Trevor, Stella Rho, Dennis Hoey, Quentin McPhearson, Antonia Brough

The story of the Red Barn Murder began in the town of Polstead in the county of Suffolk, England in 1826, when 24-year-old Maria Marten entered into a relationship with William Corder, who was two years her junior. Maria had already born two children out of wedlock, each with a different man, but the following year she gave birth to a third child, this time with Corder. Corder had hoped to keep their relationship a secret, and though the child died, Corder promised to marry Maria nonetheless. He arranged to meet her in the "red barn," which was located outside of town and known for its peculiar roof of red tiles. Telling her that she was about to be prosecuted for giving birth to children out of wedlock, he insisted that she wear men's clothes to her destination so as not to be suspected and that he would take clothes there for her to change into. Instead, he murdered her and buried her beneath the barn's dirt floor. Over the next year he moved from place to place, assuring family and friends in letters that he and Maria were happy together—though Maria, it seemed, was often too ill to write. After Maria's stepmother claimed to have received information from Maria's spirit in dreams, Maria's father went to the red barn and dug under a storage bin. There he found his daughter's body wrapped in a grain sack. Corder was swiftly apprehended and charged with murder. At first he claimed that Maria had committed suicide, but after his conviction, he confessed. On August 11, 1828, he was taken to the gallows. Sources at the time claimed that anywhere from 5,000 to 20,000 people witnessed the execution, a testimony to how well-covered the case had been throughout Great Britain.

Immediately, melodramatic plays began to pop up, casting Maria Marten as an innocent, virginal heroine victimized by the bloodthirsty William Corder. Omitted from most productions was the couple's affair and the child that resulted (which later evidence strongly hints was murdered by them). There were also questions about the stepmother's involvement in the crime; many came to suspect that she too had had an affair with Corder and that, upset with him for running away after Maria's death, told tales of nightmare visions as a way to incriminate him.

Film versions of the incident were produced in 1902 (*Maria Marten: The Murder in the Red Barn*), 1908 (*The Red Barn Crime*), 1913 (*Maria Marten, or The Murder in the Red Barn*) and 1928 (*Maria Marten*), though it is the 1935 George King adaptation that is best remembered. King's film added a band of Gypsies—including the handsome Carlos (Portman), who is both in love with Maria (Stewart) and suspected in her disappearance—but retained the portrayal of Maria as a wide-eyed innocent, changing her poor farmer father into a God-fearing minister to boot. Corder (Slaughter) is presented as a much older squire. It's difficult to believe that Maria finds him more attractive than the striking Carlos. After being invited to Corder's house, she has sex with him. Though she afterward desires marriage, he has other plans; bereft of money, he has his sights on a homely but rich heiress, a situation that necessitates the removal of the embarrassing—and pregnant—Maria. So he lures Maria to the red barn, where he dispatches her soul to Heaven and buries her body in the dirt floor—along with (unintentionally) the murder weapon that can identify him. He propagates around town the notion that Carlos is responsible for her disappearance and, believing himself to be above suspicion, settles down to his new life. When Carlos at length confronts him, however, his scheme falls apart.

Strangely missing from the film are the supernatural elements that helped propel the story from tawdry gossip to national obsession. Mrs. Marten neither dreams of murder nor is visited by Maria's ghost. Yet that omission doesn't prevent the film from crossing into horror terrain. The scene in which Corder kills Maria is set in a spooky old barn on a dark and stormy night, with thunder booming and lightning flashing. The sets have an extraordinary quality that recalls Universal's best work from the same period, though the script meanders too long after the resolution of its central mystery (with said resolution harder to swallow than the one from real life).

Milton Rosmer directed the film with some flair, but his career as an actor (he starred in Hammer's *Who Killed Van Loon?* as well as in *The Monkey's Paw*, both 1948) was much longer than his career as a director. He manages some surprisingly blunt moments here. In addition to Maria's affair with Corder—which is spelled out in no uncertain terms—and her subsequent murder at his hands, some of the dialogue comes off as startlingly adult even today. When Corder is challenged by Carlos to reveal what he's done with Maria, Corder exclaims, "Do you think I'd soil my hands with a common village slut?" The exchange sums up the film's approach to its story; on the surface, it has all the class of the Victorian stage (including wonderful performances and

Tod Slaughter starred in many horror films during Britain's film ban on the genre.

convincing costumes), but there's an undeniable aura of sleaze about the proceedings. It's no surprise, then, that the film was shorn of over 20 minutes of footage before its original release in the United States and Canada.

Maria Marten was a big success in its native Britain, where it launched a slew of barnstormers in the late 1930s and early 1940s and made a major star of Tod Slaughter (1885-1956). Born Norman Carter Slaughter in Newcastle in 1885, he made his acting debut on the stage in 1905. After serving in World War I, he changed his first name to Tod and starred in a series of Victorian melodramas featuring maniacal villains (though Slaughter usually played the heroic leads). In 1931 he starred during the day as Long John Silver in a stage adaptation of Robert Louis Stevenson's classic novel *Treasure Island* (1881-82) and at night as William Hare in *The Crimes of Burke and Hare*. His over-the-top mannerisms, leering facial expressions and nuanced vocalizations were perfect for playing diabolical, aristocratic types or insane murderers ... or amalgams of the two. Slaughter's other horror-themed films include *Sweeney Todd: The Demon Barber of Fleet Street* and *The Crimes of Stephen Hawke* (both 1936), *Never Too Late to Mend* (1937), *The Ticket of Leave Man* and *Sexton Blake and the Hooded Terror* (both 1938), *The Face at the Window* (1939), *Crimes at the Dark House* (1940), *Curse of the Wraydons* (1946) and *The Greed of William Heart* (1948).

Strangely enough, it was just after a performance in a stage version of *Maria Marten* in 1956 that he died of a heart attack. The death occurred a mere year before Hammer Film Productions—who were indebted to Slaughter's films for prepping the English in the ways of violent Gothic melodrama—revived Victorian horror with *The Curse of Frankenstein* (1957). Had Slaughter lived, he may have become a Hammer horror star alongside Peter Cushing and Christopher Lee. As it stands, he's merely a footnote in the history of British horror, one deserving of far greater recognition.

Dennis Hoey, who has a small part in the film, later moved to the United States and became a character actor for Universal, mostly portraying police inspectors. These included not only the part for which he's most famous, Inspector Lestrade in the Basil Rathbone/Nigel Bruce series of Sherlock Holmes mysteries, but similar roles in such films as *Frankenstein Meets the Wolf Man* (1943) and *She-Wolf of London* (1946). CW

Mark of the Vampire
aka **Vampires of Prague**
MGM; b/w; 60 min; U.S.

D/Co-P: Tod Browning *S:* Guy Endore, Bernard Schubert, H.S. Kraft (uncredited), Samuel Ornitz (uncredited), John L. Balderston (uncredited) *Co-P:* E.J. Mannix *C:* James Wong Howe *M:* Jack Virgil *FX:* Tom Tutwiler

Cast: Lionel Barrymore, Lionel Atwill, Elizabeth Allan, Bela Lugosi, Jean Hersholt, Henry Wadsworth, Donald Meek, Ivan Simpson, Leila Bennett, Franklyn Ardell, June Gittelson, Carroll Borland, Holmes Herbert, Michael Visaroff

Sir Karrel Borotyn (Herbert) is murdered, and the superstitious locals blame a vampire. Inspector Neumann (Atwill) scoffs at the notion but is unable to solve the crime. Borotyn's daughter Irina (Allan) moves in with her guardian Baron Otto (Hersholt), and the Borotyn family castle is abandoned. One year later, the

Bela Lugosi and Carroll Borland as the supposed father and daughter vampire duo of *Mark of the Vampire*

mysterious Count Mora (Lugosi) and his daughter Luna (Borland) inhabit the castle, though both of them are known to have died years earlier in a murder/suicide. Occult expert Professor Zelen (Barrymore) is called in to assist Inspector Neumann, who believes there is a connection between the purported undead pair and the still-unsolved murder of Sir Karrel.

Tod Browning's *London After Midnight* (1927) may be the most longed-for horror film currently considered lost (though reviews of the period suggest that it was not among the director's more accomplished pictures). It was, at any rate, a box-office success, and in 1935, Browning, still smarting from the commercial failure of *Freaks* (1932), was desperate for a hit. He sensibly decided to remake *London* as a talkie, further stacking the deck by casting Lugosi as a vampiric character, thus evoking public recollections of 1931's hit *Dracula*. (In another nod to *Dracula*, Browning also cast Michael Visaroff—the innkeeper in that film—as a superstitious landlord.)

Mark of the Vampire, then, is about as close as one can get to seeing *London After Midnight* (notwithstanding Rick Schmidlin's 2002 reconstruction of the film from vintage stills). *Mark*'s merits as a film are frequently downplayed in the process of romanticizing the original, and granted, the remake is frequently absurd and its denouement something of a "shaggy dog joke" punch line, but on the level of sheer entertainment it's in the top tier of the director's work.

Lugosi and Borland in *Mark of the Vampire*

Whereas *Dracula* is often stagy, *Mark* is terrifically stylish. The latter film also moves at a much faster clip than the former. It's known that the quick pacing can be attributed in part to studio interference; Browning's original ran about 80 minutes, but Metro-Goldwyn-Mayer demanded a number of cuts, bringing it down to exactly 60 minutes. Just precisely what was excised has been much debated. Some maintain that a back story concerning Count Mora's incestuous relationship with his daughter—ending with him murdering her and committing suicide, hence the bullet wound on Mora's temple—was too strong for 1935 audiences. It would certainly have been too strong for the Motion Picture Producers and Distributors of America, which enforced the Hays Code over most Hollywood product at the time.

It's also likely that at least some of the cuts were made to expunge bits of comedic relief injudiciously sprinkled throughout the original film. Surviving cast lists name some familiar folks (including Universal horror stalwarts Lionel Belmore and Doris Lloyd) who don't appear in the final product.

In any case, the film is a quantum leap beyond the similarly themed *Dracula* in almost every respect, with an atmosphere that's beautifully sustained throughout (whereas the former film becomes steadily less memorable after the opening scenes).

The performances in *Mark* are stronger as well. Browning is well served by a seasoned cast of veteran actors. Lionel Barrymore had worked with the director on *The Show* (1927) and *West of Zanzibar* (1929) and would do so one final time on *The Devil Doll* (1936). Barrymore attacks the role of Professor Zelen, the film's Van Helsing, with aplomb. He's not exactly subtle, but his performance suits the over-the-top tone of the film.

Lionel Atwill delivers yet another incomparable performance as the no-nonsense Inspector Neumann. And while at first glance Bela Lugosi isn't given much to do (in fact, he's robbed of dialogue altogether until the final fade-out), his presence alone is magnificently chilling. Browning and cinematographer James Wong Howe (two-time Oscar-winner for *The Rose Tattoo*, 1956, and *Hud*, 1963) give the veteran bloodsucker some wonderful moments, whether stalking through the atmospherics or charging toward the camera. Jean Hersholt (*The Mask of Fu Manchu*, 1932) is effectively neurotic as the panic-stricken Baron Otto, while Elizabeth Allan (*The Haunted Stranger*, 1958) brings class and distinction to what could have been another forgettable swooning ingénue.

Carroll Borland (1914-1994), who makes a great impression as Mora's daughter Luna, came to the film in an unusual way. She had seen *Dracula* numerous times, developed a fascination with Lugosi and written him several rapturous fan letters. (She even wrote a sequel to the story, titled *Countess Dracula*, which she sent the actor to read.) Lugosi was so touched by her devotion that he brought her to Hollywood to play his daughter in *Mark*. With her pale countenance and long jet-black hair, she reportedly served as inspiration for the character of Mortitia in Charles Addams' beloved *Addams Family* cartoons. She performed in a handful of films before abandoning acting in 1953, though she later made a couple of cameo appearances in Z-grade fare directed by Fred Olen Ray (1983's *Scalps* and 1985's *BioHazard*). She often played up her relationship with Lugosi in interviews—always emphasizing that it was strictly of the father-daughter variety—but much of what she related was and remains dubious. At any rate, she earns her place in the horror pantheon with her portrayal of Luna.

The film remains hotly contested among horror fans due to the mundane nature of its resolution. Legend has it that even the cast was disappointed, having believed for the bulk of the shoot that they were acting in a straight horror film. But that bit of apocrypha doesn't really hold water. For one thing, *London After Midnight* was less than 10 years old when *Mark* went into production. Though the silent film wasn't playing in theaters (and this was, of course, long before the days of cinematic home entertainment), it had been enormously popular and was well remembered; certainly people in the movie biz were aware of it. It also seems unlikely that the cast would have been working in the dark, as it were, doing scenes without access to the final pages of the film's scenario.

Truth be told, *Mark of the Vampire* has more in common with comedic mysteries like *The Cat and the Canary* (1927) than with overt horror outings like *Dracula*. It stands as one of the most vividly atmospheric films ever directed by Browning, who would direct only two more in his varied and interesting career: *The Devil Doll* (1936) and *Miracles for Sale* (1939). TH

Murder by Television
aka **The Houghland Murder Case**
Cameo; b/w; 54 min; U.S.

D: Clifford Sanforth *S:* Joseph O'Donnell *P:* Clifford Sanforth, Edward M. Spitz, William M. Pizor *C:* James Brown, Jr., Arthur Reed *M:* Oliver Wallace

Cast: Bela Lugosi, June Collyer, Huntley Gordon, George Meeker, Henry Mowbray, Charles Hill Mailes, Claire McDowell, Hattie McDaniel, Allen Jung, Charles K. French, Larry Francis, Henry Hall, Billy Sullivan

James Houghland (Mailes) is murdered while demonstrating a new technology for the transmission of television signals. Since he had blanketly refused to sell his invention to any of the competing television companies, there is no shortage of suspects. Chief of Police Nelson (Mowbray) is called in to investigate, and the mysterious Arthur Perry (Lugosi) seems the most likely suspect.

The conventional view is that Bela Lugosi began his series of horrendous career choices with the onset of the horror ban of the mid-1930s, when work in his genre of choice became scarce. There's little doubt that the Hungarian actor, so firmly identified with fright films, suffered greatly during that time (and even less doubt that he accepted every job that came his way). But Lugosi clunkers weren't exactly unheard of before the horror ban. Case in point: This grade-Z mystery thriller, done during the same period in which he was appearing in significantly classier genre fare for larger studios such as Universal.

Murder By Television is a movie to which the staunchest Lugosi fans have a hard time warming. Not only is it as cheap-looking as the worst of his later Monogram mad doctor pictures, its plot vacillates between confusing and flat-out boring.

It can, with a little compassion, be concluded that Lugosi manages to salvage his own dignity in this lost cause. Amid the dreck, one can barely discern a low-key and rather charming performance (in a dual role, no less). And it helps that he's surrounded by an absolutely abysmal supporting cast, including a pre-*Gone with the Wind* (1939) Hattie McDaniel as a servant required to "Lordy, Lordy!" with reckless abandon.

Production values are nearly non-existent. Indeed, parts of *Murder* appear to be actual rehearsal footage used simply because it's in focus. The screenplay is, as already alluded to, garbled beyond comprehension, though Houghland's pronouncement that television is a "great development for the betterment of mankind" is a sure-fire chuckle-drawer for contemporary audiences. Director Clifford Sanforth makes his debut with this picture; perhaps not surprisingly, he directed only a few more minor items.

While many of Lugosi's later poverty row items are indisputably lacking in aesthetic value, there's at least something fun about even the least polished of them. *Murder By Television*, on the other hand, doesn't even have "good" bad movie entertainment value. It's a low point of 1930s cinema, horror or otherwise. TH

The Mysterious Mr. Wong
aka **Mysterious Mr. Wong**
Monogram; b/w; 63 min; U.S.

D: William Nigh *S:* Nina Howatt, James Herbuveaux, Lew

Levenson *P:* George Yohalem *C:* Harry Neumann

Cast: Bela Lugosi, Wallace Ford, Arline Judge, Fred Warren, Lotus Long, Robert Emmett O'Conner, Edward Peil, Luke Chan, Etta Lee, Ernest F. Young

Based on Harry Stephen Keeler's story *The Twelve Coins of Confucius* from the collection *Sing Sing Nights* (the title story of which was the source for another 1934 Monogram cheapie), *The Mysterious Mr. Wong* is yet another Yellow Peril offering. (Apparently to confuse things further, *Wong*'s title is a twist on a third Keeler work, *The Mysterious Mr. I.*)

Wong begins with graphics informing the viewer that Confucius was "[t]he most famous of all the sages in China," and that "[t]here is a tradition that 12 coins, given by Confucius on his deathbed to 12 trusted friends, will some day [sic] come to the possession of one man and give him extraordinary powers in the province of Keelat." But the film's action doesn't take place anywhere near Keelat; rather, it's set in San Francisco's once-notorious Chinatown district, with no explanation of how not just one but all 12 coins got there.

The tale itself opens with the grisly murders of several Chinese men, each of whom has a coin stolen from his body and replaced with a sheet of paper bearing an Asian letter. The mastermind behind these weird crimes is the mysterious Mr. Fu Wong (Lugosi), who hopes that by procuring all 12 coins, he can become the powerful lord of Keelat's underworld—if not

Bela Lugosi stars as *The Mysterious Mr. Wong*.

the entire world. That 12th and final coin, however, is proving awfully hard to procure. Enter newspaperman Jason H. Barton (Ford), musing in print that the murders may not be the work of a Tong as everyone else seems to think. Barton's editorializing hits too close to home to suit Wong, even though the reporter shows no interest in doing any in-depth investigating into the matter. Nonetheless, before long, the Asian villain, who will stop at nothing to get that final coin, threatens Barton and his would-be girlfriend.

The Mysterious Mr. Wong is typical, vapid 1930s Poverty Row entertainment, but director William Nigh keeps it moving at a decent enough pace. He seems to have learned a thing or two from his previous horror outings (*The House of Mystery* and *Mystery Liner*, both 1934), neither of which has much to recommend it. There are some interesting—and somewhat gruesome—shots throughout, particularly of murdered men.

The film is pretty sadistic stuff for the period, prompting one to wonder if it got away with the violence because *foreign* types (Asian Americans), rather than white people, were the victims. In any case, xenophobia runs rampant here, as when Barton's editor asks him, "Did you ever run into a Chinaman named Wong?" and Barton responds, "If I ever run into one who ain't named Wong …" Or similarly, when Barton responds to news of a Chinese laundryman's murder with, "Oh what do I care about another laundryman; the world is full of 'em …" (This is the movie's hero, don't forget.)

He's not the only racist around, either; a police officer (O'Conner) guarding the scene of a murder gives a hint as to why he isn't actually on the case when he says, "Them Chinamen is jabberin' like monkeys. I've had to clear them away every 10 minutes." The same cop later opines, over the body of a dead Asian, "Better dead ones than live ones, if you care what's happenin …." There's also the offensively stereotypical Professor Fu (Chan), who heads up the Department of Orientology (?!?!) at a local museum.

The script provides no reason to actually watch *Wong*. There is, however, the matter of Bela Lugosi's performance. He's fun and surprisingly restrained as the eponymous villain, though one has to wonder what the various characters secretly made of Wong's thick Hungarian accent. And while never convincingly Asian, Lugosi does approach the role with just the right mixture of comic absurdity and unbridled sadism. Too bad he's undermined by the presence of Wallace Ford's relentlessly wisecracking reporter, the agony of which is compounded by a dreary romantic subplot involving him and the newspaper's switchboard operator Peg (played to perfection by the underrated Arline Judge). Not that any of this matters; apart from Lugosi, most people will forget *The Mysterious Mr. Wong* soon after seeing it.

Wong shouldn't be confused with the Monogram mystery series starring Boris Karloff, in which the great horror star portrayed an Asian detective (similar to Earl Derr Bigger's Charlie Chan) who is also named Mr. Wong.

The Mysterious Mr. Wong was shot in October and November of 1934 and released to theaters in January 1935. CW

The Mystery of Edwin Drood
Universal; b/w; 87 min; U.S.

D: Stuart Walker *S:* John L. Balderston, Gladys Unger, Leopold Atlas, Bradley King *P:* Edmund Grainger *C:* George Robinson *M:* Edward Ward, Clifford Vaughan

Cast: Claude Rains, Douglass Montgomery, Heather Angel, David Manners, Valerie Hobson, Francis L. Sullivan, Walter Kingsford, E.E. Clive, Zeffie Tilbury, Ethel Griffies, Forrester Harvey, Veda Buckland, Elsa Buchanan, George Ernest, J.M. Kerrigan, Louise Carter, Harry Cording, D'Arcy Corrigan, Anne O'Neal, Will Geer, Walter Brennan, Anne Darling, Carla Laemmle

Respected choirmaster John Jasper (Rains) is a secret opium addict with an unhealthy obsession for underage Rosa Bud (Angel). Complicating matters further is the fact that Rosa has been betrothed since birth to John's beloved nephew, Edwin Drood (Manners).

Charles Dickens (1812-1870) was in the process of writing *The Mystery of Edwin Drood* when he died of a stroke. The serialized mystery was therefore never officially solved, though there's a fair amount of evidence indicating what the resolution would have been. Still, since we'll never know with absolute certainty what the writer had in mind, *Drood*'s intended denouement will always be to some degree debatable.

The story got its first cinematic treatment in a long-lost 1909 British-made short subject, which was followed in 1914 by a U.S. version. Universal approached the property with an eye toward prestige, having recently released their first Dickens adaptation, *Great Expectations* (1934). Their *Drood* is also clearly

Claude Rains is restrained in Universal's low-key *The Mystery of Edwin Drood*.

intended to compare favorably with the lavish MGM adaptations of *David Copperfield* and *A Tale of Two Cities* (both 1935).

Stuart Walker, who directed *Great Expectations*, does the same here. From a technical point of view, *Drood* compares favorably with Universal's better-known horror productions. It makes wonderful use of some of the same village sets featured in *The Bride of Frankenstein* (1935), at the same time benefitting from sharp attention to period detail. It also manages to produce a shiver or two; the scene in which Drood's body is discovered, rendered a skeleton by quicklime, exemplifies the film's Gothic flair. Universal clearly spared no expense in mounting the production, which makes it even more unfortunate that the story itself is handled in such a predictable manner. The mystery, as presented by Walker and his screenwriters, isn't very mysterious, and while the film undeniably has its pleasures, no real suspense is ever generated.

It does do a fine job in portraying the hypocrisy of its villain, John Jasper. Claude Rains—who ended up here after passing on the part of Dr. Pretorius in *The Bride of Frankenstein*—is terrific in the lead. The audience first sees Jasper in the midst of an opium-induced stupor, from which Walker does a cheeky dissolve to the selfsame junkie leading a church choir. The juxtaposition speaks volumes about the character—to the villagers, Jasper is a beloved, upstanding individual, but beneath this respectable exterior is a wanton, perverted soul. Yet, and even taking into account the role's pedophilic subtext, Rains manages to instill a sense of mournful regret into his portrayal of the character.

The supporting cast includes an excellent Douglass Montgomery (*The Cat and the Canary*, 1939) as Neville Landless, a social outcast who also vies for Rosa's affections but who, thanks to Jasper, comes under suspicion for Drood's disappearance instead. Montgomery's good looks and easy charm make him a credible romantic lead, and he proves a skillful, engaging performer. Heather Angel (*The Premature Burial*, 1962) is equally effective as Rosa, while David Manners (*The Black Cat*, 1934) gives one of his better performances as the doomed Edwin Drood.

The film is also well stocked with familiar character actors, all of whom do well: E.E. Clive (*The Bride of Frankenstein*), Walter Kingsford (*The Invisible Ray*, 1936), Forrester Harvey (*The Invisible Man*, 1933) and Zeffie Tilbury (*Werewolf of London*, 1935). Good performances aside, the film's lack of an intriguing central mystery causes it to sag.

The Mystery of Edwin Drood was next adapted for television in 1960 as a mini-series, then in the mid-1980s as a musical. TH

The Mystery of the Ghastly Face
aka **El misterio del rostro pálido**; **The Mystery of the Pallid Face**; **The Mystery of the Pale Face**
Alcayde; b/w; length unknown; Mexico

D/S: Juan Bustillo Oro *Co-P:* José Alcalde, Alberto Monroy *C:* Agustin Jiménez *M:* Federico Ruiz

Cast: Beatriz Ramos, Carlos Villarías, René Cardona, Joaquín Busquets, Natalia Ortiz, Manuel Noriega, Miguel Arenas, Abraham Galán, José Cortéz

A horror/sci-fi hybrid, *The Mystery of the Ghastly Face* concerns one Dr. Forti (Villarías) and his assistant/son Pablo (Busquets) who, while pursuing their bizarre experiments, disappear in the jungles of South America. Years later, Pablo's former lover Angelica (Ramos), the niece of his father's housekeeper, is engaged to Luis (Cardona). Dr. Forti reappears and tells everyone that Pablo is dead, and Angelica and her aunt move in with him. Strange occurrences ensue, marked by appearances of a mysterious apparition with a pale face. It turns out that the spirit is actually the flesh-and-blood Pablo, who contracted leprosy while in the jungle. Dr. Forti tries to force Angelica to marry his leprous son, but then winds up being killed. Pablo likewise exits the story, committing suicide by jumping off a cliff, thus leaving Angelica free to marry Luis after all.

Born in 1875, Joaquín Busquets is a bit too old for the part of Pablo. (His father was played by Carlos Villarías, who was almost 20 years his junior.) Interestingly, Busquets went blind during the filming of *The Mystery of the Ghastly Face*, though he continued to act sporadically until his death in 1942 at the age of 66. Villarías is better known for playing the title in Universal's Spanish version of *Dracula* (1931).

Director Juan Bustillo Oro was no stranger to horror, having previously written *The Phantom of the Convent* and co-written and directed *Two Monks* (both 1934). Nor would *Ghastly Face* be his last effort in the genre; he went on to make *Every Madman to His Specialty* (1939) and *The Man Without a Face* (1950). Actor René Cardona was also a director who sometimes specialized in the macabre, serving up a scad of wrestler-meets-monster excursions in the 1960s and '70s.

The Mystery of the Ghastly Face was released in Mexico in October 1935 and in the United States in January 1937. CW

Night Life of the Gods
Universal; b/w; 73 min; U.S.

D: Lowell Sherman *S:* Barry Trivers *P:* Carl Laemmle, Jr. *C:* John J. Mescall *M:* Arthur Morton

Cast: Alan Mowbray, Florine McKinney, Peggy Shannon, Richard Carle, Theresa Maxwell Conover, Phillips Smalley, Wesley Barry, Gilbert Emery, Ferdinand Gottschalk, Douglas Fowley, William "Stage" Boyd, Henry Armetta, Arlene Carroll, Ray "Crash" Corrigan, George Hassell

Eccentric inventor Henry Hawk (Mowbray) invents a device that turns stone into flesh. His joy at his discovery is enhanced when Meg, a beautiful, scantily clad and adult-sized leprechaun, visits him. The two go to New York City, where Hawk uses his invention to bring statues of the Greek Gods to life.

Night Life of the Gods is adapted from the novel of the same name by James Thorne Smith. First published in 1931, it offers the same whimsical blend of humor and fantasy as his better-known *Topper* (1926). The film version is linked with the horror genre largely because of its timing; it is considered one of the initial batch of Golden Age horror films and fantasies produced by Universal between 1931 and 1936. Though thought lost by some, poor-quality bootlegs do occasionally surface.

Viewers encountering it for the first time are almost invariably disappointed. Unlike James Whale's *The Old Dark House* (1932)—another quirky Universal chiller long considered lost—it doesn't benefit from time and reflection. The story's unusual content and its blend of humor and the (vaguely) macabre required a more sensitive director than it got: one Lowell Sherman, an actor-turned-director whose career was cut short by his death from pneumonia in 1934. Released posthumously, *Night Life* was his final completed work. (As a point of trivia, Sherman was present during the Labor Day party thrown by Roscoe "Fatty" Arbuckle in 1921 that resulted in the comedian's prosecution for the rape and subsequent death of actress Virginia Rappe.)

The cast of *Night Life* includes London-born Alan Mowbray. Mowbray had established himself as a successful actor in London's West End theater district before conquering Broadway. He made his cinematic debut in 1931 and remained active in film and television until his death in 1969. *Night Life* marks one of his very few leading assignments, and given its lack of success with the public, it probably didn't improve his stock any. One of his juiciest roles is in the Basil Rathbone/Nigel Bruce Sherlock Holmes adventure *Terror by Night* (1946), in which he plays the reprehensible Colonel Sebastian Moran. TH

Obeah!
aka **Obeah**
Arcturus; b/w; 75 min; U.S.
   D/S: F. Herrick Herrick *C:* Harry W. Smith
   Cast: Jean Brooks, Phillips Lord, Alice Wessler

When an American explorer goes missing in the South Seas, a crew is sent out to find and rescue him. He is located on a small island where he's being held under a powerful voodoo spell known as obeah. The team gets him away from the natives, but the voodoo spell continues to dog them as they attempt to make it back to civilization.

This jungle melodrama was the sole directorial work of actor F. Herrick Herrick. Wisconsin-born Herrick worked more often as a character actor, albeit in a generally unbilled capacity. He appears to have been active from the mid-1930s until the early 1950s, but the spotty nature of his filmography suggests that much of his work has gone unnoticed and/or unverified. It was Herrick who devised the scenario for this melodrama, which is of note for its relatively early exploration of voodoo.

The cast includes Jean Brooks in her film debut. Blonde-haired Brooks went on to appear in many a B-film, but it wasn't until she donned a black wig to portray the haunted Jacqueline Gibson in Val Lewton's classic *The Seventh Victim* (1943) that she gained cinematic immortality.

Obeah! is believed to be lost. TH

One Frightened Night
Mascot; b/w; 66 min; U.S.
   D: Christy Cabanne *S:* Wellyn Totman *P:* Nat Levine, George Yohalem *C:* Ernest Miller, William Nobles *M:* Charles Dunworth, Francis Gromon, Josiah Zuro, Rex Bassett, Milan Roder, Oscar Potoker, Rudolf Friml, Constantin Bakaleinikoff *FX:* John T. Coyle, Howard Lydecker
   Cast: Charley Grapewin, Mary Carlisle, Arthur Hohl, Wallace Ford, Lucian Littlefield, Regis Toomey, Hedda Hopper, Clarence Wilson, Evalyn Knapp, Rafaela Ottiano, Fred Kelsey, Adrian Morris

A wonderful "old dark house" thriller with a terrific opening credit sequence, *One Frightened Night* is far superior to most similar films of the same period, including those produced by

Universal (such as *Secret of the Blue Room*, 1933, *The Great Impersonation*, 1935 and *The Black Doll*, 1938). Based on a story by Stuart Palmer, author of the Hildegarde Withers novels (which were themselves the basis for a successful series of RKO films), *One Frightened Night* has grumpy old Jasper Whyte (Grapewin) gathering his relatives in his mansion on a stormy night for a premature reading of his will, which stipulates that if his estranged granddaughter Doris Waverly ever turns up, she will inherit everything. It so happens that she drops by that very night, but there's one big problem: There are two of her, or at least two different women claiming to be her. The first—and fake—Doris (Knapp) is murdered with cyanide, making the real granddaughter (Carlisle) the killer's obvious next target.

There are thrills and chills galore—including mummified bodies, sliding panels, secret corridors and a shrunken-head-festooned study where the killer tries twice to kill the real Doris Waverly, once with a blowgun, once while wearing a grotesque monster mask. Cinematographers Ernest Miller (*The House of a Thousand Candles*, 1936) and William Nobles (*Sucker Money*, 1933) achieve some startling images on a zero budget, with the miniatures coming across as both charming and effective (though a utility pole that gets taken out by a falling tree early in the picture later mysteriously reappears intact). Christy Cabanne's (*The Westland Case*, 1937) direction is spot-on, reveling in the atmospherics of storm and shadows, and Wellyn Totman's (*Mystery Liner*, 1934) script creates real frisson while dishing out some genuinely witty one-liners for the expert cast.

Headlining that cast is Charley Grapewin (*Return of the Terror*, 1934) as Jasper Whyte, whose persona as a bitter old man turns out to be a front for a genuinely loving human being. Mary Carlisle (*Dead Men Walk*, 1943) and Regis Toomey (*The Phantom Creeps*, 1939) are believable leads, while gossip columnist Hedda Hopper (*Dracula's Daughter*, 1936) acquits herself nicely in a bigger-than-usual part as one of the greedy relatives. Wallace Ford (*The Mysterious Mr. Wong*, 1934) gets to be the brunt of everyone's jokes, a function the actor often had and here in particular seems to relish. Rounding out the troupe is Lucien Littlefield (*One Body Too Many*, 1944) as the villain, Rafaela Ottiano (*Seven Keys to Baldpate*, 1917) as the sinister maid Elvira and Arthur Hohl (*Island of Lost Souls*, 1932) as a conniving relative.

Nat Levine produced for Mascot Pictures, but he was better known for their many serials, including *The Whispering Shadow* (1933) and *Mystery Mountain* (1934). CW

Ouanga
aka **Drums in the Jungle**; **Drums in the Night**; **Love Wanga**
Terwilliger; b/w; 56 min; U.S.

D/P/S: George Terwilliger *C:* Carl Berger

Cast: Fredi Washington, Philip Brandon, Marie Paxton, Sheldon Leonard, Winifred Harris, Babe Joyce, George Spink

Clelie Gordon (Washington) is in love with Adam Maynard (Brandon), who has his own sights set on Eve Langley (Paxton). When Clelie turns to voodoo in an attempt to get Eve out of the way, Clelie's foreman Le Strange (Leonard)—whose love for his employer has itself been rebuffed—attempts to save Eve.

This independent production was shot in the West Indies with a mostly local cast. George Terwilliger goes for a triple threat here, simultaneously wearing writer, producer and director hats. And in this case the word "threat" proves especially apt, as the action unfolds slowly and his ineptitude menaces the viewer. Despite potentially interesting location shooting and an alluringly exotic theme, the film is so horribly written, photographed and directed that it seems to last an eternity even as it clocks in at under an hour.

The acting stinks, too. The cast is mostly (and justly) unknown; the only familiar face is Sheldon Leonard, known for his tough-guy routine in such 1960s television favorites as *The Dick Van Dyke Show* and *The Andy Griffith Show* (he also logged production credits on those programs, among others).

Along with *White Zombie* (1932), another independent, low-budget horror item, *Ouanga* is one of the first films to present that horror staple, the zombie; unlike *White Zombie*, though, there isn't a bit of frisson to be found here. The film is hands down among the worst horror movies of the decade; there's not a single thing to recommend it. TH

The Phantom Light
Gainsborough; b/w; 72 min; Great Britain

D: Michael Powell *S:* Ralph Smart, Joseph Jefferson Farjeon, Austin Melford *P:* Jerome Jackson *C:* Roy Kellino *M:* Louis Levy, Charles Williams

Cast: Gordon Harker, Binnie Hale, Ian Hunter, Donald Calthrop, Herbert Lomas, Milton Rosmer, Reginald Tate, Barry O'Neill, Mickey Brantford, Alice O'Day, Fewlass Llewellyn, Edgar K. Bruce, Louie Emery

Sam Higgins (Harker) runs the lighthouse outside a small Welsh village. Unwelcome guests arrive—Alice Bright (Hale) and Jim Pearce (Hunter), and his staff, led by Claff Owen (Lomas)— and Higgins regales the three of them him with tales of the place's eerie history. It's said that the previous lighthouse keepers were all driven to insanity and death by the ghosts who dwell there, and that the lighthouse has often led ships to destruction on the rocky shores.

Long before establishing himself—often in collaboration with Emeric Pressburger—as one of the most distinctive and imaginative directors in British cinema, Michael Powell (1905-1990) cut his teeth on low-budget programmers. He entered the film industry after working for the National Provincial Bank; the doldrums of such a down-to-earth profession drove the young man to despair, and he knew he needed to pursue his dream of working in the arts to find happiness. He began under the auspices of silent film pioneer Rex Ingram, whom he assisted on several projects, including *The Magician* (1925). Powell's first taste of directing came in 1930 when he stepped in to complete *Caste*, one of many films on which he contributed to the screenplay. His full-fledged debut came the following year with *Two Crowded Hours*, a film now believed lost. Throughout the 1930s, he did a number of quota quickies, low-budget second features created to fulfill quota agreements between the United States and Great Britain. *The Phantom Light* was one of these, adapted from *The Haunted Light* by Joan Roy Byford and Evadne Price.

The Phantom Light's screenplay, by Joseph Jefferson Farjeon, Austin Melford and Ralph Smart, is unremarkable, as was its source material, but Powell's direction makes it more interesting than it deserves to be. The early scenes in the Welsh village display the director's gift for establishing a sense of locale, and when the action shifts to the lighthouse, his use of framing and lighting milks the situation for all the suspense it's worth.

It soon becomes apparent, however, that something most non-supernatural is at work, and the film races toward a dud of a finale. Still, hints exist throughout of the flair that would become evident in Powell's later work. Little doubt remains that the director would have done well by a straightforward supernatural horror thriller, but his efforts here are ultimately frustrated by the machinations of a lukewarm screenplay.

After establishing himself as a major talent, Powell revisited the suspense/horror genre years later with *Peeping Tom* (1960). Though that film's provocative content effectively destroyed his career, it has in the ensuing years become recognized as a masterpiece. The same cannot be said of *The Phantom Light*, despite his best efforts and the enjoyable ensemble work of Gordon Harker, Binnie Hale, Ian Hunter and Herbert Lomas. TH

Phantom Ship
aka **The Mystery of the Marie Celeste**; **The Mystery of the Mary Celeste**; **The Phantom Ship**
Hammer; b/w; 62 (80) min; Great Britain

D/Co-S: Denison Clift *Co-S:* Charles Larkworthy *P:* Henry Passmore *C:* Eric Cross, Geoffrey Faithful *M:* Eric Ansell

Cast: Bela Lugosi, Shirley Grey, Arthur Margetson, Edmund Willard, Dennis Hoey, George Mozart, Johnnie Schofield, Gunner Moir, Ben Welden, Clifford McLaglen, Bruce Gordon, Gibson Gowland, Terence de Marney, Edgar Pierce, Herbert Cameron, Wilfred Essex, James Carew, Monti DeLyle, Alec Fraser

Hammer Productions was founded in 1934 by comedian William Hinds (whose stage name was Will Hammer). Around the same time, Hinds and fellow entrepreneur Enrique Carreras formed Exclusive Films to distribute movies made by Hammer and others. Hammer's first production was the comedy spoof *The Public Life of Henry the Ninth* (1935), designed to exploit the success of London Film Studio's *The Private Life of Henry VIII* (1933). MGM picked up *Public Life* for North American release, and Hammer quickly slapped together its first horror film, *The Mystery of the Marie Celeste* (U.S. title: *Phantom Ship*), stacking its deck by importing popular Hollywood star Bela Lugosi (*Dracula*, 1931). But when the film (and the next few that followed it) didn't mine the hoped-for box-office gold, the company went into a decade-long hiatus. Its reactivation in the late 1940s was inconspicuous, consisting at first of low-budget mysteries and crime films. Then, after an adaptation of the BBC sci-fi serial *The Quatermass Xperiment* (1955) pointed the studio in a new, more successful direction, production began on *The Curse of Frankenstein* (1957). *Curse* was Hammer's first major international hit, and thus was Hammer horror truly born.

In 1935, however, the studio's interest in the fright-film market was still tentative, with its legendary successes in the genre still a couple of decades off. Not surprisingly, *Phantom Ship* is mostly unremarkable on an artistic level. It's nominally based on the true story of the Mary Celeste, a derelict American vessel found drifting toward the Strait of Gibraltar on December 4, 1872. Its crew had vanished, though their personal belongings were found intact and the ship's cargo untouched. While mutiny

In this lobby card from *Phantom Ship*, Bela Lugosi is about to strike once again.

and piracy were both ruled out, the mystery was never solved. (Some have attributed the events that led to the ship's desertion to the Bermuda Triangle, a northern swath of the Atlantic Ocean wherein a number of ships and planes are said to have vanished under mysterious circumstances.)

Almost from the moment of the crewless ship's discovery, a mass of retro-revisionist history took shape around it. It was quickly deemed cursed, with alleged evidence "proving" that curse published *ad nauseum*. The first captain died of pneumonia aboard her, with two other captains dismissed from her for various disreputable reasons. One owner sold it after his father died aboard her; another attempted to sink her in 1885 in an insurance fraud scheme and, failing that, set her afire. Though never prosecuted for his crime (he died before authorities could do so), the presumably burned-up ship was left to sink on some reef.

There was at least one major international investigation of the world's most famous ghost ship, and in 1884 *Cornhill Magazine* published a document supposedly written by a sole survivor. Many who read the purported eyewitness account, titled *J. Habakuk Jephson's Statement*, took it for the truth, though in reality it was a short story (one admittedly heavily grounded in truth, but fictional nonetheless) by Arthur Conan Doyle. Such was its impact that, even today, his erroneous spelling of the ship's name, *Marie Celeste*, is often taken as correct.

Phantom Ship director Denison Clift (1885-1961) was an American émigré who had begun his career as a writer for Fox. He went to Britain in the early 1920s, hoping to bring some of his Hollywood panache to the British film industry. He had a love of the sea, and many of the films he wrote and/or directed were based on maritime life and incidents. These films included *The Hell Ship* (1920), *The Yankee Clipper* (1927) and *High Seas* (1929), among others. Understandably interested, then, in the true story of the Mary Celeste, he concocted this highly fictionalized account of her crew's disappearance. He even retained some of the actual crewmembers' names, though the personas themselves were radically altered (if not created from scratch). For instance, Volkert Lorenson and Gottlieb Gondeschall are

combined into Anton Lorenzen, who boards the ship under the name Gottlieb. The names of the Captain and his wife, Benjamin and Sarah Briggs, are likewise retained, though their real-life two-year-old daughter is dropped from the story and the events of their lives heavily rewritten.

The film's initial dramatic thrust comes from the friction between Captain Briggs (Margetson) and a friend, both of whom love the same woman, Sarah (Grey). Sarah chooses the captain, and after the two marry, he brings his bride along on his next voyage. Over the days that follow, he mistreats his crew, all the while pretending to be some higher moral authority (the film seems to expect the audience to see Briggs and his wife as heroic). His attitude and actions stoke a growing sense of paranoia among the crew just as members start mysteriously dying or disappearing. It's finally revealed that someone is killing the sailors off one-by-one and dumping most of them overboard. In the end only Lorenzen (Lugosi), who had been shanghaied to serve aboard the Mary Celeste years before, remains, and he throws himself overboard.

As conceived by screenwriter Charles Larkworthy and played by Arthur Margetson, Captain Briggs is indeed decidedly unlikeable; he protests shanghaiing (the practice of kidnapping or intimidating people to join a ship's crew, usually to perform hard labor tasks), yet sits idly by as people in and about the bars of New York's wharfs are intimidated into joining his ranks. Margetson's performance is, here as elsewhere, fairly one-note; he made few films in his career, with only *Phantom*, *Juggernaut* (1936) and his final film, *Sherlock Holmes Faces Death* (1943), of interest to horror fans.

Shirley Grey gives a slightly better performance as Sarah Briggs, though she's nothing to write home about, either. She was something of a scream queen in the 1930s; her other horror credits include *Get That Girl* (1932), *Murder on the Campus* (1933), *Green Eyes* (1934) and *Circumstantial Evidence* (1935). Interestingly, her film career ended in 1935, and the following year she married co-star Margetson. They later divorced, and Grey died in 1981 in Jacksonville, Florida. Grey's appearance in *Phantom Ship* seems to have been dictated by her appearance in a very similar film from 1933, *Terror Aboard*, which likewise dealt with the discovery of a derelict ship, followed by a flashback detailing how its crew was murdered.

With such weak lead performances, it's easy to see how someone of Bela Lugosi's stature could steal the show, which he easily does. And while there are indeed moments in which he horribly overacts, there are others in which he achieves an effective and pitiable sympathy. (His description of the horrors of being shanghaied, tears glimmering in his eyes, is surprisingly effective.) Though his mannerisms are frequently overwrought in the manner of silent film work, and though he tends to stress the wrong words while enunciating, his quieter moments betray some of the best acting of his career. Thus it seems strange that the film is pretty much forgotten today, with only diehard fans of Lugosi or Hammer taking much note, usually doing so with a dismissive tone

The only other performance worth mentioning is that of future Universal character actor Dennis Hoey. Hoey was better known as Inspector Lestrade in the Basil Rathbone/Nigel Bruce series of Sherlock Holmes films. He has a minor role here as one of the ship's crew.

Approximately 18 minutes of footage, mostly from the beginning and the end of the film, was cut for American release. This footage, which featured a courtroom inquiry into the case, is today considered lost. The film's top-deck and external footage was shot aboard the Mary B. Mitchell, which had been used by Great Britain during World War I as a U-Boat decoy. CW

The Raven
Universal; b/w; 61 min; U.S.
 D: Louis Friedlander (Lew Landers) S: David Boehm P: David Diamond, Stanley Bergerman C: Charles J. Stumar M: Clifford Vaughan FX: John P. Fulton
 Cast: Bela Lugosi, Boris Karloff, Lester Matthews, Irene Ware, Samuel S. Hinds, Ian Wolfe, Inez Courtney, Spencer Charters, Maidel Turner
 Dr. Vollin (Lugosi) is called upon to perform a delicate operation to save the life of ballet dancer Jean (Ware). The operation is a success, but Vollin falls in love with her. A little unhinged to begin with, his inability to capture her heart sends him over the edge. And when Jean's father, Judge Thatcher (Hinds), warns him away from her, Vollin turns to Edgar Allan Poe's macabre stories for a devious idea. The perfect opportunity for revenge

presents itself when escaped convict Edmond Bateman (Karloff) shows up on his doorstep, demanding surgery to change his appearance. Vollin disfigures Bateman and promises to repair the damage only if the felon participates in his sadistic plan for revenge against Judge Thatcher.

Following the success of the sublime *The Black Cat* (1934), Universal quickly set about looking for the next vehicle in which to pair their chief bogeymen, Boris Karloff and Bela Lugosi. The studio toyed with the notion of casting the two in James Whale's *The Bride of Frankenstein* (1935), but the director ultimately insisted on Ernest Thesiger rather than Lugosi in the role of Dr. Pretorious. The studio then decided to revisit the works of Edgar Allan Poe for inspiration. The strategy made sense; *The Black Cat* had been a big hit at the box-office, and a repeat of the Karloff, Lugosi and Poe combination seemed sure-fire.

Little did the studio anticipate the alarm that its follow-up project would generate, a wave of consternation that would effectively end the horror boom of the 1930s. *Raven*'s emphasis on torture, along with its none-too-subtle implication that Vollin derives sexual gratification from it, made the film a lightning rod for controversy in 1935. The British censor was particularly appalled, and *The Raven* helped spark the United Kingdom's ban on horror movies the following year. Universal would release only a couple more fright films that year (slashing the budget for at least one of them, *Dracula's Daughter*, and cutting Lugosi from the line-up), then cease production on them altogether until *Son of Frankenstein* (which also starred Karloff and Lugosi) in 1939.

Would that all the fuss had been over a better film! It's mildly possible, one supposes, that David Boehm's screenplay was conceived as a send-up, but the leaden direction seems geared toward shock value. Whereas *The Black Cat* captures the perverse spirit of Poe's writing, due largely to the gifted direction of Edgar G. Ulmer, *The Raven* feels like a hastily conceived knock-off. It's easily among the shoddiest of the horror films the studio cranked out during the first half of the thirties. Even the credits are sloppy, with actors Ian Wolfe and Spencer Charters listed with each other's roles.

With James Whale swearing off horror following *Bride* (and Ulmer out the door for dallying with the wife of one of studio head Carl Laemmle's relations), the studio turned to a far less capable director. Louis Friedlander had been working in film since the silent era—*The Man Who Laughs* (1928) credits him as a production associate—making his directorial debut in 1934; *The Raven* was his sixth film as a director, and probably the most famous of the 150-plus titles he worked on before his death in 1962. Under the name Lew Landers he later re-teamed with Lugosi for the not-uninteresting Columbia horror item, *Return of the Vampire* (1943).

Whereas *The Black Cat* offered Karloff and Lugosi equal screen time, *The Raven* belongs to Lugosi, a fact not reflected in the credits. He's second-billed the three times his name appears on the screen, though he does get the "surname only" treatment in an opening credit just before the film's title—as Universal had been doing, does here and continued doing with Karloff. The opening and closing cast lists dispel any doubt as to whom the studio regarded as top dog, however; Karloff is first-billed by his last name only, in the largest font, while Lugosi and the rest of the cast get the complete-name, smaller-font treatment.

Disparate treatment aside, though, Lugosi seems to have relished the opportunity to upstage his perceived rival. This is, in fact, the performance that Lugosi fans and critics argue over the most; dyed-in-the-wool Lugosiphiles regard it as his finest hour, whereas less sympathetic critics deride it as pure ham. There's little doubt that Lugosi's eager overacting is the key to the film's entertainment value, but ham is ham—and Lugosi serves up a banquet-sized helping. The actor makes no attempt to shade his character; instead he makes Vollin overtly intimidating right from the get-go. This gives his performance nowhere to go but

Bela Lugosi stars as Dr. Vollin, a mad doctor with a fixation on sadism, the works of Edgar Allan Poe and beautiful young women, in *The Raven*.

down a path of escalating melodramatics; by the last reel, he's flailing his arms and laughing maniacally. It's a classic instance of a capable actor getting carried away.

Karloff—despite, as mentioned above, being top-billed—is relegated here to a comparatively minor role, not so much a character as a plot device. He's there simply to help Lugosi in his quest for vengeance, and while he tries hard to give the character some nuance, it's all for naught. Once Bateman is disfigured, his job is pretty much just to lurk on the sidelines, scaring the dull supporting cast by glancing in their direction now and then. He's also ill served by unusually shoddy make-up from Universal's resident whiz Jack P. Pierce. Pierce had created memorable and groundbreaking designs for Karloff in *Frankenstein* (1931) and *The Mummy* (1932), but his attempt here at a partially paralyzed and wizened face are badly exposed by some overly familiar camera angles.

Both Karloff and Lugosi do manage to wring life out of some amusing lines of dialogue, notably in this famous exchange between Vollin and Bateman:

> Vollin: So you put the burning torch into his face. Into his eyes!
> Bateman: Well, sometimes you can't help things like that.

Ultimately, however, it all comes off as a bit strained and desperate. Add to this mix the presence of quite possibly the least sympathetic damsel-in-distress in Universal history (as played by Irene Ware, Jean is an addle-brained flirt who encourages Vollin's advances) and some grating comedy relief courtesy of Charters, Wolfe and Inez Courtney, and *The Raven* emerges as one of the least accomplished entries in Universal's golden period of horror films. TH

The Rawhide Terror
Security; b/w; 47 (52) min; U.S.

    Co-D: Bruce Mitchell *Co-D/Co-S:* Jack Nelson *Co-S/P:* Victor Adamson *C:* A.J. Fitzpatric, Bert Longnecker

    Cast: Art Mix, Edmund Cobb, Bill Desmond, William Barrymore, Frances Morris, George Holt, Bill Patton, Herman Hack, Tommy Bupp, Fred Parker

In the late 1890s, a group of white men posing as Native Americans (who, due largely to their cowboy outfits, look remarkably Caucasian despite their long, braided black wigs) robbed a family of settlers traveling west. The attack left the father and mother dead and the older of two sons unhinged and hiding in the mountains. Now, years later, those very same killers have taken over the town of Red Dog, and their rise to power has attracted a mysterious avenger known as the Rawhide Terror (his nickname derives from two facts: 1, part of his face is obscured by a piece of rawhide and 2, he leaves strips of the same material on his victims' bodies). The youngest son of the murdered settlers, now grown and the sheriff of Red Dog, is woefully inadequate to the task of taking down the Rawhide Ter-

DVD cover art for *The Rawhide Terror*

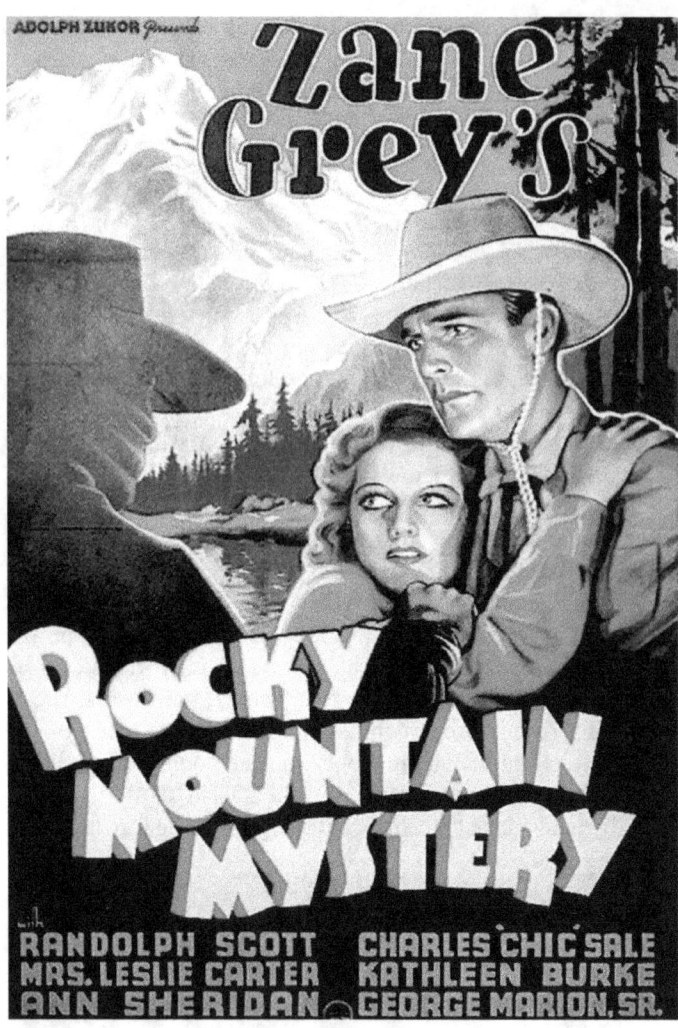

ror. When ranchowner Tom Blake is kidnapped by the maniacal killer, a young cowhand named Al (Mix, no relation to silent Western star Tom Mix) tracks him down. Al goes head-to-head with Rawhide and winds up tied to a runaway wagon headed toward a cliff. But even though he manages to escape his fetters and jump free, he vanishes from the second half of the movie, leaving the sheriff to save the day and get the girl. Oh, and as it turns out, the killer is—can you believe it—the sheriff's long-gone, crazy older brother, avenging the murder of their parents.

Cited by some film historians as the first horror Western, *The Rawhide Terror* is anything but. Cheap to make and attractive to multiple markets, weird Westerns with heavy horror content date from the early 1920s, though they did rise in popularity after the release and success of *Dracula* and *Frankenstein* in 1931. *The Rawhide Terror*, with its hyena-like serial killer and unabashed blood and violence is, however, one of the most blatantly gruesome and best known.

Though the film was produced in 1934, the lack of music on its soundtrack and its occasional use of intertitles make it seem much older. It was originally conceived as a serial, but when financing fell through it was recast as a much shorter, second-feature oater. Largely as a result of this mid-stream change, the film has numerous continuity issues, most notably a surreal confusion in character names, with more than one person starting out with one moniker and finishing with another.

Some historians cite this film as an early work from future grindhouse director Al Adamson (1929-1995), a claim where we would have to assume that he entered filmmaking at the age of five or six. In truth, Adamson's father Victor did the screenwriting and directing chores under the pseudonym Denver Dixon. Dixon was a prolific actor as well. Born in Missouri, he starred in approximately 200 films between 1910 and 1970, several of which he wrote, produced and/or directed. He died of a heart attack in 1972 in Los Angeles, California, leaving behind a body of work not dissimilar to that of Edward D. Wood, Jr., though not nearly as famous as the work of his son would become. CW

Rocky Mountain Mystery
aka **The Fighting Westerner**; **The Vanishing Pioneer**; **Zane Grey's The Fighting Westerner**; **The Rocky Mountain Mystery**
Paramount; b/w; 64 min; U.S.
   D: Charles Barton *S:* Edward E. Paramore, Jr., Ethel Doherty *P:* Harold Hurley *C:* Archie Stout *M:* Rudolph G. Kopp
   Cast: Randolph Scott, Charles Sale, Kathleen Burke, Ann Sheridan, George F. Marion, James Eagles, Mrs. Leslie Carter, Howard Wilson, Willie Fung, Florence Roberts

Pearl Zane Grey was born in Zanesville, Ohio in 1872, the son of a dentist and his wife. Though he followed in his father's footsteps and became a dentist himself, he also had a lifelong interest in writing. With his wife serving as his editor, he wrote short stories and novels set mostly in the Old West and populated by rugged heroes, swooning ladies, misunderstood Native Americans and rascally villains. It was an unrealistically romantic view of America's then recent past, yet it resonated with readers and propelled Grey's books to bestseller status again and again.

It's not at all strange that one of those standard Western adventures was given multiple film adaptations (many of Grey's books had been adapted to the big screen, some repeatedly). What is peculiar is to see a Western reworked as a horror film of the "old dark house" variety, with the clichéd setting changed to a log cabin and its nearby mill.

Paramount's *Rocky Mountain Mystery* is the third version of Grey's story *Golden Dreams*, written in short story form and

Rocky Mountain Mystery **was the only horror/Western hybrid to star Western icon Randolph Scott (right).**

adapted to the screen in 1922. A novelization of that film was in turn adapted by Paramount as *The Vanishing Pioneer*, starring Jack Holt and William Powell. Neither of these two versions bore much resemblance to each other, though *Rocky Mountain Mystery*, the third filmed version, at least bears a passing resemblance to the second film and retains some of the same character names. But lest the confusion be incomplete, this third version was shot (and later re-released) under the working title *The Vanishing Pioneer* and is today also widely known as *The Fighting Westerner*.

By whatever title, *Rocky Mountain Mystery* presents Randolph Scott as Larry Sutton, who comes to the Ballard radium mine to investigate the disappearance of his brother-in-law, Jack Parsons. There he meets Tex Murdock (Sale), who believes that Parsons murdered Ballard ranch hand Adolph Borg. Sutton poses as the Borg family's mining engineer in the hopes of solving Adolph Borg's murder and discovering what happened to Parsons. After a couple of very gruesome murders, a mysterious killer in black threatens Sutton. In the end, he solves the mystery while learning a dark secret about the Ballard family patriarch (Marion).

Neither director Charles Barton nor lead actor Randolph Scott was a stranger to the fiction of Zane Grey. Barton's directorial debut *Wagon Wheels* (1934) had been based on a Grey novel while Randolph Scott had already starred in at least eight film adaptations (including the aforementioned *Wagon Wheels*) of Grey's work, most of them for director Henry Hathaway.

Just before doing *Wagon Wheels*, Barton had won an Academy Award for Best Assistant Director. *Rocky Mountain Mystery* was only his third film, and he had not at this point gotten the knack of directing action; sequences that should be rousing come off instead as stiff and amateurish. From the 1940s on Barton worked mostly in comedy, producing and directing some of the best of the Bud Abbott and Lou Costello movies, including *Abbott and Costello Meet Frankenstein* (1948). In 1952 he made the leap into television, directing numerous episodes of various half-hour comedies and adventures. He retired in 1971 and died of a heart attack a decade later.

Scott had starred in several horror films before *Rocky Mountain Mystery*, including *Murders in the Zoo* and *Supernatural* (both 1933). He remained a leading actor in Hollywood Westerns throughout his career, which concluded in 1962 with Sam Peckinpah's *Ride the High Country*.

Mystery co-star Kathleen Burke was also a graduate of Paramount's school of horror, having made her debut in Erle C. Kenton's classic *Island of Lost Souls* (1932) as Lota the Panther Woman and following up with a terrific performance in *Murders in the Zoo* (opposite the slimy Lionel Atwill). Her exotic good looks and acting skills were not enough to keep her in the type of roles she craved, however, and at the age of 25 she retired from acting for good. Her performance in *Rocky Mountain Mystery* appears to be vintage Burke, with the woefully short amount of screen time she's given failing to do her justice. One's mind reels at the thought of her in the parts given to the much-less-talented Valerie Hobson in *The Bride of Frankenstein* and *The Mystery of Edwin Drood* (both 1935).

Rounding out the roster of supporting players were Vaudevillian Charles "Chic" Sales as the loveable Texan rube Murdock, noted Broadway performer Mrs. Leslie Anderson as the housekeeper Mrs. Adolph Borg and soon-to-be-leading-lady Ann Sheridan as Rita Ballard.

Though its horror productions were frequently polished and surprisingly scary, Paramount pretty much dropped out of the horror business after the release of *Rocky Mountain Mystery*, just as parental watchdog groups and overseas censors were turning up the heat on fright films. The forces of propriety succeeded for a time, and when Universal resurrected horror in a big way with *Son of Frankenstein* in 1939, Paramount—and Randolph Scott—were busy focusing their efforts on less controversial genres. CW

Secrets of Chinatown
aka The Black Robe

Commonwealth; b/w; 53 min; Canada
 D: Fred C. Newmeyer S: Guy Morton P: Kenneth J. Bishop C: William Beckway
 Cast: Nick Stuart, Lucile Browne, Raymond Lawrence, James Flavin, Harry Hewitson, James McGrath, Reginald Hincks, John Barnard, Arthur Legge-Willis

Secrets of Chinatown is a rarity among 1930s horror films in that it was shot in Canada rather than the United States or the United Kingdom. Scripted by Guy Morton from his novel *The Black Robe*, it presents Raymond Lawrence as Donegal Dawn, a private detective investigating a crime wave among Vancouver's Asian population. Dawn doesn't buy the common assumption that a Tong (Chinese gang) is responsible for the killings and other crimes, and, being a favorite of the police commissioner, he has the entire police department at his disposal while he sorts the situation out. His friend Robert Rand (Stuart) has fallen for a beautiful young blonde named Zenobia (Browne), who works in a curio shop owned by the sinister Chan Tow Ling (Hewitson). Rand wants to rescue the fearful girl from an unseen specter who's been oppressing her, but Dawn warns him against it, believing that any such attempt would not only fail but also imperil Robert's life to boot. It turns out that Zenobia is the high priestess of a devil-worshipping cult known as The Black Robe (though, to be fair, she appears to be entranced when performing her satanic duties). The headstrong Rand breaks into the cult's basement ceremony and is captured. Dawn, disguised as a satanist, breaks up the proceedings, but not before cult members whisk off Robert and Zenobia. Dawn manages to take one of the cultists into custody, only to learn that the man has been under the spell of the cult and can remember nothing. The private detective then tracks Rand, Zenobia and the remaining cult members to an island off the coast of Vancouver. There he rescues the pair and brings the group's leader to justice.

Though *Chinatown*'s direction is far from successful, Fred Newmeyer at least aims for originality. Scenes of violence are presented abstractly, with the action playing out in extreme closeups (of legs struggling and the like) or in silhouette. Newmeyer doesn't shy away from the creepier aspects of the story, with much of the film centered on the satanists' basement lair or on the mysterious ceremonies of the satanic cult.

Unfortunately, it's all presented through a typical-for-the-time racist lens. People of Chinese descent are to a person sinister, secretive and occultist. Newmeyer also displays a breath-

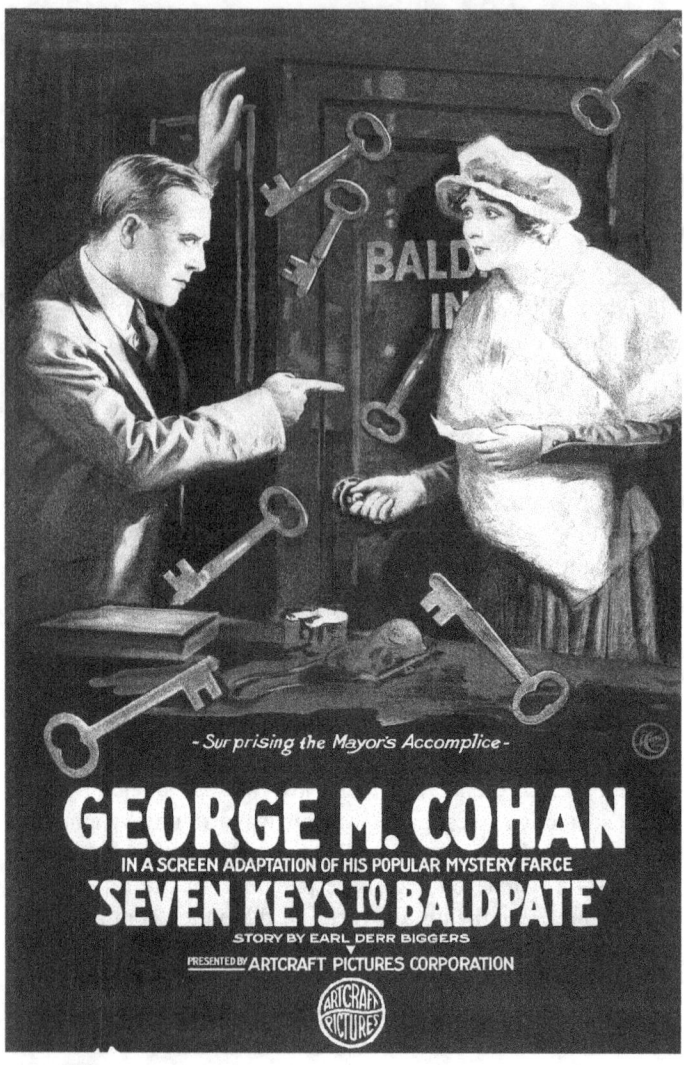

taking ignorance of the particulars of Buddhist, Hindu and even Christian belief systems. To his credit, though, the finale, set in the caves of the cult's island hideout, is fairly satisfying, and the acting he coaxes from his performers is far from the worst of its kind. CW

Seven Keys to Baldpate
RKO; b/w; 80 min; U.S.

D: William Hamilton, Edward Killy *S:* Anthony Veiller, Wallace Smith, Glenn Tryon, Dorothy Yost *P:* William Sistrom *C:* Robert De Grasse *M:* Alberto Colombo

Cast: Gene Raymond, Margaret Callahan, Eric Blore, Grant Mitchell, Moroni Olsen, Erin O'Brien-Moore, Henry Travers, Walter Brennan, Ray Mayer, Erville Alderson, Murray Alper, Harry Beresford

Writer William Magee (Raymond) goes to the secluded and deserted Baldpate Inn to finish work on his newest thriller. But as his evening progresses, a parade of strangers—all with their own key to the inn—shows up and distracts the ever-more-exasperated author.

Earl Derr Biggers' novel *Seven Keys to Baldpate* (1913) was one of his most enduring creations, second only to his series of Charlie Chan mysteries. Its popularity was further enhanced when playwright George M. Cohan adapted it into a Broadway hit the same year as its publication. Film adaptations emerged in 1916, 1917, 1925 and 1929, with the last one being produced, as was this one, by RKO Radio Pictures. Both RKO versions deviate somewhat from the Biggers/Cohan template, with the emphasis more on comedy than horror and with some of the twists jettisoned to make the work more agreeable (or, one might counter, to dumb it down).

At any rate, this is the most widely seen—and thus best known—of the earliest screen adaptations. Co-director William Hamilton was an experienced editor—among his many credits was William Dieterle's definitive version of *The Hunchback of Notre Dame* (1939). His directorial output, however, was sparse, with at least four of his handful of directorial credits shared with Edward Killy.

For his part, Killy moved from being a respected assistant director (he was nominated for the Best Assistant Director award in 1934, shortly before it was discontinued) to a body of not-so-respected work on B-pictures. *Seven Keys* is arguably the most famous title he or Hamilton ever directed (or co-directed).

The cast includes busy character actor Gene Raymond, whose filmography covers everything from *Flying Down to Rio* (1933) to Alfred Hitchcock's atypical foray into farce, *Mr. & Mrs. Smith* (1941), to guest appearances on such TV staples as *The Outer Limits* (1963) and *Ironside* (1968). Supporting players Henry Travers (*The Invisible Man*, 1933) and Moroni Olsen later reunited for Frank Capra's beloved holiday classic, *It's A Wonderful Life* (1946).

After the 1935 adaptation, Biggers' story was put on ice for over a decade. The next version was made for TV in 1946, with another cinematic adaptation, again produced by RKO, coming along later that same year. TH

She
RKO; b/w; 95 (101) min; U.S.

D: Lansing C. Holden, Irving Pichel *S:* Ruth Rose, Dudley Nichols *P:* Merian C. Cooper *C:* J. Roy Hunt *M:* Max Steiner *FX:* Vernon Walker

Cast: Helen Gahagan, Randolph Scott, Helen Mack, Nigel Bruce, Gustav von Seyffertitz, Julius Adler, Ray Corrigan, Samuel S. Hinds, Noble Johnson, Jerry Frank, Arnold Gay, Eli Mintz, Lumsden Hare

H. Rider Haggard's novel *She* has gotten the celluloid treatment numerous times since its publication in serial form in 1886-1887, with results as varied as a one-minute short by French filmmaker Georges Méliès and a Hammer vehicle for Swiss überbabe Ursula Andress (sharing the screen with the lucky John Richardson, who also starred opposite Raquel Welch in Hammer's *One Million Years B.C.*, 1966).

Most *She* adaptations came along during the silent era, with this 1935 big-budget version from the producer of *King Kong* (1933) being the first to employ sound. And while it mostly stays true to Haggard's story, there are changes to some particulars, the most immediately noticeable of which is the transplantation of Queen Ayesha's lost city of Kor. In the novel it's located in Africa, but in the film it's discovered in a frozen wasteland above the Arctic Circle. Also missing is Kallikrates, Ayesha's murdered Egyptian lover, replaced here with a backstory concerning married nobleman John Vincey, who'd discovered her lair in the

1500s and been murdered when he refused to forsake his marital vows for her. Similarly, love interest Ustane becomes the more-pronounceable Tanya, while the name of "She" herself, Ayesha, is swapped for the Egyptian-sounding Hash-A-Mo-Tep!

The film begins with the handsome Leo Vincey (Scott) being called to his dying uncle's (Hinds) estate, where he learns that equally handsome ancestor John Vincey (also Scott, but with a foppish haircut) once discovered the secret of eternal life. After the uncle's death, Leo, along with his uncle's companion Horace Holly (Bruce), retraces John Vincey's ancient footsteps to the frozen steppes of Siberia. There they meet a Russian named Dugmore (Hare) and his daughter Tanya (Mack). Dugmore agrees to be their guide through the glacial mountains and to act as an intermediary with the natives, but he's killed when he spies gold in the ice and, while trying to hack it out, causes an avalanche. It turns out, however, that the ice wall had been hiding a magma-warmed passage into the mountains. Leo, Holly and Tanya follow it and soon find themselves surrounded by hungry natives planning their next meal. Thankfully, they are rescued by Billali (Seyffertitz) and his men, who take them to an art-deco world of the distant past, there to meet the beautiful and allegedly formidable Hash-A-Mo-Tep, aka "She" (Gahagan), who tells them, "I am yesterday, and today and tomorrow. I am sorrow and longing and hope unfulfilled. I am Hash-A-Mo-Tep, She … She Who Must Be Obeyed! I am I!" One thing she definitely is, it seems, is self-impressed, though in fact she does a lot of talking and very little else.

She was a commercial failure upon its initial release in July 1935. The marketing campaign made much of its connection to *King Kong*, but apart from a lost civilization, the two films share little in terms of plot. Kids hoping for lots of giant monsters and action are bound for disappointment, as the only beastie to be seen is a Smilodon that, along with its blood-covered victim, is frozen in ice and as such not much of a threat.

The film compounds its ennui potential with far too many cornball ponderings on morality, true love and other Deep Matters, such as the appropriateness of the death penalty for the primitives who were going to eat Vincey and his friends. Vincey pleads with She to spare them and She, despite having observed reincarnation firsthand, spouts this out-of-character, out-of-context diatribe: "Would you spare them? Oh yes, a Christian. I'd

Helen Gahagan as She Who Must Be Obeyed in *She*

almost forgotten. I remember in the marketplace of Jerusalem, they spoke of a man who taught mercy and forgiveness, a man who died that others might live, as though death could beget life." Her face is tilted toward Heaven as she speaks, and her eyes contain a hopeful, faraway look. A minute or so later, she kills the transgressors. Huh?

There's also the matter of the unforgivably awkward casting of Gustav von Seyffertitz as Prime Minster Billali, his head adorned by an egregious black wig that renders preposterous his European facial features and vocalizations. Bavarian-born von Seyffertitz was a world-class actor who'd begun his career in

the teens and brought panache to almost every role he essayed throughout his career. Here, however, he adds an unintentionally comic note to the proceedings, looking as though he's just stumbled in from 1936's *Flash Gordon* (and not holding a candle to Christopher Lee in Hammer's 1965 adaptation). Less jarring but still out of his depth is Randolph Scott as the love-struck (if somewhat flighty) Leo Vincey. Similarly, Helen Gahagan fails to impress much either as She Who Must Be Obeyed.

That's not to say that the film is without stellar performances. In fact, it's the supporting players Helen Mack and Nigel Bruce who steal the show. Before his turn as Dr. Watson in *The Hound of the Baskervilles* (1939)—which forever typecast him as a bumbling buffoon—Bruce proves himself more than capable of playing a heroic man of action and intelligence. And spunky Helen Mack, who had found fame playing foil to Robert Armstrong in *The Son of Kong* (1933), proves herself worthy of icon status by breathing three-dimensional life into the role of Tanya, Vincey's naïve young lover and the object of She's jealous hatred. Whether betraying her anger at an all-powerful queen or shedding a tear over the man she believes she's lost, Mack never strikes a false note. Perhaps the film would have become a cult favorite had she, rather than Gahagan, played the film's eponymous character.

She was co-directed by Irving Pichel (whose previous genre credits include *The Most Dangerous Game*, 1932 and *Before Dawn*, 1933) and Lansing C. Holden. It's easy to see which director was responsible for the film's more striking moments: Pichel went on to a lengthy and acclaimed career as both a director and an actor, while Holden made only one more film. It's Pichel, then, who manages some striking moments in *She*, not the least of which is She's first appearance enshrouded by a beautifully moving mist. And some of the set pieces, including the collapsing wall of ice and a native attempt at carnage, do convey a certain sense of muted excitement. Too bad the film is so talky that little else matters in the long run.

In 1936 the film was nominated for an Oscar. The category? Best Dance Direction, in recognition of an overlong, Busby Berkeley-meets-Cleopatra dance sequence, replete with elementary "glee club" choreography. CW

A Shot in the Dark
Chesterfield; b/w; 69 min; U.S.

D: Charles Lamont *S:* Charles Belden *P:* George R. Batcheller *C:* M.A. Andersen *M:* Abe Meyer

Cast: Charles Starrett, Robert Warwick, Edward Van Sloan, Marion Shilling, Helen Jerome Eddy, Doris Lloyd, James Bush, Julian Madison, Eddie Tamblyn, Ralph Brooks, Robert McKenzie, John Davidson, Herbert Bunston, George Morrell, Broderick O'Farrell

Devastated college student Ken Harris (Starrett) discovers that his roommate's apparent suicide was, in fact, a murder and sets out to unmask the culprit.

Based on a book by Clifford Orr, *A Shot in the Dark* is a brisk murder mystery with some grisly elements. Much of its cast is familiar from similar films of the era. Cast as one of the world's oldest college students—until Robert Lowery came along in 1944's *The Mummy's Ghost*—Charles Starrett, who had previously portrayed one of the intrepid adventurers of MGM's ultra-kinky *The Mask of Fu Manchu* (1932), is classically handsome (though pretty wooden) in *Shot*. Edward Van Sloan is on hand as an academic type, a role he had perfected in *Dracula* (1931) and *The Mummy* (1932); he continued to crop up in horror/mystery fare until the 1940s. Busy character actor Doris Lloyd also graced many a Universal horror of the 1940s, including *The Ghost of Frankenstein* (1942), *Night Monster* (1942) and *The House of Fear* (1944).

Russian-born Director Charles Lamont made a few other horror-themed films, albeit in the spoof category. He was a regular director for Bud Abbott and Lou Costello, guiding them through arguably their finest outing, *Abbott and Costello Meet Frankenstein* (1948). Lamont was active from the early 1920s until the early 1950s, and while he never established himself as a major name, he was a reliable journeyman and craftsman.

While *A Shot in the Dark* doesn't mark a career high for any of its participants, it stands up just fine among the many B-horror/mystery hybrids that proliferated in the 1930s. TH

The Student of Prague
aka Der Student von Prague
Cine-Allianz; b/w; 86 min; Germany

D/Co-S: Arthur Robison *Co-S:* Hans Heinz Ewers, Hans Kyser *P:* Fritz Klotzsch *C:* Bruno Mondi *M:* Theo Mackeben

Cast: Adolf Wohlbruck (Anton Walbrook), Theodor Loos, Dorothea Wieck, Erich Fiedler, Edna Greyff, Karl Hellmer, Volker von Collande, Fritz Genschow, Elsa Wagner

In 1860s Prague, handsome and popular student (and accomplished fencer) Balduin (Wohlbruck) falls in love with beautiful singer Julia (Wieck), who is romantically involved with Baron Waldis (Fiedler). Balduin figures he doesn't stand a chance with her, but the mysterious Dr. Carpis (Loos) offers him a deal—in return for selling Carpis anything he asks for, Carpis will deliver Julia's love. When Balduin agrees, Carpis buys the young man's reflection.

Hans Heinz Ewers derived inspiration for *The Student of Prague* from Edgar Allan Poe's famous doppelganger tale *William Wilson*. Ewers' script served as the basis for Stellan Rye and Paul Wegener's 1913 adaptation, which was redone by Henrik Galeen in 1926 (the version today recognized as definitive). Almost 10 more years elapsed before this, the first talkie version, emerged, with Ewers' screenplay tweaked by writer/director Arthur Robison.

Chicago-born Robison worked in Germany during the silent era and there made his greatest cinematic contribution, the Expressionist horror film *Warning Shadows* (1923). None of Robison's other films come close to that distinctive achievement, which was a rare example of a silent film told entirely through visuals, without the aid of intertitles.

His respectable career drew to a close with this *Student of Prague*. He doesn't bring a great deal of creativity to his take on the story and in fact foregoes having Balduin's reflection take on a separate, imp-like identity of its own, as was the case in the earlier versions. Robison's film is closer in spirit to Oscar Wilde's *The Picture of Dorian Gray* (1890) in that Balduin's mirror image reflects its owner's baser impulses. And despite Robison's overall lack of flair, the finale in which Balduin confronts his reflection is memorably well done.

Adolf Wohlbruck gazes into his mirror reflection in *The Student of Prague*.

Student's central role is very well played by Adolf Wohlbruck, who later changed his name to Anton Walbrook and established himself in international cinema; among his most beloved screen appearances are in *Gaslight* (1940) and *Queen of Spades* (1949), and in several collaborations with Michael Powell and Emeric Pressburger, including *49th Parallel* (1941), *The Life and Death of Colonel Blimp* (1943) and *The Red Shoes* (1948). He had a knack for everything from light comedy to heavy drama, and his versatility is evident in *Student*. Balduin is a complicated character—arrogant at times, sympathetic at others—and Wahlbruck hits the right notes throughout. None of the supporting players come close to matching his versatility, though Theodor Loos is effective as the cunning Dr. Carpis.

This marked the last adaptation of Ewers' story until 2004, when another version titled *The Student of Prague* was released in the Czech Republic. TH

Trails of the Wild
Conn; b/w; 60 min; U.S.

D: Sam Newfield *S:* Joseph O'Donnell *P:* Maurice Conn, Sigmund Neufeld *C:* Jack Greenhalgh

Cast: Kermit Maynard, Billie Seward, Monte Blue, Theodore von Eltz, Fuzzy Knight, Matthew Betz, Wheeler Oakman, Robert Frazer, Charles Delaney, Frank Rice, John Elliott, Roger Williams, Rocky

Jim McKenna (Maynard) and his sidekick Windy (Knight) are dispatched to Ghost Mountain in search of a missing man. Once there, the two uncover not ghosts but a gang of outlaws.

This modest B-Western incorporates horror imagery. Like every other horror-tinged Western of its vintage, the supernatural is debunked by a more banal explanation; it wouldn't be until the 1970s, with such titles as Antonio Margheriti's *And God Said to Cain* (1970), Clint Eastwood's *High Plains Drifter* (1973) and (arguably) Alejandro Jodorowsky's impossible-to-pigeonhole *El Topo* (1970), that the Western and horror genres would wholeheartedly cross-pollinate.

Star Kermit Maynard was a mainstay in B-Westerns of the period. He started out as a double for his better-known brother Ken Maynard but eventually became a star of sorts in his own right. Kermit remained linked to the Western genre for the long run, finishing out his career doing guest stints on such television series as *Wagon Train* and *Gunsmoke*.

Director Sam Newfield, brother of *Trails* producer Sigmund Neufeld, had a long if not terribly illustrious B-movie career in his own right. He entered cinema in 1926 and soon established himself as a reliable craftsperson that could bring films in on time and under budget. He ended up doing a lot more work with his brother after the latter established the infamous Producers Releasing Corporation (PRC). Together they were responsible for such guilty pleasures as *The Mad Monster* (1942) and *Dead Men Walk* (1943), both starring fright film icon George Zucco. The brothers made their last film together, *The Long Rifle and the Tomahawk*, in 1964. Sam died that same year, while Sigmund lived until 1979. TH

The Vanishing Riders
Spectrum; b/w; 58 min; U.S.

D: Bob Hill *S:* Oliver Drake *P:* Ray Kirkwood *C:* Bill Hyers

Cast: Bill Cody, Bill Cody, Jr., Ethel Jackson, Wally Wales (Hal Taliaferro), Donald Reed, Bud Buster, Roger Williams,

After Sheriff Bill Jones (Cody) kills Joe Lang (Williams) in the line of duty, he adopts Lang's son Tim (Cody, Jr.) and raises him as his own. Sometime later, the two pass through an abandoned mining town that's reputed to be haunted. Hiram (Buster), an old friend of Bill's, is the only inhabitant, and he tells Bill that that dangerous outlaw Wolf Larson (Wales) is terrorizing the area. The three of them then hatch a scheme to use the town's haunted reputation to outwit the bad guy.

Noted B-Western specialist Bob Hill (aka Robert F. Hill) was responsible for this Western with horror undertones (he attempted a similar mixture the following year with *The Phantom of the Range*). *The Vanishing Riders* is a painfully dated affair that seems to have been aimed at children. Father and son team Bill Cody and Bill Cody, Jr. lays on the "cute" shtick painfully thick. The elder Cody plays Sheriff Bill Jones as a stereotypical square-jawed Western hero; he wears a black outfit (unusual in Westerns of the time; the good guys usually wore white), but beyond that he's a walking, talking repository of clichés. The younger Cody is supposed to come off as unusually mature for his age but is still very much a child, an obvious identification figure for the kids in the audience.

The horror elements consist mostly of talk of ghosts and spirits, but there are some shots of so-called ghouls riding through the countryside on horseback. These images anticipate Hammer's *Night Creatures* (1962), but Hill doesn't push the supernatural angle for long: It's revealed early on that it's all just a scam to catch the baddies off guard.

Screenwriter Oliver Drake later wrote *The Mummy's Curse* (1944), the last and worst in Universal's series of mummy thrillers, starring Lon Chaney, Jr. as Kharis. But that film (as well as *The Vanishing Riders*) looks accomplished compared to his 1969 directorial outing, *The Mummy and the Curse of the Jackals*, which truly defies description. TH

Werewolf of London
Universal; b/w; 75 min; U.S.

D: Stuart Walker *S:* John Colton *P:* Stanley Bergerman, Robert Harris *C:* Charles Stumar *M:* Karl Hajos, Heinz Roemheld *FX:* John P. Fulton

Cast: Henry Hull, Warner Oland, Valerie Hobson, Lester Matthews, Lawrence Grant, Spring Byington, J.M. Kerrigan, Clark Williams, Ethel Griffies, Zeffie Tilbury, Charlotte Granville, Jeanne Bartlett, Reginald Barlow, Egon Brecher, Connie Leon, Jeffrey Hassel

While searching for a rare orchid in Tibet, botanist Dr. Wilfred Glendon (Hull) is bitten by a large, howling animal of some sort. Oblivious to the implications of such an event, he finishes his mission, finding the flower and bringing it back home to London. Once there, fellow botanist Dr. Yogami (Oland) warns him that he's a werewolf, and that he's bound to kill people if he doesn't ingest fluid from the Tibetan plant. At first Glendon scoffs, but the truth of his situation quickly becomes undeniable. He also learns that Yogami is similarly infected; indeed, it was he who had attacked Glendon in the mountains of Tibet.

Barring a few silent films with promising titles like *The Werewolf* (1913) and *Wolf Blood: A Tale of the Forest* (1925),

Two werewolves (Warner Oland and Henry Hull) battle it out as they transform in *Werewolf of London.*

Universal's *Werewolf of London* marks the cinema's first true foray into lycanthropy in its depiction of the plight of a man who turns into a demonic wolf-creature when the moon waxes full.

The film was developed as a star vehicle for Boris Karloff and Bela Lugosi, but by the time the cameras rolled in 1935, both actors had been replaced. This is a sore spot among many nostalgia-minded horror buffs who believe the recasting ruined a potential classic. But the fact of the matter is that, when watched objectively, not only is it apparent that the film is quite accomplished, it's also plain that its casting of non-horror actors gives it a freshness it would have otherwise lacked.

Broadway veteran Henry Hull—already glimpsed in such horror-tinged fare as *One Exciting Night* (1922)—plays Dr. Wil-

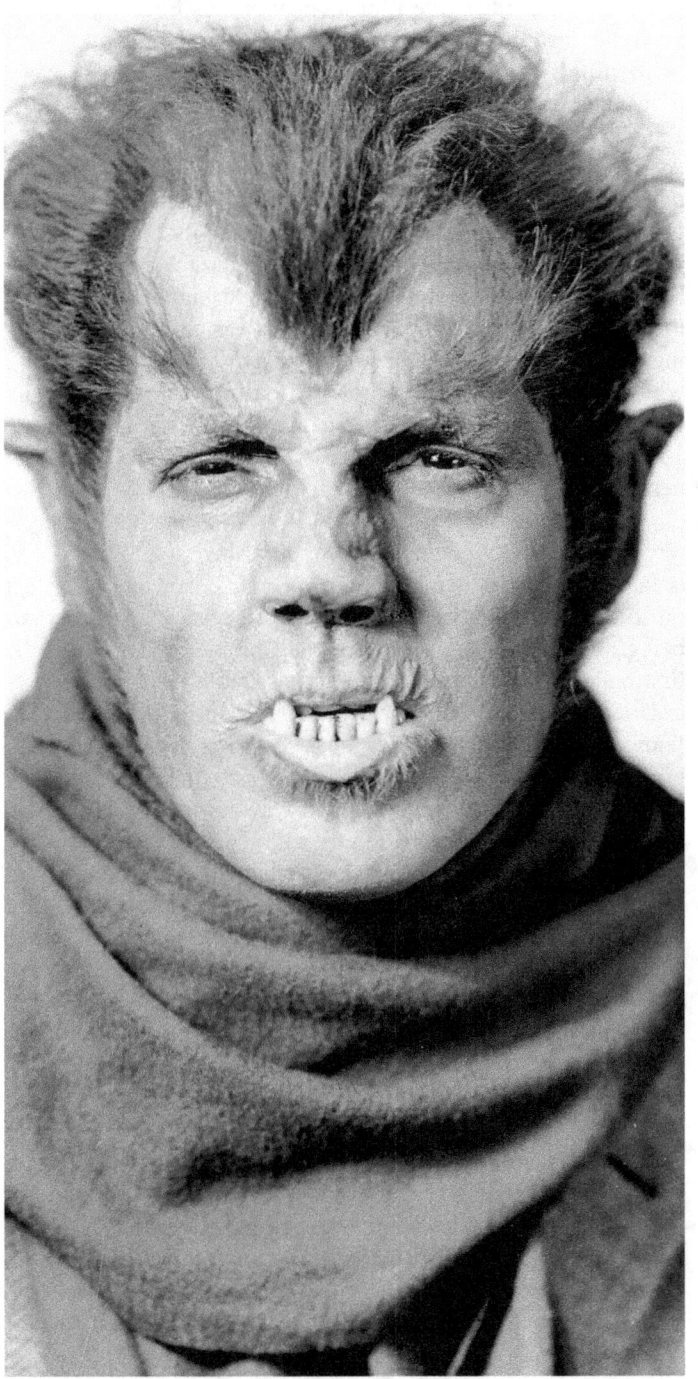

Henry Hull in Jack Pierce's Mephisthophelean make-up for *Werewolf of London*

fred Glendon. And while Karloff certainly would have done a fine job, it's also pretty likely that his interpretation would have been more sympathetic than Hull's. Yet it's precisely Hull's conveyance of social maladjustment that makes Glendon an interesting protagonist. He's not the jovial extrovert that Lon Chaney, Jr. portrayed in *The Wolf Man* (1941); Hull's Glendon is a recluse, a cold fish who barely acknowledges his wife even though he really does love her. His fixation on his work has stunted his emotional growth, and he covers his insecurities with an air of arrogant condescension. It's a skillful piece of acting, one that has never gotten the recognition it deserves.

When Glendon turns into the werewolf, Hull goes for broke, creating a frightening creature that compares well with Chaney's more iconic portrayal. The werewolf here is not quite the mindless beast of later films; instead, it's an amalgam of man and beast, more akin to Mr. Hyde than Larry Talbot's Wolf Man. The fact that Hull's werewolf stops to put on his hat and coat before going out on the town may seem a silly gaffe, but such an interpretation betrays inattention on the part of the viewer. This is a thinking, reasoning creature desiring anonymity in a crowd, which makes it all the more dangerous—and terrifying!

Jack P. Pierce's werewolf make-up is one of his crowning achievements, far outclassing Chaney's more famous look six years later. Hull's satanic look is wonderfully achieved, and special effects wizard John P. Fulton also manages to devise some ingenious man-into-beast transformations. The initial one of these—accomplished with a moving camera and rear-and-front-screen projection as Glendon walks through his house and gradually changes into the beast—is rightly celebrated; it truly is an ambitious shot for what's ultimately a low-budget affair.

Legend has it that Hull protested an earlier (and much more heavily made-up) conception of the creature, his ego being threatened by the notion of being unrecognizable. The actor, however, quite plausibly insisted that he was merely being true to the script, since the narrative calls for his character to be recognized by his wife (Hobson) toward the end of the film. A more extreme take on his appearance would have rendered that plot point incomprehensible.

Warner Oland has the role originally slated for Lugosi. Oland is best remembered for his performances as Charlie Chan, but he was also an effective villain, as evidenced both here and in his portrayals of Sax Rohmer's Asian criminal mastermind in *The Mysterious Dr. Fu Manchu* (1929) and its sequels. The Swedish-born actor may have seemed an odd fit for Asian characters, but his features lent themselves to the subterfuge; tormented by alcoholism, he died soon after mysteriously leaving the set of one of his Chan films for Fox in 1938. His portrayal of Yogami is somewhere between his heroic Chan and his devilish Fu Manchu. Yogami is by no means a completely sympathetic character, but he does have some touching moments that illustrate his inner torment.

Valerie Hobson is far more effective here than she was in *The Bride of Frankenstein* (1935), while Lester Matthews makes a more affable hero than he did in *The Raven* (1935). And director Stuart Walker does a fine job on the whole, though the pacing is at times a little slack. As in *The Mystery of Edwin Drood* (1935), he manages well within individual set pieces but has a harder time maintaining a consistent air of mystery and doom. His attempts at injecting some James Whale-styled comedy (in the form of bickering landladies played by Zeffie Tilbury and Ethel Griffies) are rather successful, however, and he deserves ample credit for having the audacity to stage Glendon's first transformation in so flashy a manner.

Too often criticized in comparison to *The Wolf Man*, *Werewolf of London* is one of the unheralded titles in the Universal horror canon of 1931-1936; it is not a masterpiece of the order of *The Black Cat* (1934) or *The Bride of Frankenstein* (1935), of course, but neither is it a poor, distant relation. TH

While the Patient Slept
Warner/First National; b/w; 66 min; U.S.

D: Ray Enright *S:* Robert N. Lee, Eugene Solow, Brown Holmes *P:* Harry Joe Brown *C:* Arthur Edison *M:* Bernhard Kaun

Cast: Aline MacMahon, Guy Kibbee, Lyle Talbot, Patricia Ellis, Allen Jenkins, Robert Barrat, Hobart Cavanaugh, Dorothy Tree, Henry O'Neill, Russell Hicks, Helen Flint, Brandon Hurst, Eddie Shubert, Walter Walker

A wealthy old man (Walker), hated by everyone in his family, has a stroke and slips into a coma (hence the film's title). His relatives gather at his gloomy mansion on a stormy night hoping that he'll die and leave them all rich. When his son Adolphe (Barrat) is murdered, the old man's caretaker, Nurse Sarah Keate (MacMahon), calls in her detective boyfriend Lance O'Leary (Kibbee) and police sergeant Jim Jackson (Jenkins) to solve the crime, though it's she who does most of the sleuthing.

While the Patient Slept is a typical 1930s murder mystery, with greedy relatives gathered in an old dark house on a stormy night. There are hidden passages, clutching hands and the obligatory "unknown" twin. What holds the film together is not the atmosphere, which it has in droves, but the performances of Aline MacMahon as the aging Nurse Keate and Guy Kibbee as her even older lover O'Leary. (This is the only Nurse Keate film to present the character as author Mignon Good Eberhart wrote her; the other five film adaptations of Eberhart's series make the lead much younger and more attractive.) At the heart of the film's frission is the wisecracking relationship between MacMahon and Kibbee, which—atypically for the subgenre—actually works.

The fact that director Ray Enright was an old hat at making quick, entertaining B-films certainly helps. Born in Anderson, Indiana in 1896, Enright moved with his family to Los Angeles when he was still a boy. In his teens he found work with Mack Sennet before entering the Signal Corps during World War I. In the 1920s he went to work for Warner Bros. as an editor, moving up the ladder to director with *Tracked by the Police* (1927), which starred America's favorite action-hero dog Rin Tin Tin. He topped off his career with several major Westerns in the late 1940s and early 1950s for the likes of Universal, RKO and Warner Bros.

Author Mignon G. Eberhart (1899-1996) had her first mystery novel, *The Patient in Room 18*, published in 1929; the book is famous for introducing the Nurse Keate character, who went on to star in a popular series of novels, resulting in Eberhart being nicknamed "America's Agatha Christie." *Patient* was the first major mystery novel to feature a female lead, and its success led directly to famed writer Christie introducing her own female sleuth, Miss Jane Marple, a year later. Nurse Keate was not so much the sleuth of Eberhart's stories (that was definitely O'Leary), but she frequently found ways to inadvertently help the man, all the while narrating the tales.

The success of Eberhart's books compelled Warner Bros. to pick up the rights, possibly to compete with RKO's acclaimed Hildegarde Withers series. Interestingly, while some critics have charged that the Warner films are rip-offs of the Withers series, the Withers character herself—a schoolteacher with a penchant for becoming embroiled in mystery—did not appear in print until two years after the first Keate novel was published, making her more likely a rip-off of Christie's Miss Marple.

While the Patient Slept was based on the novel of the same name, published in 1930. It was the second of the Nurse Keate books, though it was the first one adapted to the screen. The other films in the series were *The Murder of Dr. Harrigan* and *Murder by an Aristocrat* (both 1936) and *The Patient in Room 18* and *Mystery House* (both 1938). When Warner took a break from the character in 1937, 20th Century Fox produced their own take on her with *The Great Hospital Mystery*.

Strangely, the films had a difficult time getting the name of Eberhart's character correct, variously calling her Sarah Keate, Sara Keate, Miss Keats and Sally Keating. CW

1936

The Amazing Exploits of the Clutching Hand
aka **The Clutching Hand**
Weiss; b/w; 15 chapters; U.S.

D: Albert Herman *S:* George M. Merrick, Eddy Graneman, Leon D'Usseau, Dallas Fitzgerald *P:* Adrian Weiss, Louis Weiss *C:* James Diamond *FX:* Kenneth Strickfaden

Cast: Jack Mulhall, Rex Lease, Marion Shilling, Mae Busch, Ruth Mix, William Farnum, Robert Frazer, Robert Walker, Jon Hall, Gaston Glass, Bryan Washburn, Franklyn Farnum, Mahlon Hamilton, Gordon Griffith, Frank Leigh, Henry Hall, Yakima Canutt, Joseph W. Girard, Bob Kortman, George Morrell, Milburn Morante

Based on a novel by Arthur B. Reeve, *The Amazing Exploits of the Clutching Hand* kicks off in sci-fi terrain, with Dr. Gironda (Frazer) inventing a machine that creates synthetic gold. Before he can reveal his invention to the world, however, he vanishes. A newspaper reporter named Walter Jameson (Lease), in love with Gironda's daughter Verna (Shilling), investigates, bringing private investigator Craig Kennedy (Mulhall) on board for assistance. The proceedings veer into horror territory as a vile criminal mastermind known as The Clutching Hand shows up, hypnotizing and ensnaring people into his web of villainy and deceit. In the process he sets up a series of ingenious and diabolical death traps, though more often than not they misfire.

Despite its heavy-handed histrionics and numerous shadowy images of an upraised clutching hand—or, arguably, due to them—this overlong serial is too dull to create much tension (though the ending, if one makes it that far, *is* admittedly unpredictable). Kenneth Strickfaden's effects add at times a sense of childlike wonder to the goings-on, no surprise given how reminiscent they are of the effects Strickfaden created for James Whale's masterful *Frankenstein* (1931). Still, director Albert Herman was no James Whale, and the result here is entirely forgettable.

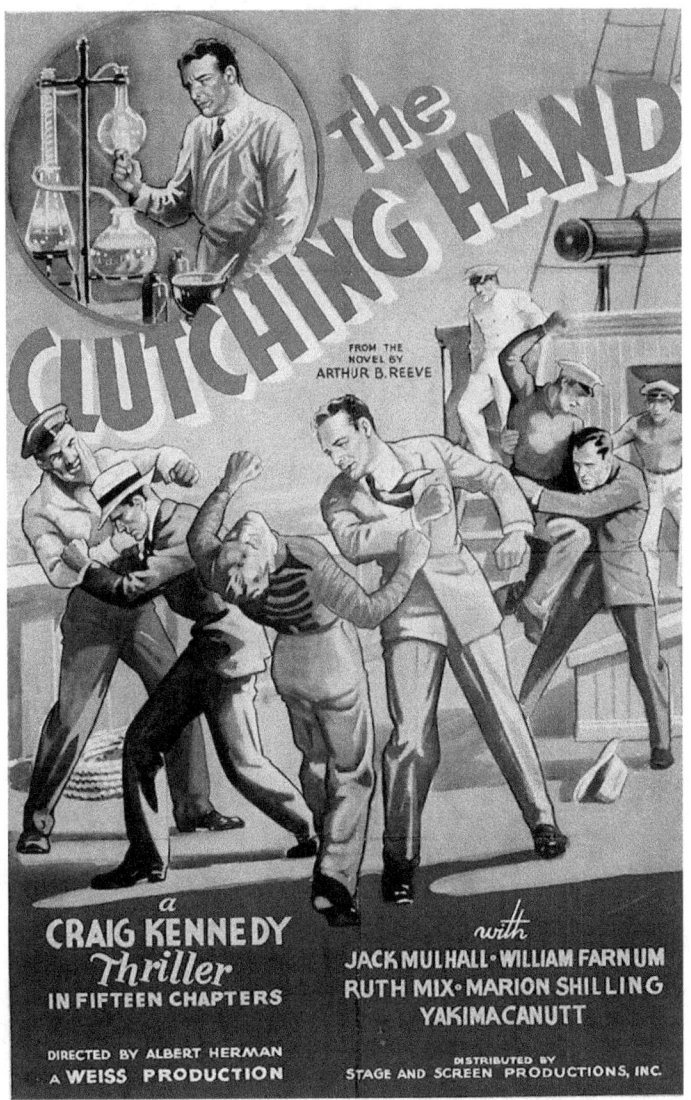

Reeve's Craig Kennedy character was popular in print and made the jump to the big screen a number of times, beginning with 1914's *The Exploits of Elaine* (starring Arnold Daly, who essayed the role three times in all). Other silent films followed, but after *The Clutching Hand*, the character was retired from the big screen and given a second career on television, portrayed by Donald Woods in the syndicated series *Craig Kennedy, Criminologist* (1952).

The Amazing Exploits of the Clutching Hand was later cut from 15 chapters to 74 minutes and re-released as a feature. It is this trimmed version that is the most easily obtainable today, but apart from its fortunate brevity, it is in no way an improvement on the original. CW

Arima no neko sodo
aka **Arima neko sodo**
Kyokuto; b/w; length unknown; Japan

D: Hakkou Nishifuji *S:* Kou Kawakami *C:* Masakatsu Taniguchi

Cast: Katsutaro Bando, Hiroko Ohara, Myoko Kohama, Kyoko Izumi, Kozaburo Arashi, Takeo Kusunoki, Renko Tae, Yozu Kojima, Sashou Ichikawa, Kotaro Isehara

When Konomo (Izumi) attempts to take over her wealthy family's estate, she drives her sister Su (Ohara) to kill herself. The spirit of Su's devoted cat then enters the maid (Tae) and carries out a murderous revenge plot against Konomo.

This was one of many films to be based on the feudal-era legend of a ghost cat that stalked the halls of Arima Castle; it also appears to have been the first produced in the 1930s. It was quickly forgotten the following year, however, when Shigeru Kito's *The Ghost Cat of Arima* was released to strong box-office and positive reviews. CW

Border Phantom
Republic; b/w; 59 min; U.S.

D: S. Roy Luby *S:* Fred Myton *P:* A.W. Hackel *C:* Jack Greenhalgh

Cast: Bob Steele, Harley Wood, Don Barclay, Karl Hackett, Horace Murphy, Miki Morita, Perry Murdock, John S. Peters, Frank Ball

A deserted, supposedly cursed hacienda is the setting for this weird Western starring popular second-string actor Bob Steele. When a shadowy figure murders an entomologist (Ball) squatting at the hacienda, his daughter Barbara (Wood) is accused of the crime as handsome cowboy Larry O'Day (Steele) and his comic sidekick Lucky (Barclay) investigate. While con-

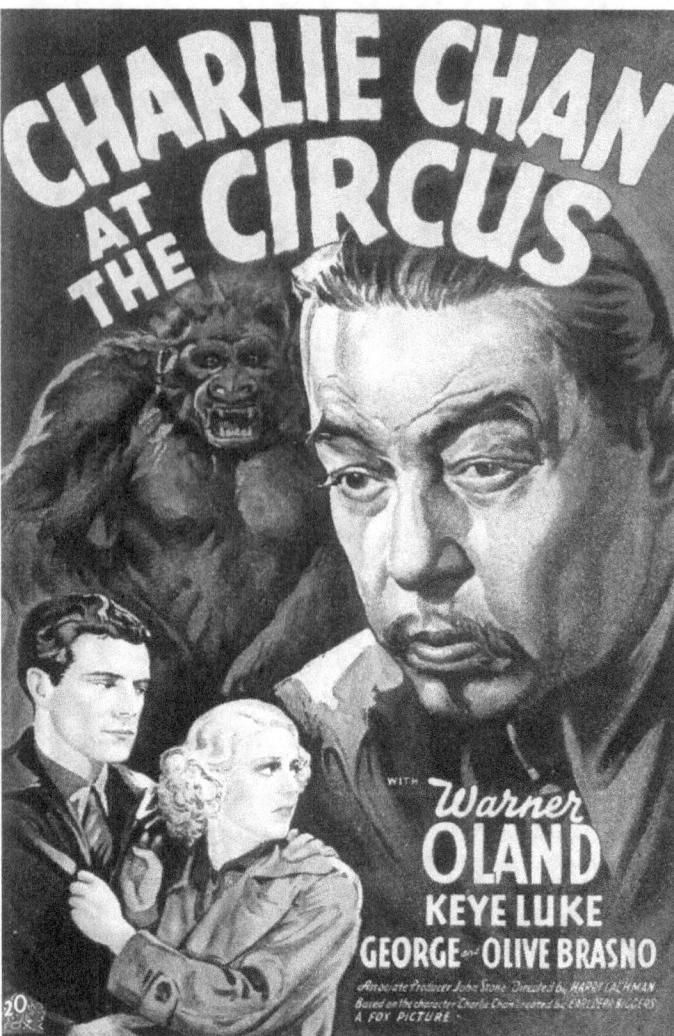

tending with a troublesome sheriff (Murphy), a second squatter named Barton (Murdoch) who has designs on Barbara, and a second entomologist (Peters) who's a bit of a thief, Larry and Lucky uncover a sex slavery ring selling young Asian "picture brides" to wealthy American men.

Though the hacienda is admittedly sinister, this film's horror is purely of the Yellow Peril variety so prevalent in 1930s cinema, with the real murderer none other than a sinister Chinaman named Chon Lee (played by Japanese actor Morita).

Thanks to Jack Greenhalgh's superlative camerawork, there are several visually interesting scenes, such as when Lucky first spots young Asian women sneaking out of feed barrels and stealing into the hacienda, or when Larry crawls through the deserted mansion's cobwebbed crawlspaces. (What would an old dark house be without a hidden passageway or two?) The shadowy imagery at times borders on Expressionistic, displaying just how much the cinematographer had grown since his first brush with the sinister, *Ghost Patrol*, in 1936. While he was no Nicholas Musuraca (an Oscar-nominated cinematographer who began his career in B-films), Greenhalgh lent a credible degree of atmosphere to a number of low-budget pictures, including *The Mad Monster* (1942), *Dead Men Walk* (1943), *Wild Horse Phantom* (1944), *His Brother's Ghost* (1945), *The Flying Serpent* and *The Mask of Diijon* (both 1946), *Lost Continent* (1951) and the legendarily bad *Robot Monster* (1953), among many others.

While some sources list *Border Phantom* as a 1937 production, it was in fact produced and released in late 1936. CW

Botan dōrō
Rengou-eiga; b/w; length unknown; Japan
  D: Akira Nobuchi
  Cast: Ryunosuke Tsukigata, Shosaku Sugiyama
This is yet another (obscure) adaptation of Sanyutei Encho's one-man play of the same title. The story had first been filmed in 1910, but it wasn't until the godfather of Japanese cinema, Shozo Makino, took on the property in 1914 that it became fodder for many generations of filmmakers to come. This version, from director Akira Nobuchi, was the second produced in the 1930s, following Teikine's 1930 adaptation of the same name.

Shosaku Sugimaya stars as the daughter of a samurai who falls for one of her father's much younger peers. The two become lovers for a time, then he deserts her and she dies of a broken heart. While traveling, he meets a second beautiful young woman and begins another affair. Each night she comes to him, carrying a lantern marked by a peony design. At some point, she reveals herself to be the ghost of his former lover, after which he dies.

Like many stories in Japanese folklore (this one was, in fact, adapted from a very similar Chinese story), morality is front and center to the piece. Similar to *Yotsuya kaidan*, the message is very clear: Men should remain faithful to the wives of their youth or face a supernatural comeuppance.

The next adaptation, *Kaidan botan dōrō*, was produced and released the following year. CW

Cat Ghost and Cherry Blossoms at Night in Saga
aka **Kaibyô Saga no yozakura**
Daito; b/w; length unknown; Japan
  D: Minoru Ishiyama
  Cast: Kusuo Abe, Futaba Kinoshita, Kodayu Ichikawa II
Some sources cite this as a 1930 production, but the best available evidence indicates that it was actually made in 1936. Whichever the case, it was based on Joko Segawa III's 1853 kabuki play *Hana Saga neko mata zoshi*, about a cat that takes on the personality of its murdered master and seeks revenge against the man who murdered him.

This wasn't the only ghost cat movie directed by Minoru Ishiyama. He oversaw *Enmadera no kaibyô* (1938) and *Kaidan Senbaya sodo* (1939), both also for Daito. CW

Charlie Chan at the Circus
Fox; b/w; 72 min; U.S.
  D: Harry Lachman S: Robert Ellis, Helen Logan C: Daniel B. Clark
  Cast: Warner Oland, Keye Luke, George Brasno, Olive Brasno, Francis Ford, Maxine Reiner, John McGuire, Shirley Deane, Paul Stanton, J. Carrol Naish, Boothe Howard, Drue Leyton, Wade Boteler, Shia Jung, Annie Mar

After circus owner Joe Kinney (Stanton) receives threatening letters, he sends free tickets for an evening under the big top to Honolulu detective Charlie Chan (Oland), his wife (Mar) and his 12 children. Kinney isn't what you'd call a nice guy, though, as is evidenced early on when he takes a whip to the circus gorilla Caesar. And it isn't just the gorilla that Kinney treats inhumanely; he's the type who thinks with his fists rather than his head, to the point that most of his employees wouldn't mind seeing him dead. And indeed, his demise occurs just after the Chan clan arrives; Kinney is found dead in his wagon, with the doors locked from the inside and what appears to be gorilla hair on the window sill. Chan suspects that the ape has been framed and that the true culprit resides a rung or two up the evolutionary ladder. And, as might be imagined, the circus is staffed with possible suspects.

A mystery with doses of humor and horror, *Charlie Chan at the Circus* has a lot going for it—from a really cool, possibly killer gorilla to an entertaining assemblage of circus "freaks" including little people Colonel Tim and Lady Tiny (portrayed by real-life brother and sister George and Olive Brasno, who were part of a vaudeville act known as "Buster Shaver, Olive and George").

Colonel Tim's discovery of Kinney's body in the boss' locked wagon is one of the film's many quietly effective moments, while the escaped Caesar's rampage through the circus evokes to good effect a common theme of horror films during that period, including First National's *The Gorilla* (1931) and Universal's *Murders in the Rue Morgue* (1932). There's also the elder Chan's brush with a venomous king cobra and an entertaining subplot involving his number one son Lee (Luke) attempting to romance a beautiful circus performer (Jung). It's all lively, suspenseful and fun, but mystery is the primary order of the day, with the exposure of a quite-human culprit bringing the proceedings to a satisfying conclusion.

Charlie Chan at the Circus was the second horror outing for J. Carrol Naish, after 1934's *Return of the Terror*. In the 1940s, the actor became a full-fledged fright-film star with appearances in *Dr. Renault's Secret* (1942), *Calling Dr. Death* (1943), *The Monster Maker*, *Jungle Woman* and *House of Frankenstein* (all 1943), *Strange Confession* (1945) and *The Beast with Five Fingers* (1946).

Chan's next brush with horror, *Charlie Chan at the Opera*, came later the same year and pitted him against none other than Boris Karloff. CW

Charlie Chan at the Opera
Fox; b/w; 68 min; U.S.

D: H. Bruce Humberstone *S:* Scott Darling, Charles S. Beldon, Bess Meredyth *C:* Lucien N Andriot *M:* Charles Maxwell, Oscar Levant

Cast: Warner Oland, Boris Karloff, Keye Luke, William Demarest, Guy Usher, Margaret Irving, Gregory Gaye, Nedda Harrigan, Frank Conroy, Charlotte Henry, Thomas Beck, Maurice Cass, Tom McGuire

Despite a 1930s ban on horror films in Britain and a growing number of family watchdog groups opposing them in the United States, American producers often gained some wiggle room by cloaking their horror pictures in other genres. Fox had pulled this off with *Charlie Chan in Egypt* (1935), and the success of that film emboldened them to try more of the same. They shuffled novelist Earl Derr Bigger's popular Chinese detective into several pictures that were horror in all but name, finally going all out with *Charlie Chan at the Opera* by putting infamous

horror star Boris Karloff on the bill as the tenor Gravelle, who has gone mad due to his wife's double-crossing ways and been placed in an insane asylum.

As the film opens, amnesiac Gravelle escapes confinement and holes up in the opera house that his diva wife, Madame Lilli (Irving), calls home. Shortly thereafter a series of murders begins. A police sergeant (Demarest, best known as Uncle Charlie in the 1965-1972 sitcom *My Three Sons*) and inspector (Usher) are certain that Gravelle is to blame, but Charlie Chan (Oland), who's visiting San Francisco from his native Honolulu with his number one son Lee (Luke), isn't so sure. Despite the racist attitudes of the city's police department, Chan uncovers evidence that solves the mystery, exposing his Caucasian naysayers as the buffoons they really are.

Charlie Chan at the Opera has been called a poor man's *The Phantom of the Opera* (1925), and it's easy to see why. In addition to the opera house settings, each involves a singer receiving death threats. Both contain murder and madness galore, with the Chan film having Karloff's shadowy Gravelle (a reinvention of *Phantom*'s Erik) haunting the San Francisco opera house, hiding out in a prop room that contains sarcophagi and wax mummies.

At the Opera is also peppered throughout with horror references, from a Mephistophelean figure (also played by Karloff) in jazz pianist Oscar Levant's original opera for the film, to a verbal reference to Frankenstein made by a stage manager. (Audiences at the time would of course have been very familiar with

Karloff's star-making turn in Universal's *Frankenstein* and its 1935 sequel, making the reference all the more appropriate.)

The film's ads proclaimed, "A fiendish killer lurks at the opera! Weird! Thrilling! The Master Minds of Crime Match Wits Against Each Other!" and the opening credits shout "Warner Oland vs. Boris Karloff" above the film's title. Both are examples of deceptive marketing, considering that Oland and Karloff appear at odds only once (in the film's best sequence), with Gravelle emerging as something of a sympathetic red herring.

For the most part it all works, although—as is usual with this sort of plot—there are simply too many musical sequences, especially for a film of such short duration. Even Karloff gets in on the tuneful action … sort of—Tudor Williams dubbed his singing.

But whatever the nits one might choose to pick, *Charlie Chan at the Opera* has gone down in history as a fan favorite, thanks to solid performances from all involved, superior art direction for a film of its size, a better-than-average score and firm direction from H. Bruce Humberstone. Humberstone had previously overseen the low-budget horror efforts *The Crooked Circle* and *Strangers of the Evening* (both 1932), but neither offered much hint of his talents as director. He seems to have found his niche in Fox's Charlie Chan series, where a slightly higher budget, a better cache of performers and longer shooting schedules apparently enabled him to focus his abilities.

Boris Karloff pretty much repeated his role here in Universal's colorful *The Climax* (1944). CW

Charlie Chan's Secret
aka **Charlie Chan in San Francisco**
Fox; b/w; 72 min; U.S.

D: Gordon Wiles *S:* Robert Ellis, Helen Logan, Joseph Hoffman *C:* Rudolph Maté

Cast: Warner Oland, Rosina Lawrence, Charles Quigley, Henrietta Crosman, Edward Trevor, Astrid Allwyn, Herbert Mundin, Jonathan Hale, Egon Brecher, Gloria Roy, Ivan Miller, Arthur Edmund Carewe

This is, without a doubt, the best of the 20th Century Fox Charlie Chan films starring Warner Oland. It's also one of the most horror oriented.

Charlie Chan (Oland) is called upon to investigate the disappearance of Alan Colby, heir to a massive fortune, while involved in a shipwreck off the coast of Hawaii. Colby's relatives, all hoping he's dead, gather at his creepy San Francisco estate with their greedy hands outstretched. Chan believes Colby is alive and contacts his aunt, Mrs. Lowell (Lawrence), a believer in psychic research who, to the chagrin of the servants, also plays with Ouija boards. She invites Chan to a séance intended to contact Colby's spirit, even though Chan insists Colby is still alive (which he was until, unknown to Chan, an assailant stabbed him in the back). The séance is conducted with the medium Carlotta (Roy) at the helm, but it's disrupted by the appearance of Colby's dead body. Lowell then entreats Chan to spend a night in the house and investigate what happened to her nephew.

After the success of *Charlie Chan in Egypt* (1935), which was heavily influenced by the Universal horror films of the previous few years, Fox shuffled their beloved Chinese detective into no less than three more horror mysteries: *Charlie Chan's Secret*, *Charlie Chan at the Circus* and *Charlie Chan at the Opera* (all 1936), the latter featuring Boris Karloff in a prominent role.

As was all the rage with horror films of the 1930s, *Secret* was an "old dark house" mystery, and an engrossing one despite the usual parade of clichés: secret passages, clutching hands and red herrings galore. The sets and photography are extraordinarily evocative of the days of silent German Expressionism, no coincidence given that the film was shot by one of silent European cinema's greatest cinematographers, Rudolph Maté.

Born in Poland in 1898, Maté began work as an assistant cinematographer in Hungary before moving to Germany to work with Karl Freund, then to Denmark to work with Carl Dreyer and then to France. In 1935 he made his final move, this time to the United States, and was immediately snapped up by Fox for their religious-themed horror film *Dante's Inferno* (1935). Relegated at first to low-budget programmers, Maté gave each film on which he worked a tone distinctly his own and was quickly promoted to big-budget, A-list pictures. By the late 1940s, however, he'd grown tired of taking orders and retired from cinematography in favor of directing. Over the next decade he shot big and small films for major producers, including the classic science fiction film *When Worlds Collide* (1951). But by 1959, most of his energy was directed toward the lesser field of television. In 1962 he produced and directed *The 300 Spartans*, his last major film, and he worked on only one further picture, *Seven Seas to Calais* (1962), before dying of a heart attack in October of 1964.

Charlie Chan's Secret also features Turkish-born Arthur Edmund Carewe in a small role as Professor Bowen, the husband of the medium Carlotta. Carewe had been a major player in the silent era and during the early 1930s, but a paralytic stroke put a damper on his career. A little over a year after the release of this, his last film, he committed suicide. Other horror films in which he acted include *The Ghost Breaker* (1922), *Trilby* (1923), *The Phantom of the Opera* (1925), *The Cat and the Canary* (1927), *Doctor X* (1932) and *Mystery of the Wax Museum* (1933). CW

The Crimes of Stephen Hawke
King; b/w; 69 min; Great Britain

D/P: George King *S:* Jack Celestin, Frederick Hayward, H.F. Maltby, Paul White, Tod Slaughter *C:* Ronald (Ronnie) Neame *M:* Colin Wark

Cast: Tod Slaughter, Marjorie Taylor, D.J. Williams, Eric Portman, Graham Soutten, Gerald Barry, George M. Slater, Charles Penrose, Norman Pierce, Flotsam, Jetsam

After opening with a vocal performance by British radio personalities Flotsam and Jetsam and moving through an introduction by the film's lead—and the nation's then-premiere horror star—Tod Slaughter, *The Crimes of Stephen Hawke* gets right to work, gifting the viewer with a stark sequence in which Slaughter's murderous "Spinebreaker" lures a boy from a garden and breaks his back.

There's nothing similar to be found in any Universal film of the same period; Slaughter's films had a particular flavor of melodramatic nastiness that at the time existed only in British horror cinema. Yet it was *Britain's* protest of *Hollywood* horror films that led to the British censor's horror ban in the late 1930s, a time during which producer George King continued racking up additional—if admittedly softer in nature—credits for Tod Slaughter.

But be all that as it may, 1936's *Hawke* goes from a chilling opening to a methodical exploration of evil in the guise of the ordinary. To all outward appearances, Stephen Hawke (Slaughter) is a kindly moneylender who spoils his adopted daughter Julia (Taylor) while warding off her less-than-desirable suitors. At night, however, he becomes The Spinebreaker and, with his one-eyed, hunchbacked assistant Nathaniel (Soutten), murders and robs rich and poor alike. When his best friend Joshua Trimble's (Williams) son Matthew (Portman) expresses an interest in Julia, Hawke balks at the notion, making it clear that his daughter will marry no man without money and social standing. After The Spinebreaker murders Lord Brickhaven, the owner of a valuable emerald, Joshua comes to suspect that his dear friend Hawke may in fact be the infamous killer, a speculation that gets him his own broken spine and causes Matthew to swear revenge on the man responsible for his father's death.

Here the film meanders as Hawke is convicted of stealing bread and sentenced to prison, thus escaping the vengeance planned for him by Matthew. A lengthy subplot kicks in at this point in which Archer (Barry)—yet another lecherous would-be suitor—blackmails Julia into marrying him. The film gets back on track when Hawke hears about the proposed marriage. Intense jealousy takes over, and he escapes from prison and murders the would-be groom before falling to his death from the roof of his own home.

Warts and all, *The Crimes of Stephen Hawke* is something of a classic horror connoisseur's dream, building on the excesses of *Maria Marten, or The Murder in the Red Barn* (1935) and *Sweeney Todd: The Demon Barber of Fleet Street* (1936). *Hawke* is the culmination of an unbridled approach to filmmaking that was prevalent in Britain prior to the ban there and in the pre-Production Code United States, before tightened standards as to what could be shown on screen in both countries.

Tod Slaughter as Hawke has an enviably meaty role, in essence giving him two very different parts: the gentle loan officer and the death-dealing Spinebreaker. While the latter role would seem to have called for a heaping helping of Slaughter's famed

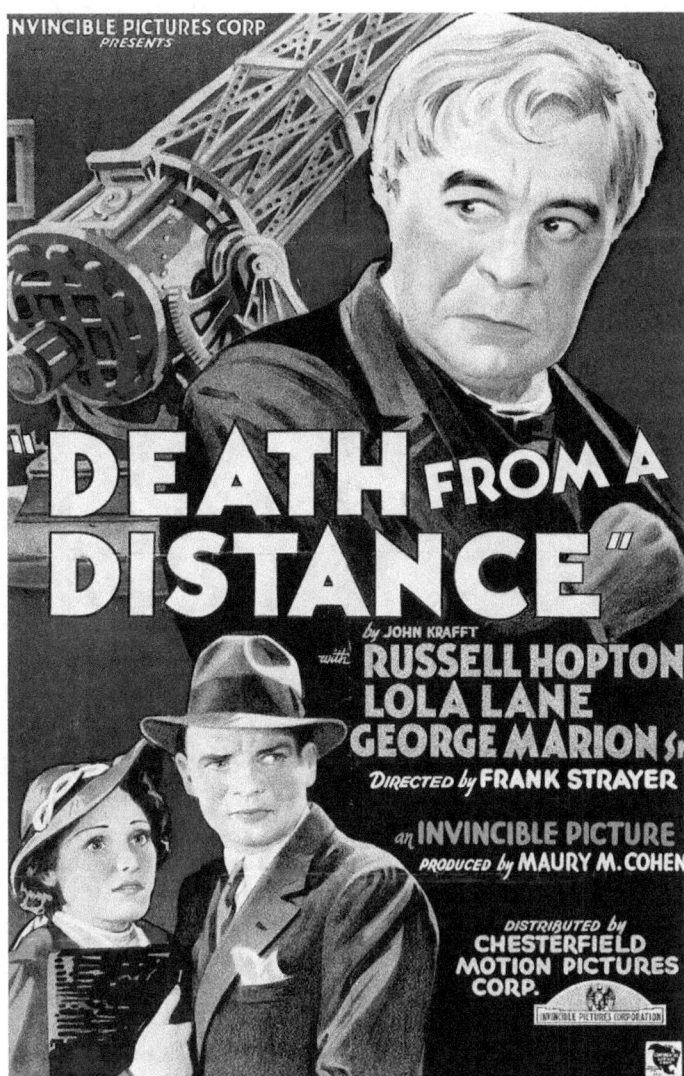

hambone theatrics, he plays the part in an unusually (for him) restrained fashion, keeping the film from toppling into campy indulgence. The performance exemplifies why Slaughter was so popular with British audiences; his unique brand of controlled histrionics made him as uniquely European as Boris Karloff or Bela Lugosi, though he never made his way to the greener pastures of Hollywood.

The only other actors in the film with a modicum of talent are D.J. Williams, who is entirely believable as the elder Trimble, and Eric Portman as the younger Matthew. Apart from a brief attempt at a film career in 1920, Williams came to acting late with the 1933 film *The Roof*. From that point until the mid-1940s, he made a career of playing essential bit parts as benevolent old men. Portman, on the other hand, was only just beginning his career at this point. He'd played a heroic role similar to the one in *Hawke* in the aforementioned *Maria Marten, or The Murder in the Red Barn*, but things didn't really take off for him until the late 1930s and early 1940s, when he hit his groove playing rugged leading man in numerous British pictures. Later in life he was a fixture on British television, remaining so until his death from a heart ailment in Cornwall, England in 1969.

The film's only other performance of note (though not in a positive sense) is that of former stage actress Marjorie Taylor as Julia Hawke. Taylor's indefinable ability to make every line

sound straight from a cue card should have doomed her career long before *Hawke*, yet for some reason King continued giving her lead roles in Slaughter's films, with this being her first and 1939's *The Face at the Window* her last. Set beside Portman's young Trimble, she comes across as remarkably dour and unappealing; nor is she particularly beautiful, leaving one to wonder just why so many men are after her hand in marriage.

Still, Philip Bawcombe's art direction is sparse but beautiful, particularly the design of the rooftop set from which Hawke falls to his death, a location which foreshadows the climax of Terence Fisher's groundbreaking *The Curse of Frankenstein* (1957). Graced with Oscar-nominated Ronald Neame's cinematography and King's vigorous direction, *The Crimes of Stephen Hawke* makes its faults digestible and emerges as a tidy little horror thriller.

Slaughter's next film was the straightforward drama *Darby and Joan* (1937), before returning to the genre that made him famous with *Never Too Late to Mend* (1937). CW

Death from a Distance
Invincible; b/w; 68 min; U.S.
D: Frank R. Strayer *S:* John W. Krafft *P:* Maury M. Cohen *C:* M.A. Andersen *M:* Sidney Cutner *FX:* Jack Cosgrove
Cast: Russell Hopton, Lola Lane, George F. Marion, Lee Kohlmar, John St. Polis, Lew Kelly, E.H. Calvert, Wheeler Oakman, Robert Frazer, Cornelius Keefe, John Davidson, John Dilson

A man is killed during the course of a lecture at a planetarium. Various people are under suspicion, and it's up to Detective Ted Mallory (Hopton) to uncover the truth. All too predictably, he does.

Prolific journeyman Frank R. Strayer (*The Vampire Bat*, 1933) was responsible for this low-budget potboiler. Its confused and confusing screenplay mixes mystery, romance, humor, sci-fi and a dash of the macabre, all to little effect. And while a more inspired director may have managed to make the script's many unlikelihoods forgivable or at least digestible, Strayer is simply not up to the task, smothering the film's action with static camera work while losing track of dialogue too pointlessly verbose to sustain interest.

Russell Hopton, a character actor who usually played much smaller roles, heads the cast. His most notable turn was that of a shifty chauffeur in Universal's much more flavorful whodunit *The Secret of the Blue Room* (1933). Here his role is pure cliché: a tough talking detective with a soft spot for the irritating female reporter (Lane) who nearly wrecks his entire investigation.

Horror buffs will also recognize Robert Frazer (*White Zombie*, 1932), whose surname is misspelled in the opening cast list as Frazier. TH

The Devil Doll
aka **The Witch of Timbuctoo**; **Devil Doll**; **The Devil-Doll**
MGM; b/w; 78 min; U.S.
D/Co-P: Tod Browning *S:* Garrett Fort, Guy Endore, Erich Von Stroheim, Richard Schayer (uncredited) *Co-P:* E.J. Mannix *C:* Leonard Smith *M:* Franz Waxman
Cast: Lionel Barrymore, Maureen O'Sullivan, Frank Lawton, Rafaela Ottiano, Robert Greig, Lucy Beaumont, Henry B. Walthall, Pedro de Cordoba, Arthur Hohl, Grace Ford, Juanita Quigley, Claire Du Brey, E. Alyn Warren

Paul Lavond (Barrymore) is framed by business associates (Greig, de Cordoba, Hohl) for murder and sentenced to life in prison. Seventeen years later he and cellmate Marcel (Walthall) escape, and the two hide out in Marcel's secluded cottage with household servant Malita (Ottiano). Marcel then reveals that he has developed a technique for shrinking humans, and this gives Lavond an idea for revenge against those who framed him.

Initially conceived as a lurid tale of voodoo and mutilation, *The Devil Doll* was softened considerably during production, its makers cowed by the anti-horror forces then gathering steam in the United States and Great Britain. Adapted by an eclectic group of screenwriters (including Erich Von Stroheim) from Abraham Merritt's 1932 novel *Burn, Witch, Burn!* (no relation to the identically titled 1960 film, which was an adaptation of Fritz Leiber's novel *Conjure Wife*), *Devil Doll* marks the final horror excursion of Tod Browning, whose career had been nearly destroyed by the disastrous reception of *Freaks* (1932) and who, despite an attempt to bounce back with *Mark of the Vampire* (1935, itself a remake of one of his silent hits, *London After Midnight*, 1927), was past his prime at the box-office.

As originally envisioned, *Doll* might well have garnered some controversy (and ticket sales), but the emasculated final product has little impact. Its gentility of approach results in a

Director Tod Browning on the set of *The Devil Doll* with star Lionel Barrymore

film more fantasy than horror. There's also an air of staleness to the proceedings, which play very much like a talking rehash of the director's silent triumph *The Unholy Three* (1925). In both films, the male protagonists (Lionel Barrymore here, Lon Chaney in the former) cross-dress to elude capture by the police. Each opens a store as a cover, and each uses his disguise to access unsuspecting households (Barrymore to take vengeance; Chaney for burglary).

That *Doll* works as well as it does—and it *is*, taken on its own, a decent piece of entertainment—is due less to its script than its innovative effects work (which goes uncredited on the release print) and also, in large part, to Barrymore's portrayal of Lavond as not merely villain but also loving father. (The scenes in which he attempts to talk to his estranged daughter, an equally excellent Maureen O'Sullivan, are genuinely touching.)

In addition to its then-sophisticated application of split screen and rear projection, Browning makes great use of oversized props to sell the idea of shrunken human beings. Precisely why mad scientist Marcel, played by Henry B. Walthall (*The Avenging Conscience, or: Thou Shalt Not Kill*, 1914; this was his final film) is experimenting with shrinking people in the first place is never clearly explained—it seems to have something to do with conserving food—but it does set up an ingenious way for Lavond to get his revenge.

Ultimately, though, one senses that too many disparate writers (with too few fresh ideas) had their hands on the enterprise. It doesn't come together very well, and it was with this production that Browning's career went into its final tailspin. His earlier successes irreparably eclipsed, he directed only one more film, the comedic mystery *Miracles for Sale* (1939), before being forced into retirement. He spent his final years resentful at Hollywood, distancing himself from the industry as well as the occasional fan who sought him out. He moved to Malibu in 1942 with his beloved wife, and when she passed away in 1944, *Variety* mistakenly eulogized him as well. (Given his dark sense of humor, Browning no doubt derived amusement from the error.) He died in 1962 from lung cancer, the same ailment that had killed his long-time collaborator Lon Chaney. Contemporary critics have tended to savage his oeuvre, but this is based more on the backlash against *Dracula* (1931)—which *was* something of a botched job, albeit an interesting one—than on any intelligent, comprehensive study of his work as a whole. TH

Dracula's Daughter
aka Daughter of Dracula
Universal; b/w; 71 min; U.S.

D: Lambert Hillyer S: Garrett Fort, John L. Balderston P: E.M. Asher C: George Robinson M: Heinz Roemheld FX: John Fulton

Cast: Gloria Holden, Otto Kruger, Marguerite Churchill, Edward Van Sloan, Gilbert Emery, Irving Pichel, Halliwell Hobbs, Billy Bevan, Nan Grey, Hedda Hopper, Claud Allister, Edgar Norton, E.E. Clive

When Bram Stoker submitted his famous epistolary novel *Dracula* (1897), his publisher deemed it too long and forced him to cut a chapter. That chapter, most likely the first, was released as the lead tale in a collection called *Dracula's Guest and Other Weird Stories*, published in 1914, two years after the author's death. *Guest* dealt with an unnamed narrator (presumably Jonathan Harker) who, somewhere near Munich on the day of *Walpurgisnacht*, leaves his hotel for what begins as a pleasant coach ride in the country. But when the narrator spies a side road on which he'd like to travel, the coachman refuses to go down it, insisting that the village at its end has long been deserted because its dead are not dead. The narrator pooh-poohs the driver and walks the road on his own. Several hours into his trek a snowstorm blows in, and the freezing cold and the sound of baying wolves prompts him to seek shelter in a nearby graveyard. The snow turns to hail, and he takes refuge in the tomb of a Styrian countess who committed suicide in 1801. Sleeping on a bier within is a beautiful woman with "rounded cheeks and red lips." A flash of lightning and accompanying thunderclap awaken the woman, and she screams. But before she can endanger the narrator, he is pulled from the tomb by what he later learns is a giant wolf. Unconscious, he is discovered by a group of men who have been out searching for him. He's taken back to his hotel, where he's shown a telegram from his future host Dracula, directing the hotel proprietor to ensure his safety and, should he be lost, to spare no effort or expense in finding him.

Realizing what the success of *Dracula* (1931) might do for an adaptation of *Dracula's Guest*, MGM producer David O. Selznick approached Stoker's widow Florence in 1933 with an offer to buy the rights. She sold them, but since Universal already owned the rights to the novel *Dracula* (and continued to until the novel fell into the public domain in 1960), including all the characters therein, Selznick's contract stipulated that any

MGM adaptation of *Guest* could not contain or reference any of *Dracula*'s cast.

Yet, despite the legalities, John L. Balderston (co-scenarist of both *Dracula* and *Frankenstein*) crafted a screenplay that included Van Helsing as a central character. Picking up pretty much where the film *Dracula* left off, the script has the wise doctor in Transylvania, where he destroys Dracula's three brides but overlooks the tomb of a fourth vampire … Dracula's daughter. Bent on revenge, the countess follows Van Helsing back to London and there victimizes an upper-class gentleman, after which Van Helsing and the man's bride try to find and destroy her. The script made much of the vampire woman's myriad (though all hetero) sexual perversions. Her home was replete with chains and whips, and her male victims were bound and degraded before being drained of blood—to their none-too-subtle enjoyment.

In 1935, Universal Pictures released *The Bride of Frankenstein*, the long-awaited sequel to their smash hit *Frankenstein*. When the returns started coming in and it was obvious that *Bride* was a resounding success, Carl Laemmle, Jr. had a brainstorm to make a sequel to *Dracula* as well. He offered the property to James Whale, who had directed both *Frankenstein* and *The Bride of Frankenstein*. Whale agreed, but only on the condition that Universal purchase the rights to *The Hangover Murders*, a novel by Adam Hobhouse, for him to adapt. The studio duly bought the rights, but once Whale completed the film adaptation—retitled *Remember Last Night* (because Joseph Breen, the head of the Production Code of America, forbade the use of the word "hangover") in September of 1935, he apparently reneged on his part of the bargain. (Some sources have suggested that Whale's treatment for *Dracula*'s sequel was so outlandish that Universal turned it down. While possible—and fun to think about—there's little evidence that this was the case.)

The same month that Whale finished *Remember Last Night*, Universal purchased the rights to *Dracula's Guest* (along with those of Balderston's MGM script) directly from Selznick for $12,500. They enlisted R.C. Sherriff, who had done the screenplay for James Whale's *The Invisible Man* (1933), to give it a major overhaul. The resulting script begins its tale in 1400s Transylvania, referencing the historical personage on whom Dracula is based before moving on to contemporary times and a visit by two couples to the wilds of the Carpathian Mountains. The two male members of the group explore Dracula's castle. One becomes insane, the other disappears, and Professor Van Helsing is enlisted to discern the missing man's whereabouts. The missing man is eventually found to be the slave of a countess … Dracula's daughter.

The British Board of Film Censors deemed that script unacceptable, and a further revision from Sherriff, while approved in Great Britain, met resistance from the U.S. Production Code. His subsequent attempts were likewise deemed unacceptable, and by January of 1936, screenwriting chores were in the hands of Garrett Fort, who had contributed to *On Time* (1924), *Dracula*, *Frankenstein* and the 1934 Boris Karloff vehicle *The Lost Patrol*. (His later credits include Tod Browning's 1936 *The Devil Doll* and the 1941 Paramount horror film *Among the Living*.)

Fort was a devotee of the Indian guru Meher Baba, and in 1937, after *Daughter*, he followed Baba to India in hopes of crafting a script about the spiritual guide's life. When that script failed to coalesce, Fort returned to the United States and resumed writing scripts for major Hollywood films. Despite his success as a writer, he died penniless in a hotel room in 1945, possibly of suicide (he overdosed on sleeping pills). His script for *Dracula's Daughter* draws upon some of the general ideas present in Balderston's original screenplay, though much of what was explicitly heterosexual in that version became implicitly homosexual, with the countess primarily a predator of beautiful young women.

The lesbian subtext of the script was not lost on the Breen office, which adamantly insisted that the film excise one particular depiction of "perverse sexual desire" in which the countess attacks a female model. The implication that the model was nude had to go, and lest anyone still entertain the idea that she had been attacked sexually, it was decreed that the character was to be immediately admitted to a hospital, where it would be "definitely established that she has been attacked by a vampire." ("And not a lesbian one, either" was, while not stated, doubtless understood.)

With James Whale categorically off the project due to his work on *Showboat* (1936), Universal assigned the picture to A. Edward Sutherland, who, though most of his films were comedies, was no stranger to horror. In fact, he was responsible for such tight little B pictures as *Secrets of the French Police* (1932) and *Murders in the Zoo* (1933). His contract for *Daughter* stipulated that he would be paid whether or not he actually wound up directing the picture, and after numerous delays (due mostly to script issues), he moved on (somewhat richer, one assumes) to do the W.C. Fields Paramount vehicle *Poppy* (1936).

Universal settled on Lambert Hillyer to take over. Hillyer is best known as a director of quick and efficient B-Westerns, though he also ended up directing the third film co-starring Boris Karloff and Bela Lugosi, *The Invisible Ray* (1936), and then, in 1943, the first live-action serial version of *Batman* (1943), based on the famous D.C. Comics character.

Originally slated to star in *Daughter* were Bela Lugosi, Jane Wyman, Boris Karloff, Cesar Romero, Colin Clive and Herbert Marshall. But by the time the film went before the cameras—in February of 1936 and still without a finished script—the cast list had changed considerably, with Lugosi now absent (though he made public appearances for the film and apparently modeled for a wax figure that made it into the final product) and Wyman, Karloff and Clive nowhere to be seen. Replacing Romero as Dr. Garth was reliable standby Otto Kruger, and in Marshall's stead as Sandor was director Irving Pichel (who co-helmed such horror entries as *The Most Dangerous Game*, 1932, and *She*, 1935). Returning for the role of Van Helsing (inexplicably renamed Von Helsing) was Edward Van Sloan.

Gloria Holden takes on her first major starring role in *Daughter* as the Countess Marya Zaleska. She went on to appear in such acclaimed films as *The Life of Emile Zola* and *The Man Without a Country* (both 1937). She also played the heroine's aunt in the Errol Flynn epic *Dodge City* (1939). And she is, it must be said, perfect here. Though alleged to have hated the role, she brings a sophisticated, alluring and appropriately butch air to her part. Make-up artist Jack Pierce pinned her hair back and painted her face in greenish make-up that made her

Countess Zaleska (Gloria Holden) exorcises her father's body in an attempt to rid herself of vampirism, in *Dracula's Daughter*.

skin look suitably colorless when shot on black-and-white film. Decked out in outfits that play down her ample bosom, she's every bit the aristocratic, rapacious lesbian that her character is written to be. Yet she's a sympathetic monster, one who deplores and seeks to overcome her baser inclinations. Holden's facial expressions reveal the character's inner turmoil; her rarely blinking, wide-open eyes and consistently upturned forehead betray her longing for help.

The film begins in the bowels of Carfax Abbey, where two Whitby police officers happen upon the dead body of Renfield. They encounter Professor Von Helsing (Sloan), who tells them that there is another body, that of the infamous Count Dracula (Lugosi's wax double) in the next room. With Dracula's staking considered murder under the law, Von Helsing is carted off to Scotland Yard and the two bodies to a local jail for safekeeping. Von Helsing asks for the assistance of one of his students, Dr. Garth (Kruger), to defend him at trial; while Dracula's body is stolen from the jail by a mysterious woman (Holden) with a hypnotic ring.

That woman, it's soon revealed, is Dracula's daughter, who has come to destroy the body of her father in a ritualistic attempt to be freed from her own vampirism. (The scene in which she consigns Dracula's body to flames while she and assistant Sandor perform the rites of exorcism is astoundingly beautiful.) Unfortunately, the rite does nothing to lessen her desires, and when next we see her, she is in London posing as Countess Marya Zaleska. She meets Dr. Garth at a party, where he tells her that psychiatry can cure even the most deviant mental

Countess Zaleska and Dr. Garth (Otto Kruger) vie for the body of his secretary (Marguerite Churchill) in *Dracula's Daughter*.

illness. Zaleska is intrigued by this and confesses to Dr. Garth that she suffers from a terrible malady. His advice is for her to meet her craving head on and defeat it. An attempt to do so results in the murder of a young Chelsea woman (Grey). At length, Garth comes to suspect the truth about the countess, and when his secretary (Churchill) is kidnapped, he follows Zaleska to her father's castle in Transylvania. There the villagers spy a light in the vampire's castle and bar themselves in their homes in terror. Garth confronts Zaleska, while Von Helsing and the police arrive to take out Sandor.

Charles D. Hall's sets are impressive, to say the least. Whether redressing those from the original *Dracula* and *Frankenstein*, or creating new ones (the moors upon which Dracula is set alight or the castle overlooking the eastern European village), he uses one of Universal's biggest budgets of that year to create a Gothic world thoroughly in keeping with the most classic of the company's output.

The most widely noted (and disputed) aspect of *Dracula's Daughter* is the above-noted, barely-veiled lesbianism of its title character. There's no doubt both that it's there and that Universal knew it when it cooked up the film's tag line, "Save the women of London from Dracula's Daughter!" When Zaleska has the model Lili pose for her, she gets the girl to remove her blouse and stares transfixed at the girl's breasts. Some maintain that it's Lili's neck at which the countess is looking, but necks aren't that low.

Actually, it takes a conscious effort to *not* read the film as an anti-homosexual diatribe (though a masterfully constructed and extremely engaging one) in which Zaleska's lesbian nature is coded as vampirism. That she makes women swoon is obvious from the moment Lady Esme Hammond (gossip columnist Hedda Hopper in a small role) first mentions her name to Dr. Garth (and in a telling detail, the countess' favorite pastime, portraiture, centers solely around female subjects). Zaleska desperately wants rid of her vampiric/homosexual inclinations and turns to the then-new science of psychiatry (which, in the 1930s, was just beginning to view homosexuality as a curable mental condition) to end her vexation. When Dr. Garth learns the truth about her, he is disgusted, a common reaction toward gays during that period.

The film is a cult classic among horror aficionados, whether gay, lesbian or straight. It's easy to see why; it is both well written and superbly crafted. Despite the occasional token nod to bumbling bobbies, comic butlers and Churchill's annoying secretary, *Dracula's Daughter* is a masterpiece of 1930s horror, an early entry in the lesbian vampire subgenre later successfully revisited by Roger Vadim's *Blood and Roses* (1960) and Roy Ward Baker's *The Vampire Lovers* (1970), among many, many others. CW

A Face in the Fog
Victory; b/w; 60 min; U.S.

D: Robert F. Hill *S:* Al Martin *P:* Sam Katzman *C:* William Hyer

Cast: June Collyer, Lloyd Hughes, Lawrence Gray, Jack Mulhall, Al St. John, John Cowell, John Elliott, Sam Flint, Forest Taylor, George Ball Trio

A misshapen killer known as "The Fiend" terrorizes members of a theater company. Newspaper reporter Jean Monroe (Collyer) catches a glimpse of the killer, putting her own life in danger. It's up to Jean and co-reporter Frank Gordon (Hughes), who also happens to be Jean's lover, to unmask the killer before it's too late.

Producer Sam Katzman (1901-1973) has something of a following among bad movie aficionados. He entered the film industry as a prop boy in 1914 (at age 13) and by the 1930s was a producer. His tightness with budgets was exceeded only by his relentless drive to get things done on time, regardless of quality. He spent the 1940s encamped at famed Poverty Row outfit Monogram Pictures, where he produced a number of grade-Z horror potboilers that occasionally starred the likes of Bela Lugosi, John Carradine and George Zucco.

Katzman wasn't too concerned with quality, but he knew what the public liked and managed to churn out a lot of it, even if it left critics scratching their heads (or turning up their noses) over the results. *A Face in the Fog* is an early example of the Katzman horror formula. It offers up a promising title ... and little else. There are admittedly faces aplenty, but no fog, as Katzman presents the audience with a tired horror-mystery—and little in the way of atmosphere, vaporous or otherwise.

Nor does the disposable cast make much of an impression. Leading lady June Collyer kicks things off with what may be the most half-hearted scream in cinema history. (Was she afraid of waking the neighbors?) She doesn't improve as the film unfolds, coming off as whiny and helpless and in the process engendering little in the way of audience sympathy. Lloyd Hughes plays her stalwart beau, a long way from his earlier success in *The Lost World* (1925). Comedic relief—really, Sam, you shouldn't have!—is provided by Al St. John, a Mack Sennett veteran whose shtick gets old really, really, *really* quick.

Production values are on a par with Katzman's later work (that is to say, almost non-existent), and the cinematography holds itself to the same standard. Canadian Director Robert F. Hill had previously worked on the screenplays for *The Adventures of Tarzan* (1921), Paul Leni's *The Cat and the Canary* (1927) and Leni's *The Last Warning* (1929). Judging by *A Face in the Fog*, Hill should have stuck to his typewriter. TH

Ferryman Maria
aka **Death and the Maiden**; **Fährmann Maria**
Pallas/Terra Filmkunst; b/w; 85 min; Germany

D/Co-S: Frank Wisbar *Co-S:* Hans Jurgen Nierentz *C:* Franz Weihmayr *M:* Herbert Windt

Cast: Sybille Schmitz, Aribert Mog, Carl de Vogt, Peter Voss, Gerhard Bienert, Eduard Wenck, Karl Platen, Ernst Stimmel, Mimi Thoma

After a ferryman (Platen) dies, his daughter Maria (Schmitz) takes over his post. One foggy night she gives a ride to a wounded man (Mog), and things take an unexpected turn when Death (Voss) comes to claim him.

Born Franz Wysbar in East Prussia (now Russia) in 1899, director Frank Wisbar entered films in 1932. *Ferryman Maria* is both his first really notable credit and his most consistently successful picture. He left Germany for Hollywood in 1939 and there established himself as an efficient craftsman. He directed two intermittently stylish B-horrors in the 1940s—*Strangler of the Swamp* (1946), a vaguely disguised remake of this picture, and *The Devil Bat's Daughter* (1946)—before moving into the then-burgeoning medium of television. Later, back in Germany, he directed several features and television films. He died in 1967.

Ferryman Maria attracted a lot of notice due to its striking visual sensibility, an outgrowth of Wisbar's interest in Expressionism; its dreamlike tone and atmosphere have been compared to that of Carl Theodor Dreyer's *Vampyr* (1932). Interestingly, these two films also share a cast member: Sybille Schmitz—who plays the enigmatic Leone in Dreyer's masterpiece and a title character here. Death is portrayed by Peter Voss, who appeared in the same year's *The Hound of the Baskervilles* as Sir Henry Baskerville.

The theme of a weary Death coming to collect a soul informs such notable titles as Fritz Lang's *Destiny* (1921) and Ingmar Berman's *The Seventh Seal* (1957). Alternate title *Death and the Maiden* bears no relation (or resemblance) to Roman Polanski's 1994 film of the same title. TH

Ghost Patrol
Excelsior; b/w; 56 (60) min; U.S.

D: Sam Newfield *S:* Wyndham Gittens *P:* Sigmund Neufeld, Leslie Simmonds *C:* Jack Greenhalgh

Cast: Tim McCoy, Claudia Dell, Walter Miller, Wheeler Oakman, Jimmy Burtis, Lloyd Ingraham, Dick Curtis

A pilot volunteers to fly a mail plane across the Shiloh Mountains in an effort to learn why there are so many crashes there. It turns out that a group of outlaws, led by the vicious Kincaid (Oakman), are using a kidnapped professor's (Ingraham) newly invented ray (actually swiped by him, one suspects, from the lab set of *Frankenstein*, 1931) to bring planes down and rob them of their goodies. Meanwhile, the professor's daughter Natalie (Dell), while pursuing her apparent hobby of compar-

Tim McCoy stars in yet another oater, this time with horror leanings, in *Ghost Patrol*.

ing newspaper clippings, discerns that it must be her father's ray that is causing the planes to crash. Using this insight as a springboard to chase down her old man, she luckily runs into cowboy Tim Caverly (McCoy) who, since he's working undercover for the Department of Justice, joins in her investigation. He cleverly pretends to be a famous criminal, also named Tim, and Kincaid's men, fooled by the ruse, take him into their trust. Tim and Natalie develop a love/hate relationship that ends happily, but only after Tim apprehends the men responsible for her father's kidnapping.

Ghost Patrol is another unintentional hoot from the brothers Neufeld, director Sam (under the pseudonym Newfield) and producer Sigmund, who specialized in just this sort of cheapie entertainment in the 1930s. Despite their guidance, Tim McCoy has a difficult time conveying any trace of emotion from beneath a cowboy hat so large that it threatens to engulf his entire head. Claudia Dell as the heroine fares a little better, though the script hardly does her acting ability justice.

The film's soundtrack seems to have garnered the most complaints from viewers/critics, perhaps because of the deafening sound the ray makes whenever it's in use (thank you, sound recordist Hans Weeren); counterproductively, it jolts one out of the pleasant nap brought on by the scenes between its appearances.

An expert in Native American folklore and sign language, Tim McCoy (1891-1978) was a leading actor in low-budget Westerns of this period. When his film career ended in the early 1950s, he hosted an Emmy-winning television program in which he taught children about history. Lloyd Ingraham, who portrays the kidnapped scientist, was a silent-film director (*The Fox Woman*, 1915) and actor (*The Midnight Warning*, 1932) who worked until 1950, six years before his death from pneumonia. Claudia Dell began her career at Warner in lead roles but petered out as the decade wore on; by the time of her last film, *Meeting at Midnight* in 1944, she was doing bit parts. While no records remain to verify this, she is believed to have been the original model for Columbia's famous logo, a fact brought to light by Bette Davis in her 1962 autobiography. CW

Hell-A-Vision
aka **Hell-O-Vision; Hellavision**
Sonney; b/w; 58 min; U.S.

D/S/P: Louis Sonney
Cast: unknown

Hell-A-Vision is a pseudo-documentary about the torments of hell, making heavy use of clips from *Inferno* (1911). An obscure oddity, it was the work of writer/producer/editor/director Louis Sonney, who was born in Italy and later immigrated to the United States. His greatest claim to fame came in 1921 when, employed as a police officer, he apprehended Roy Gardener, the so-called "smiling bandit" train robber.

He wasn't above bending the law himself, however. While a policeman, Sonney also ran a racy burlesque show on the carnival circuit. He entered cinema as a producer for the notorious exploitation filmmaker Dwain Esper, producing Esper's indescribable *Maniac* (1934) before branching off to capitalize on his own notoriety. His *You Can't Beat the Rap* (1934) provided a sensationalized portrait of how crime doesn't pay, using his arrest of Gardener to drive home the point.

Hell-A-Vision was an ambitious follow-up—ambitious on paper, that is, as the film itself was a slipshod, bargain-basement take on the terrors of hell. It's a mixture of pilfered scenes from one of the many silent versions of Dante's *Inferno* and fresh footage including risqué dashes of nudity. By way of exemplifying the souls of the damned, Sonney also works in images of John Dillinger and, you guessed it, Roy Gardener. The end result is only tenuously horror, but its low production values, preachy tone and exploitative approach make it an extremely weird example of 1930s cinema nonetheless. TH

The Hound of the Baskervilles
aka **Der Hund von Baskerville**
Ondra/Lamac; b/w; 76 min; Germany

D/Co-P: Carl Lamac *S:* Carla von Stackelberg *Co-P:* Anny Ondra, Robert Leistenschneider *C:* Willy Winterstein *M:* Paul Huhn

Cast: Bruno Guttner, Fritz Odemar, Peter Voss, Alice Brandt, Erich Ponto, Ernst Rotmund, Fritz Rasp, Lili Schoenborn-Anspach, Friedrich Kayssler, Gertude Wolle, Artur Malkowsky, Klaus Pohl, Ilka Thimm, Hanna Waag, Ernst Albert Schaach

When Lord Charles Baskerville (Kayssler) is found dead on the moors, Dr. Mortimer (Rotmund) calls upon Sherlock Holmes (Guttner) and Dr. Watson (Odemar) to investigate. Holmes dismisses the possibility of the supernatural, despite Mortimer's assertions that the Hound of the Baskervilles, which has haunted the family's estate since the days of the nefarious Lord Hugo Baskerville (Malkowsky), is responsible for Lord Charles' death. Mortimer also fears that newly arrived heir Lord Henry Baskerville (Voss) is in danger, to which Holmes agrees. Holmes sends Watson to accompany Lord Henry to Baskerville Hall, where additional mysterious events transpire.

Sir Arthur Conan Doyle's most popular Sherlock Holmes mystery gets yet another go-round in this obscure German adaptation. The film adheres somewhat faithfully to the text, though the hound's origins are explained differently than in the original tale; here the canine is the faithful companion of Lord Hugo's wife but becomes a menace when Hugo jealously strangles its mistress.

Interestingly, the filmmakers delay the arrival of Holmes for almost a half hour, taking care first to establish the atmosphere of Baskerville Hall and to provide a lengthy flashback of the death of Lord Hugo many years before. The decision works to the good, since Bruno Guttner proves to be one of the least inspiring interpreters of Holmes to date. While his hawk-like visage and lean frame give him the right look for the role, his performance is dull and colorless. Records from the time indicate that this was the last of only three credited screen appearances by the actor, and if his performance here is any indication of his talent, his short filmography is no surprise.

Also atypically, more screen time and greater emphasis is given to the character of Watson, and fortunately Fritz Odemar is just fine in the role. Odemar's interpretation is faithful to Doyle's conception of the character as a loyal, quick-witted and able-bodied man of science, which is to say that he contrasts mightily with the buffoon image popularized by Nigel Bruce in the Fox—and later, Universal—films starring Basil Rathbone as the great detective. The supporting cast is mostly nondescript, though Fritz Rasp (*Metropolis*, 1927) makes the most of his odd good guy role as the concerned servant Barrymore.

Problems with the cast aside, there's a lot to admire in the film's strong visual style. Director Carl Lamac makes excellent use of shadowy lighting and gliding camerawork to establish a nice tone of gloom, with the scenes on the moors particularly well photographed. Paul Huhn's score utilizes classical motifs and adds to the suspense, while Willy Winterstein's cinematography is accomplished throughout.

As with so many other cinematic versions of the story, however, the film stumbles badly when the hound itself shows up. The finale, where Holmes and Watson shoot the hound as it lunges at Lord Henry, is particularly risible due to an insert shot of a patently phony hound with exaggerated features.

Ultimately, the film is among neither the best nor the worst adaptations of the novel. The next screen version came in 1939, establishing Rathbone and Bruce as the big screen's most beloved interpreters of Doyle's characters. TH

The House of Secrets
aka **House of Secrets**
Chesterfield; b/w; 69 min; U.S.

D: Roland R. Reed *S:* John Krafft *P:* George Batcheller *C:* M.A. Anderson

Cast: Leslie Fenton, Muriel Evans, Noel Madison, Sidney Blackmer, Morgan Wallace, Holmes Herbert, Ian Maclaren,

Jameson Thomas, Syd Saylor, Matty Fain, George Rosener, Matty Kemp

After saving an attractive blonde (Evans) from a letch on a cruise ship to England, Barry Wilding (Fenton) becomes intent on marrying her. It can't hurt his chances that he's recently inherited a lot of money as well as a beautiful estate known as The Hawk's Nest. But while visiting his newly acquired mansion, he discovers that squatters inhabit it, including the beautiful blonde with whom he's fallen in love, Julie Kenmore, and her father, a doctor. Julie warns Barry away, insisting that her father will kill him when he sees him, and he takes up residence at a local inn. His attempts at taking back his property are met with resistance from mysterious figures as well as Scotland Yard. Matters are further complicated by the house being reputedly haunted, which seems borne out by a series of bizarre incidents involving a maniac with a hyena-like laugh and a three-fingered murderer from Chicago. And as if all this wasn't enough, there are American gangsters running around and a parchment suggesting that a pirate's treasure is located somewhere on the estate grounds.

The House of Secrets is based on a novel by British author Sydney Horler, who had become popular with the release of his first crime novel, *The Mystery of No. 1*, in 1925. *The House of Secrets* was published the following year and proved more popular. It was adapted to the stage by Horler himself shortly after the novel's debut. The screen rights were snapped up by Chesterfield, who produced a talkie film adaptation in 1929. That version proved successful enough that the company revisited the story in 1936 with this charming if redundant remake. With the release of the second film, prints of the original were pulled from circulation and haven't been seen since, while the latter became a staple of early television before falling into the public domain and finding a new audience on home video. Today it is readily available in a number of formats.

Though shot in the United States (at RKO Studios in Los Angeles, California, to be precise), stock footage of British locales are so well integrated that the foreign *milieu* proves completely believable. With its surfeit of clutching hands and secret panels, John Krafft's breezy script balances the story's "old dark house" elements with gangster badness and government intrigue. Edward C. Jewell's art direction, particularly the Gothic estate and the creepy cave below it, milks the film for all the atmosphere it's worth, while Roland R. Reed's direction never stays on any one scene or shot too long. As a result, the film plays out like a Universal horror of the period rather than the ultra-low-budget production it actually is.

Weirdly enough, Reed had begun his film career as a director with the serialized *House of Terror* in 1928 before becoming a prolific editor on such films as *The Ghost Walks* (1934), *A Shot in the Dark*, *Circumstantial Evidence* and *Condemned to Live* (all 1935). He retired from editing in the late 1930s to return to directing but made only a few features before becoming a—mostly television—producer, a role he relished until the early 1960s. He died in 1972.

The House of Secrets presents solid performances from all involved, but especially from Minnesota-born Muriel Evans, who plays the part of the enigmatic Julie Kenmore with cool assurance. Too bad she never escaped Poverty Row and was relegated mostly to minor oaters. Tired of such roles, she retired from acting in 1940, though she lived until 2000. CW

The Invisible Ray
Universal; b/w; 80 min; U.S.

D: Lambert Hillyer *S:* John Colton *P:* Edmund Grainger *C:* George Robinson *M:* Franz Waxman *FX:* John P. Fulton

Cast: Boris Karloff, Bela Lugosi, Frances Drake, Frank Lawton, Violet Kemble Cooper, Walter Kingsford, Beulah Bondi, Frank Reicher, Paul Weigel, Georges Renavent

Dr. Janos Rukh (Karloff) discovers a new element while on expedition in Africa. Conducting an experiment with his discovery, he carelessly becomes contaminated. Apart from turning his skin phosphorescent, the mishap also has the regrettable side effect of rendering his touch fatal. He turns to old adversary Dr. Felix Benet (Lugosi) who, while able to concoct a temporary antidote, warns that the drug may prove dangerous to Rukh's mind.

Janos Rukh (Boris Karloff) says good-bye to his mother (Violet Kemble Cooper) at the conclusion of *The Invisible Ray*.

For this, the third pairing of Boris Karloff (billed here, as elsewhere, simply as KARLOFF) and Bela Lugosi, Universal turned to the realm of science fiction. It's likely that the growing controversy over the horror genre played into their decision, and there's little doubt that the final product reflects a squeamishness on the part of the studio. The abundance of special effects work ensured, however, that the finished film cost more than the previous two Karloff/Lugosi vehicles (*The Black Cat*, 1934; *The Raven*, 1935) combined. And while the end result is a strange mix of high Gothic melodrama and Saturday matinee sci-fi, the stranger thing still is that it actually comes together in a coherent and entertaining manner.

There's a perpetual feud among Karloff and Lugosi aficionados concerning who was the better actor. Given that Lugosi's career was so overshadowed by that of Karloff—Karloff commanded top billing, significantly higher salaries, greater acclaim and a generally happier and more successful life—it's perhaps not surprising that many of the Hungarian actor's ardent fans are somewhat dismissive toward his British "rival." But no matter which side of the fence one is on (assuming that one feels the need to take sides), *The Black Cat* is generally recognized as the film in which both actors shine equally (it starts off as Lugosi's film, develops for a while into Karloff's, and finally allows both to face off in an acting duel that brings out the best in each).

The lines are more clearly drawn in *The Raven* and *The Invisible Ray*, with Lugosi effortlessly dominating the former and Karloff holding court in the latter. The incongruity is that while Lugosi cultists find Lugosi's full throttle emoting in *The Raven* as an example of their idol "giving his all," these same critics are quick to criticize Karloff for being a hambone in *The Invisible Ray*. Karloff does admittedly go over the top in a few scenes (such as when he shouts, "Oh, you fiends! Fiends! Fiends!"), but he does not go over the top any more so than Lugosi does in the earlier film. In the final analysis, the performances of both actors in all three vehicles are essential to their quality. Take Lugosi out of *The Raven* and it ceases to work; take Karloff out of *The Invisible Ray* and it would likely be very dull. (Remove either from *The Black Cat* and it's gone.)

The screenplay for *The Invisible Ray* was by John Colton, based on an original story by Howard Higgin and Douglas Hodges. Colton had earlier written the script for Universal's *Werewolf of London* (1935), and his thematic leanings are worth a look. Both films have been criticized as being overly talky and lumbered with unsympathetic protagonists. While the former point may be fair enough, the latter most certainly is not. In common with Henry Hull's Dr. Glendon in *Werewolf*, Karloff's Dr. Rukh is a tunnel-visioned visionary. Neither man has much time for social pleasantries, and each is trapped in a marriage that seems to have arisen out of convenience rather than passion. Given that writer Colton was homosexual, it is tempting to read his lead characters as men who've been pressured into "normal" lives against their will and who lose themselves in their work in order to preserve their sanity. Karloff's portrayal of Rukh is nowhere near as cold and stodgy as Hull's as Glendon, but he still comes off as something of a neurotic momma's boy. The fact that he constantly turns to his mother (Cooper) for comfort and guidance underscores this.

While Karloff walked through some of his later mad scientist roles, one can hardly accuse him of being on autopilot this time out. With his curly black hair and mustache, he makes a strong physical impression. (It also helps that the costume department decided to bulk him up a bit.) Karloff brings his usual flair for pathos and nuance to bear, and the character's inability to relate to others is deliberately off-putting; he comes off as something of a crackpot long before he's been infected by his precious discovery.

As for Lugosi (who looks dapper with a mustache and goatee), the Hungarian actor is saddled with a less showy role, and he responds with one of his most naturalistic performances. Critics of Lugosi have long declared that he was a one-trick pony, an actor incapable of subtlety, but *The Invisible Ray* dispels such criticisms. While some of his stauncher fans have bemoaned the fact that he was forced to play second banana, such complaints show short sightedness. Lugosi's performance is warm, believable and sympathetic; it's precisely the kind of role the actor

Bela Lugosi (Dr. Benet) and Karloff are at odds once again in *The Invisible Ray*.

longed for, and it seems unlikely that he took umbrage at losing out on the bigger, juicier mad scientist role.

The supporting cast also turns in commendable performances. Lovely Frances Drake, who'd been menaced by Peter Lorre in *Mad Love* (1935), does what she can with the sketchy role of Rukh's wife. The script is too concerned with providing her with a younger, more conventionally handsome love interest (the bland Frank Lawton, who had appeared in Tod Browning's *The Devil Doll*, 1936, though he is best known as the adult incarnation of *David Copperfield*, 1935) and as such, she comes off as a bit of a tramp. But her soulful eyes and melancholy line delivery bring more substance to the role than exists in the script; such a talented actress deserved better development of her character.

Violet Kemble Cooper was unlikely casting as Karloff's mother—in reality she was only a year older than her onscreen son—but thanks in part to Jack Pierce's make-up, she makes a terrific impression. Walter Kingsford (*The Mystery of Edwin Drood*, 1935) and Beulah Bondi (*It's a Wonderful Life*, 1946) are also fine in their roles, though venerable character actor Frank Reicher (*King Kong*, 1933) is wasted.

Director Lambert Hillyer, a veteran of countless B-Westerns, does a good job with the material. Not long after this, he replaced James Whale and Edward Sutherland on the directing chores for *Dracula's Daughter*. He displays an understanding of the Gothic genre and, along with ace cinematographer George Robinson (*Son of Frankenstein*, 1939), creates some moody and atmospheric images. The pacing lags a bit in the middle, but this is due more to the script's episodic narrative structure than to anything in Hillyer's direction.

Franz Waxman's score quotes a couple of themes from his work on *The Bride of Frankenstein* (1935) but is otherwise mostly unique to this film. It certainly enhances the film's melancholy tone. And John P. Fulton's effects work is top-notch. Making Karloff "glow" involved painting each frame of film, but the end result was worth it.

As to the evidence of squeamishness alluded to above ... though a revenge-oriented film, the actual murders are kept entirely off screen, depicted instead via newspaper descriptions. Whether this was originally intended or the result of post-production tinkering is unclear, but it does result in a curiously sedate tone, as do the sequences of Karloff training his ray on religious icons (meant to symbolize the victims of his murderous rage). In any event, warts and all, *The Invisible Ray* is a worthy and stylish addition to Universal's canon of 1930s horror films. TH

Jaws of the Jungle
aka Jungle Virgin
Jay-Dee-Kay; b/w; 60 (27) min; U.S.

D/S: Eddie Granemann P: J.D. Kendis M: Johnny Lange, Lew Porter

Cast: Cliff Howell, Gukar, Minta, Teeto, Walla

Vampire bats terrorize a peaceful tribe in Sri Lanka.

This horror-tinged film purports to be a documentary, but writer/director Eddie Granemann's attempt to pass the work off as a record of actual events is shot down by the action being so poorly faked. Still, the footage of real-life bat attacks (mostly

on other jungle creatures) does at rare moments conjure a bit of frisson.

Jaws of the Jungle was later cut by more than half an hour and re-released as *Jungle Virgin*, but the more salacious-sounding title is a cheat; the exploitation here is purely of the violent variety, with no titillation (or even an actual virgin) to speak of. To top things off, Cliff Howell's melodramatic narration pushes the whole affair into camp.

This was the only directorial credit for Granemann, a screenwriter who specialized in B-grade Westerns. TH

Juggernaut
Hagen; b/w; 61 min; Great Britain

D: Henry Edwards S: Cyril Campion, H. Fowler Mear, Heinrich Fraenkel P: Edward L. Alperson, Julius Hagen C: Sydney Blythe, William Luff M: W.L. Trytel

Cast: Boris Karloff, Joan Wyndham, Arthur Margetson, Mona Goya, Anthony Ireland, Morton Selten, Nina Boucicault, Gibb McLaughlin, J.H. Roberts, Victor Rietti

Dr. Victor Sartorious (Karloff) has tried in vain to obtain funding for his research into a cure for paralysis. Reduced to earning his living as a country doctor in a French village, he harbors a hatred for those he considers responsible for his failure. When the duplicitous Lady Yvonne Clifford (Goya) offers him the money he needs, Sartorious is overjoyed. The only hitch is that getting the financial support involves hastening the demise of Lady Clifford's ailing, wealthy husband.

After *The Walking Dead* (1936), Boris Karloff made a sojourn to his native Britain to appear in two low-budget mad scientist flicks, *Juggernaut* and *The Man Who Changed His Mind* (both 1936). And while the latter is a stylish and slyly amusing romp, the former is, frankly, pretty rough going. Karloff skulks and glowers his way across the screen, working well below his capabilities yet still far and away the most interesting thing in the picture. His performance as the irresistibly named Dr. Victor Sartorious—an apparent play on the names Dr. Victor Frankenstein and Dr. Pretorious in *The Bride of Frankenstein* (1935)—is of the "cold fish" variety that later typified his work in horror cheapies of the 1940s and '50s.

But even a disinterested Karloff is miles ahead of Mona Goya as the faithless wife engineering the murder plot. Her overwrought performance borders on camp, but without any of camp's "so bad it's good" appeal; a scene in which she lashes out at her ailing husband, for instance, seems to go on for an eternity. The even less inspiring leading man is played by Arthur Margetson, who later matched his wits against Basil Rathbone in the brisk mystery-thriller *Sherlock Holmes Faces Death* (1943; it was a role that would incidentally prove to be his last).

Juggernaut director Henry Edwards was at this point winding down a remarkably undistinguished directorial career that stretched back to 1915. (*Juggernaut* is probably the best-known film in which he was involved.) He did continue to focus on his other undistinguished career—as an actor—until his death in 1952. TH

Killer at Large
aka **Killers on the Loose**
Columbia; b/w; 54 min; U.S.

D: David Selman *S:* Carl Clausen, Harold Shumate *C:* Allen G. Siegler

Cast: Mary Brian, Russell Hardie, George McKay, Thurston Hall, Henry Brandon, Betty Compson, Harry Hayden, Boyd Irwin, Lon Chaney, Jr., Roger Gray, Billy Arnold, Harry Bernard, Alma Chester, Beatrice Curtis, Rolf Ernest, Roger Gray, Brady Kline

Linda Allen (Brian) is a detective working in a local department store. She is engaged to store clerk Tommy Braddock (Hardie). The store devises a publicity ploy in which Mr. Zero (Brandon), a self-proclaimed master of disguise, poses as a mannequin in the window. The gimmick is simple: If the customer can guess which figure is Mr. Zero, they get a discount. Passersby are, of course, intrigued, and business picks up. But when some jewelry disappears and store manager William Bentley (Hayden) is found dead, Inspector O'Hara (Hall) is called in to investigate and decides almost immediately that Linda and Tommy are behind it all. In order to clear their names, the lovers launch an investigation of their own, which leads them to a creepy cemetery and other disagreeable locales.

Killer at Large is a fairly typical B-murder mystery with a horror element here and there. It is chiefly of note for an early appearance by Lon Chaney, Jr. in what is arguably his first horror role. His presence consists of a couple of scenes in which he appears as a hulking henchman involved in the goings-on at the cemetery. He went unbilled for his efforts.

Born Creighton Chaney in 1906, Lon, Jr. decided early on to follow in his famous father's footsteps (though the elder Chaney did everything in his power to discourage his son from pursuing such an uncertain profession). After the death of his father in 1930, Creighton entered film in earnest. He initially resisted producers' urgings to change his name to Lon Chaney, Jr. but eventually gave in. After years of unrewarding character work in films such as this one and *A Scream in the Night* (1935), he at last triumphed as the dimwitted Lenny in Lewis Milestone's film version of John Steinbeck's *Of Mice and Men* (1939). And with his title role in Universal's *The Wolf Man* (1941), icon status was bestowed. Pushed by Universal as the heir to aging horror giants Boris Karloff and Bela Lugosi, Chaney the younger was put through his paces as everything from the Frankenstein monster (*Ghost of Frankenstein*, 1942) to the king of the vampires (*Son of Dracula*, 1943). At his best in "regular Joe" parts, he seemed generally miscast in monster roles. Still, he remained associated with horror films for the remainder of his career. Plagued by personal demons, he was a full-fledged alcoholic by the time he ended his career in Z-grade schlock like *Dracula vs. Frankenstein* (1971). He died in 1973 at the age of 67.

Killer's supporting cast also includes a young Henry Brandon as Mr. Zero. Brandon went on to become a fixture in Westerns, his most notable appearance being as Scar in John Ford's classic *The Searchers* (1956). He also appeared in George Pal's *War of the Worlds* (1953) and John Carpenter's superior suspense thriller *Assault on Precinct 13* (1976).

At under an hour in length, *Killer at Large* can hardly be accused of overstaying its welcome. Briskly if unimaginatively staged by director David Selman, it emerges as an agreeable time killer. TH

Lash of the Penitentes
aka **The Penitente Murder Case; El asasenato de los Penitentes**
Price; b/w; 65 (38, 45, 58, 70) min; U.S.

Co-D/Co-S/Co-P/C: Roland Price *Co-D/Co-P:* Harry Revier *Co-S:* Zelma Carroll *M:* Lee Zahler

Cast: Marie DeForrest, William Marcos, Victor Justi, Josef Swickard, José Rubio, Billy Bletcher, Zelma Carroll

Based on a "true" story, *Lash of the Penitentes* concerns a filmmaker who steals into the wilds of New Mexico and secretly shoots the goings-on at a Penitente ceremony. Trouble ensues when he befriends a young Hispanic man named Chico (Marcos), who, unknown to him, is a member of the secretive group. In the end, Marcos kills the filmmaker for defiling sacred ground.

What makes *Lash* interesting—apart from (in its uncut version) its shocking scenes of violence and nudity—is the fact that much of it consists of real-life Penitente footage shot secretly by co-director Roger Price. The particular sect he filmed was called *Los hermanos penitentes* ('the penitent brothers'), members of which "purge their guilt" through self-mutilation, whipping and cutting themselves with various torture devices. Mostly of Spanish origin, the group exists to this day in remote regions of Mexico and the Southwestern United States (New Mexico, Arizona, and Colorado). Its worldview is akin to that of the Flagellants, who date from 1200s Italy. Though ostensibly of Catholic origin, such groups have been officially denounced by the Catholic hierarchy since at least the 1850s.

Because of its unabashed presentation of the real-life excesses of the Penitentes, *Lash* met with severe criticism at the time of its original release (and the fact that the film is just plain bad couldn't have helped any). It was heavily truncated in most of its several English re-release versions. The most complete of these, the Spanish-language *El asasenato de los Penitentes*, was released in Mexico and in Spanish-speaking areas in the United States, recalling the days when Universal would produce two versions of some of its films (including *The Cat Creeps*, 1930, and *Dracula*, 1931), one for English-speaking audiences, the other for Spanish-speaking audiences. Unlike those offerings, though, *Lash of the Penitentes* plays out as a Mondo film with horror asides. CW

The Legend of Prague
aka **Le Golem; The Golem; The Golem: The Legend of Prague; The Man of Stone**
AB; b/w; 95 min; France

D/Co-S: Julien Duvivier *Co-S:* Andre-Paul Antoine, Josef Kodicek *P:* Frank Kassler, Charles Philipp, Josef Stein *C:* Jan Stallich, Vaclav Vich *M:* Joseph Kumok

Cast: Harry Bauer, Charles Dorat, Jany Holt, Roger Karl, Germaine Aussey, Truda Grosslichtova, Julien Carette, Marcel Dalio, Raymond Aimos, Alfred Bastyr, Jan Cerny, Roger Duchesne, Ferdinand Hart, Gaston Jacquet, Frantisek Jerhot

The Jews of Prague are suffering under the tyranny of Emperor Rudolf II (Bauer), an avowed anti-Semite who forces them to live in squalor in a ghetto. Rabbi Jacob (Dorat), inspired by the story of Rabbi Loew and his infamous Golem, revives the creature (Hart) to defend his people.

Talk about bad timing! *The Legend of Prague*, a French sequel to Paul Wegener's *The Golem: How He Came Into the World* (1920), began production in Germany just as Nazism—and its accompanying anti-Semitism—was on the rise. In response to the pressure, the production was moved to Czechoslovakia (where the tale is set anyway).

Too bad the final result wasn't worth all the trouble. Under the direction of co-writer Julien Duvivier, *Prague* is pure pomp and circumstance. The first section is especially tough going for viewers expecting a horror tale. Duvivier spends *way* too much time detailing court intrigue, instead emphasizing pageantry and spectacle over mood and atmosphere. He seems so in love with the massive sets and lavish production values that he doesn't even try to craft a worthy follow-up to Wegener's Expressionist gem.

The film's only horror elements are worked into its climactic scenes, but when the Golem is—finally—revived, it's a pretty sorry sight. As Phil Hardy's *Overlook Film Encyclopedia: Horror* points out, the vengeful creation looks comically like a caped Mexican wrestler. (Picture Santo turned to stone, and you'll get the idea.) There's a splash of panache here and there—some near-nudity during a seduction scene; a gruesome close-up of the Golem smashing a head with his heavy foot—but it's way too little, far too late.

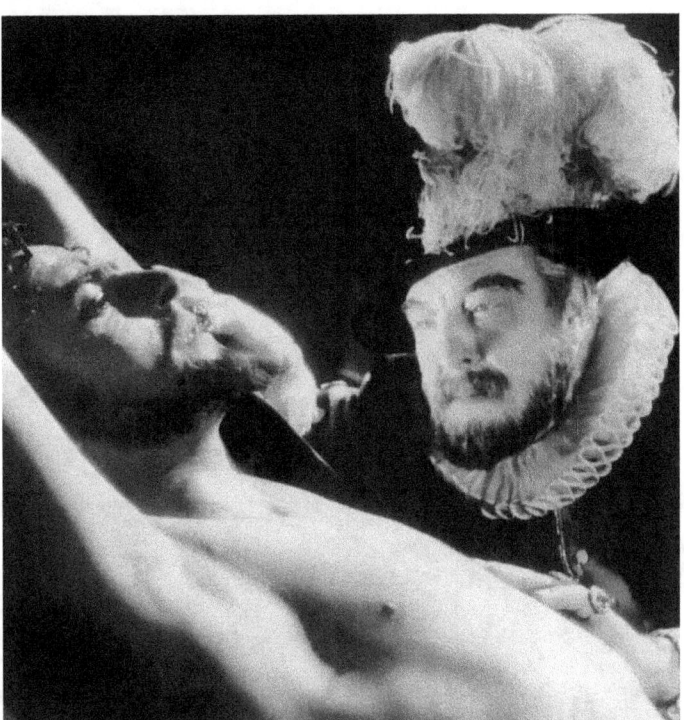

Emperor Rudolf II (Harry Bauer) tortures Jews in *The Legend of Prague.*

Shining like a diamond amid the ineptitude is an excellent performance by Harry Bauer as the despicable despot Emperor Rudolf II. Whether working himself into a petulant, childish rage or pathetically entreating the Golem to be his friend, Bauer's performance is pretty much the only thing that makes the film worth watching.

The story was revisited decades later with the British made cheapie *It!* (1967), starring Roddy McDowall. TH

The Macabre Trunk
aka **El baul macabre**
Produccions Pezet; b/w; 79 min; Mexico

D: Miguel Zacarias *S:* Alejandro Galindo *P:* Juan Pezet *C:* Alex Phillips *M:* Jorge M. Dada

Cast: Ramon Pereda, Rene Cardona, Esther Fernandez, Juanita Castro, Enrique Gonce, Manuel Noriega, Ruperto Batiz, Carlos Lopez, Victorio Blanco, Juan Garcia

Dr. Maximiliano Renan (Pereda) is desperately trying to cure his dying wife (Castro) by murdering a number of young women, whose blood he needs for his experiments.

Based on a screenstory by composer Jorge M. Dada (who also scored this film), *The Macabre Trunk* is one of Mexico's earliest horror pictures. Like even earlier entries *The Crying Woman* (1933) and *The Phantom of the Convent* (1934), *Trunk* mixes Expressionist imagery with a straight-faced approach to the fantastic. The backdrop of medical horror also anticipates such later genre fare as Riccardo Freda and Mario Bava's *I Vampiri* (1956) and Georges Franju's *Eyes Without a Face* (1959).

The cast includes future filmmaker Rene Cardona, who was then a young, personable leading man. While never achieving "major talent" status behind the camera, he did make such memorably over-the-top fare as *Night of the Bloody Apes* (1969), *Survive!* (1979) and a number of entries in the Santo and Blue

Demon masked-wrestler franchises. His best outing, *The Crying Woman* (1960), has no real connection to the 1933 Mexican horror film of the same title.

Cardona's son, Rene Cardona, Jr., went on to direct some schlock horror of his own, including the Jaws rip-off *Tintorera: Killer Shark* (1977) and *The Bermuda Triangle* (1978). Director Miguel Zacarias later switched to producing, finishing out his career with such absurdities as *The Bees* (1978) with John Saxon and John Carradine, and *Demonoid: Messenger of Death* (1981) with Stuart Whitman and Samantha Eggar. TH

The Man Behind the Mask
aka **Behind the Mask**
Joe Rock; b/w; 79 (58) min; Great Britain
 D: Michael Powell *S:* Sid Courtenay, Stanley Haynes, Ian Hay *P:* Joe Rock *C:* Ernest Palmer *M:* Cyril Ray
 Cast: Hugh Williams, Jane Baxter, Ronald Ward, Maurice Schwartz, George Merritt, Henry Oscar, Donald Calthrop, Kitty Kelly, Wilfrid Caithness, Peter Gawthorne, Gerald Fielding, Reginald Tate, Moira Fagan, Ivor Barnard

A young couple (Williams, Baxter) attends a masquerade ball. While there, things take a macabre turn when a mad scientist known as The Master (Schwartz) kidnaps the young woman.

This early directorial offering by Michael Powell reportedly melds horror, action and melodrama, but it remains a difficult film to see. Viewers who have done so nearly all report that its plot is incomprehensible, which shouldn't come as a surprise given that the original, uncut version is long gone, replaced by an abbreviated re-edit dating from just after World War II.

This same year, Powell helmed another quota quickie with horror elements, *The Phantom Light* (1936), but he wouldn't dive head first into the genre until *Peeping Tom* (1960). That film, though it kicked up a fuss that ruined his career, is now recognized as a psychologically complex, disturbed and disturbing horror classic.

The Man Behind the Mask showcases Hugh Williams, who co-starred with Bela Lugosi in the Edgar Wallace adaptation *The Dark Eyes of London* (1939). The supporting cast includes George Merritt (*Horror of Dracula*, 1958), Henry Oscar (*Brides of Dracula*, 1960) and Donald Calthrop (*The Man Who Changed His Mind*, 1936).

The British release title *Behind the Mask* should not be mistaken for the 1932 Boris Karloff vehicle of the same name. TH

The Man Who Changed His Mind
aka **The Man Who Lived Again**; **Dr. Maniac**; **The Brainsnatcher**; **Doctor Maniac Who Lived Again**
Gaumont-British; b/w; 62 min; Great Britain
 D: Robert Stevenson *S:* L. du Garde Peach, Sidney Gilliat, John L. Balderston *P:* Michael Balcon *C:* Jack Cox *M:* Louis Levy
 Cast: Boris Karloff, Anna Lee, John Loder, Frank Cellier, Donald Calthrop, Cecil Parker, Lyn Harding

Dr. Laurience (Karloff), a disgraced scientist experimenting with the transplantation of human memory, attracts the attention of newspaper magnate/philanthropist Lord Haselwood (Cellier). Haselwood offers to fund Laurience's experiments on the condition that his paper will have exclusive rights to report on his findings. Desperate for proper materials and money to work with, Laurience accepts. But when Haselwood hosts a gala event to unveil the doctor's research to the medical community, it is met with scoffs and indignation. A humiliated Laurience is forced to act quickly when Haselwood threatens to pull the plug on his experiments.

A precursor of sorts to the low-budget mad scientist vehicles Boris Karloff appeared in for Columbia Pictures in the late '30s and early '40s, the British-made *The Man Who Changed His Mind* boasts both a clever screenplay and efficient direction. The script is the work of L. du Garde Peach, Sidney Gilliat and John L. Balderston, who in tandem produce a tight science fiction story with some smart, original twists and turns. About Peach little is known; a perusal of his sparse screenwriting career reveals little of interest outside this film. However, the other two collaborators are a very different story. Balderston had a hand in many of the major genre films of the 1930s, contributing to *Dracula* and *Frankenstein* (both 1931), *The Mummy* (1932) and *The Bride of Frankenstein* and *Mad Love* (both 1935), among others. As for Gilliat, he would write one of Alfred Hitchcock's greatest British films, *The Lady Vanishes* (1938), before turning director and crafting the classic suspense thriller *Green for Danger* (1946).

In the hands of director Robert Stevenson (later Oscar-nominated for Disney's classic *Mary Poppins*, 1964), the film straddles the fine line between horror and science fiction with hardly a misstep to be found. There's not much mayhem as such, but Stevenson keeps things atmospheric with low-key lighting and judicious cutting. The pacing is brisk, and when things take a more overtly macabre turn in the second half, the suspense is wonderfully taut.

Karloff's performance as the deranged Dr. Laurience is top-notch, and *The Man who Changed His Mind* proves a far more satisfactory British vehicle for his talents than the earlier, more trumpeted return to his homeland, *The Ghoul* (1933). Chain-smoking nervously, he imbues the role with the same coiled intensity that he brought to *The Invisible Ray* (1936). Yet, whereas his portrayal of Dr. Rukh in that film sometimes bordered on camp, he is far more controlled here. The character is the typical madman with delusions of grandeur that one expects in a film of this type, but Karloff avoids caricature.

The supporting cast includes a number of fine character actors. Anna Lee (later reunited with Karloff in producer Val Lewton's *Bedlam*, 1945) brings intelligence and charm to her role as Karloff's unwilling collaborator, while John Lodge (Hitchcock's *Sabotage*, 1936) makes an agreeable would-be hero. Frank Cellier (Hitchcock's *The 39 Steps*, 1935) is amusing as the pompous, self-aggrandizing Lord Haselwood, while Donald Calthrop (Matthias in the lost 1931 version of *The Bells*) is effective as an embittered cripple hoping to benefit from Karloff's experiments. Cecil Parker (*The Brain*, 1962) and Lyn Harding (*The Speckled Band*, 1931) also appear in small roles.

The film was an early assignment for make-up artist Roy Ashton, who later did much work for Hammer Film Productions, creating memorable character looks for such films as *The Curse of the Werewolf* (1960) and *Phantom of the Opera* (1962).

Mind may appear a little tame to contemporary viewers, but its sharply drawn portrayal of switching personalities makes it essential viewing for fans of the subgenre; it's certainly one of the better Karloff mad doctor vehicles. TH

Midnight at Madame Tussaud's
aka Midnight in the Wax Museum

Steven Edwards; b/w; 62 min; Great Britain
D: George Pearson *Co-S:* Roger MacDougall, Kim Peacock *Co-S/P:* James Steven Edwards *C:* Jimmy Borger

Cast: Lucille Lisle, James Carew, Charles Oliver, Kim Peacock, Patrick Barr, William "Billy" Hartnell, Lydia Sherwood, Bernard Miles

Sir Clive (Carew) bets that he can spend the night in Madame Tussaud's infamous chamber of waxwork horrors. At the same time, he is distracted by concern over his beloved niece Carol (Lisle), who is head-over-heels in love with Harry Newton (Oliver), a man Sir Clive believes is bad news. It turns out that Clive's fears are well-founded, a fact underscored when Harry plots to take advantage of Uncle Clive's wager by sneaking into the museum to polish him off.

Less a horror film than a turgid melodrama, *Midnight at Madame Tussaud's* is of interest chiefly for its atmospheric display of the infamous wax museum. The filmmakers were granted full access to the museum and its exhibitions, and they present it in an engaging light. There's simply not enough of it. The film starts off promisingly enough, as Sir Clive is treated to a tour and makes his wager, but then it completely shifts gears to detail the relationship between Carol and Harry in what quickly becomes tedious detail. For most of its running time, in fact, it seems that the idea of Sir Clive spending the night in the creepy museum has been set aside. At the last moment, however, the film moves back to the title location for a tolerably enjoyable finale.

Still, the climactic sparks are too few and too late. Despite its short running time, *Midnight at Madame Tussaud's* emerges as padded and terribly slow-paced. Director George Pearson was nearing the end of his directorial career by the time he directed the film. His filmography, which begins with a 1914 version of the Sherlock Holmes story *A Study in Scarlet*, ends one year after *Madame Tussaud's* with the obscure thriller *The Fatal Hour* (1937).

Tussaud's performances are generally of the same caliber as the mediocre material being presented, with a few familiar faces in the supporting cast. Bernard Miles (the head heavy in Alfred

Robert Woolsey, Bert Wheeler and Barbara Pepper in *Mummy's Boys*

Hitchcock's *The Man Who Knew Too Much*, 1956) makes an early appearance as the museum's modeler, while Patrick Barr (*The Satanic Rites of Dracula*, 1973) and William Hartnell (best remembered as TV's first Dr. Who) show up as heroic newspaper reporters. TH

Mummy's Boys
RKO; b/w; 68 min; U.S.
   D: Fred Guiol S: Jack Townley, Philip G. Epstein, Charles Roberts P: Lee Marcus C: Jack MacKenzie
   Cast: Bert Wheeler, Robert Woolsey, Barbara Pepper, Moroni Olsen, Frank M. Thomas, Willie Best, Francis McDonald, Frank Lackteen, Charles Coleman, Mitchell Lewis, Frederick Burton

Fearing a death curse placed upon him for despoiling the tomb of the Ancient Egyptian pharaoh Martime, Phillip Browning (Thomas) decides to return the items he's taken from the tomb. He employs two former ditch diggers, moronic Aloysius Whittaker (Woolsey) and Stanley Wright (Wheeler)—who claim to know Egypt like the back of their hands—as guides. He also takes along his daughter Mary (Pepper). With nine of the 10 original expedition members dead, mysterious telephone calls and missives warn the expedition to turn back, and a strange man wearing a turban (an essential of any expatriated Egyptian's wardrobe) shows up at every turn. When Browning disappears, Aloysius and Stanley press on, until they find themselves entombed with a "living" mummy, at which time the real killer (Olsen) of the expedition members is revealed.

Bert Wheeler and Robert Woolsey found their initial success on Broadway in 1927 in the Ziegfeld play *Rio Rita*, which was brought to the screen by RKO in 1929. Though they were actually minor characters in the film, the two proved such a hit with audiences that RKO brought them back as the stars of a series of films, often times opposite Thelma Todd and Dorothy Lee. Something of an answer to Laurel and Hardy, Wheeler and Woolsey's early films were relatively well written and had suitable budgets, but as the series progressed, RKO spent less time and money on them, resulting in a precipitous drop in quality. The duo's partnership came to an end in 1938, when Woolsey, the older of the two, died of kidney disease, though their career together had by then pretty much run its course.

Mummy's Boys represents later-era Wheeler and Woolsey and may be the nadir of their career together. The comedic routines—mostly centered on Wright's inability to remember anything—are repetitious in the extreme. And as if dumb and dumber weren't enough, Willie Best is on board as a bumbling black guide named Catfish in yet another role as a silly, easily scared man-child. At least Moroni Olsen (*Seven Keys to Baldpate*, 1935) and Barbara Pepper (*The Westland Case*, 1937) get to play it straight; they come out all the better for it, though it strains credulity that anyone as charming and intelligent as Pepper's Mary would fall for someone as blazingly stupid as Wheeler's Wright.

Amazingly, co-scenarist Phillip G. Epstein went on to write some of cinema's most classic films, including *The Bride Came C.O.D.* (1941), *Casablanca* (1942), *Mr. Skeffington* (1944) and *The Last Time I Saw Paris* (1954). His only other semi-horror credit was Frank Capra's black comedy *Arsenic and Old Lace* (1944). CW

Pan Twardowski
aka **Pan Tvardovski**
Ultra; b/w; 85 min; Poland
   D: Henryk Szaro S: Waclaw Gasiorowski, Anatol Stern C: Seweryn Steinwurzel M: Jan Maklakiewicz
   Cast: Franciszek Brodniewicz, Kazimierz Junosza-Stepowski, Maria Bogda, Elzbieta Barszczewska, Mieczyslawa Cwikinska, Maria Malicka, Zofia Lindorf, Jozef Wegrzyn, Jan Kurnakowicz, Stefan Jaracz, Boguslaw Samborski, Stanislaw Sielanski, Tadeusz Wesolowski, Michal Znicz

Twardowski has been pursued by the Devil since adolescence but has always managed to fend off The Evil One. Now, as a young adult, he meets a beautiful young woman in love with someone else. In an effort to win her over, he offers the Devil his soul in exchange for the woman's hand in marriage. The Devil agrees but, as tends to be the case with these things, the outcome proves disastrous for Twardowski.

Pan Twardowski was based on a popular Polish legend that had already provided the basis for a 1916 Russian film from Ladislas Starevitch, *Mr. Tvardovski*, and a silent Polish adaptation also titled *Pan Twardowski* (1921), of which Henryk Szaro's 1936 film is often called a remake. This 1936 adaptation is certainly the most famous (in Europe, anyway; it's almost entirely unknown in North America, despite a 1937 release there). It's a masterful blend of horror and melodrama made not long before the Nazi occupation of Poland decimated its fledgling film industry.

Like so many films before and after it, *Pan Twardowski* was a study in sexual obsession, thematically related to *The Hunch-*

back of *Notre Dame* (1923) but with a supernatural dimension not found in most adaptations of Victor Hugo's most famous literary work (and minus the interest in deformity, though Satan's guise in *Pan* is a rather grotesque one). *Pan* is also the bastard stepchild of Goethe's *Faust*, which was one of the most popular horror inspirations during the early days of cinema.

With a gorgeous miniature opening shot of a European village, *Pan Twardowski* immediately establishes its horror credentials in an eerie tableau, with the moon casting sinister shadows over the cold stone of a dusty fortress. There, a man searches the sky with his telescope before the film cuts to a creepy shot of the Devil as he watches a young boy lying in bed, only for Old Scratch to be warded off when the boy's mother comes into his room and sings a song of beauty and spirituality.

The movie's costumes are gorgeous, the cinematography an interesting mix of influences ranging from F.W. Murnau to Edgar Ulmer, the performances strong, the lighting flawless and the special effects groundbreaking. Director Henryk Szaro achieves a guarded surrealism as he prowls the dark halls of ancient castles and monasteries, managing one truly scary moment when the alchemist Twardowski calls upon the spirit of a desiccated body; just when it appears that the rotting flesh is to be endowed with some hideous form of pseudo-life, Satan himself appears. Twardowski sits back in a chair adorned with the face of a demon, listening intently while the Devil stands enticingly over him, flames from the fireplace casting deep and undulating shadows over them both. The ending is also particularly effective as the Devil and Twardowski fight with swords, the heroine is impaled, the building surrounding them collapses and the Devil flies Twardowski into the cold reaches of outer space, where a well-timed prayer to God finally does in the Prince of Darkness.

Pan Twardowski is a masterpiece of horror made at a time when the genre was all but dead in Europe, thanks to Hitler's rise to power. It's truly past time for the film's uncanny chills to be rediscovered in the Western hemisphere, considering that it's easily better than any number of films to come out of Hollywood during the same period. CW

The Phantom of the Range
Victory; b/w; 57 min; U.S.
    D: Bob Hill *S:* Basil Dickey *P:* Sam Katzman
    C: William Hyer
    Cast: Tom Tyler, Beth Marion, Sammy Cohen, Soledad Jimenez, Forrest Taylor, Charles King, John Elliott,

Jeanne Moore (Marion) inherits an estate from a departed uncle, and it's rumored that there's a fortune buried on it somewhere. Villains plot to find and take the treasure, but Jeanne's friend Jerry Lane (Tyler) has other ideas.

Cowboys, a comic British valet, "old dark house" tropes and a buried treasure … It's all a bit disorienting when put together. Yet *The Phantom of the Range* proves a pleasantly diverting B-Western with horror overtones. The picture doesn't embrace genre elements to the same degree as later horror-Westerns such as *Curse of the Undead* (1959) or John Carpenter's *Vampires* (1998), but it still deserves credit for cross-pollinating these two very different types of film.

Leading man Tom Tyler made scores of B-Westerns, but horror buffs likely know him best as the moldering Kharis in

The Mummy's Hand (1940). Here he makes for a likable—if slightly stolid—hero. Director Bob Hill (who sometimes went by Robert F. Hill) was also no stranger to B-Westerns, and his work here is competent if unimaginative.

Producer Sam Katzman later cranked out a number of no-budget horror films under the Monogram Pictures banner. Like many Poverty Row producers of the day, Katzman didn't care much about quality—and it usually showed. TH

Pilot X
aka **Murder in the Sky**; **Death in the Air**; **Pilot X: Murder in the Sky**; **The Mysterious Bombardier**
Royer; b/w; 67 (69) min; U.S.
    D: Elmer Clifton *S:* Bernard McConville, Charles R. Condon *P:* Fanchon Royer *C:* James Diamond, Art Reed

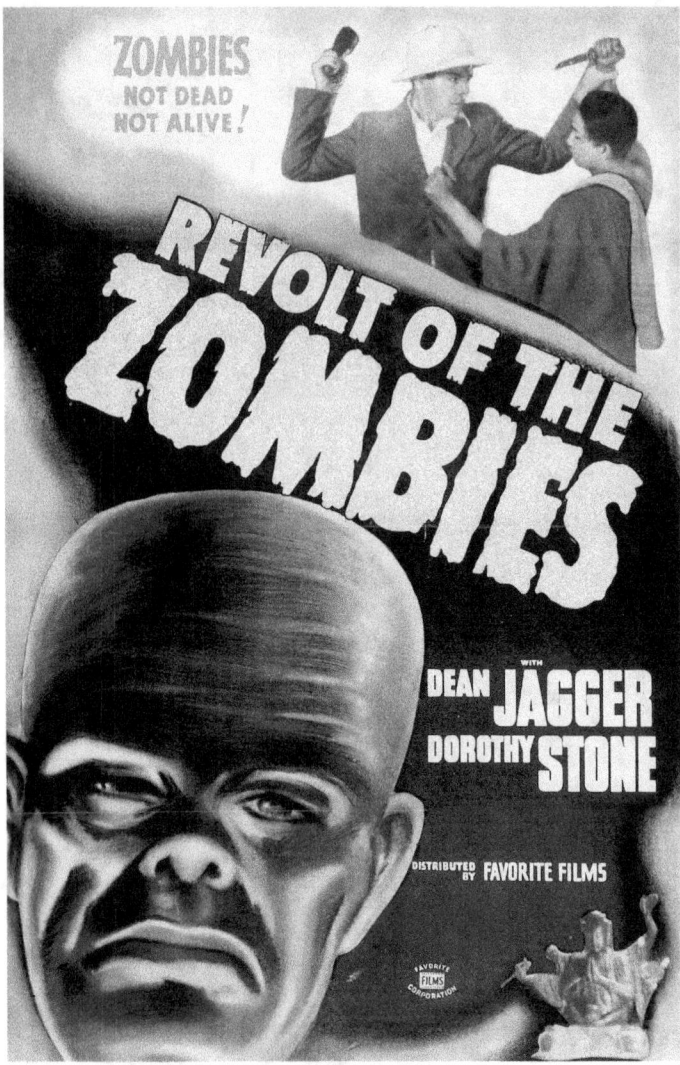

Cast: Lona Andre, John Carroll, Leon Ames, Henry Hall, John S. Peters, Gaston Glass, Pat Somerset, Wheeler Oakman, Reed Howes, John Elliott, Willard Kent

Planes are being shot down and their occupants murdered by a mysterious serial killer whose own phantom plane bears a large X on one of its wings. Dr. Norris (Elliott) believes that the killer may be an unhinged World War I pilot reliving past battles. He also suspects that the man has a split personality, "satiated for a time with his victories" but, when in need of another fix, becoming a "winged demon" of the air. His ideas are dismissed by the police but not by newbie pilot Jerry Blackwood (Carroll), who believes the killer to be one of five pilots who once worked for various militaries and are now living locally. These five men—German Baron Von Guttard (Peters), Americans Douglas Thompson (Oakman) and Lieutenant Ives (Howes), French Rene LaRue (Glass) and British Captain Saunders (Somerset)—are invited to an aircraft manufacturing plant on the pretext of brainstorming the killer's identity. But when the men begin to be murdered one-by-one, Blackwood must rethink his notions of who the killer might be.

If the film doesn't at first glance seem like a horror film, that's because of its brightly lit and unconventional setting. Many of the classic "old dark house" trappings are most definitely there, from the faceless serial killer, to the *Ten Little Indians*-style plot, to the thunderstorm that punctuates the final denouement.

Pilot X benefits from slick direction and solid production values (stock footage notwithstanding). It also has a surprisingly good script, with some sharp dialogue and a few truly unexpected twists and turns—though a tedious love triangle involving Blackwood, his nemesis Carl (Ames) and the beautiful Helen Gage (Andre) does at times slow things down. Where the film truly falters is with its performances, which range from the barely decent to the truly terrible.

Leon Ames (real name Leon Waycoff) began his career during the early sound era with a series of dashing leading man roles, among them Dupin in Universal's stylish *Murders in the Rue Morgue* (1932). In 1933 he was a founding member of the Screen Actors Guild, a union created to get better deals for actors from the major studios. (He later became its president.) Some film historians have speculated that studio resentment is what led Ames to working on Poverty Row for a period, though he did find his way back to the big leagues in his later years as a loving dad-type character actor.

Originally released under the title *Death in the Air*, *Pilot X* is a rare example of a 1930s film produced by a woman. Born in Des Moines, Iowa, Fanchon Royer entered films in 1916 as an extra. She worked as a magazine editor and actor's manager before forming her own film company in 1928, Fanchon Royer Pictures; it produced low-budget Hollywood product until 1938. In the early 1940s she moved from mainstream cinema to the creation of short films with a Catholic bent. She later served as president of the Catholic Film and Radio Guild. Her only other effort in the horror genre appears to have been *The Mystic Circle Murder* (1938). CW

Revolt of the Zombies
aka **Revolt of the Demons**
Halperin/Academy; b/w; 62 (65) min; U.S.

D/Co-S: Victor Halperin *Co-S:* Howard Higgin, Rollo Lloyd *P:* Edward Halperin *C:* Arthur Marinelli, J. Arthur Feindel *FX:* Ray Mercer

Cast: Dorothy Stone, Dean Jagger, Roy D'Arcy, Robert Noland, George Cleveland, E. Alyn Warren, Carl Stockdale, William Crowell, Teru Shimada, Adolph Millard, Sana Rayya

"Many strange events were recorded in the secret archives of the fighting nations during the world war … But none stranger than that which occurred when a regiment of French Cambodians from the vicinity of the lost city in Angkor arrived on the Franco-Austrian front …" So begins *Revolt of the Zombies*, the Halperin Brothers' belated follow-up to their wildly successful *White Zombie* (1932). Too bad nothing that comes afterward lives up to those opening words.

During the First World War, Armand Louque (Jagger) becomes obsessed with an army of "zombies" that appears to have originated in French Cambodia. Years later, certain that he can create a similar unit of unstoppable man-machines, Louque goes in search of the lost city of Angkor, where he believes he can find the secret formula for making such zombies. He hooks up with an expedition led by General Duval (Cleveland) and there meets the general's daughter Claire (Stone). The two quickly become engaged, though Claire prefers another expedition member, Clifford Grayson (Noland). What Louque doesn't know but soon learns is that Claire has only agreed to marry him to make Clifford jealous; when it becomes clear that she has a shot at Clifford, she drops Armand like a hot rock. The crazed Armand goes off on his own and, in an ancient temple, stumbles upon the secret of making zombies. His first victim is Buna (Shimada), whom he orders to kill Mazovia (D'Arcy), an expedition member who is also seeking the formula. Armand then proceeds to turn almost everyone he meets into a zombie, including many of the people in the expedition's encampment. This, he believes, will force Claire to acquiesce to their marriage.

After the successful release of the independently produced *White Zombie* by major studio United Artists, the Halperin Brothers seemed destined for the big time. The two quickly signed a contract with Paramount, where they produced and directed the low-key *Supernatural* (1933), which starred the studio's leading lady Carole Lombard. But that film's poor critical reception and box-office failure dropkicked the Halperins back into the wilderness of independents to produce their own material.

Revolt of the Zombies, a revisiting of the only theme they'd ever explored successfully, was their second production after *Supernatural*. It was nowhere near the success of *White Zombie*, which had been helped by Bela Lugosi in the lead role as the evil Murder Legendre, though *Revolt* shamefully borrows shots of Lugosi's eyes from the earlier film. That the second zombie film tanked is not due as much to its padded script as to director Halperin, whose style had hardly grown since the advent of talkies almost a decade before. Poor rear-screen projection and silent-era-style performances—Dean Jagger aside—certainly don't help matters either. Nor do the threadbare sets, the lack of atmosphere or the fact that the zombies aren't dead people brought back to life; rather, they're simply human beings under a hypnotic control made possible by an illicit drug.

Amusement Securities Corporation sued Academy (who released *Revolt*) for using the word "zombies" in the film's title. Amusement, who had reissued *White Zombie* to theaters, believed that a second film containing the word amounted to unfair competition. So *Revolt* was temporarily distributed under an alternate title while the case worked itself through the court system. That it was eventually reunited with its original title is an indication of who won that case.

Revolt has some interesting images—a zombie army being riddled with bullet holes as it moves steadily forward and a priest (Crowell) murdered while saying his prayers before a stone idol, among others—but these moments, while striking, are simply not enough to save the picture. The romantic leads come across as manipulative and insensitive, leaving the audience to side with the love-maddened and mistreated Armand. Ohio-born Jagger's performance is nuanced and sympathetic, even while the character overreaches in attempting to right the wrongs done him. It should be noted that Jagger had been a schoolteacher before making the jump to acting during the silent era. Predominantly a star of Hollywood Westerns and war films, he was nominated for a Best Supporting Actor Oscar for his role as Major Stovall in Henry King's *Twelve O'Clock High* (1949). He made only a few horror films in his career, among them Hammer's classic *X the Unknown* (1956) and John Sayles' *Alligator* (1980), before he died in 1991.

Victor Halperin's next stab at horror came in 1939 with the dull *Torture Ship*. He followed that film up with *Buried Alive* (also 1939), which, despite its title and some deceptive marketing, was nothing more than a melodrama mostly set within the cold confines of a men's prison. CW

The Rogues Tavern
aka **The Rogues' Tavern**
Mercury/Carmel; b/w; 68 min; U.S.
 D: Bob Hill *S:* Al Martin *P:* Sam Katzman *C:* Bill Hyer
 Cast: Wallace Ford, Barbara Pepper, Joan Woodbury, Clara Kimball Young, Jack Mulhall, John Elliott, Earl Dwire, John W. Cowell, Vincent Dennis, Arthur Loft, Ivo Henderson, Ed Cassidy, Silver Wolf

One dark and stormy night, Jimmy (Ford) and his girlfriend Marjorie (Pepper) arrive at the Red Rock Tavern hoping to meet up with a Justice of the Peace who will marry them. What they find instead is a gang of jewel thieves awaiting their mysterious leader (Loft) and a killer who uses fake dog teeth to frame an innocent canine (Silver Wolf) for murder. There's also a mysterious, beautiful woman (Woodbury) in a low-cut dress who claims to have visions that portend doom.

While *The Rogues Tavern* is nothing special for the period, it at least looks good, in part thanks to Bob (Robert F.) Hill's fluid direction and Bill "William" Hyer's mobile camerawork. Hill had begun his career at Universal during the silent era, but during the talkie years he was relegated almost entirely to directing poverty row productions. He did manage to make a few interesting bargain-basement items, including such horror hybrids as *The Vanishing Riders* (1935), as well as *A Face in the Fog*, *Shadow of Chinatown* and *The Phantom of the Range* (all 1936). Most, if not all, of these films were shot by Hyer, a more-than-adequate professional who understood how to add atmosphere to a film. The relationship between the two men was just what Al Martin's pedestrian script needed to bring it to life.

Some good performances here can't be undervalued. Leads Wallace Ford (*Night of Terror*, 1933), Barbara Pepper (*Mummy's Boys*, 1936) and Joan Woodbury (*Mystery of the White Room*,

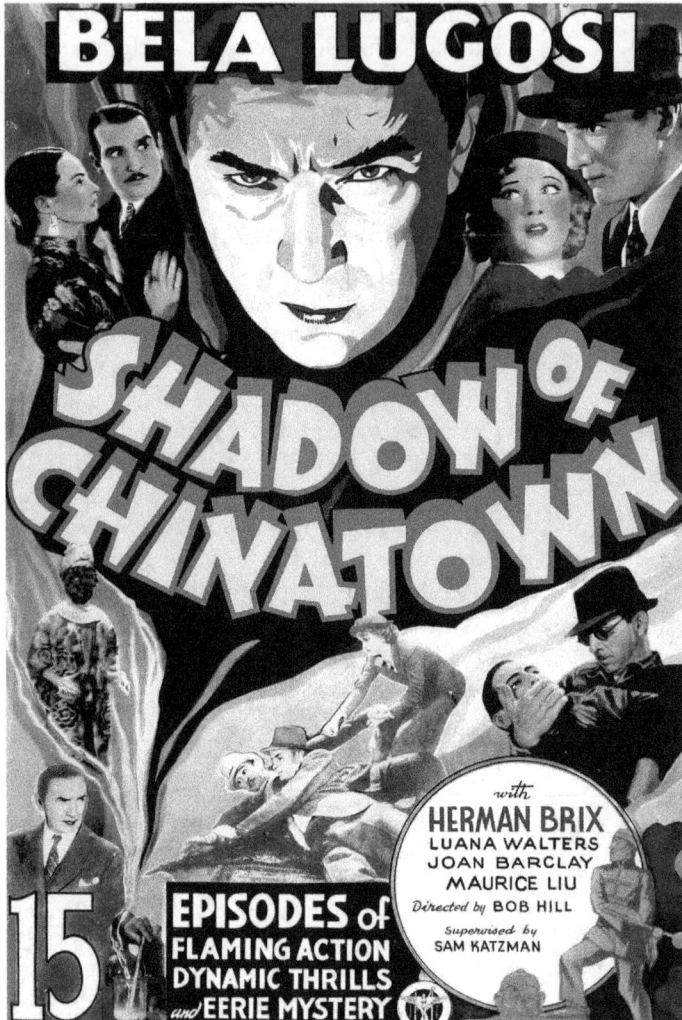

1939), the latter of whom the director seems to take an especial interest in, do well amid the sparse production values. The casting of Clara Kimball Young (*Trilby*, 1915) must have seemed something of a coup for Mercury. That's not to say that Young is particularly good, but she *is* entertaining, particularly when she gets to ham it up for the film's final, ludicrous denouement. CW

Shadow of Chinatown
aka **Yellow Phantom**
Victory; b/w; 15 chapters (281 min); U.S.
   D/Co-S: Robert F. Hill *Co-S:* William Buchanan, Isadore Bernstein, Basil Dickey *P:* Sam Katzman *C:* Bill Hyer *M:* Lee Zahler
   Cast: Bela Lugosi, Herman Brix (Bruce Bennett), Joan Barclay, Luana Walters, Maurice Liu, Charles King, William Buchanan, Forest Taylor, John Cowell, James B. Leong, Henry T. Tung, Paul Fung, George Chan, Moy Ming
   Sonya Rokoff (Walters) hires Victor Poten (Lugosi), a deranged chemist, to wipe out a group of Chinatown merchants. The racist Poten, who despises both whites and Asians, creates a deadly invisible gas to unleash on the objects of his scorn.
   This overlong and ridiculous nonsense is made (barely) tolerable by Bela Lugosi's overripe performance as a deranged and bigoted genius. His lively presence is the only life to be found in this affair (even as the script fails its star at every turn, depicting the criminal mastermind as a bungling amateur).

Like most of the actor's other serials, *Shadow of Chinatown* isn't as much a true horror item as it is a messy melodrama, with some mildly morbid bits here and there. The two-fisted hero is played by stolid Bruce Bennett, billed here as Herman Brix, who later appeared in classier fare, including *Mildred Pierce* (1945) and John Huston's *The Treasure of the Sierra Madre* (1948). He also turned up in the occasional B-horror or sci-fi item, including *The Cosmic Man* (1959), starring John Carradine and *The Alligator People* (1959), with Lon Chaney.
   Leading ladies Joan Barclay and Luana Walters had long careers in B-movies, and they both rejoined Lugosi for *The Corpse Vanishes* (1942). Producer Sam Katzman spent much of the '30s churning out serials and B-grade Westerns and went on to produce some of the most infamous no-budget horrors of the 1940s, including the aforementioned *The Corpse Vanishes* and *Voodoo Man* (1944). His lengthy tenure in Hollywood came to a close in 1973, when he died at the age of 72.
   Shadow of Chinatown was also released as a 71-minute feature. TH

Someone at the Door
Associated British; b/w; 75 min; Great Britain
   D: Herbert Brenon *S:* Campbell Christie, Jack Davis, Jr., Marjorie Deans *P:* Walter C. Mycroft *C:* Bryan Langley
   Cast: Aileen Marson, Billy Milton, Noah Beery, John Irwin, Charles Mortimer, Edward Chapman, Edward Dignon, Jimmy Godden, Laurence Hanray
   Sally Martin (Marson) and her brother Ronnie (Milton) are down and out. They return to their childhood home, which has fallen into creepy disrepair, in the hope of starting afresh. They hatch a scheme to break into journalism by faking a murder, thus giving them a potential scoop, but in the process they run afoul of a gang of thieves who has stashed its loot in the house.
   As was typical at the time, the emphasis in *Someone at the Door* is more on comedy than chills. Campbell Christie and his sister Dorothy originally wrote the tale for the stage, and the film adaptation doesn't particularly succeed in making the material more cinematic. The play was adapted again to even lesser effect in 1951 by Britain's soon-to-be-famous Hammer Film Productions.
   Director Herbert Brenon had been active since 1912, with one of his earliest credits being *Dr. Jekyll and Mr. Hyde* (1913). He made a fairly successful transition to talkies but never became more than a competent gun for hire. The cast includes American character actor Noah Beery. The brother of Academy Award winner Wallace Beery (*The Champ*, 1931) and the father of popular character actor Noah Beery, Jr. (*The Cat Creeps*, 1946), Beery senior was an old hand at playing villains, a function he serves here. His lengthy career included roles opposite such legends as Douglas Fairbanks (*The Mark of Zorro*, 1920), Cary Grant and Mae West (*She Done Him Wrong*, 1933) and John Wayne (*The Trail Beyond*, 1934).
   The most familiar British face here is the rotund Edward Chapman, who often played blustery, officious types. He had major roles in H.G. Wells' hokey but well-intended sci-fi treatise *Things to Come* (1936) and in Hammer Film Production's *X The Unknown* (1956). TH

The Super Madman
aka El super loco
P.C.E.; b/w; 65 min; Mexico

D: Juan Jose Segura *S:* Jorge Cardena Alvarez, Juan Jose Segura *C:* Lauron A. Draper *M:* Chucho Monje

Cast: Leopoldo Ortin, Carlos Villarias, Aurora Campuzano, Consuelo Frank, Ramon Armengod, Emilio Fernandez, Jorge Cardena Alvarez, Armando Roosendal, Raul Urquijo, Manuel Noriega

Dr. Deyenis' (Villaris) efforts to reverse aging yield a vicious ape-man (Urquijo) that the scientist keeps locked in his basement. Sostenes (Ortin), an inveterate alcoholic, investigates the situation with humorously gruesome results.

The Super Madman appears to have been Mexico's first horror spoof. Its comedic elements, confined mostly to the annoying antics of Ortin's alcoholic investigator, alternate clumsily with an ample amount of horrific content. Some reviewers have observed that the story melds elements of the Lon Chaney vehicle *A Blind Bargain* (1922) with a dash of Robert Louis Stevenson's *The Strange Case of Dr. Jekyll and Mr. Hyde* and a pinch of Oscar Wilde's *The Picture of Dorian Gray*.

The villainous, death-defying doctor is played by Carlos Villarias, a Spanish actor most famous for being Bela Lugosi's counterpart in the Spanish-language version of *Dracula* (1931). The doctor's anti-aging experiments anticipate Barre Lyndon's *The Man in Half Moon Street* (1945), remade by Hammer Film Productions as *The Man Who Could Cheat Death* (1959).

Madman's supporting cast includes a young Emilio Fernandez. Born in Mexico in 1904, Fernandez made his way to Hollywood in the 1920s. Movie lore has it that he was the model for the famous Oscar statue, designed by Cedric Gibbons, the husband of Fernandez's close friend Dolores Del Rio. After working as an extra in Hollywood, he returned to Mexico, where he established himself as a prolific actor and director. Known to many simply as El Indio (owing to his mother being a member of the Kickapoo Indian tribe), he is remembered today for his roles in Sam Peckinpah's *The Wild Bunch* (1969), in which he played the sadistic General Mapache, *Pat Garrett and Billy the Kid* (1973) and *Bring Me the Head of Alfredo Garcia* (1974), a horror/noir hybrid if ever there was one. TH

Sweeney Todd: The Demon Barber of Fleet Street
aka The Demon Barber of Fleet Street
King; b/w; 68(76) min; Great Britain

D/P: George King *S:* Frederick Hayward, H.F. Maltby *C:* Jack Parker

Cast: Tod Slaughter, Stella Rho, Johnny Singer, Eve Lister, Bruce Seton, D.J. Williams, Davina Craig, Jerry Verno, Graham Soutten, Billy Holland, Norman Pierce, Aubrey Mallalieu

Johanna (Lister) wants to marry Mark (Seton), but her father (Williams) protests. Mark embarks on a sea voyage, hoping to make enough money to convince Johanna's father to consent to their marriage. Meanwhile, little orphan Tobias (Singer) is sent to work for Sweeney Todd (Slaughter), a barber in cahoots with Mrs. Lovett (Rho). Todd wants Johanna for himself, and to gain her hand in marriage, he threatens to ruin her father. Not long afterward, a much-richer Mark returns, now in possession of a string of pearls given to him by a dying man. He stops on

Fleet Street to get a shave, knowing nothing of Sweeney Todd's penchant for slitting throats rather than shaving them. With a flip of a switch, the barber's chair in which Mark is sitting flips back, sending the young man through a trapdoor into Slaughter's cellar. There, he's to be finished off by the mad Mrs. Lovett, who will slice him up and sell his edible remnants in meat pies. But things don't pan out as expected.

It's a gruesome premise, certainly, but one in keeping with the serialized story upon which it's based, *The String of Pearls: A Romance*, published in an 18-issue run of *The People's Periodical and Family Library* in 1846 and 1847. This particular film adaptation retains most of the characters of the original story. Though it changes some of the situations, it keeps the original's string of pearls, as well as the plot point of Johanna disguising herself as a boy to get to the bottom of what's going on in Todd's shop. It was also the first to add the words "The Demon Barber of Fleet Street" to the title, a moniker that was thereafter synonymous with the name Sweeney Todd. As with the previous versions of the tale (both titled *Sweeney Todd*, 1926 and 1928), George Dibdin Pitt's successful play, written in 1847, shortly after the story's initial publication, became the basis for all the film versions, including this 1936 version.

While the film overall is a lot of fun, its bookends—set in a modern-day barber's shop located on the very spot of Todd's original shop—drag it down a bit. (There was neither a Sweeney Todd nor rigged-out barbershop in real life, but that hasn't stopped numerous plays and films from treating the story as if it were true.) The script was co-written by Frederick Hayward, who provided the details and settings and H.F. Maltby, who provided additional dialogue. Hayward wrote few films in his career, three of which were barnstormers for Tod Slaughter. On the other hand, Maltby was quite prolific, contributing to a number of films—both as a writer and as an actor—that are today considered classics of British cinema.

Sweeney Todd was the second film for stage actor Slaughter, who was already famous in his native Britain for starring as notorious murderer William Corder in *Maria Marten, or The Murder in the Red Barn* (1928). His performance as Todd is similar to his role in his first film, with the actor gleefully wallowing in depraved and sadistic behavior. Slaughter's next film, *The Crimes of Stephen Hawke* (1936), was more of the same, and

Tod Slaughter demonstrates why he was called "Europe's Horror Man" in this grisly murder from *The Demon Barber of Fleet Street*.

the actor wound up typecast in horror roles on the big screen and on stage until the end of his life. He was arguably Britain's first horror star, though it was only in his native country and in a few British-controlled markets that he became a household name.

Bruce Seton, who played Mark Ingerstreet, went head-to-head with Slaughter again in *The Curse of the Wraydons* (1946). His final horror appearance was as Professor Flaherty in one of Britain's few giant monster flicks, *Gorgo* (1961), which was a distant relation to *Gojira* (1954). Despite a few duds, his career was distinguished enough to earn him a knighthood.

On the other hand, this appears to have been the last film to star Stella Rho (who had played a Gypsy in *Maria Marten*). Johnny Singer, who played young Tobias, grew up in the movies; his career lasted until the late 1950s, though he lived into the late 1980s. Among his genre films were *Never Too Late to Mend* (1937)—which also starred Slaughter—and *Haunted Palace* (1949), in addition to a couple of non-horror Hammer films, *Whispering Smith vs. Scotland Yard* (1951) and *Further Up the Creek* (1958).

George King (1899-1966), whose company produced *Sweeney Todd*, made many films in the horror genre, both as producer and director. These include the aforementioned *Maria Marten, or The Murder in the Red Barn*, *The Crimes of Stephen Hawke* and *Never Too Late to Mend*, as well as *The Ticket of Leave Man* (1937), *Sexton Blake and the Hooded Terror* (1938), *The Face at the Window* (1939), *Crimes at the Dark House* and *The Case of the Frightened Lady* (both 1940).

With the passage of the Cinematograph Act in 1927—which required that a certain percentage of films shown in British theaters be actually produced in the country—King rose to dominance as a producer of "quota quickies," or low-budget films churned out simply to meet the new percentage requirement. His greatest successes came when he partnered with Slaughter, and the two made a number of B-grade horror films even after the Act was repealed in 1937.

With the coming of World War II, King jumped the horror ship in favor of so-called "respectable" films, in the process terminating his partnership with Slaughter. It may have seemed a smart move at the time, but the producer's films became increasingly infrequent until his career finally ended in 1954. He died of pneumonia in 1966, his later productions almost entirely forgotten in favor of his early horror films. CW

Trouble for Two
aka **The Suicide Club**
MGM; b/w; 75 min; U.S.

D: J. Walter Ruben *S:* Edward E. Paramore Jr., Manuel Seff *P:* Louis B. Lighton *C:* Charles Clarke *M:* Franz Waxman

Cast: Robert Montgomery, Rosalind Russell, Frank Morgan, Reginald Owen, Louis Hayward, E.E. Clive, Walter Kingsford, Ivan F. Simpson, Tom Moore, Robert Greig, Pedro de Cordoba, Leyland Hodgson

Robert Louis Stevenson's *The Suicide Club*, first published in *London Magazine* in 1878, recounted the Victorian adventures of Prince Florizel and his sidekick, Colonel Geraldine. The story was divided into three parts, with the first, *Story of the Young Man with the Cream Tarts*, placing its two heroes in a dining establishment where they meet a young man giving out cream tarts. Inquiring about this weird behavior, they learn of a secretive suicide club, which they proceed to infiltrate and break up. The club's president is arrested and dispatched to Paris in the presence of Geraldine's younger brother.

The tale's second part, *Story of the Physician and the Saratoga Trunk*, concerns a young man who meets a beautiful woman with whom he immediately becomes infatuated. She arranges to meet him later that night but fails to show, and when the young man returns to his apartment, he finds a dead man there. His physician neighbor arranges for the body to be smuggled to London in a Saratoga trunk, but once there Prince Florizel discovers it and reveals that the corpse is none other than Geraldine's brother.

This narrative dovetails into the trilogy's final tale, *The Adventures of the Hansom Cab*, in which a former military lieutenant is lured into a cab and whisked off to a mysterious party. There he meets Colonel Geraldine, who takes him to a rendezvous with Prince Florizel. Florizel has by then apprehended the president of the suicide club, and the two men duel to the death.

Stevenson's story was filmed numerous times during the silent era, first under the title *The Suicide Club* in 1909 by D.W.

Griffith in the United States, with an identically titled French version done the same year by Victorin-Hippolyte Jasset. Those initial adaptations were followed by many others, including two more under the title *The Suicide Club* (1913 and 1914), as well as *The American Suicide Club* (1910), *Polidor at the Death Club* (1912), *Simple Simon and the Suicide Club* (1913), *Batty Bill and the Suicide Club* (1914) and finally as part of Richard Oswald's *Weird Tales* (1919). When Oswald's film was remade in 1932 as *Uncanny Stories*, *The Suicide Club* segment was retained, making it the first sound feature based on the story.

In 1929 Canadian playwright Captain Hugh Abercrombie Anderson adapted the story to the stage, where it garnered positive notices. It's likely this adaptation, rather than any of the silent film versions, that led to Universal's interest in the property. The studio had found major success in 1931 with its big-screen adaptations of the horror classics *Dracula* and *Frankenstein*, in the process making stars of their lead actors (Bela Lugosi in the former, Boris Karloff in the latter). By February of 1932, *Variety* was reporting that Universal had a slate of horror productions planned, including *Cagliosto* and *The Suicide Club*, both as possible vehicles for Karloff and/or Lugosi. While portions of *Cagliostro*'s story found their way into *The Mummy* (1932), *The Suicide Club* never got past the planning stage and was eventually abandoned in favor of what was considered stronger vehicles, including two Edgar Allan Poe adaptations, *The Black Cat* (1934) and *The Raven* (1935), both of which starred Karloff *and* Lugosi.

Somewhat concurrently, in the late 1920s a dashing young actor named Robert Montgomery had made a name for himself in New York's theater district. A friendly relationship with George Cukor led him to make a career switch to Hollywood, where he was cast in films opposite such leading ladies as Greta Garbo and Norma Shearer. In 1934 he starred in his first horror-tinged film, *The Mystery of Mr. X*, about a serial killer stalking the London fog, where he played not the killer but the heartthrob.

With Universal's adaptation of Stevenson's tale dead in the water, MGM was free to move forward with its own less horrific version from a script penned by Edward E. Paramore Jr. (*Rocky Mountain Mystery*, 1935) and Manuel Seff (*Terror Aboard*, 1933), both of whom had worked on *Three Godfathers* together the year before. In the years since Universal had originally planned their adaptation, the market had fallen out from under the genre, in part because of a ban on horror films in England and pressure from watchdog groups in the United States, who maintained that Americans wanted Hollywood to reduce violence and "immoral" behavior in movies (a dubious claim given the success of such films). *Trouble for Two* appeared in the wake of the crackdown, a watered-down version of *The Suicide Club* that sought to cater to the horror market while presenting itself as mainstream fare.

Assigned to direct the project was J. Walter Ruben, the distinguished director of RKO's radio tie-in *The Phantom of Crestwood* (1932). Cast in the role of Prince Florizel was the up-and-coming Robert Montgomery, who yearned to work outside his usual genre of romance, while newcomer Rosalind Russell was cast as the heroine Miss Vandeleur, a character who did not appear in the original story. Unfortunately for Montgomery,

Robert Montgomery and Rosalind Russell star opposite each other in the romantic horror dramedy, *Trouble for Two*.

however, the role did not offer him much opportunity to flex his acting muscles; though far from a typical love story, the thrust of the film remained romance amidst an action-adventure setting, albeit with strong elements of horror and comedy.

The film opens with the words (in large type): "This motion picture is adapted from the story *The Suicide Club* by Robert Louis Stevenson. The events and characters are fictional and any similarity to actual persons, living or dead, is purely coincidental." This statement so boldly presented may seem strange today, but at that time MGM was smarting from a major lawsuit that had been filed against *Rasputin and the Empress* (1932) by real-life participants in the murder of the historical Gregori Rasputin. Though *The Suicide Club* was entirely a work of fiction based on a relatively famous (at the time) literary work, the film's European setting and period costumes were similar to those in *Rasputin*, thus leading to the overcautious disclaimer.

The viewer is introduced first to Prince Florizel (Montgomery) as he evades his nuptials to his impending bride, Princess Brenda of Irania, in a betrothal arranged by their fathers. To give his son a break, the king (Clive) sends the prince to London, assigning Colonel Geraldine (Morgan) to go along and keep an eye on the young man. Shortly into their cruise, the prince—who is traveling incognito—is called to the cabin of a lovely young woman (Russell), who claims that she's in danger and needs his assistance. A gun-toting stranger interrupts them; nobody is hurt, but after their departure from the boat, the prince cannot get the beautiful young lady out of his head. Later, when dining out with the colonel, he meets a young man named Cecil Barnley (Hayward); Barnley tells him about a mysterious club where disenfranchised people go to gamble, with their lives as the stakes. Hoping to occupy his mind with something other than the beautiful woman who continues to evade him, Florizel insists that he and Geraldine be taken to this strange suicide club, where—almost miraculously—he again sees her. They join in a game of cards in which the person who draws the Ace of Spades is to die by the hands of the person who draws the Ace of Clubs. The mysterious woman draws the murder card, while Cecil Barnley draws the death card, and the two depart alone so that the deed may be done in secret. The next night Florizel and Geraldine

Rosalind Russell incognito in *Trouble for Two*

return, and Florizel draws the death card while, as luck would have it, the mysterious woman draws the murder card (again). From there the prince and his companion are drawn into the increasingly sinister world of the suicide club.

While it definitely has its pleasures, *Trouble for Two* doesn't entirely work, largely because it tries to operate within too many genres at once without really digging into any one of them. Franz Waxman's terribly inane, zany score overwhelms the opening bits, overwrought with comedy as they are. The romantic resolution is obvious to anyone who's known someone who's read a Harlequin paperback, and the swashbuckling elements—a swordfight in particular—are well shot but simply too superfluous to count for much. The addition of political intrigue involving an enemy of the crown also helps to slow the picture down, making it feel longer than its 75 minutes.

Where the film does come alive is during its horror sequences (and that's undeniably what they are). The flight of stairs that leads up to the rooms held by the suicide club is appropriately gloomy, looking as if it were borrowed from a Universal set. And the rooms themselves, shot with low-key lighting and populated by melancholy types who wish only to die, add to the grim atmosphere. The club's president, played by noted British actor Reginald Owen, is suitably creepy in his obviously fake bald cap, which is so pronounced that it teeters between being eerie in the manner of Frankenstein's monster and being distracting to the point of silliness.

The performances from almost everyone involved are good, though Montgomery's is the standout. His Prince Florizel is charming and boyish, yet noble and upstanding. Montgomery got an opportunity to prove his dramatic mettle a year later when he took on the role of the sociopathic Danny in *Night Must Fall*, for which he was nominated for a Best Actor Academy Award. Also returning for that film was Rosalind Russell, who gave a far more nuanced performance there than she does here.

Frank Morgan heads up *Trouble*'s supporting cast as the loveable oaf Geraldine, and the aforementioned Reginald Owen plays the villainous Dr. Noel. Owen had a long and distinguished career that began in 1911 when he starred as Thomas Cromwell in the short feature *Henry VIII* and ended with the role of Jones in the television remake of *Topper* (aired in 1973, a year after his death). Rounding out *Trouble*'s lesser roles was E.E. Clive and Louis Hayward. Clive had made a career as a character actor late in life; he had small parts in several classic horror films, including *The Invisible Man* (1933), *The Mystery of Edwin Drood* and *The Bride of Frankenstein* (both 1935), *Dracula's Daughter* (1936), *Maid of Salem* and *Night Must Fall* (both 1937), *The Last Warning* (1939), and *The Hound of the Baskervilles* (1939). Hayward, on the other hand, was at the beginning of his career and went on to many leading roles. Among his few horror film appearances were those in *The Thirteenth Candle* (1933), *And Then There Were None* (1945), *The Son of Dr. Jekyll* (1951) and *Terror in the Wax Museum* (1973).

To some extent, *Trouble for Two*'s forgotten status is justified, yet it's not without its merits. And as a curio for people interested in what the horror film looked like during Hollywood's self-imposed ban, it's worthy of at least a viewing. CW

The Walking Dead
Warner/First National; b/w; 66 min; U.S.
D: Michael Curtiz *S:* Robert Adams, Lillie Hayward, Peter Milne, Joseph Fields, Ewart Adamson *P:* Louis F. Edelman *C:* Hal Mohr *M:* Bernhard Kaun
Cast: Boris Karloff, Edmund Gwenn, Marguerite Churchill, Riccardo Cortez, Warren Hull, Barton MacLane, Henry O'Neill, Paul Harvey, Robert Strange, Joe Sawyer, Eddie Acuff, Joe King, Kenneth Harlan, Miki Morita, Ruth Robinson

John Ellman (Karloff) is set up to take the blame for the murder of a judge who refused to cower before the Mafia. Ellman's mob-planted attorney (Cortez) sees to it that he is sent to the electric chair. At the same time, Dr. Beaumont (Gwenn) develops a method for resuscitating the recently deceased. After Ellman's execution, Beaumont brings the convicted felon back from the grave, and even though the returnee remembers nothing of his experience, he is driven to seek revenge on the men who framed him.

For his final Warner Bros.–First National horror film, director Michael Curtiz crafted a then-topical melding of horror and gangster melodrama. Famed aviator and inventor Charles Lindberg had recently collaborated with Dr. Alexis Carrel to create an artificial heart that enabled organs to live outside their bodies, thus allowing surgeons to perform previously undoable transplants and delicate surgeries. The five screenwriters who worked on *The Walking Dead* used the headline grabbing "Lindbergh heart" as a springboard for fancy, and the script mixes hard science with plenty of science fiction.

The film starts off like a typical Warner Bros.' gangster outing, replete with gum-chomping thugs and backroom double dealing, but once Boris Karloff shows up as the pitiable Ellman, *Dead* transcends the limitations of a typical gangster picture. Though the versatile actor had already appeared in a couple of gangster roles, notably in the Howard Hawks/Howard Hughes version of *Scarface* (1932), he is here cast in a sympathetic light that makes his work more than mere reprise. The Ellman character is an underprivileged sap, a patsy whose naïveté ensures that he is framed for a murder he didn't commit, executed and then used as a Guinea pig by an over-reaching scientist.

The fact that, upon returning from the grave, the character doesn't degenerate into a monster is indicative of Karloff's sensitivity as a performer. According to film historian Greg Mank, the original script called for the resurrected Ellman to display simian tendencies and evoke more horror than pity. Karloff nixed that idea, however, insisting that the character be developed in a subtler manner. The Ellman that results is more avenging angel than menace, though the cold-blooded gaze he shoots his enemies reminds the viewer of what a sinister presence Karloff could be. It's a beautifully structured performance, in the top tier of memorable Karloff characterizations.

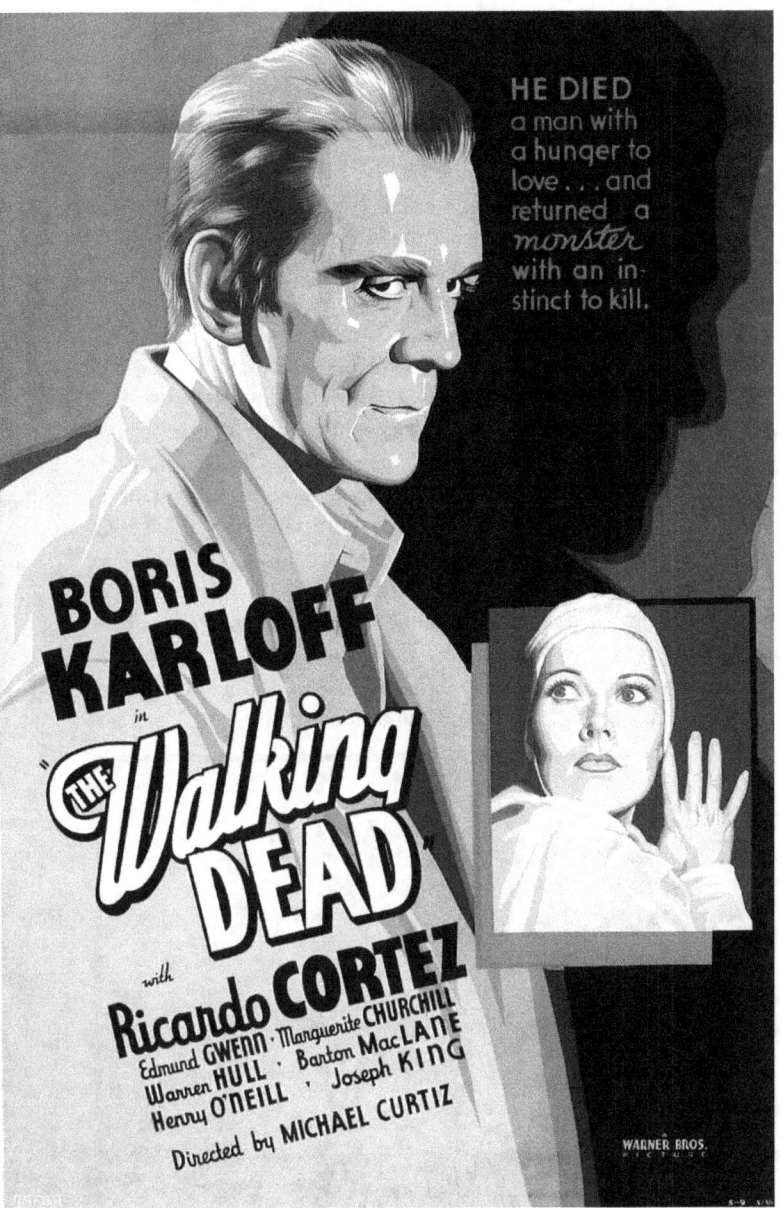

The supporting cast is generally impressive as well. Edmund Gwenn (best remembered for his Oscar-winning turn as Kris Kringle in *The Miracle on 42nd Street*, 1947) avoids caricature as the dedicated Dr. Beaumont. The character is written as callous and insensitive, driven more by morbid curiosity than a genuine desire to help mankind. In the hands of a lesser actor, he would have come across as totally unlikable, but Gwenn humanizes the part.

The obligatory young lovers are well played by Marguerite Churchill and Warren Hull. The same year as this film, Churchill went toe-to-toe with *Dracula's Daughter*, and her spunky, charming performances in both films make one regret that she didn't do more horror roles—she certainly compares well to the many shrill and basically useless horror heroines of the period. Mention should also be made of Ricardo Cortez (known for his work in *Thirteen Women*, 1932) and Barton MacLane (known for *The Mummy's Ghost*, 1943), who are effectively slimy as the central villains.

Ably assisted by Hal Mohr's shadowy cinematography, Curtiz creates some memorable images throughout. Viewers looking for more overt terror may find *The Walking Dead* to be a little soft, but it remains one of the most poignant and oddly haunting horror films of its period. TH

Yotsuya kaidan

Kyokuto; b/w; length unknown; Japan

    D: Sonoike Naruo

    Cast: Mitsusaburo Ramon, Kyoko Sakurai

This is one of numerous Japanese film adaptations of Tsuruya Nanboku IV's classic horror play *Yotsuya kaidan*, first staged in the early 1800s. The story deals with a poor samurai so desperate for wealth that he disfigures and ultimately causes the death of his wife in order to marry his beautiful mistress, a member of a wealthy and esteemed family. His former wife does not stay dead, however, returning from the grave to torment the adulterous lovers to death.

It is reasonable to conclude that Mitsusaburo Ramon starred as Iemon the samurai and Kyoko Sakurai as Oiwa, his doomed first wife. Little information about this film survives, and many film historians confuse it with a 1928 screen adaptation from Takuji Furumi, which may or may not have been the first sound version of the tale. CW

1937

Dr. Sin Fang
Victory; b/w; 60 (63) min; Great Britain
D: Anthony (Tony) Frenuelli *S:* Nigel Byass, Kaye Mason Frederick Reynolds *P:* Nell Emerald
Cast: Harry Agar Lyons, Anne Grey, Robert Hobbes, Nell Emerald, Art Ash, Louis Darnley, Ernest Sefton

Numerous sources claim that this film's plot concerns the evil Dr. Sin Fang's (Lyons) attempt to swipe a newly developed cure for cancer, a plot thwarted by Professor Graham (Ash), but British Film Institute records describe something else entirely: Having been sentenced to imprisonment (some sources assert death, though here again the BFI description doesn't support this), Dr. Sin Fang escapes and murders the judge responsible for his sentence. John Byrne (Hobbs) and the beautiful Sonia Graham (Grey) track him down and capture him.

While Harry Agar Lyons reprises his role from a 1928 six-film series of two-reelers known as the *Dr. Sin Fang Dramas*, Robert Hobbes takes over for actor Fred Paul (who had also directed the original films) in the role of John Byrne, here portrayed as a detective rather than a lieutenant. Sonia Graham (Anne Grey), the daughter of Professor Graham (Art Ash), becomes the new love interest, replacing Betty Harberry (originally played by Evelyn Arden) of the original series.

The film's producer, Nell Emerald, appears onscreen as Mrs. Higgins. This was not her first film as producer; she'd previously done *Terror on Tiptoe* and *Murder at the Cabaret*, two mysteries released in 1936. Nor was this her first encounter with actor Lyons. The two had starred opposite each other as early as 1913 in *East Lynne* and *The Grip of Iron*. CW

Doctor Syn
aka **Dr. Syn**
Gaumont British; b/w; 78 min; Great Britain
D: Roy William Neill *S:* Roger Burford, Michael Hogan *P:* Michael Balcon, Edward Black *C:* Jack Cox, Jack Parry *M:* Hubert Bath, Jack Beaver
Cast: George Arliss, Margaret Lockwood, John Loder, Roy Emerton, Graham Moffatt, Frederick Burtwell, George Merritt, Athole Stewart, Wilson Coleman, Wally Patch, Meinhart Mauer, Muriel George

Based on silent film star Russell Thorndike's popular 1915 novel *Doctor Syn: A Tale of the Romney Marsh*, this is a fast-paced action/adventure film with the odd touch of horror. Beloved Reverend Dr. Christopher Syn (Arliss) is in truth one Captain Clegg, a pirate and smuggler commonly believed hanged 20 years before. But no—he is, in fact, settled in the small village of Dymchurch in Kent, on England's southeastern coast, which, as it happens, is perfectly situated to smuggle alcohol and tobacco from France, thus avoiding heavy British taxes. Over time, Syn has taken to using his smuggling gains to assuage the village's once-high poverty rate. He's helped in this benevolent illegality by Rash (Burtwell), who also happens to be the schoolmaster, and Mipps (Merritt), the town's coffin maker.

Things liven up when Captain Collyer (Emerton) of the Royal Navy and his band of men come to town to investigate reports of smuggled goods in the Romney Marsh. When it looks as though a drunken local physician named Dr. Pepper (Coleman) might inadvertently spill the beans, Rash murders him. Things are further complicated when a loose-cannon mulatto slave (Maur), who once raped Clegg's wife (thus driving her to suicide) and had his ears and tongue sliced off in retribution, turns up to complicate matters. Romantic sparks come courtesy of Clegg's daughter Imogene (Lockwood), who has no idea who her father really is, and handsome young Denis Cobtree (Loder). Rounding things out is a group of phantom riders who warn people away from the marsh late at night, when smuggling activities are at their height.

Director Roy William Neill provides some potent images; those of the phantom riders, their faces hidden behind skull-like masks as their silhouettes block the evening sky, are quite striking. Just as memorable are shots of Syn/Clegg disguised as a solitary scarecrow, barking orders to his criminal cohorts. And the claustrophobic village sets, with their extraordinary period detail and quaint Gothic appeal, foreshadow the look and feel of many a future Hammer film.

With Neill at the helm, there's not a slow moment to be found, with the script managing to balance drawing room wordplay with rousing action. It's no wonder that Neill, who was

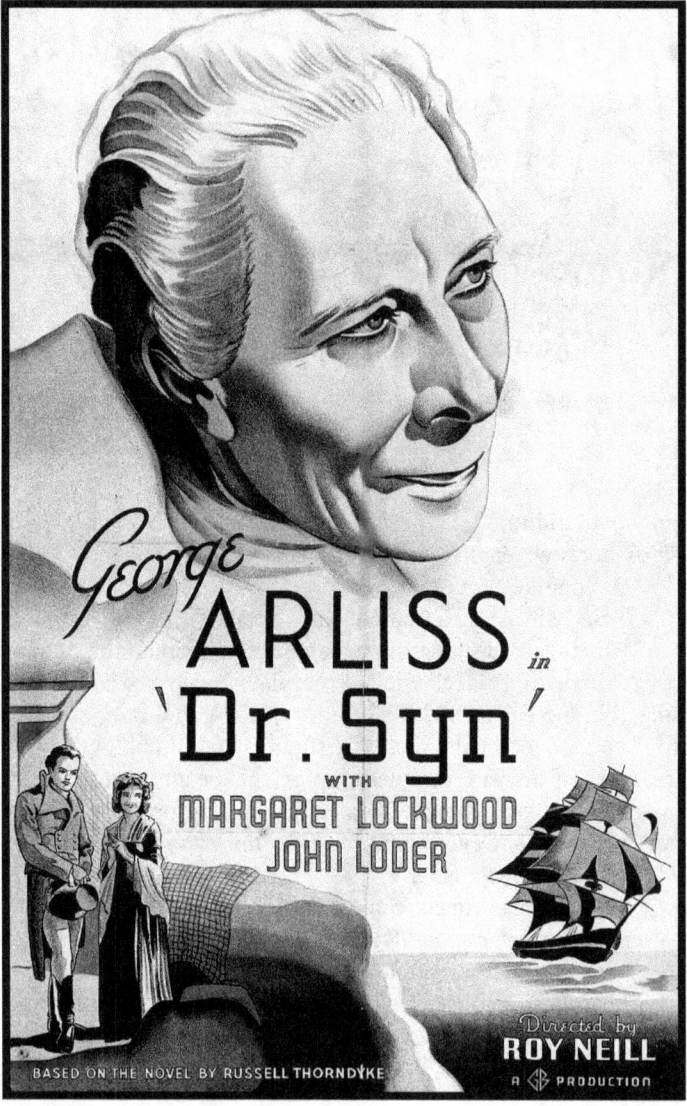

Although a famous actor in his day, George Arliss is today known as the man who discovered Bette Davis.

born in 1887 on a ship off the coast of Ireland, found such great success in the United States only a few years after this, directing Universal's iconic series of Sherlock Holmes films starring Basil Rathbone and Nigel Bruce. He also directed *The Menace* (1932), *The Ninth Guest* and *Black Moon* (both 1934), *The Black Room* (1935) and *Frankenstein Meets the Wolf Man* (1943). His career ended with his death from a heart attack in London in 1946, just four months after the release of his last film, *Black Angel*.

Apart from its visual excellence, *Doctor Syn* also boasts a terrific cast of top British thespians. George Arliss was such a sought-after star that when Warner Bros. offered him an exclusive contract, they sweetened the deal with an unheard of degree of creative control over his films (this despite the fact that he was an elderly man at the time). He was often given the privilege of selecting his co-stars; thus he can be credited with discovering the likes of Bette Davis and James Cagney, among others. At length he left Warner for up-and-comer Fox. After returning to his native London during the war years, he never returned to the United States, despite entreaties from the likes of Darryl F. Zanuck. As Dr. Syn/Captain Clegg, he is pitch perfect, a stately old gentleman with the capacity for great violence (as can be viewed by what he has done to the mulatto), held in check by his extraordinary intelligence. The role proved to be his last; he retired from film after its completion and, in 1946, died of a bronchial ailment. It's unfortunate that his barnstorming exit from cinema is overshadowed in favor of some of his more successful but less worthwhile big-studio offerings.

Likewise terrific as the young heroine Imogene, Margaret Lockwood found lasting fame the very next year as Iris Henderson in Alfred Hitchcock's megahit *The Lady Vanishes*. Born in British India (now Pakistan) in 1911, she acted until the late 1970s and retired after receiving a CBE in her native England. She died of cirrhosis of the liver in 1990. Fellow Brit John Loder fails to make much of an impression as her boyfriend, though he did eventually move to Hollywood where he became a fairly successful star alongside Maureen O'Hara (*How Green Was My Valley*, 1941) and Bette Davis (*Now, Voyager*, 1942). His other horror credits include *The Mysterious Doctor* (1943) and *A Game of Death* (1945), among others.

Despite being largely faithful to its literary source, *Doctor Syn* diverges in one major respect: In the end, Captain Clegg escapes, whereas in the book he dies. Novels in Thorndike's *Syn* series provided the basis for later films from Hammer (*Captain Clegg*, 1962) and Walt Disney (*Dr. Syn, Alias the Scarecrow*, 1964). CW

Don Juan Tenorio
Excelsior; b/w; 74 min; Mexico
   D/S: René Cardona *P:* Virgilio Calderon, Juan Pezet *C:* Ross Fisher *M:* Max Urban
   Cast: René Cardona, Gloria Morel, Alberto Martí, Jesús Grana, Consuelo Segarra, Miguel Arenas, Paco Martinez, Rafael Icardo, Mary Carrillo, Aurora Walker, Lina Santamaria, Carlos Aganza, Ina Rico, Jesús Melgarejo, Gerardo del Castillo, Enrique Gonce, Max Langler, Maria Alvarez, Georgette Somohano, José Rachini, Mayer Beraja, Murad Bettech, Jalal Zaad
   Adhering fairly closely to José Zorillo's 1844 play of the same name, director René Cardona's debut feature has Don Juan (Cardona) winning a bet with Don Luis (Martí) over who will have sex with the most women and kill the most men. The bet is extended, however, when Juan further swears that he can get both Luis' girlfriend Ana (Rico) and a nun named Inés (Morel) into the sack. Again he wins, though in the process he's forced to kill both Luis and the father of Inés. Years later Don Juan visits the grave of his victims, where he encounters Inés' ghost. When he is then killed, his victims' ghosts challenge him, but Inés saves him and whisks him to Heaven.

Cardona, who directed approximately 150 films in his career, also took on the role of Don Juan for this production. His affinity for horror led to a host of genre entries in the 1960s and '70s, including *Doctor of Doom* (1963), *Wrestling Women vs. the Aztec Mummy* (1964), *Night of the Bloody Apes* (1969) and *Santo and the Vengeance of the Mummy* (1971). Many of his later fantasy films starred several masked wrestler characters that were popular in Mexican cinema at the time. CW

The Dybbuk
aka **Der Dibuk; Between Two Worlds; Dybuk**
Warszawskie Biuro Kinematograficzne Feniks; b/w; 125 (110, 108) min; Poland
   D: Michal Waszynski *S:* S.A. Kacyzna, Andrzej Marek, Anatol Stern *P:* Zygfryd Mayflauer *C:* Albert Wywerka *M:* Henoch Kon

A young woman becomes possessed by an evil spirit in *The Dybbuk*.

Cast: Abraham Morewski, Ajzyk Samberg, Mojzesz Lipman, Lili Liliana, Leon Liebgold, Dina Halpern, Max Bozyk, M. Messinger, Gerszon Lemberger, Samuel Bronecki, Samuel Landau

Based on a 1914 Yiddish play of the same title by S. Ansky (real name: Shloyme Zanvl Rappoport), *The Dybbuk* tells the tale of two men who commit their children to marry each other despite dire warnings from a mysterious traveler. Through unforeseen circumstances the children are separated and grow up apart. Years later they find each other, but the girl has become engaged to another man. The boy determines to win her over through black magic, but his attempts result in his own death, and the girl becomes possessed by his dybbuk, or spirit.

The word *dybbuk* comes from a Hebrew verb meaning "to cling" and over time has come to denote a good or evil spirit that possesses a person. Though mainstream Judaism rejects this, the concept was part of Talmudic folklore in times past and provided the basis for Ansky's play, which was first successfully staged in 1920.

Jewish filmmakers in the border area between Poland and Russia had been creating cinema since the 1920s, and by the mid-1930s—just before Hitler's forces decimated much of Europe and ended all but patriotic German filmmaking—they had hit their creative stride. The rights to Ansky's play were a major coup for producer Zygfryd Mayflauer, and he put the property into production in early 1937. Director Michal Waszynski shot the film partially on location and partially in the studio, creating a striking balance between Old World realism and silent German Expressionism.

The Dybbuk was released theatrically in Poland on September 19, 1937 and in Yiddish cinemas in the United States on January 27, 1938. It is today acknowledged as a classic of Jewish-language cinema. CW

Enmadera no yurei
Kyokuto; b/w; length unknown; Japan
D: Teppei Yamaguchi S: Shinzabaro Ikushina C: Sadao Uemura
Cast: Katsutaro Bando, Myoko Kohama, Tazuko Suminoe, Kouji Kawada, Koutarou Isehara, Naojiro Oomidou, Inosuke Yano, Sashou Ichikawa

By all accounts, this obscure film was as much mystery as it was horror, despite its indisputable place in the venerable "ghost cat" subgenre. It concerns a man (Bando) who, obsessed with stories of a ghost cat haunting the nearby Enma Temple graveyard, sets out to investigate.

The film was released in Japan on February 20, 1937. Its title, *Enmadera no yurei*, translates as "Ghost at Enma Temple." It should not be confused with Daito's *Enmadera no kaibyô* (1938). CW

Fukushu suru shigai
Kyokuto; b/w; length unknown; Japan
D: Hakkou Nishifuji S: Sairoku Nishi C: Shizuya Matsumoto
Cast: Genzaburo Ayakuji, Myoko Kohama, Saemon Kataoka, Kenosuke Sawada, Jiro Yasokawa, Koichi Kaeda

This enigmatic Japanese horror movie was clearly inspired by Michael Curtiz's seminal 1936 horror-gangster hybrid *The Walking Dead*. Even the title is a steal; when translated, it reads "The Avenging Dead." The plot has a young man (Ayakuji) murdered and his body procured by a mad scientist named Hiraga Gennai. Gennai brings him back to life, after which the murdered man sets out to revenge himself upon his murderers.

Hiraga Gennai was the name of a real-life Japanese pharmacologist and inventor. Famed for inventing the thermometer and asbestos cloth, Gennai lived from 1728 to 1780. His appearance in *Fukushu suru shigai* evidences a long tradition in Japanese cinema of basing characters on historical personages. Another example is *Modern kaidan: 100,000,000 Yen* (1929), which cast real-life gangster Chuji Kunisada as a ghost guarding his treasure.

Fukushu suru shigai was released to Japanese theaters on July 15, 1937. CW

The Ghost Cat of Arima
aka **Kaiden Arima neko**; **Arima neko**
Shinkô Kinema Oizuni; b/w; 50 min; Japan
D: (Mokudo) Shigeru Kito S: Kenji Hata C: Tsunejiro Kawasaki
Cast: Kitseumon Arashi, Yuriko Asano, Kazuko Fuji, Mitsuko Gun, Takeko Hidaka, Omenosuke Ichikawa, Setsuko Kai, Wakako Kunitomo, Fusae Kusama, Mitsuyo Matsumoto, Atsumi Miho, Shizuko Mori, Yaeko Oe, Toshiko Okubo, Sumiko Suzuki, Masako Takamatsu, Hiroko Takayama, Yoshiko Tomei, Yoshio Tsujii, Kinue Utagawa, Masako Yanase

This is the more famous of the two mid-1930s film versions of the Japanese Arima Palace legend of a ghostly cat haunting its walls. Like *Arima no neko sodo* (1936), *The Ghost Cat of Arima* tells the tale of a murdered woman's spirit that, while inhabiting a cat, seeks revenge upon the woman's murderer (a common theme in countless Japanese "ghost cat" legends and movies).

Shigeru Kito, who also went by the name of Mokudo Shigeru, directed *The Ghost Cat of Arima*. His directorial career ended only a few years after this film's release. Kenji Hata, who wrote the script, was at the beginning of his short career, which lasted only until the mid-1940s. The film's producer, Sinko Kinema Oizuni, made films from approximately 1931 to 1939. This one appears to have been its only foray into the horror genre.

Ghost Cat was released in Japan on October 30, 1937 and is one of the few horror films from its period to exist today. Interestingly, the film's best-known movie poster, easily viewed on the Internet, was created for a 1960s re-release, not the film's original theatrical run. CW

Henge nyorai
Shinkô; b/w; length unknown; Japan
  D: Takashi Nishihara
  Cast: Hideo Otani, Sumiko Suzuki, Shizuko Mori, Kunio Kaga

When his father is murdered, young Toge Utaro (Otani) heads out to Edo (today known as Tokyo) for vengeance. There he meets an enigmatic priest named Jigen who promises to help, but only if the young man makes certain concessions to the gods.

Among this film's cast was Sumiko Suzuki, at this time edging toward the end of her distinguished career. A novel of the same name by Kikuo Tsunoda became the script's basis, and his work provided the basis for several films shot from the late 1930s to the late 1950s. This particular film seems to have been a catch all of sorts, with subplots involving a Taoist immortality drug and the Philosopher's Stone (a staple of the "science" of alchemy). One can conclude from all this that the movie was likely a mix of horror and serial-like action/adventure. CW

Honchô kaibyô-den
Makino; b/w; length unknown; Japan
  D: Kazunori Sakata S: Kyoichi Chizi C: Ihachi Omori
  Cast: Junosuke Hayama, Teruko Ouchi, Tsukie Matsura, Sume Tsuki, Sansiro Tsubaki

Released in Japan on February 7, 1937, *Honcho kaibyô-den* translates as *Domestic Legend of the Ghost Cat*. It was the first of two films, shot approximately two years apart, to bear the same title. The other came in 1939 and was produced by Daito.

This first effort was produced by Shozo Makino's home studio a decade after he died. Utilizing sound-recording equipment, which was still something of a rarity in Japan during the 1930s, it was directed by Kazunori Sakata, a relative newcomer to horror who never really took to the genre. Junosuke Hayama and Teruko Ouchi essayed the lead roles. CW

Hyaku banashi usimitsu no koku
aka 100 banashi usimitsu no koku
Shochiku; b/w; length unknown; Japan
  D: Tatsuo Osone, Taizou Fuyushima, Eji Iwata, Eji Yoshino
  Cast: unknown

This appears to have been an anthology consisting of short horror works from a variety of Japanese directors. The title translates as "Telling 100 Ghost Stories at 2:00 a.m.," which dovetails into the Japanese superstition of the *100 monogatari*, the idea that if partygoers gather and tell 100 ghost stories, with each participant blowing out a candle after he or she tells a tale, when all is said and done, something terrifying will happen.

That premise has been milked several times in Japanese cinema and television. CW

Irohagana Yotsuya kaidan
Shochiku; b/w; length unknown; Japan
  D: Shigeru Mokuto
  Cast: Sumiko Suzuki, Shinpachiro Asaka

A decade after the original *Irohagana Yotsuya kaidan* (1927), Sumiko Suzuki returned a fourth time as the ill-fated wife of a samurai (Asaka) so obsessed with bettering himself in society that he disfigures and kills his wife in favor of the wealthy daughter of a local landowner, after which his wife's spirit drives him to kill his mistress and himself (in that order, of course).

This was one of many films based upon Tsuruya Nanboku IV's infamous kabuki horror play, which had by this time entertained Japanese noblemen and peasants alike for well over a century. Of the various 1930s adaptations, none are particularly well known today, and there is no indication that prints of any of them have survived.

Shigeru Mokuto also directed the 1939 horror film *Ghost Story of a Love-Mad Tutoress*. In addition to *Irohagan Yotsuya kaidan*, another version of the story (simply titled *Yotsuya kaidan*) was allegedly made in 1937, this one starring Eigorou Onoe, but little is known about this second adaptation. Neither of these would be the last. Over the next several decades, many more adaptations were done, some as straight horror, others as romances, and still others as political allegories. CW

Kaidan botan dōrō
Nikkatsu; b/w; length unknown; Japan
  D: Toshizu Kinugasa S: Tatsuo Jinde C: Asajiro Aramoto
  Cast: Komako Hara, Kunitaro Sawamura, Fujiko Fukamizo

The title *Kaidan botan dōrō* translates roughly as *Ghost Story of the Peony Lantern*. The film tells the tale of a scorned woman named Otsuya, whose ghost lights her way with a lantern decorated with a peony pattern. In beautiful disguise, she seduces the samurai Shinzaburo, who used and deserted her years before.

Kunitaro Sawamura starred as Shinzaburo, while Fujiko Fukamizo took on the part of Otsuya. This was the last adaptation of Sanyutei Encho's *rakugo* (one-performer) play until the mid-1950s, when Akira Nobuchi's *Peonies and Stone Lanterns* (1955) was released to general acclaim and good box-office receipts. CW

Kaidan Kasane-ga-fuchi
Kyokuto; b/w; length unknown; Japan
  D: Hachiro Ogura S: Kyohiko Itama C: Shizuya Matsumoto
  Cast: Keinosuke Sawada, Kyoko Arishima, Uppei Ohata, Myoko Kohama, Saemon Kataoka, Sashou Ichikawa, Minoru Aoki, Inosuke Yano, Yoji Arima, Nojiro Omidou

Shinkei Kasane-ga-fuchi is one of several morality plays that were popular in Japan during the 19th century. (Others included *Yotsuya kaidan* and *Botan dōrō*.) All deal with men abandoning their wives for younger women, after which the

The sinister Basil Rathbone as he appeared in *Love from a Stranger*

wives die and return from the grave to take revenge upon the lovers who had done them harm. Such evil spirits were known as *grudge ghosts*, because their sole reason for returning was to even a score. *Kaidan* is the Japanese term for ghost, and *Kasane-ga-fuchi* is a reference to the area in which this particular story took place (in the swamps of the Kasane district, to be exact).

The next adaptation of Sanyutei Encho's 1860 novel came a mere two years later as *Ghost Story of a Love-Mad Tutoress*. The most famous adaptation, however, dates from the mid-1950s, when Japan's answer to Britain's Terence Fisher and Italy's Mario Bava, Nobuo Nakagawa, directed the art-house horror movie *The Ghosts of Kasane Swamp* (1956). CW

Legend of the Saga Cat Monster
aka **Saga kaibyô-den**
Shochiku; b/w; length unknown; Japan
D: Shigeru Mokuto S: Ryo Ueshima C: Tsunejiro Kawasaki
Cast: Ryutaro Otomo, Sumiko Suzuki, Setsuko Kai, Kunio Kaga

Some sources cite *Legend of the Saga Cat Monster* as being produced and released in 1931. While the date of its production is not verifiable with any degree of certainty, it does appear that the film was released in Japan on February 4, 1937. If it were shot anywhere near its release date, it would be the last adaptation of Joko Segawa III's oft-filmed 1853 kabuki play, *Hana Saga neko mata zoshi* (about the Saga Castle ghost cat), to be shot in the 1930s.

Legend starred the queen of Japan's horror industry at the time, Sumiko Suzuki, in an important role as Otoyo-no-kata. She did double ghost-cat duty in 1937, also gracing screens in *The Ghost Cat of Arima*. She made her lasting mark, however, as Oiwa, the poor wife of Iemon, in a number of adaptations of the famous kabuki play *Yotsuya kaidan* (1825). CW

Love from a Stranger
aka **Night of Terror**
Trafalgar; b/w; 86 min; Great Britain
D: Rowland V. Lee S: Frances Marion P: Harry E. Edington, Max Schach C: Philip Tannura M: Benjamin Britten
Cast: Ann Harding, Basil Rathbone, Binnie Hale, Bruce Seton, Jean Cadell, Bryan Powley, Joan Hickson, Donald Calthrop, Eugene Leahy

Carol Howard (Harding) wins a small fortune in the lottery and finds herself being wooed by the charming Gerald Lovell (Rathbone). Her friends and family worry that he's only interested in her money, but she falls for the handsome stranger and they are married. After their honeymoon, however, Gerald begins to act oddly, refusing to let Carol see her friends and confining her to their home.

Dame Agatha Christie (1890-1976) is *the* all-time most popular and celebrated female author of mysteries and thrillers. *Love from a Stranger* is adapted from her 1924 short story *Philomel Cottage*, by way of a 1936 stage play (under what would become the film's title) by character actor/playwright Frank Vosper. As an actor, Vosper is best remembered as Ramon, one of Peter Lorre's henchmen, in Alfred Hitchcock's original *The Man Who Knew Too Much* (1934). His adaptation of the Christie story was popular with audiences, and it didn't take long for it to transition to the silver screen.

Produced by the minor Trafalgar Films outfit of London, the film is an early example of the "wife in peril" subgenre. American-born Rowland V. Lee was imported to direct. He had been active as a director since 1920, and his output wound up including everything from horror (*Son of Frankenstein*, 1939) to screwball comedy (*Service De Luxe*, 1938, which featured the film debut of horror icon Vincent Price). In time Lee gained a degree of creative control over some of his U.S.–made pictures, but *Love* was cut from a smaller cloth. (A look at the mammoth excesses of his later *Son of Frankenstein* indicates that this is not necessarily a bad thing.)

Love begins as a conventional melodrama, with Carol expressing dissatisfaction with the state of her life. Then, when she wins the lottery, she revels in her chance to cut free and do everything she's ever dreamed about. The meeting between her and Gerald Lovell is too good to be true, with the suave and debonair man sweeping her off her feet. This early section is a bit slow, but once the film kicks into psychodrama, however, it establishes a firm grip and never lets go.

Lee does a terrific job of building tension. Also key to the movie's effectiveness are the central performances by Harding and Rathbone. Harding was an established film and theater actress by this time, and her billing over Rathbone indicates that the vehicle was intended for her. It is Rathbone, however, who steals the show.

Rathbone would in time come to be identified with horror/suspense roles such as the one here, but in truth his connection to the genre is tenuous at best. Though he did, of course, triumph as Sherlock Holmes—starring in a series of 14 Holmes films at 20th Century Fox and Universal—he also scored major, comparatively forgotten successes in everything from literary adaptations (*David Copperfield*, 1935) to swashbucklers (*The Adventures of Robin Hood*, 1938) to war dramas (*The Dawn Patrol*, 1938). He was, in fact, nominated twice for Academy Awards (*Romeo and Juliet*, 1936, and *If I Were King*, 1938) though he never won. A beloved veteran of countless film, stage and radio appearances, the South African-born actor finished his career making cheapies for American International Pictures, and even some of these (notably *The Comedy of Terrors*, 1963) offered him an opportunity to shine.

He was an established name by the time of *Love*, but the role allowed him to express his range like never before. His early scenes betray a character that is effortlessly charming, though one can sense that he is hiding something. As the picture moves forward, he becomes progressively more high-strung and prone to violent outbursts. The finale is a fine example of borderline camp that somehow manages to work. His showdown with the clever and resourceful Harding is a delight to watch, a wonderfully directed showstopper, brilliantly performed by both actors. (Director Lee also allowed the usually restrained Rathbone to go over the top in *Son of Frankenstein*, but it works far less persuasively there.)

The score was the work of noted English musician Benjamin Britten, with excellent use made of Sergei Prokofiev's *Peter and the Wolf*; it was among only a handful of film scores written by the composer, who spent the bulk of his career writing and performing for his self-formed English Opera Group.

Love from a Stranger was remade in 1947 under the same title. TH

Maid of Salem
Paramount; b/w; 86 min; U.S.
  D: Frank Lloyd *S:* Walter Ferris, Bradley King, Durward Grinstead, Bradley King *P:* Howard Estabrook *C:* Leo Tover *M:* Victor Young
  Cast: Claudette Colbert, Fred MacMurray, Harvey Stephens, Gale Sondergaard, Louise Dresser, Bennie Bartlett, Edward Ellis, Beaulah Bondi, Bonita Granville, Virginia Weidler, Donald Meek, E.E. Clive, Madame Sul-te-wan, Sterling Holloway, J. Farrell MacDonald, Lionel Belmore

Make no mistake about it, *Maid of Salem* is a melodrama, plain and simple. Yet, with the unofficial ban on horror films well under way, studios were keen to fill what had become a niche market without being too obvious. Paramount struck upon a real-life historical incident that was the stuff of nightmares—the Salem Witchcraft Trials of 1692, in which a group of spoiled girls accused innocent women of tormenting them through supernatural means. The result was this, Frank Lloyd's searing indictment of religious hypocrisy and violence.

Maid of Salem presents a fictional heroine, Barbara (Colbert), as the protagonist, but apart from that the film is steeped in historical fact. In Salem Village, Massachusetts, Puritan elders hold a clenched fist over their parishioners, while their children are subjected to loveless religious upbringings in which they are expected to behave like miniature adults. But since they are, despite their environment, children, it isn't all that aberrant when one of them—the minister's daughter (Granville) no less—immerses herself in fancy, pretending to be tormented by witches after listening to the South Seas tales of her father's black servant Tituba (Sul-te-wan). She's given further fuel for her imagination when she swipes a copy of Cotton Mather's infamous book about the Black Arts in New England, a tome that contains the framework for the persecution of anyone who doesn't fit into the Puritan mold (to wit: the mentally ill, elderly widows, blacks and sexually attractive young women). Not surprisingly, things get wildly out of hand very quickly, building to a shocking climax. Not, as one might expect, the deaths of its witches—which at any rate occur off screen—but rather a scene in which Barbara defies her Puritan jurists by loudly denying the existence of witchcraft and the Devil.

Even if the set-up takes a bit too long and the ending is a tad rushed, much of *Maid of Salem* feels like a very good Universal horror film in the vein of *The Mystery of Edwin Drood* (1935). This impression is further bolstered by its utilization of various Universal bit players in supporting roles. While Claudette Colbert is the indisputable star of the picture (and gives an excellent performance), Chicago-born Bonita Granville is even better as the minister's daughter, a child so emotionally starved

Donald Meek listens to Claudette Colbert, an innocent woman falsely accused of witchcraft in *Maid of Salem*.

by her parents that she turns to witchcraft fantasies as a way of empowering herself. Up to this point, Granville's career had already been marked by astonishing performances in three major films: *Little Women* (1933), *Anne of Green Gables* (1934) and *These Three* (1936), the latter being the first of William Wyler's two cinematic adaptations of Lillian Helman's subversive play *The Children's Hour*. The charming actress went on to star as Nancy Drew in a short-lived series for Warner Bros. and to shine in such vehicles as *Now, Voyager* (1942) and *Hitler's Children* (1943). (In an early example of cross merchandising, she was also the star of a young adult novel, *Bonita Granville and the Mystery of Star Island*, by Kathryn Heisenfelt.) After marrying producer Jack Wrather in 1947, she whittled down her acting career to occasional bit parts on television programs while focusing on television production herself. She died of lung cancer in 1988. Despite her many great performances in classic films, she remains a largely forgotten figure today.

Claudette Colbert, on the other hand, is anything but forgotten. Born in 1903 in Saint-Mandé, France under the name Emilie (Lily) Claudette Chauchoin, she moved to the United States and performed on Broadway in the mid-1920s under the stage name Claudette Colbert. A successful film career followed, and by 1934 she was a major draw at the box-office, winning an Academy Award for Best Actress and starring in three films nominated for Best Picture—all in that same year! *Maid of Salem* is also notable as one of seven films in which Colbert starred opposite Fred MacMurry, here playing her beau, Roger Coverman. Her last major hit, *The Egg and I* (1947), marked the beginning of her decline in popularity, and by the mid-1950s she was mostly making her living as a guest star on various television shows. Colbert's last role, for the television movie *The Two Mrs. Grenvilles* (1987), garnered her both a Golden Globe award and an Emmy nomination. She died in 1996 in Barbados after suffering a series of strokes.

Maid also offered small but important roles to future horror star Gale Sondergaard as Martha Harding and African American actress Madame Sul-te-wan as Tituba. The Salem Witchcraft Trials would be further revisited on the big screen in various adaptations of Arthur Miller's classic anti-HUAC play *The Crucible* (1953). CW

Murder at the Baskervilles
aka Silver Blaze
Hagen; b/w; 71 (65) min; Great Britain
 D: Thomas Bentley *S:* H. Fowler Mear, Arthur Macrae *P:* Julius Hagen Julius *C:* Sydney Blythe, William Luff *M:* Marcus De Wolfe
 Cast: Arthur Wontner, Ian Fleming, Lyn Harding, John Turnbull, Robert Horton, Lawrence Grossmith, Judy Gunn, Arthur Macrae, Arthur Goullet, Martin Walker, Eve Gray, Gilbert Davis, Minnie Rayner, D.J. Williams

It's been 20 years since Sherlock Holmes (Wontner) solved the case of the Hound of the Baskervilles. A still-grateful Sir Henry Baskerville (Grossmith) invites Holmes and Dr. Watson (Fleming) to his estate. The reclusive detective is reluctant to accept but ultimately relents. Once there, however, it becomes rapidly clear that this is to be no vacation. A big horse race, The Barchester Cup, is to be held not far from Baskerville Hall, but there's been a murder and the prized racehorse Silver Blaze has gone missing. Holmes is convinced that his arch-nemesis Professor Moriarty (Harding) is responsible.

The Adventure of Silver Blaze was first published in 1892. It's a trivial slice of the Holmes pie that hasn't generated nearly as much interest as many other tales in the series. *Murder at the Baskervilles*, a low-budget British production, turns the story into a sequel of sorts to 1901's novel *The Hound of the Baskervilles* and is one of only three adaptations of the story (one being an episodic television program from 1977 starring Christopher Plummer as Holmes and Thorley Walters as Watson; the other an episode of the mid-'80s Granada television series "The Return of Sherlock Holmes" starring Jeremy Brett as Holmes and Edward Hardwicke as Watson).

Murder marks the last appearance of Arthur Wontner as Holmes. A then-popular character actor who has fallen into obscurity, he first assumed the mantle of Holmes with 1931's *The Sleeping Cardinal* (aka, *Sherlock Holmes' Fatal Hour*) and revisited the role four more times: *The Missing Rembrandt* (1932, considered lost), *The Sign of Four* (1932), *The Triumph of Sherlock Holmes* (1935) and this film. Originally titled *Silver Blaze*, *Murder at the Baskervilles* wasn't released in the United States until 1941, when it was re-titled to capitalize on the success of Fox's *The Hound of the Baskervilles* (1939). The U.S. release is six minutes shorter than the original version. Though more a straight mystery than a horror film, it warrants inclusion here because of its connection to the most macabre of Doyle's thrillers.

Wontner makes a fine Holmes, sardonic and likable. He seems a bit long in the tooth this time around, but this actually works in the film's favor; this is an older, more reflective Holmes, implicitly past his glory days but still capable of rising to the occasion. Australian actor Ian Fleming (not to be confused with the creator of the James Bond series) portrayed Watson, and he teamed with Wontner in four of the actor's five Holmes' films. The exception was *The Sign of Four*, wherein Ian Hunter (*Dr. Jekyll and Mr. Hyde*, 1941) assumed the role. Fleming isn't by any stretch the most inspiring or enjoyable Watson imaginable, but he plays off Wontner reasonably well.

Arthur Wontner as the immortal Sherlock Holmes in the bloodless *Murder at the Baskervilles*

Lyn Harding played the devious Professor Moriarty, and he also played the character in *The Triumph of Sherlock Holmes*. Harding's Moriarty is a caricature, most definitely not in the same league as George Zucco (who played the part in *The Adventures of Sherlock Holmes*, 1939) or Eric Porter (in the aforementioned Granada television series starring Jeremy Brett as Holmes).

Murder at the Baskervilles is of only minor note in the cinematic Holmes canon, but it's still a briskly paced and enjoyable entry. TH

Never Too Late to Mend
aka **It's Never Too Late to Mend**; **Never Too Late**; **It Is Never Too Late to Mend**
King; b/w; 67 min; Great Britain
D: David MacDonald *S:* H.F. Maltby *P:* George King *C:* Hone Glendinning
Cast: Tod Slaughter, Jack Livesey, Marjorie Taylor, Ian Colin, Lawrence Hanray, D.J. Williams, Roy Russell, John Singer, Cecil Bevan, Douglas Stewart, Mavis Villiers

The opening credits of this film inform us that *Never Too Late to Mend* is based on the book *It Is Never Too Late to Mend* by Charles Reade, who in 1856 "so exposed the prevailing conditions in English prisons that he is generally credited with being responsible for the present reforms … After reading this work [Queen Victoria] demanded to know if such brutalities were being performed in her name and ordered an investigation which brought about the universally high standard prevailing today."

The film adaptation offers Tod Slaughter yet another turn as a conniving squire. His John Meadows lusts after Susan Merton (Taylor), the beautiful daughter of a middle class farmer (Williams). She, however, is in love with a handsome young farmer named George Fielding (Colin). When Meadows attempts to have Fielding framed for poaching, Fielding's friend Tom Robertson (Livesey) takes the rap instead and is sentenced to one-year hard labor. But unfortunately for Tom, Meadows is a Justice of the Peace with easy access to the prison, and he uses his influence to make Tom's stint as miserable as possible.

The sadistic squire, as it happens, toys with far more people than Tom. While routinely excusing prisoners who profess Christianity, Meadows delights in punishing those who commit the merest of infractions, such as singing in their cells. One underage prisoner (Singer) is given a particularly hard time for the crime of stealing bread to feed his dying mother.

Meadows revels in describing to a visiting priest (Russell) the horrors of a room in which unruly prisoners are thrown:

> That is the black hole, the most effective of all our punishments. It is dark in there, no light, no furniture and it is silent, too, as silent as the tomb. In there you are shut off from your fellow man. No sign of life reaches you. After one hour … you lose all count of time; seconds drag on and seem like hours, hours days, the days years. After one day in there, I've seen the most violent man emerge as cowed and broken as a whipped dog … and without a hand laid on him, all done by time, as it were.

Far from being impressed, the described cruelty so horrifies the priest that he begins a quest to overturn the brutal system.

A solid little horror movie dressed up as social commentary, *Never Too Late to Mend*, like many other George King productions of the period, transcends its quickie-quota limitations. The overall result is a chilling portrait of England's prison system in the mid-1800s. The film's one major flaw is that it's a bit schizophrenic. There are two very different tales being told, the first a melodramatic love triangle involving the squire, Susan Merton, and George Fielding; the second a straight-on shocker with a jarring mood that intrudes upon the first.

The art direction from Philip Bawcombe and Jack Hallwood, particularly in the opening scene in the cemetery of an old church, is appropriately atmospheric, and Hone Glendinning's cinematography frames each shot perfectly. Director David MacDonald understood the visual aspect of cinema, though he wasn't so much an action director per se; he later used what he learned from his early films on Britain's 1954 Gothic sci-fi entry *Devil Girl from Mars*.

Mend's performances are almost uniformly excellent, with British horror star Tod Slaughter leading the pack as the contemptible (and deliciously hammy) Squire Meadows. The only disappointing performance is that of Marjorie Taylor, whose tendencies toward flat, not-so-deliciously hammy portrayals marred more than one of Slaughter's barnstormers. (She also

had rather unfortunate leading roles in *The Crimes of Stephen Hawke*, 1936, *The Ticket of Leave Man*, 1937 and *The Face at the Window*, 1939).

Slaughter's next horror film was the aforementioned *The Ticket of Leave Man*, released just in time for Halloween in 1937. CW

Night Key
Universal; b/w; 67 min; U.S.
D: Lloyd Corrigan *S:* Jack Moffitt, Tristram Tupper *P:* Robert Presnell *C:* George Robinson *M:* Lou Forbes, Karl Hajos, Charles Maxwell, Arthur Morton, Charles Previn, David Raskin, Heinz Roemheld, Clifford Vaughan, Edward Ward, Franz Waxman *FX:* John P. Fulton
Cast: Boris Karloff, Warren Hull, Jean Arthur, Alan Baxter, Hobart Cavanaugh, Samuel S. Hinds, David Oliver, Ward Bond, Frank Reicher, Edwin Maxwell

Kindly inventor David Mallory (Karloff) develops a new type of security system, but an old nemesis named Steven Ranger (Hinds) buys the rights to it with the intention of suppressing it. When Mallory discovers what's up, he sets out to disarm the system with an electrical device. In the process, he falls into the hands of some desperate mob characters. Headed by The Kid (Baxter), the thieves plan to use Mallory to facilitate a crime wave.

Night Key is one of those films that horror-crazy kids in the pre-cable, pre-DVD era used to stay up late for, only to be bored into the slumber they'd been fighting. Given its year of origin—and, of course, the presence of Boris Karloff—it's even today often regarded as a minor Universal horror classic. In truth, however, it's merely an unmemorable drama with elements of suspense that don't gel. And while languishing in the same miscategorized limbo as, say, *The Man Who Reclaimed His Head* (1934), *Night Key* suffers in one additional regard: It just isn't very good.

Director Lloyd Corrigan is better known as a rotund character actor, active from the 1920s until the late 1960s. Horror buffs may remember him as an amiable inspector in Universal's bargain basement *She-Wolf of London* (1946), but he also had a brief career as a screenwriter (*The Mysterious Dr. Fu Manchu*, 1929) and director (*Daughter of the Dragon*, 1931), helming a total of 13 titles between 1930 and 1937. *Night Key* was his penultimate effort in that arena, and it's easy to see why. Though the presence of ace cinematographer George Robinson (*Son of Frankenstein*, 1939) ensures that the film is competently shot, it's nonetheless flat and, even at a little over an hour, it drags.

As for Karloff, he does a credible job under the circumstances, but his gaunt frame and stooped posture make him look older than he was at the time. There's also some unintentionally funny pantomiming at times as his character's failing eyesight reduces him to staggering about like his most famous characterization, the Frankenstein monster. Still, it's nice to see him play a good guy for a change.

The supporting cast includes prolific character actors Samuel S. Hinds (*The Raven*, 1935), Frank Reicher (*King Kong*, 1933) and Ward Bond (*The Searchers*, 1956) in small roles that, while stock, register more favorably than vapid romantic leads Warren Hull and Jean Arthur, who bring the already sluggish pace to a complete halt each time they play cute.

Karloff enthusiasts will want to see *Night Key*; others wouldn't be missing anything by steering clear. TH

Night Must Fall
MGM; b/w; 117 min; U.S.
D: Richard Thorpe *S:* John Van Druten *P:* Hunt Stromberg *C:* Ray June *M:* Edward Ward
Cast: Robert Montgomery, Rosalind Russell, Dame May Whitty, Alan Marshal, Merle Tottenham, Kathleen Harrison, E.E. Clive, Matthew Boulton

Mrs. Bramson (Whitty) is the stereotypical grouchy dowager. Bound to a wheelchair by little more than hypochondria, she lords her position over her reserved niece Olivia (Russell) and her meek servants Dora (Tottenham) and Emily (Harrison). Into her home comes the charming Danny (Montgomery), who may have had something to do with the disappearance of a woman from a nearby town. Danny may be charming, but he's also hiding something in a hatbox, and his relaxed and easy-going demeanor is obviously a cover for a tormented spirit. And though Mrs. Bramson is taken in by the young man's friendly chattiness, Olivia is not; she comes to suspect that he's hiding something, and that something may indeed be murder. Yet despite the fact that she distrusts and is afraid of him, she's also drawn by his charisma and dashing good looks. While her suspicions grow with the discovery of a headless corpse buried beneath a tree on the front lawn, so does her attraction to Danny. When an opportunity arises to alert the police, she instead saves him from being exposed. In the end (and after an additional cold-blooded murder), Olivia and Danny, inevitably, face off.

The original play by successful writer/director/actor Emlyn Williams, who also played the part of Danny on stage, was produced for the London theater in 1935 by future Hammer character actor Miles Malleson (*Horror of Dracula*, *The Hound of the Baskervilles*, both 1958; *The Brides of Dracula*, 1960). Several of the play's alums (though not Williams) went on to star in the movie version, including Whitty, Harrison and Boulton. All of them acquit themselves with aplomb.

Night Must Fall is a dramatic piece of quiet terror, driven by well-written dialogue and accomplished performances. The

film was nominated for two Oscars (Best Actor for Montgomery; Best Supporting Actress for Whitty). MGM, however, was reportedly ashamed of the picture. If true, it's easy to see why. The film's gruesome revelation, while probably not a surprise even upon its initial release, had to have seemed inappropriately blatant given what was acceptable at the time, a mere three years after the authorities had begun serious enforcement of the Production Code's stringent censorship rules.

It stands today as a nasty little production wrapped up in MGM class. As Danny describes the physical appearance of the woman for whom he once worked and who has disappeared, he notes that she had "a thick neck." At the moment he does so, his eyes take on a distant, insane glaze. While the line seems mostly innocuous when delivered, it takes on new meaning when the woman's corpse is discovered without its head, making the contents of the hatbox all too apparent. Just as daring is the not-so-subtle suggestion that maid Dora might be pregnant with Danny's baby, even though the two aren't married.

Montgomery's performance is a *tour-de-force*, a template for decades of deranged killers to come, while Dame Whitty more than holds her own with a wonderfully sly performance as the seemingly insensitive but ultimately good-hearted Mrs. Bramson. The film's only other major performance, Russell as Olivia, is fairly forgettable, not so much because of her performance, but because the character remains too staid. Had the script flirted more with her interest in Danny, then Olivia's character—a woman obsessed with murder and bloodshed though unable to come to grips with her own fascinations—and Russell's performance would have been a far more satisfying one. But given the climate of the times, the innocent and virginal heroine would never have been allowed such a fascinating indulgence.

Richard Thorpe (1896-1991), a major Hollywood director whose career lasted from the silent era to the late 1960s, manages to keep the affair moving, though there are a scattered handful of moments during which the proceedings become bogged down by adhering a little too closely to their stage-play origins. The most effective aspect of Thorpe's direction is his ability to find horror in broad daylight; in this respect, *Night Must Fall* is a precursor to the country Gothic of Thomas Tryon's *The Other* (1972) and Tobe Hooper's *The Texas Chainsaw Massacre* (1974). The film's title says it all; while the story takes place mostly during the brightness of daylight, the mood is always one of impending darkness. That night must fall is inevitable, and with it will come the terrors that darkness brings.

The story was given a more horrific facelift for the 1964 remake, produced by and starring Albert Finney and directed by Karl Reisz. CW

Noroi no madara-neko
Kyokuto; b/w; length unknown; Japan
D: Hachiro Ogura *S:* Yukie Takahara *C:* Masahiro Myazaki
Cast: Ryunosuke Kumoi, Kiko Isuzu, Fumio Shizuta, Keinosuke Sawada, Myoko Kohama, Yozo Kojima, Renko Tae, Emiko Yanagi, Ranko Mori, Kyoko Naniwa

Demonic events occur throughout Edo—the feudal name for Tokyo—and appear to be the doings of a type of grudge ghost known as a ghost cat. The spirit of a person murdered at Castle Edo some 30 years prior conjured up the beast.

Noroi no madara-neko translates roughly as "Cursed and Dappled Cat" and was one of many films to feature a ghost cat bearing antipathy born of past events. The film was released on June 3, 1937 in its native Japan, but it was quickly forgotten amidst the swelter of numerous similar films.

This wasn't the only horror film directed by Hachiro Ogura in 1937; he also helmed the obscure *Kaidan Kasane-ga-fuchi*. Though little is known about the man, he should not be confused with actor Ichiro Ogura. CW

Oh, Mr. Porter!
aka **Oh Mr. Porter**
Gainsborough; b/w; 85 min; Great Britain
D: Marcel Varnel *S:* J.O.C. Orton *P:* Edward Black *C:* Arthur Crabtree *M:* Charles Williams
Cast: Will Hay, Moore Marriott, Graham Moffat, Sebastian Smith, Agnes Lauchlan, Percy Walsh, Dennis Wyndham, Dave O'Toole

William Porter (Hay) is offered a stationmaster's position at a secluded railway station in Ireland. The only problem is … the place is reputed to be haunted, and Porter's predecessors have all gone mad.

This comedy with horror elements—apparently derived without credit from Arnold Ridley's 1923 play *The Ghost Train*, itself filmed numerous times—is primarily of interest for its production personnel, many of whom went on to establish firmer connections to the horror genre. The picture itself is a typical vehicle for popular British comic Will Hay, who starred in numerous comedies during the 1930s and '40s. Hay, who was also an accomplished amateur astronomer, is credited with discovering the planet Saturn's "great white spot" in 1933. As an actor, he had by this time achieved fame as a comedic stage and radio presence. He came to cinema relatively late in life, making his film debut in *Radio Parade of 1935* (1934) at the age of 46 and cranking out unassuming British programmers until 1943. When World War II came along, he swapped film work for a stint with the Royal Naval Volunteer Reserve. He passed away in 1949, the result of a stroke.

Oh, Mr. Porter! was one of several Hay comedies directed by Marcel Varnel, who genre enthusiasts may recall as co-director of *Chandu the Magician* (1932). Varnel's assistant on this film was 21-year-old Roy Baker. Baker would himself turn to directing with the moody *October Man* in 1947 and find his greatest commercial and artistic success by sinking the Titanic in *A Night to Remember* (1958). Tired of being confused with a sound technician by the same name, he eventually began billing himself as Roy Ward Baker, a name under which he directed some of the outstanding horror and fantasy titles of the 1960s and '70s, including *Quatermass and the Pit* (1967) and *Asylum* (1970).

The cinematographer on *Mr. Porter* was Arthur Crabtree, also destined to become a director in his own right. His two most infamous titles remain the kinky Anglo Amalgamated shocker *Horrors of the Black Museum* (1959), which contains a wonderfully over-the-top turn from Michael Gough that typecast the actor for some time. And Crabtree directed the delirious cult favorite *Fiend without a Face* (1958), which climaxes with flying brains assailing a hapless group huddled inside a farmhouse.

Porter's make-up artist was Roy Ashton, who became identified with Hammer horror in the 1950s and '60s; among his most famous work is Christopher Lee's bloodshot stare as Count Dracula in many a Hammer film, and the same actor's moldering appearance as *The Mummy* (1959). TH

The Plate-Counting Ghost of Banchō
aka **Banchō sarayashiki**
Shochiku; b/w; 40 min; Japan
 D: Taizo Fuyushima
 Cast: Kazuo Hasegawa, Kinuyo Tanaka, Sakuko Yanagi, Masao Hori

Kinuyo Tanaka stars as Okiku, a beautiful servant girl, while Kazuo Hasegawa stars as her tormentor, a samurai named Aoyama Harima. When Okiku refuses to give in to Harima's sexual advances, she is summarily dispatched by being thrown into a well, only to return as the plate-counting ghost of the film's title.

Tanaka was born in 1909 and studied to become a musician. After receiving her license to play the chikuzen-biwa (a five-string Japanese instrument), she became part of a girls' revue and from there made the leap to film. Her first film, *Genroku onna*, came in 1924, and in 1925 she became a contract player for Shochiku Studios, with which she remained for the next 15 years. She was married for a short period to director Hiroshi Shimizu. In the 1950s she directed her first film and during the

Pierre Blanchar demands the secret of the cards from Marguerite Moreno in *Queen of Spades*.

1960s made regular appearances on television. She died of a brain tumor in 1977. Her only other horror film appearance came in the 1949 classic, *The Ghost of Yotsuya—New Version*, which had two feature-length parts.

The Plate-Counting Ghost of Banchō is one of the few Japanese horror films of the 1930s (and earlier) to still exist. CW

Queen of Spades
aka **La dame de pique; Pique Dame**
Général; b/w; 87 min; France
 D/Co-S: Fyodor Otsep *Co-S:* Bernard Zimmer *C:* Louis Née, Armand Thirard *M:* Karol Rathaus
 Cast: Marguerite Moreno, Pierre Blanchar, André Luguet, Madeleine Ozeray, Abel Jacquin, Camille Bert, Raymone, Palau, Roger Legris, Jean Didier

This, the first talkie version of Alexander Pushkin's short horror story *Pikovaya Dama* (1833), follows the tale of Hermann (Blanchar), who learns from his friend Tomski (Jacquin) that Tomski's grandmother, the Countess Tomski (Moreno), is in fact the Queen of Spades, a famed master at cards. According to Tomski, the Countess learned the secret of card playing via a pact with the nether realm, and now, as she ages, she fears death and damnation. Hermann, who is deeply in debt because of his constant gambling, befriends the Countess' young niece Lisa (Ozeray) as a means of drawing closer to the old woman. At length he manages to get the Countess alone in her bedroom, but when his attempt at seducing the secret out of her fails, he threatens her with a gun instead. Out of fear that the young man will kill her, the Countess has a heart attack and dies. Her spirit soon returns from the grave, however, and Hermann learns from her the secret he seeks. But things don't pan out as he hopes.

Director and co-scenarist Fyodor Otsep (1895-1949) was no stranger to Pushkin's story, having written the 1916 Russian film adaptation. (He also wrote the famous Russian science fiction classic *Aelita* in 1924). His knowledge of the material is evident and manifests itself in the form of nuanced characters, stylistic direction, lavish sets, creative costumes and sumptuous photography. Leading man Pierre Blanchar (1892-1963) was a major draw in French theaters in the 1930s and 1940s, though his career slowed down after Germany invaded France during World War II.

The next adaptation of Pushkin's tale was made in Britain in 1949 and is the most famous, garnering a BAFTA nomination for Best British Film. CW

The Riders of the Whistling Skull
aka **Riders of the Whistling Skull**; *The Golden Trail*
Republic; b/w; 56 (58, 53) min; U.S.

D: Mack V. Wright *S:* Oliver Drake, John Rathmell *P:* Nat Levine *C:* Jack Marta

Cast: Robert Livingston, Ray Corrigan, Max Terhune, Mary Russell, Roger Williams, Fern Emmett, C. Montague Shaw, Yakima Canutt, John Ward, George Godfrey, Earle Ross, Frank Ellis, Chief Thundercloud, John Van Pelt

Shot in just eight days in late 1936 and released in January 1937, *The Riders of the Whistling Skull* is one of the most overtly horror-tinged Westerns ever made. It opens to the ominous pounding of drums as a man in a grotesque skull mask leads a Native American dance. From there it cuts to young Betty Marsh (Russell) holding a skull and reading a curse inscribed upon it. Together with a group of professors, she hopes to lead an expedition into the mountains to discover the whereabouts of her father and his friend, who went missing while seeking the lost city of Lukachukai. While the group argues about how to proceed, the Three Mesquiteers (Livingston, Corrigan, Terhune) enter the room with the father's friend Flaxon (Shaw) in tow. Flaxon has been held captive and tortured by Native Americans, and just as he takes from his pocket a gold figurine to prove that Lukachukai exists, the lights go out. When they come back on, he's dead with a knife in his back. After some cajoling, the Mesquiteers agree to act as guides for the expedition, having no idea of the perils in store.

For legal reasons, the film's opening credits claim that a novel by William Colt MacDonald that first introduced The Three Mesquiteers was the basis of the screenplay. In fact, the screenplay is adapted from an original story by Bernard McConville and *Skull*'s co-scenarist Oliver Drake (mistakenly credited on some prints as Olive Drake). Producer Nat Levine, realizing the potential of MacDonald's characters, had convinced Republic to purchase the screen rights and, beginning with 1936's *The Three Mesquiteers*, the studio milked more than 50 films out of the series. Various men portrayed Mesquiteers over the years, among them John Wayne, Robert Livingston, Ray Corrigan, Max Terhune, Syd Saylor, Bob Steele, Tom Tyler, Raymond Hatton, Duncan Renaldo, Jimmy Dodd and Rufe Davis. The films were popular in theaters between 1936 and 1943 and found an even larger audience in television syndication in the 1950s and '60s.

Riders abounds with serial/horror clichés, from a lost civilization to the massive, hollow rock skull that overlooks a mountain pass, the wind whistling eerily as it passes through it (a genuinely nice, creepy image). Inside the skull are the remains of an ancient culture, including mummified bodies, one of whom comes to life and attacks the hapless heroes. There are also murders aplenty and a native ritual intended for the sacrifice of Betty Marsh. And since all of this isn't quite enough, there's a band of outlaws searching for the Lukachukai gold.

Lest all of this make *Riders* sound like a masterpiece of horror, it should be pointed out that Mack V. Wright's direction,

though fast paced, is far from flawless, and the script suffers from an overabundance of plot holes. The acting ranges from the good to the downright terrible, and the clothing worn by the Native Americans sometimes appears to have been lifted from a jungle safari flick. Regardless of, or perhaps as a result of, these flaws, the film has garnered cult status in the years since its release and is the best known of the many Mesquiteer oaters that were produced.

The next film in the series was *Hit the Saddle* (1937). CW

Sh! The Octopus
First National; b/w; 54 min; U.S.

D: William McGann *S:* George Bricker *C:* Arthur Todd *M:* Heinz Roemheld, David Raksin

Cast: Hugh Herbert, Allen Jenkins, Marcia Ralston, John Eldredge, George Rosener, Brandon Tynan, Eric Stanley, Margaret Irving, Elspeth Dudgeon

A send-up of the works of Mary Roberts Rhinehart (*The Bat*) and John Willard (*The Cat and the Canary*), Ralph Spence's 1925 play *The Gorilla* provided the impetus for Ralph Murphy and Don Gallaher's 1928 play *Sh! The Octopus*, which ditched the gorilla in favor of an octopus and set the action in a haunted lighthouse rather than a creepy old mansion.

In *Sh!*, a woman (Ralston) who claims to have seen a body hanging from a lighthouse tower lures two bumbling detectives (Herbert, Jenkins) into investigating. An archfiend known as the Octopus happens to be on the loose, and it isn't long before numerous shady characters—the Octopus possibly among them—gather in the lighthouse on various pretexts. As the narrative unfolds, the tentacles of a remarkably dexterous octopus (rivaling in its realism the similar one in Edward D. Wood, Jr.'s *Bride of the Monster*, 1955) emerge now and then from cupboards and secret panels to clutch and grab various cast members, including a painter named Paul Morgan (Eldredge) and the sinister Captain Hook (Rosener).

Too bad comedy duo Hugh Herbert and Allen Jenkins, both successful character actors in their own right, give such relentlessly zany performances. Their constant hoots and howls, outrageous facial expressions and witless one-liners drag down a film whose inherent just-plain-badness might have otherwise made it interesting. Little of *Sh!* makes sense (despite the relatively intelligible plot synopsis above)—which, to be fair, might be intentional, since in the end the audience learns that it was all a dream. But whatever the case, it's mostly a chore to sit through.

That said, the film does manage a certain nightmarish charm at times, thanks to William McGann's admittedly creative direction. McGann had a talent for wringing suspense from trite situations (the characters wander between the lighthouse's main room and a connecting cavern in a manner betraying the film's silent-era roots in the "old dark house" subgenre, which is about as trite as cinema gets). Especially impressive is a special effects shot in which a woman transforms into a witch without a single edit or dissolve. This (black-and-white) effect appears to have been created with colored make-up and slowly shifting tinted lenses. The technique had been used to good effect in *Ben Hur* in 1925 and *Dr. Jekyll and Mr. Hyde* in 1931 and would later be utilized by Mario Bava in 1960's superior *Black Sunday*. While McGann's directing career petered out by 1944, his special effects efforts went on, and in 1946 he was nominated for an Oscar for his work on the Bette Davis vehicle *A Stolen Life*. Though he didn't win, he did go on to contribute to some of the most famous films of the 1940s, including *The Treasure of the Sierra Madre* and *Key Largo* (both 1948) and *The Fountainhead* (1949).

His other horror credits include some amazing visual work for *The Beast with Five Fingers* (1946) and the nearly invisible effects of *The Woman in White* (1948). CW

Song at Midnight
aka **Yè bàn gē shēng; Singing at Midnight; Voice at Midnight; The Phantom of the Opera**
Xinhua; b/w; 117 (113) min; China
   D/S: Weibang Ma-Xu *P:* Shankun Zhang *C:* Boqing Xue, Xingsan Yu *M:* T. Han
   Cast: Shan Jin, Menghe Gu, Ping Hu, Chao Shi, Wenzhu Zhou

A Spanish man named Galen Bocca exhibited in Shanghai (on August 11, 1896) the first film ever shown in China. The event caused a sensation, and the following year an American took advantage of the buzz by traveling around to teahouses and projecting films onto their walls. Those films were shorts, of course, actuality films that simply chronicled everyday scenes and events, though a few appear to have been trick films similar in style to Georges Méliès. By 1905 foreign cinematic product had become big business, leading Beijing photographer Ren Fengtai to build his own movie theater and shoot and present his own single-shot actuality films.

The first authentically Chinese short feature was produced in 1913, and moviegoing quickly became an integral part of Chinese life in the bigger cities. In the beginning there were only a few studios operating in China, including The Motion Picture Department and the Asia Film Company. By the 1920s, however, a burgeoning film production industry had formed, with many smaller outfits popping up to take advantage of an increasing number of theaters and growing ticket sales. The early 1920s also saw the debut of the Chinese-made feature-length film. *The Vampire* (1921) was among the first films produced to meet the demand for longer movies. Despite its title, it was not a horror

The young heroine Li is the object of a phantom's affection in *Song at Midnight*, the first horror film to be shot in China.

film; rather, it dealt with the kidnapping of a doctor by a group of women living in a cave. The title refers to the seductive powers of womanhood rather than to any literal bloodsucker (as was so often the case with the word's usage in the days before *Nosferatu—A Symphony of Terror*, 1922).

In the mid-1920s, a young graduate from the Shanghai Institute of Art named Weibang Ma-Xu entered cinema as an actor for the Mingxing Film Company and by 1926 was directing features for them. Though enterprising, his films were mostly lackluster and failed to make a mark on Chinese cinema. A standout exception sprang up in 1937—long after most of the world had bought into the vogue established by Universal's twin successes of *Dracula* and *Frankenstein* (both 1931): Ma-Xu struck a chord with filmgoers by writing and directing China's very first horror film, *Song at Midnight*. It was a major hit.

The story itself was something of a rip-off of Universal's silent super jewel *The Phantom of the Opera* (1925), which had no doubt made its way to Chinese screens in the years between its production and 1937. Regardless, audiences flocked to *Midnight*, and the message to filmmakers was loud and clear: Horror films were big business.

Midnight opens with an acting troupe coming to stay at an old, cobwebbed theater on a rainy, windswept night. A decrepit hunchback greets them and leads them through rat and snake-infested hallways to their practice room. After a particularly disappointing rehearsal, a member of the troupe, Sun, stays behind to mope about his bad performance. He hears a disembodied voice coming from above, and the silhouette of an enshrouded man approaches with a story of a young male opera singer named Song.

Song, it seems, had once been in love with a beautiful girl named Li. But Li was coveted by the wealthy merchant Tang who, to get Song out of the picture, went to Li's father, a feudal lord, and informed the old right-winger about Song's leftist politics. The feudal lord reacted by having Song whipped and sent on his way, with the warning never to see Li again. Believ-

Young hero Song befoe his face is scarred by acid in *Song at Midnight*.

ing that his way was clear, Tang hit on Li, but she refused him, professing her love for Song. Angered, Tang stalked Song as he left the theater one evening and threw acid in his face. Song's fellow actors nursed him back to health, but when Song finally unwrapped his bandaged face and saw the scarred visage beneath, he went mad with rage and became the theater's resident phantom.

Back in the present, the phantom awaits a young male singer with just the right voice to sing beneath Li's bedroom window on nights of a full moon. His hopes are that Li, who has gone crazy believing her lover dead, will snap out of her insanity when she hears Sun's voice. Later, when Li actually does hear Sun's song calling to her from the forest around her castle-like home, she follows it, believing it to belong to Song, and she does indeed return to her old self. The stage is set, Song thinks, to selflessly offer Sun to Li as a replacement husband. Unfortunately, Song learns that Sun is engaged and his fiancé works in a theater run by the degenerate Tang. When Tang attempts to accost her, Sun shows up and prevents her rape but cannot prevent Tang from shooting her. In the end, however, Song extracts vengeance for both him and Sun, and Tang gets his just reward.

Song at Midnight operates successfully in several genres simultaneously, from the musical (with songs written by composer Xinghai Xian and lyricist Han Tian), to romantic melodrama, to the horror film. In addition to the obvious references to *The Phantom of the Opera*, there are numerous other visual cues taken from other horror films of the silent and early sound era: the hunchbacked assistant is drawn from *The Hunchback of Notre Dame* (1923), and the image of the beautiful but vampiric Li, framed by her window with an entranced look upon her face, recalls *Dracula*. Sun, in black cape and black hat, brings to mind the hypnotic Murder Legendre (Bela Lugosi) from *White Zombie* (1932), while the unwrapping of Song's bandages makes one

flash on *The Invisible Man* (1933). There's also the shrouded Song approaching Sun for the first time, his candle held firmly in hand, and Li's late-night walk through the dark woods, reflecting an obvious Expressionist influence. And the film's final images of the burning theater, with the phantom trapped inside, evoke the fiery finale of James Whale's classic *Frankenstein*.

The film doesn't flinch from violent excess, such as when Song is whipped by the feudal lord's bare-chested crony. The camera first focuses on the horrified yet titillated faces of the villagers, watching intently as the whip is swung, before cutting to Song, his shirt ripped open and his chest covered in blood and torn flesh. After its initial exposure in the film's most powerful scene, the appalling image of Song's scarred face soon becomes matter-of-fact, with the camera refusing to shelter the audience from it in the way that equivalent Hollywood product from the same period usually did.

Of course, all this isn't to say that the film is perfect. Its biggest fault may be its running time, which is overly long, not because there are too many scenes, but because each scene takes so long to unfold. The expositions are too long, and as with other sound versions of Gaston Leroux's classic novel, there are too many musical numbers, most of them lasting too long. Regardless, images such as the phantom watching with sadness as Sun greets his lover, or the slow camera panning around the phantom's bowed and depressed form, are powerful, and it is moments such as these that make *Song at Midnight* a classic of the 1930s horror film.

The film proved so successful that it was followed the next year by two more Chinese horror films, *Walking Corpse in an Old House* and *The Lonely Soul*. Both were directed by Ma-Xu and contained similar elements of romance and melancholy. But it wasn't until 1941, when China was in the middle of a war with Japan, that Ma-Xu made a direct sequel, *Song at Midnight—Part 2*. That film flopped at the box-office, possibly because audiences at the time—tired of the horrors of war all around them—wanted lighter, more escapist fare. CW

SOS Coast Guard
Republic; b/w; 12 chapters (224 min/69 min); U.S.

D: Alan James, William Witney *S:* Frank Adreon, Barry Shipman, Edward Lynn, Winston Miller *P:* Sol C. Siegel *C:* William Nobles *M:* Raoul Kraushaar, Hugo Riesenfeld, R.H. Bassett, Alberto Colombo, Louis De Francesco, Karl Hajos, Nem Herkan, Arthur Kay, William Lava, Milan Roder, Leo Rosebrook, J.S. Zamecnik *FX:* Jack Coyle, Howard Lydecker, Theodore Lydecker

Cast: Ralph Byrd, Bela Lugosi, Maxine Doyle, Richard Alexander, Lee Ford, Herbert Rawlinson, John Picorri, Lawrence Grant, Thomas Carr, Carleton Young, Allen Connor, George Chesebro, Ranny Weeks

Intrepid Lt. Terry Kent (Byrd) of the U.S. Coast Guard matches wits with demented inventor Boroff (Lugosi), who has created a gas that disintegrates matter.

This busy serial offers way more action than horror, but it does feature Bela Lugosi in one of his many mad scientist roles. Republic Pictures produced this during the horror ban of the late 1930s, allowing the studio to tap into the Lugosi brand without being unduly horrific about it. Indeed, the very name

ing from *Walt Disney's Wonderful World of Color* to *The Alfred Hitchcock Hour*. His movie work, like that of James, encompassed mostly B-Westerns and serials, and he too had a hand in some of the Dick Tracy adventures. He retired in the early 1980s, after which he penned a couple of colorful autobiographies. He died in 2002 and was cited in the end titles of *Kill Bill Volume 2* (2004) as a source of inspiration for writer/director/movie junkie Quentin Tarantino.

Witney's flair for athletic action is evident throughout *SOS Coast Guard*, though it is unclear how the directorial duties were divvied up. But despite the ample smash and flash, and a formidable villain, it's pretty weak stuff on the whole. TH

Super Sleuth
Small/RKO; b/w; 70 min; U.S.

D: Benjamin Stoloff *S:* Ernest Pagano, Gertrude Purcell *P:* Edward Small, Samuel J. Briskin *C:* Joseph H. August *M:* Alberto Colombo, Bernhard Kaun, Nathaniel Shilkret *FX:* Vernon L. Walker, Russell A. Cully

Cast: Jack Oakie, Ann Sothern, Eduardo Ciannelli, Alan Bruce, Edgar Kennedy, Joan Woodbury, Bradley Page, Paul Guilfoyle, William Corson, Alec Craig, Richard Lane, Willie Best, Paul Hurst, George Rosener, Ann Hovey

Willard "Bill" Martin (Oakie) is famous for playing a detective on screen. When some of his fellow actors receive death

Boroff seems something of an in-joke, a take-off on the name of Lugosi's onscreen rival, Boris Karloff.

As is usual for serials of this sort, *SOS Coast Guard* doesn't waste much effort on characterization. Clichéd characters abound: the square-jawed hero, the wisecracking reporter, the megalomaniacal inventor, etc. Lugosi's presence is, not surprisingly, the best thing about the production. The actor tones down his trademark hamminess, delivering a performance that's positively subdued compared to his work in, say, *The Raven* (1935). He effortlessly steals the show from bland leading man Ralph Byrd, who later played Dick Tracy in a series of B-programmers, the most interesting of which was 1947's *Dick Tracy Meets Gruesome*, in which he goes toe to toe with Boris Karloff.

Directors Alan James and William Witney pack in as much hackneyed action as space allows, just stopping short of tying the heroine to a railroad track. James, who sometimes billed himself as Alvin J. Neitz, was an efficient if unoriginal journeyman. He specialized in serials and B-grade Westerns, though he did direct another horror entry, *The Phantom* (1931). His career stalled in the early 1940s, and he died in 1952.

Witney's career had far more stamina. *SOS Coast Guard* was only his second time at the helm (following brief stints as an assistant director and actor). He directed well over a hundred films and television shows, his work in the latter medium rang-

threats in the mail, Martin carries his persona into the real world by playing amateur detective. With the help of his press secretary, Mary (Sothern), and his servant, Warts (Best), Martin traces the letters to the sinister owner (Ciannelli) of a local house of horrors.

This vehicle for popular screen comic Jack Oakie is yet another spoof of the horror genre. Born in 1903, Oakie rose through the ranks, attaining popularity as "The World's Oldest Freshman" due to his success in playing college-age characters in a series of musical comedies (including *College Rhythm*, 1934, and *Rise and Shine*, 1941). He appeared in dozens of popular comedies throughout the 1930s and '40s, most of them long forgotten. Contemporary viewers are most likely to remember him for his role as Napaloni, The Dictator of Bacteria, in Charles Chaplin's classic satire *The Great Dictator* (1940). He died in 1978, having gradually phased out of films and television in the 1950s and '60s.

In *Super Sleuth* Oakie is required to play an idiot whose arrogance constantly puts him in harm's way. The film, though far from classic, does offer up a few laughs, and Oakie carries the show capably. He receives solid support from such comic standbys as Ann Sothern, Edgar Kennedy (longtime foil of the Marx Brothers) and Willie Best, the latter trotting out his usual "scared Negro" routine.

Director Benjamin Stoloff was a capable journeyman who specialized in B-Westerns and musicals; he later switched to producing and in that capacity oversaw RKO's unfortunate *Zombies on Broadway* (1945), with Bela Lugosi. TH

The Thirteenth Chair
aka **The 13th Chair**
MGM; b/w; 66 min; U.S.
  D: George B. Seitz *S:* Marion Parsonnet *C:* Charles G. Clarke *M:* David Snell
  Cast: Dame May Whitty, Madge Evans, Lewis Stone, Elissa Landi, Thomas Beck, Henry Daniell, Janet Beecher, Ralph Forbes, Holmes Herbert, Heather Thatcher, Charles Trowbridge, Robert Coote, Elsa Buchanan, Lal Chand Mehra, Neil Fitzgerald

A séance is held by medium Madame LaGrange (Whitty) to reveal the person responsible for a recently committed murder. When one of the attendees is killed during the séance, however, it's up to Inspector Marney (Stone) to get to the bottom of things.

The third screen version of Bayard Veiller's popular 1916 play—and the second produced by Metro-Goldwyn-Mayer within a span of less than 10 years—*The Thirteenth Chair* assembled an impressive cast to tell its hackneyed tale. Distinguished British stage veteran Dame May Whitty (*Night Must Fall*, 1937) plays the quirky medium Madame LaGrange, while stolid Lewis Stone (*The Mask of Fu Manchu*, 1932) took on the part of the police inspector (played by Bela Lugosi in the previous version). Dependable character actor Holmes Herbert was brought back to repeat his role as Sir Roscoe Crosby, family patriarch.

There are also a few noteworthy faces to be found among the supporting cast, among them Charles Trowbridge, who went on to be strangled by *The Mummy's Hand* (1940); Henry Daniell, who became one of the screen's premier purveyors of elegant villainy (*The Body Snatcher*, 1945) and Robert Coote, who

established himself as a specialist in upperclass British twits (*Theater of Blood*, 1973).

Director George B. Seitz and Stone later worked together in a number of 1940s Andy Hardy comedies; Steitz also directed the horror film *The Drums of Jeopardy* (1931), which starred Warner Oland as one Dr. Boris Karlov!

Following *Chair*'s 1937 release, Veiller's stage play was put on ice; this is to date the last adaptation made for the cinema, and, like the earlier versions, it's extremely difficult to find. TH

The Ticket of Leave Man
King; b/w; 71 min; Great Britain
  D/P: George King *S:* H.F. Maltby, A.R. Rawlinson *C:* Hone Glendinning *M:* Jack Beaver
  Cast: Tod Slaughter, John Warwick, Marjorie Taylor, Frank Cochran, Robert Adair, Peter Gawthorne, Jenny Lynn, Arthur West Payne, Norman Pierce, Billy Bray

Based on a 19th-century Victorian melodrama, *The Ticket of Leave Man* is pretty ho-hum stuff from producer/director George King and actor Tod Slaughter. Slaughter stars as Tiger Dalton, who takes a liking to beautiful young May Edward (Taylor), despite the fact that she's engaged to a poor bank clerk named Bob Brierly (Warwick). In a blazingly unoriginal storyline, Tiger frames Bob for counterfeiting and has him sent to prison in hopes of freeing May for himself. The plan fails; Bob's

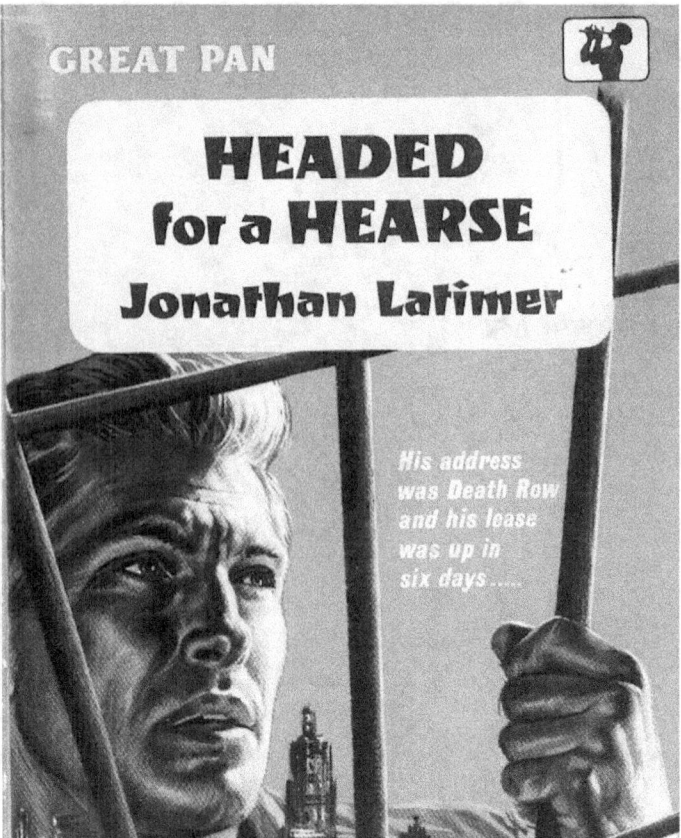

Headed for a Hearse is the Crime Club novel on which the movie *The Westland Case* was based.

good behavior gets him a "ticket of leave," or furlough, from prison (though his criminal record does make it hard for him to find work). Undaunted, Tiger cooks up a second scheme to get the young man out of the picture once and for all.

This is easily the nadir of the King/Slaughter collaborations. It apes the plot of previous outings *Maria Marten, or The Murder in the Red Barn* (1935), *The Crimes of Stephen Hawke* (1936), and *Never Too Late to Mend* (1937), all of which cast Slaughter as a killer trying to be rid of a young man in order to capture the love of a virginal young woman (in one case his own adopted daughter). And, as with those films, the villain here maintains a second, secret, identity as a kindly older man.

Director King shows little interest in the proceedings, shooting the scenes straight on without any of the fluidity of his previous endeavors. Philip Bawcombe and Jack Hallward's art direction is likewise dull and lifeless, with none of the usual flair associated with most of these barnstormers. There's also way too much talk and far too little action, with a couple of uninteresting musical interludes thrown in to bog things down even more. And to top it all off, there's a nasty streak of anti-Semitism running through the whole affair, a particularly hateful thing at a time when Hitler's Nazi Party had already forced large numbers of Jews into concentrated housing all over Germany.

At least Marjorie Taylor gives a better performance than is usual for the starlets in these pictures. Taylor was a common sight in Slaughter's horror films, but whereas usually she walked through them like a pretty but limp marionette, here she actually seems engaged in her character, with her usual silent-era histrionics (unusual for actors who began their career well into the talkie era) under firm control.

The Ticket of Leave Man is an utter timewaster that was followed in Slaughter's filmography by the slightly better *Sexton Blake and the Hooded Terror* (1938) and the definitely superior *The Face at the Window* (1939). CW

The Westland Case

Universal/Crime Club; b/w; 62 min; U.S.

D: Christy Cabanne S: Robertson White P: Irving Starr C: Ira Morgan FX: John P. Fulton

Cast: Preston Foster, Frank Jenks, Carol Hughes, Barbara Pepper, Astrid Allwyn, Clarence Wilson, Theodore von Eltz, George Meeker, Russell Hicks, Selmer Jackson, Rollo Lloyd, Thomas E. Jackson, Arthur Hoyt, Bryant Washburn, Ward Bond

Just days away from being executed for the murder of his wife, Robert Westland (von Eltz) receives a mysterious letter from someone claiming to be able to provide him with an alibi. Westland hires Chicago private dick Bill Crane (Foster) to find out who this witness is and thus exonerate Westland before the scheduled execution. There are some major facts standing between the condemned man and freedom; Mrs. Westland was murdered in a locked room, for starters, and Mr. Westland had the only other key. Nor does it help that she was murdered with her husband's rare-issue gun, or that a neighbor claims to have heard the shots while Mr. Westland was still at home. (The viewer learns much of this through a prosecutor's filmed "re-enactment," with the real participants playing themselves, offering proof to Crane and his assistant Doc Williams that Westland committed the crime.) Crane and Williams (Jenks) sort through the various possibilities but are thwarted at every turn when those with information about the case keep getting murdered. Thankfully, they solve the crime with seconds to spare.

A relatively straightforward mystery with a high body count for its time, *The Westland Case* was the first of eight films produced by Universal with its subsidiary Crime Club Pictures. All of them were cheapie productions intended for second feature status. Each was based on a separate novel published under Doubleday's Crime Club imprint, known best for its U.S. first editions of several of Leslie Charteris' *The Saint* and Sax Rohmer's *Fu Manchu* novels. The imprint also provided fodder for the later *Crime Club* radio series; though intended as competition for the popular *Inner Sanctum* series, it failed to make much of a mark and lasted only from 1946 to 1947.

As a film, *The Westland Case* works well, thanks to a tight script from Robertson White (*Mystery House*, 1938), who keeps the audience guessing while tickling them a bit with some frank sexual innuendo. For instance, when Williams suggests to Crane that they take along a sexy secretary (who also happens to be a suspect) to take dictation during an interview, Crane responds, "She doesn't take it; she gives it."

The film, adapted from the Jonathan Latimer Crime Club selection *Headed for a Hearst* (1935), was the second in the William "Bill" Crane series. Crane was a womanizing alcoholic who occasionally came out of his drunken stupor to solve crimes. Latimer's novels also provided the basis for two later adaptations in the Crime Club film series, *The Lady in the Morgue* (1938) and *The Last Warning* (both 1939).

Latimer went on to become one of Hollywood's most distinguished film noir scenarists, writing the scripts for such classics as *The Glass Key* (1942), *The Big Clock* (1948) and *Night Has a Thousand Eyes* (also 1948), as well as for the supernatural comedy *Topper Returns* (1941). He also created episodes of numerous television shows before dying of lung cancer in La Jolla, California in 1983.

Westland's performances are serviceable enough for a picture of this nature, with one actress standing out: Barbara Pepper as Agatha Hogan does her best—or worst—Mae West impression and garners laughs for all the wrong reasons. (The real mystery may be why West did not sue her.) Her performance didn't hurt her career any, however; she acted in films and television from 1933 until 1969, the year of her death from a heart attack.

The Westland Case was directed by Christy Cabanne, better known for schlocky fare such as the Bela Lugosi-starrer *Scared to Death* (1947), in addition to *Jane Eyre* (1934), *One Frightened Night* (1935) and *The Mummy's Hand* (1940). The film's editor Otis Garrett graduated to director with the second feature in the series, *The Black Doll* (1938), and helmed most of the remaining Crime Club films, including the aforementioned *The Lady in the Morgue* as well as *Danger on the Air* and *The Last Express* (both 1938) and *The Witness Vanishes* (1939). CW

Yaji and Kita's Cat Trouble
aka **Yaji Kita okazaki neko taiji**; **Yaji Kita Okazaki no neko sodo**
Daito; b/w; 60 min; Japan
    D: Misao Yoshimura *S:* Toshiko Oi
    Cast: Kaido Ooka, Tokujiro Yamabuki, Eiji Akagi, Debuko Oyama, Tomijiro Nakamura, Sadako Tani

Yaji and Kita's Cat Trouble is the first talkie adaptation of the story of the Okazaki ghost cat, first recorded in Jippensha Ikku's serialized novel *Shank's Mare* and later performed as a kabuki play in 1827. In fact, the two lead characters, Yaji and Kita, come from Ikka's comical work, making this something of a rarity in Japanese cinema: a ghost cat comedy! The original Japanese title, *Yaji Kita Okazaki neko taiji*, translates as *Yaji and Kita's Okazaki Cat Extermination*, while the secondary Japanese title, *Yaji Kita Okazaki no neko sodo*, translates as *Yaji and Kita's Cat Fuss* or, more commonly, *Yaji and Kita's Cat Trouble*. Unfortunately, only approximately 14 minutes of the film is still in existence.

This was not the first starring role for Ikku's heroes Yaji and Kita. They had previously appeared in the 1927 film *Yaji and Kita: Yasuda's Race*, which was also a comedy, and in 1937 took the lead roles in *Utau Yaji Kita Kyo-Osaka no maki*.

Ikku was famed for his shocking sense of humor. One popular story about him claims that, just before his death, he gave his students several packets and requested that they be placed on his chest during his funeral. His students did as instructed, and when his body was burned per Japanese tradition, the packets exploded into fireworks, a parting gift from the master of comedy to his beloved pupils. CW

Yurei Oman-gitsune
Kyokuto; b/w; length unknown; Japan
    D: Hideo Onoe *S:* Takeshi Kaifu *C:* Shigeki Kadono
    Cast: Genzaboro Ayakoji, Sumie Tsuki, Saemon Kataoka, Keinosuke Sawada, Kyoko Arishima, Jiro Yasokawa, Renko Tae, Jushiro Ogawa, Seiji Okada

In Japanese folklore, *yurei* are ghosts or spirits that are barred from admittance to the afterlife, generally haunting the location where they died. Some yurei are human in origin, kept Earthbound by vile deeds committed while alive, or by their anger at having been murdered or because they committed suicide. Some of these possess the bodies of animals and are able to alter the forms of their hosts to more humanlike shapes. Others, as in this tale, are animal spirits that, for whatever reason, possess the living.

The story here is of a young warrior who, as a student of the kendo style of swordsmanship, sets out for a neighboring samurai academy with plans to prove his mettle by defeating its best students. Along the way he is accosted by a girl, whom it turns out is possessed by the spirit of an evil fox.

Such tales of possession by an animal spirit provided the backdrop for numerous films during the silent and early sound years. Not all were horror; some were broad comedies, while others were fantasies or dramas.

Yurei Oman-gitsune was released in Japan on November 10, 1937. CW

1938

Ask a Policeman
Gainsborough; b/w; 83 min; Great Britain
D: Marcel Varnel *S:* Marriott Edgar *P:* Edward Black *C:* Derick Williams *M:* Clive Richardson
   Cast: Will Hay, Graham Moffat, Moore Marriott, Glennis Lorimer, Peter Gawthorne, Charles Oliver, Herbert Lomas

The sleepy village of Turnbottom Round boasts a crack police force led by Sergeant Samuel Dudfoot (Hay). Though Dudfoot takes pride in the fact that not a single crime has been committed since he took over, his superiors realize that he's simply too dim-witted to recognize a crime when one is committed. Faced with dissolution of the department, Dudfoot decides to stage a fake crime in order to get credit for solving it. In the process, he and his two equally brainless assistants encounter a headless horseman and stumble upon a smuggling ring.

The talented Sidney Gilliat (*Green for Danger*, 1946) wrote the story for this amusing Will Hay comedy. The inclusion of a headless horseman is indicative of the tentative way the British cinema was, through a fog of recently imposed censorship, fumbling its way back toward horror films. But while it would take the grim *The Dark Eyes of London* (1939) to properly reintroduce the genre, films like *Ask a Policeman* and the earlier Hay comedy *Oh, Mr. Porter!* (1937) took innocuous steps in the right direction.

Hay's favored director Marcel Varnel puts the comic through his paces here; Varnel's assistant was a young Roy Ward Baker (director of *Quatermass and the Pit*, 1967 and *The Vampire Lovers*, 1970), who had also helped Varnel on *Oh, Mr. Porter!* TH

The Black Doll
Universal/Crime Club; b/w; 66 (48) min; U.S.
   D: Otis Garrett *S:* Harold Buckley *P:* Irving Starr, Walter Futter *C:* Ira Morgan, Stanley Cortez *M:* Charles Previn
   Cast: Donald Woods, Nan Grey, Edgar Kennedy, C. Henry Gordon, Doris Lloyd, John Wray, Addison Richards, Holmes Herbert, William Lundigan, Fred Malatesta, Inez Palange, Syd Salyor, Arthur Hoyt

The wealthy Nelson Rood (Gordon) isn't well liked by his family. His nephew (Lundigan) is in need of money, but Rood refuses to help him even when the boy's mother, Rood's sister (Lloyd), begs him to do so. When *la muñeca negra*—a black doll that warns of impending danger—shows up on his study desk, a shaken Rood summons two men (Richards, Wray) to his estate, men who were once his shady partners in a crooked mining venture. The pair arrives, as does Rood's family, on a dark and stormy night, and everyone's a suspect when Rood is murdered. Additional bodies pile up as Rood's daughter Marian (Grey), her boyfriend Nick (Woods) and a bumbling sheriff (Kennedy) investigate matters. It comes to light that Marian isn't really Rood's daughter, but rather that of Barrows, a fourth shady partner who was murdered by Rood some two decades before. Afterward, Rood married Barrows' wife and adopted Marian as his own. And now someone who knows what happened is out for revenge!

In the late 1930s, Universal made a deal with Doubleday to bring the publisher's Crime Club imprint to the screen in a series of low-budget thrillers. Individual books published under the imprint had already been adapted to film (including *Murder by the Clock*, 1931, and *The Mystery of Mr. X*, 1934) with varying degrees of success.

Crime Club was Universal's first attempt at a straightforward mystery franchise, a formula that worked better for the studio in the 1940s when it adapted Sherlock Holmes' tales and the *Inner Sanctum* radio series to film. Though some cinema historians maintain that Crime Club Productions (headed by producer Irving Starr) produced the Crime Club series independently of Universal, with the larger studio only releasing the features, the films were actually co-productions between the two. This is evidenced by the fact several Crime Club players were at the time under contract to Universal, and that the stock music used in the series is indisputably from the Universal library.

The Black Doll was the second of eight Crime Club thrillers (with three additional titles, including *The House of Fear*, 1939, frequently and erroneously cited as Crime Club entries) based upon the novel of the same title by William Edward Hayes. Efficiently directed by Otis Garrett, the briskly moving film delivers some well-executed shocks, particularly the murder of Rood as his daughter watches in her dresser mirror!

Garrett had cut his cinematic teeth editing such minor horror classics as *Behind the Mask* (1931) and *The Vampire Bat*

(1933), giving him a leg up on evoking menace from what is overall a run-of-the-mill script. Garrett continued directing and also dabbled in screenwriting until his death in 1941.

Doll's morbid mood is further enhanced by Stanley Cortez's presence as co-cinematographer. The acting by C. Henry Gordon (*Rasputin and the Empress*, 1932), Doris Lloyd (*Night Monster*, 1942), John Wray (*The Cat and the Canary*, 1939) and Holmes Herbert (*Dr. Jekyll and Mr. Hyde*, 1931) fine-tunes the feel of this dark and tawdry little mystery even further. Nan Grey truly distinguishes herself as Rood's threatened "daughter" Marian. Grey had begun her career in the mid-1930s in undistinguished (and often uncredited) bit parts, but came to international attention with the role that would set the tone for the remainder of her career—as Lily, the model to *Dracula's Daughter* (1936), whose life ends with a scream. A scream that was far from her last, as it turned out: she went on to a short-lived but successful career in several classic Universal chillers, including *Tower of London* (1939) and *The Invisible Man Returns* and *The House of the Seven Gables* (both 1940).

The version of *The Black Doll* in widest circulation is an incomplete, 48-minute syndication print. CW

Cat-Ghost of the Fifty-Three Stations
aka **Kaibyô gojusan-tsugi**
Shinko; b/w; 76 min; Japan
D: Shichinosuke Oshimoto S: Ryo Kamishima C: Takenori Takahashi
Cast: Shinobu Araki, Shinpachiro Asaka, Yaeko Asano, Mitsuko Gun, Umeko Hidaka, Takeo Kawasaki, Atsumi Miho, Kyoko Mizutani, Mitsuko Mori, Toshiko Okubo, Eigoro Onoe, Hideo Otani, Isamu Sakurai, Fujiko Suwa, Sumiko Suzuki, Hiroko Takayama, Yoshiko Tomei, Yoko Umemura, Yaeko Utagawa, Eiko Wakaba

Tokaido, one of five routes designed to link, preserve and strengthen centers of Imperial Power, was the name of the first major road connecting Edo (modern-day Tokyo) with Kyoto. In 1832 an artist named Hiroshige walked the road as part of an imperial delegation. He was so impressed by the landscape that he created a series of 55 distinctive prints, 53 of which represented the landscape along the way and two of which bookended the others. The stops along the route provide the settings for *Cat-Ghost of the Fifty-Three Stations*.

Ghost cats were grudge ghosts, spirits of murdered people that entered cats and drove them to vengeance. For decades they were the central stars of the horror genre in Japan, with *The Ghost of Yotsuya* a distant second. Beginning in the 1960s, a more Earthbound approach to horror entered the mix, though grudge ghosts of various stripes began something of a comeback after the J-horror cycle begun by *Ring* (1998) wound down.

Fifty-Three Stations was released in Japan on May 4, 1938; when it was remade by Daiei Studios in 1956 using the same title, greater success resulted. CW

Chinatown Nights
Victory; b/w; 70 min; Great Britain
D: Tony Frenguelli S: Nigel Byass
Cast: Harry Agar Lyons, Anne Grey, Robert Hobbs, Nell Emerald, Arty Ash, George Mozart

This is the last film to feature the dastardly Dr. Sin Fang, who first appeared in a series of six two-reel films directed by Fred Paul (doing double-duty onscreen as Lieutenant Byrne) and written by Patrick K. Heale. The *Dr. Sin Fang Dramas* were released in 1928 and were largely an attempt by Paul to tap the market created by Stoll's 23 Fu Manchu films—the 1923 series *The Mystery of Dr. Fu-Manchu* and 1924's sequel-series *The Further Mysteries of Dr. Fu Manchu* (all 1924)—without having to purchase rights to the character or pay novelist Sax Rohmer any royalties. The individual Sin Fang entries were titled *The Scarred Face*, *The Zone of Death*, *The Light on the Wall*, *The Living Death*, *The Torture Cage* and *Under the Tide*.

The first of two Sin Fang feature films, simply titled *Dr. Sin Fang*, debuted in 1937. Though made on a minimal budget, it proved successful enough to warrant this sequel. Nell Emerald produced the first film (she stars in both as a character named Mrs. Higgins), there is no indication that she produced the second; indeed, no producer credit appears to have survived at all.

Though little is known about the plot of *Chinatown Nights*, the British Film Institute's plot description indicates that it dealt with a scheme by Dr. Sin Fang (Lyons) to extort a "silver ray" by kidnapping the sister of its inventor. One has to wonder if this is the film to which the description so often recounted for the previous film—that of Sin Fang attempting to steal a cure for cancer—truly belongs. But without known copies of either film in existence, it's impossible to know with any degree of certainty.

Chinatown Nights marked the end of Harry Agar Lyon's very narrow and unremarkable career. Director Tony Frenguelli was the Anglicized name of Italian-born Alfonso Frenguelli; he had also directed the previous film under the name Anthony Frenguelli. After his directorial career came to an end in the mid-1940s, he remained in the industry as a cinematographer in his native Rome. (It's also likely that he performed that same duty for his two Dr. Sin Fang films.) CW

Danger on the Air
Universal/Crime Club; b/w; 65 min; U.S.
D: Otis Garrett S: Betty Laidlaw, Robert Lively P: Irving Starr C: Stanley Cortez
Cast: Nan Grey, Donald Woods, Jed Prouty, Berton Churchill, William Lundigan, Richard "Skeets" Gallagher, Edward Van Sloan, George Meeker, Frank Milan, Lee J. Cobb, Johnny Arthur, Paul Lind Hayes, Louise Stanley, Elois Rawitzer, Joseph Downing

Based on the novel *Death Catches Up With Mr. Kluck* by the pseudonymous Xantippe, *Danger on the Air* is the fourth film in Universal's lowbrow Crime Club series, all of which were based on books published by the Doubleday imprint of the same name.

Radio star and dirty old man Caesar Kluck is murdered with poison gas. Suspicion falls on an assortment of shady and not-so-shady characters, including Christine "Steenie" MacCorkle (Grey), an ad writer, and Benjamin Butts (Woods), the radio's soundman. The two grudgingly join forces to solve the mystery, dodging plenty of bullets while butting heads (and winning hearts). Those they investigate include Tony (Cobb), a janitor upset with Kluck for hitting on his daughter, and Joe Carney (Downing), a gangster who had gone head-to-head with Kluck before the announcer's death. Then there's station owner Har-

ry Jones (Prouty) and Kluck's personal physician, a charlatan named Leonard Sylvester (Van Sloan). The investigation hits a snag when the janitor is found murdered in the same bizarre way as Kluck, and in a truly chilling moment, Steenie hears the voice of the radio character The Shadow warning her off the case. She nonetheless persists until she and Benjamin uncover the truth—and find love in each other's arms.

Screenwriters Betty Laidlaw and Robert Lively translate Xantippe's novel into a screwball romantic comedy cum murder mystery with dashes of horror. They also continue the tradition of lewd humor laid down by previous entries in the series. After Mr. Kluck hits on his receptionist Maria (Stanley), a young delivery boy (Hayes), hiding behind a bunch of balloons, says to her, "I've got something important to see you about when you get through." Believing him to be Mr. Kluck, the receptionist innocently asks, "What?" and he responds, "I want to see if your eyes are big enough for radio!" while he suggestively fondles a balloon.

Helping matters along are performances by Nan Grey (*The Invisible Man's Return*, 1940), Donald Woods (*The Beast from 20,000 Fathoms*, 1953), William Lundigan (*The Missing Guest*, 1938), Edward Van Sloan (*Frankenstein*, 1931) and Lee J. Cobb (*The Exorcist*, 1973). Paul Lind Hayes, who plays the delivery boy, also gets the opportunity to do vocal imitations of several successful real-life personalities of radio and screen. CW

Edo ni arawareta Kingu Kongu: Ogon no maki
aka **Kingu Kongu Zenkouhen**
Zensho; b/w; length unknown; Japan
D: Soya Kumagai
Cast: unknown

This appears to have been a sequel, or second part, to *King Kong Appears in Edo*, which is said to have been produced by Zensho earlier the same year. Both films are thought to have been directed by Soya Kumagai and to have been short horror features set in the Edo Period (1603-1868) of Japanese history. They also would have been illegal knockoffs of RKO's famous hirsute creation, which first appeared in 1933's *King Kong*. The two Edo Kong films followed Shochiku's first entry in the giant monster subgenre, *Japanese King Kong* (also 1933).

While *King Kong Appears in Edo* is believed to have been released in mid-March 1938, its follow-up is thought to have been released less than a month later, in early April. The two films are so closely related that some historians contend they were two parts of an over-arching drama in the same manner as Fritz Lang's original *Doctor Mabuse the Gambler* (1922). During this period, two-part films were fairly common in Japan. CW

Enmadera no kaibyo
Daito; b/w; 70 min; Japan
D: Minoru Ishiyama *C:* Tsuneo Tomiwaza
Cast: unknown

This is the second Japanese "ghost cat" film produced in the span of a year to be set in or around Tokyo's Enma Temple. The first, Kyokuto's *Enmadera no yurei*, had been released the previous year. It must have been successful enough to prompt this copy from Daito Studios, which is today the more obscure film of the two. While the earlier version appears to have been something of a comedy, so little is known about this one that it's difficult to pigeonhole it as comedy, horror or a hybrid of the two.

Enma Temple also provided the backdrop for another horror film, *The Hunchback of Enmei-in* (1924). CW

Every Madman to His Specialty
aka **Cada loco con su tema**; **Every Madman has His Story**
Grovas-Oro; b/w; 123 min; Mexico
D/Co-S/Co-P: Juan Bustillo Oro *Co-S:* Humberto Gomez Landero *Co-P:* Juan Bustillo Oro, Jesus Grovas *C:* Lauron Drapper *M:* Max Urban *FX:* Ismael Carrasco, Arnulfo Huerta, Manuel Munoz
Cast: Enrique Herrera, Joaquin Pardave, Gloria Marin, Antonio R. Frausto, Alberto Marti, Natalia Ortiz, Eduardo Arozamena, Adela Jaloma, Francisco Jambrina, Alberto Galan, Wilfrido Moreno, Roberto Banquells, Victoria Argota, Elvira Gosti

A shady psychiatrist, a spooky old house and greedy relatives grasping for a piece of the inheritance all factor into this obscure Mexican offering. Like the earlier *The Super Madman* (1937), it is an example of 1930s Hispanic cinema mixing its genres, with equal portions of humor, horror and mystery.

The cast includes Eduardo Arozamena, best known for his role as Professor Van Helsing in the Spanish-language version of *Dracula* (1931). Director and co-producer Juan Bustillo Oro helped dream up *Madman*'s storyline, and he also helped pen the final script. Oro had previously directed *Two Monks* (1934), one of the very first horror films shot in Latin America. He remained active as a writer and a director until the late 1960s and died in his native Mexico in 1989. TH

The Gaunt Stranger
aka **The Phantom Strikes**
Ealing; b/w; 70 min; Great Britain
D: Walter Forde *S:* Sidney Gilliat *P:* Michael Balcon *C:* Gordon Dines, Ronald Neame *M:* Ernest Irving
Cast: Sonnie Hale, Wilfred Lawson, Alexander Knox, Louise Henry, Patrick Barr, Peter Croft, George Merritt, John Longden, Patricia Roc, Arthur Hambling, Charles Eaton

The criminal mastermind known as The Ringer is believed dead, so it comes as a surprise when criminal lawyer Maurice

Meister (Lawson) receives a death threat from him. Meister at first tries to laugh it off, but it soon becomes apparent that it's no joke. The police, represented by Sam Hackett (Hale), get involved, but will they be able to find The Ringer before he kills again?

Among horror and suspense writers, Edgar Wallace (1875-1932) has been one of the most filmed, which makes it surprising that, outside of dyed-in-the-wool aficionados, he's something of a forgotten figure today. What fame he retains among the general public centers on the work he did, just before his death, on the script for *King Kong* (1933). In his day, however, he was as widely read as Stephen King is today, and film adaptations of his work began cropping up in the teens.

The Gaunt Stranger is a sequel of sorts to *The Ringer* (1931), which had also been directed by Walter Forde and which was, somewhat confusingly, also released in the United States under the title *The Gaunt Stranger*. That film aside, this *Gaunt Stranger* is a very efficient, briskly paced and cleverly plotted murder mystery with a few moments of horror along the way. Forde does a fine job of keeping the action rattling while also making the most of the quieter, moodier passages.

The cinematography is by Ronald Neame, a talented cameraman who later became a highly capable director, helping shape everything from the hilarious Alec Guinness comedy *The Horse's Mouth* (1958) to the big-budget disaster epic *The Poseidon Adventure* (1972); he also garnered Oscar nominations for his screenwriting efforts on *Brief Encounter* (1945) and *Great Expectations* (1946) and one for special effects work on *One of Our Aircraft is Missing* (1942).

The screenplay by Sidney Gilliat (*Green for Danger*, 1946) includes a fair amount of witty dialogue ("Speaking of illegitimate children, how are you?"). And even though any reasonably astute mystery buff can guess the final twist fairly early on, the story makes for believable, enjoyable entertainment.

The excellent cast deserves special praise. In one of his earliest screen roles as the oily Meister, celebrated stage and screen actor Wilfred Lawson turns in a wonderfully low-key performance. Though his career would eventually be derailed by alcoholism, he managed one final memorable characterization just before his death as the dotty butler Peacock in Bryan Forbes' *The Wrong Box* (1966).

A young Alexander Knox also steals many a scene as the sardonic Dr. Lomond. The role requires the actor to play much older than he really was—and to take on a Scottish burr—and he seems to relish the droll lines he is given. The Canadian-born actor found his biggest American success playing the leading role in *Wilson* (1944), a biopic about the 28th President of the United States; the role netted him an Oscar nomination, but he would never carry a major film again, due in no small measure, one supposes, by that film's thunderous failure at the box-office. He also teamed with blacklisted director Joseph Losey on several of the latter's British-made features, including *The Sleeping Tiger* (1954), *These Are The Damned* (1962) and *Accident* (1967)—and he squeezed in the occasional low-budget horror role, such as *The Psychopath* (1965).

Patrick Barr (*The Satanic Rites of Dracula*, 1973), John Longden (*Quatermass 2*, 1957) and George Merritt (*Horror of Dracula*, 1958) also lend solid support.

Ultimately, *The Gaunt Stranger* focuses a little more on mystery than it does horror—the final fade-out certainly takes the film out on a good-natured note—but it should still prove to be of interest to fans of the genre. TH

Ghost Cat and the Red Wall
aka Kaibyô akakabe daimyojin
Shochiku; b/w; length unknown; Japan
   D: Kazuo Mori
   Cast: unknown

This was the first sound-era adaptation of the infamous *Akakabe myojin* story (first filmed in 1918), a tale of a young female servant who, while quickly rising through the ranks of her master's household, is framed by a rival as having an affair with her master's retainer. She is wrongly executed and her body interred behind a red wall rather than being buried in hallowed ground. Unfortunately for those who wronged her, a black cat is also trapped within the brick mausoleum with her, and the animal becomes imbued with her grudge-bearing spirit.

If the story sounds similar to Edgar Allan Poe's short story *The Black Cat*, which first appeared in *The Saturday Post* (later to become known as *The Saturday Evening Post*) in August of 1843, that's because it does indeed borrow heavily from the tale. Poe's stories were so popular in Japan that one Japanese writer took on the pseudonym Edagawa Rampo (which, when spoken

slowly and with the right inflection, sounds like the name of the American horror author) and published numerous horror stories, many of which were also adapted to the screen. CW

Ghost-Cat Legend
aka **Kyobyô-den; Kaibyô-den**
Nikkatsu; b/w; 82 min; Japan

D: Kanji Suganuma *S:* Saburo Kodaiji *C:* Takeji Inoue *M:* Toranosuke Takahashi

Cast: Kensaku Hara, Komako Hara, Kobunji Ichikawa, Sayoko Kasumi, Goro Kawabe, Kaoru Nakano, Chiyoko Okura, Yoneko Sakai, Kiyoshi Sawada, Shizuko Takizawa, Emiko Yanagi, Michisaburo Segawa, Ryosuke Kagawa, Sasho Ichikawa

After several silent adaptations of the *Ghost Cat of Nabeshima* tale, Nikkatsu gave up-and-coming film editor Kanji Suganuma a break by letting him direct this talkie version. The story was based in part on historical fact and in part on a famous kabuki play about a real-life Japanese general named Naoshige Nabeshima (1537-1619). Some historians had a less-than-favorable view of the general, and a legend arose in which he murdered the lord of Saga Castle and claimed his domain, after which either the spirit of the lord or of his mother possessed a cat and stalked the castle's halls, seeking revenge.

Suganuma went on to become the somewhat famous editor of the Zatoichi films and the horror classic *100 Monsters* (1968).

The title *Kyobyô-den* translates roughly as *The Legend of the Big Cat*. It was released in Japan on April 14, 1938. CW

Ghost Cat's Mysterious Shamisen
aka **Kaibyô nazo no shamisen; Onshu nazo no kaibyô**
Shinko; b/w; 85 min; Japan

D: Kiyohiko Ushihara *S:* Kenji Hata *C:* Takenori Takahashi

Cast: Tokusaburo Arashi, Shinpachiro Asaka, Yaeko Asano, Yuriko Asano, Junzaburo Ban, Mitsuko Gun, Matsuko Hidaka, Yasumasa Jitsukawa, Taisuke Matsumoto, Atsumi Miho, Yukiko Miyagawa, Mitsuko Mori, Shizuko Mori, Shozo Nanbu, Eigoro Onoe, Fujiko Suwa, Sumiko Suzuki, Masako Takamatsu, Hiroko Takayama, Mitsugu Terashima, Yoshiko Tomei, Yoko Umemura, Kinue Utagawa, Eiko Wakaba

This is one of the few Japanese horror films from the 1930s to be widely available today, though in an incomplete form. In it, beautiful kabuki actress Mitsue (Suzuki) falls in love with a handsome musician (Shinpachiro) who plays the samisen (a stringed instrument also known as a shamisen), hence the film's title. While retrieving his black cat from a neighboring samurai's property, the musician becomes smitten with the man's eldest daughter (Utagawa), who lives there with her younger sister (Mori). This incites Mitsue to jealousy; she murders both the girl and the cat. But the murdered woman's sister avenges her death with the help of a ghostly cat.

Ghost Cat's Mysterious Shamisen was released in Japan on November 3, 1938. Director Kiyohiko Ushihara oversaw the shooting chores on numerous films between 1920 and 1950, as well as sometimes performing writing duties. CW

J'Accuse
aka **I Accuse; I Accuse (That They May Live); That They May Live**
Forrester-Parant; b/w; 125 min; France

D/Co-S/P: Abel Gance *Co-S:* Steve Passeur *C:* Roger Hubert *M:* Henri Verdun

Cast: Victor Francen, Line Noro, Marie Lou, Jean-Max, Renee Devillers, Romuald Joube, Marcel Delaitre, Paul Amiot, Andre Nox, Georges Rollin, Georges Saillard

Jean Diaz (Francen) returned from The Great War—known today as World War I—so horrified by the needless loss of life that he resolved to help prevent any recurrence of it. Twenty years afterward, with Europe again at the brink of major conflict, he ponders his experiences as a soldier and their aftermath.

Director Abel Gance claimed ignorance of politics, but he was an avowed Pacifist. Though revered today for his epic *Napoleon* (1927), there is little question that his two versions of *J'Accuse* (the first done in 1919) constitute his most impassioned work.

The 1938 remake was timed to take advantage of the conflict brewing in Europe, destined to become World War II. The early part of the story is bogged down by histrionics—the material dealing with Diaz's unresolved relationship with a comrade's widow feels particularly strained—but patience pays off as things build to their apocalyptic climax.

J'Accuse is, in fact, remembered chiefly for its finale, in which long-dead soldiers rise from their graves to remind the world of their sacrifice. Gance milks this sequence for all it's worth, deliberately leaving the viewer unclear as to whether the dead have actually returned or whether it's a hallucination. In either case, the film's anti-war message is clearly presented, though the point of heavy-handedness, and its grisly imagery, pushes the affair into full-tilt horror terrain.

The goings-on are anchored by the gripping performance of Victor Francen, who later played the ill-fated pianist in Robert Florey's *The Beast with Five Fingers* (1946). He is perfect as the cynical soldier who evolves into a haunted emissary of peace. The supporting cast performs credibly enough, though nobody else in the film hurdles the bar set by its lead.

Not surprisingly, the film underwent heavy editing for its initial American release. Approximately half an hour was removed, but it's been restored in the version widely available today.

Gance directed sporadically until 1967's *Valmy*, but *J'Accuse* was his final flirtation with the horror genre. He died in 1981 at the age of 92. TH

King Kong Appears in Edo
aka **Edo ni arawareta Kingu Kongu: Hengi no maki; King Kong**
Zensho; b/w; length unknown; Japan

D: Soya Kumagai *S:* Daijo Aoyama *C:* Yozo Okuda *FX:* Fuminori Ohashi

Cast: Ryutaro Hibiki, Reizaburo Ichikawa, Ginbei Inoue, Do Jitsukawa, Keisuke Matsudaira, Eizaburo Matsumoto, Reiko Mishima, Shojiro Ogata, Fuminori Ohashi, Shotaro Shiba, Shin Taga, Noboru Takashima, Keinosuke Yashiro, Kikutaro Yoshii

Information is thin for this film, made in the wake of 1938's successful re-release of RKO's *King Kong* (1933). An extant poster purportedly from *King Kong Appears in Edo* looks to have been faked, though a quote attributed to costume effects designer Fuminori Ohashi suggests that the film was actually made. Adding weight to its existence is a trade ad in the April 14, 1938 issue of *Kinema Junpo*, a Japanese film magazine, announcing its impending release (dubiously, this publication is said to be the source of the aforementioned fake poster). Film historians August Ragone, Stuart Galbraith IV and Simon Rowson have all testified to the film's authenticity, as has the Japanese press.

The fact that Tokyo is referenced by its former name of Edo suggests that the film was set in historical Japan sometime between 1603 and 1868, despite its reputed inclusion of modernesque painted sets along the lines of *The Cabinet of Dr. Caligari* (1919).

Like its predecessor *Japanese King Kong* (1933)—the creation of which has been improperly contested in some circles—*King Kong Appears in Edo* does not seem to have been a feature-length film. Neither production was authorized by RKO, who tightly held the rights to *King Kong* until the early 1960s, when they pimped them out to Toho Studios for *King Kong vs. Godzilla* (1962). Toho followed it up with *King Kong Escapes* in 1967. (Note that a 1966 American animated series, *The King Kong Show*, was produced by a Japanese animation studio, Toei.)

King Kong Appears in Edo was followed by an immediate sequel, *Edo ni arawareta Kingu Kongu: Ogon no maki* (also 1938), but it, too, is lost. CW

Alleged movie poster for *King Kong Appears in Edo*, a Japanese version of RKO's worldwide blockbuster *King Kong*

The Lady in the Morgue
aka **The Case of the Missing Blonde**
Universal/Crime Club; b/w; 67 min; U.S.

D: Otis Garrett *S:* Eric Taylor, Robertson White *P:* Irving Starr *C:* Stanley Cortez

Cast: Preston Foster, Patricia Ellis, Frank Jenks, Thomas Jackson, Gordon Elliott, Roland Drew, Barbara Pepper, Joseph Downing, James Robbins, Al Hill, Morgan Wallace, Brian Burke, Donald Kerr, Don Brodie, Rollo Lloyd, Gordon Hart

When the body of an unknown woman is found hanging in her hotel room, a number of people believe that she may be someone of interest to them. Detective Bill Crane and his assistant Doc Williams are hired to investigate, but the morgue attendant where the body has been taken is murdered and the body stolen. After another murder, an attempted murder and a kidnapping, Crane and Williams wind up in a creepy graveyard, where they piece together the clues and solve the case.

In the mid-1930s, Jonathan Latimer rose to fame as the author of the William "Bill" Crane series of pulp mysteries, originally published by Doubleday's Crime Club imprint. Crane was an alcoholic womanizer who also happened to be a Chicago private detective. In *The Lady in the Morgue*, first published in 1936, he was called upon to learn the identity of a woman found hung in a hotel room.

Universal had optioned several Crime Club novels to be filmed over two years, with Latimer's 1935 novel *Headed for a Hearst* being the first, produced under the title *The Westland Case* (1937). It proved successful thanks to the bickering interplay between Preston Foster and Frank Jenks as Bill Crane and his assistant Doc Williams in a tight, fun script from Robertson White.

For the third Crime Club feature, Universal gave Latimer's character a fresh go-round, this time utilizing the novel *The Lady in the Morgue*. They also sensibly brought back scenarist White and actors Foster and Jenks. The formula remained a winner, prompting Universal to try it out one last time with *The Last Warning* in 1939, also based on a Latimer novel. (For the record, Latimer went on to become one of Hollywood's most polished writers of film noir.)

White, co-writing this time with Eric Taylor, gave the film the same sort of snappy dialogue and sexual innuendo that had made *The Westland Case* so popular. In the opening scene, the police enter the hotel to seal off the crime scene, prompting the proprietor to say, "Lieutenant, you'll handle this quietly; we have a reputation," to which the lieutenant responds, "I wouldn't brag about it!"

While the movie appears at first glance to be a typical low-budget gangster-film-cum-murder-mystery, director Otis Garrett's snazzy direction takes it up a notch, keeping things moving while adding appropriate atmospheric touches at all the right times. Garrett had begun his film career as an editor, working in fact on *The Westland Case*. He quickly graduated to director with the second Crime Club movie *The Black Doll* (1938) and oversaw most of the remaining films in the series. His Universal star was still rising when he grew ill during the 1940 production of *Sandy Gets Her Man*, and he died in March of the following year, just a couple of days before his 36th birthday.

The next film in the series, also directed by Garrett, was the amusing *Danger on the Air* (1938). CW

The Last Express
Universal/Crime Club; b/w; 63 min; U.S.
   D: Otis Garrett *S:* Edmund L. Hartman *P:* Irving Starr *C:* Stanley Cortez
   Cast: Kent Taylor, Dorothea Kent, Greta Granstedt, Don Brodie, Paul Hurst, J. Farrell MacDonald, Samuel Lee, Al Shaw, Edward Raquello, Robert Emmett Keane, Charles Trowbridge, Addison Richards, Al Hill, John Miller, Frances Robinson

This fifth entry in Universal's Crime Club series remains the most obscure. It was based on a Baynard Kendrick novel, and when the rights to his work were purchased in the mid-1940s by MGM, control of the film transferred from Universal to MGM. The film disappeared from circulation and has been seen but little since.

The Last Express was the least horrific in the series, focusing on a deposition that proves gangster Frank Hoefle (Richards) murdered Tom Delaney. When the deposition goes missing, Hoefle hires two detectives, Duncan MacLain (Taylor) and Spud Savage (Brodie), to find it before the prosecutor (Raquello) does. Naturally, murder ensues.

The Crime Club series, which lasted from 1937 to 1939, was a mild hit with audiences, helping Universal to climb out of the debt left by the departing Laemmles. After the contracted eight books were adapted, however, Universal abandoned the series in favor of films starring the talented singer Deanna Durbin.

The rest of the Crime Club film series included *The Westland Case* (1937), *The Black Doll*, *The Lady in the Morgue*, *Danger on the Air* (all 1938) and *The Last Warning*, *Mystery of the White Room* and *The Witness Vanishes* (both 1939). CW

Life Returns
Scienart; b/w; 59 min; U.S.
   D/Co-S: Eugene Frenke *Co-S:* L. Wolfe Gilbert, James P. Hogan, Arthur T. Horman, Mary McCarthy *P:* Lou L. Ostrow *C:* Robert Planck *M:* Clifford Vaughan, Oliver Wallace
   Cast: Onslow Stevens, George P. Breakston, Lois Wilson, Valerie Hobson, Stanley Fields, Frank Reicher, Richard Carle, Dean Benton, Lois January, Richard Quine, Maidel Turner, George McQuarrie, Otis Harlan, Robert E. Cornish

Dr. John Kendrick (Stevens) is obsessed with reviving the dead. His experiments cost him his job and create a rift within his family. When his wife (Hobson) passes away, he finds himself estranged from his son Danny (Breakston), whom he's always neglected. As his life hits rock bottom, he reassesses the things that really matter—and makes the breakthrough that he's worked so hard to achieve.

barrel. The lead is essayed by Onslow Stevens, a usually reliable actor who seems hopelessly adrift here. Whether pitching his life-reviving theories like a used car salesman or moping about like a petulant child, he comes off as almost intentionally uninspiring. This is particularly disappointing when one considers his fine work in *Secret of the Blue Room* (1933) and *House of Dracula* (1945). Still, given the non-existent direction and the script's wet-towel characterization, maybe one shouldn't be too harsh on him.

As for the supporting cast, the less said the better, though genre buffs may be pleased to see Frank Reicher (*King Kong*, 1933) and a pitifully underused Valerie Hobson (*The Bride of Frankenstein*, 1935). Their presence has, in fact, led some to conclude that Universal had a hand in the film's production. But the studio's involvement was in distribution alone, and that was only for its initial run.

Sluggishly paced, poorly acted and curiously rambling for a film of such brevity, *Life Returns* is a dull curiosity, of interest only to the most diehard '30s horror fans. Truth be told, it barely qualifies as horror, lacking even a pleasantly demented scientist to sweeten the deal. (Dr. Cornish is worked into the padded scenario to little dramatic advantage, apparently as an excuse to utilize documentary footage of the allegedly miraculous dog revival.) Universal itself had no idea how to market the film or to whom. They foisted it upon unsuspecting audiences as a horror endeavor, then allowed the rights to lapse. The genre has been stuck with it ever since. TH

The Lonely Soul
aka **Leng yue shi hun**
Xinhua; b/w; length unknown; China
    D: Weibang Ma-Xu *P:* Shankun Zhang
    Cast: unknown

This was apparently the third horror film from Chinese director Weibang Ma-Xu, following on the heels of his successful *Song at Midnight* (1937) and *Walking Corpse in an Old House* (1938). Little is known about *The Lonely Soul* and the title gives no hint as to its plot, though it likely aped *Song at Midnight*'s formula of equal parts romance and horror. Despite its obscurity, *Lonely Soul* is not yet presumed completely lost (as is so much of Ma-Xu's early work).

In 1941 Ma-Xu followed up *Lonely Soul* with yet another horror film, a direct sequel to his first horror hit. Titled *Song at Midnight—Part 2*, it was a reaction to China's war with Japan. After it failed to leave much of a mark on audiences, Ma-Xu abandoned the genre. When Japan invaded and occupied Shanghai, Ma-Xu worked with director Bu Wancang on the pro-Japanese film *The Opium War* (1943). When Japan lost the war to China, the new Chinese government went after Ma-Xu for his wartime treachery. He fled to Hong Kong and continued his work there until 1953, after which he retired.

Ma-Xu died in 1961, but his legacy lived on, most prominently in the form of three remakes of his classic *Song at Midnight* (incidentally, the first horror film to be made in China); these were shot in 1961, 1989 and 1996. CW

The Missing Guest
Universal; b/w; 68 min; U.S.

Dr. Robert E. Cornish (1894-1963) began experimenting with techniques to revive recently deceased patients in 1933; in 1934, he revived a recently euthanized, clinically dead dog. Not surprisingly, the story became the stuff of headlines, and it didn't take long for filmmakers to display an interest in bringing it to the screen. Enter producer Lou L. Ostrow and director Eugene Frenke. The highly fictionalized result of their labors, *Life Returns*, occupies a unique (though not all that noteworthy) place in 1930s horror/fantasy cinema.

To put things plainly: Despite its real-life-sci-fi potential, *Life Returns* is pretty close to the bottom of the 1930s cinema

D: John Rawlins *S:* Charles Martin, Paul Perez *P:* Barney A. Sarecky *C:* Milton R. Krasner *M:* Charles Previn, Karl Hajos, Charles Henderson, David Raksin, Heinz Roemheld, Frank Skinner, Franz Waxman

Cast: Paul Kelly, Constance Moore, William Lundigan, Edwin Stanley, Selmer Jackson, Billy Wayne, George Cooper, P.J. Kelly, Florence Wix, Harlan Briggs, Pat C. Flick

"Scoop" Hanlon (Kelly) is a strong-minded reporter. Upon hearing the legend of the "blue room"—in which a man disappeared from an ornate room in a local mansion and was never heard from again—he investigates. Despite the passage of 20 years, people are still frightened of the place, not least because Hanlon's investigation coincides with yet another disappearance. Eventually, the flesh-and-blood culprit responsible for the disappearance is unmasked.

Erich Philippi's German horror-thriller *Geheimnis des blauen Zimmers* (1932) inspired several U.S. remakes, including this adaptation. Though produced by Universal and decked out with the usual familiar trappings (including a score that recycles elements from earlier Universal thrillers), it is far less known today than the studio's first crack at the story, *The Secret of the Blue Room* (1933). The reason for this is simple: Though a brisk and entertaining thriller, *The Missing Room* lacks the earlier film's Gothic ambience and outstanding cast. In lieu of sinister Lionel Atwill and dashing Paul Lukas, the later film is carried by smug Paul Kelly, portraying yet another in a long line of smartass journalists. The emphasis is more on comedy this time around, though director John Rawlins succeeds in creating a few mildly creepy and atmospheric moments. Rawlins went on to direct the first in Universal's modern day Sherlock Holmes thrillers starring Basil Rathbone and Nigel Bruce: *Sherlock Holmes and the Voice of Terror* (1942). He also helmed several of the low-budget Dick Tracy adventures starring Ralph Byrd, including *Dick Tracy Meets Gruesome* (1947), in which the crime fighter does battle with Boris Karloff.

Universal's *Murder in the Blue Room* (1944) revived Philippi's story one last time, further demonstrating in the process the law of diminishing returns. TH

Mystery House
Warner; b/w; 56 min; U.S.

D: Noel Smith *S:* Sherman L. Lowe, Robertson White *C:* L. William O'Connell *M:* Howard Jackson

Cast: Ann Sheridan, Dick Purcell, Anne Nagel, William Hopper, Anthony Averill, Dennie Moore, Hugh O'Connell, Ben Welden, Sheila Bromley, Elspeth Dudgeon, Anderson Lawler, Trevor Bardette, Eric Stanley, Jean Benedict

When an inquest rules her father's death a suicide, Gwen Kingery (Nagel) doesn't buy it and assembles in his home all those she suspects might have killed him. Also invited along is Detective Lance O'Leary (Purcell), whom she has secretly hired to discover the truth about what happened. O'Leary happens to be the boyfriend of Sarah Keate (Sheridan), who is nurse to Gwen's aunt Lucy (Dudgeon). When a wife (Benedict) of one of the suspects announces that she knows something about the death, she winds up dead herself, also by "suicide." Upon investigation, however, O'Leary learns that the woman was strangled to death, then shot. The murders don't stop there, and a typical trope of clichés—including a wheelchair-bound character who can actually walk and a servant with a sinister secret—is trotted out. Finally, after discovering that a gun on the study wall has been rigged to fire when the room's door is bolted, O'Leary creates a plan to force the killer (Averill) to reveal himself.

The *New York Times* once said of novelist Mignon G. Eberhart—who in the 1930s was known as "America's Agatha Christie"—that her works were invariably marked by an "atmosphere of horror and suspense." Film adaptations of her Nurse Keate novels, however, tended to be straightforward mysteries with comedy flourishes, a convention of 1930s cinema that also marred screen versions of Earl Stanley Gardner's Perry Mason books and most filmic translations of books published under Doubleday's Crime Club imprint.

Based on Eberhart's successful novel *The Mystery of Hunting's End* (1930), which received the Scotland Yard Prize in 1931, *Mystery House* atypically retains some of the creepiness that pervades its source material. Eberhart sought to provide a twist of sorts on the genre by placing it not in a typical old dark house during a thunderstorm, but in a cabin home in the woods during a snowstorm, and the film version wisely retains the setting. The result creates just the right touch of claustrophobic horror, anticipating *The Thing from Another World* (1951). This is particularly evident in an early scene in which a suicide—or murder—is telegraphed by the howling of the man's pet dog. In another, a shadowy figure outside a cabin watches through the window during the investigation of a murder victim's body.

In typical Hollywood fashion, the primary action is transferred from the book's smart and resourceful heroine Nurse Keate to her boyfriend, Detective Purcell. The script is remarkably light on humor, despite having been co-written by Robertson White, who provided wonderfully droll scripts for several of Universal's Crime Club movies (*The Westland Case*, 1937, *The Lady in the Morgue*, 1938 and *The Witness Vanishes*, 1939). Neither was *Mystery House* his first Nurse Keate script; he had also worked on *The Patient in Room 18*, which was released earlier the same year.

Mystery House was the fifth film from Warner to center on Nurse Sarah Keate; the first had been 1935's *While the Patient Slept*, which starred Aline McMahon, while the second was 1936's *The Murder of Dr. Harrigan*, with Kay Linaker in the role, now inexplicably dubbed "Sally Keating." That same year also saw *Murder by an Aristocrat*, which starred Marguerite Churchill in the role, still under the name of Sally Keating. When Warner placed its series on temporary hiatus, 20th Century Fox released *The Great Hospital Mystery* (1937) with Jane Darnell as "Miss Keats." Warner then returned to the fray in 1938 with the aforementioned *The Patient in Room 18*, which was also the first of two to star Ann Sheridan in the role, now again called Sarah Keate.

Despite the talented actresses who took on the part over the years, the success of the novels failed to translate to the screen (possibly because the film adaptations tended to ignore the books' female fan base by making the hero the male detective). Warner abandoned the series after *Mystery House* performed disappointingly at the box-office. That may have been a good thing for Sheridan, who went on to star in a series of successful films opposite the likes of John Garfield, James Cagney, Humphrey Bogart, Pat O'Brien, Errol Flynn, Robert Cummings, Ronald Reagan, Jack Benny and Cary Grant, among many, many others.

Her *Mystery House* co-star Dick Purcell (*King of the Zombies*, 1941) likewise remained active in movies until his unexpected death in 1944 at the age of 36, when we was found dead of a heart attack in a country club locker room after a round of golf. His most famous role may be as *Captain America* in the comic-book serial of 1943.

A solid supporting cast strengthened *Mystery House*, including William Hopper (*The Deadly Mantis*, 1957), who went on to star as Paul Drake in TV's *Perry Mason* (1957-1966); Elspeth Dudgeon (*Sh! The Octopus*, 1936), who had a brief but important role as an elderly man in James Whale's *The Old Dark House* (1932) and Anne Nagel (*The Mad Doctor of Market Street*, 1942), a B-movie starlet who played a likewise important role in the Perry Mason film adaptation *The Case of the Stuttering Bishop* (1937). CW

The Mystic Circle Murder
aka **Religious Racketeers**; **Mystic Circle Murder**; **Madame Houdini Speaks**
Royer; b/w; 68 (65, 70) min; U.S.

D/Co-S: Frank O'Conner *Co-S:* Charles R. Condon *P:* Fanchon Royer *C:* Jack Greenhalgh

Cast: Robert Fiske, Helene Le Berthon, Arthur Gardner,

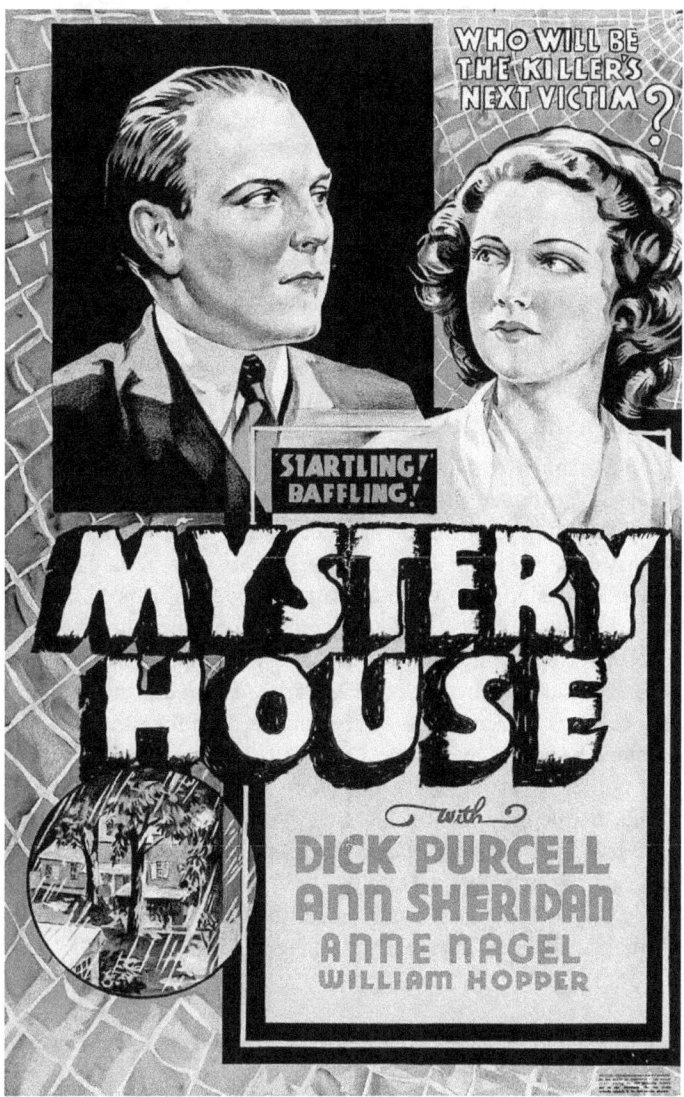

Betty Compson, David Kerman, Robert Frazer, Mme Harry Houdini

Part horror film, part would-be searing exposé, *The Mystic Circle Murder* opens with a demonstration of how phony medium the Great La Gagge (Fiske) goes about fleecing widows and orphans out of their money. When someone expresses doubt as to La Gagge's abilities, he launches into a half-cocked tirade about the science involved in contacting spirits (which, of course, spews attitude in place of testable data). The following scene features the real-life Mme. Harry Houdini, whose deceased husband had devised a plan to determine whether he could really contact her from beyond the grave, a simple scheme involving a secret code known only to the two of them and not to any mediumistic charlatans. Apparently, Harry is either really gone or keeping to himself for some reason, leading the Mrs. to conclude that there's no such thing as the supernatural. From there, it's back to La Gagge's creepy temple, where the fake fakir summons the apparent spirit of a young widow's late husband, a trick to which the woman responds by dying of a heart attack. The police are notified and put the heat on La Gagge, who plans to flee just as soon as he seduces beautiful heiress Martha (Le Berthon). Luckily for him, Martha is upset with her boyfriend, journalist Elliott Cole (Gardner), and ripe for the picking. She stupidly falls into La Gagge's trap but in the end is rescued by her estranged boyfriend.

Originally released under the title *Religious Racketeers*, *The Mystic Circle Murder* gets a bum rap from most film critics due to its low budget and preachy, heavy-handed stance against spiritism. It is, however, a more-than-decent timewaster. Granted, several of the performances are atrocious, but the film as a whole is most assuredly not dull, particularly once the action moves to Egypt, where La Gagge pretends to be a Holy Prophet of the goddess Isis, and then to India, where the faux mystic makes believe he's transmigrating his soul. There's also an interesting subplot involving La Gagge's assistant, a hood named Wilson (Kerman) who, when La Gagge falls for Martha, becomes jealous, driving the film to its dramatic conclusion.

Fanchon Royer, one of the few female producers active in the 1930s, produced *The Mystic Circle Murder*. She often wore her Catholic proclivities on her sleeve, and her disdain for non-mainstream religious thought is on full display here. The film is plainly designed to warn Christian viewers against falling in with dubious mystics. Its derisive tone doesn't in any way negate the story's entertainment value, of course, any more than the scare-tactic histrionics of 1936's *Reefer Madness* make that film any less fun (in fact, they're a large *part* of the fun). The real mystery here is why *Mystic Circle* hasn't found a comparable cult audience, especially given its ready and affordable availability on the grey market.

The Mystic Circle Murder was shot in February 1938 and released theatrically in October 1939. Although the film was made on the cheap, it actually achieves a look superior to some Universal films of comparable vintage (*The Black Doll*, 1938, for one). CW

Rasputin
aka **La tragédie impériale**
Glass; b/w; 116 (95) min; France

D: Marcel L'Herbier *S:* Marcel L'Herbier, Max Glass, Steve Passeur *P:* Max Glass *C:* Philippe Agostini, Michel Kelber *M:* Darius Milhaud

Cast: Harry Baur, Marcelle Chantal, Pierre Richard-Willm, Jean Worms, Jany Holt, Jacques Baumer, Georges Malkine, Lucien Nat, Carine Nelson, Palau, Georges Prieur, Alexandre Rignault, Gabrielle Robinne, Martial Rebe, Denis d'Ines

Grigori Rasputin (Baur) exerts a hypnotic influence over the Russian court, leading to his eventual murder by a group of assassins led by Count Igor Kourloff (Richard-Willm).

Like Adolf Trotz's *Rasputin, Demon with the Women* (1932), this film presents a decidedly sympathetic portrait of the so-called mad monk, Grigori Rasputin. Harry Baur's Rasputin is a force for positive change and a symbol of the people's revolution. Baur had already played an array of heavies (including the deranged Emperor Rudolf in Julien Duvivier's *The Legend of Prague*, 1936), so this Rasputin provided him with an opportunity to inhabit a positive, heroic characterization. Sadly, Baur himself perished in a German concentration camp in 1943; having traveled to Germany from his home in France to make a movie, he was apprehended by the Nazis, who tortured him to death because they believed his wife was a member of the Jewish resistance movement.

As had been the case with other film depictions of the almost-mythical figure's life and demise, this film was compromised by the threat of legal action by the family of Prince Felix Yusupov. The villain of the piece is therefore named Count Kourloff, leading one to wonder whether the filmmakers were having fun with a sly reference to Hollywood horror icon Boris Karloff.

The eye-popping sets make the film a visually arresting experience; the art direction came from Russian-born Eugene Lorie, who later switched to directing. Among his credits as director were the giant monster films *The Beast from 20,000 Fathoms* (1953), *The Giant Behemoth* (1959) and *Gorgo* (1961). After *Gorgo* he abandoned directing in favor of pursuing production design and art direction full time. As a designer he is best remembered for his work on Jean Renoir's *Grand Illusion* (1937); his final credits include Dan Curtis' haunted house thriller *Burnt Offerings* (1976), starring Oliver Reed, and Clint Eastwood's *Bronco Billy* (1980). Lorie died in 1991. TH

Sexton Blake and the Hooded Terror
aka **The Hooded Terror**; **The Mystery of Caversham Square**
King; b/w; 69 min; Great Britain

D/P: George King *S:* A.R. Rawlinson *C:* Hone Glendinning *M:* Jack Beaver, Bretton Byrd

Cast: George Curzon, Tod Slaughter, Greta Gynt, Tony Sympson, Charles Oliver, Marie Wright, David Farrar, Norman Pierce, H.B. Hallam, Bradley Watts

Sexton Blake was a low-rent version of Sherlock Holmes; not only were the two detectives neighbors on London's Baker Street, they each had an assistant of lesser intelligence (Holmes had Watson, Blake had Tinker) and an overly concerned housekeeper. Each suffered the chronic interference of a moronic Scotland Yard inspector, and each enjoyed a more-than-occasional puff of the pipe.

Blake first appeared in *The Halfpenny Marvel*, Issue #6, in 1893, but as it became clear that he was playing second-fiddle to Arthur Conan Doyle's more famous sleuth, Blake took on more of Holmes' characteristics, emerging at last as a lean, older gentleman with a widow's peak. Like those of his more famous colleague, Blake's stories were adapted to the stage (beginning in 1907), the big screen (beginning in 1909), radio (beginning in 1938) and television (beginning in 1967). New Blake exploits continued to appear in print until the late 1970s, with approximately 200 authors contributing to the character's 100-year history.

The first talkie adaptation of a Blake story, *Sexton Blake and the Bearded Doctor*, came out in 1935 and was produced by Fox's British arm as a quota quickie. George Curzon was cast as the dapper detective and Tony Sympson as his science-experiment-loving assistant Tinker. The film proved popular enough that Fox followed it up the same year with *Sexton Blake and Mademoiselle*, also starring Curzon and Sympson. When it became clear that the second film wasn't going to be as successful as the first (perhaps because the two were released too close together), Fox abandoned the series.

When producer George King acquired the rights to the character in 1938, he wisely retained the services of Curzon and Sympson and cast his star attraction, Tod Slaughter, as the vil-

Edgar Wallace, a prolific mystery writer, saw his novels become the basis for many horror films, most of them made in Germany during the 1960s.

lain; he also shifted the tone from grim mystery to restrained horror. But the result, *Sexton Blake and the Hooded Terror*, was as much of a commercial disappointment as *Mademoiselle* had been, and King too abandoned the character. Curzon, for the time being, continued playing Blake on radio, with Brian Lawrence replacing Sympson in the role of Tinker.

The story *The Mystery of Caversham Square* by Pierre Quiroule serves as the basis for *The Hooded Terror*. Both concern a terrorist organization known as The Black Quorum, a group of black-robed villains with serpents adorning their chests. The head of the group, The Snake (Slaughter), is in truth a stamp-collecting millionaire named Michael Larron who lusts after the beautiful Julie (Gynt). The group plans to hold a secret meeting in the Caversham Square area of London, laying plans for a city wide crime wave, but Granite Grant (Farrar) infiltrates them. After group members find him out and murder him, they learn that they have to contend with Sexton Blake.

King's directorial hand is somewhat subdued here when compared to his previous horror work with Slaughter. Slaughter likewise reins in his performance, creating a more subtle villain than he had in his barnstorming turns in *Maria Marten, or The Murder in the Red Barn* (1935), *The Demon Barber of Fleet Street* and *The Crimes of Stephen Hawke* (both 1936).

That the anticipated series reboot ended with this entry may be at least partially due to the film's uneasy straddling of mystery and horror, with the former too obvious and ham-fisted for lovers of whodunits and the latter too subtle for those seeking thrills. Philip Bawcombe's sets are excellent as usual, especially the Gothic underground lair of The Black Quorum, and Hone Glendinning's photography is appropriately atmospheric. Too bad King's approach is too sedate to take make use of these advantages; their potential for generating claustrophobia and fear remains largely untapped.

When *Hooded Terror* proved the last of the Curzon series, fans were left without a much-needed sense of closure. It wasn't the end of Sexton Blake's cinematic adventures, however. The character got a renewed lease on life in two films made by Strand in 1945, *Meet Sexton Blake* and *The Echo Murders*. Both involved wartime intrigue, with the lead character this time inhabited by David Farrar, who'd portrayed Granite Grant in *The Hooded Terror*.

King and Slaughter's next horror outing, *The Face at the Window* (1939), was a much more successful return to the macabre melodrama of their shared past. CW

The Terror
aka **Edgar Wallace's The Terror**
Associated British; b/w; 70 min; Great Britain
D: Richard Bird *S:* William Freshman *P:* Walter C. Mycroft *C:* Walter Harvey
Cast: Wilfred Lawson, Bernard Lee, Arthur Wontner, Alastair Sim, Linden Travers, Henry Oscar, Iris Hoey, Leslie Wareing, Stanley Lathbury, John Turnbull, Richard Murdoch, Edward Lexy

A criminal mastermind known as The Terror engineers a daring gold heist, then he sees to it that his accomplices (Sim, Oscar) are arrested. The two patsies swear revenge and, after serving 10 years in prison, work toward making good on their promise. The Terror, meanwhile, has established a convincing cover as a respectable member of the community, though he also moonlights as a ghost, haunting an old country house.

Edgar Wallace's popular play *The Terror* had already been adapted (one of the earliest all-talking motion pictures, in fact) in 1928. This British remake is part of a spate of Wallace adaptations that emerged from England in the 1930s. Ostensibly just another "old dark house" thriller, it nevertheless incorporates some wonderfully ghoulish touches and benefits from an excellent cast.

Top-billed Wilfred Lawson—who carried another early Wallace adaptation, *The Gaunt Stranger* (1938)—turns in his usual polished performance. He makes the most of some witty lines (when listening to the efforts of a would-be poetess who says she can't think of a word that rhymes with "drowsy," he quips, "I can!"), while playing the character with great restraint.

The same can't really be said of a young Bernard Lee (1908-1981)—here decades away from his most famous role as James Bond's testy boss M in all the 007 films from *Dr. No* (1962) to *Moonraker* (1979)—he is required to play drunk most of the time. (Lee himself struggled with alcohol throughout his adult life, though still managing noteworthy turns in everything from Carol Reed's masterpiece *The Third Man*, 1949, to Terence

Fisher's final film, *Frankenstein and the Monster from Hell*, 1972). And while he really is the hero of this piece, his "hopeless drunk" routine gets a bit old after a while. When allowed to play straight, he's far more engaging.

The real standout is the great Alastair Sim (1900-1976). Best remembered today for his definitive interpretation of Ebenezer Scrooge in *A Christmas Carol* (1951), his dry wit and unusual appearance endeared him to generations of fans. *The Terror* is one of his earliest screen appearances, and fans of his later work will doubtless be surprised to find that he looked very much the same in the late 1930s as he did decades afterward. Here he's required to play a vengeful villain, something he does with great aplomb; he also manages to work in some grim humor, which is mercifully to the film's advantage. Erstwhile Sherlock Holmes Arthur Wontner and future Hammer horror alum Henry Oscar (*Brides of Dracula*, 1960) also turn in effective performances.

Though somewhat sluggishly directed by actor Richard Bird (he directed only a handful of films before deciding to stick with acting; he appeared in a later Wallace thriller, *Chamber of Horrors*, 1940), *The Terror* is an enjoyable thriller with some atmospheric settings and cinematography. The finale is particularly well done, even if an unnecessary coda feels somewhat arbitrary and unconvincing. TH

They Drive by Night
Warner; b/w; 84 min; Britain

D: Arthur B. Woods *S:* James Curtis *P:* Jerome Jackson *C:* Basil Emmott *M:* Bretton Byrd

Cast: Emlyn Williams, Anna Konstam, Ernest Thesiger, Allan Jeayes, Anthony Holles, Ronald Shiner, Yolande Terrell, Julie Barrie, Kitty der Legh, William Hartnell

Upon being released from jail, "Shorty" Matthews (Williams) pays a visit to his ex-girlfriend, only to find her strangled to death with a silk stocking. The ex-con flees the scene, convinced that the police will blame him for her demise. When the police get wind of the murder and pursue him, he escapes into the countryside and there tracks down another ex-girlfriend, Molly O'Neill (Konstam). She believes his claim of innocence, but as the cops close in, only the intervention of the bizarre Walter Hoover (Thesiger) seems likely to save him.

Not to be confused with the 1940 George Raft vehicle of the same name, *They Drive by Night* is a forgotten gem of the British cinema. The film begins very much like a film noir, despite the fact that it predates the generally accepted period of noir cinema by several years. Then, once it's drawn the viewer in, it unfolds breathlessly, exploring deeper and deeper layers of horror.

As an examination of a psycho-sexual serial killer, it is indeed ahead of its time. (The difficulty one has in imagining a film like this emerging from this period in British cinema may, in fact, account for its obscurity.) It's easy to compare *They Drive* to an Alfred Hitchcock film (if not a mélange of them), what with its scenario of a man falsely accused, a murder with kinky underpinnings and the like.

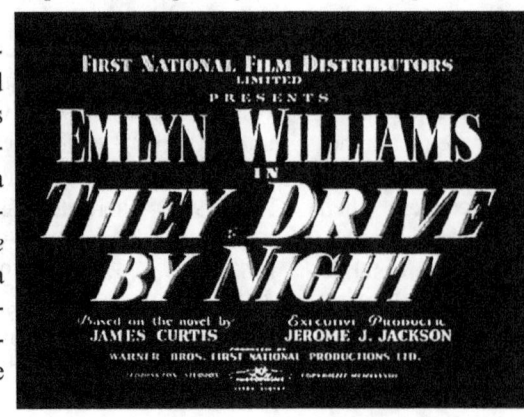

Director Arthur B. Woods (1904-1944) is a forgotten name these days, but as one watches *They Drive*, it's easy to imagine him, in some parallel universe, giving Britain's resident "Master of Suspense" a run for his money. Woods' direction here is a marvel of mood and efficiency; his use of light and shadow (and a well-placed studio-generated rainstorm or two) is effective without being heavy-handed, and he paces the film perfectly. But alas, Woods' promise was to go unfulfilled after he enlisted in the Royal Air Force during World War II and was killed, at the age of 39, in a mid-air collision.

They Drive's biggest draw for horror buffs comes during the second half, when Shorty's path crosses that of the eccentric Walter Hoover. While Emlyn Williams (famous at the time as author of, and onstage killer in, the play *Night Must Fall*) is very effective as Shorty, it can't be denied that once Ernest Thesiger as Hoover enters the picture, he steals the show. It's a brilliant characterization, witty and terrifying, and his status as a genre icon (owing principally to his casting in James Whale's *The Old Dark House*, 1932, and *The Bride of Frankenstein*, 1935) aside, Thesiger's performance alone is sufficient to prod *They Drive by Night* into out-and-out horror terrain. And while the film didn't make much of a mark upon its original release, it's certainly a title that deserves rediscovery by a wider audience. TH

Walking Corpse in an Old House
aka **Gu wu xing shi ji**
Xinhua; b/w; length unknown; China

D: Weibang Ma-Xu *P:* Shankun Zhang

Cast: unknown

In 1937 Chinese director Weibang Ma-Xu wrote and directed what is considered China's first horror film, *Song at Midnight*. The film proved a hit with the masses—though the upper classes frowned upon it—and Ma-Xu followed it up the next year with two more horror films, *Walking Corpse in an Old House* and *The Lonely Soul*. Unfortunately, information about the two latter films is sparse.

While *Walking Corpse in an Old House* sounds like something supernatural, it was likely *not* about zombies! In all probability, the plot was similar to that of *Song at Midnight* and included a similar mix of chills and romance.

Born in 1905, Ma-Xu began his career as an actor in the silent era after studying at the prestigious Shanghai Institute of Art (where he also taught for a time). He then worked for the Mingxing Film Company and began directing movies there in 1926. His films failed to make a mark until the aforementioned *Song at Midnight*.

Though he can fairly be called China's first horror director, he didn't stick with the genre long, abandoning it after the failure of *Song at Midnight—Part 2* (1941). He continued film work even after Japan's occupation of Shanghai during World War II, though his choice to cooperate with the Japanese film industry (even going so far as to help make a pro-Japanese film) led to his flight to Hong Kong when the Chinese later regained Shanghai. In 1949 he made what is generally considered his best feature, *The Haunted House*—which, despite the title, was a drama about a maid, not a horror film. CW

1939

Beware Spooks!
Columbia; b/w; 65 min; U.S.

D: Edward Sedgwick *S:* Richard Flournoy, Albert Duffy, Brian Marlow *P:* Robert Sparks *C:* Allen G. Seigler *M:* M.W. Stoloff, Leigh Harline, Louis Silvers, William Grant Still

Cast: Joe E. Brown, Mary Carlisle, Clarence Kolb, Marc Lawrence, Don Beddoe, George J. Lewis, Charles Lane, Byron Foulger

Bumbling cop Roy Gifford (Brown) is humiliated when he accidentally lets a robber get away. Determined to repair his reputation, he sets out to find the thief, a pursuit that leads him to a final showdown in a carnival "spook house."

Beware Spooks! offers up the ever-popular scenario of an idiot who accidentally makes good, with its negligible horror elements coming into place only during the finale. Richard Flournoy adapted the screenplay from his own stage play.

The film was a vehicle for popular comic actor Joe E. Brown. Born in Ohio in 1892, Brown entered show business by pursuing a then-common childhood fantasy—he actually ran away from home and joined the circus. From there he entered vaudeville, where he honed his shtick as a rubber-faced comedian. He made his first film in 1928 and by the mid-1930s had become a fixture in mainstream cinema. He is fondly remembered today as the inept millionaire who falls in love with a cross-dressing Jack Lemmon in Billy Wilder's *Some Like it Hot* (1959). He also had a cameo appearance in Jacques Tourneur's all-star horror romp *The Comedy of Terrors* (1964). He died in 1973.

Though popular in its time, Brown's persona hasn't aged well. His style of humor today seems forced and badly dated. The supporting cast of *Spooks!* includes Marc Lawrence, a pockmarked character actor who made a career out of playing thugs and mob underlings; his other genre credits include *The Monster and the Girl* (1941) and *Night Train to Terror* (1985). Director Edward Sedgwick also contributed the action-packed finale to *The Phantom of the Opera* (1925), albeit without credit. TH

The Cat and the Canary
Paramount; b/w; 72 min; U.S.

D: Elliott Nugent *S:* Walter DeLeon, Lynn Starling *P:* Arthur Hornblow, Jr. *C:* Charles Lang *M:* Dr. Ernest Tolch

Cast: Bob Hope, Paulette Goddard, John Beal, Douglass Montgomery, Gale Sondergaard, George Zucco, Elizabeth Patterson, Nydia Westman, John Farrow, George Regas

A family gathers at a creepy New Orleans mansion for the reading of a will. The sole heir turns out to be Joyce (Goddard), provided she isn't murdered before she can collect.

In 1927 Paul Leni filmed John Willard's popular stageplay *The Cat and the Canary* to great effect. With the coming of sound, Universal Pictures—the same company that had produced Leni's film—did a dual remake (one version in English, one in Spanish) under the title *The Cat Creeps* (1930), both versions of which are today lost.

This, the next film adaptation, emerged nine years later from Paramount as a star vehicle for up-and-coming comedian Bob Hope (1903-2003). Born in Britain, Hope had moved with his family to Cleveland in 1907. Eventually he made his way to New York, where he top-lined a few forgotten short films. After being lured to Hollywood, he made his major motion picture debut in *The Big Broadcast of 1938* (1938). It was the following year's *The Cat and the Canary*, however, that made Hope a star, ensuring that his brand of nervous, wise-cracking humor would be a film and television staple for decades to come.

A striking publicity photo features Bob Hope (far right) and Paulette Goddard (second from the left) from *The Cat and the Canary*.

Director Elliott Nugent lacked Leni's flair for orchestrating atmosphere and shock effects, but he created some memorable sequences, notably the prolonged scene of heroine Paulette Goddard being stalked through dimly lit corridors. It's also clear that Nugent studied the 1927 film, since one of the big shocks—the discovery of Lawyer Crosby's corpse behind a secret panel—is shot in exactly the same manner, right down to the corpse seeming to fall into the camera.

After 17 years of stage and film performances, Willard's story was probably drained of surprises well before this version, yet this *Cat* remains a well-paced piece of entertainment. It was frankly no real stretch to rework the story as a showcase for a comic actor. Even Leni's film, which was quite suspenseful at times, contained heavy doses of humor (and Hope's style of humor is downright sophisticated compared to the antics of Leni's bespectacled Creighton Hale). It helps, too, that much of the humor is actually funny. Indeed, the fact that Hope's character (a radio actor) is well versed in melodramatic conventions (and thus able to predict plot twists before they unfold) anticipates the celebrated self-reflexive nature of Wes Craven's *Scream* (1996) by about 60 years.

The impressive supporting cast includes two superb character actors: Gale Sondergaard and George Zucco. Sondergaard's slinky persona later became immortalized when she portrayed one of Sherlock Holmes' most ruthless antagonists in *The Spider Woman* (1944), while beady-eyed Zucco went on to portray a long line of demented scientists in the 1940s. Neither of the two has a great deal to do here, but they add to the film's spooky atmosphere with their mere presences.

Soft-core filmmaker Radley Metzger directed the next official remake under the same title in 1979. TH

Charlie Chan at Treasure Island
aka **Charlie Chan at the World's Fair**
Fox; b/w; 74 min; U.S.

D: Norman Foster *S:* John Larkin *P:* Edward Kaufman *C:* Virgil Miller *M:* Samuel Kaylin

Cast: Sidney Toler, Victor Sen Yung, Cesar Romero, Douglas Fowley, Pauline Moore, Donald MacBride, Wally Vernon, Douglass Dumbrille, Sally Blane, Charles Halton, Billie Seward, June Gale, Trevor Bardette, Louis Jean Heydt, Gerald Mohr (uncredited)

The Zodiac Killer was an infamous serial murderer who operated in northern California during the late 1960s and early 1970s; though he claimed credit for almost 40 murders, only five were ever confirmed. His *modus operandi* included sending cryptograms and taunting letters to the police and to media outlets, sometimes enclosing items taken from his victims. Based on the Zodiac's writings and his one solved cryptogram, it is known that he was a fan of classic movies, particularly RKO's *The Most Dangerous Game* (1932) as well as *Charlie Chan at Treasure Island*, one of several Charlie Chan movies to incorporate stylized horror elements.

Charlie Chan (Toler) is escorting his son Jimmy (Yung) to college when the detective runs across an old friend, author Paul Essex (Heydt), on the plane from Hawaii to San Francisco. After the flight, it is discovered that the usually chipper Essex has apparently committed suicide. While conferring with the police, Chan is introduced to two men, magician Rhadini (Romero) and reporter Peter Lewis (Fowley). The duo is on a campaign to expose phony mediums, including one Dr. Zodiac (Mohr), whom they believe is responsible for a number of murders disguised as suicides. Believing that Zodiac might be behind Essex's own "suicide," Chan pays a visit to the spiritualist, who is disguised under heavy layers of clothing, make-up and a mask. Later, while partying at the International Exposition on Treasure Island in San Francisco Bay, Chan observes firsthand the uncanny abilities of mind reader Eve Cairo (Moore), who is closely associated with Rhadini and Lewis. Returning to Dr. Zodiac's lair, Chan finds and burns the files the spiritualist was using to blackmail others, then sets a trap (involving Eve's psychic powers) to capture the criminal mastermind. But all is not as it seems, and while Chan's plan does result in outing the real Dr. Zodiac, it also results in murder.

In addition to bearing the same name as his movie counterpart, the Zodiac Killer also wore a bizarre costume in his attack on two young people at Lake Berryessa that, with its zodiacal images, was similar—though not identical—to his namesake's accoutrements. Both Zodiacs wrote letters to the media and the police. And both the movie character and the real-life murderer were obsessed with the occult.

Charlie Chan at Treasure Island is one of Sidney Toler's more interesting outings as the ingenious Charlie Chan, a role first made famous by Swedish actor Warner Oland. While Oland had had every intention of continuing to play the part (as he had done already in 16 films for Fox), he walked off the set of *Charlie Chan at the Ringside* in 1937. An alcoholic, he was at the time undergoing a stressful divorce that prevented him from either accessing his wealth or traveling to his birthplace of Sweden, where many family members still lived. Although under contract with Fox to star in additional Chan films, Oland did return to Sweden upon the settlement of his divorce, and there he contracted pneumonia and died on August 6, 1938. *Ringside* was never completed, and the scenes already filmed were later integrated into one of Peter Lorre's Mr. Moto movies, *Mr. Moto's Gamble* (1938).

After Oland's departure and death, Fox launched a nationwide search for a new Charlie Chan, finally choosing Sidney Toler from his screen test. Toler was noted mostly as a silent-era stage actor, having worked with such future luminaries as Humphrey Bogart and Katharine Hepburn. He entered the movies in 1929 as a character actor, but it wasn't until he was cast as the humble but brilliant Asian detective that he found everlasting

Sidney Toler, Douglas Fowley, June Gale and Cesar Romero in *Charlie Chan at Treasure Island*

fame. He was a more-than-competent actor who stepped admirably into a role strongly associated with Oland and, through his own skill, made it entirely his own, so that today his name is as synonymous with the character as is Oland's. Toler's first Chan film, *Charlie Chan in Honolulu* (1938), was an immediate success, and the actor was quickly shuffled into *Charlie Chan in Reno* and *Charlie Chan at Treasure Island* (both 1939).

According to news reports of the time, *Treasure Island* was to have included performances by Joyce Compton and John Carradine; neither, however, appears in the final film. It's tantalizing to fantasize about just which part Carradine would have played (most likely either Rhadini or Dr. Zodiac). Instead, we get heartthrob Cesar Romero as Rhadini. Romero went on to portray The Joker in 21 episodes of ABC's popular *Batman* television show in the late 1960s.

Variety, on August 23, 1939 gave *Treasure Island* a generally positive review, saying that it was slow in spots but held up well to the standards set by previous Charlie Chan pictures. Picking up on the horror angle, the magazine noted correctly that the film contained many "weird and spooky episodes." Numerous scenes in the film are indeed horror-tinged, not the least of which is a séance involving the appearance of a ghostly woman.

The Treasure Island of the film's title is an artificial island constructed in 1936 and '37 from landfill dredged up from San Francisco Bay, where the island is in fact located. Originally intended as the site of an airport, it wound up being used for the World's Fair of the Golden Gate Exposition in 1939 and '40 before being converted to Naval usage during World War II. It is during that Expo where *Treasure Island* is set, providing an incidental snapshot of a very brief but fondly remembered period in San Francisco's history. Today, the island is home to a few film and television studios, as well as various other types of business. CW

The Dark Eyes of London
aka **The Human Monster**
ABP/Argyle; b/w; 76 min; Great Britain

D: Walter Summers *Co-S:* Patrick Kirwin, Walter Summers, Jan Van Lusil *P/Co-S:* John Argyle *C:* Bryan Langley *M:* Guy Jones, C. King Palmer

Cast: Bela Lugosi, Greta Gynt, Hugh Williams, Edmon Ryan, Wilfred Walter, Alexander Field, May Hallatt, Bryan Herbert, Arthur E. Owen, Charles Penrose

A series of "accidental" deaths is occurring in a home for the blind run by Dr. Orloff (Lugosi). Inspector Holt (Williams) and his American colleague Lieutenant O'Reilly (Ryan) are convinced that the deaths are anything but accidental and that Orloff is in some way responsible. Using Diana (Gynt), daughter of one of the victims, as an undercover agent, they attempt to expose Orloff before he kills again.

Based on Edgar Wallace's 1924 novel of the same name, *The Dark Eyes of London* gives Bela Lugosi his first top-line role in a British production since Hammer's *Phantom Ship* (1935). And although it was the British who spearheaded the horror ban of 1936-1938, they entered the resurgence enthusiastically with *Dark Eyes*, in part because it marked the establishment of a new certificate (*Dark Eyes* was awarded the first "H" for horror) to distinguish horror films from more mainstream fare. It's a rating *Dark Eyes* certainly merits; it contains scenes that outdo anything in the same period's Hollywood films in terms of sheer cruelty.

Lugosi dominates the picture. His portrayal of Orloff is nicely understated (by Lugosi standards), and he makes a properly vile villain throughout. (It's difficult to discuss his performance further without giving away the film's mystery, so spoilers follow.) The Hungarian actor dons a fake moustache, wig and dark glasses to play the kindly, supposedly blind Professor Dearborn, as well as the sinister villain. The filmmakers even dubbed the character in an attempt to keep the audience in the dark, a waste of time since Lugosi's facial structure is so distinctive. As it stands, one is left wondering not whodunit, but rather how Orloff is able to disguise his voice so effectively.

The film also showcases some very capable supporting performances. Greta Gynt is a spunky and intelligent heroine, a notch above the typical screaming-and-fainting heroines offered

Dr. Orloff (Bela Lugosi) threatens the daughter (Greta Gynt) of one of his murder victims in *The Dark Eyes of London*.

impresses—despite an awkward make-up job—as the brutish Jake, whom Orloff uses to do his dirty work.

It has been remarked that the dynamic between Jake and the pathetic Lou (an uncredited Arthur E. Owen, required to play both blind and mute) is similar to that between Lugosi's Ygor and Boris Karloff's monster in that same year's *Son of Frankenstein*. Given that *Dark Eyes* was released after *Son*, it's indeed quite possible that the earlier film might have influenced the British film, which did tremendous box-office. In any event, the relationship fleshes out the character of Jake, otherwise presented as a Neolithic brute, and gives some pathos to the proceedings.

The Dark Eyes of London was one of a number of Wallace adaptations produced in England in the 1930s. It's arguably the most horrific of the bunch, but many of the others have their moments of horror as well. Director Alfred Vohrer later filmed Wallace's novel as *The Dead Eyes of London* (1961), part of a series of even more horrific *krimi* (crime) thrillers produced in Germany between 1959 and the early 1970s. TH

Daughter of the Tong
Metropolitan; b/w; 54 (56) min; U.S.

D: Raymond K. Johnson *S:* Alan Merritt, George H. Plympton *P:* Lester F. Scott, Jr. *C:* Elmer Dyer

Cast: Evelyn Brent, Grant Withers, Dorothy Short, Dave O'Brien, Richard Loo, Dirk Thane, Harry Harvey, Budd Buster, Robert Frazer, Hal Taliaferro

Making for a refreshing change of pace—though ultimately not enough of one—*Daughter of the Tong* eschews the usual wisecracking reporter and his dame girlfriend for FBI agent Ralph Dickson (Withers) and a woman, Marion Morgan (Short), whose brother is being held hostage by racketeers. But despite this, and despite some unusually good performances, the film is entirely pedestrian. Its plot concerns FBI attempts to crack down on Carney (Brent), the female leader of a dangerous criminal gang known in Asian circles as a Tong. Obviously based on Sax Rohmer's Fah lo Suee (the daughter of Fu Manchu), Carney's supposed Asian heritage is telegraphed solely by her choice of clothing; apart from that, she's obviously and completely Caucasian, despite the lead's charming assertion that she looks like "a slant-eyed lady like Mrs. Fu Manchu …"

Though released in 1939, *Daughter* plays out like a film of much older vintage, a vibe created largely by its lack of dramatic music and its clumsy recycling of stock footage from the silent and early talkie eras. The performances, as noted above, are quite good, with Dorothy Short faring far better here than in her other horror outing, the terrible *Spooks Run Wild* (1941), and Robert Frazer (*The Vampire Bat*, 1933) making a brief but welcome appearance as an FBI chief. Grant Withers (*The Vampire's Ghost*, 1945) also does quite well as the agent in pursuit of the femme fatale, while silent superstar Evelyn Brent (*Paramount on Parade*, 1930) delivers Carney's awful dialogue with such relish that she actually manages to bring the character to life.

Raymond K. Johnson was one of many pseudonyms used by Bernard B. Ray, a writer, director, producer and cinematographer of low-budget melodramas in the 1930s and '40s. His direction here is flat, and he shows little understanding of how to shoot action sequences. (His sole strength appears to have

up during the period by the likes of Universal, Paramount, RKO and Warner Bros. Hugh Williams and Edmon Ryan appear to have a good time playing off each other, while Wilfred Walter

Ken Maynard stars in yet another weird Western, *Death Rides the Range*.

been drawing out good performances from his actors.) Thankfully, he doesn't overload *Daughter* with comedy relief, though a fair amount of unintentional comedy manages to creep into the proceedings now and then. One other thing the director does manage to get right, mostly because he doesn't try anything that can't be pulled off with so small a budget, is a car chase that comes at the film's climax. The film is also helped along by a thankfully short running time, and at least its bad dialogue is largely free of unnecessary padding.

While mostly a boring crime drama, *Daughter of the Tong* warrants inclusion in a book about horror films because it fits within the Yellow Peril subgenre, a staple of horror at the time. CW

Death Rides the Range
Colony; b/w; 58 min; U.S.

D: Sam Newfield *S:* William (Bill) Lively, Oliver Drake *P:* Arthur Alexander, Max Alexander *C:* Art (Arthur) Reed *M:* Lew Porter

Cast: Ken Maynard, Fay McKenzie, Ralph Peters, Julian Rivero, Charles King, John Elliott, William Castello, Sven Hugo Borg, Michael Vallon, Julian Madison, Kenneth Rhodes, Richard Alexander, Bud Osborne, Wally West

Ken Baxter (Maynard) and his two comedic sidekicks, Pancho (Rivero) and Panhandle (Peters), become embroiled in a mystery when a wounded archaeologist, Dr. Wahl (Vallon), stumbles into their camp with a horrifying tale of being thrown over a cliff. Later, after Wahl is taken to a trading post, he begins to describe a cave and a secret stash of some sort when the lights go out and he's murdered. When the sheriff refuses to investigate, Baxter, with the assistance of a second archaeologist, Dr. Flotow (Castello), takes on the task. He finds the cave and, in the process, also examines a creepy graveyard and a moaning chimney in a decrepit ranch. Eventually, he finds that the cave connects to a chamber containing helium gas, which foreign agents want for fueling their dirigibles.

Death Rides the Range is another in a long line of weird Westerns starring Indiana-born Ken Maynard, whose work also includes *The Haunted Ranch* (1926), *The Phantom City* (1928), *Tombstone Canyon* (1932) and *Smoking Guns* (1934), as well as *Mystery Mountain* (1934) and *Phantom Rancher* (1940). It was a remake of sorts of the Tom Mix oater *The Fourth Horseman*, which had been shot at Universal, Maynard's one-time studio home, in 1932. The budget for Maynard's unofficial version has been estimated at a mere $15,000, peanuts even by 1939 standards and a far cry from the kind of budgets the actor commanded when contracted to Universal.

Despite the fact that *Death Rides the Range* is considered Maynard's picture, the real star of the show is his horse Tarzan, which exhibits the intelligence to untie ropes and pick its master's hat from the ground!

Though some sources cite the film as a 1940 production, it was actually produced in 1939 and released theatrically on December 14 of that same year. CW

The Devil's Daughter
aka **Devil's Daughter**; **Pocomania**; **Daughter of the Isle of Jamaica**
Lenwal/Sack; b/w; 52 (67) min; U.S.

D/Co-P: Arthur H. Leonard *S:* George Terwilliger *Co-P:* Harry M. Popkin *C:* Jay Rescher *M:* John Killam

Cast: Nina Mae McKinney, Ida James, Jack Carter, Hamtree Harrington, Willa MacLane, Francine Larrimore, Emmett Wallace, Leon Lee

After a lengthy opening sequence involving a dance and a cockfight, *The Devil's Daughter* continues to take its sweet time in setting up its premise, which turns out to be something of a rehash of George Terwilliger's *Ouanga* (1935). Filmed on location in Kingston, Jamaica, *Daughter* has New Yorker Sylvia Walton (James) returning to her island home to take control of the family business, a large plantation that has been under the control of her bitter half-sister Isabelle Walton (McKinney). Picking up quickly that sophisticated, successful city-girl Sylvia is weirdly superstitious, Isabelle pretends to be a practitioner of Obeah (a type of West Indies folk magic) and tries to scare Sylvia off by threatening to sacrifice her to the dark gods.

The ill-paced proceedings are padded with a couple of ill-paced subplots, the first involving Isabelle's obsession with plantation foreman Phil (Carter), who in turn pretends to love Sylvia in order to swindle her out of her inheritance. What little entertainment value this (or the main storyline, for that matter) might have had is thoroughly undone by a second, very unfunny subplot about a bumbling cockfighter, Percy Jackson (Harrington), who has been led by a servant named Elvira (MacLane) to believe that he shares his soul with a pig.

Arthur H. Leonard's direction is no more effective here than Terwilliger's was for *Ouanga*, and Jay Rescher's camerawork is

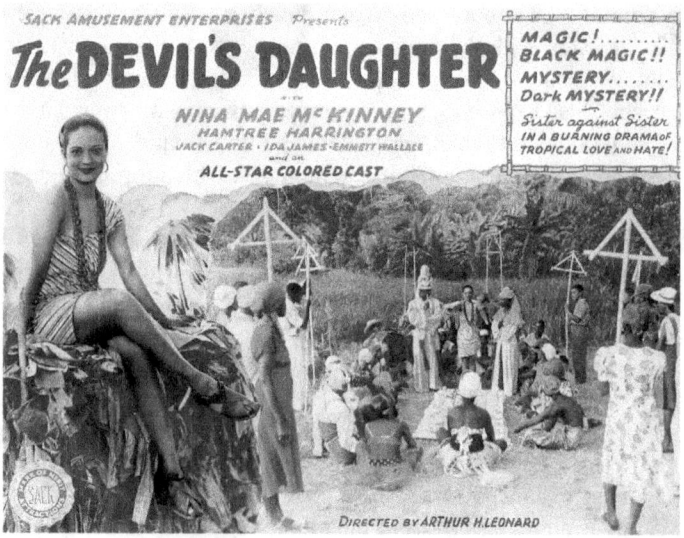

The Devil's Daughter was one of only a few black exploitation horror movies made during the 1930s.

strictly stationary; nobody involved takes the slightest advantage of the exotic locale. The script, as already touched upon, is poor, with a finale (in which the sisters are reconciled and the villainous Phil banished) that is a bit hard to swallow.

On the plus side, several members of the film's all-black cast manage decent performances. Nina Mae McKinney impresses as the jealous Isabelle, as does Ida James as the kind-hearted and soft-spoken Sylvia. McKinney has become something of a legend among purveyors of 1920s and '30s black cinema; her good looks and charming personality (neither of which, incidentally, is on particular display here) have earned her something of a positive reputation, further bolstered by an ability to immerse herself in her roles. And singer Ida James' sweet-natured humility here prefigures a similar performance from Simone Simon in *Cat People* (1942) by three years.

The Devil's Daughter was released to black cinemas in big cities and in the South; it was also served up to the midnight-movie crowd in predominantly white theaters. The word "pocomania," which is not only used by a character in the film but was also one of the film's alternate titles, describes a religious sect that combines some aspects of Christianity with West African traditions and customs, with spirit possession being among its favored tenets. It can also refer to the specific moment when the spirit of a dead person possesses a living person (enchanted by the sound of drums and frenzied dancing). CW

The Face at the Window
King; b/w; 65 (70) min; Great Britain
D/P: George King *S:* A.R. Rawlinson, Ronald Fayre *C:* Hone Glendinning *M:* Jack Beaver
Cast: Tod Slaughter, Marjorie Taylor, John Warwick, Leonard Henry, Aubrey Mallalieu, Robert Adair, Wallace Evennett, Kay Lewis, Bill Shine, Margaret Yarde, Harry Terry

"France 1880: A series of unsolved murders—a country panic-stricken—fantastic stories of Le Loup—a wolf man. A wave of terror which inspired this melodrama of the old school—dear to the hearts of all who unashamedly enjoy either a shudder or a laugh at the heights of villainy." So begins the best film adaptation of *The Face at the Window*, F. Brooke Warren's infamous 1897 stage play.

After George King's success at turning an unknown actor named Tod Slaughter into a full-blown horror star (in his native country, anyway), he turned to Warren's play in hopes of continuing his winning streak—and in so doing created the best version of *Face* to date. The play was a perennial favorite with British theatergoers, so it was a given that it would find an acceptable audience on the big screen. By 1939 there had already been three film adaptations (1919, 1920, and 1932), all of them made in England. Some sources state that versions were also made in 1910, 1912, 1913 and 1915, but it turns out that, while all of these are identically titled, none are actual adaptations of Warren's play (one is a drama, one a gangster thriller, one a Western and so on). Nor are there, as some of those same sources state, 11 film adaptations in all.

Though the film attains a degree of Gothic horror not achieved again on film until Hammer's heyday in the 1950s, it contains an interesting science fiction angle that allows for a dead man to come briefly back to life to finger the identity of The Wolf, a notorious murderer who announces his crimes with a howl.

Of course, in actuality The Wolf is none other than Chevalier Lucio del Gardo (Slaughter), a rich miser who lusts after the beautiful but much younger Cecile de Brisson (Taylor). Naturally there's a problem. She's engaged to marry a near-destitute bank clerk, Lucien Cortier (Warwick), so The Wolf plots to frame the clerk for a crime he didn't commit and, once he's sentenced to prison, make his own move on the unsuspecting girl.

If this all sounds familiar, that's because it is: It's the overall plotline of at least four Slaughter films before it—*Maria Marten, or The Murder in the Red Barn* (1935), *The Crimes of Stephen Hawke* (1936), *Never Too Late to Mend* (1937) and *The Ticket of Leave Man* (1938). Slaughter and Marjorie Taylor reprise their roles from those previous films, while John Warwick repeats his role from *Ticket*. But what sets *The Face at the Window* apart from the earlier films is that it's the most overtly horrific of Slaughter's films up until that time. It was also one of the most successful, pointing the direction in which Slaughter would go for nearly another decade to come.

The film intentionally apes the excesses of Universal's most violent and sadistic 1930s pre-Code fare, one-upping Universal in the process with a level of period detail rarely seen in the bigger company's slicker output. To that end, Philip Bawcombe outdoes himself as art director, creating a number of period sets, including an external Parisian street, a garden with ornate stone steps and numerous internal dwelling places, all of which are effective in establishing the Gothic mood (and making the film appear much more expensive than it really was, as do superior costumes and set decoration). The faux authenticity of the not-so-mad scientist's lab equipment prefigures by almost 20 years Baron Frankenstein's life-creating paraphernalia in *The Curse of Frankenstein* (1957).

In addition to the eerie call of an unearthly howl, the film's horrific touches include the titular face at the window, a beastly visage that portends death. (Said face doesn't belong to Slaughter's Wolf, however; it belongs to his deformed sidekick/brother, played by Harry Terry as a drooling, hirsute monstrosity with bad teeth.) And the finale, in which The Wolf's murdered victim, his body flowing with electricity, appears to write the name of his murderer on a note pad beneath his hand while lying on his deathbed, is a beautifully morbid sequence.

Tod Slaughter is believably slimy as del Gardo. He avoids excessive hamminess, a tendency that mars some of his lesser performances. Likewise good is his regular co-star Marjorie Taylor as Cecile de Brisson. She had been terrible in the aforementioned *The Crimes of Stephen Hawke* and *Never Too Late to Mend*, but by the time she starred in *The Ticket of Leave Man* she began to show some maturity. This culminated in *The Face at the Window*, with the actress giving her most natural performance to date. Weirdly, after finally developing the ability to act, she seems to have done one more (uncredited) role before vanishing from the industry altogether.

Rounding out the cast is John Warwick as Lucien Cortier, giving the same sort of effective but forgettable performance he gave in *Ticket*. Born in 1905 and beginning his cinematic career in 1932, Warwick continued acting into the 1970s on both the big and small screens. Among his few horror appearances were roles in *The Case of the Frightened Lady* (1940) and *Horrors of the Black Museum* (1959). He died of a heart attack in 1972 in his native Australia, and his last film was released posthumously in 1975.

The Face at the Window was not released in the United States until October 1940, right before Halloween. That same year also saw the release of Slaughter's next horror film, *The Crimes at the Dark House*, the most grisly adaptation of Wilkie Collins' *The Woman in White* (1859-1860) ever produced. CW

Ghost Story of a Love-Mad Tutoress
aka **Kaidan kyoren onna shisho**
Shinkô; b/w; length unknown; Japan

D: Shigeru Mokuto

Cast: Sumiko Suzuki, Shintaro Nanjou

This is one of the last horror films to feature popular Japanese actress Sumiko Suzuki, who stars as a tutor in love with a blind masseur. When she learns that her man is having an affair with one of her students, she offs herself—then comes back from the grave to do in her erstwhile lover and his mistress.

As the 1930s gave way to the 1940s, film production all but stopped in Japan, with the government allowing only propaganda to be produced. Big-screen horror was nixed as the horrors of war took center stage in day-to-day life (unlike in the United States, where moviegoers turned to horror films to escape the war). It wasn't until the mid-1950s that horror films once again took their rightful place among Japan's most popular cinematic expressions. CW

Ghost Story of the Mother Tree
aka **Kaidan chibusa enoki**
Zensho; b/w; length unknown; Japan

D: Kanenori Yamada

Cast: Toshiko Myagawa

This is the third known adaptation of Sanyutei Encho's tale *Kaidan chibusa no enoki*. The story concerns a painter's assistant, Isogai, who falls in love with Oseki, his master's wife. Isogai murders his master, only to contract a horrific (and presumably rare) disease in which birds incubate in his chest. Eventually, the birds pop out and cause the death of his wife, after which he dies, not from an exploded chest, but at the hands of his former master's five-year-old son.

The story was adapted again to greater acclaim in 1958 by Goro Kadono under the title *The Mother Tree*. CW

The Ghost Train
aka **De spooktrein**
Filmex; b/w; 70 min; Netherlands

D: Carl Lamac S: Kees Bruynse, Nico De Jong P: Rudolf Meyer C: Otto Heller, Bryan Langley M: Max Tak

Cast: Jan Musch, Jan de la Mar, Louis Borel, Adolph Engers, Cissy Van Bennekom, Sara Heyblom, Chris Baay, Lies de Wind, Lau Ezerman, Nico De Jong, John Gobau, Piet Rienks, Hans Tiemeyer

Passengers at a reputedly haunted railway station are frightened by ghostly goings-on, but it turns out that the whole thing is a smokescreen to draw attention away from a band of smugglers.

Arnold Ridley's 1923 play *The Ghost Train* inspired a number of cinematic adaptations in the 1920s and 1930s. The director of this one, Carl Lamac, had a lengthy—if not terribly distinguished—career that lasted from 1919 until his death in 1952; his only other noteworthy horror credit is his 1931 version of Edgar Wallace's *The Squeaker*.

Ghost Train's cinematography is credited to Bryan Langley and Otto Heller. Langley also photographed the lurid Bela Lugosi vehicle *The Dark Eyes of London* (1939), and he is rumored to have done some uncredited special effects work on Jacques Tourneur's brilliant *Curse of the Demon* (1957). Heller went on to become one of Britain's top cinematographers, shooting everything from Michael Powell's classic *Peeping Tom* (1960) to the gaudy Hammer horror *The Curse of the Mummy's Tomb* (1964) to the 1966 box-office hit *The Ipcress File*.

Ridley's story got another go-around in 1941. TH

The Gorilla
Fox; b/w; 66 min; U.S.

D: Allan Dwan S: Rian James, Sid Silvers P: Harry Joe Brown C: Edward Cronjager M: David Buttolph, David Raskin, Alfred Newman, Cyril J. Mockridge

Cast: Jimmy Ritz, Harry Ritz, Al Ritz, Lionel Atwill, Bela Lugosi, Patsy Kelly, Anita Louise, Joseph Calleia, Edward Norris, Wally Vernon, Paul Harvey, Art Miles

A killer known as The Gorilla threatens to make Walter Stevens (Atwill) his next victim. Stevens laughs off a menacing letter from the psychopath, until his servant Peters (Lugosi) reminds him that previous recipients of such death threats were all dead within 24 hours of receiving them. Stevens hires three detectives (the Ritz brothers) as protection, but their ineptness proves more of a hindrance than help.

Ralph Spence's Broadway hit *The Gorilla* was filmed in 1927 and again in 1930, with both versions now considered lost. There was an unauthorized British rendering titled *Sh! The Octopus* in 1937, but 20th Century Fox made the next official adaptation in 1939. On an artistic level, the studio needn't have bothered. The better-than-average production values don't near-

Bela Lugosi plays another suspicious butler in *The Gorilla*.

ly compensate for the misstep of crafting the film as a vehicle for the then-popular Ritz Brothers. The erstwhile vaudeville performers had made their film debut in 1934's *Hotel Anchovy*, and their frantic antics proved popular enough that a series of mindless comedies followed, including this adaptation of Spence's stage play.

Fox is clearly hedging its bets here, surrounding an established comedy team with the trappings of a horror movie, including genre stalwarts like Lionel Atwill and Bela Lugosi. For Lugosi, the film proved portentous; he famously moved on to a career playing ill-defined servant characters and red herrings, managing top billing mostly in Poverty Row drek. To their credit, Lugosi and Atwill play their roles with tongues planted firmly in cheeks; their performances are far and away the most appealing aspect of the production. Atwill is particularly good as the shifty would-be murder victim, imbuing his limited screen time with oily duplicity. Lugosi's appearance is likewise truncated, but he manages a few wryly amusing moments, mostly in his interactions with the Brothers Ritz.

As for the Brothers themselves, well … suffice it to say that their comedy stylings are an acquired taste. They mug mercilessly and obnoxiously in a desperate attempt at laughs. Almost everyone else in the cast provides welcome relief from their forced zaniness, including gifted character actor Joseph Calleia (*Touch of Evil*, 1957) in a small role as a shady investigator. There's also an appearance by comedienne Patsy Kelly (*Rosemary's Baby*, 1968), who gives the Brothers a run for their money in the "enthusiasm" department.

Director Allan Dwan had a string of successes in the silent era (including the 1922 Douglas Fairbanks version of *Robin Hood*), and his prolific career lasted into the early 1960s. It should be noted that in 1914 he directed *The Forbidden Room*, an early horror vehicle offering Lon Chaney a role as a murder victim.

Ultimately, *The Gorilla* is a disappointment. The laughs are few, the chills sparse and the mystery smothered by slapstick foolishness. TH

Honchô kaibyô-den
Daito; b/w; length unknown; Japan
   D: Houzou Nakajima
   Cast: Sozaburo Matsuyama, Teruko Sanjo, Sumire Shiroki

This was the second film to bear the name *Honchô kaibyô-den*, which translates roughly as *Domestic Legend of the Ghost Cat*. Like its predecessor, it dealt with a ghostly cat manifestation, carrying out the vengeful will of a grudge ghost.

Ghost cat movies were extremely popular in Japan from the silent era into the 1960s, at which time they gave way to the more erotic horror of Edogawa Rampo and the irradiated *daikaijū eiga* ("giant monster") horrors unleashed by the atomic bomb in the form of Godzilla and his cohorts. CW

The Hound of the Baskervilles
Fox; b/w; 80 min; U.S.
   D: Sidney Lanfield *S:* Ernest Pascal *P:* Gene Markey, Darryl F. Zanuck *C:* J. Peverell Marley *M:* David Buttolph, Charles Maxwell, Cyril J. Mockridge, David Raskin
   Cast: Basil Rathbone, Nigel Bruce, Richard Greene, Wendy Barrie, Lionel Atwill, John Carradine, Morton Lowry, Barlowe Borland, Beryl Mercer, Eily Maylon, Ralph Forbes, E.E. Clive, Nigel de Brulier, Lionel Pape

Dr. Mortimer (Atwill) consults Sherlock Holmes (Rathbone) in hopes of preventing a tragedy. The recent, violent death of Sir Charles Baskerville has convinced Mortimer that the legendary Hound of the Baskervilles is stalking the moors. The youthful Sir Henry Baskerville (Greene) is poised to inher-

Basil Rathbone in his trend-setting role as Sherlock Holmes in *The Hound of the Baskervilles*

it Baskerville Hall, and Mortimer wishes to protect him from meeting the same fate as Sir Charles. Holmes, though skeptical, sends his faithful friend and companion Dr. Watson (Bruce) to the Baskerville estate to watch over the young lord.

Sometimes an actor is so perfectly cast in a role that he or she becomes identified with it for all time. It doesn't matter what else said actor ever accomplishes; it's impossible for him or her to completely escape the image of that particular character. Boris Karloff as the Frankenstein Monster comes to mind, as does Sean Connery as James Bond and Anthony Hopkins as Hannibal Lecter. The same can be inarguably said of Basil Rathbone, who began his association with Sir Arthur Conan Doyle's immortal sleuth Sherlock Holmes in this 1939 adaptation of *The Hound of the Baskervilles*, a novel first serialized in Britain's *Strand Magazine* in 1901 and 1902.

Filmmakers recognized the cinematic potential of Doyle's mysteries early on, but none of the individual stories have been filmed as frequently—and with such mixed results—as *Hound*. By 1914, the French and the Germans had adapted it for the screen, while the British took their first crack at it in 1921. Most of those early versions are lost, the earliest known extant rendering being the 1936 German one.

There's little doubt that this first U.S. take on the tale is the most famous version of all. This is, however, arguably due more to its introduction of Rathbone's Holmes than it is to its technical merits as a film. That's not to say that it isn't accomplished—far from it—but it does fall short of its source material.

For one thing, Sidney Lanfield's direction is slow and stodgy. The absence of a music score (only the titles and a lengthy flashback sequence are scored) also seems a missed opportunity. The overall feel of the film is more drawing room mystery than moody horror film, though there are a few world-class set pieces studding the near-mediocrity.

Rathbone, of course, is perfect as Holmes. It's a role the actor would grow to resent—an air of detached boredom crept noticeably into his later portrayals—but such was not yet the case here. He goes through his paces with precision and sly wit, making one regret that, per the novel, he is required to be absent for the movie's mid-section.

The casting of Nigel Bruce as Watson has for decades angered the more canonical Holmes buffs, but he's a perfect match for Rathbone's Holmes. Whereas Rathbone is sleek, acerbic and perceptive, Bruce's bumbling Watson is rumpled, flustered and easily distracted. It's a complete bastardization of Doyle's intelligent man of medicine, no argument there, but it just as undeniably makes for wonderful screen chemistry. Bruce's blustery delivery and huffs of anger are a delight to watch, and the fact that Holmes so obviously enjoys needling him adds a level of humanity to their relationship.

Richard Greene (who found fame in the '50s as TV's *Robin Hood* before starring in such fright flicks as 1968's *The Blood of Fu Manchu* and 1972's *Tales from the Crypt*) is an agreeable Sir Henry, while John Carradine as the sinister butler Barryman (changed from the book's Barrymore) and Lionel Atwill become wonderful red herrings. Neither actor, if one pays close attention, is given much to do, but the presence of each adds immeasurably to the film's entertainment value.

It's also worth noting that of all the 14 Holmes films to team Rathbone and Bruce, this is one of only two—the other being *Sherlock Holmes and the Secret Weapon*, 1942—that makes reference to the detective's drug habit; the film's fade out finds a weary Holmes calling out to his colleague, "Oh Watson ... the needle!"

Rathbone and Bruce immediately re-teamed for Fox's *The Adventures of Sherlock Holmes* before moving to Universal for 12 further adventures (set in contemporary times to accommodate lower budgets). Most of those were flat-out murder mysteries, but some, including *The Scarlet Claw* (1944) and *The Spider Woman* (1944), incorporated enough creepiness and tension to qualify as horror.

The Hound of the Baskervilles would next be filmed in Germany in 1955, and then in 1958 (but released in 1959) by Hammer Film Productions, with Peter Cushing as Holmes and Andre Morell as Watson. TH

The House of Fear
Universal; b/w; 65 min; U.S.
D: Joe May *S:* Peter Milne *P:* Edmund Grainger *C:* Milton Krasner *M:* Charles Previn
Cast: William Gargan, Irene Hervey, Dorothy Arnold, Alan Dinehart, Robert Coote, Harvey Stephens, Walter Woolf King, El Brendel, Tom Dugan, Jan Duggan, Donald Douglas

When actor John Woodford (Douglas) is killed while performing on stage, the police are baffled. The killing goes unsolved, and the theater closes down due to bad publicity. A short

time later, ambitious detective McHugh (Gargan) poses as a producer and re-opens the theater in an attempt to nab the killer.

The Last Warning (1929) was the last film completed by Paul Leni, the gifted German émigré lured to Hollywood after the success of *Waxworks* (1924). While *Warning*'s script was awfully creaky stuff, Leni's imagination transformed it into an engaging, comedic horror-mystery. When Universal decided to remake the film, they turned to another German émigré, Joe May (1880-1954). May had a distinguished reputation in the silent German cinema scene, where he'd infamously clashed with his part-time scenarist Fritz Lang over directing duties for *The Indian Tomb* (1921). The story goes that Lang had written the screenplay and planned to direct, and when May got the job instead, a furious Lang vowed never to work with him again. (Lang did find closure with his own gaudy color remake in 1959.)

That incident aside, May's reputation was already eclipsed by Lang's well before the rise of Nazism prompted both men to seek refuge in the United States. While Lang's arrival on American shores resulted in a major studio offering (*Fury*, 1936, produced by MGM), May found success more difficult to come by. He eventually landed at Universal, where he helmed three horror-tinged properties. A *Last Warning* remake called *The House of Fear* was the first of them. It's also the most obscure, and for reasons easily discerned. It has no recognizable names, and it's a remake of a film that is relatively obscure. But most significantly, it's far and away the most half-heartedly done of the three. If the story was clichéd and predictable when Leni filmed it, there was nothing in the decade that followed that made it less stale. And it's topped off by a finale that's, in a word, predictable.

The sparseness of a music score is sorely felt. While Universal's resident composer Charles Previn composed opening and end title music, the bulk of the film unfolds with no score at all. Compare this to the other Universal horror fare of the same year, *Son of Frankenstein* and *Tower of London*, both of which benefit from rousing soundtracks (though, truth be told, the latter film's music is basically a re-orchestrated score from the former's).

It doesn't help that May's direction is too heavy for comedy and too tentative to make much of the "killer on the loose" angle. The cast also lacks color, even if the performers do mostly capable jobs. William Gargan is effective as the no-nonsense detective masquerading as a theater producer; he had earlier played a key role in Lang's *You Only Live Once* (1937). Gargan isn't exactly leading man material, but he does all right with the role. The supporting cast includes an early appearance by British character actor Robert Coote, who later played one of the snobby critics murdered by Vincent Price in *Theater of Blood* (1973). Faux Swede and alleged funnyman El ("Yumpin' Yiminy!") Brendel is also inexplicably on hand for (thankfully) occasional comic relief.

Milton Krasner's cinematography makes good use of shadow, but May did a much better job on his next Universal assignment, *The Invisible Man Returns* (1940).

This film has no connection to *The House of Fear* (1945), which was a part of the Basil Rathbone Sherlock Holmes series produced by Universal. TH

The Hunchback of Notre Dame
RKO; b/w; 116 min; U.S.
D: William Dieterle S: Sonya Levien P: Pandro S. Berman C: Joseph H. August M: Alfred Newman FX: Vernon L. Walker
Cast: Charles Laughton, Sir Cedric Hardwicke, Maureen O'Hara, Edmond O'Brien, Thomas Mitchell, Harry Davenport, Walter Hampden, Alan Marshall, George Zucco, Katherine Alexander, Fritz Leiber, Etienne Giardot, Helene Whitney, Minna Gombell, Arthur Hohl, Curt Bois, George Tobias, Rod La Rocque, Spencer Charters, Kathryn Adams, Diane Hunter, Siegfried Arno, Louis Adlon, George Barrows, Vangie Beilby, Lionel Belmore, Barlowe Borland

Hunchback Quasimodo (Laughton), bell ringer at Notre Dame Cathedral, is in love with beautiful Gypsy Esmeralda (O'Hara). When she rejects the affections of Frollo (Hardwicke), the Chief Justice of Paris, he takes revenge on her by killing her lover Phoebus (Marshall) and framing her for the murder. Just as she is about to be executed, though, Quasimodo rescues her and whisks her to sanctuary in the cathedral. Insane with jealousy, Frollo demands that the King (Davenport) revoke Notre Dame's sanctuary status, but a group of beggars led by Clopin (Mitchell) has other plans.

Victor Hugo's 1831 novel had been filmed several times during the silent era, most notably in 1923 by Universal Pictures, with Lon Chaney giving an indelible portrayal of its pathetic title character. With the coming of sound, however, the tale became ripe for a remake. The producers at RKO assembled a massive cast and spent millions replicating Notre Dame Cathedral and its surrounding streets, the end result being the most expensive picture the company had produced to date, eclipsing even *King Kong* (1933).

William Dieterle (1893-1972) was selected to direct. Dieterle, whose first name was actually Wilhelm, was born in Germany, where he got his start in the industry as an actor, appearing in, among many other films, Paul Leni's *Waxworks* (1924) and F.W. Murnau's *Faust* (1926), two of the stand-out titles in the history of Expressionism. He dabbled in movie directing in his native land, but didn't focus on it in earnest until he immigrated to the United States in 1930. *The Hunchback of Notre Dame* is generally considered his masterpiece, though he made other noteworthy films, including the Oscar-winning *The Life of Emile Zola* (1937), *The Devil and Daniel Webster* (1941) and

Portrait of Jennie (1948). His career was derailed in the 1950s by the McCarthy witch hunts; though never officially blacklisted, good assignments became fewer and far between. The late-period Ginger Rogers outing, *Quick, Let's Get Married* (1964), was a forgettable end to his otherwise distinguished career.

Dieterle's background in German cinema is evident throughout *Hunchback*, both in its use of strong chiaroscuro lighting and in his handling of large crowd scenes, evocative of Fritz Lang's *Metropolis* (1927) or E.A. Dupont's *Variety* (1925). And while the Chaney version of the story suffers from Wallace Worsley's wooden staging, such criticisms can hardly be leveled at Dieterle's efforts. The film is beautifully realized on every level.

Charles Laughton gives a classic, heartfelt performance as Quasimodo. Though the actor shunned the sort of grotesque make-up utilized by Chaney (make-up quite faithful to the etchings accompanying the initial pressing of Hugo's novel), he enlivens the character with depth and nuance. He speaks little, but when he does it's with a slur that suits a character for whom words are of little use. He's also jarringly sinister when it's called for, such as when he's put on display for a mocking crowd to jeer, or when Frollo sends him to kidnap Esmeralda.

Sir Cedric Hardwicke is also at his best as Frollo, a character that can most gently be described as despicable. Interestingly, Hardwicke got the role after RKO failed to secure the services of Basil Rathbone, who was working for Universal on back-to-back productions of *Son of Frankenstein* and *Tower of London* (both 1939), but then hopped aboard Universal's Frankenstein saga, playing a son of Frankenstein himself in *The Ghost of Frankenstein* (1942).

Making her American film debut, Maureen O'Hara is ideal as Esmeralda. She captures the character's inner strength and naiveté with quiet intensity. Laughton had previously worked with the actress on Alfred Hitchcock's minor period drama *Jamaica Inn* (1939) and was reportedly instrumental in getting her the lead female role here, which proved the beginning of her long-running Hollywood career.

The supporting cast includes Edmond O'Brien (*The Wild Bunch*, 1969; *Hunchback* was his film debut), Harry Davenport (*The Ox-Bow Incident*, 1943), Thomas Mitchell (*Stagecoach*, 1939) and George Zucco, later to lend class to many a B-picture.

The film was nominated for two Academy Awards, one for sound, the other for Alfred Newman's superb score; it won neither. The year 1939 is often referred to as the finest year in the history of movies, and given the stiff competition, it's not surprising that the film failed to net more nominations, though Dieterle, Laughton and Hardwicke were all more than deserving of Oscar recognition for their work here.

Despite some pacing issues in its mid-section, Dieterle's *Hunchback* remains the gold standard by which all other versions are judged. The next version emerged for the big screen in 1956 (*The Hunchback of Notre Dame*, an Italian/French co-production starring Anthony Quinn), though there was also a two-part dramatization for the *Robert Montgomery Presents* TV series in 1954. Other adaptations (both big-screen and television) were made in the 1970s, 1980s and 1990s. TH

Kaidan Senbaya sodo
Daito; b/w; length unknown; Japan
 D: Minoru Ishiyama
 Cast: Sozaburo Matsuyama, Teruko Sanjo
 An angry ghost haunts Senbaya Temple.
 Little is known about this lost horror item from the Golden Age of Japanese cinema. Minoru Ishiyama directed; he also oversaw *Cat Ghost and Cherry Blossoms at Night in Saga* (1936) and *Enmadera no kaibyô* (1938). Actors Sozaburo Matsuyama and Teruko Sanjo starred together in another 1939 film, *Honchô kaibyô-den*.

Production company Daito Eiga was no stranger to horror, having also produced such early examples as *Yaji and Kita's Cat Trouble* (1937), in addition to the titles listed above. CW

The Last Warning
aka **The Dead Don't Care**
Universal/Crime Club; b/w; 62 min; U.S.
 D: Albert S. Rogell S: Edmund L. Hartman P: Irving Starr C: George Meehan
 Cast: Preston Foster, Frank Jenks, Joyce Compton, Kay Linaker, E.E. Clive, Frances Robinson, Ray Parker, Robert Page, Albert Dekker, Roland Drew, Clem Wilencheck, Orville Caldwell, Richard Lane
 Private investigators William "Bill" Crane (Foster) and Doc Williams (Jenks) are called to the estate of John Essex (Parker), who is being threatened by mysterious letters. The primary suspect is Steve Felson (Lane), a gangster to whom Essex owes money, but when Felson dies, it becomes clear that anyone could be the murderer. There's Essex's sister Linda (Robinson), who seems innocent enough, and also an aspiring actress named

Preston Foster stars in Universal's Crime Club entry, *The Last Warning*.

Dawn Day (Compton). Then there's Paul Gomez (Drew), who is obsessed with Linda, or rather her money, along with Carla Rodriguez (Linaker), Tony Henderson (Page) and Higgs the butler (Dekker). When Carla is murdered and Linda is kidnapped, Crane and Williams realize just how much work solving the case is going to be.

Not to be confused with Paul Leni's horror classic of 1929, *The Last Warning* is an entry in Universal's Crime Club series, a group of films based on novels published under Doubleday's imprint of the same name. It was the seventh in the string and the third to be based on a novel by Jonathan Latimer, in this case, *The Dead Don't Care* (1938). It was also one of three Crime Club movies to be included in Screen Gems' *Shock Theater* package, a collection of horror and mystery films sold into television syndication in 1957. (The other two were *Mystery of the White Room* and *The Witness Vanishes*, both 1939.) Latimer himself went on to a successful career as a writer for film (*Alias Nick Beal*, 1949) and television (*Perry Mason*, 1958-1965).

The Last Warning is an amusing thriller with a solution that's difficult to see coming. Despite its plot, it's hardly an "old dark house" chiller, though director Albert S. Rogell does manage to conjure some creepiness here and there as he integrates comedy, mystery, and mild horror elements into a cohesive whole. It must be said, however, that his direction is flatter than that of Crime Club's usual director Otis Garrett. Rogell was a thoroughly second-string director who never rose above B pictures. He got his start in the silent era, and by the 1940s his cinematic career was winding to a close, though he continued to work in television until the late 1950s. His other films of interest to horror enthusiasts include the weird Western *The Phantom City* (1928), starring Ken Maynard, and the entertaining but ultimately empty *The Black Cat* (1941), with Basil Rathbone and Bela Lugosi. Also a songwriter and musician, he died in 1988 of cancer, 30 years after directing his last program, an episode of the television Western-adventure series *Broken Arrow*.

Star Preston Foster remained a lead actor in films through the 1940s and settled into lesser parts in the 1950s. Among his most famous roles were parts in *My Friend Flicka* (1943), *The Harvey Girls* (1946), *I Shot Jesse James* (1949), and *Tomahawk* (1951). He also had a supporting role in *Doctor X* (1932).

Though *The Last Warning* was shot in October 1938, it wasn't released to theaters until January 1939. CW

Maboroshi-jô no bakeneko
Kyokuto; b/w; 40 min; Japan
 D: Seiji Suzaki S: Juro Kanbara C: Sadao Uemura
 Cast: Ryunosuke Kumoi, Myoko Kohama, Saemon Kataoka, Kyoko Arishima, Kuzaburo Arashi, Sayoko Mori, Koji Kawada

A Japanese Samurai named Myamoto Musashi lived from 1584 to 1645. His skill with a sword was legendary even during his lifetime; he both developed a new and enduring style of swordsmanship and wrote a book on the subject that is still widely read in his native country. In 1939 he became a character in an otherwise fictional Japanese film, *Maboroshi-jô no bakeneko*, which translates as "Ghost Cat in Iyama [or Illusion] Castle." The story has Musashi, along with his assistant Benji, investigate sundry and sinister doings in an ancient castle. The perpetrator? None other than—surprise, surprise—a ghost cat!

The film was released in Japan on May 4, 1939. It was one of at least three ghost cat movies produced that year; the others were *Honchô kaibyô-den* and *Silver Cat's Curse*. CW

A Macabre Legacy
aka **Herencia macabre**; **La traicionera**; **Macabre Heritage**
Productora de Peliculas; b/w; 83 min; Mexico
 D: Jose Bohr S: Jose Bohr, Xavier Davila, Eva Liminana C: Jack Draper M: Jose Bohr, Manuel Esperon
 Cast: Miguel Arenas, Consuelo Frank, Ramon Armengod, Luis Aldas, Aurora Walker, Agustin Isunza, Jose Rubio, Manuel Fabregas, Maria Virginia Navarro Schiller, Alberto Galan, Fanny Schiller

Famed plastic surgeon Dr. Duarte (Arenas) believes that unattractive people are inherently evil and that altering their physical appearance can turn them into good people. His devotion to his work prompts his wife Rosa (Frank) to seek solace in the arms of his associate Eduardo (Armengod). The furious Duarte takes revenge by injecting the young man with a virus, disfiguring Rosa, and locking her in his private laboratory. Then, as a final act of spite, he drags the dying Eduardo to see Rosa, the shock of which gives his wife's lover a fatal heart attack.

There's ample melodrama and teeth gnashing in *A Macabre Legacy*, presented in an (intentional, one hopes) over-the-top manner. This surgical thriller appears to have cribbed elements from Universal's *The Raven* (1935), in which crazed plastic surgeon Dr. Vollin (Bela Lugosi) makes the claim that being ugly on the outside will also make a person ugly on the inside.

Director Jose Bohr's credits stretch from the silent era until 1969. He wore a number of hats on this production: he also co-wrote the script and music score and served as editor. He died in 1994.

Curiously, the film failed to secure release in its native country until 1945. It's possible that censorship issues caused the hold-up, as it played American theaters as early as 1940. Production records establish that the film was made in 1939, however. TH

The Man They Could Not Hang
Columbia; b/w; 64 min; U.S.

D: Nick Grinde *S:* Karl Brown *P:* Wallace MacDonald *C:* Benjamin H. Kline *M:* Morris Stoloff, R.H. Bassett, Joseph Nussbaum, Ben Oakland, George Parrish, Karol Rathaus, William Grant Still, Gregory Stone

Cast: Boris Karloff, Lorna Gray, Robert Wilcox, Roger Pryor, Don Beddoe, Ann Doran, Joe De Stefani, Charles Trowbridge, Byron Foulger, Dick Curtis, James Craig, John Tyrrell

Dr. Savaard (Karloff) conducts a dangerous experiment on one of his students to prove the effectiveness of his new artificial heart. The student participates willingly, knowing the risks involved, but Savaard's nurse (Doran), afraid of what may happen, alerts the police. The experiment is interrupted, the boy dies and Savaard is condemned to hang for murder. Before he is executed, he instructs his assistant Lang (Foulger) to use the artificial heart to restore him to life. Lang believes Savaard will use his miraculous revival to prove the effectiveness of the invention, but Savaard has vengeance in mind instead.

The Man They Could Not Hang was the first of several low-budget mad scientist films Boris Karloff top-lined for Columbia Pictures. Being the first, it benefits from a feeling of freshness missing from later examples of the subgenre (though it's doubtful that any of them will ever be embraced as a classic). Karloff gives a solid performance as the well-meaning medico driven to vengeance. Despite a none-too-convincing wig (since Karloff wasn't bald, why he was saddled with it is anybody's guess), he appears genuinely committed to the material, and he brings some nice details to the performance, particularly the strange posture and body language he adopts after the character returns from the dead.

The supporting cast can't hope to compare with his efforts, though prolific character actors Byron Foulger and Charles Trowbridge (both of whom would rejoin Karloff for Columbia's *The Man With Nine Lives*, 1940) put in capable performances as, respectively, the naïve Lang and the judge who sentences Karloff to death.

Director Nick Grinde never made much of a name for himself, despite turning out a prolific number of titles between 1928 and 1945; he also guided Karloff through two of the later Columbia titles—*Before I Hang* (1940) and the aforementioned *The Man With Nine Lives*. Though he never seemed to have much flair for the genre, *The Man They Could Not Hang* does benefit from his no-nonsense, briskly paced aesthetic. TH

The kindly Dr. Savaard (Boris Karloff) murders an innocent victim in his quest to create an artificial heart, in *The Man They Could Not Hang.*

The Midnight Ghost
aka **El fantasma de media noche**; **The Midnight Phantom**
Rex Films; b/w; 72 min; Mexico

D/P: Raphael J. Sevilla

Cast: Victoria Blanco, Sergio de Karlo, Carlos Lopez Moctezuma, Emma Roldan, Natalia Ortiz, Miguel Weimer, Crox Alvarado, Ricardo Mondragon, Amalia Ferriz, Victorio Blanco, Manuel Sanchez Navarro, Parkey Hussain, Humberto Rodriguez

Lolita (Blanco) is being raised by her godparents, due to her father's murder. Her father's spirit materializes during a séance and insists that she marry Juan Antonio. Because the identity of this mysterious man is unknown, the scheming Blas (Moctezuma) tries to pass himself off as Lolita's intended. He is eventually discredited when the kindly Arturo (de Karlo) is revealed to be the real Juan Antonio. The two are married, and Lolita's father is able to rest in peace.

This is a melodrama with suitably grim overtones. The usual array of plot twists is on display, but thankfully the filmmakers resist the urge to discredit the supernatural. Producer/director Raphael J. Sevilla broke into films in 1931. He also worked as an editor, production designer and occasional actor, but he found his niche in directing. He worked steadily until the early 1960s, closing out his career as an assistant to various American filmmakers on low-budget U.S./Mexican co-productions. He died in 1975.

The obscure *The Midnight Ghost* appears to have been one of Sevilla's few fantasy credits. It was not released in Mexico until 1940. TH

Midnight Shadow
Randol/Sack; b/w; 53 min; U.S.

D/P: George Randol *C:* Arthur Reed

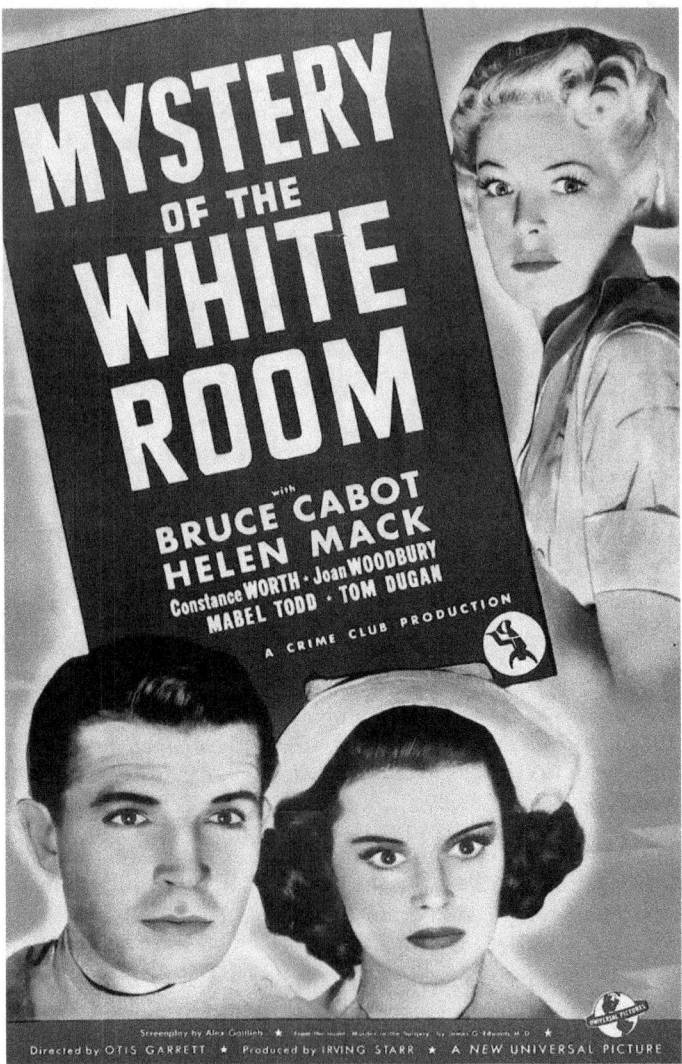

Cast: Frances Redd, Buck Woods, Richard Bates, Ollie Ann Robinson, Clinton Rosemond, Jesse Lee Brooks, Edward Brandon, John Criner, Peter Webster, Ruby Dandridge, Napoleon Simpson

In the southern part of our country lies that great land of romance and sunshine known as the Old South. Here amid fertile fields, vast areas of timber, oil lands and rippling rivers live millions of black men and women in the most highly concentrated area of Negro population in America. Here, in certain communities, the like of which is found nowhere else in the world, these people of darker hue have demonstrated their abilities in self-government by the orderly processes of law of which they are capable when unhampered by outside influences. It is in a community such as one of these that the scene of our story is laid, and the events which follow are depicted.

So begins *Midnight Shadow*, a mystery film with minor horror elements, released by Sack Entertainment, a company that specialized in low-budget movies with all-black casts aimed at African American audiences. The tale begins with the turbaned, mind-reading Great Alihabad (Criner) convincing the Wilson family that he must stay with them rather than at a hotel because only in a private home can he get the quiet stability he needs for his work. While there, he falls for the Wilson's beautiful daughter Margaret (Redd), but Mother Wilson (Robinson) is concerned about their dalliance, especially given that there's a local boy named Buster (Brandon) who is single and interested. After Father Dan (Rosemond) rather cluelessly reveals to Alihabad that he's giving an oil well to his daughter when she weds, he and his wife are attacked, Dan is killed and the deed to the well is stolen. Two bumbling would-be detectives, Junior (Bates) and Lightfoot (Woods), show up and take on the case.

A typical homespun mix of sinister shadows, deerstalker caps and mystery infused with equal parts comedy and horror, *Midnight Shadow* is unmemorable fluff with little to distinguish it from any number of other Poverty Row programs. The direction is bland, the uncredited writing lifeless and the camerawork dull. The performances are on the same level, though the appearance of Ruby Dandridge is of interest to those eager to see the mother of future leading player Dorothy Dandrige. CW

Mystery of the White Room
Universal/Crime Club; b/w; 58 min; U.S.

D: Otis Garrett *S:* Alex Gottlieb *P:* Irving Starr *C:* John Boyle

Cast: Bruce Cabot, Helen Mack, Joan Woodbury, Constance Worth, Thomas E. Jackson, Tom Dugan, Mabel Todd, Roland Drew, Addison Richards, Frank Reicher, Don Porter

This is the seventh film in Universal's Crime Club series and one of three to be included in the *Shock Theater* package, a group of horror and suspense movies sold into television syndication in 1957 to capitalize on the theatrical success of Hammer's *The Curse of Frankenstein* (1957). Like the other CC films, *Mystery of the White Room* was based on a novel published under Doubleday's Crime Club imprint, in this case *Murder in the Surgery* by James G. Edwards.

During routine eye surgery, the operating room lights go out and the patient, Dr. Finley Morton (Richards), is murdered. There are of course suspects aplenty. Two younger doctors were vying for a position as assistant to Dr. Morton; one of them, Dr. Kennedy, had refused out of cowardice to operate on a terminally ill child, while the other, Dr. Clayton (Cabot), had recently had an ugly altercation with Morton. Nor are they the only ones with a reason to want Morton dead; among others, there's Dr. Thorton, who believes that Morton left him on the operating table with a paralyzed arm in order to take his position. Police investigator Mack Spencer (Jackson) steps in and strong-arms his way through the hospital, browbeating anyone who even remotely resembles a suspect. Unsurprisingly, he comes to have his strongest doubts about Dr. Clayton, the film's obvious hero. When a hospital attendant (Puglia) accidentally comes upon the real murderer, he is blinded by acid thrown into his face. Dr. Clayton transplants the cornea from the deceased Morton to the attendant, who is then able to identify his attacker—a young nurse (Woodbury) who had been jilted by the doctor.

Though it's certainly no masterpiece, *Mystery of the White Room* largely works due to a surprisingly efficient script and a cast of dedicated actors. By setting his story not in an old dark house but rather a brightly lit (if implausibly threadbare due to lack of budget) hospital, novelist Edwards crafted a startlingly creepy tableau in which to set murder, much like Robert Bloch did with the shower in his novel *Psycho* (1959).

Alex Gottlieb's script wrings an additional helping or two of tension out of the premise, and Otis Garrett's direction conjures some effective scares. In one scene, for instance, a killer, who appears only in silhouette, threatens a nurse (Mack); the audience sees the nurse from over the killer's shoulder rather than the killer from the nurse's point of view. It's a refreshing change from the usual for this sort of vintage mystery fare. There's also a fair amount of sexual innuendo and grisly atmosphere that keeps things moving while distracting viewers from the occasional plot hole.

Helping things along are performances from such old standbys as Frank Reicher, reuniting with his *King Kong* (1933) co-star Bruce Cabot, and Frank Puglia. Roland Drew, who made quite the career out of B-horror movie appearances in the late 1930s and early 1940s, is also on hand and holds up his end of things well. But it's Helen Mack (*The Son of Kong*, 1933) who really shines as Clayton's love interest, Nurse Carole Dale. Too bad her role is rather limited (despite being second billed) by a screenplay that requires little of her apart from screaming now and then.

The next film in the Crime Club series, *The Witness Vanishes* (1939), was also the last before Universal abandoned the series altogether. CW

The Phantom Creeps

Universal; b/w; 12 chapters; U.S.

D: Ford Beebe, Samuel L. Goodkind *S:* George Plympton, Basil Dickey, Mildred Barish *P:* Henry MacRae *C:* Jerome Ash, William A. Sickner *M:* Frank Skinner, Karl Hajos, Franz Waxman, Hein Roemheld, Clifford Vaughan

Cast: Bela Lugosi, Robert Kent, Dorothy Arnold, Edwin Stanley, Jack C. Smith, Regis Toomey, Edward Van Sloan, Dora Clement, Anthony Averill, Hugh Huntley, Monte Vandergrift, Frank Mayo, Jim Farley, Eddie Acuff, Reed Howes, Ed Wolff

Dr. Zorka (Lugosi) both develops a gadget that can render him invisible and harnesses the power of a meteorite strong enough to destroy the world. He plans to use these discoveries—along with a giant robot (Wolff)—to take over the world, but his schemes become complicated when the authorities get involved. Finally, driven by madness, he fakes his own death and uses his invisibility device to move among his enemies undetected.

During the British horror film ban of 1936-1939, Bela Lugosi found Hollywood employment hard to come by. The venerable performer had been typecast as freaks and vampires, and with horror on hiatus few producers cared to bother with him. Even Universal studios, where he had scored a major triumph with *Dracula* (1931), treated the actor shabbily. They refused him quality roles and underpaid him for the third-rate work they did send his way. Against all odds, he launched what should have been a comeback in Universal's lavish *Son of Frankenstein* (1939)—thanks in no small measure to producer/director Rowland V. Lee, who kept Lugosi on the payroll for the entire shoot by expanding his role—but despite a first-rate performance, he shortly thereafter found himself back on the short end of the stick.

That's not to say that *The Phantom Creeps* short shrifts Lugosi in terms of screen time. On the contrary, this 12-chapter serial features plenty of him. But the role itself is a walking chestnut—another in a long line of megalomaniacal, cackling Lugosi villains—and the serial is so shoddily produced that it wears out its welcome early on. The actor does what he can with the idiotic clichés he's given to spout, but that's not much; nor does the god-awful fake beard he sports in the earlier part of the story help the cause.

The supporting cast does provide a bright spot in the form of Edward Van Sloan, best remembered for his paternal roles in *Frankenstein* (1931) and *The Mummy* (1932) and for going head-to-head with Lugosi in *Dracula* (where he plays Professor Van Helsing). Van Sloan struggles with a poorly realized, ill-defined character—the stern ringleader of a group of spies out to steal Lugosi's inventions—but he does have a moment that would have done Moe Howard proud when, reacting to news of his underlings' latest flub, he raises his hand threateningly and sputters, "You blockheads!" Nyuk-nyuk-nyuk …

The film cannibalizes pieces of scenes from earlier Universal efforts. A sequence of Lugosi extracting material from his meteor, for instance, is actually unbilled footage of Boris Karloff from *The Invisible Ray* (1936). The soundtrack is similarly cobbled and recycled, wallpapered with cues from *The Bride of Frankenstein* (1935), *Werewolf of London* (1935), *The Ra-*

The original graphic design for the cover of the French DVD of *The Phantom Wagon*

ven (1935), *Dracula's Daughter* (1936) and *Son of Frankenstein* (1939), music that reminds one of Universal's better days but grows tiresome here.

Co-director Ford Beebe later directed Lugosi in the far-more-interesting *Night Monster* (1942), a film noteworthy for providing the fading horror star with his last instance of top-billing at Universal. *The Phantom Creeps,* though, is so much "sound and fury signifying nothing." It's basically a 12-chapter chase scene, with the good and the bad guys running back and forth between one location and another, "another" most often being Zorka's lair. The robot (credited as "The Iron Man") may be the most laughable in cinema history—not only is it clearly a man in a suit, but it does nothing even remotely useful to Zorka or anyone else. TH

The Phantom Wagon
aka La Charette Fantome
Columbia; b/w; 93 min; France
 D/Co-S: Julien Duvivier *Co-S:* Alexandre Arnoux *P:* Harry Cohn, Paul Graetz *C:* Jules Kruger *M:* Jacques Ibert
 Cast: Pierre Fresnay, Marie Bell, Micheline Francey, Louis Jouvet, Jean Mercanton, Ariane Borg, Alexandre Rignault, Robert Le Vigan, Palau, Rene Genin, Marie-Helene Daste, Philippe Richard, Georges Mauloy, Joffre, Marcel Peres

Though once a prosperous family man, David Holm (Fresnay) has become an embittered alcoholic whose vices have driven his loved ones away. When he dies at the stroke of midnight on New Year's Eve, a phantom coachman picks up his spirit, informing Holm that he is to assume soul-collecting duties for the next year. As he does so, he is given glimpses of what his life could have been like, and a longing grows in him for a second chance. He then finds out that he has, in truth, just narrowly escaped death, and he works to restore his past happiness.

This is a remake of Victor Sjostrom's *The Phantom Carriage* (1921). Writer/director Julien Duvivier sticks relatively close to the earlier film, but the mixture of the distressing and the sentimental doesn't work quite so well this time around. The film's somber tone feels forced and artificial, and the heavy sermonizing compares unfavorably with the more subtle and low-key approach of Sjostrom's original. Still, Duvivier does create some impressive images, notably in the fogbound forest and the visions of the titular vehicle.

Duvivier entered the film industry in 1918 and made his debut as a director in 1919. For almost 50 years thereafter, he was an active and prolific talent. Shortly after *The Phantom Wagon*, he relocated to the United States and paid his dues in the Hollywood studio machine. This was followed by a brief tenure in England before a final return to his native France. Renowned for such films as *Pepe le Moko* (1937) and *Anna Karenina* (1948), Duvivier died at the age of 71 in a car accident in 1967. His only other horror credit was *The Legend of Prague* (1936).

Leading man Pierre Fresnay had a distinguished career in his own right, working with such luminaries as Jean Renoir (*Grand Illusion*, 1937), Alfred Hitchcock (*The Man Who Knew Too Much*, 1934) and Henri-Georges Clouzot (*Le Corbeau*, 1943). Entering films in 1915, he quickly found success and acclaim, and he remained active in cinema until shortly before his death in 1975. TH

The Return of Doctor X
aka The Return of Dr. X
Warner/First National; b/w; 62 min; U.S.
 D: Vincent Sherman *S:* Lee Katz *P:* Bryan Foy, Hal B. Wallis, Jack L. Warner *C:* Sidney Hickox *M:* Bernhard Kaun
 Cast: Wayne Morris, Rosemary Lane, Humphrey Bogart, John Litel, Dennis Morgan, Lya Lys, Huntz Hall, Charles C. Wilson, Vera Lewis, Howard C. Hickman, Olin Howland, Arthur Aylesworth, Cliff Saum, Creighton Hale, John Ridgely

Reporter Walter Garrett (Morris) teams up with Dr. Mike Rhodes (Morgan) to investigate a series of murders. The two men follow a trail of clues to the mysterious Dr. Xavier (Bogart), who is conducting a series of experiments involving the creation of synthetic blood.

This belated, in-name-only sequel to Michael Curtiz's *Doctor X* (1932) is notable chiefly as the only horror film appearance of Humphrey Bogart, who had found success a couple of years earlier playing the heavy in Archie Mayo's *The Petrified Forest* (1936). The actor was mortified to find himself in the film, feeling it far better suited to Bela Lugosi or Boris Karloff. (Warner Bros. had in fact tried to secure Karloff for the film, but when he passed it fell to contract player Bogart to don the white face paint and portray the eponymous ghoul.)

And, against all odds, it works! Bogart's performance is, in fact, an undiluted pleasure. He may have hated the role, but from the moment he takes the screen (stroking a pet rabbit on a typical "mad doctor" laboratory set), he's wonderfully—and believably—sinister.

Humphrey Bogart stars as Dr. X in *The Return of Dr. X*, his only horror film.

Regrettably, the remainder of the cast isn't up to his level; indeed, "funny" leading man Wayne Morris proves to be the film's major flaw. Lee Tracy may have had his groaner moments in the original *Doctor X*, but he looks like Charlie Chaplin compared to Morris.

The film marks the directorial debut of former actor and screenwriter Vincent Sherman. He later made more prestigious fare, including *Mr. Skeffington* (1944) and *All Through the Night* (1941), the latter also featuring Bogart in a more conventional tough guy role. His direction on *Return* is slick and efficient, though it doesn't evoke much in the way of atmosphere.

Apart from Bogie, there are scattered moments of quality in the film, notably the stylized studio "exteriors," but it's safe to say that this *Return* would have gone unheralded had it not been for the film's casting coup. TH

Sanjusangen-do no yurei: Oryu onryo
Shinko; b/w; length unknown; Japan
  D: Kumahiko Nishina
  Cast: Sumiko Suzuki, Eigoro Onoe, Setsuko Kai, Kunio Kaga

A ghost haunts the Buddhist temple of Sanjusangen-do in Kyoto, Japan in this forgotten Japanese horror tale. Its exact plot is as lost as the film itself, but it does seem that the story was first filmed as *Sanjusangen-do no yurei* in 1910 by Shozo Makino, with actor Matsunosuke Onoe in the lead. In this 1939 adaptation of the tale, Japanese scream queen Sumiko Suzuki essayed the lead female role.

The temple at Sanjusangen-do is one of Japan's major attractions because it houses one thousand life-sized statues of a Japanese deity called Thousand Armed Kannon. Only 129 of the figures are original, however, as the rest were destroyed in a fire that swept the building in 1249. Near-perfect replicas replaced the ruined images. CW

The Sign of Death
aka **El signo de la muerte**
CISA; b/w; 69 min; Mexico
  D/Co-S: Chano Urueta *Co-S:* Jose Benavides Hijo, Francisco Elias, Jose Martinez de la Vega, Salvador Novo *P:* Pedro Maus, Felipe Mier *C:* Victor Herrera *M:* Silvestre Revueltas
  Cast: Cantinflas, Manuel Medel, Elena D'Orgaz, Carlos Orellana, Tomas Perrin, Matilde Corell, Max Langler

A cult seeks virgins to sacrifice to the Aztec god Quetzalcoatl, believing that this will spark a return of the Aztecs to their land. The group is led by a museum curator (Orellana) who, when his own daughter is up for sacrifice, defects. He is slain, and the sacrificial women are rescued.

This Mexican entry is notable as the first horror film to use Quetzalcoatl as a narrative lynchpin. The flying serpent deity later appeared in such fare as *The Flying Serpent* (1946) with George Zucco, as well as in Larry Cohen's tongue in cheek *Q: The Winged Serpent* (1982).

The cast is graced with the presence of soon-to-be-popular Mexican actor Cantinflas. Born Mario Moreno in 1911, he adopted the single-name moniker soon after entering films in 1937. It was a character he would remain identified with for the remainder of his career, a baggy-pants comedic figure also played for pathos similar in style to Charlie Chaplin. *The Sign of Death* appears to have been the actor's first appearance as Cantinflas, though he plays things relatively straight here. A prolific actor, writer and singer, the man retired in the early 1980s and died in 1993.

Director Chano Urueta went on to direct some of the most outrageous Mexican horror films of the 1960s, including *The Brainiac* (1962) and *The Living Head* (1963). He also worked sporadically as an actor, appearing in small roles in Sam Peckinpah's *The Wild Bunch* (1969) and *Bring Me the Head of Alfredo Garcia* (1974). TH

Silver Cat's Curse
aka **Noroi no ginbyo**
Zensho; b/w; 46 min; Japan
  D: Kanenori Yamada *S:* Shutaro Nachi *C:* Yozo Okuda
  Cast: Ryutaro Amatsu, Kimie Hayashi, Ryutaro Hibiki, Toshiko Miyagawa, Shiro Naruto, Kihachiro Oshiro, Shimizu Utaji, Kikutaro Yoshii

A publicity shot for *Son of Frankenstein* that features Basil Rathbone's image dominating Bela Lugosi and Boris Karloff.

This is one of numerous films produced in the silent and early sound eras telling the tale of the "Ghost Cat of Nabeshima," also sometimes referred to as "The Ghost Cat of Saga Castle." Like most of the others, Yamada's film took a real-life Japanese war general and made him the culprit in a murder story. He gets *his*, though, and *good* when a cat that's possessed by the spirit of one of his victims avenges his black deeds. The film was released March 30, 1939. CW

Son of Frankenstein
Universal; b/w; 99 min; U.S.
 D/P: Rowland V. Lee *S:* Willis Cooper *C:* George Robinson *M:* Frank Skinner *FX:* John P. Fulton
 Cast: Basil Rathbone, Boris Karloff, Bela Lugosi, Lionel Atwill, Joseph Hutchinson, Donnie Dunagan, Edgar Norton, Emma Dunn, Lawrence Grant, Michael Mark, Lionel Belmore, Perry Ivins, Gustav von Seyffertitz, Caroline Frances Cooke, Lorimer Johnson, Tom Ricketts, Clarence Wilson, Ward Bond

Baron Wolf von Frankenstein (Rathbone) returns to his ancestral home to vindicate the memory of his father, the late, infamous Dr. Frankenstein. He encounters the broken-necked graverobber Ygor (Lugosi), who explains that his father's creation (Karloff) is not really dead. Against his better judgment, Wolf revives the creature, hoping to prove that it is not the murdering brute of village lore. But the vengeful Ygor—who, it turns out, has a mental hold over the monster—uses the creature to carry out a series of murders.

James Whale's macabre masterpiece *The Bride of Frankenstein* (1935) was a big hit at the box-office, but the British horror ban of 1936 put an indefinite halt to the series. Then, in 1938, a triple bill of *Dracula* (1931), *Frankenstein* (1931) and *The Son of Kong* (1933) attracted record numbers in Los Angeles. Universal smelled the money and came to its senses, realizing that there was still a strong market for horror, and they decided to revive their most successful fright franchise.

Son of Frankenstein was first conceived as a big budget, all-star, Technicolor extravaganza, marketed to be the Frankenstein film to end all Frankenstein films. It only made sense to do it up big. After all, Whale had outdone his original with *Bride*, and doing a small-scale follow-up to such a baroque extravaganza would have been bad form (though that was indeed the direction the series later took).

Whale was unlikely from the beginning to have been offered the third Universal Frankenstein film (and was equally unlikely to have been interested had he been asked). A lot had changed at the studio since 1935; for starters, the Laemmles had sold it all in 1936, leaving the director without the creative control that had made *Bride* possible. And though his successful *Showboat* (1936) ensured him a respectable budget to make 1937's *The Road Back* (the sequel to 1930's *All Quiet on the Western Front*), Whale's uncompromising vision of war ran afoul of censors and studio. The film was mutilated for general release, and when it flopped, the director caught all the heat. It was a professional blow from which Whale never recovered, though he did helm an occasional picture of interest (*The Great Garrick*, 1937; *Wives Under Suspicion*, 1938).

By the time *Son* was on the schedule, Whale's time as Universal's golden boy was over; the assignment was given to producer/director Rowland V. Lee. Lee had been directing since 1920 and had achieved a position of prestige at Universal, with creative autonomy comparable to what Whale had enjoyed between 1931 and 1936. Lee's prior experience in the horror genre was limited—he'd done *The Return of Dr. Fu Manchu* (1930) and *Love from a Stranger* (1937), along with some uncredited work on *The Mysterious Dr. Fu Manchu* (1929)—but he attacked *Son* with enthusiasm.

The idea of color was nixed early on, with Lee later maintaining that he'd never intended to shoot the film in anything but black-and-white. There were no corners cut with the acting talent, however, and *Son* wound up with one of the most impressive casts in the Universal canon. After Claude Rains turned down the title role (reportedly out of fear of being typecast in horror movies), the studio set its sights on Peter Lorre. But director Lee had someone else in mind: Basil Rathbone, who likely was sought specifically because of his performance as the disturbed Gerald Lovell in Lee's *Love from a Stranger*. The studio relented (despite the fact that Rathbone was more expensive than Lorre), and Lee pulled a second high-strung, neurotic performance from the normally relaxed actor.

The character of the monster was, of course, offered to Boris Karloff, who consented to return to the role out of gratitude toward what the character had done for his career. His acceptance was not without misgivings, for he feared (and justifiably so, as it turned out) that *Son* would begin the reduction of the Monster to a mere prop. After this, Karloff donned the make-up on screen only once more, for an episode of the popular 1960s TV show *Route 66* that united him with fellow heavyweights Peter Lorre and Lon Chaney, Jr. And while the screenplay limits Karloff's performance, he makes the most of what he's given; his reaction to Ygor's death, for example, is as touching as anything in the first two films.

The role of Ygor was reportedly proffered by Universal solely for the publicity Bela Lugosi's presence in the film would bring. Lee, however, absolutely loved the actor's work. Suspecting at one point that the studio, in a panic over budget, was gunning to get Lugosi's scenes in the can in order to cut his fees, Lee enlarged Lugosi's role. The decision was artistically dead-on; Lugosi was never better than he is here. Ygor gives him a chance to shine as a character actor, and he meets the challenge with style and flair. Lugosi was too often just "the Lugosi character," but here he becomes Ygor; it's a fascinating performance, alternately funny and chilling.

Lionel Atwill plays Inspector Krogh, the dour, one-armed head of police in the village of Frankenstein. This marked his first genre assignment for Universal since 1933's *Secret of the Blue Room*. He makes a tremendous impression, effortlessly upstaging Rathbone whenever the two share the screen. Kenneth Mars, in Mel Brooks' *Young Frankenstein* (1974), parodied Atwill's wooden-armed constable quite memorably.

Josephine Hutchinson (*North by Northwest*, 1959), Edgar Norton (*Dr. Jekyll and Mr. Hyde*, 1932), Lawrence Grant (*Werewolf of London*, 1935) and Lionel Belmore and Michael Mark, both of whom had appeared in Whale's *Frankenstein*, round out the stable of supporting players quite nicely. Ward Bond, who went on to appear in many John Ford films, has a bit part as a policeman guarding Castle Frankenstein who tells Ygor to "Shut up!"

All of this acting excellence stands in disastrous contrast to Donnie Dunagan's performance as the Frankensteins' young son Peter. Dunagan's grating delivery and Southern twang are ludicrous in and of themselves, but given that his parents are stiff-upper-lipped Brits, the lad's incongruities become surreally comic. Inexplicably, Lee indulges the child actor, giving him far too many scenes.

On a technical level, the film delivers the best that money could buy. Cinematography is by George Robinson (*Tower of London*, 1939), who brings a dash of German Expressionism to the proceedings and went on to shoot three more entries in Universal's Frankenstein saga. The imposing set designs by Jack Otterson are similar to those of *The Cabinet of Dr. Caligari* (1919), but with actual sets instead of painted backdrops. Add to this a rousing score by Frank Skinner (recycled mercilessly for subsequent Universal horrors), and *Son of Frankenstein* emerges as one of the most polished of the studio's productions in any genre.

The trade-off is that Lee, for all his good intentions, simply lacked the imagination, wit and sense of poetry that made Whale's films so special. While there is nothing major inher-

Ygor (Bela Lugosi) and Wolf von Frankenstein (Basil Rathbone) look over the Monster (Boris Karloff) in *Son of Frankenstein*.

ently wrong with the film, it does stand as something of a poor relation to its parents. The director's attempts at adding class to the picture also bog it down somewhat. The pace is too deliberate, with too much conversation, particularly in its mid-section. At 99 minutes, the film classifies as "prestige" in a way that the later, shorter sequels do not, but it's just too long.

Rathbone didn't speak well of *Son* in his memoirs, calling it a "penny dreadful." The description is, in truth, more aptly applied to the next in the series, *The Ghost of Frankenstein* (1942). TH

Torture Ship
Neufield; b/w; 57 min; U.S.

D: Victor Halperin *S:* Harvey Huntley, George Wallace Sayre *P:* Ben Judell, Sigmund Neufeld *C:* Jack Greenhalgh *M:* David Chudnow

Cast: Lyle Talbot, Irving Pichel, Jacqueline Wells, Sheila Bromley, Anthony Averill, Russell Hopton, Julian Madison, Eddie Holden, Wheeler Oakman, Stanley Blystone, Leander De Cordova, Demetrius Alexis, Skelton Knaggs

Dr. Herbert Stander (Pichel) is indicted on charges related to illegal medical experiments. He flees from law enforcement and resumes his work on a privately chartered cruise ship, with a motley gang of criminals and psychopaths as his subjects, in the hopes of making the breakthrough that will vindicate his name.

If ever the term "one hit wonder" applied to a filmmaker, that filmmaker was Victor Halperin. Halperin had directed Bela Lugosi in the memorable Poverty Row horror item *White Zombie* (1932), a film that overcame its air of cheapness to establish itself as one of the most memorable horror movies of the 1930s. Halperin tried several times thereafter to prove that the artistic success of the film was no fluke, but none of his attempts gelled. *Torture Ship* was his last foray into the genre that provided him with his flash-in-the-pan success.

Nominally based on Jack London's short story *A Thousand Deaths*, the film plays like a macabre forerunner to the television series *The Love Boat*, with Irving Pichel's low-key mad doctor in the Captain Stubing role. Pichel, unforgettable as the pale-faced servant of *Dracula's Daughter* (1936), here gives a performance so understated as to border on the somnambulistic. He doesn't seem all that *mad*, really. Just sleep-deprived.

The supporting cast includes Lyle Talbot (*The Thirteenth Guest*, 1932) and Jacqueline Wells (*The Black Cat*, 1934) as the obligatory couple in distress. Interestingly, Wells (who later changed her name to Julie Bishop) is named Joan here, just as she was in *The Black Cat*. Pichel's group of misfits includes at least one familiar visage: the aptly named Skelton Knaggs, a craggy-faced British character actor who made several horror film appearances in the 1940s (including in *Ghost Ship*, 1943, and *House of Dracula*, 1945).

Ultimately, while *Torture Ship* is more enjoyable than some of Halperin's earlier attempts to recapture the magic of *White Zombie* (notably the abysmal *Revolt of the Zombies*, 1936), it's still pretty heavy going. Halperin directed only two more pictures after this (including *Buried Alive*, 1939, which, despite its title, is not a horror film) before leaving the business for good. He died in 1983. TH

Tower of London
Universal; b/w; 93 min; U.S.

D/P: Rowland V. Lee *S:* Robert N. Lee *C:* George Robinson *M:* Frank Skinner *FX:* Jack Cosgrove, Russell Lawson

Cast: Basil Rathbone, Boris Karloff, Barbara O'Neil, Ian Hunter, Vincent Price, Nan Grey, Ernest Cossart, John Sutton, Leo G. Carroll, Miles Mander, Lionel Belmore, Rose Hobart, Ronald Sinclair, John Herbert-Bond, Ralph Forbes, Francis Robinson, G.P. Huntley, John Rodion, Walter Tetley, Donnie Dunagan

Sometime around 1591, William Shakespeare penned his famous tragedy *Richard III*, about the evil Duke of Gloucester's rise to power. Though it purported to be based on fact, it was likely highly fictionalized, though Shakespeare may have believed much of its fiction at the time of its writing.

The Duke of Gloucester, Richard III (1452-1485), was the brother of King Edward IV. Edward died in April 1483, leaving the throne to his son, 12-year-old Edward V. But Richard desired said throne and had his brother's marriage to Elizabeth Woodville annulled and his young nephews Edward and Richard of Shrewsbury declared illegitimate. Both of his brother's young sons were placed in the White Tower building of the Tower of London, and it is said that Richard murdered them there.

Sir Thomas More, a crony of Henry VIII (son of Henry VII, who replaced Richard as King of England), first alleged the double murder. Centuries later, bones were found at the foot of a stairwell in the Tower, seemingly lending credence to the story. However, in the years since their discovery, at least some of the bones have been determined to be those of animals. Many scholars now believe that More, who had an axe or two to grind with Richard, made up the story. But while scholars at one time claimed that More was likely to have exaggerated Richard's infirmities, falsely claiming him to be deformed of body, with a hunched back and a clubfoot, the recent discovery of Richard's remains prove otherwise.

Shakespeare's play was filmed at least three times during the silent era (in 1908, 1911 and 1912), if not more, and it inspired several silent horror films focusing on the fate of the princes in the Tower (*The Little Princes in the Tower*, 1909; *The Children of Edward IV*, 1910 and *The Crown of Richard III*, 1914). But as of 1939 it had yet to receive a talkie adaptation, despite a series of successful adaptations of other Shakespearian works. This made it ripe for the picking when Universal perused the great writer's plays. They assigned the classic to Rowland V. Lee, who had put the studio back on the horror map with his 1939 hit *Son of Frankenstein*, starring Boris Karloff, Basil Rathbone and Bela Lugosi (a film which ended Hollywood's so-called horror ban of the late 1930s with a bang).

Lee, who had a great deal of autonomy on his pictures—he frequently co-wrote, produced, and directed them—read the play and became fascinated with its eponymous character. Inspired, he did his own exhaustive research and created his own take on the tale, which he believed (probably correctly) to be more historically accurate than Shakespeare's play. It was definitely much darker. He co-wrote an original screenplay with his brother Robert N. Lee. Richard's hunched back was retained (albeit reduced to the point of being almost unnoticeable), and his clubfoot was taken from him altogether and given to the local executioner. What remained was a handsome and urbane man with the cunning of the devil. And no longer was Edward IV a sickly wimp; rather, he emerged as a strong, willful and sometimes humane ruler. For his part, the Duke of Clarence's noble and heroic nature was quashed in favor of a more realistically impudent and petulant alcoholic.

After completion of the horror-tinged screenplay, Lee immediately turned to the two men who had contributed so greatly to the success of *Son of Frankenstein*: Basil Rathbone and Boris Karloff. The handsome Rathbone, who had starred in such popular films as *Love from a Stranger* (directed by Lee two years before) and *The Adventures of Robin Hood* (1938), was chosen to play Richard, while Karloff was cast as the vicious and club-footed executioner Mord. Newcomer Vincent Price, who had made his film debut the previous year in Lee's *Service de Luxe* (1938), was picked to portray the Duke of Clarence, setting in stone early his standing as a horror icon. (Interestingly, Price twice again essayed roles related to Richard III: in the 1962 Roger Corman remake of *Tower of London* and in the Grand Guignol classic *Theater of Blood*, 1973.) Other actors of note included Ian Hunter (*A Midsummer Night's Dream*, 1935), Nan Grey (*Dracula's Daughter*, 1936), Leo G. Carroll (*A Christmas Carol*, 1938 and NBC's *The Man from U.N.C.L.E.* TV series, 1964-1968), Lionel Belmore (*The Vampire Bat*, 1933) and Rose Hobart (*Dr. Jekyll and Mr. Hyde*, 1932).

Vincent Price is about to be murdered, drowned in a vat of wine, in *The Tower of London*.

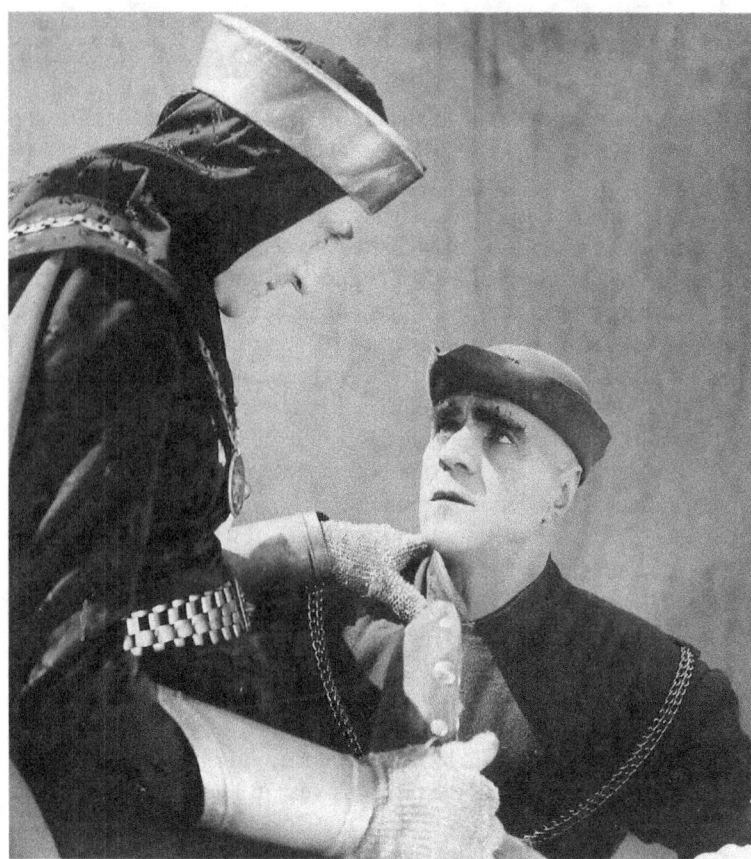

Basil Rathbone as the evil Richard III and Boris Karloff as his club-footed executioner in *The Tower of London*

Intended to be shot during August 1939, the film was hit with a number of setbacks—most notably the shooting of the battle sequences, which were beset by either heavy wind or terrible summer heat, depending on the day. The production wound up 10 days over schedule and $80,000 over budget when shooting finally wrapped on September 4. Further issues popped up when, at a preview screening in early November, Universal executives were displeased over the film's lack of an original score (Lee had gone with stock period music). With the film scheduled for release later the same month, it was too late for a new score to be composed, leaving Universal's executives to recycle much of Frank Skinner's original score from *Son of Frankenstein*.

When the film was finally released on November 17, 1939, it proved a success. And no wonder! It's a lurid slice of horrific historicity with enough court intrigue for mature audiences and a touch of ham for the matinee crowd. It begins with the words: "No age is without its ruthless men—who, in their search for power, leave dark stains upon the pages of History. During the Middle Ages—to seize the Tower of London was to seize the throne of England. In 1471 this has been done by Edward IV—who has violently deposed the feeble Henry VI and holds him prisoner. Within the deep shadows of the Tower walls lives the population of a small city—some in prison cells and torture chambers; some in palaces and spacious lodgings, but none in peace. A web of intrigue veils the lives of all who know only too well that today's friends might be tomorrow's enemies ..."

The film then follows Richard (Rathbone), Duke of Gloucester, as he deviously ascends to the throne of England. To this end he constructs a miniature set containing replicas of everyone standing between him and the crown: current King Edward IV (Hunter), former King Henry VI (Mander), the Prince of Wales (Huntley), Edward's two nephews (Sinclair, Herbert-Bond) and the Duke of Clarence (Price). There's a figure for Richard himself too, of course. As each one is dispatched, the corresponding figure is destroyed, and the figure of Richard III is moved closer to the throne. It's an ingenious touch, setting the film squarely within the provenance of horror.

Richard kicks off his plans by slaying the Prince of Wales in battle. He then has Mord (Karloff) murder Henry VI and, with the further aid of the executioner, he drowns his brother, the Duke of Clarence, in a butt of malmsey wine. Several years pass; King Edward grows ill and dies, but just before the end he declares that Richard should act as father to his two sons, Edward V and Richard of Shrewsbury. Richard "protects" the two boys by placing them in the Tower of London. There, Mord murders them both and buries them in a shallow grave, at last clearing the throne of England for Richard. It is then up to the exiled John Wyatt (Sutton), who loves Edward IV's daughter Alice (Grey), and the exiled Henry Tudor VII (Forbes) to set it all to rights.

Lee's misplaced tendency to intrude upon the action with moments of light comedy mars the film at times. It does work beautifully in the opening, however, as a warmly lighthearted scene in which the queen grooming her children gives way to Mord (Karloff) sharpening his executioner's axe, his face a twisted mask of evil.

Much of *Tower* wallows in violence and depravity, including decapitations, stabbings, drownings, whippings, suffocation and impalement, much of it subtly and all of it effectively shot. The top-notch mayhem is accompanied by strong performances from all involved, particularly Rathbone, who here tones down the histrionics so prevalent in *Son of Frankenstein*. The sets, aided by George Robinson's superb camerawork, betray a larger budget than was usual for Universal films of the time, clearly making this an A-feature rather than the standard B-fare.

Tower of London was not the first film, as mentioned above, to be set in or around the infamous White Tower, which provided the location for England's political executions. On the non-horror front there was also a "documentary" titled *The Tower of London* (1926), part of producer George J. Banfield's *Haunted Houses and Castles of Great Britain* series.

A remake of Lee's film followed over 20 years later. Directed by Roger Corman, it pales next to Lee's magnificent and imposing masterwork, which is today considered a classic of the horror film. CW

Trunk Crime
aka **Design for Murder**
Charter; b/w; 60 min; Great Britain
   D: Roy Boulting *S:* Francis Miller, Edward Percy *P:* John Boulting *C:* Wilkie Cooper
   Cast: Manning Whiley, Barbara Everest, Michael Drake, Thorley Walters, Hay Petrie, Eileen Bennett, Lewis Stringer, Ian Fulton, Tom Gil

Director Roy Boulting (left) behind the scenes on the set of *Trunk Crime*

Bentley (Whiley) is fed up with being mocked by his classmates, so he formulates a horrific plan for revenge. He drugs his tormentors' ringleader, Grierson (Drake), and buries him alive in a trunk. The proverbial race against the clock ensues to save the endangered young man.

John and Roy Boulting, born in 1913, were twin brothers whose names remained intertwined throughout their cinematic careers. Entering the film world in 1937, John usually served as producer while Roy directed and often co-wrote. Occasionally they'd switch roles, with John directing and Roy producing, and they likewise mixed it up with genres, often to memorable effect. *Trunk Crime* was one of their earliest outings, and it remained their only foray into horror/suspense for many years. And while their film *The Risk* (1960) was an interesting suspense offering, they didn't revisit outright horror until the ghoulish *Twisted Nerve* (1968). John passed away in 1985 and Roy in 2001.

The supporting cast of *Trunk Crime* includes character actor Thorley Walters in one of his earliest screen appearances. He later graced a number of British horror and fantasy films, including *The Phantom of the Opera* (1962), *Frankenstein Must Be Destroyed* (1969) and *Vampire Circus* (1971). Cinematographer Wilkie Cooper was, in 1939, at the beginning of his illustrious career, which eventually encompassed such fantasy and horror titles as *The 7th Voyage of Sinbad* (1958) and *Maniac* (1963). TH

Die unheimlichen Wünsche
Tobis; b/w; 99 min; Germany

D/Co-S: Heinz Hilpert *Co-S:* Kurt Heuser *C:* Richard Angst *M:* Wolfgang Zeller

Cast: Olga Tschechowa, Käthe Gold, Elisabeth Flickenschildt, Hans Holt, Ewald Balser, Paul Dahlke, Heinrich Troxbömker, Aribert Wäscher, Axel von Ambesser, Franz Pfaudler, Armin Schweizer, Oskar Schättiger, Ellinor Hamsun, Eva Sommer, Friedrich Maurer, Wolfgang Dohnberg, S.O. Schoening

Rafaél de Valentin is contemplating suicide when he finds a shagreen (a tanned hide, in this case that of a wild ass) in an old antique shop. Learning that it has the power to grant wishes, he buys it and uses it to become successful beyond his wildest dreams. But as it shrinks with each usage, Valentin loses a portion of his own soul, growing physically weaker in the process.

Based on the novel *Le Peau de chagrin* by Honoré de Balzac, *Die unheimlichen Wünsche* stars Hans Holt as the Marquis Valentin, Olga Tschechowa as his mistress Feodora and Käthe Gold as Pauline, the confidante who loves him.

Olga Tschechowa was a popular actress in Nazi Germany. There's an apocryphal tale that she once upset the Nazi Minister of Propaganda, Josef Goebbels, by telling him during a dinner party that she did not think Germany's invasion of Russia would succeed. Later, when Heinrich Himmler planned to arrest her, she called him up and asked if he'd wait until after she'd had her morning coffee. He complied, and when his men arrived at her home and knocked on the door, it was an angry Adolf Hitler—who, it seems, was not exactly a stranger at Olga's place—who answered. After the war ended, the Soviets compensated Tschechowa financially as it is believed she may have served as a secret agent.

The next version of Balzac's tale was made in Argentina in 1943 under the title *La piel de Zapa*. CW

We Want Our Mummy
Columbia; b/w; 18 min; U.S.

D: Del Lord *S:* Searle Kramer, Elwood Ullman *P:* Jules White *C:* Allen G. Seigler *M:* Leigh Harline, Ben Oakland, William Grant Still

Cast: Moe Howard, Larry Fine, Curly Howard, Dick Curtis, Bud Jamison, Eddie Laughton, Theodore Lorch, James C. Morton, Robert Williams

A museum curator (James C. Morton) hires the Three Stooges to go to Egypt in search of the mummy of King Rootin-Tootin. If they are successful in their quest, they stand to gain a $5,000 reward. Unfortunately for them, they face some not-very-sporting competition.

The Three Stooges are a peculiar phenomenon. Revered by a generation of fans (mostly male), they relied almost exclusively on sadism and violence to elicit belly laughs. Their fans adore them precisely because their laughs are pure surface: There's nothing to think about; all one has to do is sit back and watch them slap the hell out of each other. Conversely, those who are immune to their charms find them to be a waste of celluloid. The trio seems to be a "love 'em or hate 'em" institution, with few people if any coming down in the middle.

We Want Our Mummy is representative Stooges fare, though the inclusion of horror elements is relatively rare in their oeuvre, unlike, say, Abbott and Costello, who at one point rekindled their dwindling popularity with a string of horror-themed comedies.

The Stooges troupe got their start in the vaudeville circuit in 1925, when comedian Ted Healy (best known to horror buffs as the wisecracking reporter in Karl Freund's *Mad Love*, 1935) formed "Ted Healy and His Stooges." Brothers Moe (1897-1975) and Shemp Howard (1895-1955) were part of the act, with Larry Fine (1902-1975) joining them later on. The team made their silver screen debut in *Soup to Nuts* (1930), but when the brass at Fox offered up a contract, they excluded Healy from the deal. Healy never recovered professionally from the snub, but the Stooges soared to ever-lasting infamy. Shemp left the act for a time for fear of retaliation from the volatile Healy and was

The Three Stooges—Larry, Moe and Curly—dip their toes into the horror arena with their short, *We Want Our Mummy*.

replaced by another Howard brother, Jerry (1903-1952), who adopted the nickname Curly.

The group underwent further changes over the years, with Shemp rejoining the act when Curly was forced to retire due to a series of strokes. Shemp's passing resulted in Joe Besser filling the third slot, though Joe DeRita (aka "Curly Joe") replaced him when it was time to do feature films. Their shtick proved surprisingly enduring, with the act not petering out until the early 1970s, after Fine suffered a stroke.

Critics never really warmed to the Stooges crude blend of mirth and mayhem, although to this day there are audiences who beg to differ. *We Want Our Mummy* was one of several comedies that spoofed the mummy subgenre made popular by Universal's classic *The Mummy* (1932), starring Boris Karloff; another was the Wheeler and Woolsey comedy *Mummy's Boys* (1936). The inevitable *Abbott and Costello Meet the Mummy* followed years later, in 1955, but failed to bring anything fresh to the formula. TH

The Witness Vanishes
Universal; b/w; 66 min; U.S.
D: Otis Garrett S: Robertson White P: Irving Starr C: Arthur Marinelli
Cast: Edmund Lowe, Wendy Barrie, Bruce Lester, Forrester Harvey, Walter Kingsford, J.M. Kerrigan, Barlowe Borland, Boyd Irwin, Vernon Steele, Reginald Barlow, Levland Hodgson, Robert Noble

Years ago, Lucius Marplay (Borland) was tricked into relinquishing ownership of his newspaper the *London Sun* to his four business partners, who then had him secretly placed in an insane asylum. Now his American-raised daughter Joan (Barrie) shows up in England searching for him. After threatening to kill the men responsible for his predicament, Lucius fortuitously escapes, and sure enough, they begin to die one by one, each death foretold by a premature obituary in the paper. With the help of a journalist (Lester), Joan uncovers the truth—that Lucius isn't the killer after all; rather, it's one of the newspaper's unscrupulous owners (Lowe) taking advantage of Lucius' status as insane to eliminate the other partners.

Shot in July 1939 and released in September of that same year, *The Witness Vanishes* was the last entry in Universal's Crime Club series. It was based on the book *They Can't Hang Me* by James Ronald, which in turn was based on a work bearing publisher Doubleday's Crime Club imprint. *Witness* is one of the more horror-oriented films in the series but also the least interesting, sacrificing the wit and sexual innuendo of earlier entries in favor of a more toned-down approach typical of the period. Some of the murders are admittedly creative, but not enough so to save the film. And while parts of the film have a Val Lewton feel to them (indeed, one scene in a creepy, old dark house anticipates a similar scene in Lewton's *The Seventh Victim*, 1943), *The Witness Vanishes* is pretty pedestrian stuff, belonging more to Universal's 1940s horror cycle than to that of the 1930s.

Nor do the performances offer much reason to recommend the film. Edmund Lowe (*Chandu the Magician*, 1932) is top billed but barely appears, taking a back seat to Wendy Barrie (*The Hound of the Baskervilles*, 1939). Hong Kong-born Barrie does a good job in ditching her British accent, though it was in such roles that her short-lived theatrical career was made. She later hosted her own daytime television talk show, one of the first for a former movie star.

Universal's next attempt at a mystery series was a takeover of the Fox Sherlock Holmes series that had begun with the aforementioned *The Hound of the Baskervilles*, starring Basil Rathbone as the famous detective and Nigel Bruce as his dimwitted assistant Watson. The studio also adapted the popular mystery/horror radio franchise *Inner Sanctum*, but that one failed to leave much of a mark, and with interest in horror waning as WW2 wound down, Universal abandoned suspense in favor of comedies featuring Abbott and Costello, Ma and Pa Kettle and Francis the Talking Mule. CW

Youjutsu Takiyasha-hime
Kyokuto; b/w; length unknown; Japan
D: Seiji Suzaki S: Sadashi Fumino C: Yoshihiko Kadono
Cast: Jusaburo Ichikawa, Sumie Tsuki, Saemon Kataoka, Myoko Kohama, Jushiro Ogawa, Kotaro Isehara

This revenge fantasy serves up the Tarano Family, the father of which, Masakado, is murdered in cold blood. Eldest brother Yoshikado (Ichikawa) sets out to avenge his father's death but his own physical and intellectual limitations hamper him. He convinces his sister, Princess Takiyasha (Tsuki), to use her mastery of the magic arts to help him.

The title, which translates as *Magic Princess Takiyasha*, refers to the sister, a character played by popular Japanese actress Sumie Tsuki. Her biggest claim to fame may have come when she played the daughter of a noodle shop owner in Jiro Kawate's *Saikun nero: Katei sogi no maki* (1934). CW

Index of Film Titles

100 banashi usimitsu no koku, see *Hyaku banashi usimitsu no koku*, 1937
6 Hours to Live, see *Six Hours to Live*, 1932
9th Guest, The, see *The Ninth Guest*, 1934
Adventures of David Gray, see *Vampyr*, 1931
After Dark, 1932
Alraune, 1930
Amazing Exploits of the Clutching Hand, The, 1936
Amazon Head Hunters, 1932
Amore e Morte, see *Love and Death*, 1932
Andere, Der, see *The Other*, 1930
Ang Aswang, 1933
Ape, The, see *House of Mystery*, 1934
Ape, The, see *King Kong*, 1933
Arima neko, see *The Ghost Cat of Arima*, 1937
Arima neko sodo, see *Arima no neko sodo*, 1936
Arima no neko sodo, 1936
Asasenato de los Penitentes, El, see *Lash of the Penitentes*, 1936
Ask a Policeman, 1938
At the Villa Rose, see *Mystery at the Villa Rose*, 1930
Atlantide, L', 1932
Autre, L', 1930
Banchō sarayashiki, see *The Plate-Counting Ghost of Banchō*, 1937
Barton Mystery, The, 1932
Bat Whispers, The, 1930
Baul macabre, El, see *The Macabre Trunk*, 1936
Beast of Borneo, The, 1935
Beast, The, see *King Kong*, 1933
Before Dawn, 1933
Before Midnight, 1933
Behind the Mask, 1932
Behind the Mask, see *The Man Behind the Mask*, 1936
Bells, The, 1931
Bells, The, see *The Polish Jew*, 1931
Between Two Worlds, see *The Dybbuk* 1937
Beware Spooks!, 1939
Big Calibre, 1935
Black Abbot, The, 1934
Black Cat, The, 1934
Black Doll, The, 1938
Black Moon, 1934
Black Robe, The, see *Secrets of Chinatown*, 1935
Black Room, The, 1935
Black Room Mystery, The, see *The Black Room*, 1935
Blood Sucker, see *The Vampire Bat*, 1933
Border Phantom, 1936
Botan dōrō, 1930
Botan dōrō, 1936
Brainsnatcher, The, see *The Man Who Changed His Mind*, 1936
Bride of Frankenstein, The 1935
Bucket of Blood, see *The Tell-Tale Heart*, 1934
Burgomaster, The, see *The Burgomeister*, 1935
Burgomeister, The, 1935
Cada loco con su tema, see *Every Madman to His Specialty*, 1938
Campanile Murders, The, see *Murders on the Campus*, 1933
Case of the Missing Blonde, The, see *The Lady in the Morgue*, 1938
Case of the Missing Coffins, The, see *The Living Dead*, 1934
Castle of Doom, see *Vampyr*, 1931
Castle Sinister, 1932
Cat and the Canary, The, 1939
Cat Creeps (Spanish version), The, 1930
Cat Creeps, The, 1930
Cat Ghost and Cherry Blossoms at Night in Saga, 1936
Cat-Ghost of the Fifty-Three Stations, 1938
Chandu the Magician, 1932
Charette Fantome, La, see *The Phantom Wagon*, 1939
Charlie Chan at the Circus, 1936
Charlie Chan at the Opera, 1936
Charlie Chan at the World's Fair, see *Charlie Chan at Treasure Island*, 1939
Charlie Chan at Treasure Island, 1939
Charlie Chan in Egypt, 1935
Charlie Chan in San Francisco, see *Charlie Chan's Secret*, 1936
Charlie Chan's Secret, 1936
Chéri-Bibi, see *The Phantom of Paris*, 1931
Child Monster, see *Tiyanak*, 1932
Chinatown After Dark, 1931
Chinatown Nights, 1938
Chloe, see *Chloe, Love Is Calling You*, 1934
Chloe, Love Is Calling You, 1934
Circumstantial Evidence, 1935
Clairvoyant, The, 1934
Clutching Hand, The, see *The Amazing Exploits of the Clutching Hand*, 1936
Condemned to Death, 1932
Condemned to Live, 1935
Conga, see *Kongo*, 1932
Creeping Shadows, see *The Limping Man*, 1931
Crime of Dr. Crespi, The, 1935
Crimes of Dr. Mabuse, The, see *The Testament of Dr. Mabuse*, 1932
Crimes of Stephen Hawke, The, 1936
Criminal at Large, see *The Frightened Lady*, 1932
Crooked Circle, The, 1932
Crying Woman, The, 1933
Curse of Kali, The, see *House of Mystery*, 1934
Dame de pique, La, see *Queen of Spades*, 1937
Danger on the Air, 1938
Dangerous Affair, A, 1931
Dante's Inferno, 1935
Dark Eyes of London, The, 1939
Daughter of Dracula, see *Dracula's Daughter*, 1936
Daughter of Evil, see *Alraune*, 1930
Daughter of the Dragon, 1931
Daughter of the Isle of Jamaica, see *The Devil's Daughter*, 1939
Daughter of the Tong, 1939
Dead Don't Care, The, see *The Last Warning*, 1939
Dead Eyes of London, The, see *The Dark Eyes of London*, 1939
Dead Reckoning, see *Terror Aboard*, 1934
Dead Speak, The, 1935
Death and the Maiden, see *Ferryman Maria*, 1936

Death from a Distance, 1936
Death in the Air, see *Pilot X*, 1936
Death Kiss, The, 1932
Death Rides the Range, 1939
Death Takes a Holiday, 1934
Death Valley, see *Mystery Ranch*, 1932
Death Watch, see *Before Dawn*, 1933
Demon of Doom, see *Condemned to Live*, 1935
Desert Phantom, 1935
Design for Murder, see *Trunk Crime*, 1939
Devil Doll, The, 1936
Devil-Doll, The, see *The Devil Doll*, 1936
Devil in a Bottle, The, see *Love, Death and the Devil*, 1934
Devil in the Bottle, The, see *Diable en bouteille, Le*, 1934
Devil's Daughter, The, 1939
Diable en bouteille, Le, 1934
Dibuk, Der, see *The Dybbuk*, 1937
Dr. Jekyll and Mr. Hyde, 1931
Dr. Jekyll and Mr. Hyde, 1932
Dr. Mabuses Testament, see *The Testament of Dr. Mabuse*, 1932
Dr. Maniac, see *The Man Who Changed His Mind*, 1936
Doctor Maniac Who Lived Again, see *The Man Who Changed His Mind*, 1936
Dr. Sin Fang, 1937
Doctor Syn, 1937
Dr. Syn, see *Doctor Syn*, 1937
Doctor X, 1932
Don Juan Tenorio, 1937
Doomed to Die, see *Smoking Guns*, 1933
Dos monjes, see *Two Monks*, 1934
Double Door, 1934
Dracula, 1931
Drácula, 1931
Dracula's Daughter, 1936
Dracula—The Spanish Version, see *Drácula*, 1931
Drums in the Jungle, see *Ouanga*, 1935
Drums in the Night, see *Ouanga*, 1935
Drums O'Voodoo, 1934
Drums of Jeopardy, The, 1931
Dybbuk, The, 1937
Dybuk, see *The Dybbuk*, 1937
Edgar Wallace's The Terror, see *The Terror*, 1938
Edo ni arawareta Kingu Kongu: Hengi no maki, see *King Kong Appears in Edo*, 1938
Edo ni arawareta Kingu Kongu: Ogon no maki, 1938
Eighth Wonder, The, see *King Kong*, 1933
Enmadera no kaibyo, 1938
Enmadera no yurei, 1937
Every Madman has His Story, see *Every Madman to His Speciality*, 1938
Every Madman to His Specialty, 1938
Evil Mind, The, see *The Clairvoyant*, 1934
Excess Baggage, 1933
Face at the Window, The, 1932
Face at the Window, The, 1939
Face in the Fog, A, 1936
Fährmann Maria, see *Ferryman Maria*, 1936
Fantasma de media noche, El, see *The Midnight Ghost*, 1939
Fantasma del convent, Il, see *The Phantom of the Convent*, 1934
Fantômas, 1932
Ferryman Maria, 1936
Fighting Westerner, The, see *Rocky Mountain Mystery*, 1935
Five Deadly Vices, The, see *The Murder in the Museum*, 1934
Five Sinister Stories, see *Uncanny Stories*, 1932
Flames of Conscience, see *The Burgomeister*, 1935
Flaming Signal, The, 1933
Florentine Dagger, The, 1935
Forbidden Love, see *Freaks*, 1932
Forced to Sin, see *The Vampire Bat*, 1933
Forging Ahead, 1933
Frankenstein, 1931
Freaks, 1932
Frightened Lady, The, 1932
Fukushu suru shigai, 1937
Fünf unheimliche Geschichten, see *Uncanny Stories*, 1932
Gaunt Stranger, The, 1938
Geheimnis des blauen Zimmers, 1932
Get That Girl, 1932
Ghastly Tales, see *Uncanny Stories*, 1932
Ghost Cat and the Red Wall, 1938
Ghost Cat of Arima, The, 1937
Ghost Cat's Mysterious Shamisen, 1938
Ghost of John Holling, The, see *Mystery Liner*, 1934
Ghost of the Convent, see *The Phantom of the Convent*, 1934
Ghost Patrol, 1936
Ghost Story of a Love-Mad Tutoress, 1939
Ghost Story of the Mother Tree, 1939
Ghost Train, The, 1931
Ghost Train, The, 1933
Ghost Train, The 1939
Ghost Valley, 1932
Ghost Walks, The, 1934
Ghost-Cat Legend, 1938
Ghoul, The, 1933
Gläserne Fluch, Der, see *Love, Death and the Devil*, 1934
Golden Trail, The see *The Riders of the Whistling Skull*, 1937
Golem, Le, see *The Legend of Prague*, 1936
Golem, The, see *The Legend of Prague*, 1936
Golem: The Legend of Prague, The, see *The Legend of Prague*, 1936
Gorilla, The, 1930
Gorilla, The, 1939
Great Impersonation, The, 1935
Green Eyes, 1934
Gu wu xing shi ji, see *Walking Corpse in an Old House*, 1938
H.G. Wells' The Invisible Man, see *The Invisible Man*, 1933
Hands of Orlac, The, see *Mad Love*, 1935
Haunted Gold, 1932
He Lived to Kill, see *Night of Terror*, 1933
Hell-A-Vision, 1936
Hellavision, see *Hell-A-Vision*, 1936
Hell-O-Vision, see *Hell-A-Vision*, 1936
Henge nyorai, 1937
Herencia macabre, see *A Macabre Legacy*, 1939
Herrin von Atlantis, Die, see *Queen of Atlantis*, 1932
Hidden Corpse, The, see *Strangers of the Evening*, 1932

Honchô kaibyô-den, 1937
Honchô kaibyô-den, 1939
Hooded Terror, The, see *Sexton Blake and the Hooded Terror*, 1938
Horror, The, 1932
Houghland Murder Case, The, see *Murder by Television*, 1935
Hound of the Baskervilles, 1932
Hound of the Baskervilles, The, 1936
Hound of the Baskervilles, The, 1939
Hounds of Zaroff, The, see *The Most Dangerous Game*, 1932
House of Danger, 1934
House of Doom, The, see *The Black Cat*, 1934
House of Fear, The, 1939
House of Mystery, 1934
House of Secrets, The, 1936
House of Unrest, The, 1931
Human Monster, The, see *The Dark Eyes of London*, 1939
Hunchback of Notre Dame, The, 1939
Hund von Baskerville, Der, see *The Hound of the Baskervilles*, 1936
Hyaku banashi usimitsu no koku, 1937
Hypnotized, see *The Burgomeister*, 1935
I Accuse (That They May Live), see *J'Accuse*, 1938
I Accuse, see *J'Accuse*, 1938
Immediate Possession, 1931
Imp in a Bottle, The, see *Love, Death and the Devil*, 1934
Ingagi, 1930
Intruder, The, 1932
Invisible Man, The, 1933
Invisible Ray, The, 1936
Irohagana Yotsuya kaidan, 1937
Island of Lost Souls, 1932
It Is Never Too Late to Mend, see *Never Too Late to Mend*, 1937
It's Never Too Late to Mend, see *Never Too Late to Mend*, 1937
J'Accuse, 1938
Jane Eyre, 1934
Japanese King Kong, 1933
Jaws of the Jungle, 1936
John the Drunkard, see *The Horror*, 1932
Juggernaut, 1936
Juif polonaise, Le, see *The Polish Jew*, 1931
Jungle Virgin, see *Jaws of the Jungle*, 1936
Kaibyô akakabe daimyojin, see *Ghost Cat and the Red Wall*, 1938
Kaibyô gojusan-tsugi, see *Cat-Ghost of the Fifty-Three Stations*, 1938
Kaibyô nazo no shamisen; Onshu nazo no kaibyô, see *Ghost Cat's Mysterious Shamisen*, 1938
Kaibyô Saga no yozakura, see *Cat Ghost and Cherry Blossoms at Night in Saga*, 1936
Kaidan botan dōrō, 1937
Kaidan chibusa enoki, see *Ghost Story of the Mother Tree*, 1939
Kaidan Kasane-ga-fuchi, 1930
Kaidan Kasane-ga-fuchi, 1937
Kaidan kyoren onna shisho, see *Ghost Story of a Love-Mad Tutoress*, 1939
Kaidan Senbaya sodo, 1939
Kaiden Arima neko, see *The Ghost Cat of Arima*, 1937

Killer, The, see *Mystery Ranch*, 1932
Killer at Large, 1936
Killers on the Loose, see *Killer at Large*, 1936
King Ape, see *King Kong*, 1933
King Kong, 1933
King Kong, see *King Kong Appears in Edo*, 1938
King Kong Appears in Edo, 1938
Kingu Kongu Zenkouhen, see *Edo ni arawareta Kingu Kongu: Ogon no maki*, 1938
Kong, see *King Kong*, 1933
Kong, The Eighth Wonder, see *King Kong*, 1933
Kongo, 1932
Kyobyô-den; Kaibyô-den, see *Ghost-Cat Legend*, 1938
Lady Beware, see *The Thirteenth Guest*, 1932
Lady in the Morgue, The, 1938
Lash of the Penitentes, 1936
Last Express, The, 1938
Last Warning, The, 1939
Law of the Tong, 1931
Legend of Prague, The, 1936
Legend of the Saga Cat Monster, 1937
Leng yue shi hunl, see *The Lonely Soul*, 1938
Liebe, Tod und Teufel, see *Love, Death and the Devil*, 1934
Life Returns, 1938
Life Sentence, see *Condemned to Live*, 1935
Limping Man, The, 1931
Living Dead, The, 1934
Living Dead, The, see *Uncanny Stories*, 1932
Llorna, La, see *The Crying Woman*, 1933
Loch Ness Mystery, The, see *Secrets of the Loch*, 1934
Lodger, The, see *The Phantom Fiend*, 1932
Lonely Soul, The 1938
Lost Atlantis, The, see *Mistress of Atlantis*, 1932
Louisiana, see *Drums O'Voodoo*, 1934
Love and Death, 1932
Love Captive, The, 1934
Love, Death and the Devil, 1934
Love from a Stranger, 1937
Love Wanga, see *Ouanga*, 1935
Lucrèce Borgia, see *Lucrezia Borgia*, 1935
Lucrezia Borgia, 1935
M, 1931
Maboroshi-jô no bakeneko, 1939
Macabre Heritage, see *A Macabre Legacy*, 1939
Macabre Legacy, A, 1939
Macabre Trunk, The, 1936
Mad Genius, The, 1931
Mad Love, 1935
Madame Houdini Speaks, see *The Mystic Circle Murder*, 1938
Maid of Salem, 1937
Man Behind the Mask, The, 1936
Man of Stone, The, see *The Legend of Prague*, 1936
Man They Could Not Hang, The, 1939
Man Who Changed His Mind, The, 1936
Man Who Dared, The, see *Behind the Mask*, 1932
Man Who Lived Again, The, see *The Man Who Changed His Mind*, 1936
Man Who Reclaimed His Head, The, 1934

Maniac, 1934
Maria Marten, or The Murder in the Red Barn, 1935
Mark of Terror, see *Drums of Jeopardy*, 1931
Mark of the Vampire, 1935
Mask of Fu Manchu, The, 1932
Medium, The, 1934
Menace, 1934
Midnight at Madame Tussaud's, 1936
Midnight Ghost, The, 1939
Midnight in the Wax Museum, see *Midnight at Madame Tussaud's*, 1936
Midnight Mystery, 1930
Midnight Phantom, The, see *The Midnight Ghost*, 1939
Midnight Shadow, 1939
Midnight Warning, 1932
Missing Guest, The, 1938
Misterio del rostro pálido, El, see *The Mystery of the Ghastly Face*, 1935
Mistress of Atlantis, 1932
Monkey's Paw, The, 1933
Monster Show, The, see *Freaks*, 1932
Monster Walked, The, see *The Monster Walks*, 1932
Monster Walks, The, 1932
Monster, The, see *The Horror*, 1932
Moonstone, The, 1934
Most Dangerous Game, The, 1932
Muertos hablan, Los, see *The Dead Speak*, 1935
Mummy, The, 1932
Mummy's Boys, 1936
Murder at Dawn, 1932
Murder at Midnight, 1931
Murder at the Baskervilles, 1937
Murder by Television, 1935
Murder by the Clock, 1931
Murder in the Museum, The, 1934
Murder in the Old Red Barn, see *Maria Marten, or The Murder in the Red Barn*, 1935
Murder in the Red Barn, see *Maria Marten, or The Murder in the Red Barn*, 1935
Murder in the Sky, see *Pilot X*, 1936
Murder on the Campus, 1933
Murders in the Rue Morgue, 1932
Murders in the Zoo, 1933
Mystère de la Villa Rose, Le, 1930
Mysterious Bombardier, The, see *Pilot X*, 1936
Mysterious Mr. Wong, The, 1935
Mystery at the Villa Rose, 1930
Mystery House, 1938
Mystery Liner, 1934
Mystery of Caversham Square, see *Sexton Blake and the Hooded Terror*, 1938
Mystery of Edwin Drood, The, 1935
Mystery of Mister X, The, see *The Mystery of Mr. X*, 1934
Mystery of Mr. X, The, 1934
Mystery of the Ghastly Face, The, 1935
Mystery of the Marie Celeste, The, see *Phantom Ship*, 1935
Mystery of the Mary Celeste, The, see *Phantom Ship*, 1935
Mystery of the Pale Face, The, see *The Mystery of the Ghastly Face*, 1935
Mystery of the Pallid Face, The, see *The Mystery of the Ghastly Face*, 1935
Mystery of the Wax Museum, The, 1933
Mystery of the White Room, The, 1939
Mystery Ranch, 1932
Mystic Circle Murder, The, 1938
Nature's Mistakes, see *Freaks*, 1932
Never Too Late to Mend, 1937
Never Too Late, see *Never Too Late to Mend*, 1937
New Adventures of Dr. Fu Manchu, see *The Return of Dr. Fu Manchu*, 1930
Night Key, 1937
Night Life of the Gods, 1935
Night Must Fall, 1937
Night of Terror, 1933
Night of Terror, see *Love from a Stranger*, 1937
Night Rider, The, 1932
Ninth Guest, The, 1934
Noroi no ginbyo, see *Silver Cat's Curse*, 1939
Noroi no madara-neko, 1937
Not Against the Flesh, see *Vampyr*, 1931
Obeah!, 1935
Oh, Mr. Porter!, 1937
Oiwa nagaya, 1931
Old Dark House, The, 1932
On the Stroke of Nine, see *Murders on the Campus*, 1933
One Frightened Night, 1935
Other, The, 1930
Ouanga, 1935
Pan Tvardovski, see *Pan Twardowski*, 1936
Pan Twardowski, 1936
Paramount on Parade, 1930
Pays du scalp, Au, see *Amazon Head Hunters*, 1932
Penitente Murder Case, The, see *Lash of the Penitentes*, 1936
Phantom, The, 1931
Phantom Broadcast, The, 1933
Phantom Creeps, The, 1939
Phantom Express, The, 1932
Phantom Fiend, The, 1932
Phantom Light, The, 1935
Phantom of Crestwood, The, 1932
Phantom of Paris, The, 1931
Phantom of the Convent, The, 1934
Phantom of the Opera, The, see *Song at Midnight*, 1937
Phantom of the Range, The, 1936
Phantom Ship, 1935
Phantom Strikes, The, see *The Gaunt Stranger*, 1938
Phantom Train, The, see *The Ghost Train*, 1933
Phantom Wagon, The, 1939
Picture Brides, 1934
Pilot X, 1936
Pilot X: Murder in the Sky, see *Pilot X*, 1936
Pique Dame, see *Queen of Spades*, 1937
Plate-Counting Ghost of Banchō, The 1937
Pocomania, see *The Devil's Daughter*, 1939
Polish Jew, The, 1931
Procureur Hallers, Le, see *L'Autre*, 1930

Profanación, see Profanation, 1933
Profanation, 1933
Queen of Atlantis, 1932
Queen of Spades, 1937
Quest of the Perfect Woman: The Vampire of Marrakesh, 1933
Rasputin, 1938
Rasputin, see Rasputin, Demon with Women, 1932
Rasputin and the Empress, 1932
Rasputin, Dämon der Frauen, see Rasputin, Demon with Women, 1932
Rasputin, Demon with Women, 1932
Raven, The, 1935
Rawhide Terror, The, 1935
Religious Racketeers, see The Mystic Circle Murder, 1938
Return of Chandu, The, 1934
Return of Doctor X, The, 1939
Return of Dr. Fu Manchu, The, 1930
Return of Dr. X, The, see The Return of Doctor X, 1939
Return of Frankenstein, The, see The Bride of Frankenstein, 1935
Return of the Terror, 1934
Revolt of the Demons, see Revolt of the Zombies, 1936
Revolt of the Zombies, 1936
Riders of the Whistling Skull, The, 1937
River House Ghost, The, 1932
Rocky Mountain Mystery, 1935
Rogues Tavern, The, 1936
Saga kaibyô-den, see Legend of the Saga Cat Monster, 1937
Sanjusangen-do no yurei: Oryu onryo, 1939
Satan, see Satanas, 1932
Satanas, 1932
Scotland Yard Mystery, The, see The Living Dead, 1934
Secret of the Blue Room, 1933
Secret of the Blue Room, see Geheimnis des blauen Zimmers, 1932
Secret of the Chateau, 1934
Secret of the Loch, The, 1934
Secret Service, see Behind the Mask, 1932
Secrets of Chinatown, 1935
Secrets of the French Police, 1932
Secrets of Wu Sin, The, 1932
Seven Keys to Baldpate, 1935
Sex Maniac, see Maniac, 1934
Sexton Blake and the Hooded Terror, 1938
Sh! The Octopus, 1937
Shadow, The, 1933
Shadow of Chinatown, 1936
She Devil, see Drums O'Voodoo, 1934
She, 1935
Shin Yotsuya kaidan, 1932
Shivers, 1934
Shot in the Dark, A, 1933
Shot in the Dark, A, 1935
Shriek in the Night, A, 1933
Sign of Death, The, 1939
Signo de la muerte, El, see The Sign of Death, 1939
Silver Blaze, see Murder at the Baskervilles, 1937
Silver Cat's Curse, 1939

Singing at Midnight, see Song at Midnight, 1937
Sinister Hands, 1932
Six Hours to Live, 1932
Smoking Guns, 1933
Someone at the Door, 1936
Son of Frankenstein, 1939
Son of Kong, The, 1933
Song at Midnight, 1937
SOS Coast Guard, 1937
Spanish Dracula, see Drácula, 1931
Spanish Version of Dracula, The, see Drácula, 1931
Speckled Band, The, 1931
Spectre Vert, Le, 1930
Sphinx, The, 1933
Spider, The, 1931
Spooktrein, De, see The Ghost Train, 1939
Strange Adventure, A, 1932
Strange Adventure of David Gray, The, see Vampyr, 1931
Strange People, 1933
Strangers of the Evening, 1932
Student of Prague, The, 1935
Student von Prague, Der, see The Student of Prague, 1935
Sucker Money, 1933
Suicide Club, see Uncanny Stories, 1932
Suicide Club, The, see Trouble for Two, 1936
Super loco, El, see Super Madman, The, 1936
Super Madman, The, 1936
Super Sleuth, 1937
Supernatural, 1933
Svengali, 1931
Sweeney Todd: The Demon Barber of Fleet Street, 1936
Tales of the Uncanny, see Uncanny Stories, 1932
Tangled Destinies, 1932
Tell-Tale Heart, The, 1934
Terror Aboard, 1934
Terror in the Night, see Night of Terror, 1933
Terror, The, 1938
Testament des Dr. Mabuse, Das, see The Testament of Dr. Mabuse, 1932
Testament of Dr. Mabuse, The, 1932
Thark, 1932
That They May Live, see J'Accuse, 1938
They Drive by Night, 1938
Third Clue, The, 1934
Thirteen Women, 1932
Thirteenth Candle, The, 1933
Thirteenth Chair, The, 1937
Thirteenth Guest, The, 1932
Tianak, see Tiyanak, 1932
Ticket of Leave Man, The, 1937
Tiyanak, 1932
Tombstone Canyon, 1932
Tomorrow at Seven, 1933
Torture Ship, 1939
Tower of London, 1939
Tragédie impériale, La, see Rasputin, 1938
Traicionera, La, see A Macabre Legacy, 1939
Trails of the Wild, 1935

Trenul fantoma, see *The Ghost Train*, 1933
Trick for Trick, 1933
Trouble for Two, 1936
Trunk Crime, 1939
Two Monks, 1934
Uncanny Stories, 1932
Unheimliche, Der, see *Uncanny Stories*, 1932
Unheimliche Geschichten, see *Uncanny Stories*, 1932
Unheimlichen Wünsche, Die, 1939
Unholy Quest, The, 1934
Unholy Three, The, 1930
Unsterbliche Glück, Das, see *Love, Death and the Devil*, 1934
Vampire Bat, The, 1933
Vampires of Prague, The, see *Mark of the Vampire*, 1935
Vampyr, 1931
Vampyr – Der Traum des Allan Grey, see *Vampyr*, 1931
Vampyr, ou l'étrange aventure de David Gray, see *Vampyr*, 1931
Vanishing Body, The, see *The Black Cat*, 1934
Vanishing Pioneer, The, see *Rocky Mountain Mystery*, 1935
Vanishing Riders, The, 1935
Voice at Midnight, see *Song at Midnight*, 1937
Voluntad del muerto, La, see *The Cat Creeps (Spanish version)*, 1930
Voodo, 1933
Walking Corpse in an Old House, 1938
Walking Dead, The, 1936
Wasei Kingu Kongu, see *Japanese King Kong*, 1933
Wax Museum, see *The Mystery of the Wax Museum*, 1933
Wayne Murder Case, The, 1932
We Want Our Mummy, 1939
Werewolf of London, 1935
Westland Case, The, 1937
What a Night, 1931
While the Patient Slept, 1935
Whispering Shadow, The, 1933
White Zombie, 1932
Will of the Dead Man, The, see *The Cat Creeps (Spanish version)*, 1930
Witch, The, see *Ang Aswang*, 1933
Witch of Timbuctoo, The, see *The Devil Doll*, 1936
Witching Hour, The, 1934
Witness Vanishes, The, 1939
Woman Condemned, The, 1934
Yaji and Kita's Cat Trouble, 1937
Yaji Kita okazaki neko taiji, see *Yaji and Kita's Cat Trouble*, 1937
Yaji Kita Okazaki no neko sodo, see *Yaji and Kita's Cat Trouble*, 1937
Yè bàn gē shēng, see *Song at Midnight*, 1937
Yellow Phantom, see *Shadow of Chinatown*, 1936
Yotsuya kaidan, 1936
Youjutsu Takiyasha-hime, 1939
Yurei Oman-gitsune, 1937
Zane Grey's The Fighting Westerner, see *Rocky Mountain Mystery*, 1935
Zwei auf Hawai, see *Love, Death and the Devil*, 1934

If you enjoyed this book,
write for a free catalog of
Midnight Marquee Press titles
or visit our website at
http://www.midmar.com

Midnight Marquee Press, Inc.
9721 Britinay Lane
Baltimore, MD 21234
410-665-1198
mmarquee@aol.com

www.ingramcontent.com/pod-product-compliance
Lightning Source LLC
Chambersburg PA
CBHW081719100526
44591CB00016B/2424